minority problems

minority problems

SECOND EDITION

ARNOLD M. ROSE
AND
CAROLINE B. ROSE
EDITORS

HARPER & ROW, PUBLISHERS
NEW YORK, EVANSTON, SAN FRANCISCO, LONDON

Minority Problems, Second Edition

Copyright © 1965 by Arnold M. Rose and Caroline B. Rose. Copyright © 1972 by Caroline B. Rose.
Printed in the United States of America. All rights reserved. No part of this book may be used or reproduced
in any manner whatsoever without written permission except in the case of brief quotations embodied in
critical articles and reviews. For information address Harper & Row, Publishers, Inc., 10 East 53rd Street,
New York, N.Y. 10022.

Standard Book Number: 06-045573-X

LIBRARY OF CONGRESS CATALOG CARD NUMBER: 72-7608

contents

preface

A book of readings needs some explanation. The purpose of this book is to look for universal propositions about the relations among groups, particularly when some of those groups are in a dominant position and others in a subordinate one. This takes far more knowledge than any two people have and is the justification for drawing upon the expertise of a large number of scientists and observers.

The focus of the book is largely on modern industrial societies and more specifically on the United States. All modern societies are mosaics of groups having a variety of relations with one another. It is the belief of the authors that conflict is inevitable among these groups as each jockeys for power and for the ability to express its needs. Conflict is viewed as a basic social process that decides who gets what. The only way in which group conflict can be stopped is for some group to mobilize sufficient power to force other groups out of conflict with it by suppressing them; this the reader will recognize as a description of an absolute dictatorship.

If these statements about conflict are accepted, the problem for democracy then is two-fold: The first is to prevent any group from dominating all others. This may involve deliberately strengthening the weaker groups so that they can take part in conflict on an equal basis with other groups. There is an assumption here that any group can express its own needs and arrange its own affairs better than anybody else can, "better" meaning to the satisfaction of the group members. If the group then can enter into conflict on an equal or almost-equal basis, the needs of the group are most likely to be met.

The second problem is to provide effective means of nonviolent conflict. It is by no means certain that all violence can forever be avoided in any society; but to the extent that members of groups in conflict feel that they have some chance of winning at least some of their demands through law, politics, or restructuring society, violence will be reduced. These two themes run through the entire book, expressed as the choice between cultural pluralism and assimilation.

The structure of the volume is suggested by the Contents. Part I seeks to define the nature of minority problems and sketches the historical origin and present status of American minority problems. Part II applies this approach to minority problems in countries other than the United States. Part III explains the range of specific types of discrimination against minority groups. Part IV takes up the group life of minorities and their reactions to minority status. Part V examines the varied efforts to explain the causes of the problems. Part VI considers various philosophies and techniques of changing the situation.

This book should be of primary value to teachers of college courses in intergroup relations, minority problems, or "race relations." Many teachers will find that they can use it as their sole text; others will prefer to use it as a supplement to one of the existing texts in the field. Although the volume is organized around problems and processes, it can easily be used in a course centered on the specific minority groups simply by asking the student to read all the selections on blacks and on race at one time, then all the selections on nationality groups and immigration, and so on. Those concerned with ameliorating intergroup relations will find selections from much of the basic theoretical literature in the field as well as many of the practical suggestions offered by social scientists and practitioners.

The editors are deeply grateful to all the authors and publishers who have permitted their contributions to be included. Some deserve particular thanks for the kind comments with which they granted permission.

The first edition of this book had two editors, Arnold Rose and Caroline Rose; and together, they worked out the purpose and plan of the book. Arnold Rose died in 1968, and the second edition was completed by Caroline Rose. Because the basic plan of the book and its theoretical structure were joint products and have been maintained, the book is published under both names even though only about a third of the original text remains.

Caroline B. Rose
University of Minnesota

I.

the nature of minority problems in the united states

introduction: some definitions

The term *national minorities* came into use in Europe to describe the particular social position of some people in relation to the rest of the population. In European countries with a long history, people with a certain cultural background frequently had an ancient attachment to a given piece of land. They were known as a nationality group, and the land they occupied bore their name. But in the course of many wars, political trades, and migrations, small groups of people frequently found themselves within political boundaries in which the majority group was of a different nationality. That is, the territories covered by political nations ceased to be exactly the same as the territories inhabited by the historical nationality groups.[1] Not only did these nationality groups sometimes occupy only small pieces of territory, but also they sometimes were dispersed by place of residence and occupation throughout the territory of the majority group. Since the modern conception of a political nation included a belief that it was to serve the interests of a particular nationality, the smaller groups within the physical boundaries of a nation became known as minorities. Most nations had laws to establish the political conditions of existence of their minorities. Sometimes the minorities were enjoined to live within a certain area; sometimes they were restricted to certain occupations; sometimes they sent their own group representatives to the national parliament instead of voting as individuals; and so forth. In nearly all countries, they were regarded as a group apart.[2] For example, a Slovak living in the Austro-Hungarian Empire would never be regarded as an Austrian or Hungarian, even though he was a subject of the emperor; and a Ruthenian would never be regarded as a Pole, even though he was a citizen of the Polish Republic. Each person was a member of a nationality group determined by his ancestry, not by the country within whose borders he happened to dwell. If his nationality group was dominant in the political control of a nation, he was a member of a majority group. If his nationality group was not dominant, he was a member of a minority group and had a different status determined both by law and by custom.

The United States grew up with a different political ideology. There was no conception that a single historical nationality was to be the politically dominant group. It was expected that people of various nationalities and religious faiths would migrate to this country and form a new nationality called American. As a matter of fact, after about 1830, no one nationality group from Europe had either a political or a numerical dominance in the population. By numerical count, a large number of people of German or of English background would be found in this country, but even they would not form a majority. Since the United States has a democratic form of government, and since few groups are denied access to the ballot box, no one group has political control. Nor are there special laws to govern the political status of each of the nationality groups. In other words, there are no national minorities, in the European sense of the term, in the United States.

Rather, the term *minority group* has come to be applied to those groups in the United States who face certain handicaps, who are subject to certain discriminations, and who are the objects of the prejudices of most other people. There is no one *majority group* with a distinctive history and a special claim to the land.[3] Any numerical majority would consist of a heterogeneous mixture of historical nationalities, with few intergroup attitudes in common except an antagonism toward some particular minority group. Many of the people who have a common European nationality background and who today are not the objects of any discrimination as a group (the Germans or the Swedes, for example) were once minority groups in this country. They were looked down on and felt themselves to be discriminated against. But in the course of time, these groups were no longer regarded as minority groups and no longer tended to think of themselves as such. They were no longer Germans or Swedes; they were now Americans. Being a member of a minority group in the United States, then, is a function of the state of mind of the general population and of the person himself, rather than a function of his ancestry only. Some groups are allowed and encouraged to merge their distinctiveness and identity into the general body of Americans, but certain other groups (the blacks, for instance) are not permitted to do so. Thus, throughout American history, there seem to have been both permanent and temporary minority groups.

Minority groups in the United States today can be objectively distinguished by one or another of four different characteristics: race, nationality, language, and religion.[4] A minority group in the United States is thus either not of the white race, not of American nationality, not of the Protestant faith, or does not use primarily the English language. These traits characterize the dominant majority group when considered on grounds of race, religion, nationality, or language alone. Before delimiting and illustrating these terms, it should be noted that by no means all groups distinguishable by race, religion, nationality, or language are minority groups. During most of the eighteenth and nineteenth centuries, Jews were not a religious minority group in this country.[5] At the present time, Americans of Irish descent are no longer a nationality minority, although they once were. A group is a minority group if it is the object of prejudice and discrimination from the dominant groups and if the members think of themselves as a minority. It is not a minority merely because its members have a distinctive racial or nationality background or because its members adopt a certain religion or language, although minority status in the United States is attached to at least one of these four characteristics.

Race is a biological category; the people of a given race have certain inherited physical features that distinguish them from any other race. There is variation within the race, and there is overlap in regard to some of the specific features among the races, but a certain combination of physical features on the average distinguishes one race from another. These unique inherited features have resulted from thousands of years of endogamy, so that a racial group has a common and distinguishable ancestry. Among the racial minorities in the United States are the blacks, the Chinese, the Japanese, the Filipinos, and the American Indians. These groups are not pure biological races, since many people in each of them have some Caucasoid (i.e., "white") ancestry. Also, the dominant white race in the United States has a certain proportion of people with Negroid or Mongoloid ancestry. It is not strictly on biological grounds, therefore, that a person is classified as belonging to a racial minority. For example, a person will be called black even though he has only one grandparent who was black and three grandparents who were whites. A black is defined in the United States as any person who has any known Negroid ancestry.[6]

The term *race* has been applied to many groups that are not biological races at all. Many people ignorantly, and some maliciously, speak of the "Jewish race" or the "Italian race," although these are, respectively, religious and nationality rather than racial designations. Certain people thus are regarded as members of racial minorities even when they are not scientifically distinguishable on the basis of a certain combination of physical features. Also, occasionally, a group that scientists call a race on the basis of physical features is not regarded by the general population as a racial minority. The Mexican people in the United States, for example, are predominantly of Indian ancestry and therefore are predominantly members of the Mongoloid race, at least to the same extent that American blacks are of the Negroid race. Yet there is a strong tendency in most parts of the United States to regard an assimilated person of Mexican ancestry as a "Spaniard." Race, then, is at once a basis for distinguishing scientifically a biological category of persons and an epithet applied to certain peoples to designate their membership in minority groups.

The nationality groups are mostly from Europe, although Americans generally consider some of the peoples from Asia Minor and Latin America as nationality groups also. The European nationality groups that are minorities in the United States are all predominantly white, although there has been an admixture of Negroid ancestry in some people from Spain and Sicily and some Mongoloid ancestry among some of the Russians. Although the nationality groups have a distinctive common ancestry, their separation from one another does not extend back into history for the hundreds of thousands of years necessary to differentiate racial groups. The nationality groups, as already suggested, are characterized mainly by a distinctive culture and a sense that they are a distinctive people with a distinctive history. Since the various peoples of Europe and Asia Minor have had a good deal of cultural contact, at least over the past 2,000 years, they have many cultural traits in common. It is their unique cultural traits to which most attention is paid, however. These range from food preferences to the pattern of mutual obligations within the family. Usually a distinctive language is associated with a given nationality, but occasionally two or more nationalities use the same language. (The Germans and Austrians, for example, both use the German language.) Most immigrants gradually learn to speak English, and their children usually grow up speaking two languages. In other respects, too, immigrants of the second generation are part of two cultures: the minority culture of their ancestors and the dominant culture of the United States. By the third and subsequent generations, the language and cultural patterns tend to be predominantly those of the dominant group. Since there are no permanent physical features associated with their minority status, the third and subsequent generations among the nationality minorities are usually no longer considered to be members of a minority group.

There are some major exceptions to this pattern. Some members of the various nationality minorities live and work in isolated rural areas. Out of contact with the dominant Americans and therefore not faced with the necessity of adopting a second set of cultural practices and values, they maintain the ways of their ancestors for generation after generation. Such is the situation, for example, among a few of the German and Scandinavian groups that live in Wisconsin, Minnesota, and the Dakotas. Although they may be third-generation Americans and exercise fully the privileges of citizenship, they speak the language of their grandparents or great-grandparents and maintain a cultural life not too different from that of Sweden or Germany some seventy-five years ago. These groups are not minorities by virtue of discrimination and prejudice (although some seem to feel hostility from other minority nationalities living not far away) but by virtue of their physical isolation and the consequent lack of opportunity to adapt to dominant American culture patterns and absence of pressure on them to do so.

Similar to the nationality minorities are the language minorities. They can be differentiated from the former mainly by the fact that they are not composed of recent immigrants. They are distinguished by having retained a language other than English over many generations. They also have some other distinctive culture traits. One of the largest of these groups is the so-called Hispano group concentrated in New Mexico and southern Colorado. These are Spanish-speaking people whose ancestors migrated from Spain to America many hundreds of years ago. Most of their ancestors were incorporated into this country after the United States defeated Mexico in the war of 1846-1848. They are similar to some of the European national minorities in that the political jurisdiction over the land they occupied changed, but their nationality did not. Their isolation in the sparsely populated Southwest has allowed them to maintain their traditional uniqueness. Although subjected to a certain amount of discrimination when they come in contact with a large number of "Anglos" (as English-speaking Americans are known to them), their isolation prevents most of them from suffering legal or political disabilities. Most of them are poor, but their poverty stems from the sparse soil on which they choose to live, rather than from discrimination from the outside. Except for their retention of the Spanish language and some archaic Spanish-Mexican folkways, their cultural uniqueness and their economic backwardness are reminiscent of the hillbillies of English or Scottish descent who live in the mountain regions of Kentucky and Tennessee.

The religious minorities in the United States include the Jews, the Eastern Orthodox, the Moslems, members of certain small sects that have broken away from the major Protestant or Orthodox faiths, members of the major Asiatic faiths, and in certain respects, the Roman Catholics. Each of these groups has a heterogeneous composition of race, nationality, or language background. Discrimination and prejudice against them on the part of the dominant groups in the United States are associated with their religious faith and the historical background of that faith. Most of their members have acquired their faith from their parents, but some have adopted it themselves. This indicates that one can join a minority; it is not necessary to be born into one.

The Jews constitute a fairly unique minority in that there is no adequate single basis for categorizing them. Their racial, nationality, and language characteristics and backgrounds are about as diverse as possible. Many, perhaps more than half, do not today adhere to the Jewish faith. The most satisfactory way of describing them is to say that for all of them, their recent forebears are known to have believed in the Jewish religion. As already mentioned, many ignorant or malicious persons think of Jews as a race, but this mistake is also made, although perhaps to a lesser extent, about other religious or nationality minorities.

This introduction has attempted to define a minority group and to indicate what minority groups there are in the United States. The first group of readings offers further descriptions of several of the specific minorities, including all the larger ones. The minorities selected for inclusion illustrate all the bases on which minorities are distinguished in the United States. Although many facts are presented about the characteristics of each minority as a group, the main emphasis is on the history of their relations to the dominant groups in the United States and the nature of the problems arising out of those relations. Primary interest, then, is not so much in the groups themselves as in intergroup relations and the discrimination and prejudice that make certain people into minorities.

NOTES

[1] Failure to understand this point led President Wilson to proclaim the ideal of "self-determination for nationalities." Since political self-determination for one nationality was incompatible with political self-

determination for other nationalities, as well as being incompatible with economic and military needs, the statement of this aim led to endless friction.

[2] After World War I, a body of international law came into existence to protect national minorities within the boundaries of both the defeated nations and the newly created nations.

[3] Closest to such a group, on the basis of historical attachment to the land, would be the American Indians. But the Indians are relatively few in number, and they are the objects of considerable discrimination from the dominant majority.

[4] Sex is a fifth characteristic distinguishing a minority group.

[5] Jewish immigrants might have been temporary minority groups, but then it was on the basis of their nationality background rather than their religious affiliation. There was a period in which German Jews were a minority group, and then Jews from eastern Europe, but not all identifiable Jews.

[6] Southern state laws used to define *Negro* with fictitious precision (e.g., as having one-fourth or one-eighth Negroid ancestry), but in practice the law enforcement officials treated as black anyone with any known Negroid ancestry. In other countries, such as Brazil, racial characteristics by themselves tend to be ignored; whereas in South Africa, the mixed population is placed in a third category, distinguished from both "natives" and "Europeans."

1
cultural pluralism in the united states

OSCAR HANDLIN

When foreigners analyze the United States, they frequently complain that Americans are conformists, that everybody is like everybody else, and that Americans do not have the variety of cultures and life-styles which they value in their own countries. It is true that most American cities look alike, that Americans wear similar clothes and eat silimar foods bought at supermarkets, all the result of mass production. Americans have also probably thought of themselves as similar in values and life-styles. For many decades, this similarity was regarded as desirable and through schools and mass media everybody was encouraged to adopt the manners and morals of the dominant American group. This philosophy was known as the melting pot *theory.*

For historical reasons, the language and law of the United States is Anglo-Saxon in origin, even though the explorers and settlers of the country were mainly French, Spanish, and Dutch, as well as English. Great pressure was and is put on immigrants to learn English and to adopt what today is called the "white middle-class culture." Those who did not or could not were deprived of many of the good things in American life. Some groups (the American Indians, for example) did not want a white, middle-class style of living. Others (blacks, for example) were kept from acquiring this life-style so that they could be kept out of the mainstream of American life. Religion and geographical isolation separated out other groups. Increasingly, it could be observed that the United States was less of a melting pot than a mosaic of groups, with different amounts of power, different statuses in the society, and hostility toward other groups. Some people welcomed the diversity of the society while deploring hostility between groups. The theory that the preservation of different cultures was desirable and would in the end make for a stronger social bond was first put forth by Horace Kallen, writing in the early 1920s; he called his theory cultural pluralism.

Both the melting pot theory and the theory of cultural pluralism present a number of difficulties in practice; these shall be examined in the remainder of the book. The essay that follows is a short survey of cultural pluralism in the United States; it raises but does not solve the problems involved in adopting either theory. The author, Oscar Handlin, is Winthrop Professor of History at Harvard University.

Abridged from Oscar Handlin, *Out of Many: A Study Guide to Cultural Pluralism in the United States,* 1964. Reprinted by permission of the Anti-Defamation League of B'nai B'rith.

PEOPLE IN MOTION

Americans have much in common—citizenship, a democratic way of life, values that emphasize human dignity, and a concern for the individual personality. But they are also divided by genuine differences. The Texan does not speak quite the same language as the Maine Yankee; Negroes and whites do not look alike; the Baptist does not worship in the same church as the Roman Catholic; and different music may move the grandsons of Italian and German immigrants. Yet they are all equally Americans.

What in the experience of this nation has enabled these heterogeneous people to live harmoniously together, to accept rather than attempt to wipe out the differences among themselves?

A clue to the answer lies in the willingness of Americans to recognize the central fact of their past. They are not all descended from common ancestors; nor have they always been rooted in the places which are now their homes. To some degree they are all immigrants or the offspring of immigrants. And even today, when foreigners no longer cross the borders in former numbers, Americans feel free to move about the vast land they occupy in search of individual advantage.

A HERITAGE OF DIVERSITY

From the start there was space within which many types of men could move about. In the seventeenth-century forests, the Indians watched the English come to New England and the Chesapeake colonies; they watched the Dutch come to New Netherland and the Swedes to the Delaware. As settlement spread, it became more diverse; German and Scotch-Irish farmers advanced toward the frontier; French-Hugenot and Jewish merchants took up trade in the towns; and a growing number of African slaves stocked the expanding plantations. These people could not simply shed the habits and beliefs, the practices and customs nurtured by their diverse origins. What then enabled them to live and work together?

No doubt the emptiness of the land permitted accommodations that reduced frictions. There was room for strangers to settle either in communities of their own or among the earlier arrivals; and no one could deny that the crying need of the country was for men—no matter where they came from. Furthermore, the very fact of migration was a common experience. Though they had departed from many different

regions of Europe, all these people knew what it meant to leave home, to risk the hazards of the ocean and the wilderness, and to face the social and psychological problems of an unfamiliar environment. To the extent that those trials influenced their character, they all became Americans.

The independent nation that emerged from the Revolution recognized this situation. It did not make place of birth or descent the test of citizenship. Anyone who wished to do so could participate in the life of the Republic; and any free man could migrate to the United States to enjoy its advantages on terms of complete equality with those already settled. Free institutions and open opportunity, it was confidently believed, would convert people of any background into Americans. That was the heritage of a past which had taught the residents of the New World to live with differences.

The eighteenth-century formula left one exception—the Negro who was not free but a slave. Although, in 1776, most Americans hoped that bondage would ultimately disappear, they could not envisage the terms upon which blacks and whites would live together. The inability to do so would long remain troublesome. Meanwhile the Constitution attempted to limit the problem by ending the importation of more slaves.

THE GREAT MIGRATIONS

The receptive attitude toward newcomers proved enormously stimulating as the United States entered upon the unparalleled territorial and economic expansion of the nineteenth century. The promise of freedom, opportunity and equality drew millions of Europeans across the Atlantic to help conquer the vast empty spaces west of the Appalachian Mountains, to build great industrial cities and to develop a culture that met the challenge of a rapidly changing world.

Almost immediately after the end of the Napoleonic wars in 1815, a tide of immigration began to flow toward the New World. It continued almost without interruption for more than a century and brought well above 35,000,000 Europeans to America.

Great social and economic transformations in the Old World cast adrift the population that would pour into the New. Industrialization and the modernization of agriculture broke up traditional households and left no places for thousands of artisans and peasants. The landless poor were crowded out of their villages and were hastened on their way by recurrent famines.

The movement to America came in four great waves. From 1815 to the Civil War, western Europe was the source of most of the newcomers, for England, Scotland, Wales, Ireland and southwestern Germany were the first countries to feel the shock of modernization. The volume of the movement mounted steadily from a few thousand a year to a peak of more than 400,000 in 1854. The flow then subsided and was cut off by the Civil War. But by then some 7,375,000 Europeans had come to the United States, in addition to smaller contingents from China and from across the Canadian border.

A second wave took form shortly after the Civil War and continued until about 1890. It included many people from the countries of former migration, but the movement had by now also spread to northern Europe and drew along substantial numbers of Norwegians, Swedes, Danes and Finns. In all, about 8,000,000 persons made the journey in less than three decades.

Migration reached its climax in the years between 1890 and 1924, when more than 20,000,000 new arrivals swelled the population of the United States. The countries of western and northern Europe still contributed to the flow, which however now expanded with additions from the east and the south, where economic and social changes were now also setting millions adrift. Out of the old Austrian Empire came aggrieved subject peoples—Czechs, Slovaks, Hungarians, Slovenians, Serbs, and Poles. From the territories of the Russian Czar came other Poles, as well as White Russians, Ukrainians and Ruthenians. Some 2,000,000 East European Jews were swept along in the migration to join co-religionists who had earlier arrived from England, Holland and Germany. Almost 4,000,000 peasants fled from Italy. Portugal added a sizable group; and there was a smaller exodus from Rumania, Greece, Turkey, Albania, and Syria. By 1900, the tendency was

world-wide. The United States had become the land of hope also for Mexicans and Canadians, for Japanese, Filipinos, and East Indians. All this while, of course, the native Americans themselves were on a move that subdued the frontier and filled up a continent.

Between 1924 and 1945, the great migrations subsided under the pressures of our own restrictive legislation, of war, of world-wide depression, and of the policies of European totalitarian regimes. Only 200,000 refugees, about half of them Jews, found asylum in the New World. The only important movements then were internal, from South to North, from East to West and from country to city.

The fourth movement which began shortly after 1945 and lasted for about fifteen years differed from its predecessors. It consisted largely of refugees displaced by the war, of skilled technicians needed in the American economy, and of the brides of servicemen who had married overseas. Together these sources produced about 2,000,000 newcomers. They were therefore less important than the internal shifts of population which, in the same years, directed southern Negroes and Puerto Ricans to the industrial cities and pulled millions of other Americans to the Pacific Coast and the Gulf states. That internal reshuffling of population still continues.

Their long history of migration forced Americans to wonder about their own character and identity. Few indeed could take it as a matter of course that they were what they were because they and their parents and grandparents had lived in a fixed place or had inherited a stable culture. What kind of nation was it that remained restlessly in motion? What did nationality mean if it took in people descended from migrants from every part of the world?

THE AMERICAN IDENTITY

Already in the eighteenth century before the Revolution, these problems had begun to elicit discussion. The colonists by then were no longer Englishmen. What were they? Independence lent greater urgency to these questions for it emphasized the separateness of the new nation from the former mother country. Down to the middle of the nineteenth century the answer was generally confident. The American was a new type of man, a mixture of all the stocks of the Old World; he would develop, in time, a completely new character shaped by his free environment. Whatever problems existed for the moment could be postponed for the future.

By 1850, however, it was no longer possible to speak in such confident terms. The mixture was not growing more homogeneous; differences persisted. The New England Yankees were by no means becoming more like the cavaliers in Virginia; westerners were not similar to either; and the immigration of Irish and Germans had added new ingredients not readily dissolved. As the century advanced and the country expanded, the concern about national character deepened.

By 1900, the explanation of the failure of various groups to fuse into a single type had polarized in two directions. Some Americans continued to believe that their nation was a melting pot which would ultimately create from the ingredients poured into it a single, purer and better stock. But it was necessary more consciously to assimilate the immigrants by teaching them the manners, the habits, the language and the faith of those long established in the land. Others believed that the task was hopeless. The melting pot did not work because the various races were biologically distinct from one another and could not fuse. Therefore it was necessary to exclude all further immigration except for that which added strength to the original Anglo-Saxon element.

Neither explanation was satisfactory. The one could not account for the fact that the groups did not dissolve, but retained their identity for generation after generation. The other, by stressing racial homogeneity, denied historical tradition and the actuality of diversity.

Such men as William James, Charles W. Eliot and Randolph Bourne therefore began to question the melting pot concept itself. They saw no value to uniformity as an end in itself and pointed out that the immigrant and other groups could serve the nation most effectively if they retained their identity and enriched the culture of the whole with their own unique contributions. Horace M. Kallen drew an analogy to the orchestra, the instruments of which did not play in unison, but joined in a general

harmony by following each a melodic line appropriate to its own character. American character, from this point of view, was a product of the cultural pluralism of its people.

The concept of cultural pluralism was valuable insofar as it recognized the diversity of the American population and stressed the values of group life. But, as it was formulated fifty years ago, it also raised important questions. Were the groups to which Kallen referred fixed and unchangeable? What would happen to them when they were no longer sustained by immigration? Would inter-marriage dissolve them? Could an individual belong to no group, or to more than one? Were all the forces which created these divisions of equal weight; that is, was it the sentimental attachment to the land of his grandparents that made an Irish-American as important as the color that made a Negro? These are still important problems today.

ETHNIC GROUPS AND AMERICAN FREEDOM

These questions are more comprehensible when viewed in the perspective of American free institutions.

Characteristically, in the United States, men do not turn to government to supply all their social needs. In great areas, they prefer to act voluntarily and cooperatively rather than through the instruments of compulsion controlled by the state. The most important is religion, from which the Constitution altogether separates the government. But the economy, culture, education, philanthropy and family life of the nation offer similar scope for voluntary associations.

Some associations define themselves by function. The medical society includes physicians; the museum enrolls as members all those interested in art; and the Red Cross appeals to the benevolence of all. Others attract only a segment of the whole population; not everyone wishes to join Trinity Church or Temple Emmanuel, the Ancient Order of Hibernians or the Sons of Italy. Some parents wish their children to attend Yeshiva University, others Holy Cross and still others St. Olaf's. Such preferences are largely shaped by values which descend from generation to generation through the family; that is, by ethnic values. Those who adhere to these values and form associations to sustain them behave as ethnic groups.

In our society, migration has generated three kinds of indifferences which draw men into such groups. The strangeness that results from a move away from the place of one's birth—or even the memory of an ancestral move—induces Kentucky hillbillies in Chicago or Yankees in California or Italians in New York to act together. Color—particularly when associated with an inferior status—separates Negroes and Indians from others. And diverse creeds and practices keep Catholics and Baptists, Jews and Mormons from worshipping together.

The ethnic group thus serves an important function in organizing a complex society. It enables each individual to find an appropriate affiliation free of interference either from others or from the government. How these groups operate in practice will emerge more clearly from an examination of those which rest upon the most common difference, that of religion.

RELIGIOUS ASPECTS OF CULTURAL PLURALISM

Any listing of churches in the typical American city directory will show how wide are the distinctions generally accepted. Well over 400 distinct religious bodies operate side by side in the United States. However deeply they differ among themselves in articles of faith, they have learned to tolerate each other in daily life. And the ability of their members to work together is an essential part of the social order.

Sectarianism as a Quality of American Protestantism

Toleration, however, was not always a feature of the religious life of the New World. It was not a principle transferred from Europe but a practice that grew out of the conditions of settlement.

Almost all the seventeenth-century newcomers expected to establish churches with close ties to the government and to exclude dissenters. Neither the Puritans of New England nor the Anglicans of the Chesapeake colonies had any intention of encouraging heretics to live in their midst. But controls were too loose

to permit any group to maintain its hegemony; Anne Hutchinson and Roger Williams who were persecuted in Massachusetts could find refuge in Rhode Island. Furthermore, the demand for population made toleration advantageous. Hands were so short in the wilderness that few could afford to be sticklers about creeds for very long. After 1680 when the new colony of Pennsylvania, established by a Quaker, thrived by openly adopting freedom of worship as a policy, its competition had to follow.

As a result, no denomination had a monopoly of religious life. By the time of the Revolution a multitude of sects were free to follow their own inclinations; and the separation from England strengthened the tendency by dissolving most of the remaining ties between church and state. Thereafter no legal favor put any group at an advantage over the others; each was equally free to take what form it wished.

Some denominations were the products of immigration. The Congregationalist, Anglican and the Dutch Reformed churches thus originated in the Old World. They were later followed by German Lutherans and Scotch-Irish Presbyterians. Still later Lutheran Norwegians, Danes, Swedes and Finns insisted on forming their own synods; and the Greeks, Welsh, Russians, and Armenians also insisted on transplanting Old Country ways of worship. The Negroes too are mostly communicants of churches of their own.

Other sects arose from frequent schisms that reflected differences of theological opinion, as when the Unitarians divided from the Congregationalists. Still others arose when great social issues divided the people, as when attitudes toward slavery splintered the Methodist and the Baptist churches. Finally, a succession of native prophets attracted significant followings through the nineteenth and twentieth centuries—Joseph Smith and the Church of the Latter-Day Saints, Joseph Miller and the Adventists, and Mary Baker Eddy and the Christian Scientists, for example.

The designation Protestant therefore applies to hundreds of different sects. They have in common a vague theological heritage; they are Christian and refuse to accept the authority of the Roman Catholic Church. But on most doctrinal matters, they diverge radically. On the other hand, their ethnic character establishes connections among them. Each individual is, of course, free to worship in the church of his choice. But most remain affiliated with the denomination of their parents; and the Protestants, as a result, have some degree of social unity despite the creedal differences among them.

American Catholicism

Two large religious groups stand apart by virtue both of their faith and their social origins.

Toleration was not readily accorded to the handful of American Catholics in the colonies. In part that was due to lingering suspicions inherited from Reformation England. In part it was due to fear of the hostile French and Spanish along the borders who seemed to be allied with the Church of Rome. In any case, a group which still accepted the discipline of a foreign potentate then seemed alien. Catholics labored under some disabilities until after the Revolution and a residual prejudice against them existed until well into the twentieth century; and that itself kept them apart.

Furthermore, the Church was largely a product of late immigration. Its greatest period of growth came in the middle of the nineteenth century when it received millions of new Irish and German communicants. Still later, its numbers swelled with the arrival of Italians, Poles, French Canadians, and Mexicans. Immigration which added strength to the Church also made it seem foreign and increased the difficulties of adjustment to the American environment.

The Church, however, was neither as monolithic nor as detached from American life as it seemed to outsiders to be. Its members did not deviate from the central doctrines of the faith. But the Irish, the Italians and the Poles each wished to retain the distinctive features of worship they had known at home. Furthermore, age-old practices did not quite fit the new conditions and led to disputes over such important questions as the role of lay trustees, the control of education and attitudes toward republican institutions.

Americanization involved changes by which the Church accommodated itself to both kinds of problems. It insisted upon retaining its unity; but it permitted national parishes to serve the needs of each group it embraced. In time also it adjusted to its situation as one among many religious bodies that co-exist in a pluralistic society. It therefore became not simply the arm of a foreign body operating in the United States, but an American institution.

Judaism in the New World

The comparable process that transformed Judaism in the New World was modified by its lack of a central source of authority. Each congregation of Jews was completely independent and entirely controlled by its members. Each was free to interpret the tradition of the Torah in its own fashion.

The few thousand Jews in the colonies on the eve of the Revolution were already divided by nationality and by mode of worship; and divisions among those of Spanish, Portuguese, German, English and Polish descent long persisted. Indeed immigration in the nineteenth century introduced even more complexities, as newcomers arrived from eastern Europe, the Levant and North Africa.

The divisions bred by recollections of place of birth would ultimately subside when immigration ended and left an even larger proportion of Jews native-born. But before that happened other groupings based on religious policy had appeared. A Reform movement sought to reshape Judaism to modern conditions by stressing the ethical rather than the ritual aspects of faith. In reaction the Orthodox insisted on maintaining the traditional law. And a Conservative element took an immediate position, seeking gradual changes under the control of some authoritative body. The result at present is three quite clearly defined sects among American Jews. In addition smaller groups like the Hasidim insist on going their own way; and a large number of Jews remain formally unaffiliated, yet continue to identify themselves as Jews either out of loyalty, sentiment or cultural attachments.

Americanizing Tendencies

All the faiths have been subject to the pressure of Americanizing tendencies which have left similar impressions on them. All operate, after all, in the same society and feel the influence of the same environment. Science, the mass media and the educational system subtly created similarities in the patterns of worship, in the round of social activities that center in the church, and in the basic assumptions of the members. There was a tendency in all to expand the role of the laity who increasingly shared the attitudes and views of people in other denominations.

Yet paradoxically, Americanization did not make all the groups alike or destroy their ethnic quality. Not only did diverse traditions retain their strength, but the very conditions of co-existence in a pluralistic society created the assumption that each man would adhere to the faith of his fathers.

Every religion, to some extent, felt a missionary impulse. Each conceived itself as the custodian of the truth and the sole path to salvation; and each wished to spread its gospel as widely as possible. Yet as a practical matter, in the United States, it was impossible to assume that people of other faiths, with whom one lived and did business, whom one elected to office or chose as a doctor, would be damned. Even the most exclusive churches found some way out of the dilemma to spare the heroes of the past and the friends of the present. Furthermore, since these were social as well as religious organizations, there was no urgency to bringing in great numbers of strangers. "Live and let live" was the preferable formula. Each man was to go to the church of his choice which, it was assumed, would be that in which he was raised. On this basis it became possible for the various denominations to work with, rather than compete with, one another.

The Functions of Faith

The fact that the churches take for granted the common antecedents of their members permits them to serve an important function, in addition to that of divine worship; and conversely that further emphasizes their ethnic character. These bodies are the custodians of tradition and of the sacred objects, rituals and forms of expression which men cherish. When faced with the significant incidents in human life—birth, marriage, and death—people wish

to have the emotional assurance of a connection with the ancestral past. At such moments the church and the family converge in an association which cements ethnic loyalties.

Religion too is the custodian of ethical values. In a general sense, Americans share a common moral position derived from their Judeo-Christian heritage. But the practical expression of their ethical impulses through philanthropy still is likely to fall within ethnic and religious lines.

As a consequence, these groupings are likely to retain their identity for a long time. Their deep roots in the past and their functions in the present give them a strong hold on our society. Along with the other kinds of groupings which are the products of migration —those created by color and nativity—they establish pluralistic modes of action as normal in the United States. That is a source of great social strength; and also of serious social strains.

PLURALISTIC GROUP LIFE
Can There Be Minorities Without a Majority?

Homogeneous societies can readily define a minority. The community to which the majority belongs acts through a government, a church, a school system and an array of philanthropic, cultural and social institutions. The minority stands apart insofar as it does not participate but supports autonomous activities of its own.

In the United States, there is no majority; and, except for the political order which involves every citizen, there is not a single set of institutions of which most people are members. Instead, society consists of a multitude of groupings and associations, which operate on a parity and none of which, therefore, is, properly speaking, a minority. Legally, none has either a privileged or a disadvantaged position, for the law recognizes only individuals whom it aims to treat on the basis of equality.

With one important exception, each person is free to choose his own affiliations. He may change his name or religion, contribute to what charities and join what clubs he likes. He may remain entirely detached if he prefers. Most men do prefer to be members of some group—for simple fellowship and sociability, for mutual assistance, and for cooperation in meeting the cultural and religious needs no individual can satisfy in solitude. Generally, similar people act together in these matters. Therefore the groups to which they belong fall within ethnic lines. But the act of belonging is itself voluntary. A man can, if he wishes, forget the origins of his ancestors or he can change his faith just as he can move from one section to another. He can be a member of both Jewish and Russian-American or Catholic and Italian associations, for there is no reason why these groupings need be exclusive or make a total demand on his loyalties.

The one exception arises from color. The history of slavery and of contact with the Indians in this country created a special sensitivity to color which is regarded as an indelible sign of the individual's identification. Some people do pass, but the great majority of Negroes, Indians and Orientals lack that choice. Membership in their groups is not merely the result of a voluntary decision; it is thrust upon them by the prejudice of the whole society. What significance that has in the functioning of these ethnic groups will become clearer from a survey of some of the types that operate in American society.

Types of Ethnic Groups

Ethnic groups differ not only in the element that sets them off—whether color, nativity, or religion—but also in other important respects. Their size determines whether they will be able to carry on a round of activities complete enough to satisfy their members. The extent to which the group is concentrated in a single social and economic position and the level of that position influence the regard in which the rest of the society holds it. Most important of all, these groups differ in the degree to which membership is voluntary.

The people of color stand at one extreme. Most of them lack any choice whatever; they are born what they are and can rarely divest themselves of their affiliation. Furthermore, the prejudice of the rest of society stamps them as inferior. Some states forbid miscegenation by law; and almost everywhere discrimination limits these men to restricted residences, occupations and educational op-

portunities that further bind them to the group. As a result their own loyalties are mixed with resentment. They may be proud of their color, but they cannot help but regard it also as a badge of shame.

Most immigrants are also limited in their choice. The Italian or Puerto Rican who lands in New York, the Mexican who arrives in El Paso or Los Angeles knows that he is different from the natives. He moves into a community of people who speak his own language, stand at his own social level and share his ideas and tastes. The group is helpful because it provides continuity with his past and aids in the adjustment to the new environment. The exceptional few, who become mobile either through gaining wealth or through talent or education, can leave the group or retain whatever degree of affiliation they desire.

The second generation has more problems. It is born into an immigrant group but is marginal in the sense that it acts both inside and outside the world of its parents. To the extent that its members seek to advance, they often find the old community a handicap and wish to break away. To the extent that they encounter prejudice and are rebuffed they may be driven back into it. An ethnic group of which many members are in this position is often unstable and torn by conflict.

In the third generation and after, these difficulties subside. Such people are more secure, better adjusted, less torn by divided values. Their ethnic associations are reduced to cultural, sentimental or religious bases, compatible with their full participation in the wide opportunities of the whole society. They have great latitude in making choices and fewer conflicts than their parents.

The group which rests entirely upon a religious foundation is the most secure of all, for such differences are universally recognized as valid in the United States and indeed are protected by constitutional guarantees.

Prejudice thus has an important effect upon the health of ethnic groups. The hostility of the outer society strengthens rather than weakens affiliations, but it does so by restricting the choices of the members. It thereby emphasizes the negative rather than the positive aspects of belonging. The victims of prejudice come to regard their group as a prison that curtails their freedom rather than a means of serving their individual needs.

The Values of Difference

The effects of prejudice are unfortunate because they obscure the means through which the group can assist the individual in adjusting to the mass society in which we live. We have moved beyond the point in which the community consists entirely of similar people, all known to one another. More than 200,000,000 Americans are bound together by the ties of a highly complex industrial society. No man can remain alone or stay put in the same place or avoid frequent contact with strangers. Yet the necessity of frequent moves, of continual exposure to unknown faces and to unfamiliar ways, puts a great strain on the individual.

When it is voluntary, the ethnic group can act as a buffer between the lonely man and the whole society. It provides him with a meaningful round of activities among people he knows; it supplies him with continuity to his personal past; it strengthens his family life; and it helps him understand himself and his problems.

The ethnic group also contributes to the welfare of the whole society. It lends diversity to, and thus enriches, our culture so that all of us can profit from the combined heritages of the various strands of our population. Even more important, by relieving individual tensions, it contributes to the welfare of the whole society. People who enjoy a sound group life are not as likely as others to become disorganized or to find themselves dependents or social problems.

The Problems of Co-Existence

It is no easy task to achieve harmony among so many diverse groups; and in the past Americans have not always been able to avoid bitter conflicts. Sometimes contact has led to competition rather than cooperation; at other times the very desire to strengthen the group has tended to injure those not in it. In a free society, it is necessary to be vigilant in the watch for such potential sources of dissension.

Since all groups co-exist in the same society, the contacts among them are always in danger of deterioration. Each seeks to develop its own leaders, but must be careful lest it become the tool of personal ambition. The appearance of a machine or the impression of bloc voting creates resentment because the group then seems to put its own narrow interests above those of the whole community. Different views about such issues as birth control or prohibition also generate hard feelings out of the suspicion that one element is trying to impose its philosophy of life on the whole population. There are times when economic and ethnic problems intermesh to produce a combustible situation, as they did in the case of slavery or in the case of the relations of capital and labor early in this century. Even foreign policy can lead to bitterness as when sympathies were divided over American attitudes toward the war between 1914 and 1917, or over the isolationism of the 1930's.

More subtle pressures also create difficulties which may smolder for a long time before they erupt into conflict. Each group develops institutions and habits of action which add to its comfort. It then becomes anxious to maintain its strength by holding the loyalty of its own members, by keeping the next generation within the fold, and by excluding outsiders. All these tendencies imperceptibly generate prejudice against those who do not belong. It is quite natural that similar people should wish to live together, that friends should favor one another on the job or in the business, and that parents should wish to see their children marry within the group. In each case, however, there is but a short step between those desires and the restrictive residential covenant, discrimination in employment, and the belief that various racial stocks are biologically divided from one another. It is not a necessary step, but care is needed to avoid it, for prejudice is a disease to which a pluralistic society is always exposed.

We can guard against such ill effects by remembering that a community which consists of a multitude of groups can only operate effectively when the members of all of them are treated equally. No group in the long run can protect itself by its own efforts; it will only be safe if it helps to create the general conditions under which all will thrive. And no group justifies itself as an end in itself, but only to the extent that it furthers the interests of its individual members and of the whole society.

UNITY OR UNIFORMITY:
THE CHOICE FOR AMERICANS

Is it worthwhile to be different? This is a question Americans are sometimes tempted to ask. Would not our major problems dissolve if we could wash away the vestiges of the past and arrive at a situation in which we shared the same beliefs and practices, even looked alike in outward appearance? Then we could escape all the difficulties created by prejudice and discrimination and avoid all necessity for choice.

Some forces in our society do operate in that direction. Mass production and mass communication impose similarities upon us all. Millions of people all over the country watch the same television program or read the same magazine and learn to talk and think alike. The same media shape their behavior and the economy supplies them with the ready-made clothes and homes that impose an almost identical appearance on them all. But not quite. We are still far from the mass society that some observers think they have made out. But this certainly is one of the most powerful tendencies in our lives. Is it altogether good?

This is a part of the price we pay for the relative abundance we enjoy. It is better to have discount-house suits and shoes than not to have any at all. But we must limit the cost and to do so we must take account of what might be lost if we were to go all the way to uniformity.

What would it be like if everyone were just an American, pure and simple, nothing else? It would mean that each individual would have only one role in society, that of the citizen, and would belong to only one organization, the state. All would then be equal and alike.

All the intermediate organizations in society would disappear. For if there were no important differences, there would be no need for separate churches, hospitals, philanthropic associations and cultural institutions. The individual would become an atom, isolated among millions of others, with but one loyalty—to the government.

We have encountered such people before and know that they were unhappy in their loneliness. When the depression of the 1930's dislodged millions of Americans from their accustomed moorings, they sought an alternative mode of belonging. They provided attentive audiences for the demagogues who then tried to lure them into silver-shirted and other fascist organizations. Earlier social dislocations had produced the membership of the Ku Klux Klan and its counterparts which fed off the eagerness of men without connections to be part of something meaningful. In the United States, such movements flowered but briefly before they withered away; a pluralistic society proved unfertile soil for them. But the fact that other, more homogeneous cultures did offer the ground on which totalitarian tendencies could thrive should alert us to the importance of the saving element in our own situation.

Man is a social being. He cannot live alone. At all the critical moments of his existence he needs the support and involvement of a group. The question is whether it shall be one single overarching group imposed on him or whether he shall be able to choose from among a variety that which best comports with his individual inclinations. In the past, the diverse heritage of the Americans gave a pluralistic answer to that question with consequences reflected in our whole way of life. And whatever we can discern of the future that lies before us would indicate that pluralism retains its value for a people who still wish to be free.

2
indians in the united states

GORDON MACGREGOR

It is not easy to assess the attitudes of non-Indian Americans toward Indian Americans. People who live near the reservations are likely to think of Indians as poor, shiftless, and alien. The Indians number under 800,000 and until recently lived for the most part in the remote areas of only a few states. Most non-Indians had no contact with Indians except as tourists in the West or through the westerns on television and in the motion pictures. The Indian was either the enemy, the ever-present danger on the frontier, or the romanticized noble savage.

Recently, the Indians have emerged in the national consciousness as a repressed and depressed minority. Indians have been migrating to the cities, where, like other poor and under-educated rural migrants, they do poorly in school and require welfare assistance. At the same time, younger, often college-educated Indians have been organizing their compatriots to protest the policies of the Bureau of Indian Affairs and to demand that more assistance be given to the schools and welfare agencies of the cities.

Professor Macgregor surveys the situation of the Indian today and outlines the history that produced the present situation. Professor Macgregor is chairman of the Department of Anthropology at American University, Washington, D.C.

THE PROBLEM OF INDIAN EDUCATION

The education of the American Indians in federal schools began as a means of bringing about their rapid assimilation into American society. Putting the children in boarding schools, teaching the adults the techniques of farming, and Christianizing young and old were the first techniques employed. Little thought was given to the wide differences in the ways of life that tribes had developed in their various natural environments. Less attention was given to the family and tribal customs

First published as "The Context of American Indian Education," in *The Status of American Indian Education: An Interim Report of the National Study of American Indian Education to the Office of Education, U.S. Department of Health, Education and Welfare* (January 1970), Chapter 1.

of child training directed to young boys and girls in becoming Pawnee, Cheyenne, Hopi, or members of other tribal groups and to retaining native customs, ideas, or personality types.

As a result, education did not bring about assimilation and the elimination of Indian life as anticipated. Some acceptance of various aspects of the imposed life did occur and continues. But the holding to many Indian ways and striving to maintain Indian identification and attitudes also goes on.

Indian people have undergone much change, and reservation life has brought about a type of life that is neither Indian in the indigenous sense nor thoroughly American. Their situation is unfortunately an anomaly marked by poverty and great unhappiness and by community and personal deterioration. It can be called a "culture of dependency." This is the context which now must be fully understood and recognized in providing relevant and effective education.

On the federal government's assumption that assimilation of Indians had already gone far and that the association of Indian, white and other children of America would be beneficial, the majority of Indian children have been placed in public schools. Under present policy federal schools are continued only where public schools are inaccessible.

No one can question the principle that early mixing of children of different racial and cultural backgrounds in public schools is desirable from a social and linguistic point of view. But in practice Indian children have frequently experienced the problems of ethnic minorities in largely white American student bodies, such as the lack of administrative concern for the quality of schools in poor communities and poor teacher selection for meeting Indian children's needs.

The value of public school education for reservation Indian children must be judged on its appropriateness and effectiveness in meeting these particular needs and problems of Indians. The causes and nature of their special needs and problems are discussed in this chapter.

HISTORICAL BACKGROUND

American Indians once hunted, fished or farmed in all parts of the United States. They made ecological adjustments to the local natural resources, developing different styles of culture. As colonial and American settlers spread across the country, eastern and middle western tribes were persuaded or forced to give up their original territories for unsettled areas of the West. The focus of this transplantation of population was the Indian Territory that became the state of Oklahoma. A period of concentration on reservations followed, limiting the Indians to small segments of their former territories.

This movement upset the indigenous adjustments of the Indians to their lands. It was also accompanied by pressure to adopt the customs and occupations of the white man. Over time the policy of Indian administration has been variously designated as civilization, assimilation, and participation of the Indians.

With greater sensitivity to the worth of Indian cultures and the rights of Indians to decide on their own destiny, the change process has become more persuasive and permissive than coercive. As a result the periods of eviction and military suppression, of subordination and political control have been followed more recently by an Indian community renaissance.

The processes of change in Indian ways of life have resulted in a great variety of tribal and individual adaptations ranging from complete absorption to rejection of American life. This great variation in adaptation is the fundamental and most complex problem facing Indian education today.

The different Indian responses to introduced change place upon Indian education a need not only to provide for the usual intellectual, psychological and social preparation, but also a need for special understanding and for giving guidance to the Indian child from families and communities still seeking a satisfactory adjustment to the outside world. The objectives of Indian education so perceived require that planning, substantive curriculum formation, guidance and participation with Indian parents and communities must be flexible and adapted to the particular stage of social change of each reservation community.

INDIAN BACKGROUND

To understand these educational problems facing different groups of American Indians today, recognition should be made of the varying cultural backgrounds and historical experiences that have largely determined contemporary Indian conditions.

The problems are made more complex by diverse cultures and ecological adaptations in their background. The Indians formed no great social or political entity nor were they biologically or racially uniform. They spoke two hundred or more languages and sublanguages that belong to sixteen or more language families.

The North American tribes have been classified by anthropologists into culture areas based on common ecological adaptations. Within the United States and Alaska, Indians are grouped on the basis of their subsistence on: (a) hunting sea animals (Eskimo), (b) hunting caribou (Eskimo and Alaskan Indians), (c) deep sea and river fishing (Northwest coast tribes of Alaska and Plateau Indians of Washington, Oregon, Idaho), (d) wild seed and small game hunting (California and in the Great Basin between the Sierra Nevada and Rocky Mountains), (e) buffalo hunting (the area of the Great Plains), (f) limited farming combined with woodland hunting which varied in the intensity of practice by tribes throughout the eastern United States (east of the Mississippi and from the Great Lakes to the Gulf of Mexico), and (g) the intensive agricultural production of corn, beans, squash and other foods by settled village tribes and pueblos (the Southwest). Tribes adopting these ecologies were not exclusive in these areas. Some tribes, such as the Navajo and Apache who invaded the Southwest, became herders and farmers only in early historic times.

In association with the variety of these subsistence patterns, American Indian groups developed different social, political and economic structures, religions, and views of the world and the meaning of life. These differences underlie the great complexity of the differences of groups faced with the necessity of adapting to American civilization which has overwhelmed them. The dispossession of much of their natural resources—two-thirds of that originally given in treaties—and the depletion of wild food resources thrust upon most Indians an immediate need for new ways of making a living. Agricultural Indians who retained land, in Oklahoma and the Southwest, could carry on subsistence practices without conflict. Northwest coast Indians could in time turn to commercial salmon fishing with a new technology. But for the most part the native technologies and lifeways were no longer viable.

Undermining of the economic base of the Indian groups led to dysfunctioning of their social and religious institutions. The breakdown was hastened by the nature of reservation existence and by the strains created by strong governmental and missionary pressures for assimilation. The gradual course of adjustment to a changed environment, which many Indians might have pursued if left free, was interfered with by shifting and confusing government policies. The recent stated desire of Indians "to regain some measure of adjustment they enjoyed as the original possessors of their native land," expressed in the Declaration of Indian Purpose made at the American Indian Chicago Conference in 1961,[1] is predestined to failure if this adaptation is perceived as the whole Indian population becoming dependent on the land and natural resources. The adjustment will come only with increasing participation in the American economy.

Commercial irrigated farming, commercial cattle herds, wage work in industries and businesses located in Indian communities, tourism, government service and professional life for limited numbers appear to provide the most likely opportunities. The continued adoption of new technological and economic practices, in all probability, will continue to influence traditional family and kinship organization, childhood experience, religious life and other native institutions and outlooks. Further adjustments in the context of the dominant culture seem likely. But Indian communities can continue. These changes need not affect individual identification as a tribal member or as an Indian. Indian culture in all likelihood will persist in many forms beyond mere ceremonies and rituals for sentimental purposes. Communities of Indians can and will endure for a long period just as other ethnic communities continue to thrive in our culturally pluralistic society

TREATY PERIOD

The taking possession of Indian lands coupled with early harsh attempts at "civilization" of Indians were only two of the procedures for elimination of the Indians as a barrier to the winning of the continent. Indians proved more tenacious than anticipated in the defense of their territories and their way of life. In order to remove the Indian as a barrier to the westward expansion of white Americans, other methods were employed. Among the early efforts to reduce the resistance of Plains tribes particularly were military attacks and government encouragement of extermination of the buffalo on the Plains.

Until 1871 the United States dealt with tribes on a treaty basis in an attempt to avoid continuing military conflict and to establish Indian territories. In negotiating with tribes as independent nations the Indians were recognized as having political equality. To the Indians, treaties indicated a cessation of invasions and protection of their lands that they could not achieve by fighting. But among those tribes where raiding, stealing and achievement of personal prestige through fighting was a cultural pattern, there could be no expectation that they would give up this integral part of their way of life.

In this treaty period the underlying concept of establishing land reserves where Indians would be restricted was to make remaining lands available to settlers from the eastern United States. The technique was originated by the English who, in the eighteenth century, attempted to take over lands of the Scottish and Irish clans for settlement and exploitation. While the Indians were very much like these clansmen in resisting and retaliating against the English settlers, they were entirely unlike them through not being peasant agriculturalists who might be turned into farm labor or tenants.

THE PERIOD OF GUARDIANSHIP

In 1871 Congress decided no longer to negotiate with tribes on a treaty basis. Instead, a period of guardianship commenced under which the Indians were subordinated. Every educational effort was directed to a rapid assimilation of Indian children and to the conversion of adult hunters and warriors into small farmers. The program of homesteads then being established for easterners and peasant farmers from Europe was projected for the settlement of Indian families.

Beginning in 1869 and for approximately a half a century lands were allotted but held in trust for all members of tribes until few undivided reservations remained. This policy was destined to almost complete failure. The small size of allotments in areas of limited rainfall, the poor quality of the soil, the erosion that followed plowing up natural grassland ranges, the timbered allotments too small for productive operation, the rocky, infertile soil, and even in California allotted lava beds, led to non- or inefficient use. Rental of allotments proved

the only feasible solution for aged, women and child allottees. The federal practice of granting rights to, but no ownership of, inherited lands further stalemated the allotment-for-assimilation policy.

The strongest barrier, however, was the cultural resistance shown among the great number of non-agricultural tribes. Farming was an unknown technique. Long days of unaccustomed manual labor providing no social reward or status had little appeal to former warriors. Life could be lived, although meagerly, on rations issued to those tribes who had lost their lands and means of subsistence.

Farming and cattle raising came to be accepted, in time, among later reservation-born and more acculturated Indian generations motivated to earn money and obtain a better level of living. Between 1900 and 1916 many Indian families were producing wheat to be ground in the local flour mill and winning prizes in county fairs for displays of farm products and preserved foods in competition with white farm families.

This development of individual and tribal cattle enterprises was severely weakened by a shift in federal policy allowing a rapid increase in the sale and rental of allotments and tribal lands. The justification given was the need for more intensive and efficient beef production on Indian lands for the men overseas in World War I. Although farming and cattle raising were resumed by many Indians after the war, the severe drought and economic depression brought to an end this period of adopting agriculture.

Throughout the reservation history positive Indian efforts to assimilate to the white man's economic system failed because of shifting federal policies which defeated Indian achievements before they became stabilized. New policies thought to encourage assimilation of Indians were not always formulated with the Indians in mind. They were derived from legislative efforts to improve the economic development of the nation. The application of these policies to the Indian came as an afterthought. The shifting from farming to cattle raising to farming and then to subsidized wage work in the Indian projects of the Civilian Conservation Corps program established in the 1930's all reflected these national economic changes.

The so-called CCC-ID program gave many Indians their first experience with regular wage work on their own reservations. The opportunity to live in their own camps and for Indian married men to live in their own homes while being employed in congenial gangs in the out-of-doors provided an occupational pattern that has since become the most desired model of economic activity on reservations. This economic experience also demonstrated the strong Indian preference for wage work and residence in their own communities. But the subsidized character and trend toward permanent dependency have been overlooked by its supporters.

THE PERIOD OF REVIVAL

In 1928 "The Problem of Indian Administration," known as the Meriam Survey, was published. This document was concerned with the appalling conditions on Indian reservations. It revealed the shocking poverty, ill-health, poor education and widespread desperation to which Indians had fallen under the coercion to accept the dominant white civilization. Assimilation policies of sixty years had failed. Yet, more significantly, the supposedly vanishing Indians were not only remaining but increasing as a race. Indian cultures and values, although badly crushed and upset, were persisting. The assimilation policies and the assumptions of the necessity for and of the ease of bringing about cultural change on which these policies had been based were acknowledged as tragic blunders.

In the more liberal and socially aware atmosphere of the New Deal from 1932 to World War II, a turning point occurred in national Indian policy. It was based on a deep recognition of the dire effects of the clash of white and Indian cultures. The Indian Reorganization Act of 1934 and the sensitive leadership of John Collier as Commissioner of Indian Affairs and his associates for sixteen years brought a new approach to bringing Indians into the American economy, society and culture. Decisions were made based on consultation with tribes and operation of new economic enterprises were shifted to Indian leadership. Indian tribes and reservation groups were encouraged to adopt constitutions and charters of incor-

poration, elect councils and enter into business and agricultural enterprises. Loans were made available for corporate and individual economic activities, and funds were established for the higher education of young men and women. A permissive attitude toward surviving Indian life and customs and the right of freedom of worship were adopted.

Not all groups accepted the Indian "New Deal." For the others there were frustrating periods of learning and factionalism. Political conservatives and progressives appeared. Sometimes elected leaders exploited their positions for individual or family benefit. But despite these growing pains a new spirit of hope and confidence now pervaded reservation societies.

The most immediately valuable economic features of the new policy were the cessation of allotting Indian lands, the restoration of surplus marginal federal lands once separated from tribal holdings and a moratorium on selling of individual Indian land holdings. Although this last practice has continued where feasible for some families, the process has been recognized as disastrous for the welfare of the community and has been significantly slowed down.

World War II and the preceding years of national return to prosperity terminated the CCC-ID relief program. Some 25,000 Indians participated in the war, many with great distinction. Older men and women left reservations for employment created by the sudden manpower demands of war-time construction and industry. Indians were employed in various efforts from building munition depots near reservations to welding ships in coastal ports. These off-reservation experiences in the white man's economy and communities brought new awareness of the outside world. The end of war brought many of those in the military forces and employed in civilian war efforts back to the reservation. New knowledge and attitudes acquired led to dissatisfaction with living conditions and with limited education found at home. Returned veterans became a force in demanding literacy, high school training and more economic opportunities. Many achievements toward these goals have since been made by the Bureau of Indian Affairs and by Indian leaders and councils.

In 1951 a reversal of the government's

Indian policy directed at curtailing Bureau activities and eventually terminating all federal protection sent a new wave of anxiety and suspicion of the white man's intent over the Indian country. The economic and political developments and activities of Indian communities were retarded or obstructed. Two reservations exceedingly rich in timber resources were eventually severed from the services of the Bureau of Indian Affairs. Residents of one reservation who accepted huge financial payments for the loss of tribally owned resources received little permanent benefit. Tribal members moved into lower class white neighborhoods and re-formed Indian groups, but they lost the potential of their income from timber and their own lands on which to work out a new community life.

The forced termination program was short lived. The Department of Interior, realizing its policy was undemocratic and extremely unpopular, withdrew to a position of promising that no further termination actions would be taken without the consent of the Indians. However, many national and state politicians still regard the supposed efficacy of rapid termination of the services of the Bureau of Indian Affairs and the sale of Indian reservations as the most efficacious way of "assimilating" the American Indian and solving the "Indian problem."

With the change of administration in 1961 a new approach has been taken in national policy of Indian matters. This stemmed from the report of a task force on Indian affairs which consulted with many Indian leaders over the country, former commissioners and other experts on Indian life. Members of this task force attended the American Indian Chicago Conference where representatives of most tribes, of the National Congress of American Indians, and one hundred fifty non-Indian specialists met under the sponsorship of the University of Chicago. The object was to conduct a major inquiry into present-day Indian conditions and Indian points of view for future federal policy. In this meeting the greatest significance was given to the broad and considered participation of Indians in shaping the direction that future policy should take. Moreover, great importance was also placed on the process and timing of adjustment to allow for their survival as Indians. These steps and the appointment of a new commissioner, a student of Indian life and a member of the task force, restored a more favorable climate of opinion among the Indian people.

The policy of abrupt termination of services has been set aside and a new course adopted promoting the objectives of maximum economic self-sufficiency, full participation in American life and equal citizenship privileges and responsibilities for Indians. The task force has emphasized that Indian support was crucial to the attainment of these objectives and that this should be secured before projects were to be commenced. It was recognized that "Indians can retain their tribal identities and much of their culture while working toward a greater adjustment" and, that for the further enrichment of our society, "it is in the nation's as well as the Indian's best interests to encourage them to do so."

This most recent federal policy returns to the earlier New Deal approach of permissiveness and tolerance of Indian culture and communities. However, it does not reveal altogether a thorough awareness of the complexities and difficulties of the processes of adjustment and attaining stability or of maintaining cultural plurality in a larger dominant society. This latter interest of Indians will be very difficult in a society still committed to the idea of the melting pot for all alien or culturally different peoples. Ultimate assimilation of Indians remains a basic assumption of the new policy, although it seems to be expected that it may take a different form than did the assimilation of the European immigrant in an earlier era.

"Participation in the mainstream of American life"—the phrase used to describe the primary objective of the new policy—cannot take place without economic and social change and acceptance of new values and attitudes and modifying personality structure. This is already taking place in the process of acculturation as individuals move through the stages of native, transitional and assimilated orientation.

Although some Indian groups have adopted cults reviving Indian custom and attitudes, none appear to have reconstructed a truly new and integrated culture. The Pueblos remain traditionally organized and oriented although a steady adoption of Anglo-American customs and attitudes takes place. Young, educated Navajo as an assimilated elite lead their tribesmen toward becoming an economically and politically assimilated community. Navajo young people are moving into the American labor pool and far less frequently continuing their own agricultural operations. Other tribes are undergoing a parallel development.

The Peyote cult, incorporated in some states with the Native American Church, is an attempt to resolve problems of culture conflict and change by amalgamating Indian and white religious practices and belief and establishing standards for moral conduct. However, as an attempt to restore or create new Indian cultures, it is not truly a revitalization movement. It follows the pattern of seeking supernatural power to meet the present-day culture conflict. Peyotism intermingles customs and ideas from many tribes, essentially those of the Plains, with the addition of the ritual consumption of the non-narcotic or non-habit-forming peyote or cactus button. This trait was borrowed from Indians of Mexico. In its general orientation the Peyote cult gives support to the growing Pan-Indian movement.

The National Congress of American Indians gives political expression to Pan-Indianism. The various annual ceremonials inviting the participation of members of all tribes, including the election of a Miss American Indian, encourage amalgamation of all Indians. However, these trends toward a generalized Indian cultural pattern are more symbolic of the Indian desire for group identity and prestige rather than indicative of formation of an Indian subgroup in the larger population.

THE CONTEMPORARY CONTEXT

This summary review of historical events has been presented to underscore the nature of the social and psychological impact of the federal government upon the Indians as the bearers of different cultures. The additional impact of private individuals and groups on Indians has not been as well documented. However, certain trends are apparent. There has been a continual legal and extra-legal appropriation of Indian resources by outsiders. Early attitudes of fear of Indians changed to contempt as the Indian hostility was suppressed. Strong prejudice and exclusion from public facilities have characterized relationships with the dominant white group. Missions have had a socially disrupting effect in the conversion of individual Indians to Christian belief and morality.

At the same time, many associations for the protection and social advancement of Indians have worked assiduously for improved conditions and the advancement and full recognition of Indian rights. While these efforts have been helpful, their varied purposes and representations of the white man's ideology and customs have contributed to both confusion and doubt about their true character and intentions.

Conditions have improved over those which were described in the Meriam Survey, but serious economic problems still exist. In general, Indians are poor and a too-high percentage is unemployed or unemployable. On reservations with agricultural resources, only a minority participate in farming and stock raising. Incomes are supplemented by periodic wage work, subsidized poverty program employment and general welfare assistance. Introduction of new industrial plants and urban relocation of families have not significantly alleviated the poverty problem. In fact, urban relocation has contributed to the growing concern over difficulties of urban Indians. In many of our large cities, many families do not make a satisfactory adjustment to this new environment. Many unemployed create demands on welfare agencies and problems for schools which urban agencies are often reluctant to assume.

Great improvements have been made in medical care and health education services but the incidence of disease particularly of the infectious type of tuberculosis remains high. Life expectancy is much lower than for the general population. Infant mortality rates have been reduced but are still excessive.

The educational level of the Indian populace has improved annually and on some reservations matches the eleventh grade median for the states in which they are located. Participation in state and national political affairs has accompanied the raising of educational levels and the acquisition of English. Many Indians fully recognize the important role of politics in their affairs and they are increasingly articulate and active in communicating their desires and opinions. Indians became citizens in 1924, but widespread interest in becoming active participants by assuming citizenship responsibilities has developed only since World War II.

In their attempts to cope with and to find their place in modern society, Indians have responded differently toward efforts to assimilate them into the larger society. The stages of development and the forms of acculturation still reflect the variety of cultural and historical backgrounds. Recalling the diversity of Indians of the various cultural or ecological areas, it is not surprising that the adaptation to change has gone through several and often a combination of lines of development.

The Navajo with their extensive and mainly unallotted area have been able on a group basis to incorporate new ways from the outside world. But when the Bureau of Indian Affairs attempted to direct changes which focused on the individual and which led to his separation from his society and culture, it was done without a realization that it counteracted the constructive nature of the Navajo process of group adaptation.

The Pueblo peoples have under great duress made significant changes. However, they have, through a closed society and a secret religion, channeled these changes into the secular cr economic and social segments of their culture. This remains well integrated and receives group support. This life faces an internal challenge from the younger generation to the degree that the religious structure and ritual demands interfere with jobs, careers and acculturation in the outside world.

The small bands of the far western states have been more easily assimilated, since their aboriginal cultures were primitive in terms of human cultural development and because poverty and starvation were frequent. Yet many are not fully integrated into the neighboring economy or society. When unemployed they reside in small rancherias of their own as marginal and excluded people.

All Indian groups now appear to be increasingly drawn into the economic and social life of white society, but some aspects of custom change more rapidly than others. This means weakening of the integration of the ways of life developed over centuries. Technology, social organization, religion, ideology and language are abandoned at different rates.

Many Indian communities have not yet found or created satisfying replacements. New and innovative cultural institutions will undoubtedly be developed as Indian groups discover new social ways that are meaningful and functional in their changed situation. But as the aftermath of these losses, individual distress, apathy, frustration and antagonism appeared where power, autonomy, status and prestigious roles once functioned to give life meaning. Unreliable means of obtaining subsistence and the inability to cope with a dominant and often prejudiced society have become common. These are essentially symptoms of the difficulty of adaptation when little or no opportunity for obtaining guidance or insight into the nature of the change process was provided.

If schools, and this applies to public, private, and missionary as well as to federal schools, are to be successful in the education and socialization of Indian children and youth in contemporary American society, they must recognize and respect the vast basic differences among the Indian peoples. Moreover, the schools must support the efforts of these peoples to retain those aspects of their cultural identity that they still value. The schools, to the extent possible, also must assist the Indian peoples to develop new social and political institutions to help them in the process of adapting their community life to contemporary society.

American Indians on reservations today still comprise many distinct groups primarily conditioned by two factors: their location and resources and their degree of adaptation to white American life. To view American Indians otherwise, especially as a single minority group in the population of the United States requiring uniform programs for development, is to be oblivious of the complexity of the issues and problems affecting them. Policy, services, transition can only be realistically effected within the framework of the existing tribal or reservation community groups.

WELFARE DEPENDENCY

For many tribes the loss of their original hunting territories and game thrust them into extreme poverty and dependency upon federal rations, social services and more recently upon the welfare payments for the aged, the blind and dependent families and general assistance. For some families financial aid or subsidized employment on the reservations has continued for generations. No accurate history or measure of the extent of welfare assistance that has been paid out or is being paid out annually to Indians can be established. Federal records of categorical aids are not kept according to the race of recipients. At least eight states with sizeable but not the largest Indian populations provide general welfare assistance to Indians on the same basis as it is granted to other needy families.

It is estimated that more than twice as many Indians are helped by state and county welfare funds than are assisted by the Bureau of Indian Affairs. The Bureau gave general assistance funds to 15,330 households with 53,770 individuals for varying periods of need during the fiscal year of 1968.[2] In addition, 3,893 received foster home or institutional care for the handicapped. A relatively high proportion of Indian children, with the exception of Navajo and some Alaskan children, are orphans or half orphans. Many are emotionally or psychologically disturbed cases from broken homes and extremely poor social environments. Many of these cases are placed in Bureau of Indian Affairs boarding schools.

The so-called welfare case load dramatizes the negative character of the change experience upon child training and development. A high proportion of Indian children within the welfare group are growing up ill-nourished, in poverty-stricken homes with disorganized family life. Child care is frequently inconsistent and irregular. Such home environment produces anxious, insecure personalities frequently suffering from deep and complex psychological problems early in life. Many other children become confused from the early childhood experiences received from traditionally oriented Indian child-training practices by older adults. Other children have emotional difficulties arising from the partially understood American child-training practices taught to young parents by white teachers, visiting nurses and social workers. The conflicting patterns derived from different child-training traditions or disorganized family life lead children to question what is right or wrong and good or bad, both in terms of behavior and of moral imperatives.

Funds will continue to be needed for the unemployable, physically and socially handicapped, but demands for more welfare assistance will increase unless some other attack is made on the problem of dependency and negative social adjustment of many reservation families.

This need to strengthen personality formation through child training challenges education. But it must not be considered the total responsiblity of schools and pre-school programs. It should be seen and understood as a need for better socialization of Indian children by parents and community members. Children require consistent and constructive preparation for their social, spiritual, psychological and economic life. This responsibility falls back on the Indian community and their men and women leaders who would help in overcoming the problems of cross-cultural transition. Coordination of efforts by community service agencies and Indian leaders to deal with this problem has barely begun.

ACCULTURATION AND ASSIMILATION

Although it is widely recognized that the American Indian population today is derived from many aboriginal cultures and linguistic stocks, this fact is frequently forgotten or ignored in the programs established to assist them in their adaption to the larger society. The common term "Indian" allows educators and administrators to fall into the common assumption that all unassimilated Indians are relatively alike and share common problems. National policy, legislation and federal services "for Indians" reinforce this view.

In the sense that many Indians such as the Navajo have borrowed material elements and adopted customs from the surrounding

American society which have displaced or added to the native Indian cultural life, we may speak of them as acculturated. They have continued a degree of cultural and social stability but further change is inevitably leading them to adopt behavioral patterns and attitudes closer to those of American life. Other tribes have virtually lost or are in the process of losing their native customs and institutions and are nearly assimilated. These social processes have not been ones of simple cultural aggrandizement or substitution from one cultural pole to another. Individuals have experienced cultural change at varying rates and with varying results. Many suffered from the loss of the traditional customs, social institutions, social roles and the satisfaction afforded by their former existence and the non-acceptance of new ways enforced upon them. Others are midstream in the process, fluctuating at times toward Indian behavioral and attitudinal patterns and at other times toward white American social norms. Still others have, from family training, school and employment experiences, and a high motivation to make a living and gain social status, become personally adapted by permanently moving away from Indian community membership.

The stages of adjustment have led to at least four groups within the spectrum of the social-change process. Adopting the classification made by George and Louise Spindler of the Menominee of Wisconsin,[3] there is first a *native-oriented type* brought up as Indians within the contemporary Indian pattern. The contacts with whites and the life outside the reservation are only marginal and irregular. People in this group think and act as Indians. These are frequently spoken of as full-bloods although they may have mixed racial antecedents. A second group form is the *transitional type.* This consists of individuals who, to varying degrees, are moving out of Indian life but have not fully accepted white American society customs. They are marginal and from their culturally impoverished condition often act in unpredictable and asocial ways. They can be alternately passive and violent, apathetic or emotional.

A third type is the *acculturated Indians* who, through personal qualities and educa-

tion, change in personality characteristics, accept new social patterns and move into the white American lower-class society. A few may move in the direction of other ethnic or racial groups (for example Mexican-American) with whom they live and intermarry. Within this general type is an essentially *assimilated elite group* of individuals who not only have adopted the white American middle-class cultural patterns, but have acquired attitudes and values that reflect the high value placed upon achievement characteristic of the success-oriented, middle-class American personality and status. Among these people are those who have left the reservation voluntarily to work and especially to enter federal employment where they are a favored group finding greater security in government service. They pursue roles providing financial and social advancement, but still enjoy recognition as Indians.

Social science studies have also shown that Indian tribes of several of the major cultural groups share some psychological characteristics that sharply distinguish them from white native-born Americans. These widely exhibited Indian psychological features include non-demonstrative emotionality and reserve accompanied by a high degree of control, autonomy of the individual, ability to endure pain, hardship and frustration without an outward show of distress, and a positive value on bravery and courage expressed to different degrees in aggressive behavior in military exploits, and usually a particular fear of the natural world as dangerous.[4] The degree to which these features appear varies with cultural groups.

From the point of view of education and understanding the diversity of Indian adjustments under the direct and indirect pressures to assimilate in the white American society, recognition of the nature and stability of this psychological pattern becomes extremely important. Among the native- or traditionally oriented the Indian personality structure and attitudes have persisted through group retention of early child-training customs. Those in the transitional group, in spite of showing a superficial acculturation in dress, language, food and housing habits, retain the basic characteristics of Indian personality. Understanding these personality characteristics helps to explain the stoicism, unwillingness to speak up in groups or publicly compete or seeming irresponsibility of parents over the relatively autonomous Indian child—characteristics which have so long baffled and often angered white teachers and other service personnel.

Extensive psychological or personality transformation appears to be associated with the well-acculturated Indian who adopts the demands for status achievement, the time patterns and work habits leading to success and rewards in white American society. When existing barriers to achievement are reduced and new motivations appear under new and rewarding economic and social conditions, reformulation of Indian life goals and personality configurations can be expected to emerge.

Acculturation and assimilation as culture change are not the only dimensions by which contemporary Indians are to be evaluated. Biological change, *although this is difficult to ascertain and should not be measured by the degree of "blood quantum,"* and psychological change, which is broadly measurable in personality configuration, need to be new concepts considered in developing new educational and socialization procedures.

CONCLUSION

One comes to the end of this description and analysis of the situation facing the education of Indians with the conclusion that the educational need is not just one of preparation of the Indian individual for participation in the outside world and for understanding himself, but also one of providing understanding of the social context and the problems and processes of cultural change from which Indians can determine their social and economic adjustment. In this sense the challenge to Indian education is the guidance in socialization of the Indians in the context of living in two social worlds and not the single one of continuing pressure for assimilation. If they are to be helped in making personal adjustments and in the development of a better community life, they must be provided with the knowledge and skills with which to arrive at decisions of their own making for their future.

NOTES

[1] Nancy O. Lurie, "The Voice of the American Indian: Report of the American Indian Chicago Conference," *Current Anthropology* 2:5 (December 1961), 478-500.

[2] Unpublished data, Bureau of Indian Affairs, January, 1969.

[3] George D. and Louise S. Spindler, "American Indian Personality Types and Their Sociocultural Roots," *Annals of the American Academy of Political and Social Science* 311 (May 1957), 147-157.

[4] Spindler, *op. cit.*, 153-156.

3
newcomers from the southern mountains

ROSCOE GIFFIN

To most Americans, the term minority group *calls up a picture of people racially different from the majority of Americans, such as the blacks, the Indians, and the Orientals. Or it may suggest a group with a different religion, such as the Jews, or with a distinctive culture, such as immigrant Hungarians or Turks. It may come as a surprise to find a white Protestant group of English ancestry, which has lived in the United States for 200 years, regarded as a minority group. Yet the people from Appalachia show all the traits associated with groups more conventionally regarded as minorities. The mountain regions from which they come are poor. Educational standards are low. When the mountaineers migrate to the cities, they immediately become a problem. Their children do poorly in school and are prone to juvenile delinquency. The men are unskilled and thus susceptible to unemployment. Many are on the relief rolls. The family structure is unadapted to urban living. They meet with prejudice and discrimination; they retaliate with hostility and suspicion.*

The resemblance of the problems of the southern mountaineers to those of migrant rural blacks, Indians, and Mexicans points up the fact that in part at least, minority problems result from the nature of American society rather than from the traits of the minority groups. Rural America of the nineteenth century was a patchwork of differentiated groups earning their livings locally and in unskilled work and segregated from one another by law and custom. An industrialized society requires standardization among its members. They must have the education and skills necessary to get jobs in a technical economy. They must learn how to live in urban areas without becoming socially disorganized. They must be mobile enough to go where the jobs are and flexible enough to adjust to living conditions different from those they were raised in. They need to consume on a high level to achieve the "American standard of living" and to bolster the market economy with their consumption.

Roscoe Giffin evaluates the problems and strengths of the southern mountaineers in this frame of reference. Until his death in 1962, Mr. Giffin was professor of sociology at Berea College, Kentucky, in the southern mountains. He had firsthand acquaintance with the people of Appalachia and their social situation.

Reprinted from Roscoe Giffin, "Newcomers from the Southern Mountains," paper delivered at the Institute on Cultural Patterns of Newcomers (Chicago: Welfare Council of Metropolitan Chicago, 1959), pp. 15-40. Reproduced by permission of the author and publisher.

Some people stoutly maintain that there is nothing which distinguishes Southern Mountain people from any one else in the U.S. I submit that going to church on Saturday night in the summer time plus families of eight and ten children in 1957 are indicators of significant cultural differences.

Despite this evidence and much more which is available, people of and from this area are often very resistant to being given any specific identification. For purposes of this presentation they will be identified as Southern Mountain Newcomers. . . .

There are important variations among the approximately 7,000,000 people in the Appalachian South which complicates the task of making valid generalizations. And a third difficulty is the lack of adequate research data to document some of the hypotheses.

Magnitude and Causes of the Migration from the Southern Mountains

The Southern Mountain States have long been an important source of population for such industrial states of the Midwest as Illinois, Michigan, Indiana, and Ohio. I have estimated that nearly 800,000 people have moved out of the counties in the Appalachian South between 1950 and 1956. Not all of these have come north by any means for Southern cities are also growing. But there is much evidence that the road north has attracted a great many of them.

Many factors are involved in this population movement. Perhaps if we classify them by area of origin and area of destination, the factors can be summarized readily. Within the mountain states in which these people originate the following factors are operative. First, dissatisfaction with the possibilities of life there is increasing as a result of receiving and accepting the knowledge and values of urban living. Second, the population-carrying capacity of the resources of the area are already strained to such a point that further population increases will reduce the already low levels of living. The area as a whole is characterized by high birth rates, declining agricultural resources, and only a few opportunities for industrial employment. A third cause of the outmigration is the rapid mechanization of coal-mining and the declining demand for coal. . . .

Most of the [migrants] are young and in reasonably good health. They thus offer many years of productive labor. Despite all the handicaps for urban living which their situational background imposes upon them, we can take encouragement from the evidence that, like most people, they have a capacity to learn the ways and demands of a new environment.

They have no responsibility for the fact that they are "Old American" stock, but in the scales of group membership by which people are judged in America, the balance is tipped in favor of such groups. I have received numerous favorable reports of the work of Southern Mountain men in factories and with machinery. This particular strength comes almost as a "natural" to men who have been reared on the near-subsistence farm of the mountains or who have worked in mines and logging woods. Their ability to keep their elderly cars and trucks operating is evidence of a mechanical ability and ingenuity which few people I know possess.

Places of Residence Are Dominantly Rural and Relatively Isolated in a Mountainous Region

The social, economic, and political manifestations of a rural background have been noted frequently in recent research studies, such as those of the Detroit Area Study.

A recent Indianapolis study showed that the limited capacity of Southern migrants to make new friends constituted one of their major sources of adjustment difficulty.

For many, . . . concerned with the adjustment problems of such migrants as these, the difficulties are those of involving them in programs of churches, neighborhood centers, or helping their children develop a feeling of belonging in large urban schools. The areas of our great cities in which the Southern Mountain people concentrate are generally lacking in active churches. The building may be there, but their congregations have moved away. In many cases the staffs of such churches have done all they knew to get the newcomers to participate.

I know of a Cincinnati case where only one family from the hills attended church after seven years of concentrated effort by the church staff. Finally, the staff gave up and turned to the task of ministering to its own membership. But I'm sure it will not be long before this church moves out to the suburbs where its membership is.

There are no easy remedies for this problem. One difficulty seems to be the tendency of rural people to define large impersonal organizations as unfriendly. Also, there is the fact that they simply are not accustomed to regular church attendance as are many urban people. For many in the mountain areas, going to church has been something you do only in the summer while the revivals are being held. . . .

Most of the Area Must Be Characterized as One of Low Economic Productivity

The meaning of a thin economic base for urban adjustment can perhaps only be understood as we get some comprehension of the effects of poverty upon attitudes and behavior. Although most of our understandings of this are derived from studies of urban poverty, there are many insights which can be appropriated and applied to the case of rural poverty.

Not all mountain families have adequate food, nor are their houses always warm in winter despite the general abundance of fuels. Allison Davis has shown how from such circumstances come anxiety patterns which may show up as excesses of eating and getting warm when resources are abundant instead of rational budgeting for future needs. I wish I had a nickel for every time I've heard a middle-class mountain person of secure income condemn the improvidence of coal-mining families. Poverty seems to develop a certain defensive hardening and insensitivity which James Plant interprets as a product of insecurity and deprivation. There is no reason why we should not expect to find all of these manifestations among the Southern Mountain Newcomers. . . .

The Relatively Large Families Perform Numerous Functions Through a System of Roles Allocated by Age and Sex in Which the Father Is Generally the Authority Center and Mother the Affection Center

Both in terms of structure and function the extended families to which this proposition refers are in conflict with the need to prepare children for migration. In place of rigid systems of role allocation, there is a need for flexibility; and instead of activities mainly in concert with other members of the family, there is a need

for variety of personal contacts. Rather than seeking to bind its members to it by continual involvement in activities centering in the family, a major function should be to prepare children emotionally for leaving home by a gradual process of separation and new experiences.

But the ties that pull these people toward their childhood home are not those only of family. There are also the bonds to place, to the beauty and serenity of the hills. As one who left behind the mountain grandeur of Colorado in exchange for those broad, green plains of Urbana, Illinois, I think I can empathize with the writer of "The Hills of Home." And also with the mountain man who left a good Indiana farm to return to Kentucky because he just couldn't get along without some hills to "lean his eyes agin" when he got up in the morning. . . .

Child-rearing Practices Are Generally Permissive in the Early Years of Life and Continue for Boys as Regards Their Outside Activities and Choices of Age-related Activities

Research studies on this point are few and far between, but the writings of various novelists and able observers all seem in line with my own numerous observations on the permissive character of parent-child relations. One of the most interesting documents in this field was written by a former New York City nursery school teacher, Claudia Lewis, in her book, *Children of the Cumberlands.* Perhaps such permissiveness is but a general characteristic of families with numerous children, crowded living quarters, and limited and uncertain incomes. Numerous studies of lower-class urban families point to this conclusion. . . .

In the hills the children seem to be rather free to roam about the roads, woods and streams doing much as they please. This is not necessarily a healthy pattern, but does not exist amidst the variety of dangers of the city. Transplanted to the city such permissiveness becomes neglect. In view of the small living quarters available to most of these newcomers and their own behavioral patterns, there is an obvious need for play areas, made safe both by absence of traffic and by the presence of adult supervision.

Houses Are Generally Small and Cheaply Constructed

Both in absolute size and more importantly in terms of the number of persons per dwelling unit, the houses of the area must be classed as "small." I have run some data through my slide rule and come up with a few figures which might be thought of as an Index of Crowding. For the mountain counties of Kentucky the index ranges from 100 up to nearly 125, but for the urban counties it ranges around 70. In the Midwestern states the index stands at about 60. It is no exaggeration to say that living space per occupant in Leslie County, Kentucky, is less than half that available on the average in Illinois.

In such crowded houses there is an obvious problem of order. How families of four, six, eight children even keep out of each other's way in such small quarters remains a mystery to me. In my own interviewing experience in the mountains, I've yet to enter a home in which the beds were not made, regardless of the time of day. And remember living room and bedroom may all be the same.

There is some evidence that such order is purchased at the price of harsh authoritarianism which demands conformity from the children, and the repression of hostility among the family members. The scope of this authority among farm families extends also to the work-sets. One careful student of mountain culture who lived in many homes while gathering his data has offered the hypothesis that the displacement of repressed feelings may explain the widespread bickering, lawin', and various forms of conflict which are so obviously present in Southern Mountain neighborhoods.

Religious Beliefs and Practices Are Dominated by the Fundamentalist and Literalist Interpretations of the Bible, and, Though Not Promoted by Active Church Organizations, These Beliefs Permeate the Society

It is considerably easier to provide evidence for the low levels of church participation than for the idea of religious beliefs permeating the society. Membership rates in the eastern mountain areas of Kentucky are probably not much above 20 percent of the population, and when we note further the infrequency of services for rural churches and the general shortage of pastors, it is evident that participation rates will be well below those of our urban areas.

The degree to which religion permeates the society is difficult to measure. It's something you learn about as you listen to and talk with people, as you listen to school children, note the signs along the highways and in the country stores. The following summarizes the matter well: "To an outsider coming in, it is a source of wonder how universally religion is recognized in the mountains. Practically everyone acknowledges its claims, whether he does anything about them or not. Almost no one opposes or deprecates religion."

Emphasis on a hereafter, lovely in its promise of tangible goods and a reversal of the ranks of the present society, has been noted frequently by observers of religious behavior among the poor. Rural church services in the mountains among the various "holiness" groups are noted for their extremes of emotional display. To interpret this as a culturally acceptable outlet for normally restrained emotions would seem to be a logical extension of the preceding analysis.

Education Through the Schools Has Been Serving the Rather Minimal Needs for the 3 R's in a Family-centered, Low-Productivity Economy Infused with Other Worldly Values

Throughout the rural farm areas of the Southern states the proportion of adults, 25 and over, whose formal schooling stopped before the completion of the 8th grade averages close to 75 percent. In rural non-farm regions two-thirds is a fair approximation.

In recent years much interest has been focused on the dropout problem. In one study of the percentage of children enrolled in the fifth grade in 1943-44 who graduated eight years later from high school, Wisconsin topped the list with 80 percent; Illinois was 65, well above the national average of 52. The Southern states with mountain counties ranged from a low in Georgia of 22 percent to 41 in West Virginia. The Kentucky figure of 35 percent means that only 35 out of every 100 in the fifth grade as of 1943-44 finished high school within eight years. We are on the upward road in this regard but the vista that I see ahead is long and steep.

Such data can only mean that the vast majority of the Southern Mountain Newcomers will have received inadequate formal education, judged by urban standards. For both the teachers of children and those who would find some way to involve the older newcomers in adult education, getting acceptance of the value of schooling is a difficult undertaking. Most of our schools are probably oriented to the values of the middle class and taught by representatives of this class. Such values are not part of the experience world of most people from the mountains, and their values are by the converse not part of the experience world of their teachers and those who would help them.

The present concern with dropouts, and the discovery of the extent to which this is concentrated among lower-status persons has intensified the concern of educators to find some way to bridge these cultural worlds. We have plenty of evidence that these people have adequate learning capacity. The problem is one of diffusing to them the values and experiences which the educational system has to offer.

The Leisure Time of Adults and Children Is Not Usually Organized Around Competitive Activities

Rural life in the mountains has a relaxed quality about it which may lead one to the erroneous conclusion that they never work hard. This is far from the truth as anyone knows who has shared in the tasks of a household of numerous children but devoid of running water, automatic heating, and the like. The largely unmechanized agriculture requires a large output of energy, and those who cut the timber from precipitous mountain slopes or mine the coal are hardly engaged in sedentary occupations. Such activities surely do not call for a game of golf or tennis, when the day's work is over. "Jus' settin'" on the porch is much more appropriate. . . . .

It Is Expected that Fear, Pain, and Hardship Will Not Be Expressed, and Demonstrations of Affection and Joy Are Subject to Cultural Controls

I have no statistical measurement of the extent to which mountain people are conditioned to repress open expression of the feelings associated with hardship, pain and fear. Pride is of course involved in these phenomena, but one psychiatric social worker has written of the way in which coal miners drive themselves back to the mines, never admitting their fears, until for some the repressions come forth as a characteristic neurosis.

And then I recall a conversation with a Red Cross worker in Hazard, Kentucky, during the great flood there last January and February. She spoke of having worked in disaster situations in many parts of the nation, but she had never encountered people so unwilling to reveal the extent to which they had been damaged by the flood. Perhaps some of the high rejection rates noted by Selective Service in this area is a result of the patterned emphasis on not admitting the need for medical care and taking steps to get it. . . .

The need the children show for openly expressed affection is an observation which has been impressed on me repeatedly and which others who visit mountain schools notice. To get close to a warmly affectionate adult, to touch the person—these seem experiences of great value to mountain children. From what I know of their family life, this search for affection is understandable.

The Rights of Individuals to Independence of Belief and Action Are to Be Vigorously Defended Against Criticism and Interference by Others

The two aspects of this proposition probably find their best documentation in novels and stories of mountain life, plus the daily newspapers of the region. Both the independence and vigorous defense of this independence probably have their cultural roots in isolated rural living, historic rebellion against the landed classes of the seaboard states, and the cotton economy of the South, and the permissiveness of child-rearing practices.

I find such independence manifesting itself in the "right-to-differ." One expects this right for himself, and extends it to others. But those who differ must adopt a laissez-faire attitude toward each other's differences. Among many examples of this spirit let me cite a few. On learning about a unique way of house construction proposed by a visitor whose idea had been subject to much scoffing by urban acquaintances, one mountain man remarked, "It's a free country, ain't it? A man's got a right to do what he wants." . . .

Racial integration in schools has taken place in numerous mountain counties of eastern Kentucky and West Virginia without serious difficulties. For about 30 years following the Civil War the student body of Berea College was about equally divided between white and Negro, and our integration today, though on much smaller scale, has been without difficulty. I submit that such events as I have mentioned could not have occurred unless the culture of these people gave them the expectation of accepting the different.

To have someone out of the South make such a statement today must indeed give rise to honest doubts. I am aware that there are thousands of low-status whites coming into Northern cities bearing a heavy load of prejudice toward all sorts of differences. But I do not believe my mountain neighbors have been the victims of this spiritual disease quite so intensively. Those responsible for programs calling for integration where Southern Mountain Newcomers are involved can, I believe, act with confidence that clearly stated and well-administered programs will be accepted with tolerance.

Conclusion

As with other migrant groups who have come to Chicago a considerable amount of acculturation of the newcomers is to be expected; many of their children will lose most evidences of their mountain background. But many of them will simply exchange the status of "newcomer from the Southern Mountains" for the status of lower class.

We have every reason to expect the continuation of this migration-stream if the following assumptions hold true: first, the continued growth of employment opportunities in the Chicago metropolitan area; second, the continuation of the high effective fertility rate now present in the mountains.

One economic analyst has concluded that eastern Kentucky has presently twice as many people as can be adequately employed. There is good reason to believe this applies to much of the rest of the mountain South. Presently most of these people are deeply attached to the values of land ownership and farming. Industrial employment will not attract them except on terms far beyond what employers would be willing to offer. If ever the expectations of these people rise above the level which can be met by staying on their small farms, the potential stream of out-migrants will have expanded greatly.

The satisfactoriness both for the newcomers and the old-timers of future movements of population groups such as this one would seem to depend upon the following conditions. First, if helping agents can obtain and make use of insights into not only the cultural background of the newcomers but also the meaning of the urban situation for them, then a more beneficial adjustment for all can result. Second, I believe there is no doubt that a better solution must be found for the problems of housing and residential areas than has yet been achieved. Third, the youngsters in the mountains need to be prepared for urban adjustment through improving and extending their formal education, through diversifying their social and cultural experiences with other people, and through orienting and training them for the possible kinds of employment the city has to offer.

The accomplishment of this tremendous task requires resources far beyond those which can be supplied by any of the states from which these folks come. Is it possible that those states which get the best years of the newcomers' lives might transfer resources to the states which are responsible for preparing them for adult living?

4
being female in america today: the consequences of cultural images

CYNTHIA FUCHS EPSTEIN

Women are not a racial or an ethnic group and certainly not a numerical minority; indeed, they are a slight majority in the United States. Why, then, include them in a book on minority problems?

Despite their numbers and despite some special protection they have in law, women are in an inferior position; they are discriminated against in jobs and in higher education; they play an unimportant part in the economic and political life of the nation.

According to the Women's Bureau, Fact Sheet on the Earning Gap *(Washington, D.C., April, 1971):*

Comparison of the median wage or salary incomes of women and men who work at full-time jobs the year round reveals that while those of women are considerably less than those of men, the difference was less in 1969 than it had been in recent years. The gap, however, was wider than it was 10 to 15 years ago. For example, in 1955, women's median wage or salary income of $2,719 was 64 percent of the $4,252 received by men. By 1966 the proportion had dropped to 58 percent, where it remained through 1968. But in 1969 women's median earnings of $4,977 were 60 percent of the $8,227 received by men. . . .

The educational background of a worker often determines not only the type of work but also the level of job within an occupation for which he or she can qualify. However, a comparison of the incomes of fully employed women and men workers by educational attainment reveals that women earn substantially less than men who have the same amount of education. Among workers who had completed grade school or 1 to 3 years of high school, women's incomes in 1969 were only 56 percent of men's. Among those who had 5 years or more of college, the proportion was 67 percent. . . .

The gap in earnings varies by major occupation group. It is largest for sales workers (women earn only 41 percent of what men earn) and smallest for clerical workers and professional and technical workers (women earn 65 percent of what men earn). Women's wage or salary incomes showed almost the same relationship to those of men in 1969 as in 1968 for all occupation

Reprinted from *Quadrille* 2, no. 5 (June 1968), pp. 1-3, 9-12. Reproduced by permission of the author and publisher.

groups except service workers outside the home, where the percentage increased from 55 to 59 percent. . . .

Another measure of the gap in the earnings of women and men full-time year-round workers is a distribution of these workers by earnings levels. For example, 14 percent of the women but only 6 percent of the men earned less than 3,000 in 1969. Moreover, 51 percent of the women but only 16 percent of the men earned less than $5,000. At the upper end of the scale, only 5 percent of the women but 35 percent of the men had earnings of $10,000 or more.

A number of people have compared the position of women with that of blacks. This is, I think, misleading in most respects because women do not meet nearly as much discrimination; but the comparison is valid in terms of self-attitudes. Men regard women as inferior in everything except child-rearing and housekeeping, and women have come to regard themselves in the same way. Similarly, there are jobs regarded as suitable only for blacks, and blacks are thought not to be able to do efficiently the higher-paying, more prestigious jobs. The self-hatred of women and blacks is very similar; both have love-hate attitudes toward the superordinate group (men or whites); both regard themselves with contempt; both suffer from low morale and staying power as a result of self-doubt.

The following essay, an address delivered by Cynthia Fuchs Epstein at Bennington College, examines in more detail how feelings of inferiority on the part of women are caused by cultural attitudes toward them. Dr. Epstein is a sociologist at Queens College.

We are living in revolutionary times in which it is getting O.K. to talk sex, to have sex, and as well to be black, to be Jewish or Catholic, Italian, Greek or Chinese—or soon it will get to be so. Rights to do and be are related. The world today, with the exception of some groups of die-hards, finds the notions of freedom and equality attractive and finds it necessary to pay at least lip-service to the ideals. All cultures are beginning to share and place a positive value on freedom and individual rights to self-realization. Yet there is a certain paradox in these ideological advances. The female half of the world's population is holding back in pressing for its share. The further paradox is that women's advance is slowest in the societies with most freedom of expression and opportunity. In 70 years their proportional representation in positions of influence and professional activity has remained the same. The women are conforming to cultural images which direct them away from opportunity.

But you may disagree. You have been well educated. You believe you can do almost anything you want to. But most of you won't want to—and this is a reflection of a cultural image which begins in the cradle and may have begun before you were born. If you are first-born, for example, chances are your parents forced themselves to do a mental flip to cancel their disappointment at not having a boy.

Even in equal America, our cultural preference is for boy babies and it seems to be a universal preference. Wherever infanticide has been practiced the girl babies are the victims along with the deformed or illegitimate.

Note it is the mothers who choose to nurture their boys rather than their girls—the female of the species has entered the conspiracy which rates the male life as more important than the female life.

In affluent societies life takes on a different meaning. We have enough to nourish the bodies of all, even the deformed. Yet being female often means being selectively undernourished. Even most of our best are deprived of the wide assortment of nourishment which stimulates all the knowledge and emotional zones necessary for operating at fullest potential. Like many people who are selectively fed starches and sweets, and get fat in the wrong places and become sedentary, women have grown lumpy and complacent, fed on a host of secondary gains—big homes, false eyelashes, and power in the PTA. Like the overweight they accept their lot and argue it's just one of those things they were born with. Biology is destiny and once more they like it and it's enough for them. The women can lean on the rationalizations supplied by the Freudian psychologists, the popular media and the generations of males who have a certain vested interest in keeping the women believing them. As Mirra Komarovsky of Barnard pointed out, they are willing to take jobs but not to have careers—they wave the banner of feminity and treat it as if it is some filmy coating which is easily damaged by contact with the spheres so long labeled as male. The women are afraid. At all levels they are afraid, and they are defensive about that fear.

Past college they are afraid to venture to graduate school; if they get that far they are afraid to opt for certain specialties; they are afraid to be lawyers or doctors. If they choose the arts they may be less afraid—but perhaps only in the theatre can they expect to be able fully to achieve their promise if they truly wish to push for it.

Examine yourselves, and your own desires and ambitions and see to what extent you permit them to deviate from common cultural expectations. You are the most elite, well-educated, avant-garde women in the United States at this moment—sharing with just a few others the most "emancipated" outlook, greatest sense of personal freedom and greatest determination to achieve the goals of the great and free society. You will fight for the rights of the blacks to share in the rewards and honors of white society; you are against tyranny, oppression and degradation. You are one of the manpower reserves, a source of talent, in this society. You are the creative, the innovative. If a woman is ever to compose a great symphony she may come from here. If there is to be another Laurencin, Hodgkins, or Marietta Tree, she is apt to come from here. But you don't need to know much about the laws of probability to know that most of you will abort the fetus of creativity, ambition, or even simple productive competence. You'll root it out before it starts growing or won't permit it to be born—you'll drown it in six loads of wash in your two-hundred-dollar washing machine, bury it under a ton of manure on your lawn in Shaker Heights or

even Georgetown, or let it wither in the shade of a stronger force.

Today, or next year, or in five years at most, you and your sisters at other universities will be looking for, or will have found, a man to live with—you hope he will be smarter than you, taller, and certainly you will want him to have more talents and prospects for success. You will then cheerfully look up to this man, defer to his wisdom in the big issues, reserving for yourselves decision in some circumscribed areas of home and child care, be grateful if he treats you as an alert, thinking person. You will cheerfully type his thesis, and thus be too exhausted to think about yours, you'll take a job to see him through law school or through a career in quantum mechanics (and, if you are especially bright, do the statistics for his study). Later you'll keep the kids out of his hair, be charming to his boss or the dean, and subtly play up his talents—and having done all this this you will consider yourself an effective and fulfilled woman. You will be happy in your deference and accept your place without anger, inner hostility, and hopefully without the symptoms of the tired housewife syndrome. You will take a modern dance class once a week, or a sculpting lesson or maybe even give the class yourself.

You certainly will not be Victorian Woman. After all, you know about freedom. You will therefore demand, but subtly, that your sexual needs must be fulfilled by your husband as you fulfill his. Actually neither will have to demand anything since you will both have accepted that love-making, as loving, must be based on equality of concern and delight. It is tacitly agreed that your orgasm may be as good as his.

But you will also agree that you will be not equal, but subordinate in the other things that count—your job will give way to his, you will not make more money than he does, you will not ask him to move to a city where your prospects for work are best. I don't denigrate the victory for equality in the bedroom and concede that there are still good battles yet to be fought. It only seems strange that its champions do not look beyond to the greater arena. But outside the bedroom being a woman in America is an impossible state of being. My advice is not to be one.

You can't help but fail. The culture makes it so.

Your failures, in fact, contribute to the equilibrium of society. Your compliance is necessary not to rock the boat. Perhaps stability cannot be achieved without you all doing your part to depress your desires or propensities at being whole people, and to keep being womanly women as the culture defines it.

If you think I am being overly cynical, again explore your own feelings at this moment. At 40 or 50 I'm sure you will all fight your bigotry and at least welcome to your house the black date of your daughter if you are white, and the white date of your daughter if you are black. If you object you will spend sleepless nights wrestling with the problem, trying to exorcise from your psyche the evil you know lurks within. Before that you'll buy your daughter a Negro doll to help her learn that black skin is only a matter of pigmentation. But will you also buy her a chemistry set, or an erector set? Will you encourage her to climb as high on the monkey bars as her brothers? Was this your experience? Since you are a segment of the best, perhaps so. Women today are being appealed to by the intellectual community and the public sphere and from internalization of those messages by the proddings of their personal psyches to *do*. Once more they find they must measure success in life by the standards of the *entire* society, the standards which in the last few generations have been applied to men alone. Perhaps only the hippies avoid them. Therefore what they do to gain recognition and fulfillment must get them over to the male sphere, yet the culture creates problems of *definition* (what is men's work and what is women's work), problems of *competition* (will "success" spoil chances for marriage or a good marriage), and problems of *feasibility* (how to manage time schedules to fit children and work and hopes and dreams, making love and chicken curry and computer programs).

You are, in a sense, new women in a new America. If you were in college even 15 years ago you would have graduated with concern primarily for the homemaking roles you would hope to acquire and play for only a stopgap job. As part of what Jessie Bernard calls the Mother's Mission, you would be apprehensive about being a proper Spockian mother. Yet you would get few social honors for it.

The person who wishes to achieve notice, power or wealth must produce commodities that the culture deems important goods, or scientific discoveries, or paintings. Although we have steered women away generally from these product-producing activities we have not given her an alternative route to success and honor by rewarding her efforts as homemaker or child-rearer. . . . If she wants honor she must get it the man's way and in the man's world. In the years of the motherhood mania (1946-57) she dropped out of graduate education, work and politics. As a society we try to solve the problem by convincing women that they need not have success. They should be happy to look on as the men in their environment—their fathers, their husbands and often their sons—work for it, and bask in the reflected glory.

But even that doesn't work. Again, paradoxically, women are reared in the culture which sends out the same messages to boys and girls—at least in the early years—to learn, to work hard, to produce, and to expect rewards for thrift, honesty, ability and so on. And then they realize that the rewards are not given in the same way as they are for men—whether it be the reward of advancements, the reward of more money or simply the reward of fulfilling and challenging work.

What to do in the face of these messages, contradictory messages? Most do nothing. The early voting studies showed that non-voters were those people who were often under cross-pressures, for example, from on the one hand a spouse who selected the Republican candidate and a strong parent who selected the Democrat. Rather than weighing the issues and deciding on one, the poor individual would not vote at all. Women are non-voters, and non-deciders. They meet conflict by copping out, by doing nothing, or doing the minimum.

Most of you are pretty militant today, I imagine, on the subject of Negroes' rights to free and equal opportunity to the entire occupational spectrum. I suppose many of you would picket even so sacred an institution as the Wall Street law offices of Cravath, Swaine and Moore if they rejected a black candidate because he was unreliable and wouldn't "fit in" with the crowd there. But do you know— and this is by the profession's own admission— that Wall Street law firms are more likely to hire a Negro than a female, even if both present equally outstanding credentials? Many of you, after four years of fine education, will sit in some employment agency asking for a job which uses your creative abilities and then, without many murmurs, accept a job as a "gal Friday," a common euphemism for secretary-typist, for some ad man or publishing executive who is probably not as smart as you are. In short, you will become, without revolting, the servants of a privileged class, a class you will hope to enter through marriage, not by equal right. You have been conditioned to accept the definitions of the system. You will suspect the women who push too hard of having personal problems.

I imagine many women prefer the home-centered life, feel no great drive to conquer the environment—who think that writing about the virtues of Ajax isn't much more exciting than cleaning the bathrooms with it. But the virtues of the alternatives are not at issue here; what is important is the boundaries on freedom to decide which alternative one would like to pursue. And the fact that those who believe in freedom somehow accept the lack of freedom for themselves and others in their social category. There are many paradoxes in the care and treatment of women. The Barry, Bacon, Child studies of sex-differences in socialization indicate that in a majority of the world's cultures, girls are reared to be nurturant, obedient and responsible. Boys are reared to be self-reliant and to achieve. Thus girls all over the world are bred to be docile and accepting—to be good rather than innovative. In American society, Aberle and Naegele showed that middle-class fathers are proud if their boys have a "bit of the devil" in them but want their daughters to be sweet and pretty. No one wants a "bossy" daughter. Women are bred, therefore, to keep in their place. Women should know their place and we know where their place is.

I do not mean to paint the picture all black. A lot of my college companions put me

to shame today, the women as well as the men. The women who have made the best of both the female and male worlds responded to another set of cultural images which are also available, but underutilized in our society. The doing, the achieving according to personal promise.

But there are enormous problems in doing this and I do not underrate them. Women must face many demands. Consider the role demands on the woman as wife in today's America. (The spinsters have nearly died out as a social category.) The problems are not just problems of image, but of real role expectations—structural demands as the sociologists call them. Those demands which attach to the wife role will lead to conflict with her possible or actual occupational or political role.

First, the American family system in which the husband, wife and children are separated from their kin heavily weights the obligations of the woman's role. The obligations of the mother/wife role are rigorously demanding of the woman.

Unlike the extended family system in which a division of household labor is possible among numbers of kin, the primary responsibility for the conjugal family household falls on the wife. Even though some paid domestic help often is feasible, she must administer the household and, as a manager, is responsible for a very large number of tasks. These responsibilities become *more* numerous with income, class position and number of children. They also seem to proliferate in the middle years of the life cycle. Whether or not all the tasks are essential or could be successfully eliminated does not detract from the fact that they demand decisions and are of a character usually not easy to delegate to others.

Note, too, these tasks are not confined to certain times; food must be planned daily, children's activities occur throughout the day, and in the evening the husband's needs for a sympathetic companion must be met. In clear conflict with this schedule, the professional needs large blocks of uninterrupted time— snatches of time taken here and there are not additive, and snatches of time are all that the housewife can usually muster.

Alternative means of performing household functions assigned to the wife/mother must be sought out if the woman is to be free to enter other activities. First, there are few institutional arrangements on which anyone can really rely (day-care centers for children or bonded housekeepers, for example) and, in addition and perhaps most important, few norms exist governing and legitimizing their use. Second, the woman cannot turn to her husband *automatically* to fill in for her. If a woman's work requires that she travel occasionally or attend professional meetings or if she should simply wish to attend social get-togethers which might bring in clients or provide an arena to air her work problems, she must personally make arrangements for the home to run smoothly in her absence. It is probably rare that a woman can depend on her husband for the same kind of overall supervision of house and children that the husband can be sure of when his wife is home. The wife who works, alas, could use a *wife* (or she could use a change in the cultural view of the husband's role). There have been changes in the definition of children's roles and mothers' roles which create intense demand on the woman. Children's roles have changed so that offspring are dependent *longer* on the family, or the family at least feels responsible longer for its youth. Thus, even though families are now smaller, many child-caring activities have been prolonged. The middle-class mother of recent vintage has also been so sensitized to her role in the development of the child that she is always conscious of the consequence of her habits, techniques and emotions, making the mother-child relationship pervading and depleting her energies. Perhaps this is good and perhaps not—kids today are running from home to escape their over-scrutinizing mamas.

Further, American women's roles often include tasks which are *extensions* of their husbands' occupational roles. Women may become informal (and thus *unpaid*) but necessary members of a work team (like the ambassador's wife, the corporation executive's wife must socialize, become knowledgeable about the work world of her husband and operate within its perscribed patterns). Margaret Helfrich has outlined the basic duties and norms of the executive's wife as:

1. to care for the home, husband and children
2. to manage so that the husband gets a portion of the wife's time
3. to entertain his business associates and their mutual friends
4. to participate in social and civic affairs

Perhaps women who seek this kind of work should have their accomplishments recognized—give Lady Bird [President Johnson's wife] a salary for her efforts to beautify America and be the nation's first hostess and let IBM give the corporation wife a salary for keeping its executives in good spirits and good repair. Either that, or free her to do her own work.

Let us consider American attitudes toward the economics of work and women's place in the occupations.

Since it is common in American society to regard work as a means of livelihood rather than as an avenue for self-expression or self-realization, the case against the middle-class married woman who works is often couched in economic terms. Thus the question often posed is "Does it *pay* her to work?" The reply is expected to be measured in terms of the high expenses incurred by the woman for child-care services, added clothing, daily work expenses, domestic help, expenditure for high-cost convenience foods, and the difference between the costs saved on all items by the full-time housewife's comparison shopping versus the convenience shopping of the working woman.

Working women are taxed at the same rate as men and often at higher rates if their incomes are added to those of their husbands, as they are on most family tax returns. Although the cost of child-care is the most fundamental of a working mother's "business" expenses, no tax relief for child-care is available to any except those women in the very lowest economic strata. Child-care alone can consume a considerable portion of the working mother's salary. (Although much has been said publicly on this issue, including a recommendation of the President's Commission on the Status of Women to liberalize existing provisions for tax exemptions, no legislative action has been taken to implement the suggestion. This suggests that the question is given a rather low priority by the culture.)

Thus work *pays* only those women who *must* work (and perhaps depend on free baby-sitting from kin) and the rare highly paid women professional. When the family books are balanced, the woman's work, at its early stages, is not likely to show a sizeable economic return. In addition, little or no thought is given to the fact that the investment necessary early in many women's careers for child and household care is likely to be returned with interest as the woman advances in her work. Thus, while a male doctor expects to go into debt to buy the equipment for an office or to pay for his training, a woman doctor may not feel as free to borrow to pay a housekeeper, an essential part of the "equipment" she needs to build a practice. It is also probably true that if her family did not have resources, a bank would not give a loan for this purpose, though perhaps this has not been tested. Most likely she would drop or delay her work because she could not afford to be free to work.

The problem varies, however, with the type of work and profession. It is likely that a doctor will receive a relatively good income in the early years of practice; attorneys, however, may not reach this level until their practices are well established, and perhaps not until late middle age. Thus, the woman doctor may have a far better economic reason to stick to her practice than the woman lawyer who knows that economic reward still is far away. It is precisely in the years that a woman *most* needs household help that she is also most apt to make the *least* money. Unless she plans well ahead and has vision and confidence she may be unable to succeed.

But there is no doubt that the career-oriented woman who does make an early investment can make working pay. Almost any professional or business woman makes more money than a domestic employee and each additional year she spends at it, work widens the economic gap between them. American women do not invest in themselves or in their futures, *because they are not taught to*

think that way. Since they do not prepare, train, or plan toward marketing a skill, they most often wind up as secretaries or trainees for relatively low-level jobs. With specialized training, however, it is easier to get a good first job, and be able to get back into the job market should you decide to leave. We can learn this lesson well from other societies.

Perhaps the first rule for the advisor of an American woman about a career is to urge that she at least complete *training* and obtain whatever certification her field requires before taking a leave of absence for childbirth. Since there are few pressures in our society to urge women to think about the time when they will want to work, this is a crucial step.

The life-style of Americans, especially with regard to housing and the character of American geography—its vastness, its rural-urban configuration—also has many consequences for women's work habits.

Women do not display the same mobility patterns as men; unlike bachelors, single women do not travel to find work opportunities. This is partly because women are not given resources by their families to travel and seek careers, and once married, they usually must stay with their husbands and follow them in their moves. Although women situated in large economic centers have more opportunity to train and work, one cannot postulate that the nearer a female lives to the center of the city the more likely it is that she will work. One might postulate, however, that the further she lives from the city, the less likely it is she will train or work.

The fact of geographic location has direct consequences for the life patterns of educated middle-class women, most of whom live in suburbia. The most common contrast with the American suburban pattern is the Swedish. But the Swedes do not share our feelings that we "deprive" our children if we bring them up in the city. A vacation shack in the country generally satisfies the Swedish apartment-dweller's bucolic longings.

I'm sure by now that my "pitch" is quite apparent to you. Not only does society define certain jobs as appropriate for a woman in the occupational sphere; it defines what her jobs shall be in the sphere of home and family, including how she should feel about these jobs. Attitudes toward work and the reasons for working; attitudes about how and where one should live; attitudes regarding how high one may aspire—all these act on young and older women, channelling and directing them in and out of the work world.

David Riesman, speaking here at Bennington some years ago, said it was immoral for a society to insist that one's sex must predetermine one's vocation and even one's style of life. That, even if one assumed that there were "feminine" gifts, these should not dictate the choices of women who possess those gifts, let alone those of women who possess "masculine" gifts (since traits overlap and there will always be women more interested in masculine things than some men and vice versa). It is a part of freedom, he noted, to be able to decide the vocational outcome of one's gifts. I don't know if very much has happened in ten years to make the problems he spoke of then less relevant or his words less applicable. But even if women succeed in skirting these problems or making the personal adjustments (and they will be personal since there are few institutional aids to help them out) and seek to act out their talents, the specters will still arise.

My study of women lawyers indicates that there is room at the top for the small percentage of outstanding women who not only have the highest I.Q.'s, personalities, drive, fortitude and absence of work blocks, but that those who are normal and perhaps who are better than normal but not the best, will still face the imposing gatekeepers who cling to their belief that women will taint the purity and productivity of the male clubs which control the elite professions. It is not that they discriminate against women (although a *Harvard Record* poll showed a few years ago that the persons considered most objectionable—running neck and neck with students who received the lowest grades in their schools—were women) but that the best jobs, the most honored and prestigious, have been held by male networks for so long, that women truly *don't fit in.* There are few norms for treating or dealing with women in law and medicine and even in Ivy League academia. The men are embarrassed by the presence of women,

and as a result, or in an interactive process, the women do act odd. They try to overcompensate by being too feminine or too masculine; they are rate-busters or don't carry their load. They act, in short, as the insecure minority group that they are, and thus provide that kernel of truth which usually supplies the rationalizations for most stereotypes. And perhaps, worst of all for themselves, and their sisters and daughters, they define themselves as being inappropriate there.

A great many of the women lawyers I interviewed in the course of my studies claimed they loved their work, and had all the qualities necessary to perform it well, but they tended to agree with the men, that it was a man's work and only the unusual woman could hope to accomplish it. If the women lawyers themselves accepted this, how can we hope that young women considering occupational alternatives would choose law equally with teaching or interior design?

There is also a good deal of self-hatred among women in the professions and hatred directed at them by women outside. Home-based women want all women to stay home. If you work they will remind you that children of working mothers tend toward delinquency, homosexuality and more frequent colds. Your professional sisters may, I am told (though this has never been my personal experience), be upset that you are dislodging their exclusive niche in the male society. They don't want equality, they prefer being the only women around.

Women are everywhere bombarded with images of what they should do, often being damned if they do and damned if they don't. Yet I wonder if women will ever have freedom, and even if given freedom will accept it. I don't know if they can have freedom without radical changes in this society.

I think we are living in changing times, although the statistics still don't show it. Let me outline a few changes generally which should affect all women *personally.*

1. Schools are recruiting from a wider social base. This means that more young people have a chance for professional training and that the experience of studying with fellow

students from varied backgrounds will prevent future professionals or occupational gate-keepers in other elite spheres from expecting to work with colleagues with the same old school tie. Having accepted a Negro colleague, perhaps the establishment will try a female colleague.

2. And of course, young men are more at ease with educated women. The men are no longer being raised in all-male environments through the Ivy League establishment from prep school through graduate school. Separatism in education is breaking down and this should make men less resistant to working with women.

3. Even though women haven't increased their proportions in professional spheres, for example, changes in absolute numbers (and there are more of them) can provide significant changes in image. Although women still are the same old six percent of the medical profession they were twenty years ago, there are 15,000 of them now as opposed to 7,000 then.

4. There are pressures to utilize our huge resource of wasted talent—perhaps even in our affluence we cannot afford the luxury of the conspicuous waste of our woman-power lest we lose the race we enjoy with other world powers in science, especially, but in other spheres as well. (I must note here that the other superpower—the USSR—takes a different view of its women's potential and utilizes their talents heavily in technology and the professions.)

5. And again, the ideological changes and challenges to the establishment. Nobody would let the Bar Associations in New York City ban women with the excuse that there are no women's rest rooms there. (By the way, this excuse was used up until 1960 in Queens. It was also used by Princeton University to keep women from graduate education there, and by Oxford University in England.) I think our mass education and mass higher education will pay off in added sophistication.

But, evolution, as we know, is not necessarily progressive, and many lines of development simply die out. Being a woman is never, and has never been solely a biological state anywhere. What it means today and tomorrow will depend on what people think and our ability to make them think what we want them to think. It is the nature of images that they may be recast.

5
origins of anti-semitism in the united states

OSCAR and MARY F. HANDLIN

In many respects, the Jewish immigrant's experience is similar to that of Christian immigrants from the central and eastern European countries from which most American Jews' ancestors came. The major difference is that European Jews were urban and literate and thus able, as a group, to rise faster in the United States than their rural, mainly illiterate Christian compatriots. In the strength of their family structure, the Jews resembled the Chinese and Japanese immigrants. All three groups have been able to resist the disorganization prevalent in the urban slum areas where immigrants first settle.

The Jews, however, have met with one problem other immigrants have not faced. Toward the end of the nineteenth century, the Jews began to be slandered for their religious beliefs and traditions. Since the end of World War I, the United States has had a full-blown development of anti-Semitism.

Oscar Handlin, professor of history at Harvard, and his wife, Mary F. Handlin, also a historian, describe the development of anti-Semitism in America.

FIRST IMPRESSIONS

The first two centuries of American experience were almost completely free from expressions of hostility to the Jews. This favorable condition grew out of the high place held by them in American society and out of the Christian concept of the mission of Israel, widely accepted in the United States

As late as 1800 there were only a few thousand Jews scattered through American cities. Their role as merchants and the general cosmopolitan air of the towns in which they

lived brought them into close, friendly contact, on equal terms, with their neighbors. In this social environment there was little room for prejudice.

Furthermore, the Christian idea that a remnant of Israel would bear witness to the truth of the gospels also contributed to that favorable position. In the United States there had always been a pronounced millennial feeling, a feeling that the day of final judgment was soon approaching. In the process of salvation, the Jews were to play an important role; their conversion would herald the great day. Naturally they were to be treated in such a manner as would hasten their redemption.

More generally, among Christian Americans, veneration for the Bible created respect for the "People of the Book." The prevailing attitude toward the Jews early in the nineteenth century was set down by John Adams:

They are the most glorious Nation that ever inhabited this Earth. The Romans and their Empire were but a Bauble in comparison of the Jews. They have given Religion to three quarters of the Globe and have influenced the affairs of Mankind more, and more happily than any other Nation ancient or modern.

The only problems in the relations of Jews with their neighbors were those that survived from the colonial and English connection of church with state. In some places an established religion was supported by taxpayers' funds; elsewhere religious oaths were prerequisites to voting and to holding office. Atheists, Jews, Catholics and even some Protestant sects were thus discriminated against.

But already in the eighteenth century, the American atmosphere was inhospitable to such anachronistic relics. After 1700 the freedom to worship was almost everywhere recognized; and, year after year, the trend toward religious liberalism grew ever more pronounced.

The revolutionary movement that culminated in Independence also stressed individual rights, including the right to religious equality. Virginia took the lead in this respect, and its example was soon followed by the other states and by the federal government.

The same movement necessarily gave an impetus to the severance of the ties between church and state in such matters as support of religious activities by public funds and clerical control over education. By the third decade of the nineteenth century, the campaign for public education separated from sectarian religious controls had been won; everywhere, then, men of all beliefs stood on an equal footing in the eyes of the law. The struggle for liberty and freedom had given Jews, Catholics, and dissenting Protestants the same rights as other American citizens.

A PEOPLE COMING INTO BEING

The prevailing attitude toward the Jews changed as the nineteenth century advanced, but was no less favorable than it had been earlier. In fact, it would be more proper to say that there really was no attitude toward the Jews as such in this period.

Americans still thought of themselves as a new folk. They did not regard themselves simply as descendants of one or another of the old nations, but rather as a people just coming into being. In the process of evolution, all sorts of men were expected to join on equal terms. Ralph Waldo Emerson hoped that the "Irish, Germans, Swedes, Poles, and Cossacks, and all the European tribes," would construct here a new race, uniting the best qualities of all the old. The Jews were one of many strains that would enter into the "smelting pot" to contribute to the new and finer culture.

There was some discussion of such questions as the propriety of holding public school sessions on Saturday. But there was no acrimony over the subject. If there were any traces of anti-Semitic prejudice in this period, they were in the realm of the idiomatic slur, figures of speech that described the supposed characteristics of a whole people. Jews, like Yankees, were identified as peddlers and were often endowed, as a group, with the Yankee peddlers' traits. Every other distinctive group had a similar verbal reputation to live down—the drunken Irishmen, the stingy Germans, the haughty Southerners, the uncouth Westerners.

Although such characterizations generally went unheeded, they could nevertheless become dangerous. The Irish reputation proved a convenient tool in the hands of Know-Nothing agitators. Similarly, in the heat of the Civil War, General Grant ordered Jewish traders away from the Union lines in terms that reflected upon their loyalty and honesty. Although the command was almost at once rescinded, it illustrated the strength of the impression left by these slurs.

Such incidents were significant for the habits of mind they revealed. But they were more often the products of lazy minds than of a clear intention to discriminate. So William Dean Howells planned to make one of the unpleasant characters in *The Rise of Silas Lapham* a Jew. He changed his plan when the implications of such a step were called to his attention.

Indeed, this situation remained the same as long as the Jews were regarded merely as communicants of another American religion. In view of the prevailing latitudinarianism, the attitude that any religion that taught good morals was good, any overt discrimination on religious grounds would have disturbed the delicate balance among all the sects in the United States. . . .

FIRST FRUITS OF RACISM

By 1920, a full-fledged racial ideology colored the thinking of many Americans. Yet, the conquest of opinion was by no means complete; the traditional American attitude of tolerance still acted as a brake upon the headlong sweep of these new ideas. What was ominous was the occasional demonstration of racist thought at the practical level.

Significantly, in practice as in theory, the Jews were not the only group singled out. The racist also viewed as enemies all the colored peoples, the Latins, and the Slavs. If the Jews were often the first to draw fire, that was because local circumstances sometimes made them the most prominent targets.

The Pattern of Exclusion

Social mobility has always been an important characteristic of the American social ideal. A great deal of freedom in the economic structure has made room for the free play of talents and has permitted newcomers to make their way from the lower to the higher rungs of the occupational ladder. In the absence of an heriditary aristocracy, social position has generally accompanied economic position.

Those who occupied the higher places, of course, always resented the competition from those who climbed up from the lower places. More than a hundred years ago, newspapers were already carrying the injunction over their help-wanted ads, "No Irish Need Apply!"

But the democratic nature of American society made it difficult permanently to establish such barriers. In the nineteenth century these artificial restraints had always broken down beneath the pressure of the necessity for cooperation at all levels in the community. Furthermore, constant expansion in the economic and social structure of the nation made room for newcomers without lowering the positions of those already well established. In fact, it often happened that a rise in the level of the immigrants and their children lifted the positions of all those above them.

The earliest encounters of the Jews with this feature of the American social system were not unlike those of members of other ethnic groups who passed through the same process. In adjusting to the American economy, however, some groups moved upward much more rapidly than others. The Jews were among those who advanced most quickly in earning power and in social position. Their special difficulties arose from the fact that they seemed to rise so much faster than other peoples of recent immigration origin. This success in mobility came at a time when the earlier immigrant groups of the later eighteenth and early nineteenth centuries had chosen to forget their own swift rise and extraordinary accumulation of the great fortunes characteristically found among them.

All who mounted the economic ladder earned the resentment of the well-established; but, because of the rapidity of their climb, the Jews seemed interlopers, more distinctly out of place than earlier outsiders moving in the same direction.

Economic power in America was usually accompanied by certain symbols of prestige and position—good family, membership in the appropriate churches and associations, residence in select districts, and participation in communal activities. Success by Jews was resented, not only because the success of every new arrival seemed to leave less room for those already entrenched, but also because success in their case was not graced with the proper symbols, did not take the proper form.

Furthermore, the rapidity of the climb heightened the sense of difference between Jews and non-Jews at the upper economic levels. Some Jews reached positions of economic power and influence within a single generation, a time-interval too short for adequate social adaptation. The contrast in behavior was therefore particularly noticeable. In the case of Jews, "high society" and its lowlier imitators could ascribe its discomforts to the difference in manners rather than to an inherent unwillingness to make room for competitors. The Jew was in the same category as other minorities in every manifestation of prejudice. But his exceptional mobility made him the more prominent and the more vulnerable target.

Exclusion was first prominently expressed in areas that involved the use of leisure-time facilities, that is, in vacation places, in clubs, and in social groups of various kinds. Such activities, being less formalized than, say, those of business or politics, were open to intimate personal contacts. Here, then, the strangers' presence was felt more sensitively. What is more, these activities involved the whole family. Unlike the office or the workshop, where each man could deal impersonally and almost anonymously with individuals as individuals, the resort or dance drew in the members of his family and made him more conscious of questions of background and origin.

Toward the end of the nineteenth century, many places began to close their doors to Jews. The incident in Saratoga Springs in 1877 when Joseph Seligman was refused accommodations at the Grand Union Hotel was a dramatic precursor of a pattern that would become more familiar in succeeding decades. In the 1890's also appeared a large number of hereditary prestige societies, which based their membership upon descent from eighteenth-century American ancestors. These societies excluded most Jews as well as most other Americans descended from immigrants who arrived after 1800.

These social slights ultimately had an effect upon other activities. To the extent that business and political contacts often were made within the realm of the club or society, those who were excluded from the club or society were automatically discriminated against.

And soon that discrimination became more direct. After 1910, as the sons of the immigrant Jews entered more keenly and more noticeably into competition for professional and white-collar places in the American economic system, the weight of such prejudice became formal and more open. Newspaper advertisements began specifically to exclude Jews from consideration for certain positions. Access to many professions was arbitrarily if informally limited.

Uneasily, many Americans accepted this pattern of discrimination. Although not a few

were still conscious enough of their heritage of freedom and equality to protest against the tendency, all too many, lulled by the racist justification of ineradicable differences, were disposed to acquiesce. The formation of the American Jewish Committee in 1906 and of the Anti-Defamation League of B'nai B'rith in 1913 to fight these trends indicated a growing awareness of the seriousness of the problem.

Georgia Blood Bath

What drew attention to the potential menace of all these developments was a sudden eruption that displayed the ugly turn the forces of racism could take. Appropriately enough, the eruption came in the South, the source of so much of the festering venom; and appropriately enough, it came in the New, not the Old, South, in industrial Atlanta rather than on the romantic plantation.

Among the disorganized masses of men thrown together in the American cities, seeming grievances with no hope of redress from "legal" channels often led to violent outbursts of mob action. Many people did not trust their governments, were ready to believe that their police departments and courts had sold out to special interests, and, under provocation, were willing to take direct action themselves.

Distinctive minorities were particularly subject to violent reprisals when their actions seemed to run against the cherished patterns of the community, yet involved no clear infraction of the law. In the 1890's, Italians in New Orleans and Irishmen in Boston had suffered the harsh effects of mob violence.

In 1915 the blow fell upon Leo Frank, a Jewish resident of Atlanta, Georgia. Accused of the murder of a fourteen-year-old girl and convicted on the flimsiest grounds, he was taken from jail and lynched the day after the governor of the state had commuted his sentence.

Many factors combined to draw the web of hatred around Frank's neck. He was a Northerner and an employer of labor, and earned a full share of mistrust on those grounds alone. As a Jew he inherited all the dislikes stirred up by the racist writers of the period, and also the murky suspicions about Jewish blood murders left over from the agitation of the Beiliss case a few years earlier. Finally, the widespread indignation following his conviction, and the ultimate commutation of the sentence by the governor raised the suspicion that justice was being frustrated through the intercession of powerful hostile outsiders. Under skillful manipulation, these became the goads that prodded the mob into action.

The manipulation came from Tom Watson. By 1913 this man had a long political career behind him. A sympathizer with the cause of the poor in his own region, he had been prominent as a populist and as a leader in the progressive movements at the turn of the century. But the years after 1900 were a long series of frustrations, not so much in terms of personal ambitions, but in terms of the success of the program for which he fought. "The world is plunging Hellward," he complained.

In common with many other men of his period, Watson blamed this deterioration upon the interference of outside interests. At first his hostility focused upon the traditional objective of fundamentalist America, the Roman Catholic Church, and he engaged in a long, bitter campaign of vilification through his journals and books.

But in practice as in theory, prejudice was not easily limited to one group. The Frank case offered an alternative, and Watson transferred the identical arguments he was using against the Catholics to the Jews. He rallied his followers with the argument that Frank must be executed to eliminate outside Jewish interference from Georgia.

In an immediate sense, Watson was successful. Frank died, and Watson himself rode to continued political power on the basis of his leadership in the anti-Semitic campaign. Local bitterness raised by the issue persisted for many years.

Yet the very violence of the terms Watson used, the very barbarity of the methods of his mob revolted the great mass of Americans outside his state. The rude gallows at Marietta, Georgia, cast a somber shadow across the land, a grim warning of what might develop.

Then came the war and, for a time, the presence of an enemy from without seemed to still internal dissensions. Jews contributed with their fellow citizens to the winning of the struggle, and their participation was officially recognized by the government through such agencies as the Jewish Welfare Board. What was more, the very slogans in terms of which the war was fought seemed to rebuke those who promoted intolerance at home.

THE CONSEQUENCES OF WAR AND OF DEPRESSION

Although the war brought peace, peace itself unloosed the bitter passions of disappointment and betrayal. The outcome of the conflict was so different from the aims for which sacrifices had been made that millions of Americans felt cheated and turned against those aims.

In the five years after the armistice, the United States seemed to wish to draw back into a chauvinistic isolation, to cut its ties with the rest of the world, to forget not only the phrases but also the ideals that had sparked the war effort. Rejection of the League of Nations and the World Court, and the high tariff system were symptoms of this deep drive.

Perhaps even more important was the final reversal between 1920 and 1924 of the historic immigration policy. In those years, the number of new entrants was not only cut drastically, but cut in terms of a crude racist philosophy that set up standards of desirability for all the people of the world, counting some high, some low, almost exactly as Madison Grant had counselled.

The consequences for the American social and economic system were drastic. With no more newcomers, expansion slackened, and before long there was a noticeable contraction in the range of opportunities. Between 1920 and 1940, for instance, the number of practitioners in certain professions remained almost stationary. This meant that competition for the desirable places became sharper than ever. If the number of doctors did not grow, every new Jewish doctor deprived the son of a gentile of his place.

In the 1920's almost every leading American college and university, formally or informally, adopted a quota system for Jewish students. Unofficial regulatory agencies made it difficult for Jews to enter almost every profession. In 1944 and 1945, some representative groups in the fields of dentistry and psychiatry went so far as openly to propose a quota system in those fields. Everywhere, the difficulty of securing desirable employment constantly became more oppressive.

In those years, too, the pattern of exclusion extended into the field of housing. Through voluntary covenants of real estate owners, whole areas of many cities were abruptly closed to persons of "Hebrew descent."

While the effects of such practices were still being felt, the depression after 1929 struck a blow at the American economy from which there was no recovery for almost a decade. Through the thirties, close to ten million unemployed men and their families lived by the insecure margin of public relief or of charity, and remained the prey of all sorts of demagogues ready to capitalize upon their fears.

"The International Jew"

Immediately after the first world war, xenophobia seemed to seep into every corner of American life. Naturally, it affected the Jews. Hostility toward them centered on their "foreign" qualities.

The most flamboyant preachers of 100 per cent Americanism were the members of the latter-day Ku Klux Klan. This obscure organization had started in the South shortly before the war. It assumed the title of the old Reconstruction bands, made popular by a film that had just swept the country, D. W. Griffith's *Birth of a Nation*. At first the new Klan operated as a simple racket form fleecing the gullible through fancy prices on sheet-uniforms. But between 1920 and 1925 the Order grew and spread, until it attained a membership of close to four million, heavily concentrated in the North, and particularly in the states of Oregon, Ohio, Indiana and Illinois.

The Klan found its leading antagonist in the Pope; in that respect it fell into the tradition of confusing issues by identifying Catholicism with internationalism. But it had hatred left over for the Jews, also touched by international affiliations, and for the Negroes who were vulnerable enough to be attacked without a pretext.

Undoubtedly, the Kluxers were influenced in their anti-Semitism by the circulation in this country of the *Protocols of the Elders of Zion*. This little volume, an obvious forgery that we now know was used by the Czarist secret police, purported to record the proceedings, in Prague, of a secret body, plotting to capture the world on behalf of international Jewry. That this flimsy story, so clearly fraudulent on the face of it, should pass through edition after edition and find credence among thousands of well-intentioned, if uncritical, American citizens may seem amazing. It is perhaps a commentary upon the insecurity and uncertainty of the world in which they lived, a world in which truth was difficult to separate from fiction and in which promise did sometimes lead to betrayal.

By 1928, however, people, no matter how insecure, were no longer likely to phrase their fears in terms of an international menace to the United States. Disarmament treaties and the Kellogg Pact, after all, had made the nation safe from attack from without; prosperity kept it sound against attack from within. A token of this turn of events was the disintegration of the once-powerful Klan.

The Shadow of Hitlerism

The advent of the Nazis to power had a double effect. It was one of the disturbing elements that upset the stability of Europe and the world and that revived all the old American fears of involvement in foreign quarrels. More directly, the accession of the national Socialists to power gave control of a sovereign government to a group that was aggressively interested in spreading anti-Semitic ideas throughout the world.

In the United States, Hitler's primary agents in this mission were rigidly organized German-Americans. Large numbers of Germans, many veterans of the Kaiser's army and many still imbued with national pride, had come to the United States in the 1920's under the quota laws of 1920-24 which had granted the Germans a high percentage of entrants.

Some of these people had joined patriotic societies such as the Teutonia; but these groups had been small in number and short in purse. After 1932, however, they had the support of agencies of the German government, from which they secured organizational leadership, funds, and a steady stream of propaganda to be spread through the United States.

Many German-Americans were first drawn to these societies through simple fraternal and nationalistic motives. But as the German government plunged ever deeper into the path of anti-Semitism, to the horror of the rest of the civilized world, the defense of Germany tended to become the defense of anti-semitism. Before long it seemed the only way to uphold the good name of the Germans, wherever they were, was to stand by the Fatherland, to convince others that the Nazi persecution of the Jews was necessary to save Western civilization from the menace of world Jewry.

Hitler had not been in power for a year when the American societies were reorganized and centralized in the Friends of the New Germany, later known as the German American Bund. Under the successive leadership of Heinz Spanknoebel, Fritz Gissibl, Fritz Kuhn, and Wilhelm Kunze, the Bund set itself the task of popularizing the doctrines of Hitler's new order. Through newspapers and books inspired from abroad, the stock libels about the Jews were given currency. Camps maintained the morale of the members, and public meetings served to infect outsiders.

A great part of the early financial support for these activities came from the German government. In this respect, the Bund was a Nazi agency. In furthering Hitlerite objectives, it performed, on the direct operational level, the same function that was being performed, on a more respectable level, by George Sylvester Viereck through his Nazi-front publishing house, Flanders Hall.

Elements of American Fascism

Hitler did not have to rely exclusively upon Germans to do his work for him in the United States. There were native tools at hand willing, for their own interests, to serve his purposes.

Among the insecure groups rendered more insecure by the depression were millions of men ready to be enlisted in a crusade, men awaiting some call to salvation. Mostly, they wanted something about which they could be enthusiastic, something in which they could believe, and which would bring the promise of security. Out of such cravings came support for all sorts of new movements untouched by any trace of anti-Semitism, the Townsend Plan, for example, or EPIC in California.

It was significant that the vast majority of men who participated in such drives did not respond to bigoted appeals, and labored to attain their economic ends without relying upon the support of group hatred. Yet, in this inchoate mass of distressed people, a small proportion did respond to appeals that were clearly fascist in nature and that were often oriented around anti-Semitic programs. Between 1933 and 1939 some hundred organizations, large and small, drew together the Jew-haters into a potentially dangerous force.

Confusion and inconsistency characterized all these groups. While their members were insecure people the sources of their insecurity were markedly diverse.

There were some, for instance, who carried on in the spirit of the twenties, chauvinists, foes of the "international" Jew, striving for purity of the American race, hostile to anything alien. These people were most numerous in the South and Middle West, the old Klan territory. They were Protestants, often fundamentalist in religion, and terrified at the disappearance of an American way of life that actually had never existed. They joined William Dudley Pelley's Silver Shirts and the revived Klan, or became the audience of Gerald L. K. Smith (leader of the Christian Nationalist Party) and the late Reverend Gerald B. Winrod (publisher of *The Defender*).

Another fund of discontent was different in origin but similar in expression. The Catholics, particularly of the second and third generation, had the same economic difficulties as other marginal groups in the thirties, and emerged with the same feelings of insecurity, the same search for an alternative. But the Catholics had a long history of experience with bigotry in the United States, and had strong reasons for distrusting this aspect of the American spirit. Despite this, anti-Semitism made some headway among them.

A leader in this movement was Father Charles E. Coughlin, who had gained an enormous radio audience before 1936 by focusing his sermons on economic questions, and by support of the New Deal. Shortly after his break with President Roosevelt, Father Coughlin used his radio time and his newspaper, *Social Justice*, to attack the Jews. His stock in trade was the old international plot of communists and bankers to hand over the world to the Jews. In 1938, Father Coughlin's followers gathered into organizations which subsequently became the Christian Front. Among the leadership were Father Curran, often referred to as Father Coughlin's Eastern Representative, John F. Cassidy and Francis P. Moran. The Christian Front not only spread the then-current anti-Semitic propaganda, but also held provocative meetings. The war later drove such groups to cover.

The diversity of the sources from which these anti-Semitic groups sprang helps to account for the fact that they were never able to unite, to eliminate rivalries among their leaders, or to pool interest and support. While some of these organizations were able to draw upon substantial financial support from time to time, their total effects tended to cancel out each other. Most of them did not survive the war, which cast the suspicion of disloyalty upon them.

They were not without effect, however. Even in more respectable groups there was, in the years before Pearl Harbor, an unprecedented willingness to raise the Jewish issue as such, in reference to politics and to international affairs. Month after month in 1941, the prospect of war became more real, many well-meaning people, committed to keeping the country neutral, succumbed to the temptation of using a fictitious Jewish issue for their own ends. Men like Charles A. Lindbergh and Senator Nye expressed themselves in terms that raised questions as to their motivations.

It was shocking in 1933 to hear Congressman MacFadden of Pennsylvania use the halls of the Capitol as a sounding board for anti-Semitic charges. But eight years later, it was commonplace to find Congressmen Thorkelson and Rankin, in the boldest terms, ascribing American participation in the war of 1941 to nefarious Jewish influences.

EVERY PERSON'S COUNTRY

An ugly stain appears upon the fabric of American society. The stain is out of harmony with the complexion of the whole fabric. It jars. It will not stay as it is.

The stain was not always there. It was not woven in with the warp and woof of the cloth, but imposed later. How and why, we know.

Still the cloth is no longer the same, and cannot stay as it is. Will the whole cloth be dyed to match the color of the stain? Or can we, in time, eradicate the stain? A good deal depends upon the answer.

"We know, properly speaking, no strangers. This is every person's country." Such was the boast of Americans a century and a half ago. Jews no less than others, no differently from others, found their home here.

This tolerance, this open attitude toward new ideas and new influences, was founded upon confidence. Americans believed in the destiny of their country and of its institutions. They knew they had nothing to fear save ignorance and fear. Who was their enemy when they were every man's friend?

Little more than fifty years ago, that confidence was shaken. There were men in the United States who no longer had faith in what the future might bring. And their fears bred dark and atavistic hatreds.

The consequences have since unfolded before us—at home and across the ocean.

But how are we to remove the stain? Do we have enough faith in America, once more to say, "We know no strangers. This is every person's country"?

6
john xxiii, vatican ii, and american catholicism

EUGENE C. BIANCHI

Only an obtuse person, indeed, could be unaware of the great changes that have been taking place in the Roman Catholic church. The church is an international organization, and its history stretches back 2,000 years. Thus, many of its provisions have been particularly difficult for American Catholics to live with in their attempts to adjust to modern industrial life.

Although Catholics were among the first immigrants to the United States, Maryland and Georgia both having been settled by Catholics, the bulk of the Catholic population arrived in the nineteenth century from Ireland, Italy, and central Europe; in the twentieth century came the Puerto Ricans and Mexicans. Most of the Catholics were peasants—poor, illiterate, and subject to prejudice and discrimination in the United States. As these groups have assimilated into American life, they have desired changes in the church structure. Of primary importance has been the ban on most contraceptive methods. The American hierarchy has failed to support anticontraceptive laws, and the Catholic population itself seems to practice birth control as much as others do, if education and recency of migration are held constant. But the Vatican has held firmly to its anticontraceptive postion, which must have produced a great strain in the American church.

Parochial schools that satisfied an older generation of Catholics are no longer regarded as competitive with public schools, and the cost of meeting the standards of public schools is prohibitive. Parochial schools are being consolidated or closed down, and the Catholics are asking for public funds for busing and other fringe benefits for the schools. This runs headlong into both anti-Catholic prejudice and those provisions of state constitutions that ensure the separation of church and state. The young, both in the laity and the hierarchy, have espoused civil rights and peace, often in open conflict with the older church members.

Dr. Bianchi examines in more detail the changes in the American Catholic church and their possible effects. Dr. Bianchi is professor of religion at Emory University in Atlanta, Georgia.

It is hardly an exaggeration to say that the last decade has been the most momentous in American Catholic history. At the time that European immigrants were beginning to come into their own as an accommodated and reflective American community, the Second Vatican Council brought unexpected challenges. Pope John XXIII, as a churchman and as a man, spoke to the hearts and imaginations of Americans across denominational barriers. But it was

Reprinted from "The Sixties: Radical Change in American Religion" (Philadelphia: *The Annals of the American Academy of Political and Social Science* 387 (January 1970), pp. 31-40. Reproduced by permission of the author and publisher.

his Council that unleashed in American Catholicism both new creativity and deep tensions. In this writer's opinion, we are only beginning to witness the latent consequences of Vatican II. It is, therefore, precarious to speak too boldly about what has happened to the American Catholic church during the last ten years. Yet, the new accomplishments, anxieties, and hopes are clear enough to describe in a limited way, although we are still too close to the watershed of Vatican II to do more than indicate various directions that new currents are taking.

For purposes of analysis, it is helpful to employ a typology of clashing world views that have become more acutely separated during the 1960's. A classical-conservative outlook is frequently coming into conflict with a historical-progressive viewpoint in areas of Catholic theology, cult, polity, and morals. Of course, a complex spectrum of attitudes and reactions exists between these two poles, but the manifestations of division are clear and numerous enough to support the working typology. This article will be an attempt to understand the ongoing ferment in American Catholicism in the light of the above polarity. In the American church, persons representing the conservative pole are largely bishops, older clergy, religious, and laity; the progressive side consists mainly of lower clergy, younger religious, and college-educated laity. Difference in age, however, though generally indicative of the split, is not a decisive factor; differences of temperament, education, and life-style are also important determinants.

Vatican II and the biblical-liturgical developments preceding it stimulated a redefinition of the nature of the church itself. The new stress on the church as a historical, pilgrim people tended to play down the long-dominant tradition of the church as chiefly hierarchy. Progressives understand the church with a greater sense of relativity: it is historically conditioned, imperfect morally and religiously, a learning community being taught by the Spirit through continuing historical experiences. Conservatives, though nodding assent to the theory of Vatican II, cling to a notion of the church as a basically finished, perfect institution with clear lines of juridical authority from the top

down. This view is more absolutist, centralist, legal, and self-contained; progressives emphasize the church as decentralized (local), horizontal-fraternal, charismatically oriented, and searchingly open. For the most part, the former vision of the church is more monarchical-paternalistic, while the latter is more democratic-participational.

Closely related to these contrasting conceptions of the church is a new questioning of who belongs to the church and where it is to be found. In the recent past, Catholics were able to mark off rather clearly in creed, code, and cult the lines of demarcation between the "one, true church" and other groups. But with the renewed theology of baptism, all Christians are somehow included in the ecclesiastical body; the "somehow" has not been well worked out, but modern ecumenism has toned down, in theory at least, rigid distinctions between Christian communions. Moreover, contemporary theology, as reflected at Vatican II, has corrected previous dichotomies between the natural and the supernatural, the world and the church. Inasmuch as all reality is now seen as graced in Christ, especially humane endeavors toward justice and freedom, the distinctions between Christian and non-Christian have become somewhat blurred. Thus, considerable discussion has arisen about the terms "anonymous Christian" and "anonymous" or "latent church."

THEOLOGY AND TENSION

It would be a mistake to dismiss these theological problems as unrelated to the tensions of the 1960's between conservatives and progressives. For example, such theoretical positions underlie the growing criticism, during this decade, of new building programs. Progressives maintain that church resources ought not be used to build a haven church apart; rather, resources should be employed, the progressives hold, for humanistic reconciliatory works in society. Conservatives tend to interpret such criticism as a deflection from the church's task of evangelization, a watering down of the gospel for do-good humanism. Similar theological attitudes have been just below the surface of the widespread role-identity crises among priests and nuns in recent years. Unprecedented numbers of clergy and religious are leaving convents, orders, and dioceses for more directly secular and humanistic involvements. Not only is the suitability of monastic life-styles and outlooks being called into question, but social, psychological, and political roles in secular society are interpreted as more significant ways of Christian ministry. Thus, tremendous strains are produced between conservatives and progressives, because different theological appreciations of the nature and purpose of the church inevitably lead to serious disagreements over the use of material and human resources in the church.

Another theological area revealing the struggle between permanence and change in Catholicism is that of development of doctrine. Catholics of the classical viewpoint were raised in a doctrinal tradition that insisted on dogmatic immutability and clear continuity. In a world of increasing subjectivity and relativity, these Catholics were proud of the security provided by the teachings of the ecclesiastical magisterium (papal and episcopal teaching authority). Even Cardinal Newman's creative position on development, which threatened the non-historical outlook of Catholic officials in the past, seemed tame in comparison with progressive attitudes toward development in recent years. During the last five years, Pope Paul VI has repeatedly warned against new theological opinions which menace traditional Catholic doctrine. These papal anxieties and admonitions have been faithfully echoed by American bishops. At the same time, liberal theologians have been radically rethinking doctrines on original sin, the meaning of Christ's incarnation and redemption, the eucharist, eschatology, the ministry, and the place and authority of pope and bishops.

While many conservatives are theologically and psychologically upset by this questioning, progressives hold that it is not only legitimate but necessary to revise the most cherished doctrines. The latter base their deep probings and reformulations on a keener sense of the historical conditioning of doctrinal language, the radically altered world view of modern man, and the evolutionary processive development of man's religious consciousness. Contact with Protestant theology, progressive

and existentialist forms of philosophy, contemporary psychology, and new historical-biblical learning has freed progressive Catholic thinkers from static, scholastic, and supernaturalistic interpretations of doctrine. In this ferment of re-evaluation, the Catholic doctrine of infallibility is being seriously questioned. Vatican II shifted the focus of infallible teaching from a papal perspective toward the infallibility of the whole praying, believing, witnessing church community. But since the Council, a number of Catholic thinkers reject the notion of infallibility and argue for the need of negating past symbolizations of faith in a dialectical fashion in order to come to more adequate understandings of religious doctrine. Yet, these theologians of discontinuity also grapple with the problem of continuity, striving to found it on more basic understandings of the nature of religious faith in a historical community. Moreover, progressive theologians point with more certainty to actual profound changes in Catholic teachings of the past in matters of both faith and morals. In American seminaries and universities over the last decade, large numbers of young Catholics have been exposed to this post-Vatican II theology. While this new theological learning has a liberating effect for many Catholics, it also places them at odds with great numbers of their coreligionists and evokes policies of official retrenchment.

Such tensions between conservatives and progressives have come to world-wide attention since the publication, in July 1968, of the birth-control letter, *Humanae Vitae,* in which Paul VI reiterated the ban on contraceptives, against the advice of a majority of his own birth-control commission. As never before in modern Catholic history, voices of dissent from papal teaching have been heard from clergy and laity. Yet, before dealing explicitly with the novel phenomenon of strong dissent from official doctrine and its consequences, it is important to explore the changing understandings of structure and authority in contemporary Catholicism. For the protest of the Catholic University (Washington, D.C.) theologians and the resignation of Bishop James Shannon of St. Paul over the birth-control encyclical must be seen in the light of the expectations issuing from the renewed theology of Vatican II about church structure and authority.

Through biblical and historical research, progressive theologians have been coming to a deeper awareness of the historical relativity of the monarchical, paternalistic, pyramidical structure of Catholicism. This polity structure, with its maximizing of the papal role, is seen as largely reflecting the styles of government and culture of feudal-medieval Europe and later monarchies. Such structures were sacralized as divinely instituted and shored up with an elaborate Roman canon law and the hierarchical thought-forms of scholasticism. Vatican II represents a compromise attempt to maintain the older structure, while at the same time opening the church to more democratic-participational structures. Thus, the conciliar doctrine of collegiality between pope and bishops recovers the vision of communal government characteristic of primitive Christianity. Since the Council, the desire for significant participation in decison-making has spread to religious orders and to many dioceses where lower clergy and laity call for a share in collegiality. The latter groups in America have also been more fully influenced than their Catholic elders by present-day movements in secular society for political participation and self-determination. That the controversy between monarchical and collegial forms is far from subsiding in the Catholic church was evidenced in May 1969, when Cardinal Leon Suenens of Belgium, in a widely published interview, criticized the Roman Curia for continuing its imperialistic ways in defiance of coresponsibility in the church.

AUTHORITY AND DISSENT

Closely linked to the tensions over church structure among Catholics is the issue of authority. In the award-winning book, *Authority in the Church*, the American Jesuit, John L. McKenzie, elaborated, from a New Testament perspective, the sense of authority characteristic of the documents of Vatican II. McKenzie contrasted the biblical view of authority, as humble, charismatic service based on love, with the dominative and legalistic exercise of authority in the church. The book was pilloried by Archbishop Robert E. Lucey of San Antonio and praised by the Catholic Theo-

logical Society of America. Two other incidents in recent years portray an authority based on highly sanctioned edicts from Rome rather than on inspirational guidance that respects diversity of judgment and personal conscience. One such affair was the heavy-handed suspension from the ministry of a group of priests in Washington, D.C., by Cardinal Patrick O'Boyle for their public dissent from the birth-control encyclical. The other event near the American scene was the Roman inquisition of Monsignor Ivan Illich and the banning of his center for the study of Latin American society and language in Cuernavaca, Mexico.

The 1960's might be termed the decade of critical, public dissent among American Catholics in the wake of Vatican II.[1] Such dissent is often viewed by conservatives as disloyalty to ecclesiastical authorities, to Catholicism, and to God. Thus, it is seen as destructive disobedience stemming from the sinful pride of the dissenters. The latter interpret their criticism as a service to the church, which especially tends to turn finite forms and ways of thinking and acting into absolutes. The dissenters point to the need for prophets who speak out against religious idolatry, and the critics also invoke the doctrine of Christian eschatology, according to which the imperfect structures and life of the present church should be judged in the light of the hoped for future Kingdom.

The spectrum of dissent among Catholics during the 1960's extends from complete and variously articulated rejection of Roman Catholicism to moderate varieties of criticism within the structure of the church. An American example of radical abandonment of Catholicism is found in James Kavanaugh, a former priest whose book, entitled *A Modern Priest Looks at His Outdated Church,* became a best seller. English theologian Charles Davis presented a more scholarly rejection of Roman Catholicism in his *A Question of Conscience;* Davis exerted considerable influence on the American scene through his writings and public talks. Others choose to occupy a middle position; rather than sever all ties with the church, these dissenters, sometimes operating outside church laws, take a critical stance on the periphery of official Catholicism. In this category, the National Association for Pastoral Renewal conducted a broad educational campaign for optional celibacy among Catholic priests. A somewhat more radical group is the Society of Priests for a Free Ministry, a loosely organized group of priests, most of whom have left clerical structures. This group fostered liturgical and other experiments in the "underground church." The latter phenomenon, supported by progressive laity and clergy within and outside of official structures, constitutes a significant dissent movement in American Catholicism of the 1960's. For the most part, underground church movements sought to realize more meaningful liturgical communities, although most of this experimentation was opposed by episcopal authorities.

In addition to the older voices of dissent among Catholic publications such as *Commonweal* and certain learned journals, the *National Catholic Reporter* (NCR) became, during the 1960's, the most significant weekly newspaper in American Catholic history. The NCR, edited by competent and independent laymen, acted as both a mirror and a goad toward radical reform in the church. NCR was either loved or hated, but it was rarely ignored. Its pages reflected the ferment and polarization of postconciliar Catholicism on such issues as birth control, democratization of the church, reform of religious orders, critiques of Catholic education, and broader analyses of tensions between church and world. For the most part, diocesan papers remained house organs whose critical scope was limited by episcopal control. The major Catholic publishing houses also contributed significantly to theological progress and polarization. Through translations and in original English editions, these houses provided the arsenal of thought-provoking religious writing which supplied the Catholic opposition to the conservative establishment in theory and practice. The growing independence of these publishing houses from ecclesiastical supervision was evidenced in a frequent disregard for obtaining an imprimatur and in the publication of officially controverted books like the Dutch Catechism. Such conduct in the literary field both manifested the lessened efficacy of ecclesiastical dictate and sanction and underscored a heightened awareness of an author's

rights and freedoms. An important factor in bringing about this freer environment for Catholic authors in the last decade has been the undoing of ecclesiastical secrecy by the rapid and widespread publication of Catholic happenings in the secular press. Such news arouses response in liberal circles and embarrassment among conservative authorities.

Vatican II has gradually released among the American Catholic laity a spirit of public frankness and constructive dissent. Characteristic of this attitude is the National Association of Laymen, with its numerous affiliates around the country. The outspokenness of these groups on matters of church finance, birth control, liturgy, and many other topics, is in marked contrast to the tradition of loyal subservience of Catholic organizations in this century. In the past, lay groups might take moderately progressive stands (as did the hierarchy) in social and political matters, but since the days of Catholic modernism, early in this century, the American layman has been successfully trained to submission on theological and ecclesiastical questions. Most Catholic lay organizations continued the tradition (inculcated in Catholic schools) of an accepting obedience. Often apathy or secular enticements lure the laity altogether away from church interests. But the newer breed of "emerging laymen," who are more aware of themselves as also constituting the church, are beginning to seek decision-making participation in its life.

TOWARD COLLEGIALITY

The movement at Vatican II toward collegial government has given a new emphasis to episcopal and sacerdotal bodies. Regional and national conferences of bishops have become important in a way not previously experienced in the centralized style of preconciliar Catholic polity. The National Conference of Catholic Bishops is slowly striving to gain a sense of American Catholic identity in order to cope more adequately with national issues. The direction of this episcopal organization is toward a slightly more autonomous administration of American affairs, which, in the past, were handled by direct communication from individual bishops to the Roman Curia. Little creative innovation, however, has come from this body since the Council. In liturgical, disciplinary, pastoral, and theological matters, the generally conservative American bishops preserve older procedures and listen faithfully to Vatican promptings. The closed manner of selecting American bishops has been controlled by a conservative episcopal elite, which has largely succeeded in perpetuating its own kind. Thus, the typical American bishop continues to be a reasonably good financial manager and bureaucratic administrator and a person thoroughly schooled in loyal obedience to Rome. The more charismatic and inspirational leader in the American clergy rarely passes through the selection filter that determines entrance to the episcopal college. This situation engenders mounting frustration and resentment among younger clerics, who often see little hope of altering the "system."

The formation of priest's senates and other associations also manifests the collegial direction of the postconciliar American church. Although the official senates of priests mark the start of democratic organization for representation, participation, and pressure, these groups enjoy only an advisory capacity, and they are usually moderate or conservative bodies. Yet, the fact that religious and diocesan priests are commencing to take an active part in various commissions dealing with every phase of their lives is, in itself, a significant development of the 1960's. The local priests' senates have, moreover, formed a National Federation of Priests Councils, whose officials attempt to represent the interests of priests at the bishops' conferences. In a few places, such as Chicago and San Francisco, priests have formed independent associations without the expressed approval of their bishops. These associations display a disillusionment with the official senates, which are seen as conservative bodies under the domination of the local bishop. The independent groups call for far-reaching reforms in priestly life and pastoral activity.

NEW LITURGIES

The renewal of sacramental and liturgical theology in the years after the Second World War reached the stage of implementation and experimentation under the impulse of Vatican II. In sacraments and liturgy, the direction has been away from individualism, mysteriousness, and the hieratic, and toward communal participation, intelligibility, and a sense of fraternity. This newer orientation is not simply a recovery of the distant Christian past, but rather a response to the wider demand in modern society for a needed experience of personal identity and intimate community. The impersonal and seemingly uncontrollable dimensions of advanced technological societies create desires for a sense of belonging and purposiveness. Thus, American Catholics in the 1960's, challenged by the cultural pluralism and relativism of values characteristic of the times, have attempted to find fresh religious meaning in postconciliar liturgical reforms.

Because Catholicism is such a highly cultic religion, changes in liturgical attitudes and actions are both indicative and productive of important tensions and developments. Many saw in the changes a new hope for liturgical involvement and meaning. They rejoiced at the vernacular mass; greater lay participation in word, song, and action; and the gradual diversification and simplification of liturgical form and architecture. Yet, those of more conservative bent saw in the changes a vulgarization of worship and a loss of what they had come to think of as important Catholic traditions. A minority traditionalist movement to restore the Latin Mass and other devotional customs of the past, headed by Father Gomar DePauw, represents the extreme Right among American Catholics. The official church has attempted to run a middle course by ordering a variety of changes in the direction of communal participation. Large numbers of liberal and radical Catholics, however, have been dissatisfied both with the formalistic ineptitude of implementation and the tardiness of official reform.

Such dissatisfaction with the pace of reform coupled with a new spirit of liturgical freedom have motivated many younger clergy and lay persons to experiment with worshiping in unprecedented ways. Episcopal attempts to limit experimentation meet with partial success, at best. In private homes and in university communities, innovations continue: at times a member of the laity chooses the readings and leads the discussion homily; vestments are abandoned; the whole assembly recites the consecration prayers (sometimes they are improvised by the celebrant); communion (ordinary bread and wine is used) is received under both species and in the hands of the recipients.

These concrete examples of new liturgical forms are indicative of an underlying attitude that is becoming more common among progressive American Catholics. It is basically a democratic attitude about worship that is at odds with the hierarchical concepts of the recent past. The better experimental liturgies strive to preserve the important dimensions of traditional worship, but the criterion of adaptation has shifted. The standard is no longer permission from Rome, but, rather, the changing circumstances of worship and the varying needs of the worshiping community. As young Catholics experience more satisfactory liturgies in unofficial ways, new problems are created when they return to less-advanced parochial worship. These college-educated Catholics often find little meaning in the sermon or the ceremony of the parish church.

It is still too early to determine the results of this confrontation between the new expectations of the progressives and the old ways and mentalities of the established church. This growing polarization could produce discouragement and defection from the official church, or it could result in the building of parallel communities disassociated from parish structures, but not from the Catholic tradition. Or the liturgical tensions could produce a kind of healthy dialectic with the official church that would move the latter into a more progressive orientation. But whatever the future holds for liturgics, the 1960's will be viewed as a major turning point in the worship experience of American Catholics.

RENEWED MORALITY

In addition to the tensions and polarizations in creed, structure, and cult, American Catholics experienced, during the last decade, an upheaval in moral teaching and discipline. The new morality, with its emphasis on subjectivity, situationalism, and pluralism, is part of the larger ferment in American mores. But the clash of the new morality with the traditional legalism and casuistry of much Catholic thinking has been particularly intense. The much-publicized controversy over *Humanae Vitae* is a major public example of the conflict between official dictate and personal conscience. But, in a more silent way, the general falling-off in the practice of private confession is still another indicator of the irrelevance of the morality of the older code, with its own set of motivations and sanctions.

Much of the older morality was externally imposed by moral theologians with hierarchical backing. The foundations of this morality were said to be faith and reason. The former consisted largely of canonical interpretations of biblical ethics. This morality was circumscribed and rigidified because of the limitations of Catholic biblical and theological research and because of the narrowing effects of a code of morality fashioned for the use of confessors. The rational basis of much Catholic morality rested on an overly fixed interpretation of natural law. Instead of seeing natural law as right reason used flexibly for the individual and general welfare, it was understood in a much more deterministic sense. The laws of nature were not interpreted as possibilities for creative becoming, but rather as permanent rules written in the biological and cosmic order of things.

The new morality, which is becoming more prevalent among Catholics, stresses the internal determination of conscience over externally imposed edicts. Whether it be a question of Sunday-mass obligation, the use of contraceptives, or conscientious objection to military service, a broader spectrum of criteria is employed for the formation of personal conscience. Official church statements constitute only a part of this spectrum of standards for an ethical decision. Also to be considered are the shifting demands of the situation, both private and public, the opinions of other thinkers, perhaps at variance with official decrees, and the intentions of the deciding individual. Thus, right reason and the ethical models of scripture operate in a more flexible way as guidelines for personal options rather than as intransigent norms of conduct. The broader spectrum of criteria for moral decision-making was not completely foreign to the older

Catholic ethic, but the emphasis in the past was much more clearly placed on obedience to edict, rather than on the risk of informed personal decision.

Because most American Catholics in the 1960's had been trained in the ways of the older morality, a feeling of anomie and confusion has beset them. The movement from a code-book morality to the more relative and precarious morality of the personal search has created new strains for Catholic confessional practice. The quantification of sinful acts and the anonymous priestly absolution have ceased to be a central concern of the contemporary theology of penance. The latter focuses on the long-term growth and orientation of the persons, a more communal sense of repentance, and the priest as counselor rather than judge, Moreover, Catholic morality has, in recent years, stressed the social dimensions of Christian living over the individualistic preoccupations of the previous sinful-act morality, with its special concentration on sex. Because these moves in ethical thinking have been relatively recent and sudden, the above-mentioned liberal-conservative polarizations are often acutely evident in Catholic homes, schools, and churches on moral questions.

The ferment in Catholicism has also significantly affected the extensive American parochial school system. Although attendance has not fallen off greatly, the motivations for sending children to Catholic schools have shifted notably. Reasons of social (and, at times, racial) class maintenance seem to motivate parents more than the religious and ethnic values that previously urged them to send their children to these private schools. Severe economic pressures have also forced the closing of some schools, and these financial strains augur many more school closings in the next decade. Rising costs and diminishing numbers of church professionals promise a very uncertain future for Catholic parochial education. Moreover, among college-educated Catholics, there is widespread questioning about the value of preserving the church school system at great costs, when quality public education can be supplemented by other forms of religious education.

ECUMENICAL STEPS

The last decade marked the entrance of the Catholic church into the modern ecumenical movement. The presence of Protestant and Orthodox observers at Vatican II and the Council's Decree on Ecumenism were in stark contrast to the negative Roman Catholic attitudes on ecumenism expressed in Pius XI's encyclical, *Mortalium Animos,* published in 1928. The differences between these two documents depict profound changes in the Catholic church's understanding of itself and its relation to separated Christian and non-Christian bodies. Yet, the ecumenical exhilaration of the early 1960's has largely faded and given place to plodding efforts of theologians and church bureaucrats as they inch toward greater Christian unity. Ecumenism has failed to reach the majority of churchgoers in the grass-roots churches in any significantly energizing way. The ecumenical elan of Vatican II has given way to a certain discouragement about institutional inertia and fear of change in the churches.

It would be very shortsighted, however, not to recognize the ecumenical gains of the last decade. In America, attitudes changed importantly: Catholics put aside their hostile defensiveness toward Protestants and began regarding them as separated brothers. American Protestants, influenced by the remarkable historical convergence of Pope John XXIII and John F. Kennedy, were overcoming their long-standing fears of the Roman Catholic menace. Theological advances were also impressive: a new understanding of how other Christian bodies were part of the one church universal, and a richer evaluation of the life, ministry, and witness of separated churches. These insights opened new and as yet unexplored avenues of possible rapport among the churches.

Three general paths toward unity were encouraged by Vatican II: prayer, study and mutual action. Ecumenical worship services became customary, especially during Church Unity Week in January. But intercommunion remained a stumbling block between various Christian bodies. Although such intercommunion has, in actual practice, been restricted to underground and experimental groups, its theoretical justification has received much support on both Catholic and Protestant sides. In scholarly circles, studies of other church movements in history are conducted without polemics and distortions, and many Catholic colleges have developed ecumenical programs. The American Catholic hierarchy has launched a number of study commissions meeting with Christian and Jewish bodies. On the grass-roots level, a few attempts have been made to initiate dialogues between separated Christians on religious issues, but enthusiasm for this has been difficult to maintain.

Cross-denominational participation in social movements concerning race, peace, and poverty has produced one of the most fruitful ways toward unity among religious groups in America. Catholics, Protestants, and Jews have collaborated in significant civil rights demonstrations, anti-Vietnamese war protests, and efforts on behalf of the poor at home and abroad. Such secular ecumenism is drawing Americans together in spite of denominational barriers. In secular ecumenism, Catholics and Protestants often find that they are closer to one another in theological theory and actual practice than they are to members of their own denominations. This ecumenical discovery may, in the future, lessen the importance of separations between Catholics and Protestants and foster a diversified cross-denominational life in areas of worship and theology, as well as

in social involvements. Thus, at the beginning of the new decade, the ecumenical movement is a mixture of frustration and hope, of ecclesiastical doldrums and creative possibilities.

CONCLUSION

We have briefly examined areas of conservative-progressive polarization in the Roman Catholic church today. Each area—the nature of the church, doctrinal development, and forms of polity and authority, liturgy, morality and ecumenism—has its own configuration of problems in the polarizations described above. Yet, underlying all these tensions is a basic conflict of over-all outlook and commitment. We have called this a difference of world view couched in theological-ecclesiastical symbols. The conservative view embraces hierarchical order and control, conceptual permanence, monarchical-paternal direction, patterned prayer, a repressive-edict morality, and clear lines of ecclesiastical demarcation. By contrast, the progressive Weltanschauung stresses community and communion, developmental symbols, charismatic-fraternal leadership, freer worship, subjective-situational ethics, and ecumenical diversity. The polarities could be even more sharply drawn between "nay" or "yea" attitudes toward theoretical-institutional change and personal-communal self-determination. Catholic structure and life in the future will be determined by which voice prevails.

NOTES

[1] The 1950's witnessed the mild origins of inner Catholic criticism in the writings of Thomas O'Dea, John Tracy Ellis, and Joseph H. Fichter.

7
mexican americans

LUIS F. HERNANDEZ

As of November, 1969, the census issued a special report on persons of Spanish origin in the United States. Nine million persons identified themselves as of Spanish origin: 55 percent classified themselves as Mexican; 16 percent as Puerto Rican; 6 percent as Cuban; 6 percent as Central or South American; and 17 percent as "Other Spanish." The census showed that 79 percent were born in the United States, the Commonwealth of Puerto Rico or in outlying areas of the United States; 61 percent lived in Arizona, California, Colorado, New Mexico, and Texas.

Spanish is currently spoken in the homes of about one-half of the population of Spanish origin, which makes Spanish the most widely spoken language after English in the United States. The population thirty-five years old or older had completed only 8.5 years of school, compared with 12.0 years in the general population of the same age; but among young adults twenty-five to thirty-four years of age, the median level of education was 11.7 years compared with 12.6 among others. The income of families of Spanish origin was, on the average, $5,600, about 70 percent of that of other families; their unemployment rate was 6.0 percent, about 1.7 times that of all other persons in the labor forces. Only 25 percent of the employed Spanish-origin men and 41 percent of employed Spanish women held white-collar positions, in comparison with 41 percent for all other men and 61 percent for all other women. (These statistics are from U.S. Bureau of the Census, Current Population Reports, Series P-20, no. 213, "Persons of Spanish Origin in the United States: November 1969," U.S. Government Printing Office, Washington, D.C., 1971).

The following article examines the situation of the Mexican Americans, and the Puerto Ricans are discussed in Chapter 9. Something should be said here about the Cubans. The majority of Cubans are refugees who fled from Castro. At first, they settled in Miami with the expectation of returning to Cuba when Castro was ousted. As it became clear that Castro would remain in power, the Cuban refugees began to migrate to other large cities and to attempt to integrate themselves in American life, although there are now almost half a million Cubans still in Miami. Many were educated urban people and adjusted rapidly; many opened small stores and made the same kind of adjustment as earlier European immigrants had made. Although they have met discrimination, they have not had the same difficulties as the Puerto Ricans or Mexican Americans.

Mr. Hernandez is assistant professor of education at San Fernando Valley State College and is consultant to the Mexican-American Studies program of the Los Angeles city schools.

What is a Mexican American? The answer to this question is as complex as the definition of what an American is. Indeed, Mexican Americans themselves find it difficult to define who they are. There are those who say, "I am an American of Mexican descent." Others say, "No, I am a Latin American," or ". . . a Spanish-speaking American," or ". . . a

Adapted from Luis F. Hernandez, *A Forgotten American*, 1969. Reprinted by permission of the Anti-Defamation League of B'nai B'rith.

Spanish-surnamed American," or ". . . an American of Mexican parentage," or ". . . an American Mexican." Some may even call themselves "Mexican American without the hyphen." Still other terms exist, some more recent than others, such as Chicano or Brown People. Each term expresses a particular philosophy or an attitude regarding self-identification. To consider Mexican Americans a homogeneous group with a given set of characteristics and qualities is therefore to stereotype.

Further analysis of Mexican Americans in terms of location, origin, history and culture will lead to the insight and understanding that they are culturally distinct from the dominant society as regards language, customs, heritage, attitudes and values.

The majority of the nearly 4,000,000 Mexican Americans are to be found in the southwestern part of the United States, with the largest concentrations in Los Angeles and San Antonio Yet large groups also live in Chicago, Detroit and Gary, Indiana. It is likewise significant to note that Mexican Americans vary from state to state, from community to community. The differences are based on local "in" and "out" attitudes, the economic resources and size of the community, whether it is rural or urban and whether the leadership is to be found on a local or state level.

The origin of the group is another major factor in determining the various ways in which Mexican Americans identify themselves. Some may be the descendants of the original settlers of an area, such as the people in the Chama River valley in New Mexico, settled in 1598. A simple review of place names in the West and Southwest gives ample indication of the presence there of a Mexican-American population dating back to the period of Spanish and Mexican exploration and settlement: San Francisco, Atascadero, Pecos River, Colorado River, Amarillo, Santa Fe, Los Alamos, Alamogordo, Nogales, Pueblo, San Joaquin Valley, Sacramento. (A closer study of the map also demonstrates a variance in the concentration of Spanish names. Thus, in Texas and Arizona there are fewer such names than in California or New Mexico, indicating that the former areas were not as attractive for settlement.) It is estimated that 1,333,000 Mexican Americans are descen-

dants of Mexicans who were residents of the West and Southwest as far back as 1848.

Of the remaining 2,667,000 Mexican Americans most are recent migrants or else first- and second-generation Americans. There have been three large waves of migrants from Mexico, the first of which began in 1910 when the country went through its great political-social upheaval. The United States encouraged this immigration because of the need for agricultural labor created by World War I.

During the 1920's, there was a second wave of migration, again due to the political and economic insecurity of Mexico. It is estimated that, all told, nearly 1,000,000 Mexicans emigrated to the United States between 1910 and 1930.

After World War II a third group of migrants came to the United States, attracted once more by the agricultural labor market.

It must be understood that for a large number of Mexicans there has never been the cultural and psychological wrench generally associated with migration. Many simply consider it a "returning," an attitude which has existed among Mexicans for centuries. For example, early Mexican California families considered themselves to be residents of both California (Alta and Baja) as well as the Mexican states of Sonora or Sinaloa, and had land holdings equally divided among these areas. As a consequence, with the annexation of California by the United States in 1850, many of them considered that a political rather than a territorial differentiation had taken place. Today, too, Mexicans continue to hold this attitude. Many have residences on both sides of the border; many work in one country and live in the other, regardless of their nationality.

A broad study of Mexican history is imperative for a thorough understanding of the Mexican American. However, such a study is beyond the scope of this resource unit. What we shall discuss here are those historical events which are of crucial importance in comprehending the differences that exist among Mexican Americans.

The first of such events is the Treaty of Guadalupe Hidalgo, signed on February 2, 1850, at the end of the Mexican-American War. As a result of this treaty Mexico acknowledged the annexation of Texas by the United States and ceded to the Americans the territory that is presently represented by California and most of Arizona and New Mexico. In addition, Mexican nationals were given one year to decide whether they wanted to move to Mexico, or remain in their homes and become citizens of the United States. Finally, along with the provision of citizenship, the treaty guaranteed the property rights of these nationals as well as freedom of religion and choice of language. (Incidentally, studies of the struggle of Mexican Americans to establish property rights, especially in California, reveal the names of unscrupulous Anglo-Americans who used their position to further themselves politically or materially. For further information, see *Decline of the Californios* by Leonard Pitt.)

The approximately 75,000 Mexicans who decided to remain and receive American citizenship were as varied a group as exists today in any area. However, they reflected those differences typical to Mexico, not to the United States; for built into their group was the system of social stratification that under Spanish rule had controlled Mexico for more than three hundred years.

If we picture this system as a pyramid, at the apex were the peninsulares, those individuals born in Spain who had come to the New World as government, religious or military leaders. This group, overthrown during the Mexican revolution for independence in 1821, was subsequently replaced by the criollos, or creoles, i.e., Mexican-born people of Spanish parents. The criollos, typifying all that was Spanish—physical appearance in particular— were truly "white," unless they had some Moorish blood. To all intents and purposes they became la gente bien (the people who are well off), la gente de razon (the people who reason), la gente decente (the decent people) and los quien mandan (the people who command).

Mexicans of the highest social class owned large land holdings throughout the Southwest, particularly areas that were suited to cattle grazing or farming. When the Anglo-Americans began to move into these newly annexed areas, many of them married into Mexican families in order to secure land for development of new industries or expansion of old ones. In this way, they either inherited land or received large sections as dowry. (In this connection it is a matter of interest to note the number of Anglos who, when fiesta days come to their communities, point with pride to their Mexican ancestors. An even more striking phenomenon is that these ancestors, both Anglo and Mexican, become retrospectively more aristocratic with the passing of the years.)

Below the criollos were the mestizos, those of mixed Indian and Spanish blood, now popularly known as La Raza. The majority group, the mestizos, were established not only socially but economically. Though limited at first in terms of the areas of work or service they could enter, with the Mexican revolution their position greatly improved. A greater freedom was theirs; they could achieve higher social levels. Notwithstanding this, a great deal was dependent on their appearance and coloring; obviously it was easier for el blanco (the white) to "make it" than for el moreno (the dark one).

Below the mestizo was the lowest class, the Indian—the indio, the indígeno. The Indian, together with the uneducated or impoverished mestizo, were the laborers, the soldiers, the artisans, the vaqueros (cowboys) in the class system, and vertical movement on the social scale was difficult for them. Yet the Indian was able to look down upon the Negro, who by 1850 had been nearly completely assimilated into the Indian and mestizo groups.

(During the period of Spanish rule there had been one other grouping, the zambo, a mixture of Negro and Indian. But by the nineteenth century this sub-stratum had vanished.)

The significant fact implicit in the foregoing discussion is that social stratification was basic to Mexican culture and that, when the Southwest became part of the United States, this aspect of Mexican culture was an accompanying element. (In fact, some Mexican Americans still place value on one's social position, skin coloring and type of employment.) Yet class lines were not so markedly drawn as they were in the large cities of Mexico itself. After all, the Southwest bordered on Mexico and, as on any frontier, a great many differences could be overlooked and certain conventions of prejudice modified.

Another event in Mexican history which played a key role in the development of the Mexican American was the Mexican revolution of 1910-1922. During this period there was a mass migration of Mexicans to the United States. Many were political refugees, but the majority came as displaced people who had been victimized by the fast-changing governments and the indiscriminate destruction wreaked by the armies of the revolution.

Those immigrants who came as political refugees generally represented la gente bien, i.e., they were educated and accustomed to living well. A number of them managed to escape with some material wealth which sustained them for a time. Once having decided to remain in the United States (probably because the world they once knew was gone), they were able to integrate into the dominant society because of their education and financial means. At the same time, they retained a pride in their Mexican heritage.

As for the displaced people who came to the United States during this period, they sought asylum and a new hope for the future. They offered little in terms of skill, other than manual; they were handicapped by unfamiliarity with the English language, and they had little formal education. Many, too, were experiencing urban living for the first time.

Both groups, however, had one thing in common—at least in the beginning: they felt their residency in the United States was a temporary one. Therefore, they clung to those aspects of Mexican culture that reinforced their Mexican identity, and this slowed down their assimilation into the dominant culture.

During this period, which just predates World War I, the United States had expanded the agricultural industry of the Southwest. The demands of the war coupled with the resultant curtailment of European and Oriental immigrant labor led to the opening up of the Mexican border. The minimal qualifications regarding literacy and health required for entry into the United States diminished as the labor shortage increased, thus bringing into this country thousands of workers from the farming areas of Mexico. It was these laborers who established the great agricultural industry of the San Joaquin, Imperial, Salt River, Mesilla and lower Rio Grande Valleys. (A close study of the growth of the agricultural, mining and railroad industries of the Southwest inspires one with an appreciation not only of the fortitude of these people but of their contribution to the rapid progress of these areas.)

This migration came to a halt during the Great Depression. In order to alleviate the pressures created by unemployment, the government adopted the simple and cheap expediency of deporting Mexican laborers. Federal, state and local agencies sent carloads of them back to Mexico. In thousands of cases their legal rights were overlooked, and, in the enforced exodus, many who were United States citizens by right of birth were summarily deported. The criterion that was generally used was one of visual identification or stereotype.

From 1940 to the present represents yet another period of immigration, with agricultural labor being the main attraction. In recognizing the importance of such labor to the U.S.A., the two countries signed an agreement, popularly called Los Braceros Program, which brought to the United States thousands of Mexican nationals. Thousands of other Mexicans have waded across the Rio Grande (such action being the origin of the term "wetbacks") and entered this country illegally. In either case, both groups have come seeking enough money to make it possible for them, on their return to Mexico, to improve their socio-economic position.

What is important to understand here is not the details of this latest migration (although they play a role in shaping the attitudes many Mexicans have developed toward Anglos), but the fact that the migration has provided a constant reinforcement of Mexican culture. The majority of Mexican laborers who enter the United States legally come with limited education, skills or language ability, which places them at a great disadvantage in terms of assimilation into the mainstream. These same limitations force them to cluster together in communities (barrios or colonias) which, instead of offering them new experiences, only reinforce the culture they have brought with them

From this rather brief analysis, certain broad generalities about Mexican Americans emerge. These can be summarized as follows:

1. Mexican Americans are a heterogeneous group.
2. Mexican Americans have a strong heritage that reflects Spanish influence.
3. Many Mexican Americans are descendants of original settlers of the West and Southwest.
4. The proximity of Mexico has provided a labor market for the United States.
5. The growth of many industries in the Southwest has been due to Mexican labor.
6. There has been a constant migration of Mexicans to the United States, especially since 1910.
7. Most migrants have come to the United States as laborers.
8. Most migrants reflect a strong rural background.
9. The limited skills and educational background of the migrant have worked against his assimilation.
10. The migrants' limited knowledge of English has forced them to cluster together in communities—barrios or colonias.
11. Living in barrios or colonias has provided a constant reinforcement of Mexican culture and values.

CONFLICT OF VALUES

Any attempt to understand Mexican Americans depends upon recognition of the fact that they possess a set of values different from those of Anglo-Americans. It is this difference in values that constantly creates misunderstanding, resulting in lack of empathy for, sensitivity toward, and acceptance of the Mexican American. Some teachers try to compensate for these differences in values by imposing on their students values that reflect their own personal background. However, such teachers are inevitably at a disadvantage, for, in the imposition of their own values, they are implying that they do not recognize Mexican American culture as an entity or consider it worthy of recognition. Consequently they cannot expect success with their teaching.

It has already been shown that Mexican Americans are heterogeneous; that most of them are rural in origin; that they vary in their stage of acculturation. Therefore, any study of their values must be based on the premise that the degree to which these values are reflected in their lives is dependent on their stage of acculturation and individual differences.

The value system characteristic of most Mexican Americans is based on the development of Mexican rural society. It follows, then that many of these values are traceable to Spanish tradition and the social caste system developed by the Spaniards in their New World colonies, an analysis of which has already been presented.

Spanish Catholicism played an important part in the development of attitudes of fatalism and resignation. In addition, the rural people's closeness to the land, which led to greater awareness of the capriciousness of nature and man's dependency on natural phenomena beyond his control, also fed the development of such attitudes.

Closely tied to religion is authority or leadership, another factor which shaped cultural values. Many decisions or directions were based on interpretations received or learned in the church. Leadership came as well from those members of the family who were in authority. But what carried the greatest weight was the patron system. This system had been established by the Spaniards during the period of colonization and remained in force until recent times. The system depended on a paternalistic boss who made decisions and gave direction; thus laborers rarely had an opportunity for democratic decision-making. Similarly, the social positions created by this boss-worker relationship were seldom altered; therefore, there was little opportunity for change. What adjustments were made in this relationship were almost invariably on a personal basis.

Since most Mexicans were rural in origin, they lived in some degree of isolation. This isolation limited social intercourse which in turn limited cultural exchange. Many aspects of the industrial revolution were late in reaching the rural areas, and major social changes took place very slowly. Instead, there continued to be a consistent reinforcement of the traditional way of life.

This traditionalism helped create a society in which innovation was not important, a society which did not progress or plan for the future. In short, things were the way they were always going to be.

The basic skills of reading and writing were largely absent from this society, for there was no need for them in maintaining the status quo. Furthermore, education was hard to come by in most rural communities.

Isolation and traditional living made for a greater emphasis on the family unit as the source of security and emotional satisfaction. Living in these isolated communities made for an uncomplicated daily pattern, and the various roles that an individual played in such a community were few in number.

Even less complicated was the attitude toward time. To the rural Mexican, there was simply a season for one thing and a season for another. A day's work was regulated by the amount of light available. Some jobs were to be done today, others tomorrow.

In communities of this kind there were some tasks, of course, that required a given skill. That skill was carefully passed from father to son, and it was generally understood that both the skill and the attendant tools were the property of one person or family. However, most families were nonetheless quite self-sufficient. In these communities, people asked, "Quién es?" (Who are you?) not "Que hace?" (What do you do?). In other words, the emphasis was on being, not doing.

Though the above is an over-simplication of Mexican rural society, it does make easy the contrast between Mexican-American and Anglo-American values.

Mexican-American values can be said to be directed toward tradition, fatalism, resignation, strong family ties, a high regard for authority, paternalism, personal relations, reluctance to change, a greater orientation to the present than to the future and a greater concern for being than doing.

The contrasting Anglo-American values can be said to be directed toward change, achievement, impersonal relations, efficiency, progress, equality, scientific rationalization, democracy, individual action and reaction and a greater concern for doing than being.

These contrasting values can be broken down into the following conflicts:

rural vs. urban
isolation vs. cultural exchange
slow vs. rapid social and scientific change
personal vs. impersonal association
authoritarian vs. democratic action
simple vs. complex labor relations
established dependence vs. independence
sacred vs. secular emphasis
concern for the present vs. concern for the future
set social organization vs. social mobility

It must be emphasized again that this is only a cursory evaluation of Mexican values. When the rural Mexican immigrates to the United States, he brings these values with him, and it is these values which come into conflict with those of the Anglo-American. It must also be reiterated that the degree of conflict is determined by the individual's place on the continuum of acculturation.

THE FAMILY

Knowledge of the Mexican-American family structure provides an insight into many problems which may be faced by teachers in the classroom, such as the absence of either interest or desire to be involved in school, shown by both parent and student; student dependency on being told what to do and how to do it; an overall lack of initiative; truancy from school, and so forth.

Vastly more than the school, the family unit provides a foundation for the Mexican-American youngster of emotional and material security that remains with him through his entire life. Therefore, the family will always come first. The family gives the Mexican American a sense of being—an identity. Once this fact is understood by the teacher, he will at the same time understand that school then is not a stage in the Mexican-American youngster's life so much as a means toward an end. It means, too, that many concepts and organizations originating in the school, such as P.T.A., school clubs, school spirit and so forth, are Anglo-American middle-class values, and as such have little meaning to the Mexican-

American youngster—at least until he has progressed well across the continuum of acculturation.

At this point, a brief discussion of the basic organization of a Mexican-American family is in order. The organization is patriarchal. The father is the head of the family and is the ultimate authority. He is the provider; he establishes his position in the family and the community by how well he provides. Traditionally, all men are considered to be superior to women. A girl looks forward to the day she will fulfill her role as a woman through motherhood. As a mother she then becomes the center of the home, where her first duty is to serve her husband. On her shoulders fall the responsibilities of raising the children. The boys are brought up to emulate the father, the girls to follow in the mother's pattern. Thus, there is an early division of labor within the home based on sex differences, which makes for certain work that is done only by a woman, and work that is done by a man.

In addition, in most Mexican families there is the so-called extended family, which may consist of grandparents, maiden aunts, unmarried males or compadres. (Compadres are individuals who have earned a place in the family through any one of innumerable reasons.)

The family is a sanctuary; it is strength; it is identification. As such, the family comes before the individual. A Mexican or Mexican American is thought of first as a Gonzalez or a Sanchez, and only secondly as a Francisco or a Dolores.

In the process of acculturation, many families undergo circumstances which upset or seriously disrupt this orderly pattern. Often the father is unable to provide an income that will support such a structure, and the mother must go to work. In such a situation, the father's machismo (maleness) suffers and his role as head of the family becomes nominal. At the same time, the mother, with the new importance that she achieves as a contributor to the family income, begins to take on a more dominant role in family decision-making. As for the children, they are more and more unsupervised, and gradually lose the sense of security in the home and of parental control

and authority. Thus the entire traditional structure inevitably collapses. To the teacher, seeking to understand causes for certain student behavior, such disintegration of the family unit provides explanations for absenteeism, failure to come to class prepared, lack of cleanliness, poor health, emotional disturbances, early dropouts, etc.

Each youngster mirrors the degree of acculturation of his family, most noticeably in his mastery of language. Though the majority of Mexican-American youngsters are bilingual, the level of bilinguality varies with their position on the continuum. If a student is on the Mexican end of the continuum, he is expected by his family to speak Spanish in the home. This expectation, and even insistence, reduces the reinforcement of English he is learning in school. Generally a youngster from such a family has a more limited vocabulary in both languages than many of his peers, and his speech and pronunciation are adversely affected. Naturally, these handicaps have an adverse effect on such basic language skills as comprehension, speaking, listening, reading and writing.

As a corollary to the above, children of such background tend to demonstrate attitudes and behavior patterns that are basically Mexican in origin. Among these may be particular attitudes regarding time, the importance of an academic education, personal reaction to the teacher, and so forth. As for the parents of this group they have a great tendency to expect more from the school than the school may be capable of doing. They have no real understanding of the process of education. They feel that learning takes place by magic. They find it difficult to understand why their child "hasn't learned anything—he can't do anything—he can't earn a living yet and he's been in school ten years." Many times these parents also oppose concepts that their youngster learn in school. Instead, they fall back on a practical approach to problems based on their personal experience and resist the theoretical, conceptual or academic approach taught in the schools.

The parents' general attitude toward their youngster when he enters high school is more formal and authoritarian. The father is especially intolerant of "deviations in behavior," and the parental solution to such behavior (which is seen as reflecting on parental control and authority) is the use of corporal punishment. However, this punishment becomes especially difficult to administer to mature boys who are aware of their manhood —their being macho.

Often parents stimulate their youngsters to efforts to raise the family level through socio-economic gains. But many times this encouragement proves ultimately detrimental to the family unit, for it demands a greater acculturation on the part of the youngsters. Parents do not realize that the loss of some of the basic Mexican identity is part of the price of such acculturation, while certain young people who acculturate rapidly and identify with the dominant culture find they are increasingly embarrassed by their parents' provincialism.

Mexican-American youth is often burdened by this effort to straddle two cultures. On the other hand, parents who either fear loss of identity and authority or who are not ready to accept the "new ways" do not hesitate to instill feelings of guilt in their children.

It is obvious, then, that youngsters in a state of transition from one culture to another carry many burdens which directly affect their role in the classroom. Their progress is slowed by minimal reinforcement of classroom learning in the home; lack of understanding on the part of parents for school activities which go beyond that of learning; forced decisions in terms of a career or future when there are no clearly defined points of reference, or where high achievement is unreasonably expected by parents who do not or cannot provide an environment which is conducive to building proper study skills; and by the guilty realization that, instead of studying, they should perhaps be contributing materially to relieving the pressures created by the low incomes of their parents.

Knowledge of these encumbrances on the part of a school staff should lead eventually to viable programs to relieve the situation. These should include teacher sensitivity to the lack of home participation in school activities, to an awareness of the lack of motivation of many students, and to the reasons for their dropping out of school. Teachers must learn to accept the limited development of student study skills as a logical outcome of limited space, materials and equipment for study.

The size of the Mexican-American family is a major factor that must also be considered when working with students. In large families with low incomes the oldest child carries the burden of home responsibility at a very early age, and parents generally expect them to contribute to the family income. (This contribution may be in the form of supplying their own clothing and "extras.") In situations where one parent is absent, for whatever reason, the premature responsibility that falls on the eldest becomes easily evident, either through the student's attendance record or his dropping out altogether. Often girls in their early teens manage a whole household, while boys of a similar age may be expected to fill the vacancy left by the absent father—a role for which they have no preparation or training. Nonetheless, prepared or not, the youngster is the head of the house.

The value that education has for the Anglo-American is not the same for the Mexican American. To the latter, it may offer a way out from a future of low status such as his parents had. Because the Mexican-American youngster often has this expectation, he expects that the effects of an education will be immediately perceptible. He wants rapid results. When the fruits of education are slow in coming, he becomes impatient, frustrated and tends either to consider school valueless, or to blame himself for lack of success. This attitude is a commonplace among most disadvantaged groups. Clearly, the implication exists as to the necessity for providing a classroom situation that will in some way be applicable to the youngster's need—especially in terms of content, certainly in terms of opportunity for achievement. In other words, Mexican-American youngsters must taste the fruits of success often.

One should not conclude this section without pointing out that the needs of many Mexican-American youngsters are even more complex than those mentioned above. Generally, they stem from interpersonal kinds of problems—problems quite separate from either the community or the family. In addition to being culturally different, they also carry the pains and sorrows that accompany growth and development. Puberty in any culture is not without its traumas. These youngsters also are subject to all the other variables that exist in any classroom situation, such as the ability spectrum, health, family crises, physical appearance, etc. For the Mexican-American youngster, these factors are exaggerated because of the inevitable comparison and contrast with the Anglo-American enclave in the public schools.

CHICANO POWER

The present-day Mexican American can be described as being in a stage of an upheaval which has taken much of its inspiration from the civil rights movement. Perhaps the major consequence of this recent development has been to give to the leaders within the various Mexican-American communities of the Southwest (the majority of whom are young) the courage to voice their dissatisfaction with the inequalities, discrimination and lack of status which have been the lot of the Mexican American for the last hundred years. These leaders have found that an organized community has a strong voice which can be heard not only in the legislative chambers, but also in the caucus room of political parties.

Mexican-American leadership has taken many forms—from extreme conservative to extreme radical. There are those who advocate compromise, expecting that a slow and gradual recognition of the Mexican American will lead to his eventual assimilation. There are those, too, who can envision a day when Mexican-American identity will be recognized and accepted, without its necessarily being conditional to the assimilation of Mexican Americans. Some groups work for the complete and immediate overhauling of those areas which are responsible for discrimination and inequality. Still others express their determined purpose by joining forces with highly militant Negro groups. In fact, these last have gone so far as to establish a color rather than a cultural identity: the Brown People.

Because, as has been pointed out, the Mexican-American community is segmented into many groups, each with a slightly different interpretation of what a Mexican American is, it is not surprising that the name or label each group gives itself (or another group) reflects this difference in interpretation. However, there is one label which only a generation ago was considered by some as being disparaging and has now come to have general acceptance —Chicano. Since education is patently the key change in social status, education has been the focal point of most Chicano groups.

The increase in the number of Mexican Americans who have attained an education, have achieved success and are returning to the community (if not to live, at least to serve) has swelled the number of leaders and authoritative voices. Many have attained their education through the G.I. Bill. Thus, what could never have been done by an individual or his family has been done through federal aid—but only after military service is completed.

At the same time, a new feeling of personal worth has arisen among Mexican-American youth, especially those in the larger urban communities. To be a Chicano is to be not only of Mexican descent but, more important, it is to be an American. As Americans, Chicanos have a place within the national community. They are a determining factor in the economic market, on the political scene, on the military front. This new sense of worth has given them the strength to demand changes in an educational system that has not yet considered either their individual differences, or the difference in their needs and those of their Anglo-American counterparts. To them, the school is a foreign enclave in their community, an established system that has imposed itself on that community. Recent student walkouts clearly show the new character of Mexican-American youngsters that is developing. An analysis of their grievances and demands demonstrates that they have insight into their problems, and are thoroughly cognizant of their own shortcomings and handicaps. Of greater consequence, still, is that they do not want to be isolated; that they want to be contributing members to the constant development and progress of American society.

These youngsters have quickly learned to use the many tools developed by the other great minority, the Blacks, in achieving change. Close communication with the school as well as with the local community brings immediate knowledge of the young people's activities. In addition, they employ "underground" newspapers, form student organizations on college and high school levels and participate in group action such as picketing, marches, political rallies. More and more, these young people are upsetting the stereotype of what a Mexican American is.

A great awakening has likewise taken place among young Mexican-American parents who are not willing to settle for the same education for their children that they received. Their children, they feel, must be better prepared than they were to cope with the problems and handicaps created by their cultural difference. These parents fully realize the disadvantages created by not having a greater command of the English language. They also understand the gap created by a cultural lag. It is these parents who participate actively in Head Start programs.

Adults who have lived under the disadvantages of not having been properly prepared vocationally are attending adult education programs in even greater numbers. Others are seeking a better knowledge of the English language. Increasingly, there is a feeling in Mexican-American communities that all its citizens must have a more active role in determining their future. In short, the people are developing a broader time orientation.

The preceding has many implications for teachers. In a time of change, not all members of the community are necessarily involved in the change. Once again the prime determinant of mobility is the place the individual occupies on the continuum of acculturation. Movement across this continuum may well be faster because of current legislation that provides beneficial innovations, such as bilingual education. Likewise, new programs at secondary and college levels, sponsored by federal aid, take into account the cultural differences of the Mexican American.

The teachers' contribution to bringing about this change can take many forms. They may make adjustments within established curricula that clearly provide for cultural differences. They may leave the confines of the school altogether and step into the community. They may strengthen language skills. They can adopt new methods of teaching that do not violate the basic principles of learning —i.e., first comprehension, then speaking, then reading, and finally writing.

The forces which have motivated the Mexican American in the direction of change, or "Chicano Power," cannot be dismissed. It is therefore the responsibility of all involved to accept the change, to encourage the development of the individual, and most of all to understand that the Chicano wants and intends to play his role as he best sees it.

8
new york's italians: a question of identity

RICHARD SEVERO

This is a journalist's report on a large and important ethnic group in our biggest city. The author reports that Italian-Americans are torn between wanting to assimilate and the feeling that they have not been rewarded for the attempts they have already made to do so. The diversity of opinion in the Italian community is also revealed. Some Italians are quite at home with their ancient culture and do not feel it threatened in the United States; others feel that Italian culture is being diluted and is less vigorous in the third generation. Almost everybody is worried about the lack of solidarity and organization.

A report on Polish-Americans, Greek-Americans, or any recently immigrated group would reveal the same problems. These groups have not been in the United States long enough to have become part of the "old Americans," but they are getting there. Because of their language, their peasant background, their Catholicism, they have met prejudice. They have tried to overcome it by learning English, educating their children, modernizing their church, and engaging modestly in politics. Economically, they are mostly at the lower end of the middle class, a position they have attained only with great effort; they feel their economic position to be precarious. The decline of the cities (where most of them live), the increase in homeowner's taxes, and above all the direct competion for jobs with groups newly arrived in the city (southern blacks, Puerto Ricans, Mexican-Americans) increase their sense of insecurity.

One cannot help but feel that those who have left the cities have placed the burden of helping new migrants into the city upon the European ethnic groups who are still urban residents and who are scarcely more economically secure than the new arrivals. It may be that the economic and political threats they feel encourage an emphasis on the older cultural traits as a way of increasing solidarity within the group. If this is so, it is an example of how cultural pluralism can enhance conflict.

Mr. Severo is of Italian descent and is a reporter for The New York Times.

The Italians of New York do not agree about who they are, what progress they have made since the great migrations of half a century ago and where they should be going. And yet this people whose identity is so difficult to define has recently been thrust very much into the public eye.

In June, thousands of them gathered in Columbus Circle to protest use of the term "Mafia" as an affront. Later, homeowners from the Corona section of Queens protested the city's plans to take their land for a new school and playground.

Then, in pursuit of what some political observers feel is faltering Italian political "clout," several Democrats of Italian extraction announced their support for the re-election of Governor Rockefeller. Among them were former Mayor Vincent R. Impellitteri and two former City Controllers, Lawrence E. Gerosa and Mario A. Procaccino.

VIEWS ON COHESION

Because of such activity, and because they frequently call themselves "Italian," many of their fellow New Yorkers think of them as being a cohesive group. But Italians themselves say they are far from it.

"There is no one life-style you can point to as being theirs," says Dr. John A. B. Faggi, a historian and director of Columbia University's Casa Italiana.

They are not a closely knit group in any sense. The two great characteristics of the descendants of the immigrants is the pride—frequently unarticulated—they take in being part of the great Romano-Italian civilization, although many of them know very little about it. But mostly, they share an overriding sense of responsibility as American citizens and in that, they are not Italian.

There is disagreement over the number of people of Italian ancestry in the United States, but the best estimate is between 15 million and 20 million with perhaps 1.5 million in and around New York City. Most are the descendants of immigrants who arrived penniless and illiterate from southern Italy more than half a century ago.

THE CINEMATIC IMAGE

Who are these people and what have they become?

Perhaps their identity has been more defined by motion pictures and television than by anything that might be considered truly Italian. The cinema has presented them as brown of eye, black of hair and red of temper. So great was the demand for swarthy Italian gangster styles some years ago that an Irishman named J. Carroll Naish made a fortune portraying them in Hollywood.

Many Americans retain an extraordinary image of the Italian immigrant and his descen-

dants as cultural aberrations who sing tenor and peddle fish, and who are romantic, oily, prudish, devious, faithful, sexy, clannish, open-minded, tolerant, intolerant, brilliant, anti-intellectual, unambitious and industrious—all at the same time.

In New York, Italians are stereotyped as garbage collectors who adorn their lawns with plastic flamingos and who sit behind aluminum storm windows in Queens and talk of how Negroes and Puerto Ricans must wait until they are qualified before they get good jobs. The image of the barber who keeps the Madonna on his dashboard remains alive and well.

These impressions have not been altered by the fact that anticlericalism is an older tradition among the Italians than dashboard Madonnas, or by the fact that a survey on race relations conducted recently for the Urban League suggests that Americans other than Italians are far more reactionary.

Whatever his image, the Italian from his very beginnings in America prided himself on how rapidly he was assimilated. Some immigrant parents refused to speak Italian in front of the children so that they could become American that much faster.

DISPLAY OF UNITY

But on June 29, a remarkable thing happened to the people who have been described as being more American than the Americans. About 40,000 of them, according to the police estimate, gathered at Columbus Circle and waved the Italian tricolor. Perhaps the only Italian word many of them knew was "ciao," but they wore red, white and green buttons calling for "Italian power." After melting in the melting pot for all these years, they looked like they wanted to climb out.

Here was a group New York had taken for granted. But it was also a group that never really considered itself a group, for the Italians and their descendants are notoriously independent of one another. Even in the early days, when they worked for nickels and dimes and were called wops by the immigrants who had gotten there before them, their self-help societies had been weak.

But here they were, reflecting the American proclivity for group defensiveness, joining blacks, Puerto Ricans, Jews, Arabs, Mexicans, Indians, welfare recipients, the aged, conservatives, women, policemen, the New Left, drug advocates, homosexuals and Yippies in protesting for their rights.

If the speech-making at Columbus Circle was taken at face value, those who attended came because they felt that use of the word "Mafia" had smeared them and made them suspect. And there is no question that many Italians, even those who did not go to the Unity Day rally, are upset by the use of the word.

But beneath the rhetoric and the goals expressed by the Italian-American Civil Rights League was a dissatisfaction that went much deeper than use of a label that is not central to Italian culture or the Italian experience in this country.

The dissatisfaction was essentially nurtured by a disagreement with the priorities of city government, an awakening to the fact that Italians have at best been a weak pressure group and a belief that the city now responds only to strong pressure groups. It was dissatisfaction with what Italians see as a double standard.

Why, Italians wonder, is it no longer permissible in respectable circles to use pejoratives to refer to Negroes, Puerto Ricans and Jews, but almost fashionable to direct the same vulgarity at Italians and expect them to laugh at "wop," "Guinea," "dago," and other terms.

LITERARY OUTPUT

A frequent observation about the Italians and their descendants in America is that they have not written much about themselves. Nor have they wanted to read about themselves. The Jews, on the other hand, have shown a desire to read about the Jewish experience. It is a desire at least in part born of oppression and is a striking element of the cohesiveness among Jews.

The Italians were oppressed for centuries, too, but mostly by their own kind. And even when they suffered under the French, Austrians or Spanish, it was on their own soil. The harsh realities of New York at the turn of the century did not arouse in the Italians the feeling of identity through oppression that Jews share.

Pietro di Donato, the son of an immigrant laborer who became a bricklayer himself, wrote an acclaimed work on the Italian immigrant experience more than 30 years ago— "Christ in Concrete." But Mr. di Donato concedes that few Italians bought the book. He feels they have turned their backs on the dignity of the immigrant and what he represented.

"The Italian has become homogenized," he said recently.

He does not compare with the original immigrant. My father took me to the Metropolitan Opera when I was 5, and he had concrete on his shoes. The Italians then were full of legends; they were self-regulating and self-entertaining.

But now the species has degenerated. The Italian-American has become a vociferous, rotund breed; endomorphs in the anarchy of freedom over freedom. A good people gone wrong.

Mr. di Donato is especially critical of working-class Italians for not being able to overcome some of the limitations associated with a lack of education and motivation: "There are few things they enthuse over, except football and baseball. This is the age of the ugly people and the Italians are adapting to it." In a sense, Mr. di Donato is accusing the Italians of being American, which is precisely what they have become.

At the same time, he contends that despite their assimilation, Americans of Italian descent still suffer from a "consciousness of unbelonging."

WHAT'S IN A NAME?

"America has always been an embarrassment for Guiseppe Mozzarella," Mr. di Donato says. "He is attempting to be an American but he does not have the image. For what is an American? He changes his name and he gives his children names like Debra and Gary. If a boy's name is Walter Nash or Bill Tudor, that is American. If it is Guiseppe Mozzarella, it is something else."

It is on this point that substantial disagreement arises among descendants of Italian immigrants.

John Ciardi, poetry editor of the *Saturday Review,* whose parents were immigrants, feels no unbelonging and thinks that "within another 10 years you won't even be able to classify the Italians as an ethnic group."

Alfred Drake, who was born Alfred Capurro in Brooklyn and who went on to win acclaim in such musicals as "Kiss Me, Kate," says he detests the Italian-American label. "I don't like hyphenated nationalities."

He loves to talk about his Italian background, is not offended when he sees "Mafia" in print and insists there is no need for Italians to even consider joining defense groups.

Asked the inevitable—why he changed his name—Mr. Drake laughed and recalled the time an agent told him "Capurro" would be hard for Americans to remember and pronounce. He selected "Drake" he recalled, because as a young man in Brooklyn, he used to walk by the Drake secretarial school. Later, he changed his name legally to Alfred Capurro Drake.

TRYING TO ADAPT

The concert violinist Ruggiero Ricci was born in San Francisco and given the name "Woodrow Wilson Rich" by parents eager to adapt to a new land. Later, they bowed to the American preference for brevity and christened him Roger Rich. A few years later, after they were told their son was a musical genius, they decided he could afford the luxury of an Italian name and Roger became Ruggiero.

Mr. Ricci admits that there are times when he feels like a "displaced Italian." When he is in America, people think he is Italian. When he is in Italy, people know he is not Italian because he cannot speak the language.

Although the Columbus Circle rally raised the question of whether the Italians can form a workable self-help organization, the evidence seems to suggest that they really don't want to.

PROPOSING SOME IDEAS

John Carbone, a Brooklyn insurance broker, has spent fruitless years trying to get Italians to agree on projects that might benefit them. He recalls how he sought to win interest in starting an Italian home for the aged about 10 years ago.

"Every time I'd mention it to an Italian he'd look at me suspiciously and say, 'Who's behind it?'"

Mr. Carbone's Neapolitan father, Amadeo, who is 80, says that a club to which he belongs, Fiore di Boro Park, had 600 members when it started in 1928 and paid $1,000 to women after their husbands had died. Now he says, membership is down to 130, the clubhouse is up for sale and widows get only $500.

"I think that any sort of Italian defense organization is doomed to fail," John Carbone said. "You could not get two Italians to agree on anything."

Still, there are groups that try to organize and represent Italians. The Italian-American Civil Rights League, which organized the Columbus Circle rally, now claims a national membership of almost 30,000. It is attempting to acquire land in Brooklyn for a 400-bed hospital, a narcotics treatment center and community youth center run on a nonethnic basis.

DOUBT ON ETHNIC VOTE

To raise money for the project, it is sponsoring a benefit concert at the Felt Forum on November 20. Tickets to the event are $100, $150 and $200 and those scheduled to appear include Frank Sinatra, Sammy Davis, Jr., Ed McMahon, Godfrey Cambridge, Ross Martin, Vic Damone and Connie Francis and others.

A league spokesman says the artists have donated their talents. But many Italians say they are suspicious of the league because of reports that it has received some support from Italian criminals.

Another group, the Americans of Italian Descent, has been in existence for four years, and also claims a membership of 30,000. Its executive director, Joseph Jordan, admits that it is extremely difficult to enlist Italians in group action.

Political pundits often talk of an "Italian vote" and some Italian-American politicians, among others, tend to reinforce that proposition, since it would suggest they are forces to be reckoned with. And although there are Italians who vote for people with Italian names. there is increasing evidence that the practice is dying, especially among the second and third generations. Sometimes Italians show little interest in voting for anyone.

"The Italians are not really motivated politically," says Barbara Galgano Young, a former reporter for *The Villager* who watched the decline of Carmine G. De Sapio among Italian voters long before De Sapio was ever accused and convicted of conspiracy to bribe a city commissioner. "They are cynical about politicians, Italian and otherwise. They think politics is sordid and unproductive and filled with hacks."

There has been a growth of conservatism among the working-class Italians, as there has among other working-class groups, and this was quite evident in the election just past. But if the experiences of Representative Edward I. Koch, a liberal Democrat, are any indication, the Italian identification with conservatism has its exceptions.

When Mr. Koch ran for the City Council in 1966 a key group of Italians was fearful that he would lose votes in 10 predominately Italian wards in the South Village because he supported a civilian-dominated review board to handle complaints about the police. Such a board was finally established, and then voted down by an overwhelming majority of New Yorkers.

SUPPORT IN "VILLAGE"

Since Mr. Koch refused to tone down his views on the board, his Italian supporters devised a little speech to make him attractive to Italians in the South Village. According to versions supplied by Mr. Koch and Emanuel P. Popolizio, a lawyer who supported him, it was delivered in dozens of tenements and went something like this:

Hello, Mrs. Verdi. I'm Wally Popolizio. You remember me? I used to deliver ice here with my father. Listen, I want you to vote for my friend, Ed Koch. Ed is in favor of good schools and clean streets and he is really interested in this neighborhood. He really cares.

O.K., so he's a little nuts about the civilian review board, but what the hell, vote for him anyhow.

Mr. Koch carried the 10 predominately Italian districts by a huge plurality. And this June, when as a Representative of the 17th District, he faced Paul Rao, Jr., an Italian-American, in the primary, he got 89 per cent of the vote.

"They are a truly remarkable people," says Mr. Koch. "They forgive me when I say things they don't approve of. They are much more understanding and tolerant than the so-called liberals, who turn on me when I express my doubts about something they believe as dogma."

Is there discrimination against New Yorkers with Italian names? If there is, it would appear to be diminishing and the Italians themselves are skeptical when one of their own complains.

And, as if to underscore their lack of defensiveness, the third generation is increasingly marrying non-Italian, especially the Catholic Irish and Poles, but also Protestants, Jews and Puerto Ricans, according to parish priests.

DISPUTES DISCRIMINATION

Manhattan's chief assistant district attorney, Alfred J. Scotti, says: "The banner of discrimination is frequently waved to conceal ineptitude and as a rationalization for one's deficiencies. There may be some discrimination, but I do not believe it is pervasive."

One area in which high-ranking Italians are conspicuously few is the Roman Catholic Church in the United States, in which the prominent Italians in the hierarchy are the Most Rev. Joseph Pernicone, Auxiliary Bishop of New York, and the Most Rev. Francis J. Mugavero, Bishop of Brooklyn.

"The Italians are not a sensitive people like our own," complained the Rev. B. J. Reilly in a letter to John Cardinal Farley on March 4, 1917. "When they are told that they are about the worst Catholics that ever came to this country they don't resent it or deny it. If they were a little more sensitive to such remarks they would improve faster. The Italians are callous as regards religion."

Some Italians think they still have not convinced the Irish of their devoutness.

FIRST IN 400 YEARS

"We still enter the church with the cloak of anticlericalism around us," said the Rev. Mario Zicarelli, assistant pastor of Our Lady of Mount Carmel in the Bronx. "I am the first priest in my family in 400 years and when I did it, my uncle accused me of ruining the family name."

At any rate, Italians still control the Papacy, and the Irish here have observed that if an Irishman became Pope, an Italian would probably stand a greater chance of becoming a Cardinal in New York.

Italians and their descendants have apparently had more success in achieving hegemony in organized crime rivaling the Irish, Jews and Anglo-Saxons. But now an argument has arisen as to whether Italian criminals are a highly organized society that could be called the Mafia.

The Federal Bureau of Investigation, after years of avoiding such a description, decided that Italian-organized crime could be called "Cosa Nostra," which means "Our thing." Now they have been asked by the United States Attorney General not to use any labels.

Ralph J. Salerno, a retired New York police detective of Sicilian extraction who is frequently called a "Mafia expert," says that nothing that could be called a Mafia has existed in New York since 1931. However, he does think that Italian-organized crime is different from that run by non-Italians because it re-quires membership limited to people of Italian blood. He feels it could be called "Cosa Nostra."

QUESTIONS LABELS

But District Attorney Frank S. Hogan of Manhattan, who has won a national reputation for battling organized crime, says that both "Mafia" and "Cosa Nostra" have no basis in fact. He contends that while Italians in organized crime maintain liaison with each other and with non-Italian criminals, there is not a tight-knit organization limited to Italians.

How has the Italian in America fared?

Dr. Faggi of Columbia's Casa Italiana feels that "they have begun to be prosperous, but not spiritually and intellectually."

And State Senator John J. Marchi says that the problems faced by Italians and other ethnic groups in New York are bound to occur in any heterogeneous society, but that they can be solved without special help or defense-group thinking.

In this transitional period for the Italians in New York, many of them remain hopeful about their future in America by taking comfort in the past, and in the enormous vitality the Italian people have shown over the centuries.

"We will endure," Mr. Popolizio said. "We can go to the Anglo-Saxon and say: "You see this road in Scotland? We built it 2,000 years ago."

"I look at a building and I see a Roman arch. I go to court and I know the law I practice stems from something the Romans started. We gave the fork to the French when they were eating with their hands. Even our humble pizza has become American. So, we will be patient."

9
the puerto ricans: protest or submission?

MANUEL MALDONADO-DENIS

When most Americans think about Puerto Ricans, they think of the migrants from the island to the mainland, but they seldom think about Puerto Rico itself. Puerto Rico is part of the United States; its status is that of a commonwealth, which means that the Puerto Ricans have a choice of remaining in that status, of becoming independent, or of becoming the fifty-first state. Puerto Ricans are divided on which choice is most desirable.

Because Puerto Rico is a commonwealth, Puerto Ricans govern themselves, hold American citizenship, and are less taxed than other Americans; but because it is an economically undeveloped country, they are heavily under American economic influence. If Puerto Rico became a state, the Puerto Ricans would have increased political rights but also more economic responsibilities. If Puerto Rico became an independent state, they would have all the political rights of citizens of any sovereign state and complete economic independence if they wanted it.

Although he represents a minority position at present, Professor Maldonado-Denis also thinks that Puerto Ricans would commit cultural suicide by choosing anything except complete independence. It is, of course, a question that the Puerto Ricans will have to decide for themselves; but it is well for other Americans to know the choice that some Puerto Ricans would like to make and why they prefer it.

Dr. Maldonado-Denis is professor of political science at the University of Puerto Rico.

Among the minority groups in the United States, Puerto Ricans are the latecomers. In what constitutes an impressive mass exodus after World War II, nearly a half-million Puerto Ricans emigrated to the United States between 1945 and 1959. As a noted demographer has indicated, from 1940 to 1960 the Island lost nearly a million persons as a result of this mass migration.[1] The majority of these Puerto Rican emigrants have settled in New York City, where an estimated three-quarters of a million live at present. They are concentrated mainly in East Harlem or Spanish Harlem—"El Barrio," as Puerto Ricans are fond of calling it. A recent study has pointed out that since the mid-1950's there has been a reverse flow of migrants to Puerto Rico, estimated to number at least 145,000.[2] Ease of communication with the Mainland, the absence of immigration requirements (Puerto Ricans have been American citizens since 1917), and the spur of economic necessity help to explain the reason why "at least one out of every three persons born in Puerto Rico has experienced living in the United States at some time in his life."[3]

Furthermore, it is the declared policy of the Commonwealth's government to foster this mass migration as an "escape valve" that will help to ease the pressures of a population

Reprinted from "Protest in the Sixties," *The Annals of the American Academy of Political and Social Science* 382 (March 1969), pp. 27-31. reproduced here by permission of the author and publisher.

growing at an annual rate of 2.1 per cent (as of 1966). This migration tends to be among those age groups whose economic productivity is greatest. According to Dr. Vazquez Calzada, in the decade from 1950 to 1960, 70 per cent of the migrants were persons ranging from 15 to 39 years of age. The Island's labor force faces an acute unemployment problem. Government economist Hubert C. Barton has estimated it at 30 per cent, while other economists estimate it at around 14 per cent. But the situation facing the Puerto Rican migrants in the United States is hardly any better. An Associated Press dispatch, quoted in *The San Juan Star,* May 22, 1968, points out that Labor Department official Herbert Bienstock indicated that a 1966 survey had shown that the subemployment rate for Puerto Ricans in slum areas in New York is 33.1 per cent, while the unemployment rate is 10 per cent. In this respect, one need only read Patricia Cayo Sexton's *Spanish Harlem: Anatomy of Poverty* or Helena Padilla's *Up from Puerto Rico* to understand that the lot of the Puerto Rican ghetto-dweller in New York is hardly any better than that facing the "lumpenproletariat" in the slums of San Juan, so vividly described by Oscar Lewis in his controversial book *La Vida.* But, notwithstanding Puerto Rican participation in the Poor People's March on Washington, and some sporadic outbursts of rebellion, it can hardly be said that Puerto Ricans in the United States—as a group that faces the prejudices and hardships of a nonwhite group in a racist society—have achieved, in their struggle for liberation, a level of consciousness and of militancy similar to that of Afro-Americans.

Island and Mainland Puerto Ricans: Similarity of Problems

It would be a grievous mistake, however, if the problems facing the Puerto Ricans in the United States were to be seen as abstracted from the situation of the Puerto Ricans who live in Puerto Rico. The essence of the matter really lies in the relationship that exists between Puerto Rico and the United States.

Puerto Rican Nationality and United States Colonialism

It is my contention that Puerto Ricans are a colonial people with a colonial outlook, and that, as such, they have not been able, so far—as the Afro-American groups are increasingly doing—to achieve a true "decolonization," either in the political or in the psychological sense of the word. This holds true for Puerto Ricans both in Puerto Rico and in the United States. All the problems faced by Puerto Rico as a colony of the United States are found— and magnified—in the American metropolis: the question of identity, the problem of language, and the achievement of political power commensurate with numerical strength. And, yet, an attitude of acquiescence, of passive submission, seems to characterize the Puerto Ricans both here and in New York City, with the exception of those groups within the Puerto Rican population which have mounted a persistent protest against the perpetuation of colonialism in our country ever since 1898. I refer in this instance to those sectors of our population which have carried on the struggle for independence from American domination.

Puerto Rico exhibits a distinct nationality. And Puerto Ricans—including those who live in the Mainland—are a people with a culture, a language, a tradition, a history. Nevertheless, the colonization of Puerto Rico under the American flag has meant the gradual erosion of our culture and the slow but persistent destruction of the Puerto Rican's sense of identity. This means, in effect, that, as the late nationalist leader Pedro Albizu Campos stated on one occasion, the essential goal of any colonial regime is the cultural assimilation of the colonized people. The process is not yet complete because Puerto Rican culture has shown a certain resilience, a certain capacity for survival and resistance, that has forced the colonial legislators and administrators to pause before continuing in their course.

As Frantz Fanon—the most perceptive and articulate writer speaking for the colonized, not the colonialists—has pointed out, colonialism creates in the minds of colonial peoples a sense of inferiority, a feeling of impotence and self-destruction, a desire to negate themselves by becoming more like the colonialists. Thus, aggressiveness tends to take the form of internal aggressiveness, an aggressiveness against one's own group. The situation is very similar to that of the black people living

in a white man's world. They are faced squarely
with the problem of either asserting their own
"negritude" or assimilating to the ways of the
whites. Accordingly, one of the responses to
colonialism may be, not liberation, but submission to the colonizer: assimilation, not the
struggle for identity. This, I submit, has been
the case of the Puerto Ricans. It is only because there are groups within our society which
fight for the survival of our nationality that it
has survived to the present day. Otherwise,
Puerto Rico would have disappeared as a nationality, to become another ingredient within
the American melting pot.

Proindependence Movements

American occupation of the Island in
1898 dealt a grave blow to those Puerto Ricans
who believed that the United States would not
impose upon the Puerto Rican people a colonial regime similar to that which had governed
the Island during the four centuries of Spanish
rule. And, in 1904, independence was adopted
—together with statehood and autonomy—as
one of the definitive solutions to Puerto Rico's
political status by the Partido Union de Puerto
Rico, the most powerful political party at that
time. However, the struggle for Puerto Rican
independence reached its highest peak in this
century during the decade of the 1930's, spear-
headed by the Puerto Rican Nationalist party,
under the leadership of Pedro Albizu Campos.
Proindependence sentiment was strong in
Puerto Rico at the time, and both Albizu
Campos and Luis Muñoz Marín (who later was
to reject the ideals of his youth) were outspoken in the defense of independence. After
several violent encounters with the police, and
the killing of the chief of police (an American)
by members of the Nationalist party, all of its
top leaders were jailed under a "conspiracy"
statute of the federal government (1936). On
Palm Sunday of 1937, the police carried out—
under orders from Governor Blanton Winship—
what is known as the "Ponce Massacre," in
which the police shot unarmed demonstrators
of the Nationalist party in the City of Ponce.
With their leaders jailed, the Nationalist movement entered into a state of disarray, and
official repression gained momentum.

Repression reached its peak in 1950 and
1954, as a consequence of the Nationalist uprising of October 30, 1950, the attempt to kill
President Truman, and the shooting of several
congressmen by four Puerto Rican Nationalists
in 1954. As a result, Albizu Campos spent the
rest of his life in prison, or under police detention in the hospital, where he was interned
following a stroke, until he was released by
Executive order shortly before his death. Many
of his followers were jailed or killed as a result
of these acts, and there are, at present, seventeen political prisoners in Puerto Rican and
American jails, some of them serving sentences
of up to 460 years. It is fair to say that police
persecution of Nationalist party members and
the jailing of the leaders of the party were successful enough to blunt the effectiveness of the
Nationalist party as a political force in Puerto
Rico.

It was also in the 1930's that the Popular
Democratic party (PDP) was founded by Luis
Muñoz Marín. Although originally committed
to independence, social justice, and the liquidation of colonialism, the PDP, once it achieved
power in 1940, veered its course in such a way
that it is, at the present moment, the arch-
enemy of independence. As a result, a group of
the disenchanted founded the Puerto Rican
Independence party in 1946, a party devoted
to the search for independence through the
ballot box. This party reached its greatest
strength in the 1952 elections and then started
to decline to its present all-time low. Dissidence
within its ranks led to the creation, in 1956, of
the Pro-Independence Movement (PIM), at
present the most militant and radical of all
proindependence groups in Puerto Rico.
Although there are at least three other proindependence groups—the Puerto Rican Independence party, the Nationalist party and the
Socialist League—the PIM is undoubtedly the
one which, by its policy of confrontation,
exhibited through resistance to the military
draft, alliance with United States New Left
groups, and attendance at the Organization for
Latin-American Solidarity (OLAS) Conference,
as well as through political activism guided by
a radical ideology, has been able to carry on
the protest movement in Puerto Rico most
successfully at the present time.

Contemporary Conflicts

Puerto Rican youths are compulsorily drafted into the United States Army, as a result of the fact that, in 1917, Congress imposed American citizenship on the Puerto Rican people. A movement has emerged, particularly among university youth, for the purpose of refusing to serve in the United States Armed Forces. About a year ago, more than a thousand Puerto Rican youths signed a public statement declaring that they would refuse to enter the United States Army under any circumstances. The United States District Attorney in San Juan has already indicted about fifty youngsters, but the number of opponents to the draft keeps increasing. So far, the policy of the United States government seems to be one of intimidation, but none of the cases has come up before a court. The matter is generally disposed of by means of a technicality.

University students have also expressed their protest by battling the police on the campus at the University of Puerto Rico on October 28, 1964, and, more recently, on September 27, 1967. In May of 1967, more than a thousand students successfully disrupted a parade of the Reserve Officers Training Corps (ROTC) at the University of Puerto Rico, as a means of demonstrating their protest against militarism. The leaders were suspended as a result. Many of them now face indictments for the events of September 27, 1967, when the police shot at the students on two occasions, killing a man who happened to be on campus at the time as an innocent bystander.

"Repressive Tolerance" and the Colonialist Syndrome

As an American colony, Puerto Rico illustrates very clearly what Professor Marcuse has called "repressive tolerance." The Puerto Rican is allowed to express his views about "the System," insofar as he does not endanger it. Indeed, "the System" itself fosters the kind of dissent that can be shown as a confirmation of its members' own "generosity" and sense of "fair play." In this respect, the colonial elite that rules Puerto Rico on behalf of the American power elite has been successful, so far, in muting Puerto Rican discontent or in suppressing it altogether by incorporating or assimilating it within the existing structures. The same holds true—with rare exceptions—with Puerto Rican leaders in New York. The Puerto Rican youngster is taught an official interpretation of our history that denigrates or ignores the independence movement and its tradition. Private schools in Puerto Rico—out of which come the future numbers of the colonial elite —indulge in the antipedagogic practice of teaching everything in English. The mass media are almost totally controlled by Americans. Indoctrination to imitation of American middle-class values is constant in the mass media. Add to these factors the influence of absentee ownership of most of our industry (78 per cent is owned by Americans), commerce, and financial institutions; the occupation of more than 13 per cent of our tillable land by American Armed Forces; and the drafting of our youth into the United States Armed Forces, and the picture will emerge more clearly. Puerto Rico is a country that is threatened at its very roots by the American presence here, the rhetoric of "a bridge between two cultures" and "bilingualism" notwithstanding. After seven decades of American colonial rule, what is really surprising is that there is still a hard core of Puerto Rican culture and identity that holds out against the American culture's penetration.

And yet, the most pervasive, the most significant, tendency that one finds among the Puerto Rican population, both in the Island and in the United States, is what one might call the "colonialist syndrome": that aggregation of attitudes, orientations, and perceptions which magnifies the power, wisdom, and achievements of the colonizer while minimizing the power, wisdom, and achievements of the colonized. No one illustrates this attitude better than the completely "Americanized" Puerto Rican, who, in his quest to be more "American", seeks to identify as closely as possible with the patterns of culture of the metropolis. The grotesque aspect of this syndrome may be found in the "men" (as he is called), or cultural hybrid, resembling the Mexican "pachuco," whose sense of identity is so blurred that he—like his Mexican counterpart described so brilliantly by Octavio Paz in *The Labyrinth of Solitude*— has no roots and no bearings: a cultural schizophrenic who does not know what he is.

The "colonialist syndrome" is, of course, played down by the elite that helps it on its way, but it is nurtured by an almost complete dependence on the United States Congress as the main source of legislation for Puerto Rico, as well as by other federal aid programs extended to Puerto Rico and administered directly by the federal bureaucracy. As long as Puerto Ricans themselves do not control the decision-makers who determine their fate on a day-to-day basis, the attitudes and orientations characteristic of colonial subservience to the wielder of power will continue to prevail in Puerto Rico and among Puerto Ricans in the Mainland. Today, the Puerto Rican protest is limited to a minority of the population, while the majority remains acquiescent, perhaps more out of a sense of impotence than out of approval of the present situation.

A Puerto Rican protest will only be effective when Puerto Ricans free themselves from the mental bonds that, more than anything else, hold them in submission. The real problem now is how to crystallize the Puerto Rican protest effectively, so that more and more groups within the population, here and in the Mainland, will come to understand, at the conscious level, that their true interest lies, not in assimilation and dissolution, but in assertion and identity. "Puerto Rican power" should be a welcome complement to Black Power, to the extent that it sees Puerto Ricans—as the Afro-Americans are increasingly seeing themselves—as a nationality that is faced with the threat of extinction within the framework of a colonial situation. This can only mean—as the one fruitful way of achieving "Puerto Rican Power"—that charity begins at home, that is to say, that Puerto Ricans must achieve total power in Puerto Rico.

Independence Versus Assimilation

The definitive triumph of colonialism would be the total assimilation of our population into the American union. Insofar as the Puerto Rican protest movement is an anticolonialist one—and so it has traditionally been—it will have to be attuned to the currents that are at present shaking the world with the demands of "the wretched of the earth." This means no more, and no less, than that the only way in which a protest movement can be successful in Puerto Rico is through the espousal of independence as a first step toward the achievement of economic independence. This struggle is at present being carried out by the Pro-Independence Movement of Puerto Rico, but also by other proindependence groups in the Island. The message is being carried to the ghettos of New York and elsewhere. Colonialism as an institution is dead the world over. Puerto Rico cannot—will not—be the exception to this rule. Otherwise, we may be faced with a situation similar to that of New Mexico; cultural hybridization and eventual assimilation to American culture. This prospect—insofar as Puerto Ricans achieve consciousness of its real implications—should be enough to deter them from committing cultural suicide by becoming the fifty-first state of the American union.

NOTES

[1] José Luis Vázquez Calzada, "La emigración puertorriqueña:" solución o problema?," *Revista de Ciencias Sociales,* Vol. VII, Núm. 4 (Diciembre 1963).

[2] José Hernández Alvarez, *Return Migration to Puerto Rico* (Berkeley: University of California, 1967), p. 40.

[3] *Ibid.,* p. 40.

10 distribution of minorities in the united states

  The preceding sections have described some of the important minority groups in the United States. Table 1 gives a more detailed picture of racial and ethnic minorities, and Table 2 does the same thing for religious groups. Unfortunately, this book is being written before detailed material on minority groups is available from the 1970 census. For a number of groups, it has been necessary to use 1960 figures. Although the figures may not be precise, the relative percentages are. The figures in Table 2 should not be taken too seriously. Because the Constitution provides for the separation of state and church, the census does not ask questions about religion. The figures come from church organizations. Some groups count as members all those baptized in the church; others count only those who formally join as adolescents or adults. Some groups are very stable; some split frequently. Only the larger, more stable groups are reported on in Table 2; and although the actual figures are unreliable, the relative percentages are accurate.

  Notice that 37 percent of the American population does not belong to any church. Nothing is known about this group; they may have always been unchurched (church membership in the United States has been increasing over the past fifty years) or they may have been raised in Catholic, Protestant, or Jewish homes.

TABLE 1. Minority Groups in the United States

Date	Group	U.S. total	Percent total of population	Other data
1969[a]	Negro	22,300,000	11.0	Negroes in South, 52% Negroes in North, 41% Negroes in metropolitan areas, 64%
1968[b] (est.)	Indian, Eskimo, Aleuts	680,000 28,078	0.3 —	Indians in selected states: Arizona, 15.9%; Oklahoma, 12.4%; New Mexico, 10.7%; Alaska, 8.1%; California, 7.5%; North Carolina, 7.3%
1969[c]	Spanish origin Mexican Puerto Rican Cuban Central or South American Other Spanish	9,230,000 5,073,000 1,454,000 565,000 556,000 1,582,000	5.0	Population of Spanish origin in five southwestern states (Arizona, California, Colorado, New Mexico, Texas), 61%
1960[d]	Japanese	464,332	Less than 1%	Japanese in selected states: California, 34%; Hawaii 44%
1960[d]	Chinese	237,292	Less than 1%	Chinese in selected states: California, 40%; Hawaii, 16%; New York, 16%
1960[d]	Filipino	176,310	Less than 1%	Filipinos in selected states: California, 37%; Hawaii, 39%
1969[e]	National origin of selected groups of the white population German English Irish Italian Polish Russian	19,961,000 19,060,000 13,282,000 7,239,000 4,021,000 2,152,000	10.1 9.6 6.7 3.7 2.0 1.1	

[a]U.S. Bureau of the Census, *Current Population Reports*, Series P-23, no. 29, "The Social and Economic Status of Negroes in the United States, 1969" (Washington D.C.: U.S. Government Printing Office, 1970), pp. 3, 7.

[b]Estimates made by the Bureau of Indian Affairs, Herbert A. Aurback *et al.*, "The Status of American Indian Education," *An Interim Report of the National Study of American Indian Education*, (University Park, Pa.: Pennsylvania State University, January 1970), p. 21.

[c]U.S. Bureau of the Census, *Current Population Reports*, Series P-20, no. 213, "Persons of Spanish Origin in the United States: November, 1969" (Washington, D.C.: U.S. Government Printing Office, 1971), Table 1, p. 4.

[d]U.S. Bureau of the Census, *Statistical Abstracts of the United States: 1970*, 91st ed. (Washington, D.C., U.S. Government Printing Office, 1970), Table 31, p. 29.

[e]U.S. Bureau of the Census, *Current Population Reports*, Series P-20, no. 221, "Characteristics of the Population by Ethnic Origin: November, 1969" (Washington, D.C.: Government Printing Office, 1971).

TABLE 2. Membership in Major Religious Groups, United States

Date	Group	Number in sub-groups	Number in main groups	Per cent of all churched
	Major Baptist groups		22,419,000	17
1967	Am. Bapt. Convention	1,455,000		
1965	Nat'l. Bapt. Conv. of America	2,669,000		
1958	Nat'l. Bapt. Conv. U.S.A., Inc.	5,500,000		
1969	Nat'l. Primitive Bapt. Conv. Inc.	1,465,000		
1968	Southern Bapt. Conv.	11,330,000		
	Churches of Christ		4,433,000	3
1968	Churches of Christ	2,400,000		
1968	United Churches of Christ	2,033,000		
1968	Disciples of Christ		1,593,000	1
1968	Church of Jesus Christ and Latter Day Saints (Mormons)		2,180,000	2
1968	Episcopal		3,374,000	3
	Lutherans		8,638,000	7
1968	American Lutheran	2,576,000		
1968	Lutheran Church in America	3,280,000		
1968	Lutheran Church, Missouri Synod	2,782,000		
	Presbyterians		4,185,000	3
1968	Presbyterians	962,000		
1968	United Presbyterian Church in the U.S.A.	3,223,000		
1968	United Methodist		10,991,000	9
1951	African Methodist Episcopal		1,166,000	1
1968	Total Protestants		69,424,000	54
1969	Greek Orthodox Archdiocese of North and South America		1,875,000	1
1969	Russian Orthodox Greek Catholic Church of America		1,000,000	1
1969	Roman Catholics		47,873,000	37
1966	Jews		5,780,000	5
1968	Membership in all religious bodies		128,470,000	

Per cent of total population

				63
1968	Unchurched			37

SOURCE: U.S. Bureau of the Census, *Statistical Abstracts of the United States: 1970*, 91st ed. (Washington, D.C.: U.S. Government Printing Office, 1970), Table 50, pp. 41-42.

II.

minority problems in other parts of the world

introduction: some definitions

Because of its racial, religious, and ethnic diversity, as well as its peculiar history of racism, the United States exhibits an unusually complex array of problems in intergroup relations. But these problems are also to be found in other parts of the world. Few countries are so homogeneous that they do not have the possibility of intergroup hostility, although it should be understood that not every heterogeneous nation experiences this. The migration of peoples and political upheavals have been especially productive of situations in which racial, religious, and ethnic groups clash. Part II presents examples of such conflicts outside the United States.

The principles drawn from observations about the United States, included in the introductions to the other parts of the book, apply equally well to this one, so there is no need for a separate discussion. It is especially important to draw attention to the introduction to Part V, where the diverse sources and causes of intergroup antagonism are analyzed.

11
the comparative study
of intergroup conflict

ARNOLD M. ROSE

Many societies in various parts of the world and at earlier periods have had problems of intergroup relations, although most have not had the racist prejudice that underlies the American situation. These societies have had a considerable variety of forms of government, economy, family structure, and other aspects of social organization, and it is interesting to see what kinds of minority problems have developed under these social forms. This is the topic of the present selection, and it provides an introduction to the other readings in Part II, which describe specific minority problems in countries other than the United States. This study will be referred to again in Part V, which systematically examines the sources of intergroup conflict, prejudice, and discrimination.

The comparative study of cultural behaviors has taken two forms: (1) a description of one or a few other societies, implicitly or explicitly contrasted with what is assumed to be our own; (2) a systematic comparison of a limited set of related behaviors in a great range of societies. The present study uses the latter approach. Outstanding previous users of this approach have been those who have worked with the Human Relation Area Files at Yale University. Our study differs methodologically from the Yale studies in that practically all of our data come from literate societies, while practically all of the Yale data come from preliterate societies. Most of the literate societies known to the author in which separable and distinctive minorities are or were living in a majority population were included in the analysis. The U.S. was omitted to avoid the possibility of bias. Sometimes a society changed so much in historical time that it was analyzed as two separate societies. Data were collected by 240 senior and graduate students at the University of Minnesota as term papers in the course on intergroup relations. Only the more adequate papers were used in the analysis and in a number of cases there was more than one paper on a given society. The minority groups and the societies compared in the analysis are the following:

Moslems in India
Falashas in Ethiopia
Negroes in Brazil
Chinese in Malaya
Marranos in Spain
Parsis in India, twelfth to sixteenth century, seventeenth century to present
Doukhobors in Canada
Negroes in contemporary France, Germany, and England
Irish in England, seventeenth to nineteenth centuries
Lapps in Sweden
Mongols in China, thirteenth to sixteenth centuries
South Tyrolese in Italy since 1918
Karens in Burma
Huks in the Philippine Islands

Reprinted from *The Sociological Quarterly* 1 (January 1960), pp. 57-66.

Protestants in Italy (including Waldensians)
Swedish-speaking people in Finland
Eta people in Japan
Maoris in New Zealand
Negroes in South Africa
Jews in Russia
Old Catholics in Germany
Hindus in South Africa
Mennonites in Paraguay
Negroes in British Africa
Indians in Middle and South America
Arabs in France
Arabs in Israel
Druses in Lebanon and Israel
Kurds in Turkey
Jews in Medieval Russia
Ainus in Japan
Christians in Ancient Rome
Albigensians in Medieval France
Greeks in Ancient Rome
Moors in Spain
Catholics in England
Bantus in Rhodesia

Our study is focused on intergroup conflict, discrimination, and prejudice even though some of our cases were not characterized by a significant amount of these things. Most of the theories offered to explain problem relationships between groups are in terms of a conflict of interests, ideological (including religious) opposition, specific historical traditions such as racism, and individual psychological mechanisms (such as frustration-aggression or the "authoritarian personality"). Without in the least denying the validity of these theories, we shall attempt in this paper to relate intergroup problems to a purely sociological variable, namely, aspects of the social structure characteristic of the majority and minority group. The question posed is: Are specific patterns of intergroup conflict, discrimination, and prejudice associated with certain forms of the social structure? Our ability to answer this question is limited by (1) inadequacies in the literature, which usually fails to describe objectively many aspects of the social structure; (2) inadequacies in the sample and coverage of material partly due to our own lack of knowledge of intergroup relations and social organization in many parts of the world; (3)

inadequacies on the part of the student readers who sometimes could not perceive how they were to answer. Because of these inadequacies, the conclusions of this paper should be regarded as tentative. Because of the significance of its subject matter the study is worthy of more systematic replication.

In considering the dependent variables of conflict, discrimination and prejudice, the concept of "severity" or "intensity" will be used to describe the measure or index employed. Examples of forms of discrimination on a scale of decreasing intensity are execution, torture, destruction of property, restriction of activities, segregation without additional restraints, unfavorable attitudes. While correlation tables will be used to indicate an association, no effort will be made to calculate an exact coefficient of correlation. The somewhat arbitrary methods necessary in a study of this sort, used to select cases and to fit only partially complete descriptions of them into categories, render unjustifiable any exact statistical correlation. The tables to be presented make comparisons and suggest patterns of relationship; they do not provide measurable data.

Discriminations, conflicts, and prejudice were classified for the purposes of this study into five categories: economic, political, personal, religious, and social. These rubrics may best be defined in terms of the major types of behavior categorized into each:

Economic Discrimination. Destruction or confiscation of property, restrictions on land or property ownership or business practices, discriminatory employment practices.

Political Discrimination. Withholding of citizenship, the right to vote, or positions of political authority.

Individual Discrimination or Persecution. Physical violence, execution, imprisonment, requiring registration or identification, curfews, suppressing press or schools.

Religious Discrimination or Persecution. Desecration or preventing building of place of worship, forcing disobedience of religious

TABLE 1. Forms of Discrimination Reported in Societies with a Feudal Economy (Number of Societies Reported)

	Economic	Political	Personal	Religious	Social
Extremely harsh	1	1	8	1	1
Relatively harsh	2	–	3	1	1
Moderate	2	1	3	–	7
Little or none	–	–	–	–	–

TABLE 2. Comparison of Forms of Discrimination Reported in Societies with Slave Economies and Slavery in Recent Past (Number of Societies Reported)

	Economic		Political		Personal		Religious		Social	
	S	PS[a]	S	PS	S	PS	S	PS	S	PS
Extremely harsh	1	–	1	–	5	–	1	–	–	–
Relatively harsh	–	4	–	–	2	–	1	–	1	–
Moderate	3	3	–	4	1	–	–	–	3	7
Little or none	–	–	–	–	–	6	–	–	–	1

[a]S, slave economies; PS, recent past.

rules, penalizing worship or other religious practices.

Social Discrimination. Forbidding social intercourse, segregation, physical isolation, suppressing "culture," relegating to socially inferior positions, restricting public (but nonpolitical) roles, unfavorable attitudes.

The findings of the study are the following.

Discrimination in Feudal Economies (Table 1). The literature gives greatest attention to personal discrimination, and in feudal economies most of it tends to be harsh. Economic patterns tend to be fixed, and the consistency modifies some of the harshness of treatment of minority groups. Social segregation exists, but it is not a main source of harshness of treatment of minorities in feudal economies.

Discrimination in Slave and Former Slave Economies (Table 2). The pattern described above for feudal economies applies also to slave economies. There is a great difference in intergroup relations, however, for societies that have abolished slavery. Harsh personal treatment has been largely abandoned; social and

political discriminations are somewhat abated, it is economic discrimination that is most likely to continue. It may be that the proper interpretation of this is that economic exploitation can be maintained even where slavery is abolished and along with it much of the personal mistreatment and other deprivations incidental to slavery. While this might be a cynical Marxist interpretation in one respect, it recognizes the non-Marxist fact that many important group behavior patterns can be changed without changing a basic economic exploitation of minorities.

Discrimination in Societies with Different Forms of Government (Table 3). The greatest harshness toward minorities seems to occur in absolute monarchies, especially in regard to personal violence and economic exploitation. There is not much difference in patterns of discrimination between societies with other forms of government, except that religious discrimination seems to be avoided in democratic societies.

Discrimination in Societies in Which Religion Is Integrated with Government (Table 4). In theocracies or in societies in which the rulers

TABLE 3. Comparisons of Forms of Discrimination Reported in Societies with Varying Forms of Government (Number of Societies Reported)

	Economic					Political					Personal					Religious					Social				
	AM	T	CM	DA	DL[a]	AM	T	CM	DA	DL	AM	T	CM	DA	DL	AM	T	CM	DA	DL	AM	T	CM	DA	DL
Extremely harsh	1	–	–	–	–	–	1	–	–	–	10	1	–	–	–	1	–	–	–	–	1	1	–	–	–
Relatively harsh	7	–	2	1	–	1	1	1	–	–	3	2	–	1	–	3	1	–	–	–	–	–	–	–	–
Moderate	6	2	4	1	2	2	2	3	2	–	6	2	3	2	2	–	–	–	–	–	6	11	1	1	4
Little or none	–	–	1	–	1	–	–	–	–	–	–	–	–	–	–	–	–	–	1	1	–	–	–	–	2

[a] AM, autocratic monarchy; T, totalitarian; CM, constitutional monarchy; DA, democratic form with authoritarian rule; DL, democratic form with much individual liberty.

TABLE 4. Forms of Discrimination Reported in Societies Where Religion is Closely Integrated with Government (Number of Societies Reported)

	Economic	Political	Personal	Religious	Social
Extremely harsh	–	6	5	–	1
Relatively harsh	8	–	3	3	3
Moderate	7	3	7	–	12
Little or none	–	–	–	1	–

TABLE 5. Forms of Discrimination Reported in Societies Where Dominant Group Feels Strong Nationalism (Number of Societies Reported)

	Economic	Political	Personal	Religious	Social
Extremely harsh	–	–	–	–	–
Relatively harsh	1	–	1	–	4
Moderate	2	3	3	–	4
Little or none	–	–	–	1	–

TABLE 6. Comparison of Forms of Discrimination Reported in Societies Where the Discriminated Group is Perceived as an Economic Threat and as a Political Threat (Number of Societies Reported)

	Economic E	P[a]	Political E	P	Personal E	P	Religious E	P	Social E	P
Extremely harsh	–	1	–	2	2	7	–	1	–	–
Relatively harsh	3	1	–	–	1	3	1	2	1	1
Moderate	6	5	1	1	3	3	–	–	2	6
Little or none	1	–	–	–	–	–	–	–	1	–

[a]E, economic threat; P, political threat.

claim divine sanction, and where the religious and political authorities are combined, there tends to be an emphasis on political discrimination, and to a somewhat lesser extent on religious discrimination, against minorities (which are presumably mainly differentiated on the basis of religion). Personal discrimination (including violence) is extreme in some of these societies, but moderate in others.

Discrimination in Societies in Which the Dominant Group Is Highly Nationalistic (Table 5). There seems to be no evidence from the literature that there is harsh discrimination in any respect against minorities in those societies in which the dominant group feels a strong sense of nationalism.

Discrimination in Societies in Which the Minor- ity Is Perceived as an Economic Threat or as a Political Threat (Table 6). There is some slight evidence that political discrimination is greater where the minority is perceived as a political threat, but not that economic discrimination is greater where the minority is perceived as an economic threat. The intensity of personal attacks tends to be greater when the minority is seen as a political threat.

Discrimination in Societies Where There Is Strong Respect for Law and in Societies Where Respect for Law Is Weak (Table 7). There seems to be a greater likelihood of personal attacks on members of the minority in societies where respect for law is low or casual, as might be expected. But there is no evidence that respect for law is associated with intensity of other forms of discrimination.

TABLE 7. Comparison of Forms of Discrimination Reported in Societies with Deep or Moderate Respect for Legal Authority and Casual Attitude or Disrespect for Legal Authority (Number of Societies Reported)

	Economic H	Economic L[a]	Political H	Political L	Personal H	Personal L	Religious H	Religious L	Social H	Social L
Extremely harsh	–	–	1	1	–	6	–	–	–	–
Relatively harsh	4	3	–	1	2	3	1	1	1	2
Moderate	4	4	3	2	2	3	–	–	7	5
Little or none	1	–	–	–	–	–	1	–	1	–

[a]H, respect for legal authority; L, casual attitude or disrespect.

TABLE 8. Forms of Discrimination Reported in Societies with Well-defined Class Systems (Number of Societies Reported)

	Economic	Political	Personal	Religious	Social
Extremely harsh	–	3	10	1	2
Relatively harsh	5	–	4	2	2
Moderate	7	2	4	–	10
Little or none	–	–	–	–	–

Discrimination in Societies with Well-defined Class Systems (Table 8). Personal discrimination seems to be the most frequent form of intergroup antagonism in societies with well-defined class systems. Social discrimination might have been expected to occur frequently in such societies, but such does not seem to be the fact. It may be noted that social discrimination was judged as moderate for most of the societies examined throughout this study. Social discrimination seems to be especially characteristic of societies in which the ideology of racism appears as a dominant cultural trait. There are not many such societies in existence. Included in our study as racist societies were only South Africa and Germany (the United States was deliberately excluded from the analysis).

12
divided ireland: persistent trauma

JEANNE ROCKWELL-NOONAN

Although the groups fighting in Ireland are racially the same, in some ways the conflict resembles the hostility between blacks and whites in the United States. First, it is a long-standing conflict. It smolders for decades, then breaks out in violence that, when it subsides, leaves a residue of bitterness. In Northern Ireland, the Protestants are a numerical majority; and the Catholics, like American blacks, complain of discrimination in jobs and housing. All over the rest of the world, Catholics and Protestants are coming together as they have not since the Reformation; it is tragic that ancient religious prejudices should be so tenacious. Again, as in the American South, the potentialities for a more economically prosperous life are sacrificed to deep and irrational animosities, and nobody seems able to explain or moderate the hatred.

Mrs. Rockwell-Noonan is a free-lance writer who has lived in Ireland. In the following essay, she carefully delineates all the issues involved.

HARD LINES DRAWN

Peace in Northern Ireland[1] seems to be no more substantial than the will-o'-the wisp over the Tullamore bogland. The ruling Protestant majority in the six northeastern counties, affiliated with Great Britan since the 1920s, has repeatedly given notice that even should Her Majesty's troops now on hand to keep peace be withdrawn and all political ties dissolved, it would try to go it alone rather than unite with the independent 26-county Republic of Ireland (Eire), where Protestants constitute only 5 per cent of the population.

It is possible, but not probable, that an agreement for unification could be worked out. But it was the prospect of political domination from Dublin that led to the drawing of the present demarcation line across the island. The truce with Britain which ended intermit-

Reprinted from *The Christian Century* 80, no. 47 (19 November 1969), pp. 1494-1498. Copyright © 1969 Christian Century Foundation. Reproduced by permission.

tent civil war and was followed by partition almost fully satisfied the predominantly Protestant north, but in the Catholic south determined "united Ireland" elements and particularly the hard core of the Irish Republican Army (officially outlawed) never accepted the concept of a divided island.

Listen to statements typifying the two positions: "Republican rule is Rome rule," sneers the militant member of the Order of the Orange (formed by Protestants almost two centuries ago to watch over their interests); "we will fight it." "Draw lines as you will," a long-time nationalist vows. "It doesn't matter. Ireland has been occupied now for three and a half centuries. We will end what Cromwell began."

"TROUBLES"–1969 VERSION

In the current eruption of civil strife in Northern Ireland political and religious issues are inextricably mixed. Attitudes of hatred and bigotry are passed down from parents to children and are reinforced by a school system that rigidly separates Protestant and Catholic pupils.

Social and economic issues also play their part. Unemployment is chronic among both the Protestant and the Catholic poor. But it wreaks particular hardship on Catholics because of alleged job discrimination and because their families are usually large. Ironically, the political and economic ties with Britain that Catholics want severed make possible broader welfare and educational services and higher unemployment and retirement payments than the Republic of Ireland can offer its citizens. But when these benefits are cited to the champion of "one Ireland," he counters with examples of discrimination in employment and housing ("You have to be a Protestant Unionist party member to get a council house") and of gerrymandering—apparently successful, if one is to judge by the fact that the Unionist party has been in power for 50 years.

At this writing the 1969 riots have resulted in a toll of nine dead, more than 800 injured and property damage to the extent of millions of pounds. A local official estimates that in Belfast (the capital city) alone as many as 5,000 persons have been made homeless. The resulting increase in anger and bitterness is immeasurable. Shortly before returning to her Londonderry home to help man the barricades, member of Parliament Bernadette Devlin (at 22 already hailed by her like-minded compatriots as Ireland's Joan of Arc) summed up the Catholics' feeling when she told her fellow M.P.s at Westminster: "There is no place for us in this society of gentlemen because we have nothing and they are the ones who have everything."

It is being predicted that in the wake of the bloodshed and flames widespread economic boycotts will ensue, with Catholics refusing to patronize Protestant businesses and Protestants taking their trade only to their fellow religionists. Predicted also is emigration by unhappy moderates, weary of the bigotry and intransigence on both sides. But most Irishmen agree that emigration is no answer, that at best it can be but a sad and desperate expedient.

TRAGIC MISTRUST

Of many examples of bitterness on both sides that could be cited, consider these:

A Protestant teacher complains: "We pay high taxes to build their schools, and the main subject of study is 'Throw Out the Queen.' Is that fair?"

Performing their calisthenics under a priest's supervision, Catholic schoolboys in Belfast mark the rhythm with chants: "Kill the Prods"; "Up the Pope"; "Down with Old King Billy." Such slogans, dating from as far back as the Battle of the Boyne in 1690, inflame the followers of Ian Paisley, the fundamentalist minister who, unrecognized by the dominant Presbyterian Church of Ireland, has formed his own denomination and who because of his inflammatory activities is often in jail—but not for long.

In full view of incoming ships' passengers in Belfast are ten-foot-high slogans—freshly painted in white each year on the gray stone quays of the Harland & Wolff shipyards. "No Pope Here," they proclaim.

A woman who lives in a prosperous middle-class suburb, not far from the fire-blackened blocks of Belfast's Ardoyne section, advises bitterly: "If they want so badly to live in a Roman Catholic country, let them go south to the Republic and see how they like it."

As indicated above, the militant Irish Republican Army is outlawed in Eire. But that its terrorist elements are illegally active is suggested by the state of buildings housing the customs posts on the northern side of the border. Those at the two points at which I crossed recently contrasted markedly with the large, durable buildings on the south side of the demarcation line. They were jerry-built, sand-bagged, surrounded by barbed wire. Why? They were designed to be rebuilt quickly after bombings. And in the hills roundabout redoubts were guarded by tanks and equipped with long-range guns manned by units of the British armed forces and the Ulster police.

REVERBERATIONS ABROAD

Americans are reaping criticism in Northern Ireland for failing to understand the depth and complexity of the Irish problem. Protestants commonly believe that arms for the I.R.A. terrorists are being purchased with funds supplied by groups of second- and third-generation Irish-Americans. They feel that those who contribute funds do not realize that they are supporting militants who have no interest in a constitutional resolution of the problem posed by a divided Ireland. As in Vietnam, the fighting in Northern Ireland has assumed overtones of "Catholics vs. others."

Naturally, the riots have resulted in diminution of the tourist business. Also affected is the effort (previously marked by success) to attract outside industrial firms to Northern Ireland. A U.S. group calling itself the American Congress for Irish Freedom has sent leaflets to U.S. manufacturers advising them not to establish plants in Northern Ireland.

Government officials, disturbed by such adverse publicity abroad, insist that a comprehensive review of the record of the ruling party and the government would reveal that it has sparked progress in housing, voting rights, employment and industrial training programs.

The new prime minister, James D. Chichester-Clark, professes commitment to reform and to relief of many of the grievances voiced by civil rights groups. At the same time he appears to be adamant on two points: maintaining order and keeping the present government intact. "No surrender"—an echo from the past—is still the watchword of his Unionist party.

GRIEVANCES ACKNOWLEDGED

Moderates of all creeds hope to strengthen the rising New Ulster Movement (NUM). That there are legitimate grievances on both sides (but particularly on that of the minority Catholics) was confirmed in the report issued after the onset of the riots by an investigative commission that had been set up some time previously under the chairmanship of Lord Cameron, a Scottish judge.

The commission found justified many Catholic complaints—for instance, those about inadequate (and unfair allocation of) housing, discrimination in employment, deprivation of voting rights through "deliberate manipulation" of electoral boundary lines and restrictions on the franchise, abuses perpetrated by the "B Specials," paramilitary forces recruited exclusively among Protestants. The commission.

acknowledged the part played in the rising tension by Protestant fears that unrestricted access to the ballot box by the rapidly increasing Catholic population (now one-third of the total) would threaten Unionist control of the government.

AN END TO ECUMENISM?

In the climate of ecumenism stimulated by the example of Pope John XXIII, Irish Protestants and Catholics—particularly the young—were at long last able to consider together the challenges facing their homeland. It began to seem that moderation might win the day, that a peaceable solution to partition was possible. Meanwhile, the Republic of Ireland was beginning to cast off the shackles forged by a puritan priest-dominated society. The old inward-looking, narrowly Catholic isolation was being breached by television, air travel abroad, new industries and an increase in foreign trade, particularly with Brit..in. Some of the same factors were of course operating in Northern Ireland.

Now, with the advent in Rome of what seems to be renewed conservatism, what many see as the "death of ecumenism" is arousing bitterness, particularly among the university-educated young people both Protestant and Catholic. They despair at the lack of moderate leadership, at the strange wedding in Ulster of radical left and Catholic militancy at one end of a political spectrum whose other end is occupied by rigid, reactionary Protestants. They are distressed to find themselves forced to take sides, since the only alternative to unreserved support of the government seems to be alignment with the civil rights militants bent on redress of grievances even at the cost of martyrdom and the possible destruction of the civil regime.

Subserviency, schism and factional strife, all in the name of religion, have for centuries drained the energies of Ireland's people. After the reduction of native opposition in the 16th century Ulster was declared forfeit to the British crown and "planted" with Scots and English to ensure its loyalty. In later years the settlers' descendants (largely but not entirely Protestant) were active in agitation for home rule. And though today the Protestants among them insist on maintaining ties to the British crown, they feel that the land in which they were born and where they now live is theirs, that their government is representative and that its legal position is not to be questioned.

THE LAND REMAINS

Ireland is a fruitful country, hauntingly beautiful. It may be a fatal flaw that love of the land so captures the spirit that more people are born than the land can support. Plans are under way for more careful nurturing of the land—for reforestation and agricultural improvements. But such measures are not enough to deal with the problem of overpopulation. A majority of the Irish Protestants, and some Catholics in the north as well, believe that family planning is essential if a viable economy and a decent standard of living are to be maintained. Indeed, the possibility that such planning might be forbidden haunts Protestants when they dare think the unthinkable; a takeover by Catholics, either by force of arms or by victory at the polls as the result of broadened voting rights. As an example of what might happen they cite the law that forbids the importation of contraceptives into the Republic. Some Catholic moderates are among those who say that so long as the Roman Catholic Church can so deeply affect social policy in the Republic, any chance of a united Ireland is remote.

Despite all the current tensions, despite the drab cities marred by areas of burned-out and boarded-up shops and the presence of army posts surrounded by barbed wire and tanks, there is still the land—the beautiful countryside that remains as awe-inspiring and lovely as it appears in the dreams of the most homesick expatriate.

The land is seen by all Irishmen as a bounty from God. To protect that gift from the spoliation that comes when men and women spill blood in the name of religion will take all the strength, intelligence, patience and determination every segment of Irish society can muster—today and in the future.

NOTES

[1] "Ulster," the term popularly used by Protestants in the north, is resented in the south because not all of the ancient kingdom of Ulster lies within Northern Ireland's borders.

13
apartheid 1948-1969: the politics of dehumanization

LESLIE RUBIN

A great tragedy is being enacted in South Africa, an independent republic, once part of the British Empire, which lies at the southern tip of the African continent. As of 1960, the population of South Africa consisted of 15,841,000 people: 10,808,000, or 68 percent, were black or Bantu-speakers; 1,488,000, or 9 percent, were of mixed white and nonwhite ancestry, called Colored; 477,000, or 3 percent, were Asian; 3,068,000, or 19 percent, were whites, of which 60 percent were Afrikaans-speaking and 40 percent were English-speaking. All these groups, except some of the Asians, have lived in South Africa for many generations; and South Africa is their only home.

In 1948, the Nationalist party came to power and has won every election since. It is composed mainly of Afrikaners. The opposition, the United party, is composed mainly of the English. Other groups are disfranchised. The Nationalist party has pursued a policy of apartheid, or separation of the black, colored, and Asian groups from the whites in every sphere of life. The spokesmen from the Nationalist party say that apartheid means separate but equal development of each racial group. In practice, this is not true. All but the whites are excluded from the government. Every nonwhite must carry a passbook, which he must present on demand and without which he can be imprisoned and denied employment.

South Africa is the richest and most industrialized country in Africa, the original capital having come from the exploitation of gold and diamond mines. South Africa cannot maintain its present standard of living except by increased industralization and with the labor and purchasing power of its nonwhite population. In addition, the great majority of the population is opposed to apartheid, including a large portion of the English-speaking whites and the Anglican church. To enforce apartheid, the government has had to resort to increasingly repressive measures that, in turn, have provoked riots and violence. South Africa has become a police state under constant threat of internal conflict. Freedom of assembly, of protest, of speech, and of the press are increasingly restricted for everyone.

Internationally, South Africa has been subjected to great pressure to renounce apartheid and to develop a plan for a state in which all groups might participate equally. The pressure comes mainly from the black African nations in the United Nations and from India; at every session, they seek to have other nations condemn South Africa and apply economic sanctions

Reprinted by permission from the July 16, 1969, issue of *The Christian Century*, pp. 947-950. Copyright © 1969 Christian Century Foundation.

against her. They are usually unsuccessful, but there have been other sanctions, usually in the field of sports.

South Africans, at least the government spokesmen, do not seem to be at all moved by either threats or appeals. Occasionally they try to explain themselves, but they are more likely to withdraw from an international organization as a response to censure.

The following selection is a more detailed presentation of the history of apartheid from its inception until 1969. Dr. Rubin is a professor at American University in Washington, D.C.

The world has now had almost 21 years to observe apartheid in practice, to assess South Africa's claim of freedom for the 15 million nonwhite peoples (within their own areas) and to determine what actually has happened to those people's civil rights, economic opportunities and potential for advancement. No student of the South African situation should have serious difficulty in making such an assessment.

South Africa's answer to the charge that the nonwhite is denied fundamental human rights is that each nonwhite group will enjoy those rights within its own separate area. But the record of separate development in practice through the past two decades does not support this contention.

In 1948 an official statement described the new policy of apartheid as one "based on the Christian principles of justice and reasonableness" whose aim was "the maintenance and protection of the indigenous racial groups as separate communities with prospects of developing into self-supporting communities in their own areas, and the stimulation of national pride, self-respect and mutual respect among the various races of the country." But when the policy was presented to the electorate for approval it took the form of a naked appeal to the white minority's fears. Addressing a public meeting Daniel F. Malan (later to become prime minister) said that the forthcoming election would determine whether the white race would be able to "maintain its rule, its purity and its civilization or float along until it vanished forever in the black sea of South Africa's non-European population."

During the next ten years no steps were taken toward fulfilling the election promise of separate development in their own areas for "the indigenous racial groups." Instead, the period saw the enactment of harsh laws separa-

ting the races and restricting nonwhite activity in the white areas.

"SEPARATE DEVELOPMENT" INITIATED

Finally, in 1959, the government enacted the Promotion of Bantu Self-Government act, implementing part of a carefully constructed plan to retribalize 12 million Africans. The act abolished parliamentary representation for the Africans and provided for the "gradual development of self-governing Bantu national units." This summary disfranchisement of four-fifths of the South African population was justified officially by two arguments: (1) The existing representation was "the source of European fears of being swamped by the Bantu in the political sphere." (2) The "legitimate needs and desires" of the Africans would receive better attention under the proposed new system.

The new system of "self-government" was based on the proposition that the Africans of South Africa "do not constitute a homogeneous people, but form separate national units on the basis of language and culture." These national units are entitled to "homelands" covering an area amounting to 13.7 percent of the country's area. The homelands are reserved exclusively for the 12 million Africans and, according to declared government policy, will never be increased. The remaining 86.3 percent of the area of South Africa is reserved exclusively for the 3 million non-Africans. The act recognized eight national units: North Sotho, South Sotho, Swazi, Tsonga, Tswana, Venda, Zhosa and Zulu. But this is an arbitrary classification; the October 1968 issue of *Scope,* published by the South African Information Service, omits the Swazi from a list of "Bantu nations" and adds West Sotho, Ndebele and a tenth group labeled "Others."

The act also established legislative

powers for the territorial authority (consisting of chiefs and other tribal representatives) in each national unit. In 1962 Prime Minister Hendrik Verwoerd announced the government's intention to grant "self-government" to the Xhosa national unit. In 1963 the Transkei Constitution act was passed, creating the first homeland or "Bantustan." Two more homelands were established in 1968, and several more are planned for 1969.

"SELF-GOVERNMENT" IN PRACTICE

The description of this first Bantustan as "a self-governing territory within the Republic" is misleading. For one thing, the self-governing areas do not cover the whole of the Transkei. There are significant exclusions, among them Umtata (the capital), part of which is reserved for white ownership and occupation and Port Saint Johns, the site of the only harbor. For another, though the Transkei legislative assembly consists of 64 chiefs and 45 elected members, all the chiefs are appointed, paid and may at any time be removed from office by the government of the Republic of South Africa.

The assembly can legislate in matters relating to taxation, inferior courts and public works. But it lacks authority in most important matters. For example, it cannot legislate on foreign affairs or communications, and it does not have the right to refuse admission to South African police "charged with the maintenance of public peace and order, and the preservation of internal security," or to control the police once they have entered. Amendment of the constitution is prohibited, and no law passed by the assembly can take effect unless it is approved by the president of the Republic of South Africa.

Contests for the "elected" seats in the Transkei legislative assembly were farcical. Emergency regulations prohibited meetings of more than ten Africans without special permission and authorized arrest and detention of persons without warrant. Republic of South Africa laws permitted issuance of "banning orders" against opponents of government policies and detention of persons for an unlimited number of 90-day periods. One prospective candidate—Hammington Majija, a member of the Liberal party and a known opponent of "separate development"—was prevented from contesting the election by "banning orders" which, affixed to the door of his home in Cape Town, prohibited him from leaving the area where he lived or attending any gatherings. Although the voting resulted in overwhelming support for Chief Victor Poto, who opposed apartheid and stood for a policy of multiracialism, his opponent, Chief Kaiser Matanzima who supported apartheid, received most of the vote of the 64 government-controlled chiefs and thus despite his rejection by the electorate, became chief minister. In October 1968 new elections were held and Matanzima obtained a majority.

A Transkeian police force was established early in 1966, but in August of that year 828 members of the South African police force were still stationed in the Transkei. When two Africans were appointed as magistrates in the Transkei in January 1968 they were not permitted to try cases in which whites were either the complainants or the accused.

Normal industrial growth is inhibited by the fact that while the Republic of South Africa refuses to permit white capital and initiative within the homeland, it offers inducements to whites to establish "border industries" nearby, using cheap labor from the homeland region. Thus the Transkei can provide employment for only a handful of its citizens, while hundreds of thousands continue to be employed in the mines, farms and factories of the republic. Unemployment problems in the Transkei are aggravated by the influx of Africans who have been forcibly removed from their work and homes in the Western province to their supposed "homes" in the Transkei, where there is no work for them. The annual per capita income is $48, of which only $36 is "disposable cash income."

The 3.5 million citizens of the Transkei, far from being masters of their own fate, continue to be as effectively under the control of the white government of the republic as they were before. When it promises all nonwhite groups complete freedom in their own areas, the policy of separate development reeks of fraud; when it encourages the belief that the present realities of South African life can ever make such freedom possible, it reeks of fantasy.

THE APARTHEID LAWS

When the Nationalist party coined the term "apartheid" in 1948, it was not clear what the precise nature of the new policy would be. But there was much in the past record of the party to arouse fears that it would be both authoritarian and racist.

Soon after the rise of Hitler in Germany the Nationalist party began to express nazi sympathies, to espouse anti-Semitism and to cooperate with the Greyshirts, a paramilitary fascist group which closely followed the nazi model. During World War II the party opposed the Smuts regime's participation on the side of Britain and her allies, avowed support for Germany and attempted to undermine South Africa's war effort by violent means.

After the Nationalist party came to power the fears proved to be justified. With a ruthless contempt for all opposition the new government proceeded to construct an apparatus of laws and administrative procedures designed to bring about complete separation between white and nonwhite and to ensure white domination, as well as to repress forcibly all nonwhite opposition to the new policies. Since the party has been in power it has ignored mounting international criticism and the hostility of independent black Africa, even to the extent of imposing apartheid in South-West Africa (Namibia), which has been declared to be under the control of the United Nations. The systematic exclusion of 15 million non-whites from all normal rights and opportunities in South Africa has been intensified, and the government continues to assert its determination that apartheid shall continue.

Only in South Africa is racial discrimination enforced by law. Color is the criterion which determines the place of every man in the life of the country. What are known as civil rights in the Western world tend more and more in South Africa to mean privileges accorded to the citizen at the discretion of an official—a government inspector, the superintendent of an African township, a policeman.

The machinery for keeping the races separate rests on the Population Registration act, which requires every citizen to be classi-

fied in a national register as a white person, an African or a Colored person (a person of mixed descent) and to carry a corresponding identity card.

A "white" is defined as

a person who in appearance obviously is a white person and who is not generally accepted as a Coloured person, or is generally accepted as a white person and is not in appearance obviously not a white person, but does not include any person who freely and voluntarily admits that he is by descent an African or a Coloured person, unless it is proved that the admission is not based on fact.

Among the factors considered in determining "general acceptance" as a white person are "habits, speech, and deportment in general." An African is defined as "a person who in fact is or is generally accepted as a member of any aboriginal race or tribe of Africa." A Colored person is defined as one "not a white person or an African."

WHAT "CLASSIFICATION" CAN MEAN

Even after one has been classified as "white" and issued with the appropriate identity card, he may later be reclassified as a "Colored" person. The lives of many families are tragically disrupted by application of this law. Take the case of Sandra Laing who, unlike her "obviously white" father, mother and two brothers, has a dark skin and crinkly hair. In 1966, when she was 11 years old, she was removed from a school she had attended for four years and escorted home by school officials accompanied by a policeman. She had been reclassified "Colored." An appeal to the Supreme Court against that classification was unsuccessful. When the law was amended her classification was reversed because both her parents were white, but the school from which she had been excluded would not readmit her. Finally after being out of school for almost two years, she was accepted by a church school.

Alan Paton has written: "I could tell of a man who lived as 'white' and then was declared to be 'coloured,' who lost not only his job and his wife, but also his children, who fled from him in hatred and anger; yet they cannot really flee from him, for they are now coloured' too."

Two especially vicious apartheid laws deserve to be singled out for attention. In the Reservation of Separate Amenities act of 1953 South Africa declared its recognition of the doctrine of "separate and unequal" in its treatment of different races. This law has meant that beaches, parks, bridges, railway stations and post offices are adorned with notices reading "Whites Only." Further, if there is only one waiting room in a railway station it is lawful for the stationmaster to reserve it for the exclusive use of white persons. A nonwhite person entering it is guilty of a criminal offense punishable by a fine of not more than $140 or imprisonment for not longer than three months, or by both fine and imprisonment.

The Bantu (Urban Areas Consolidation) act of 1945, as amended makes it a criminal offense for an African woman to live with her husband for more than 72 hours without a permit to do so. It also empowers the minister of Bantu administration and development, whenever he decides that the number of Africans in a city is "in excess of the reasonable labour requirements" of that area, to require the city council to remove from the city such Africans as he may determine, irrespective of the amount of time they have lived and worked there. The official term for such Africans is "redundant Bantu."

NO DISSENT!

Attempts to oppose apartheid have been met with a series of increasingly ferocious laws designed to curb dissent. For example, under the General Law Amendment act of 1962 any person who breaks the window of a building in the course of a demonstration calling for the grant of increased political rights for the African people is guilty of sabotage and liable to the death penalty—unless he can prove that

his act was not intended to encourage feelings of hostility between whites and Africans. Under the Terrorism act of 1967 a person who has written letters to Africans likely to "encourage feelings of hostility between the white and other inhabitants of the Republic" is guilty of the offense of "terrorism," which is punishable by death—unless it is proved that he did not intend to encourage such feelings. Incredibly, this law is retroactive.

The number of executions in the republic is among the highest in the world. In the latter half of 1966, 66 persons were executed (1 white, 19 colored and 46 African). Corporal punishment of nonwhite prisoners is common; prisoners, suspects and witnesses have been assaulted, tortured and kicked to death. In 1968 Gabriel Mbindi, a 68-year-old African, brought proceedings against the South African government, alleging that he had been detained in custody for eight months without any charge being formulated against him, and that during his detention he had been handcuffed to an iron water pipe so that his feet barely touched the ground, had been blindfolded, kicked and beaten. The South African government settled the case out of court, paying $4,200 toward costs of the trial.

There is today no expectation of change within South Africa. Prime Minister Balthazar J. Vorster has made it clear that there will be no change whatsoever in the present status and treatment of nonwhite groups within South Africa. Meanwhile the continued practice of apartheid means that the nonwhite people of that republic are suffering progressive dehumanization.

In an address to the United Nations on March 21, 1967, U.S. Ambassador Arthur Goldberg described apartheid as "one of the greatest offenses against human rights still existing in the world." Certainly to those who seek to build a world free from fear and strife, it is our time's greatest moral challenge.

14
the asians of kenya

VINCENT CABLE

When Kenya became independent, she offered citizenship to the white settlers from Britain and to other groups who were not native to Kenya but who lived there; the ideal was a multiracial state. When the British Empire was disbanded in favor of a commonwealth, all British citizens from outlying areas were allowed to immigrate freely to Britain. Inasmuch as Britain is a small, densely populated country in the throes of a continuing economic crisis and the Commonwealth has millions of poor, unskilled potential immigrants, this was a quixotic gesture at best. Eventually, in 1968, Britain limited immigration from Commonwealth countries, and at this point the Asians from Kenya were caught between Kenyan and British policies.

Most Asians in Kenya had kept their British passports. When Kenya, in response to its own economic and other internal pressures, asked Asians to leave, they expected to go to Britain rather than back to India or Pakistan; but this route was now closed to them by the British immigration rules, and they became stateless people.

In the next selection, Mr. Cable analyzes the events leading up to this tragic situation and indicates that even the most enlightened policies cannot always be realized in the face of economic problems. Mr. Cable is from the University of Glasgow.

Until the passing of the British Immigration Act of 1968 and the publicity which surrounded it, the Asians of East Africa had lived in comparative obscurity, attracting little political interest since the 1920s, and little study apart from a few descriptive booklets.[1] Recent contributions by Ghai[2] and Morris[3] have remedied this to some extent, but the long preoccupation of sociologists and anthropologists with rural and tribal groups has left its mark in a dearth of information on one of the most dynamic and important elements in East African society.

Thus we are badly equipped to answer the kind of questions which have been raised by those whose interest has been stimulated by the events of the last 18 months. Why is it that East African Asians are apparently so

Reprinted from *African Affairs* 68, no. 272 (July 1969), pp. 218-231. Reproduced by permission of the author and publisher.

communalistic and exclusive in their social behavior? Is this a carry-over from the conservatism of traditional India or due to racial segregation which was imposed upon Kenya particularly by the British? How does one explain the apparent paradox, (highlighted by Bharati), of a high degree of technical skill, material success and exposure to "western"[4] education co-existing with the old taboos of religion and caste and firm loyalties to extensive networks of kin? Successful trading communities are normally associated with a distinctive and work-orientated philosophy of life, e.g., the "protestant ethic"—and some adaptation of the family structure; but the Asians, with the possible exception of the Ismaelis, have clung to traditional Indian religion and appear to make good use of their extended families. Müller[5] and Desai[6] have given us some insight into this problem but it remains something of a mystery. On a less theoretical level why do Africans dislike Asians so much—or do they? This leads us to a basic questioning of policy; is it, or was it, reasonable to expect that the Asians would thrive in East Africa after independence?

It was frequently argued at the time of independence, and after, that adaptation to the new situation could be achieved given a reasonable amount of mutual goodwill. Y. P. Ghai concludes the book *Portrait of a Minority*:

> *One must continue to hope that this great experiment in social engineering will succeed and that Asians will be accepted and will play a positive role in the new societies in East Africa.*[7]

These hopes are now substantially deflated and considerable mutual recrimination has followed. Those who felt that freedom of manoeuvre lay with the minority have criticised the Asians for their racialism and unwillingness to integrate, for holding on to their British passports "like leeches"[8] and general myopia. Others have described the Kenya government as "the villain of the piece."[9] Paul Theroux in a recent article "Hating the Asians" writes; "Africans . . . now in Kenya for example hold the banner of bigotry high . . . racial insult now approaches the proportion of fashion."[10] Closer examination would reveal that these accusations are not only unfair and exaggerated but, worse, that they conceal one of the fundamental problems of East African society, namely stark class inequalities based essentially on racial differences. There is mass under-employment among Kenya's 10,000,000 Africans. Differences in incomes and wealth are enormous and conspicuous. There are high, and largely unfulfilled, expectations amongst the vast majority of the educated or semi-educated poor who form the bulk of Kenya's population. To have expected an expanding and successful community of alien merchants, even if only 180,000 strong, to have quietly integrated in such a society once power was in the hands of the majority was somewhat naïve. If most of the Kenyan Asians had responded to the offer of citizenship they could very easily have provided the fuel for a pogrom in the 1970s. The massacre of Zanzibari Arabs, although in ad-

mittedly different circumstances, was not a cheering precedent.

While it is easy to have the wisdom of hindsight, it is now fairly clear that there were only two logical solutions. One was a severe egalitarian policy of taxation, nationalisation and the elimination of privilege as perpetuated through the educational system. The other was the gradual expulsion of substantial numbers of Asians, leaving behind a manageable minority to enjoy full civil rights and to continue working as before; the policy that Kenya in effect has followed. Much the same prospect confronted the white settler farmers and the British government wisely expedited the process by offering assistance to carry out a large amount of land transfer and by keeping open the option of a return to Britain under the terms of the Kenya Independence Act and a series of British Nationality Acts.[11] Britain, however, offered no economic assistance to help to introduce a programme of Kenyanisation of the Asian-dominated commercial sector, nor has the British government honoured its obligations to guarantee free-entry rights to Britain. As a result of this abdication of responsibility a serious racial situation could have been created in Kenya were it not for the other "safety valve" of immigration to India and Pakistan.

However before assuming too easily the inevitability of the Asian exodus it is important to look in more detail at the Asian "problem" as Kenya inherited it.

First, who are the people classified as Asians in colonial racial taxonomy? It is in fact a very mixed category: Hindu Indians from Gujerat and the Punjab, Muslim Pakistanis, Goans and even Arabs. The categorisation disguises a considerable diversity of faiths (Muslim, Hindu, Sikh, Catholic), language, sect and caste which constitute the bases of commercial organisation and social activity. While the distinctions which proscribed Asian landownership, which segregated schools, hospitals and public amenities; which arbitrarily grouped Catholic, Portuguese-speaking Goans on the same salary scales and voting rolls as Muslim, Urdu-speaking Pakistanis, were inconvenient rather than brutal, they nevertheless helped to form the basis of misleading and facile racial stereotypes. Very rarely, for example, do public attacks on Asians for not taking citizenship and persisting in their traditional ways ever bother to exclude the Ismaelis for whom these accusations have no relevance. Nor do references to business behaviour usually exclude the largely clerical Goans. Most of the stereotypes are built around the Gujerati Hindus who make up about 70 per cent of the total Asian population.

The basis of Kenya's "class" structure can be clearly seen in the mal-distribution of income and wealth, and in the bias towards certain types of occupation. Asians generally occupy "middle-level" jobs. The over-concentration of Asians in commerce and private manufacturing (over 80 per cent of those economically active) stems from the restrictions on land-holding, and from salary discrimination and obstacles to promotion in the higher ranks of the civil service. In the Manpower Plan of 1964-1970,[12] it was shown that whereas Asians occupied only 16 per cent of Grades A and B (professional and semi-professional) with Europeans contributing 26 per cent and Africans 58 per cent, in Grade C (skilled workers and clerks) Asians occupied 40 per cent of the posts, Africans 46 per cent and Europeans 15 per cent. In unskilled jobs the Asian proportion falls to a negligible fraction. Asians are, therefore, for historical reasons, in the position of providing much of Kenya's stock of skilled and semi-skilled labour, while at the same time being in jobs largely vulnerable to the pressures of African secondary school leavers.

The Manpower Plan, however, does indicate that Asians are far more than petty traders. They provide the largest number of medical and legal professional staff, many engineers, teachers, draughtsmen, electricians, much of the executive officer class of the bureaucracy and large numbers of accountants, clerks, bookkeepers, business executives and manufacturing entrepreneuers in the private sector. The "middle-class" nature of the Asians is even more clearly shown in the figures for income distribution. From figures published in 1967,[13] 62 per cent of Asian men earned less than £720 per annum, in comparison with approximately 32 per cent of Europeans and 98 per cent of Africans. A more meaningful guide would be data on family and corporate wealth, but in the absence of comprehensive capital taxation, it is only possible to guess that this would improve the relative prosperity of the Asian group.

Thirdly the Asians in Kenya are mostly urban: in 1962, 85 per cent lived in the five largest towns.[14] This is largely due to restrictive ordinances and practices under which Asians were effectively precluded from owning land and trading outside certain towns and townships, although some (10 per cent) do trade in rural areas. This concentration has had very important implications for their social organisation. As there were no indigenous urban communities—a feature of East African historical geography strongly contrasting with West Africa—they created Kenya's towns, dominated them and to a considerable extent were limited to serving each other. This physical concentration and introverted network of economic activity limited both their contribution to the national economy and their interaction with other races, a factor that must have helped to lead to much of the disliked "clannishness" which is normally regarded as "typically Indian."

While it is difficult to generalise in retrospect, there is strong evidence that this is not how the Asians wished to develop. The early arrivals, traders who both preceded and followed the white man's "discovery" of Africa, were pioneers in the truest sense, opening up East Africa to trade and working in dangerous and tough conditions, which most white men were not prepared to accept. The popular history of East Africa tends to emphasise the rugged European settler, explorer and missionary braving the wilds; a story in which the Asian has little or no role. However soothing to later prejudices, this idea was very misleading and contemporary records[15] do much to rehabilitate the Asians from their reputation as "city slickers" or "coolies."

As can be seen, Kenya's society was characterized by certain economic divisions based upn race and also by a system of stereotypes and myths which helped to reinforce them. As described by Elizabeth Hopkins,[16] these ideas helped to maintain the "social distance" necessitated by the "superiority" of the European minority after the Indians had fought unsuccessfully to preserve their right to own rural land and command political authority in proportion to their relatively superior numbers. The history of Asian-European conflict was long and complex and no attempt will be made here to analyse it. Suffice it to say that the settlers eventually persuaded the administration to limit the Asians' rights and representation and to tolerate what amounted to de facto apartheid. This led to a vicious circle. The communal nature of politics brought to the fore those who were more concerned with group interests than with the society as a whole and these interests were almost invariably conservative; urban segregation strengthened traditional ties; segregation in schools in particular provided a cocoon in which the essentials of religious and ideological continuity could be maintained; ambitions to strive for equal rights in the larger community thus became stunted.

The other important function of the isolation of the Asians as a race was their potential usefulness as intermediaries. Indians could perform the vital retail and clerical functions, not only eliminating the need for training Africans but attracting the natural unpopularity of petty traders and bureaucrats, siphoning off hostility from the administration which could thus appear detached, impartial and disinterested and even protective of native interests.

Given a framework in which they could move up only with difficulty, the economically weaker Asians were led to protect themselves from encroachment from below; the family and community could help them by employment in a family firm, or nepotism in an office. Business management and ownership were confined to members of the community, so excluding Africans. Desai also shows that such an exclusive policy facilitates debt-settlement and early deliveries where moral suasion could be employed.[17] Asians developed their own strong prejudice against Africans which, while it is based partly upon European example, and partly on the strong if subtle colour-consciousness of the Indian caste system, must at least partly be explained by their role in the "pecking order"; their insecurity about African competition is rather like that of the "poor whites" of southern Africa.

It might be argued that all this is very deterministic. Surely the Asians should have rebelled and made common cause with the Africans? There was in fact resistance in the 1920s and 1930s and as a by-product—though an accidental one—the colonial government was led to accept "the paramountcy of native interests."[18] Some Asians did try to promote a radical policy against the colonial government—Makhan Singh and Pio Gama Pinto are examples—but the prevailing mood appears to have been one of quiescence or support for the main lines of colonial policy, even during the period of the anti-colonial movement in India. This could have been simple unenlightened economic self-interest. But Tandon[19] and others have explained there was probably a whole complex of reasons. First the Asians had no effective weapon. They did not have numerical strength as they had in Guyana or Fiji, for example; the settlers had the backing of British authority and while later India was prepared to intercede on the Asians' behalf the Government of India's influence was distant and diplomatic. Above all their economic power was double-edged: it would have hurt them as much as or more than the government if they had struck or closed their shops because, at least in later years, there were increasing numbers of Africans waiting to compete.[20] Thus being both relatively privileged and lacking sanctions they could achieve little and lose a great deal.

Colonial restrictions and segregation were of course resented by the sensitive, the able, and the ambitious, but they were felt to be uncomfortable rather than vicious. Their relative security was a basis for successful business and as Y. P. Ghai points out[21] many Indians were recent immigrants, anxious to fit in and adapt as painlessly as possible. Lastly the Asians, knowing that at best they could only marginally help in the African struggle for power, might be culpable for not having backed the winner sooner, for not having offered more financial assistance to the nationalists, but it has to be remembered that their equivocal attitude was not dissimilar to that of the KADU minority tribes or the African "loyalists" of the Mau Mau emergency period, both of whom are now reintegrated into Kenyan political life. Even the "hard-core" white settlers seem to have buried their history. The fact that the Asians alone have not done so seems to indicate that the problem has deeper roots than an identification with colonial authority.

What have the Asians done since the Lancaster House Conference to make themselves more acceptable in independent Kenya? Rothchild in his article[22] discusses the test of citizenship which he considers to have been a crucial factor. The provisions for non-Africans to assume Kenyan citizenship were in fact quite liberal. A Kenya-born non-African with one parent also born in Kenya could qualify automatically for citizenship and for the others there was an opportunity for naturalisation by application within two years of independence, that is before December 1965. There was a striking lack of interest. Of the 180,000 or so Asians in 1963 only 20,000 applied for citizenship and those mostly in the last few weeks allowed for this procedure. In addition about 50,000 qualified automatically. This was widely regarded by Kenyans as "fence sitting," or a lack of confidence in Africans' ability to run Kenya. If what now constitutes the non-citizen, Asian population intended to remain in Kenya their lack of commitment has done them enormous harm.

To reduce the matter to the citizenship question is something of an over-simplification, however. It should be noted that the European response to voluntary naturalisation was even smaller—less than 2,000 out of 60,000 applied —while one Asian sub-group, the Ismaelis, applied almost without exception. This has not altered Kenyan attitudes to either group. Secondly, the rights of citizenship are limited in some respects: citizens can be deported under certain circumstances if they are naturalised; racial discrimination in the Civil Service, moreover is accepted practice. On the other hand non-citizens enjoy important rights: protection of property from confiscation without adequate compensation, "approved"status for certain manufacturing industries, and freedom

to own land—although since 1967 additional purchase can take place only with Presidential approval. While it might have been expected that unskilled and semi-skilled work could be limited by immigration legislation to citizens, most highly skilled workers and professionals looked forward, like the farmers, to a long uninterrupted stay.

Thirdly, it was not altogether clear at that time that the government believed in its own liberal policy on citizenship. Perhaps the main cause for concern was the policy of favouring "black Africans" in the Civil Service to redress the "historical imbalances." As the number of non-African citizens in the administrative class was very small before December 1965 and Asians suffered a similar exclusion before this time, this seems in retrospect to have been rather unnecessary, though there would have been a problem if most Asians had taken citizenship. Fourthly, the general political climate of 1963-64 and even later was hardly propitious for committing one's life and one's family to a future in Kenya. The Zanzibar massacres of the much more "integrated" Arabs, memories of the Congo troubles, and Kenya's own recent history were all unconnected phenomena, but all conspired to create a vague unease in an already insecure minority. The fact that Kenya is now regarded as one of the most stable countries in black Africa is a tribute to the achievements of the Kenyatta government, just as it reflects on the misrule of others. Taking all the factors into account, the poor Asian response was understandable, and the British government was probably justified in leaving open the "back door" of British citizenship, which was in itself a major reason why waverers did not commit themselves to Kenya.

Apart from the citizenship question, the next major question was that of business practice and ownership. The Kenya Asians generally have suffered from the reputation of the trading sector of their working population. While the Asian traders were regarded by the 1953-55 East Africa Royal Commission as—

mainly responsible for stimulating the wants of the indigenous population even in the remotest areas by opening to them a shop-window on the modern world and collecting for sale elsewhere whatever small surpluses are available for disposal,[23]

they have been more commonly regarded locally as "bloodsuckers" or "exploiters."

It is perhaps worth looking at some of the alleged practices; overcharging, giving under-weight, making speculative gains, rudeness, dilution of quality (the last exemplified by a common belief that Indian doctors inject their patients with coloured water). Many of these allegations are attributed to all trading communities, but in East Africa they have to be seen against the fact that while most of the small traders doubtless charge what the market will bear, they also work long hours, operate on low margins and maintain a remarkable diversity of stock. Neither Europeans or Africans have ever been able to compete. As Marris has observed,[24] the question of "discrimination" or lack of credit only very partially explains the uncompetitiveness of African trade, which is rather based on a whole complex of factors relating to inefficient business practices and inexperience. If Indians had not been kept from competition in the rural areas in colonial times their predominance might have been much greater. The experience of credit organizations such as the Industrial and Commercial Development Corporation has been extremely mixed, with embryo African traders frequently defaulting on loans.[25] Co-operatives have encountered even greater problems.[26] It might also be added that the functions of the trader as a money-lender and purchaser of agricultural products developed in the absence of rural organized credit, bulk buying and adventurous banking policies, and have served as a partial substitute. The persistent criticism from high levels about Asian traders who show lack of respect for poor African customers and obvious deference for rich white ones, while felt as an insult, is probably explained by a natural tendency amongst shopkeepers who wish to obtain and keep rich careless customers who will not bother to haggle over prices and discounts. In fact most of the complaints are those which would be employed against all retailers in a poor society and particularly against traders who retain a bargaining system (the government is very

sensibly trying to enforce fixed prices, which will probably be higher but which will eliminate the constant fear of being cheated). The choice facing the Kenya government has been a clear one: an efficient retail system owned by aliens and attracting resentment because of it, or a locally owned network which is less efficient—at least in the short term.

There are three other practices which have caused particular anger. One related to "extortionate" rents and racial discrimination in property transactions. The high rents are mainly due to the chronic shortage of housing in towns where property, both residential and commercial, is owned to a large extent by Asians. As in Britain, the government has sought to tackle the symptom rather than the cause by rent-control legislation, with the result that landlords have responded by demanding larger pre-payments. Racial discrimination by landlords is widely believed to be common but the cases brought to prominence in the press usually involve Europeans. The absence of tough legislation against racial discrimination in Kenya is an unfortunate omission as it allows the perpetuation of a vague feeling of injustice which cannot be redressed and encourages random acts of retaliation, such as the action of the Nairobi City Council in excluding all Asian tenants (both citizen and non-citizen) from the urban market. Another "malpractice" refers to exchange-control evasion, mainly by non-citizens. Since exchange control was instituted in 1965, the capital outflow has been stemmed to some extent; though there is undoubtedly considerable evasion by false reporting of import-exports, black-market dealing—especially since the United Kingdom's devaluation—and in the tourist trade. Nevertheless there is no evidence that this involves Asians any more than Europeans and it certainly does not involve the small trader who has little access to import-export channels.

Finally, the "clannishness" of Indians has been regarded as a major obstacle to Africans entering business or even employment. Some gestures have been made; some genuine partnerships have been created; Asian organisations such as Africindo, sponsored by the Indian High Commission, have been set up to help African traders with credit and advice; a big family concern, the House of Manji, went public and offered 40 per cent of its share to Kenyans on the local stock exchange. Other Asian concerns have made or are making big investments in manufacturing industry—rope and twine, razor blades, hessian sacks, textiles, steel rolling, caustic soda and plastics—all with a considerable impact on the Kenyan economy and with a greater visible impact than can emerge from commerce. For some reason this appears to have back-fired. Not only has the effort been grossly inadequate for the government, hence the Trade Licensing Act, which limited trade in certain products and certain areas to citizens, but the offers of co-operation have been mistrusted. Mr. Arap Moi called upon African businessmen at a rally to be wary of "unscrupulous Asian businessmen who take in African partners only as figureheads."[27] In fact the worsening political climate has hindered better business practices. The impossibility of being tough with defaulting debtors increases the propensity to deal only with relations, while the shortening time horizons increase the tendency to make quick profits and repatriate them where possible. Regarding Asian business practices in general, and given an ideological climate, as in Kenya, where private commerce is acceptable in principle, it is difficult to see how a radically different situation could have evolved as long as Asian domination remained.

The other major area in which Asians were expected to change was in the field of social relationships, where clannishness and arrogance were to give way to "integration." The main problem here has been that there has been no clear indication of what they should do; "assimilate" or "integrate," intermarry or keep to themselves. The fragmented nature of Asian society is a big-enough obstacle; when people are unused to marrying out of caste or associating out of community, they are singularly ill-prepared for the greater barriers of race relations. But there is some evidence of greater adaptation by marginal groups like the Ismaelis and the Goans, and this is especially important as most Ismaelis are Kenyan citizens. Quite a lot of activity goes on, however superficially, in the multi-racial chari-

ties, at cocktail parties, and in cultural organisations. Also it is important that Asians are frequently criticised not for refusing to "integrate" but because the form which integration takes occasionally smacks of insincerity or sycophancy and is of the rather clumsy "back-slapping of Ministers" variety. But pre-judging all efforts as insincere does not help. The example of KANU party politics will illustrate the dilemma. On the one hand Asians are expected to contribute to party funds and to appear at political rallies, but on the other hand they are expected not to "interfere" in politics—especially where it involves showing sympathy with the opposition. Nor however must their loyalty take the form of currying favour.

One sphere in which one might have expected to see an improvement was the educational system, where African pupils are now entering the formerly "Asian" and "European" schools. A lot of factors militate against quick results: the dominance of expatriate staff, age and educational differences between African and non-African in the same forms, political interference in school affairs, and parental attitudes. Consequently it is far too early to say whether the next generation will be integrated more happily. The University is not regarded by many as a successful experiment in multi-racial living, mainly because of conflict between African and Asian students. Much the same considerations, however, apply to all but a small minority of Europeans and, given the enormous differences in living standards between the minorities and the bulk of the population, this is not surprising.

Given the constraints which have limited greater adaptation by the Asians, one might ask what has been done by the government to ease the process. It is most important to bear in mind the problems which Kenya has to face, mainly in the urban areas. First, there is chronic unemployment; population is rising at a rate of 3 per cent per annum and the level of employment in 1966, even though it was the highest since 1961, was below the average figure for 1957-60. School leavers are entering the labour market at the rate of somewhere around 80,000 a year while employment is rising by only a fraction of that amount. Many will find their way into the towns to add to the backlog of visible unemployed. Secondly, Kenya's political problems are acute, in particular tribalism and a radical opposition, both of which, in different ways, greatly limit the government's freedom of action. The government must produce "results" quickly, and spread them about widely. To create employment opportunities in the short term by evicting "foreign" traders and public employees is an obvious line of least resistance. Thirdly, the government is much less able to resort to a paternalistic form of administration than its colonial predecessor. An afternoon in parliament will convince anyone that it is uncomfortably close to public opinion. The temptation to find an easy way out, or to find a scapegoat, is great. To a large extent this has not been done. The government in its Development Plan has embarked on a development strategy which makes good use of expatriate private capital and immigrant skills, despite the resentments which this has frequently aroused. It is of course easy to find, as Theroux has done, selective quotations to demonstrate the "racialism" of Ministers, but it is equally important to remember the unrecorded cases when Ministers run the gauntlet of an angry parliament in refusing to answer the innumerable questions on the "racial composition" of this or that firm or government department, or replying in terms of "citizens" and "non-citizens" to hoots of derision.

For the unemployed and the school leaver, the Asian clerk and semi-skilled worker is in the way, and when he is a non-citizen there are obvious pressures to remove him. The Kenyanisation policy which has been developed over the last year has been explicitly defined in terms of citizenship. Non-citizens have to hold a work permit which is granted only if Kenyans are not available to do the job and this also involves the payment of a deposit to cover the holder's eventual departure. It is easy to bring economic arguments to bear against the Kenya Immigration Act.[28] They are basically two-fold: that overrapid Kenyanisation will seriously jeopardise the growth targets and ultimately employment levels, and that at least in the more skilled jobs Kenyanisation is unnecessary due to an overall shortfall in supply. The latter point is implicitly

acknowledge by the government and Kenyanisation is taking place largely in Group C of the Manpower Plan categories—skilled office and manual workers. At these levels the impact of Africanisation is very difficult to assess: on one hand the government has taken perhaps a rather cavalier attitude towards the accumulated skills of such groups as clerical workers, telephone operators and registry clerks, with the result that the administrative standards of many offices have fallen to a rather low level— perhaps temporarily. On the other hand, as one defender of the government has pointed out,[29] the scope for on-the-job training and learning-by-doing has probably been underestimated. And, as the same writer has argued, ultimately the question is not an economic one and certainly not a moral but a political one. One may point out that the policy may lead to falling output per man and eventually falling investment and falling employment but, provided that discrimination against citizens is not involved, an independent Kenya is surely fully entitled to, and even perhaps sensible to, trade off a redistributive policy at the expense of aliens against a certain amount of economic growth—as it has done previously over land transfer.

Nor are the measures introduced as severe as is sometimes argued. Some of the more exacting requirements of the Immigration Act—the need to put down a deposit for dependents—have been eased and as far as can be seen the delays in the relevant government departments and a concern to preserve at least minimum standards of efficiency will act as an effective brake. By September-October 1968 fewer than 10,000 applications had been dealt with and many had been accepted. As far as this Act is concerned most Asian non-citizens with a profession or an irreplaceable skill can look forward to a few more years in Kenya. The Traders Licensing Act, which looked so draconian on paper, has been used mainly against non-citizens in rural areas—under 10 per cent of the total—and in one town, Kitale, which is being used as an experiment; though the 3,000 who have had licenses refused—in January 1969—include many from the main shopping centres. The ban on non-citizen trade in basic "African products," maize, khirgas, second-hand clothes, salt, tin-roofing, etc., will be limiting but not prohibitive. The Kenyanisation measures must be regarded as restrained and necessary given the Kenyan context.

The Kenyan government's attitude to its Asian citizens has been severely criticised. Discrimination in the Civil Service has been mentioned and it might be noted that this practice was discontinued in Tanzania several years ago. Several Asian Kenyan citizens have been deported. The Nairobi City Council—which is not part of the central government—excluded non-African citizens from the central market, though appeals were subsequently upheld in court and the decisions reversed. Above all there has been resentment over the slow rate at which citizenship applications, most of which arrived in the last weeks of 1965, have been processed. Several thousand are still outstanding. The Home Affairs Minister has promised to hurry matters along but the affair reflects badly upon his department. The whole question of the Kenya government's attitude to citizenship is something which should attract the interest of future historians. The initial offer was very generous, stemming perhaps from a genuinely idealistic view of race relations in the new Kenya. But if Asians and Europeans had responded in very great numbers, the government would have been exceedingly embarrassed, and with the inequalities which are so marked in Kenya the pressure for upward mobility for Africans would sooner or later have had to be met by overt discrimination. Since then the government has rather obviously felt that citizenship was acquired too easily, and this has led to the "go-slow" on new citizenship applications and to attacks on Asian citizens who "are only here for what they can get." This feeling probably explains the occasional cases of semi-official discrimination. Asian citizens frequently complain of the difficulties of getting jobs in government and the local City Council, even in such politically innocuous fields as engineering, while white expatriates later come in to do the same jobs at far larger salaries. It would perhaps have been much better if the government had been stricter from the outset, restricting citizenship to more carefully sifted applicants and those with long residence qualifications, and then

taking a liberal approach to all those accepted and perhaps even as a gesture extending the application period by two or three months. In this way obligations towards a small number of non-African citizens could have been honoured without limiting the scope of promoting the interests of Africans. However, insomuch as the decisions taken in 1963 were irrevocable, the government has largely avoided encouraging overt racialism. There is one possible exception to this generalisation and that relates to the occasional broadcasts on the "Voice of Kenya" on the "Asian question." In August 1966, at the time of the deportation of several Asians, a speaker said:

Kenya's whole Asian community stands indicted by the actions of some of its members.

A subsequent broadcast in September 1967 claimed that—

the Government was niether instrumental in bringing those disgruntled Asians into the country nor is it bound to stop their exodus. Moreover this is not its responsibility. . . . The Asians have stuck to their British passports like leeches.

No apology was subsequently forthcoming and one must conclude that this represented an official line. Theroux relies heavily on these broadcasts to document his thesis that racialism in Kenya is the responsibility of those in authority who should know better. While these V.O.K. broadcasts are an exceptional lapse they are nonetheless unfortunate.

It is important to distinguish between official policy, which in general is fair, and unofficial statements, which usually are not. MPs who are not members of the government have been particularly virulent in their efforts to speak for the man in the street—in much the same way as Enoch Powell in the United Kingdom. One recently asked that an Asian crematorium be moved on the grounds that it was "an insult to our people who do not burn their bodies."[30] There are innumerable racial questions of this unsophisticated type; about the driving and dining habits of Asians; their "inso-

lence"; their birth rate. MPs are strongly representative of a new class of Kenya Africans who
are moderately prosperous, small landowners,
partly educated, and with aspirations towards
commerce. They articulate the frustrations of
the up-and-coming retailers who are dependent
on Asian wholesalers and are struggling against
Asian competition. They successfully lobbied
for the Traders Licensing Act and are keen to
expand schemes such as that of the ICDC for
promoting African shareholding. They also
give vent to the grievances of the poor and
sometimes confused electorate which is easily
convinced that the rich foreigners in their
midst are the source of Kenya's, and hence,
their own, problems. Another anti-Asian group
are the trade-unionists, who speak for the
manual workers and urban consumers and who
are concerned with pay-differentials and factors
which influence the cost of living like rising
rents and food prices. Such things are more
easily explained by "Asian exploitation" than
by remote events such as tariff increases or
rises in shipping costs. What is significant is that
the worst anti-Asian feeling usually comes from
those Africans who are struggling up the social
ladder—traders, university students, semi-skilled
workers, clerks and politicians—rather than
those right at the bottom, the landless agricultural workers and subsistence farmers.

These factors help to explain why Asians
are finding themselves more unpopular than
Europeans at least amongst those more ambitious and mobile individuals for whom Asian
economic power is an obstacle and Asian prosperity an object of envy. There are clearly
other aspects to the problem as well. Europeans undoubtedly benefit from the general
respect which is afforded to European education—and to white teachers—and to much of
the European way of life and religion. Little
interest is shown in things oriental; indeed,
Hindustani broadcasts, Diwali, celebrations,
Muslim public holidays and other "Asian"
features of Kenyan life are slowly being re-

moved. These cultural elements, however,
would have been of minor importance if the
basic causes of friction with the white population—colonial authority and inequality based
upon the ownership of the land—had not been
tackled directly by the resettlement of 1½ million acres of the former "scheduled areas"
(White Highlands) with African farmers and
the Africanisation of key posts in the Civil Service. As a side effect many of the more intolerant Europeans have left. Only two-thirds of
the 60,000 in Kenya at independence remain.
By way of contrast nothing was done until
1967 to limit Asian domination of most
"middle-class" employment. There were far
more of the Asians—over 180,000—and the
numbers increased after independence. Generous British aid and freedom to return to the
United Kingdom provided a safety valve for
the Europeans and removed much of the un-
pleasantness in relations between European
and African. This is frequently acknowledged
and Kenya's Africans show great willingness to
forget the past and interpret favorably any
constructive gesture. A KANU official stated
at a press conference: "Europeans have identified themselves completely with the new Kenya"[31]—a generous overstatement that would
never be applied to Asians.

To conclude: The largely economic basis
of Kenya's immensely difficult problem of race
relations meant that, even if much more had
been done by the Asians to "integrate" and by
the government to welcome them, the problem would have remained. For the majority of
Kenya Asians the alternatives were emigration
or systematic impoverishment in Kenya. The
failure of the British government to find a way
of easing the process of Kenyanisation as it did
for the farmers, and the failure to honour its
obligation to admit into Britain those forced
to leave, put great obstacles in the way of a
humane and painless resolution of the problem.
It is indeed fortunate that this has resulted in
hardship rather than bloodshed.

NOTES

[1] e.g., L. W. Hollingsworth, *The Asians of East Africa* (London, 1960); George Delf, *Asians in East Africa* (London, 1963).

[2] Y. P. Ghai (ed.), *Portrait of a Minority: Asians in East Africa* (London, 1965).

[3] H. S. Morris, *The Indians in Uganda* (London, 1968). See also his article, "Communal Rivalry among Indians in Uganda," *British Journal of Sociology* 8 (1957).

[4] A. Bharati, in Ghai, *Portrait of a Minority*, pp. 13-63.

[5] J. Müller, in *South African Journal of Economics* (1965), p. 114-130.

[6] R. H. Desai, in *Racial and Communal Tensions in East Africa* (Nairobi, 1966).

[7] Ghai, *Portrait of a Minority*, p. 152.

[8] Quoted in Paul Theroux, "Hating the Asians," *Transition* 33 (October/November 1967).

[9] Editorial in *Spectator*, 1 March 1968.

[10] Theroux, *Transition* 33, loc. cit.

[11] Its effects are examined by Morgan in *New Society* 11 (November 1965); and by Carey Jones in the *Geographical Journal* (June 1965).

[12] *High-level Manpower: Requirements and Resources, 1964-1970*, Ministry of Economic Planning (Nairobi, 1965).

[13] *Statistical Abstract*, Ministry of Economic Planning (Nairobi, 1967).

[14] *Kenya: Census of Population, 1962* (Nairobi, 1964).

[15] e.g., W. S. Churchill, *My African Journey* (London, 1908). This early period is described in detail in C. Wrigley's Chapter V of the *History of East Africa* (Oxford, 1965), Vol. II, edited by V. Harlow, E. M. Chilver and A. Smith, "Kenya: the Patterns of Economic Life, 1902-1945."

[16] Elizabeth Hopkins, in S. Diamond and F. Burke (eds.), *The Transformation of East Africa* (New York, 1966), pp. 83-153.

[17] Desai, in *Racial Tensions*, loc. cit.

[18] For a full account see G. Bennett's Chapter VI, "Settlers and Politics in Kenya," in *History of East Africa*, Vol. II.

[19] Y. Tandon, in Ghai, *Portrait of a Minority*, pp. 65-90.

[20] As happened in 1963 when many Asian employees resigned from the East African Common Services Organization in protest against terms of service. To their dismay their resignations were accepted.

[21] D. P. Ghai and Y. P. Ghai, "Asians in East Africa: Problems and Prospects," *Journal of Modern African Studies* 3, 1 (1965).

[22] D. Rothchild, "Kenya's Minorities and the African Crisis over Citizenship," *Race* 9, 4 (1968).

[23] *Report of the East Africa Royal Commission*, Cmd. 9475 (London, 1955), p. 65.

[24] e.g., *New Society*, March 1968; and *Occasional Papers of the Institute of Development Studies* (Nairobi, 1968).

[25] ICDC *Annual Reports*, 1964-66.

[26] See inter alia the Van Arkadie *Report on Land Settlement in Kenya, 1967*.

[27] Quoted in Theroux, *Transition* 33, loc. cit.

[28] As do a group of economists in *East African Journal* (March 1968).

[29] See for example J. Wells, in *East African Journal* (April 1968).

[30] Reported in *East African Standard* 13 September 1967.

[31] Sammy Maina, quoted in J. S. Roberts, *A Land Full of People* (London, 1967), p. 160.

15
the australian aboriginal: what white australians know and think about him – a preliminary survey

J. S. WESTERN

In the eighteenth century, when Europeans first came to Australia, there were about 300,000 people already living there. Their culture was Stone Age, in this respect quite different from the original inhabitants of North and South America, some of whom lived in cities; none of those people had Stone Age cultures. Despite the more advanced technologies of the Americans, the history of the native inhabitants of Australia and of the Americas is similar. Europeans wanted land for agricultural use; the natives were nomadic. Conflict resulted, and the more efficient weapons and military organization of the Europeans prevailed.

The Australians have, like Americans, alternated between trying to assimilate the aborigines (a word which means "original inhabitants") and providing a separate life for them on reserves. As time has passed, the government has been more concerned about their welfare. In 1958, a Federal Council for Aboriginal Advancement was established, and free and compulsory education was provided for all detribalized aborigines. In 1959, the aborigines came under the federal social welfare laws, which are quite extensive in Australia. In 1960, the policy of reservations was abandoned, and in 1962, aborigines were permitted to enroll themselves as voters if they so desired. Some of the group have entered modern Australian life, usually as laborers, mechanics, and stockmen on cattle ranches; but in 1966, the first aborigine graduated from an Australian university. Some groups, however, prefer their communal tribal life and have not availed themselves of the educational and voting privileges. In 1961, there were 40,081 full-blooded aborigines and 30,000 of mixed ancestry.

In this article, Mr. Western, who teaches political sociology at the University of Queensland, investigates the attitudes and knowledge of white Australians toward the remaining aboriginal population.

Reprinted from *Race* 10, no. 4 (April 1969), pp. 413-434. Reproduced by permission of the author and The Institute of Race Relations, London.

INTRODUCTION

The attitude of Australian whites to aboriginal Australians could probably most accurately be described, until very recent times, as one of indifference. The aboriginal was no economic threat, it would be hard to conceive of one's daughter as likely to marry him, and one would be unlikely to find him taking up residence next door. Indeed, for the majority of Australians the aboriginal was probably not as visible as his counterpart, the American Indian, and his fate was of no greater concern.

In recent years, however, the picture has changed somewhat and is even now still changing. Partly this has been due to the rise to prominence of certain aboriginals, partly to the energies of a few, who, recognizing that aboriginals shared the same human attributes distributed in much the same manner as others were somewhat disconcerted to learn that their social relationships with whites seldom reflected this basic equality, and partly to the few, who insisted, often in quite an embarrassing manner, on publicizing the basic social inequalities that the aboriginal experienced in his day-to-day existence.

But if indifference is not now the attitude of white Australians to their black contemporaries, what is? Is it one of hostility as R. and C. Berndt[1] would seem to suggest, or is it one of patronizing concern or genuine interest, to mention but three by no means exhaustive alternatives? Fay Gale, in *A Study of Assimilation*,[2] suggests that unfavourable attitudes towards aborigines are more common in residents in smaller country towns, in older and less well educated people, and among those who are economically depressed—remarkably similar conclusions to those coming from studies of Negro-White relations in the United States. Jeanne MacKenzie,[3] on the other hand, in describing visits to towns where aborigines lived and worked, has stated that she did not see obvious signs of colour prejudice. Several Gallup Polls, too, in the last decade have reported generally favourable attitudes towards aborginals. And more recently still, Ronald Taft,[4] in an as yet unpublished paper, demonstrates that the environment in which an individual lives affects his attitude towards aborigines.

It would appear that persons brought up in the tolerant atmosphere of Perth are intellectually not only pro-aborigine, but are also resistant to the pressures to the contrary in country towns. On the other hand, persons raised in the country, interstate or overseas tend to be comparatively unfavourable to aborigines and these unfavourable attitudes increase under the influence of living in the towns.

Clearly a body of data is gradually being built up around this topic but the findings stemming from it are far from conclusive. The study reported in this paper does not pretend to be any more definitive than those that have gone before, although it does try to answer several questions that have been raised in the earlier work.

CHARACTERISTICS OF THE STUDY

It has sometimes been claimed (by Asch,[5] for example) that attitudes have a cognitive and experiential basis; that is to say that the attitudes a person holds on a particular topic are in no small part determined by his knowledge about that topic and his experience of it. The present study, while not espousing some sort of inflexible determinism, looks particularly at the relationship between attitudes to aboriginals, knowledge about aboriginals and contact with them. As well, it tries to determine whether the attitudes that are held about aborigines are in some sense unitary, that is whether individuals tend to have a generally more or less favourable attitude or whether they tend to be favourable on some issues and unfavourable on others. Finally, it takes up the problem of the relationship between attitudes and such background factors as age, education, social class and sex.

The study was conducted in two communities separated by about 300 miles. The first is a small, although allegedly sophisticated city of some 80,000 situated approximately 190 miles from Sydney, the capital of New South Wales and 400 miles from Melbourne, the capital of Victoria. It contains no aborigines. The second is a small country town of New South Wales with a population of about 1,000. It has a "sizeable" aboriginal population although not even the most knowledge

TABLE 1. Age of Urbania and Bush Town Residents

Years	Urbania (%)	Bush Town (%)
17-20	7	9
21-30	25	32
31-40	29	20
41-50	24	11
51-60	12	10
Over 60	3	18
Total number	132	125

able could put a figure to it. A sample of approximately the same size of white Australians was interviewed in each centre, although the method of their selection differed. In the first centre, Urbania, the sample was selected in the following way. First, the suburbs comprising the city were divided into two groups: those to the north of an artificial lake, which has been held to either divide or unify the town, and those to the south. Then each of these groups was further divided into "new" and "old" suburbs. Within each of these four groups a series of streets was randomly selected. Within streets five dwellings were selected by taking every second from a random start. Within dwellings any person over seventeen years of age normally resident there and having lived in Australia more than fifteen years was regarded as an appropriate subject. The interviewers were instructed to select one such person from each house visited, the normal device being to select the person first coming to the door.

In the second centre, Bush Town, the first step in the selection of the sample was to divide the town into twenty approximately equal areas, the number corresponding to the number of available interviewers. These areas were quite small, normally, no more than one or two streets of some twenty or so dwellings, and the interviewers were required to select dwellings distributed representatively throughout the area, again from a random start. Within dwellings the same criteria applied as in Urbania.

All told 257 successful interviews were held; 132 of these were in Urbania, and the remaining 125 in Bush Town. There were relatively few refusals to co-operate; in Urbania twenty people declined to be interviewed, while in Bush Town the figure was slightly higher, at thirty.

THE SAMPLE

Of the total sample, 156 or 58% were female. These proportions remained roughly constant across the two communities: 60% of the Urbania sample were female, as were 57% from Bush Town. The Bush Town respondents were both older and younger than those from Urbania. As Table 1 shows, 41% of the country respondents were 30 or less, while only 32% of those from Urbania came in this category. As well, 18% from Bush Town were over 60, compared with just 3% of the Urbanians. Educationally, as might be expected, the two groups were quite different: 58% of the Urbanians had had some post-secondary education compared with only 14% from Bush Town. Bush Town residents, too, were much more likely to have only received primary schooling. The details are presented in Table 2.

The distribution of occupations in the two communities is also quite different. As can be seen in Table 3, 44% of the Urbania sample come from upper-white-collar and professional backgrounds while only 8% of the Bush Town respondents do. As well, working-class backgrounds are much more common among the Bush Town residents. A second index of class affiliation, the social class the respondent perceives himself as belonging to, presents somewhat different distributions in the two communities (Table 4). Those with a

TABLE 2. Educational Level Reached by Urbania and Bush Town Residents

	Urbania (%)	Bush Town (%)
Primary school only	5	22
At least some secondary education	37	63
Tertiary education (teaching diploma, accountancy qualifications, university degree)	58	14
No answer	—	1
Total number	132	125

TABLE 3. Occupation of Head of Household

	Urbania (%)	Bush Town (%)
Managerial and professional (individuals occupying responsible managerial positions or engaged in professional activities)	20	2
Upper white collar (white-collar workers with supervisory functions, including commissioned officers of armed forces)	24	6
Lower white collar (white-collar workers without supervisory functions)	21	23
Skilled manual workers and supervisors	10	17
Semi-skilled and unskilled workers	14	26
Farmers and graziers	3	13
Pensioners, students, housewives	8	8
No answer	1	2
Total number	132	125

TABLE 4. Perceived Class of Urbania and Bush Town Residents

	Urbania (%)	Bush Town (%)
Upper class	2	1
Upper middle	27	20
Lower middle	14	12
Middle class undifferentiated	20	16
Working class	31	46
Other (denies existence of classes, don't know, no answer)	7	6
Total number	132	125

working-class background are still found more commonly among the Bush Town group, 46% consider themselves working class compared with 31% from Urbania, but there is not as great a discrepancy in the number of middle-class respondents in the two communities as Table 3 might perhaps have led us to believe. This is largely due to the fact that the graziers, separated out in Table 2, almost all regard themselves as members of the upper middle class.

It is clear from this brief account that there are quite marked differences between the two groups. Not only are we dealing with an urban group relatively isolated from aborigines, and a rural group in quite close contact with them, but we are as well dealing with a relatively well educated middle-aged and

TABLE 5. Amount of Contact with Aboriginals by Residents in Both Communities

	Urbania (%)	Bush Town (%)
Never held a social conversation with an aboriginal	41	11
Know no aboriginals by name	57	12
Never visited an aboriginal home	83	68
No aborginals among personal friends	86	68
Belong to organization for assimilation of aborigines	3	6
Total number	132	125

TABLE 6. Contact "Scores" for Urbania and Bush Town Residents

Contact Score	Urbania (%)	Bush Town (%)
0	66	13
1	14	17
2	8	28
3	10	21
4	2	18
5	0	2
Total number	132	125

middle-class group and a less well educated working-class group that contains fewer middle-aged but more who are young and old. We will have to be cautious therefore in attributing any difference we find to an urban-rural difference, or to differences in contact with aboriginals until we have examined the effects of these other variables.

CONTACT AND KNOWLEDGE

To ascertain how much actual contact with aboriginals the members of the two samples had had, a number of questions focussing on contact were asked early in the interview.

Among the Urbanians 41% had never had a conversation with an aboriginal, and 57% knew none by name. In Bush Town on the other hand only 11% had never held a conversation with an aboriginal and only 12% knew none by name, not surprising differences when the contexts of the two groups are considered. When we move from these purely formal contacts to more personal ones the differences become less marked. Thus while 83% of the Urbanian sample had never visited an aboriginal home, and 86% of them claimed no aboriginals among their personal friends, the figures for Bush Town are a relatively high

68% in each instance. Finally, on a question enquiring about membership of organizations for the assimilation of aboriginals, positive responses are given by four Urbanians and six of their Bush Town contemporaries. The data are summarized in Table 5.

To summarize this information still further we gave the members of the sample a score of one point every time their response indicated contact. Thus having held a social conversation with an aborigine counted one point, as did knowing an aboriginal by name, having visited an aboriginal home, having aboriginal friends and belonging to an organization for the assimilation of aborigines. The maximum score possible therefore was five, and the minimum was zero. Table 6 details the way in which the sample was distributed over this "scale." As the earlier results had already suggested, there are quite considerable differences between the groups: 66% of the Urbanians score zero while only 13% of those from Bush Town do, 20% of those from Bush Town get four points or more while only 2% of the Urbanians do. When we come to the question of knowledge about the status and rights of aboriginals, however, the picture is somewhat different. The residents of Urbania

TABLE 7. **Responses to a Series of Factual Statements Concerning the Position and Status of Aboriginals**

	URBANIA (N = 132)			BUSH TOWN (N = 125)		
	True (%)	False (%)	Don't know (%)	True (%)	False (%)	Don't know (%)
All Australian full-blooded aborigines have full citizenship rights. (False)	13	73	14	32	55	14
In some states Australian half-caste aborigines do not have full citizenship rights. (True)	45	24	31	52	18	30
Aboriginal workers are paid wages equal to those of white people doing the same work. (False)	13	72	15	51	38	11
Aborigines have the right to vote in state and federal elections. (False)	18	66	16	49	35	16
All aborigines have the right (by law) to drink in any Australian hotel. (False)	26	63	11	63	30	7
In some states there are literacy tests which aborigines have to pass before they are entitled to certain rights. (True)	34	13	53	29	18	53
There are no restrictions imposed on the buying of land by aborigines. (False)	20	38	42	45	20	35
In some states control is exercised over how aborigines spend their wages. (True)	41	22	37	25	41	34
Aborigines living on reserves are free to leave when they wish. (False)	46	29	26	62	21	15
There are no restrictions imposed on the land which the Welfare Board may buy for aboriginal settlements. (False)	14	38	47	53	28	45

appear far better informed than those from Bush Town. The questions asked ranged from general enquiries about citizenship rights to quite specific questions about issues such as the land the welfare board is permitted to buy for aboriginal settlements. Considerable attention was paid to wording the questions in precise and unambiguous terms, and the respondents were simpy requested to indicate whether they regarded each statement as true or false or whether they were unable to say.

The item which was answered accurately by the greatest number of each group concerned citizenship rights. To the statement: "All Australian full-blood aborigines have full citizenship rights," 73% of the Urbania sample correctly answered "false" as did 55% of the Bush Town group. However to the corollary: "In some states Australian half-caste aborigines do not have full citizenship rights," only 45% of the Urbania sample gave the correct response "true" while 52% of the Bush Town group responded in the same way. Interestingly, this is the only item on which the Bush Town group was more accurate than the Urbanians.

Three quite specific items on which the groups differed markedly concerned wages, voting and drinking. Seventy-three per cent of the Urbanian sample stated correctly that the

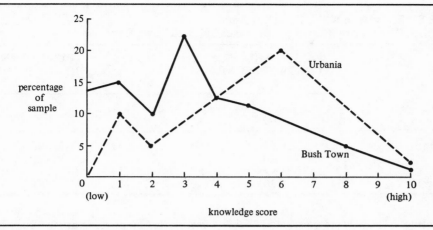

FIGURE 1. Differences Between Urbania and Bush Town Residents in Knowledge Scores

assertion: "aboriginal workers are paid wages equal to those of white people doing the same work," is false, while only 38% of those from Bush Town gave the correct answer; 66% of the Urbanians knew that not all aboriginals had the right to vote in state or federal elections, while only 35% of the Bush Town group were aware of this. Again, only a minority of the Bush Town residents, 30%, were aware that all aboriginals did not have the right by law to drink in any Australian hotel, while a majority of the Urbanians, 63%, knew this to be the case.

On four further items the differences in correct response were not so marked, principally because only a minority of both groups knew the correct answers. But even on these items, concerned with the notion of literacy tests for aboriginals, the freedom of aboriginals to buy land, spend their wages as they wish and depart from reserves when they wish, the Urbanians consistently gave more correct answers, and interestingly were slightly more prepared to admit they did not know. All the details can be found in Table 7. On a final item concerned with land the Welfare Board may buy for aboriginal settlements, the same pattern of differences was maintained.

Again it is possible to summarize this information by scoring each respondent's answers and so arriving at a total score. The

procedure we adopted was a very simple one: giving a score of one point to each item correctly answered. This procedure, of course, lumps together those who admit they do not know the answer to a particular question and those who actually answer the question incorrectly. To determine whether it was in fact justified to proceed in this way we adopted an alternative scoring procedure as well and compared the results. The alternative procedure was to score as plus one correct answers, minus one incorrect answers, and zero don't know responses. On correlating scores obtained by the two procedures a correlation coefficient of the order of 0.95 was obtained, and so in the analysis which follows a measure, or index, based on the simpler scoring procedure will be employed.

With ten items scores could range from zero to ten, and in Figure 1 we show the manner in which the two groups were distributed over this range. The differences are quite striking, with the Urbania group very much ahead in knowledge scores. In general terms, then, it would seem that proximity to aboriginals is not related to knowledge about them. But how does actual contact with them affect knowledge? Do those individuals in the two samples who have more to do with aboriginals have greater knowledge of their rights, or again is our specific measure of contact not related

TABLE 8. The Way in Which Knowledge and
Contact Are Related for Urbanian and Bush Town Residents

Knowledge score	URBANIA CONTACT SCORE (%)			BUSH TOWN CONTACT SCORE (%)		
	0	1-2	3-5	0	1-2	3-5
0-2	20	13	6	31	36	38
3-5	40	40	44	50	43	50
6-10	40	47	50	19	21	12
(Number)	(85)	(30)	(16)	(16)	(56)	(54)

to knowledge? The data are presented in Table 8. The trends are inconclusive. For the Urbania sample the pattern is much as might be expected; knowledge and contact are positively associated; with increasing contact, knowledge of aboriginal rights increases. For example, among those with no contact 20% have low knowledge scores and 40% have high scores, while among those with a considerable degree of contact only 6% have low scores and 50% have high scores. However, among the Bush Town residents this orderly pattern does not exist and it would seem that contact makes virtually no difference to knowledge. Clearly the answer is not a simple one.

ATTITUDE TO ABORIGINES

In order to assess their attitude to aboriginals the two groups of respondents were presented with a series of statements concerning aboriginals and asked to indicate the extent of their agreement with each. The statements were included in a list, containing, also, items from established Liberalism and Dogmatism scales,[6] which was prefaced by a request for their opinion on these social issues. The distribution of responses to the statements relating to aboriginals is shown in Table 9.

The first seven statements are positive, an "agree" response indicates a favourable attitude, while the remaining thirteen are negative, a "disagree" response indicating a favourable attitude. Within each group the statements have been arranged in descending order: those most likely to elicit a favourable response come first. A quick glance at the table

reveals that on no items are the Bush Town respondents more favourable than those from Urbania. As well, while there are no items eliciting unfavourable responses from a majority of the Urbanians, in seven instances Bush Town respondents give more unfavourable than favourable responses: aborigines expect more out of life for nothing than whites, they give neighbourhoods a typical aboriginal atmosphere, they will always adapt the white man's materials to their old ways, aborigines are pretty much alike, restrictions should be placed on aborigines to protect them from their own lack of responsibility, races cannot merge because white culture is more advanced, and manual work is best for aborigines. Interestingly, these items are all negative and all bear on the stereotype of the aboriginal as inherently inferior, shiftless, dirty and lazy. Of the items which are likely to elicit favourable rather than unfavourable responses from both groups a number are concerned with the rights aboriginals should be accorded: aborigines should be encouraged to join local organizations where they live, they should possess Australian citizenship automatically, rates of pay for whites and aborigines should be the same, aborigines should have full use of public facilities used by whites, and it is a criticism of Australia that aborigines do not possess equal rights.

Although the Urbanians are more likely than those from Bush Town to give favourable responses to all items there are, nevertheless, patterned differences within the whole group. Thus, on the items already referred to which focus on aboriginal rights (1, 3, 4, 6 and 7) the percentage of favourable responses ranges from 94% on item 1 to 72% on item 7, while on the items concerning the aboriginal stereotype, the percentage of favourable responses is markedly lower ranging from a maximum of 64% on items 13 and 19, down to 49% on item 20. Both groups it seems are more likely to have a favourable attitude to aboriginal rights than they are to reject the stereotype that aboriginals are inferior, shiftless, dirty and lazy.

This preliminary appraisal has been based on the responses of the two groups to the separate issues; whether the structure suggested above can be derived by more systematic procedures will be examined now. Initially, responses to the 21 items were given weights as follows:

a. positive items:	strongly agree	1
	agree	2
	not sure	3
	disagree	4
	strongly disagree	5

b. negative items:	strongly agree	5
	agree	4
	not sure	3
	disagree	2
	strongly disagree	1

A factor analysis was then performed using Kaiser's varimax technique[7] and four factors were extracted. The percentage of the total variance accounted for by each factor is shown in Table 10, and the factor loadings of each item on the four factors in Table 11.

The items with the highest loadings on factor 1 are, in descending order: 14, 17, 15, 12, 16, 19, 18, 13, 21 and 20. After item 20, which had a loading of −0.455, there is a considerable drop to item 9 with a loading of −0.343, and a further drop to item 8 which loads −0.218. From an examination of the items with the high loadings it seems clear that factor 1 has to do with the stereotype mentioned earlier and we propose to think of these items as tapping an aboriginal image dimension. At one extreme of this dimension are those who hold to the view that aboriginal culture is inferior to that of whites, that the aboriginal must be protected because of his own lack of responsibility, that attempts to introduce aboriginals into white communities will result in a lowering of the living standards of those communities and that it is in the interests of all for the races to be kept apart. At the other extreme are those who disagree that aboriginal culture is inferior, who reject the notions that the aboriginal must be protected, that the aboriginal is likely to lower the living standards of white communities and that the races should be segregated.

Factor 1 accounted for 18.404% of the variance; factor 2, the only other factor accounting for a sizeable proportion of the variance, 11.079%, is the only other interpretable factor. The items with high loadings on this factor, again in descending order, are: 8, 2, 3, 4, 9, 6, 1 and 10. From an examination of these items it seems clear that this factor has to do with aboriginal rights, and we propose to think of them as tapping an aboriginal rights dimension. Again, at one extreme are those who feel that the rights an aboriginal should be accorded by virtue of his status as an aboriginal should be no different than the rights accorded a white Australian by virtue of his status as a white Australian. At the other extreme are those who see the statuses of aboriginal Australian and white Australian as distinct; the net result of which is to socially disadvantage the aboriginal. Or, to put it slightly differently, at one extreme there are those who hold that racial characteristics should neither qualify nor disqualify individuals for occupancy of the status of Australian citizen, while at the other there are those who claim that racial characteristics should serve as either qualifiers or disqualifiers for the status.

The net result of the factor analysis, therefore, was the identification of two dimensions, an aboriginal image dimension and an aboriginal rights dimension. The next task to be faced was that of allocating members of the sample to positions on the two dimensions. Two main alternatives appeared open: the first and the simpler procedure would simply have been to give each respondent a weighted score, employing the weights described earlier, on

TABLE 9. Responses to a Series of Opinion Statements About Aborigines

		EXTENT OF AGREEMENT (%)[a]					(NUMBER)
		I	II	III	IV	V	
1. Aborigines should be encouraged to join local organizations so that they can play their full part in the life of the town in which they live.	U	33	61	3	2	1	(132)
	BT[b]	11	76	4	8	1	(125)
2. If I had decided to vote along party lines in an election I would still vote for my party if they elected an aboriginal.	U	26	65	6	1	1	(132)
	BT	12	76	5	7	0	(125)
3. All aborigines should possess Australian citizenship automatically.	U	34	55	4	6	1	(132)
	BT	30	60	4	6	0	(125)
4. There should be no difference between rates of pay for aborigines and whites engaged in the same work.	U	36	54	1	8	1	(132)
	BT	25	60	5	8	1	(125)
5. Given the same opportunities aboriginal children will do as well at school as white children.	U	23	62	7	6	1	(132)
	BT	24	55	3	17	1	(125)
6. Aborigines should have full use of all public facilities which are used by whites.	U	23	59	7	11	1	(132)
	BT	16	60	9	13	2	(125)
7. It is criticism of Australia as a democratic country that aborigines do not possess equal rights.	U	19	53	10	14	4	(132)
	BT	13	54	10	23	0	(125)
8. If an aborigine sat next to me in a bus or train I would feel uncomfortable.	U	1	2	3	57	37	(132)
	BT	0	6	2	64	27	(125)
9. I have nothing against people of another culture but allowing aborigines to vote and to drink in public places is going a little too far.	U	1	11	3	50	35	(132)
	BT	1	13	4	62	20	(125)
10. I have nothing against aborigines but can never see myself being really friendly with one.	U	3	14	8	53	23	(132)
	BT	6	29	5	49	10	(125)
11. Although I have nothing against aborigines there is something about their physical appearance which is basically unattractive.	U	1	22	6	50	21	(132)
	BT	3	30	10	57	0	(125)
12. The incorporation of aborigines into our communities could well lower our standards of hygiene.	U	1	23	8	49	20	(132)
	BT	3	26	14	49	8	(125)
13. Aborigines expect to get more out of life for nothing than white people.	U	1	20	16	44	19	(132)
	BT	5	42	8	40	5	(125)
14. The trouble with letting aborigines into a nice neighbourhood is that they gradually give it a typical aborigine atmosphere.	U	1	18	19	44	18	(132)
	BT	7	35	17	36	5	(125)
15. Because the aborigine can never escape from the limits of his culture, he will always adapt the white man's materials to his old ways.	U	1	17	17	50	14	(132)
	BT	2	43	13	37	4	(125)

TABLE 9. Responses to a Series of Opinion Statements About Aborigines (Continued)

		EXTENT OF AGREEMENT (%)[a]					(NUMBER)
		I	II	III	IV	V	
16. There may be few exceptions but in general aborigines are pretty much alike.	U	2	20	20	44	14	(132)
	BT	9	49	7	33	2	(125)
17. Restrictions should be placed on the aborigine to protect him from his own lack of responsibility.	U	3	30	9	44	14	(132)
	BT	7	48	6	37	2	(125)
18. No matter how much one might support it on idealistic grounds, there have been too many unfortunate consequences of racial mixing for me to be willing to agree with it.	U	1	17	16	53	13	(132)
	BT	3	35	23	37	1	(125)
19. One reason white and black races can never merge is because the white culture is so much more advanced.	U	3	21	11	53	11	(132)
	BT	4	46	7	38	6	(125)
20. Manual labour and unskilled jobs seem to fit the aborigines' nature and ability better than more skilled or responsible work.	U	5	40	6	40	9	(132)
	BT	7	48	7	35	2	(125)
21. When all is said and done aborigines probably prefer not to mix with whites.	U	4	36	15	40	5	(132)
	BT	10	62	6	21	1	(125)

[a] I = strongly agree; II = agree; III = not sure; IV = disagree; V = strongly disagree.
[b] U = Urbania; BT = Bush Town.

TABLE 10. Variance Accounted for by the Four Factors Extracted Using a Varimax Technique

Factor	Variance	% of variance	Cumulative %
1	3.865	18.404	18.404
2	2.327	11.079	29.483
3	0.993	4.730	34.213
4	0.804	3.828	38.041

the basis of his responses to the items which appeared to define the two dimensions. Although this is quite a common procedure, the work reported by Moseley and Kleitt in *Psychological Reports*[8] and by Horn in *Educational and Psychological Measurement*[9, 10] suggest the appropriateness of a more rigorous approach. Consequently the decision was made to obtain factor scores for all respondents on the first two factors. The least squares technique advocated by Horst[11] was adopted and

the factor scores and scale score equivalents which were set up are given in Table 12. It should be noted that in both cases a positive factor score, and so a high scale score, means an unfavourable position on the dimension concerned. For instance, a positive factor score on the image measure means a relatively unfavourable image of the aboriginal, while a positive factor score on the rights measure means that restricting the rights of aboriginals is generally favoured. To repeat: the higher the scale

---

TABLE 11. Factor Loadings of Items Concerned with Attitudes to Aboriginals

Item	FACTOR LOADINGS[a]			
	Factor 1	Factor 2	Factor 3	Factor 4
1. Aborigines encouraged to join local organizations.	136	−395	−303	349
2. Vote for aborigine if party elected him.	050	−553	−075	105
3. Aborigines should possess citizenship automatically.	091	−502	−369	181
4. No difference between rates of pay for whites and aborigines.	087	−464	−128	076
5. With same opportunities aborigines and whites do equally well at school.	169	−314	−050	511
6. Aborigines should have full use of all public facilities.	424	−437	077	230
7. Criticism of Australia that aborigines do not possess equal rights.	167	−241	−420	085
8. Feel uncomfortable if aborigine sat next to me.	−218	586	030	−015
9. Letting aborigines vote and drink in public places going too far.	−343	450	285	−199
10. Never see self being friendly with aborigines.	−433	373	098	−061
11. Aborigines basically unattractive.	−418	233	355	073
12. Aborigines lower standards of hygiene.	−583	295	−085	−149
13. Aborigines expect more for nothing.	−484	282	−052	−200
14. Aborigines give nice neighbourhoods aboriginal atmosphere.	−641	198	017	−235
15. Aborigines always adapt white man's materials to old ways.	−590	063	322	−086
16. Aborigines much alike.	−577	146	180	−015
17. Restrictions on aborigines to protect from lack of responsibility.	−618	068	129	−149
18. Unwilling to agree to racial mixing.	−507	221	101	012
19. Races cannot merge because white race much more advanced.	−559	138	358	−011
20. Manual work best for aborigines.	−455	081	120	−335
21. Aborigines prefer not to mix with whites.	−474	013	161	−060

[a]For convenience the decimal points have been omitted.

---

score the more "unfavourable" the attitude, and the lower the scale score the more "favourable" the attitude.

The first question we need to ask, of course, is how do the two groups differ on the two dimensions. And, as far as the image measure is concerned, the answer is quite marked. The data are presented in Figure 2. It is clear that the members of the Urbania sample have a much more favourable image of the aboriginal than do those from Bush Town. However, on the aboriginal rights measure (Figure 3) there is virtually no difference and a fairly even distribution over the nine scale points is obtained for both groups. The inference would seem to be that while all agree that

TABLE 12. Factor Scores and Scale Score Equivalents for the Aboriginal Image and Aboriginal Rights Dimensions

ABORIGINAL IMAGE			ABORIGINAL RIGHTS	
Factor score	Frequency	Scale score	Factor score	Frequency
−0.27 - −0.10	25	1	−0.27 - −0.08	28
−0.09 - −0.07	30	2	−0.07 - −0.05	28
−0.06 - −0.05	22	3	−0.04 - −0.03	40
−0.04 - −0.03	34	4	−0.02	22
−0.02 - −0.01	30	5	−0.01 - 0.00	33
0 - 0.01	22	6	0.01 - 0.02	28
0.02 - 0.03	30	7	0.03 - 0.05	30
0.04 - 0.05	22	8	0.06 - 0.08	30
0.06 - 0.08	22	9	0.09 - 0.36	24
0.09 - 0.36	26	10	—	—

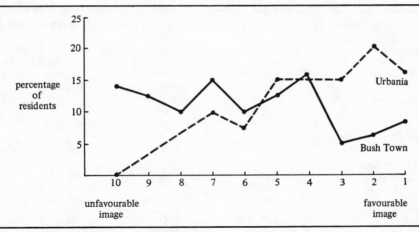

FIGURE 2. Differences Between Urbania and Bush Town Residents on the Aboriginal Image Dimension

aboriginals should be accorded some rights, only a minority in each sample feels that these should mirror those possessed by white Australians.

These trends provoke more questions than they answer. Are, for instance, the differences between Bush Town and Urbania on the image measure due to differences in contact with aboriginals, or are they due to the fact that there are substantial differences between the members of the two communities in such variables as age, education and occupation? What accounts for the variability in the aboriginal rights measure? There are no community differences, it is true, but perhaps there are differences again due to contact and background factors. In the analysis which follows we will try to sort out the picture and offer some suggestions as to why the groups should be quite different on one measure yet very similar on the other.

ATTITUDES, CONTACT AND KNOWLEDGE

We will start by looking at the way in which contact and knowledge are related to the aboriginal image measure, and because our analysis will involve examining the way in

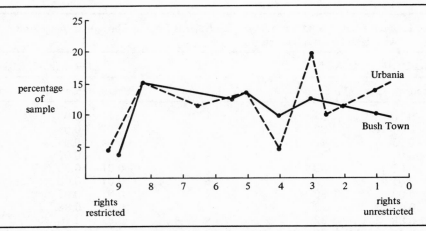

FIGURE 3. Differences Between Urbania and Bush Town Residents on the Aboriginal Rights Dimension

TABLE 13. Relationship Between Contact with Aboriginals and Image of Aboriginals for Urbania and Bush Town

| Aboriginal image | URBANIA | | BUSH TOWN | |
	High contact %	Low contact %	High contact %	Low contact %
Favourable (scale score 1-3)	62	41	20	5
Moderately favourable (scale score 4-7)	31	45	46	49
Unfavourable (scale score 8-10)	7	14	34	46
Total	100	100	100	100
(Number)	(26)	(106)	(88)	(37)

which more than two variables interact, we will dichotomize both the contact and knowledge measures. As far as contact is concerned we will distinguish between those who have had no contact with an aboriginal and those who have had one instance of contact, and the remainder, who reported at least two instances of contact. With respect to knowledge we will arbitrarily distinguish between those who get a score of zero to four on our measure and those who score five or more. The relationship between contact and scores on the aboriginal image measure is shown in Table 13.

The initial differences between the two groups remain. The Urbanians are clearly more favourable, but within each group contact makes a difference: those who have had the greater contact with aboriginals are likely to have the more favourable image of them. Among the Urbanians 62% of those with high contact scores have a favourable image while only 41% of those with low contact scores do. Among the Bush Town residents 20% of those with high contact scores have a favourable image while this is true for only 5% of those with little contact.

The relationship with knowledge is shown in Table 14. The pattern is remarkably similar, although not quite as orderly. In the Urbania sample, those with high knowledge

TABLE 14. Relationship Between Knowledge and Image of Aboriginals for Urbania and Bush Town Residents

	URBANIA		BUSH TOWN	
Aboriginal image	High knowledge (%)	Low knowledge (%)	High knowledge (%)	Low knowledge (%)
Favourable (scale score 1-3)	49	37	13	16
Moderately favourable (scale score 4-7)	42	43	58	44
Unfavourable (scale score 8-10)	9	20	29	40
Total	100	100	100	100
(Number)	(81)	(51)	(31)	(94)

TABLE 15. Percentage of Residents Possessing a Moderately Favourable or Favourable Aboriginal Image, Classified According to Amount of Contact with Aboriginals and Knowledge of Aboriginal Rights

	URBANIA		BUSH TOWN	
	High contact (%)	Low contact (%)	High contact (%)	Low contact (%)
High knowledge	100 (14)[a]	89 (67)	75 (16)	67 (15)
Low knowledge	83 (12)	70 (39)	64 (70)	46 (24)

[a]The figures in the parentheses are the totals on which the cell percentages were based.

are more likely to have a favourable image than those with low (49% compared with 37%) while in the Bush Town sample the trend is not as marked, although if we simply compare those with an unfavourable image with the rest the effect of knowledge becomes much more regular, and the pattern is almost identical with that observed in Table 13.

So knowlege and contact both make a difference to an individual's image of an aboriginal. While it is generally true that the Urbania residents have a more favourable image than their Bush Town counterparts it is also true that within each group those with more knowledge about aboriginals, and those who have had more contact with them tend to have a more favourable image of them. Now, we saw in Table 8 that for the Urbania sample at least there was a relationship between contact and knowledge: those with more contact tended

to have more knowledge. Is the effect of knowledge on the image measure, therefore, simply due to this relationship? The answer would seem to be no, and as Table 15 reveals knowledge and contact appear to have quite an interesting interactive effect. But before suggesting an interpretation of the data a word of explanation and caution: in Table 15 we have combined the moderately favourable and favourable groups; the numbers with which we are working are, nevertheless, very small, and so our findings should be regarded solely as suggestive of trends which a more extensive investigation might confirm, rather than as firmly established conclusions. To return to the data: when knowledge of aboriginal rights is high, and when contact with aboriginals is high then the likelihood that the image of the aboriginal will be at least moderately favourable is greatest. When knowledge and contact are both

low an image which is at least moderately favourable is least likely. When there is discrepancy between knowledge and contact the
picture is quite interesting: a favourable image
is more likely with high knowledge and low
contact than it is with the reverse. Apparently
high knowledge in a sense "makes up" for low
contact, while high contact fails to "make up"
for low knowledge.

When we come to the second dimension,
concerning aboriginal rights, the picture is by
no means as clear. We have already seen that
there is almost no difference between the two
groups on the rights measure. A fairly detailed
analysis of the relationship between knowledge
and contact and this measure failed to reveal
any consistent trends. Initially we examined
the relationship between the three variables
for the total group; we felt the initial finding
of no difference between the samples justified
this procedure. However, when no meaningful
pattern emerged we looked at the relationships
for the two groups separately. Again the findings were inconclusive, although a couple of
trends which did appear are perhaps worthy
of note. Firstly, among the Urbanians those
most likely to favour restricting the rights of
aboriginals were the sample members who had
high contact scores, but low knowledge scores,
a finding which, intuitively, does not seem to
make much sense. These findings are powerful
reminders that with very small samples results
can at best be suggestive of relationships which
large-scale studies are needed finally to establish. When the findings that the data do provide reinforce our intuitions, or perhaps
prejudices, we are inclined to lose sight of
their tentative nature; it is often only when
we are at a loss to account for them that we
start questioning their reliability.

Let us take time for a brief review. We
have been concerned in the last two sections
with the differences in attitudes to aboriginals
of two samples, one urban and one rural, and
with the way in which knowledge about the
position and status of aboriginals and contact
with aboriginals affects attitudes towards
them. We suggested initially that there were
two attitude dimensions, one we called the
aboriginal image dimension, and the other the
aboriginal rights dimension. There were marked

differences between the groups on the image
measure but not on the rights measure. There
were as well differences within the groups on
the image measure depending on knowledge
about and contact with aboriginals, although
knowledge and contact seemed not to affect
in any systematic way the rights measure. One
additional point is perhaps in order here. It
should be clear from the preceding analysis
that we have not attempted in this section to
account for the initial differences observed
between Urbania and Bush Town. Rather our
analysis has, in the main, attempted to account
for the variability within the two groups. And
the fact that the same variables, knowledge and
contact, operate in the same way in the two
groups suggests that we have been at least
partially successful in doing so. The significance of knowledge and contact for the rights
measure is a much more open question of
course.

We are left then with two unanswered
questions. How do we account for the initial
differences between the two groups on the
image measure, and how do we account for
the variability in the rights measure? Are the
differences in the image measure due largely
to the fact that there are very marked differences between the two samples in certain
social characteristics, or, are they due to the
fact that we are dealing on the one hand with
a small rural community with a sizeable aboriginal population on its outskirts, and on the
other hand with a sophisticated urban group
literally miles from the nearest aboriginal? Or
are they due to the intangible "urban-rural"
differences that the literature speaks about so
frequently?

The analysis which follows will enable
us to say with some confidence whether or
not differences in social characteristics are
related to differences in the image measure;
it will not enable us to choose between the
second and third alternatives; the results of a
replication of the present survey in a country
town without an aboriginal community would
need to be known before we could do so.

The second unanswered question, what is
variability in the aboriginal rights measure due
to, is even more difficult to answer. It is fairly
clear that it is unlikely to be due to factors

TABLE 16. Relationship Between Educational Background and
Scores on the Aboriginal Image Measure

Aboriginal image	URBANIA SCHOOLING			BUSH TOWN SCHOOLING		
	Primary (%)	Secondary (%)	Tertiary (%)	Primary (%)	Secondary (%)	Tertiary (%)
Favourable (scale score 1-3)	0	47	47	3	19	22
Moderately favourable (scale score 4-7)	80	35	44	47	45	55
Unfavourable (scale score 8-10)	20	18	9	50	36	22
Total	100	100	100	100	100	100
(Number)	(6)	(51)	(73)	(28)	(78)	(18)

such as those mentioned above, on which the two communities differ, rather it is likely to be due to some underlying variable which is distributed in much the same way in the two centres. In the section which follows these various alternatives will be investigated.

ATTITUDES AND SOCIAL CHARACTERISTICS

It will be remembered that the initial differences we found between the members of the two groups were with respect to age, education and occupation. Urbanians tended to be middle-aged, better educated and likely to be engaged in white-collar work. Bush Town residents tended to be both younger and older, less well educated and more likely to be engaged in manual work. Now, if the differences in the image measure between the groups are simply a reflection of the differences in social characteristics, we would expect to find, for instance, the small, well-educated group in Bush Town holding similar attitudes to the larger, similarly educated group of Urbanians. As well we would expect the small, less well educated group of Urbanians to resemble in attitude the large, poorly educated group of Bush Town residents. In other words we would expect differences in educational, age and occupational categories to exist across communities.

The relationship between education and the aboriginal image measure is shown in Table 16. As can be seen the main differences are

still those between the two communities rather than between respondents differing in educational background. In other words, the Urbania group, at all educational levels possesses the more favourable image. It is worthy of note that within groups education appears to make a difference to the image measure: those with only primary schooling are the least favourable, those with secondary are somewhat more favourable, while those with tertiary education are the most favourable of all. But this is still a "within groups" phenomenon and does not account for the differences between them.

With age the situation is somewhat the same (Table 17). It makes a difference to the Urbanian group: a favourable image is most likely among the young, not so likely among the not-so-young, and less likely still among the oldest group. However, among the Bush Town sample it apparently has little effect; favourable images are relatively uncommon at all age levels. Again it fails to account for differences between the groups, but contributes a little to our understanding of within-group differences.

Now, it is a well-established fact that the young are the better-educated so the differences we have observed in Tables 16 and 17 may be due simply to either age or education rather than to both variables. To clarify the situation we will look at the relationship between education and image measure for "young," 35 and under, and "old," over 35, groups separately. A section of the data is presented in Table 18. It

TABLE 17. Relationship Between Age and Score on the Aboriginal Image Measures

Aboriginal image	URBANIA			BUSH TOWN		
	17-25 years (%)	36-45 years (%)	Over 45 years (%)	17-25 years (%)	36-45 years (%)	Over 45 years (%)
Favourable (scale score 1-3)	52	47	36	14	15	17
Moderately favourable (scale score 4-7)	38	43	43	49	47	45
Unfavourable (scale score 8-10)	10	10	21	37	38	38
Total	100	100	100	100	100	100
(Number)	(29)	(70)	(33)	(35)	(47)	(72)

TABLE 18. Percentage of Residents Possessing a Favourable Aboriginal Image, Classified by Age and Education

	URBANIA		BUSH TOWN	
	35 years and under (%)	Over 35 years (%)	35 years and under (%)	Over 35 years (%)
Primary education only	0 (0)[a]	50 (6)	0 (8)	4 (21)
Secondary education	55 (22)	40 (25)	13 (46)	27 (31)
Tertiary education	53 (40)	45 (38)	15 (13)	33 (6)

[a]The figures in the parentheses are those on which the percentages were based.

TABLE 19. Relationship Between Class Position and Aboriginal Image for Bush Town and Urbania Residents

Aboriginal image	URBANIA[a]				BUSH TOWN[a]			
	Upper white collar (%)	Lower white collar (%)	Manual workers (%)	Farmers and graziers (%)	Upper white collar (%)	Lower white collar (%)	Manual workers (%)	Farmers and graziers (%)
Favourable (scale score 1-3)	54	52	40	0	37	10	16	18
Moderately favourable (scale score 4-7)	37	36	43	75	26	60	37	47
Unfavourable (scale score 8-10)	9	12	18	25	37	30	46	35
Total	100	100	100	100	100	100	100	100
(Number)	(56)	(25)	(33)	(4)	(11)	(30)	(54)	(17)

[a]The samples are slightly smaller than has been the case for the other tables; housewives, pensioners, and those who declined to answer have been omitted.

is clear that for both groups age is more important than education, but paradoxically its effect seems to be reversed in the two centres: in Urbania it is the young who are more likely to possess a favourable image, while in Bush Town it is their elders. Clearly a more extensive analysis with larger samples is needed before we can come to any definite conclusions.

We have strayed somewhat from our primary intention in the last paragraph or so, and it is time now to examine the remaining variables which distinguish the two communities. These, it will be remembered, are our two indicators of social class: occupation of the household head, and perceived class. The data relating to occupation are presented in Table 19. Again the major differences are between the two groups. The upper-white-collar workers, managers, executives and professionals in Urbania are more likely to have a favourable image than their counterparts in Bush Town. This also holds true for the lower-white-collar workers, clerks and salesmen, and for the manual workers both skilled and semi-skilled. The trend breaks down when we come to farmers, but we cannot assert much with confidence here as there are only four of them in the Urbanian sample. Again within the groups there is something approaching a regular pattern; in both centres the upper-white-collar workers are the most likely to have a favourable image while the manual workers are least likely (we are excluding graziers and farmers in this comparison). The pattern is slightly different in the two centres, however, as the main difference in Urbania is between white-collar workers and manual workers, while in Bush Town it is between upper-white-collar workers and the rest. With perceived class as our indicator the pattern is much the same so we will not consider it further at this point.

We have answered the first question posed at the beginning of this section. The difference between Urbania and Bush Town residents in their image of the aboriginal are clearly not due to differences in age, education and social class, nor are they due to differences in the extent of social contact with aboriginals, although and perhaps paradoxically, all these variables are to a greater or lesser extent related to the image the two groups of respondents have of the aboriginal.

It is as if the two groups start off from a different "base line," and once this has been established, variability in response pattern can be accounted for relatively satisfactorily. But what accounts for the initial differences is still an open question. Perhaps it is something to do with rural-urban differences or perhaps, and more probably, it is due in the one instance to the presence of an aboriginal community on the outskirts of the town and in the other to a complete lack of close contact. The implication of this hypothesis, of course, is that proximity means an unfavourable image, yet our measure of contact indicates that greater contact, of the type defined by the items comprising the measure, means a more favourable image. It is stating the obvious to say that the problem is a complex one, yet it is clear that it is. Intuitively one can see how an unfavourable image of the type found in Bush Town develops. The town's aboriginal population is housed mainly in shanties on its outskirts; the aboriginals are mainly service and unskilled manual workers, and they have all the characteristics of an underpriviledged and deprived group. It is not unusual to find communities attributing the causes of such deprivation to the groups themselves: "if they really wanted to be different they would," as one rather garrulous respondent reported. Perhaps this is the fact that accounts for the different "base lines" of the two groups. However, it is one matter intuitively to feel that this may be the case, it is something rather different to demonstrate empirically that in fact it is.

We come to the second question posed earlier, namely, how to account for variability in the aboriginal rights measure. We should say at the outset that we have no satisfactory answer to this question. There seeme to be slight relationships between sex, age, education and the rights measure but there is no consistent patterning of the data and the findings are at best equivocal. However, for what they are worth we will describe them briefly. Table 20 documents the relationship between sex and the rights measure. The differences between the Urbanians and Bush Town residents were negligible, so the two groups have been combined. The differences between the groups in the table are small yet consistent: the

TABLE 20. Relationship Between Sex and Aboriginal Rights Measure

Aboriginal rights	Male (%)	Female (%)
Favourable (scale score 1-3)	42	34
Moderately favourable (scale score 4-7)	41	46
Unfavourable (scale score 8-9)	17	20
Total	100	100
(Number)	(100)	(154)

TABLE 21. Relationship Between Age and Aboriginal Rights Measure

Aboriginal rights	35 and under (%)	Over 35 (%)
Favourable (scale score 1-3)	39	36
Moderately favourable (scale score 4-7)	44	44
Unfavourable (scale score 8-9)	17	21
Total	100	100
(Number)	(127)	(126)

TABLE 22. Relationship Between Education and Aboriginal Rights Measure

Aboriginal rights	Primary schooling (%)	Secondary schooling (%)	Tertiary schooling (%)
Favourable (scale score 1-3)	32	36	40
Moderately favourable (scale score 4-7)	50	43	40
Unfavourable (scale score 8-9)	18	21	20
Total	100	100	100
(Number)	(34)	(129)	(91)

women are slightly more likely to have an unfavourable image, and slightly less likely to have a favourable one. When one reflects on the items in the rights measure, sitting in buses next to aborigines, aborigines drinking in hotels, belonging to clubs, making full use of all public facilities, this finding, intuitively at least, perhaps makes some sense.

The relationship between age and the rights measure, although marginal also, intuitively seems to make some sense. As can be seen from Table 21 there is a slight tendency for the younger respondents to adopt a more favourable position on aboriginal rights: 39% of them are in the most favourable category compared with 36% of the older respondents who also are a little more likely to adopt an unfavourable position.

However, it is not all old respondents nor all female respondents who are in favour of limiting the rights of aboriginals. When we examine the way in which the three variables are related we find that there is very little difference between the views of both groups of men and young women. In each case approximately 40% come in the favourable category, and about 16% in the unfavourable category. For the older women, however, the picture is rather different; only a third of them obtain a scale score of one to three, and just 25% come at the other extreme of the dimension. The effects of sex and age apparently are due largely to this one group.

The significance of education for the aboriginal rights measure is shown in Table 22. Again the relationship is marginal but it does appear that the more education an individual has, the more likely he is to be favourably disposed towards rights for aboriginals. Again, a finding which makes some sense.

Clearly we have been able to say less about the aboriginal rights measure than we have about the image measure. Partly this is due to the fact that the rights measure is not as strong a scale as the image measure. This means that our measurement is not as reliable as it might have been with a stronger instrument and so statistical regularities are more difficult to demonstrate. Partly it is also very probably due to the fact that we have not asked some of the right questions. It is hard to accept that variability in response to the sort of items that comprise the rights scale is not due to some social and personal characteristics of individuals. But what these may be, other than those we have already seen are marginally related to aboriginal rights, must remain a question for further investigation.

There is little more to add. This paper has been concerned with examining the nature of attitudes towards aboriginals and how these attitudes are affected by two classes of factors: the first having to do with contact and knowledge about aboriginals, and the second concerned with some of the social and personal attributes of the individuals comprising the samples under investigation. Within the limits of the data it would appear that these intentions have been reasonably met.

NOTES

[1] R. and C. Berndt, *The World of First Australians* (Sydney, Ure Smith, 1964).

[2] F. Gale, *A Study of Assimilation* (Adelaide, Library of South Australia, 1964).

[3] J. MacKenzie, *Australian Paradox* (Melbourne, Cheshire, 1961).

[4] R. Taft, "A Survey of the Attitudes of Western Australian Whites toward Aborigines" (unpublished, 1966).

[5] S. E. Asch, *Social Psychology* (New York, Prentice Hall, 1952).

[6] D. S. Anderson and J. S. Western, *An Inventory to Measure Students' Attitudes* (Queensland, Queensland University Press, 1967).

[7] H. F. Kaiser, "The Varimax Criterion for Analytic Rotation in Factor Analysis," in *Psychometrika* (23, 1958), pp. 187-200.

[8] E. C. Moseley and C. J. Kleitt, "An Empirical Comparison of Factor Scoring Methods," in *Psychological Reports* (14, 1964), pp. 179-84.

[9] J. L. Horn, "A Note on the Estimation of Factor Scores," in *Educational and Psychological Measurement* (24, 1964), pp. 525-27.

[10] J. L. Horn, "An Empirical Comparison of Various Methods of Estimating Concern Factor Scores," *Educational and Psychological Measurement* (25, 1965), pp. 313-23.

[11] P. Horst, *Factor Analysis of Data Matrices* (New York, Holt, Rinehart and Winston, 1965).

16
a debate on the position of the soviet jews

SAMUIL ROZIN
MOSHE DECTER

The views presented in this debate on the position of the Jews in Soviet Russia are those of Moshe Decter, an American who is director of Jewish Minorities Research, and Samuil Rozin, a Soviet author and journalist associated with the Novosti News Agency. Both men are Jews.

Mr. Decter is operating with American definitions. In the United States, to practice a religion is regarded as good. The government is constitutionally prohibited from interfering in any way. The government is also completely unconcerned about the expression of subcultural traits. Insofar as this expression involves publishing a newspaper or producing plays in a foreign language, the government is again enjoined from interfering by the constitutional protection of free speech and a free press. The production and sale of religious articles is completely free and of no concern to anyone but their producers, sellers, and buyers.

Mr. Rozin, on the other hand, accepts the right of a government to proscribe religions of all kinds, to control the press and the stage as it sees fit, and to manage the production and sale of goods.

Soviet Russia has a constitution, however, and some Jewish spokesmen have said that Russia violates her own principles. Mr. Decter, for example, claims that nonreligious individuals of Jewish ancestry meet discrimination in access to education and government positions. He claims that the expression of secular (Yiddish) culture has been restricted. He even states that the government has resorted to outright and vicious anti-Semitism.

These articles were written in 1963, at which time Jewish-Soviet relations were in crisis. They were so again in 1971. This time the question was whether Soviet Jews should be allowed to migrate to Israel. Many Soviet Jews, particularly religious ones, would like to; but they have not been allowed to do so in any numbers. It should be pointed out that the restraints on emigration have also applied to other Soviet citizens.

What exacerbated the situation in 1971 was the tension between Israel and the Arab nations, which were being supplied with arms and otherwise supported by the Soviet Union. Israel, which is a small country, would like very much to receive immigrants from the Soviet Union; and there is no doubt that if they were permitted to leave, a very large number of Soviet Jews would do so. A few Jews from other countries, particularly the United States, have formed an organization called the Jewish Defense League, which harasses Soviet officials and has thrown

Reprinted from: Samuil Rozin, "I Speak as a Soviet Jew," *The Minority of One* 5, no. 5 (May 1963), pp. 13-15; and Moshe Decter, "The Truth About Soviet Jewry," *The Minority of One* 5, no. 7 (July 1963), pp. 15-17. Reproduced by permission of the authors and The Minority of One, Inc., New York.

bombs on occasion into Soviet embassies. The American Jewish community has strenuously condemned this violence, and the culprits have been caught and punished; but strain between the Soviet Union and Jewish communities everywhere has been intensified.

A very recent Soviet census shows that the Jewish community has dropped from 3,000,000 to 2,500,000; since Jewishness is a self-designation in the Soviet Union, this fact may support either Mr. Rozin or Mr. Decter. It may be that Jews are becoming assimilated and no longer wish to be a separate community, or it may be that life has been made so uncomfortable for Jews that they prefer to keep their Jewishness private.

Samuil Rozin

Moshe Decter's article in the January issue of *Foreign Affairs* purporting to depict the life of Jews in the Soviet Union prompts me to offer a counterview from the pages of *The Minority of One.*

At the beginning of his article, Mr. Decter declares that although the Soviet Constitution recognizes the right of all nationalities within Soviet borders to cultural freedom, "actual Soviet policy toward the Jews clearly violates these principles." I propose to counter this generality with an observation rooted in my life-long experience as a Soviet citizen: All the peoples of the Soviet Union enjoy equal rights —both legally and in reality. This is true in everyday life, in work, in public affairs, in access to the material and cultural wealth of the Soviet society. The Jews are no exception. The new social relations which prevail in our country put no premium on ethnic or racial discrimination; there are no forces at work which would benefit from the subservient or secondary status of any particular group of citizens. This reality necessarily has a humanizing impact upon the Soviet man. Intergroup brotherhood has become, under these circumstances, a natural property of men's attitudes rather than the heroic and exceptional achievement of the few.

It is in the light of this historic change that the place of the Jewish population in the community of Soviet nationalities should be considered.

Is There A Need For "Passing"?

Mr. Decter seems totally oblivious of these factors, which are usually among the first to strike the foreign visitor to the Soviet Union. It is therefore not surprising that he misconstrues and misinterprets certain phenomena of Jewish life in the U.S.S.R. He writes, for instance, that during the 1959 census the Jews were given the opportunity for "passing," i.e., for identifying themselves as members of nationalities other than Jewish. This is presented pretty much as a terrible sin of the Soviet authorities. Actually Soviet citizens are free to give any answer they choose when questioned as to their nationalities, without having to give any proof. Mr. Decter presents the democratic spirit of the census as the opposite of what it is: freedom of man's cultural and ethnic self-identification is, according to him, an exercise in state coercion.

Mr. Decter's real objective is evident. He seeks to convince his readers that the Soviet Jew has such a hard lot that many Jews choose to "pass" as non-Jews. That is why, in his opinion, only 2,268,000 Jews identified themselves as such in the census, although "the total number more closely approximates 3,000,000."

Mr. Decter speaks of "forcible assimilation" as practiced in the U.S.S.R. for decades. He bases this serious allegation on the fact that only 472,000 Soviet Jews have identified Yiddish as their mother tongue. If we accept Mr. Decter's line of reasoning, we would have to conclude that "forcible assimilation" of Jews is nowhere pursued with greater vigor and determination than in the United States of America. Indeed, if claiming Yiddish as his mother tongue is an indication of a Jew's effective freedom to identify himself as a Jew, and if we consider the proportion of American Jewry to Soviet Jewry, there would have to be roughly 1,000,000 American Jews proclaiming Yiddish as their mother tongue in order for the U.S.A. to be able to claim that degree of "Jewish liberty" which prevails in the Soviet Union. In fact, however, not only the proportional but even the absolute numbers of those who speak Yiddish are higher in the U.S.S.R. than in the U.S.A.

It is also relevant to note that in the U.S.A., unlike the Soviet Union, Yiddish is spoken only in the "corridors" to the American society. In the United States it is primarily the language of immigrants who are not yet acclimatized. The Yiddish-speaking Jews of the Soviet Union are not new arrivals in the process of shedding "imported" cultural leftovers. Their Yiddish has survived many generations, and the Soviet environment gives them the option to maintain their cultural heritage.

Voluntary vs. Forcible Assimilation

Mr. Decter's mistake lies in confusing voluntary and natural assimilation with forcible assimilation. In the Soviet experience, assimilation is a completely normal phenomenon. It has nothing in common with minority persecution. It does not follow state ordinances as in Czarist Russia, where Jews often converted to Christianity as a means of gaining access to higher education, or in order to acquire the right to live outside the Jewish pale. In the Soviet Union, doors are always open to Jews just as to other citizens.

The drawing together of the cultures of various peoples of the U.S.S.R. is a democratic process set in motion, not by group exploitation, but by group cooperation made possible by the prevailing economic relations and interests.

Mr. Decter is aware that Jews in the Soviet Union are spread throughout its vast territory. They take an active part in the economic, political and cultural life of all the Soviet republics. This brings them close to other Soviet peoples, with whom they live side by side, with whom they make friends, intermarry, rear children and build a future.

The very factors Mr. Decter invokes to "prove" coercion prove the opposite: that Jews are unquestioningly accepted as an integral part of Soviet society and culture.

Culture and Religion

Mr. Decter displays no less confusion when he discusses matters pertaining to religion. He states: "The Jews are also regarded

. . . as a religious group. This complicates their status and makes it even more precarious." It seems to me that in drawing this conclusion Mr. Decter is misled by a prejudice quite common in the United States. The U.S. Constitution speaks of separation of church and state; but in actuality the American state apparatus is actively involved in promoting religion. Its "neutrality" in matters of religion is confined to inter-denominational affairs, disputes and differences, and not directed to religion as such. It is perhaps for this reason that Mr. Decter has difficulty in recognizing the line we in the Soviet Union draw between ethnic and religious ties. Peoplehood and religious community are two separate sociological phenomena. That in the case of the Jews the two aspects have coincided for long periods in history does not contradict this independence. Perhaps a personal statement will help to clarify this: I am myself a Jew; I cherish the history of my people, their best traditions, their culture; but I have nothing to do with religion. Whoever wants to believe may believe. This is a matter of personal decision and conscience. But what does the status of Jews in the Soviet Union have to do with their religiosity or beliefs?

Seeking to prove that Judaism in the U.S.S.R. "is subjected to unique discrimination," Mr. Decter turns to comparative statistics: there are so-and-so many churches and so-and-so many priests for the Orthodox Christians, Lutherans and Baptists, whereas the Jews have only 60 or 70 synagogues and rabbis for as many as a million Jewish believers. That this phenomenon reflects a greater portion of voluntary nonbelievers among Jews is not even considered by Mr. Decter. And the fact that Jewish atheists like myself find intellectual satisfaction in this phenomenon conclusively proves that it is not the result of external anti-Jewish coercion.

Jewish Worship

The Great Synagogue in Moscow is attended during the holidays by as many as 1500-2000 worshippers. In addition to the synagogues reported by Mr. Decter, there are numerous small prayer houses with an attendance of less than 100. Thus there are sizeable numbers of Jews who continue to worship. Those who do not are not deterred by any external pressures or prohibitions; they act in accordance with their individual philosophies and consciences. Perhaps the number of Yiddish-speaking Jews in the Soviet Union is an indication of the proportion of believers among Soviet Jews? If so, Decter's guess that there are as many as a million believers in the Jewish religion among Soviet Jews seems utterly unjustified.

When I spoke with Rabbi Judah Leib Levin of the Great Synagogue in Moscow, he denied that he had announced in the synagogue, as Decter contended, that matzah-baking had been prohibited. The Rabbi said he could not have made any such announcement, since matzah-baking has never been prohibited. Jewish believers bake it in their homes and in private religious establishments. This particular accusation of Mr. Decter's is based on nothing more than the fact that state bakeries produce neither matzah nor ritual Greek Orthodox wafers. Thus Soviet adherence to the separation of Church and State is misrepresented by Mr. Decter as discrimination against Soviet Jews.

Mr. Decter's pursuit of his erroneous thesis leads him to ultimate absurdity. He speaks of the Jews' "dual character," which allegedly distinguishes them from other groups in Soviet society. He would have us believe that "they have come increasingly to be considered an alien group in a land where they have resided for more than a thousand years." It is not surprising that Mr. Decter offers not a single shred of evidence to bear out this allegation; for such evidence is non-existent. The Jews in the Soviet Union have deep roots; they have soaked this land with their sweat and blood; they have given many of their numbers for its defense. I am a Soviet Jew; and if introspection is to tell us about the attitude of Soviet Jews toward their homeland, it is not unreasonable that my feelings about the Soviet Union and not those of Mr. Decter be viewed as typical. That he feels a stranger, and a hostile stranger at that, in relationship to the Soviet Union is probably as typical a result of his environment as my identification with the Soviet land is of the attitude of Soviet Jews.

Jewish Literature and Theater

Mr. Decter contends that the Jews in the Soviet Union are "deprived of the basic cultural rights." To bear this out, he says that works by Jewish writers are put out "mostly for foreign consumption." This is not so. Most of the Yiddish books published in the U.S.S.R. are sold in the U.S.S.R. Books by Jewish authors, in both Yiddish and Russian, are available in bookstores in Moscow, Kiev, Leningrad, Odessa, Minsk, Vilnius, Riga and many other cities. Just recently, in Bookshop No. 100 in Gorky Street, the central avenue of Moscow, I ordered a Hebrew-Russian dictionary and an anthology of Israeli verse. These are due to come off Soviet presses this year.

The Jewish magazine *Sovietish Heimland* can be bought in all parts of the country, and all post offices accept subscriptions for it. The cultural coverage of this Jewish magazine is indicated by the fact that its first ten issues carried 320 works by more than a hundred Jewish writers. These works included novels, short stories, plays, poems, songs and literary reviews.

Decter's ignorance of facts is quite consistent. He would have his readers believe that all that remains in the Soviet Union of Yiddish theatrical culture is a handful of amateur troupes subsisting on a marginal basis. Actually, Yiddish theater and concert companies headed by Anna Guzik, Emil Gorovets, Benjamin Shvartser (Moscow), Esther Roitman, Zinovy Kaminsky (Leningrad), Nekhama Lifshits, Benjamin Kaitovsky (Vilnius), Dina Roitkop (Riga), Sidi Tahl (Chernovtsi), and others, are members of state cultural societies and concert-tour organizations. All their members are subsidized by the state. The state also covers their expenses in obtaining performance premises, stage settings, etc. The actors draw fixed salaries and thus do not depend on fluctuating box office receipts.

Professional Yiddish troupes are not confined to their home ground but perform in other cities throughout the country. Early this year, for example, Nekhama Lifshits sang in Leningrad, while Benjamin Khaitovsky gave concerts in Birobidzhan. The new company headed by B. Shvartser, whose success was reviewed in the February 14, 1963 *New York*

Times (Int. Edition) went on a two-month tour of the Ukraine and Central Asia. Its performances had a total attendance of about 25,000.

In addition, there are many amateur Jewish artistic societies. The Theatrical Society in Vilnius, for instance, which has more than 50 members, stages with great success plays by Sholem Aleichem. It has performed in various cities in Lithuania as well as in Riga, Leningrad, Minsk and other cities. Equally popular in Vilnius is the Jewish choir, with more than 50 members, and the Jewish orchestra, with 40 musicians. Well-deserved fame is enjoyed by the Jewish choir of Riga, which has more than 100 participants.

Jews in Higher Education

Decter's "factual" survey continues to be inaccurate when he remarks upon the declining number of Jews in higher education, science and culture. His statistical jugglings obscure the fact that, according to official Soviet statistical manuals, there were 28,966 scientific workers of Jewish nationality in 1958; 30,633 in 1959; 33,529 in 1960; and 36,173 in 1961. Jewish participation in science is therefore constantly growing. Among Soviet scientists, Jews rank third among all Soviet nationality groups, although the total Jewish population ranks only 11th in the country.

Decter laments that among students in higher education Jews comprise "only" 3.1 per cent (the actual figure is 3.5 per cent), whereas thirty years ago their percentage was higher. What Decter chooses not to mention is the phenomenal educational development of all the national groups in the U.S.S.R., which has naturally caused increased representation in the scientific community of those nationalities which thirty years ago were much less educated. Even so, Jewish representation of 3.1 or 3.5 per cent is exceptionally high and certainly disproves, rather than confirms, any discrimination against Jews. Then too, does not the fact that every year there are more and more Jewish scientists prove that every year there are necessarily more Jewish students?

Decter is also inaccurate when he contends that Jews have a strong position only in teacher-training schools, music conservatories and institutes of journalism. The access of Jewish students to higher education in all branches is unrestricted. In fact, it is precisely within the technical areas of higher education that the bulk of Jewish students is found. I find it quite unnecessary to discuss this matter in greater detail; for whatever the facts, I fail to see why Soviet authorities should be held responsible for the career preferences of individual Jewish students.

The Press Which Doesn't Exist

Decter also discusses alleged "popular" anti-Semitism in the Soviet Union. He labels as anti-Semitic whole regions of the country in which the majority of the Jews reside. He contends that from the press "the image of the Jew emerges in traditional anti-Semitic stereotypes." He does not even try to substantiate these assertions; apparently, he senses the futility of such an attempt. He can refer to no newspaper and cite no quote to bear out his libel. Instead, he enumerates eight themes of atheistic articles in the Soviet press as "evidence." . . .

I challenge Mr. Decter to name at least one Soviet newspaper which portrays the Jews as "money worshippers." Since such a Soviet newspaper does not exist, I am certain that this challenge will be ignored. The truth of the matter is that the Soviet press is imbued with a spirit of international brotherhood and friendship, and to present it in the opposite light is outright malice and falsehood.

But the truth is also that Soviet newspapers *do* print atheistic articles. It stands to reason that the religious are not exactly in enthusiastic accord with such articles. If and when an atheistic article critically discusses a particular dogma of the Jewish religion (as they often do discuss dogmas of any religion), those perpetually on the lookout for anti-Soviet propaganda jump to "substantiate" the claim of "Soviet anti-Semitism." One must ask: Since when are *bona fide* philosophical discussions prohibited on pain of stigmatizing the participants?

Immunity for Criminals?

In Decter's claim that anti-Semitism plays a part in prosecutions for economic crimes there is an inherent blackmail. Unless Soviet authorities grant immunity from prosecution to criminals who happen to be Jews, they are branded anti-Semites. I will leave it to sociologists and criminologists to investigate the links between certain ethnic groups and the incidence of certain types of crime. As for the Soviet courts, however, I am absolutely satisfied that in meting out justice to those brought before them, they are not concerned with the national origin of the accused, but only with the injury to society. I will quote from N. S. Khrushchev's relevant reply to Bertrand Russell: "The punishment for every one of those who have committed crimes is determined by the nature of their particular crime and, of course, has nothing to do with their nationality."

A Mishmash of Facts

I have not touched upon many questions raised by Decter. The consistent inaccuracy of his "facts" and the obvious malice of his misrepresentations absolve me of the duty of taking each of his allegations seriously. His intellectual frivolity is well manifested in such gross errors as his "liquidation" of several Soviet autonomous republics. He states that the Chechans, Ossetians and Komis do not have their own territories. The Komis *do* have their own autonomous republic, and so do the Checheno-Ingushes. There is a North Ossetian Autonomous Republic; and there is a South Ossetian Autonomous Region.

Equally inaccurate are Decter's comments regarding Yevgeny Yevtushenko's poem, "Babi Yar." Decter has the audacity to assert that "Soviet authorities have been consistently silent about the nature, dimensions and even the very existence of the unique Jewish tragedy during the Second World War." I have never before been confronted with a more cynical misrepresentation. It is so obvious that I hardly see a need to counter it with all the wealth of available evidence. It will suffice to mention the press conference held by the Soviet Foreign Ministry this winter in connection with the trial in Koblenz. I attended that press conference. Much was said about the fascists' atrocities in Byelorussia, with emphatic stress on the tragic fate of the ghetto in Minsk.

Among the speakers there were Jews, victims of Nazi crimes. The press conference was broadcast over radio and television. All Soviet newspapers gave it extensive coverage.

As to Yevtushenko's poem, the poet himself said that only 30 out of the 20,000 letters he received after the publication of "Babi Yar" expressed discontent. How then can Moshe Decter fail to appreciate the boomerang effect of the myth of anti-Semitism in the Soviet Union?

The factual inaccuracy of Moshe Decter's article is hardly surprising; it is an unavoidable characteristic of any dissertation that assumes the existence of Soviet anti-Semitism. When you depict a make-believe house, the walls, the gates and the windows you describe cannot possibly be real.

Moshe Decter

I wish first to express my appreciation to the editor for the privilege of replying to Samuil Rozin, whose article, "I Speak As A Soviet Jew," appeared here in May. This openness does honor to the integrity of the ideals of the editor and of TMO and, incidentally, of the country which guarantees his right to be in the minority of one.

The debate centers on my article, "The Status of the Jews in the Soviet Union," in the January 1963 issue of *Foreign Affairs*. In it, I demonstrated that Soviet Jewry is subjected to rank discrimination in vital areas; (1) that Soviet Jewry, though officially considered a nationality, is deprived of virtually all the cultural rights enjoyed by all other Soviet nationalities; (2) that, even within the context of the official antireligious policy, the Jewish religion suffers unique disabilities; (3) that Jews are discriminated against in important areas of education and employment; (4) that Jews have been singled out for capital punishment in the campaign against economic abuses; (5) that the Jew is portrayed in the Soviet press in noxious, incitatory anti-Semitic stereotypes.

This policy reflects the distrust felt by the authorities toward the Jewish group as such, and ineluctably sets in train a vicious circle in which distrust feeds upon itself. The consequences must alarm all men touched by moral concerns: through attrition, Jewish culture is being strangled; through deprivation, Jewish identity is being pulverized; through intimidation, the Jewish community is being atomized; through incitation, grass-roots anti-Semitism is being stimulated.

Now Mr. Rozin charges me with "consistent inaccuracy . . . obvious malice . . . misrepresentation . . . falsehood." Though I am pleased to note that he makes these accusations in a restrained manner, he invariably fails to meet my contentions head on. His refutations are pathetically inadequate, based as they are on flimsy evidence, exaggerated claims, tendentious analysis and distorted imputations. He accomplishes his mission skillfully enough, however, to make an ostensibly persuasive case for those not intimately familiar with the problem, and his Panglossian asseverations about this tragic situation require meticulous dissection.

Preserving a Heritage?

Mr. Rozin assures us that "the Soviet environment gives them [the Jews] the option to maintain their cultural heritage." Precisely how?

There are surely vast numbers of Soviet Jews who, as Mr. Rozin claims for himself, "cherish the history, best traditions and culture" of the Jewish people, and who would wish to have educational institutions through which to perpetuate them. Yet the simple, undeniable, tragic fact is that this is not possible for Soviet Jews. How can a cultural heritage be maintained without the opportunity to learn, teach and transmit it?

Soviet law stipulates that a minimum of ten parents may organize instruction for their children in their own language. Would Mr. Rozin seriously contend that in a city like Moscow, where more than 600,000 Jews live, there are not at least ten parents who wish to have their children learn something of their Jewish heritage? Is this conceivable . . . in a country where 472,000 people cited Yiddish as their native language?

Yet there is not a single institution—no school, no classroom, no course, no lectureship, no textbook—whether in Yiddish, Hebrew or Russian—in which Soviet Jews may acquire and transmit to their children knowledge and understanding of their history, literature, language and moral traditions, and the decent self-respect and pride that go along with such knowledge and understanding especially under Soviet circumstances.

All other nationalities—no matter how small, primitive or dispersed—are provided such opportunities, and are encouraged to be proud of their language, culture and history. Why not also the Jews?

Actually, for the first two decades of Soviet rule, a vast network of such institutions, on the elementary, high school, university and research levels, did exist. No matter how restricted in content, these institutions produced many scores of thousands of educated Jews, and Jewish teachers and scholars thrived. But during the Great Purges of 1936-38, all this was destroyed: the institutions were forcibly and arbitrarily shut down, and their leading spirits permanently disappeared. Since then, Soviet Jews have been forbbiden to reconstruct any institution of Jewish secular learning, and are thus deprived of a cultural leadership without which a group's culture can survive only with the greatest hardship. Is this an environment in which Jews have "the option to maintain their cultural heritage"?

Nevertheless, as I clearly indicated in *Foreign Affairs,* a considerable array of other types of Jewish cultural institutions did survive. But even these were violently shut down in 1948; their leaders unjustly imprisoned and done to death in 1948-53—at the height of what Soviet parlance characterizes as "the period of the personality cult." (Like Mr. Khrushchev, Mr. Rozin does not see fit to mention these crimes against many individual Jews and against the Jewish people and culture.)

From 1948 to 1959, all was deathly silence—a great desert in Jewish cultural life. Since then, a handful of tokens have been grudgingly, but with great fanfare, granted to the huge Soviet Jewish audience that thirsts for full-bodied cultural creativity. It is these pitiful remnants, truly ruins of what was once a vast and rich cultural enterprise, which Mr. Rozin disingenuously seeks to palm off on unsuspecting outsiders as a flourishing Jewish culture.

Jewish Literature

Mr. Rozin is able to mention just one Yiddish literary magazine, the bimonthly *Sovietish Heimland.* (I mentioned it too; in fact, I welcomed it.) It was established only in late 1961, with a circulation of 25,000. But even if not one copy were ever sent abroad, can it be maintained that an edition of 25,000 supplies the want of the 472,000 whose native language is Yiddish?

Mr. Rozin notes with justified pride that "its first ten issues carried 320 works by more than a hundred Jewish writers. These works included novels, short stories, plays, poems, songs and literary reviews." For me this demonstrates the vitality of Yiddish writers, who answer with a courageously resounding "Yes" to the challenge of adversity. No less does it demonstrate that they have an eager audience —of at least 25,000.

Yet—if they write in Yiddish for a Yiddish magazine and a Yiddish-reading audience— how is it that not one novel, not one play, not one volume of their short stories or poetry or critical essays has ever appeared as a Yiddish book?

The fact is that from 1948 to 1959, *not one* was published. From 1959 to 1961, a grand total of *six* were published in editions of 30,000 each. And since then—the stillness of the desert. Like *Sovietish Heimland,* many thousands of these volumes found their way abroad; but how many actually were available at home? The fact that they may *also* be found in the major centers of Jewish population (which Mr. Rozin takes care to list in detail) is only one more indication of the potent cultural hunger among Soviet Jews.

The uninitiated reader would be mistaken to feel encouraged by the inference ever so slyly insinuated by Mr. Rozin that Hebrew has suddenly found favor with the Soviet authorities. That language has been cruelly proscribed for over four decades in the land where its modern usage was first pioneered. No, the anthology of Israeli verse to which Mr. Rozin refers has actu-

ally been announced as a translation into Yiddish (which is, naturally, a gratifying innovation, but no substitute for Hebrew which thousands of Soviet Jews crave). As for the Hebrew-Russian dictionary, it too will be very welcome indeed . . . when it appears.

It is good to read that these particular volumes are "due" this year. We have had announcements of their imminent publication for several years now, and it is only to be hoped that the date will not coincide with the time, in Mr. Khrushchev's famous adage, "when shrimps will whistle."

A further note about Yiddish book publication. One is pulled up short by the glaring contrast between the six meager volumes published in 1959-61 and the scores published in the immediate postwar years when the country, and not least its surviving Jews, was desperately trying to emerge from devastation. In 1945, fourteen Yiddish books were published; in 1946, nineteen; in 1947, fifty-two; in 1948, the year the guillotine descended, sixty. Did the Jews lose interest overnight in 1948? And have their cultural needs been met by the silence since 1961?

What of the hundreds of artists who wrote, were published, and were exceedingly popular, *in Yiddish* during the decades of Soviet rule until 1948? One slim, inadequate volume of selections from the work of the great novelist, David Bergelson (judicially murdered in 1952 and never publicly rehabilitated), *has* appeared. But why has not one volume by Markish, Kvitko, Feffer, Kulbak, Der Nister, Hoffshtein, Kharik, Dobrushin— to mention only the most luminous—appeared since 1948 in the language in which they wrote?

To take a characteristic contrast: In 1959-60 when the six Yiddish books were published, more than 600 books were published in their native languages for such small, primitive peoples as the Yakuts and the Bashkirs. Since then, while no Yiddish books have appeared, many hundreds were again published in Yakut and Bashkir.

The appearance of books of minority nationalities in translation is certainly a good thing. But the Jews, and their creative elements, are the only ones condemned to the shadowy half-world of existence in translation, which is no existence at all for a people and its culture.

Jewish Theater

Mr. Rozin insults the intelligence of his readers if he expects them to believe his glowing account of Jewish theatrical life in the U.S.S.R. He notes that there are "many" amateur Jewish dramatic and choral societies—and he is able to mention precisely three. . . . Far more painful to witness is his egregious distortion of the Yiddish "professional theater." Once indeed there was such a thing. Until 1948, there were a number of distinguished professional, permanent repertory Yiddish State Theaters in Moscow and other cities; some of them even had schools to train young professional actors. As I wrote in *Foreign Affairs,* they were one of the great prides of Soviet culture. But like all other Jewish cultural institutions, they were brutally liquidated in 1948, and their most brilliant personality, Honored People's Artist of the Soviet Union Shlomo Mikhoels, murdered by Stalin's henchmen. (None of this, naturally, is fit to be printed in Mr. Rozin's catalogue of glories.)

All that remains is individual artists, many of them old and broken-down, of varying degrees of talent (many survived simply because they were not deemed prominent or gifted enough to be eliminated) who, alone or in small groups, travel the circuit giving "concerts" of Yiddish dramatic readings, skits and folk songs. These wandering, homeless artists are the remnants of a once-glorious tradition. (Mikhoels' *Lear* was as celebrated in the U.S.S.R. as Barrymore's *Hamlet* was here.)

Even the Gypsies—all 132,000 of them throughout the Soviet Union—have a professional repertory theater housed in its own building in Moscow. But the Jews . . . ?

The Problem of Assimilation

I did not in my article, and I do not now, wish to be drawn into a polemic contrasting Jewish cultural rights and practices in the U.S. and the U.S.S.R. But since Mr. Rozin presses the issue, I should make just one point. I leave aside the thousands of schools in which hundreds of thousands of American Jewish children are learning Hebrew, Yiddish and Jewish history and culture; I leave aside also the proliferation of Jewish cultural, social, religious and philanthropic institutions and organizations which American Jews voluntarily support; and I leave aside, finally, the question of their long-range vitality and prospects.

Here I only wish to note that the Jewish Communists in the United States have a daily Yiddish newspaper (the *Morgen Freiheit,* the only Communist daily, by the way, published in this country in any language), and scores of Yiddish-language schools with thousands of pupils. Why, then, Mr. Rozin, cannot the Jewish Communists of the U.S.S.R. have a daily Yiddish newspaper and Yiddish-language schools? And on what better basis, in fact, than the one Mr. Rozin so aptly states—because "not only the proportional but even the absolute number of those who speak Yiddish are higher in the U.S.S.R. than in the U.S.A."?

But Mr. Rozin wants to eat and have his cake. On the one hand, he assures us that these pathetic shards constitute a thriving Jewish culture. On the other hand, he ignores or explains away all the deprivations, all the lacks, with the word "assimilation." In an unworthy effort to blame the victim rather than the victimizer, he calls this "normal," "natural," and "voluntary": "The drawing together of the cultures of various peoples of the U.S.S.R. is a democratic process. . . . "

He neglects to point out that in the case of no other Soviet nationality has this process resulted in the virtual elimination of any of them. Quite the contrary. Only for the Jews it has evidently been decreed that "assimilation" should mean cultural extinction.

None of the factual or analytic statements above are "inventions" of mine (TMO's editor to the contrary notwithstanding). They have all been voiced, in one form or another, by Communists themselves. And I hereby make an offer: I shall gladly send to any TMO reader who requests them the text of some of these Communist accusations and protests.

Religious "Freedom"

As a secular Jew, Mr. Rozin is clearly more interested in secular Jewish matters; but he does have some things to say in criticism of my *Foreign Affairs* analysis of the disadvantaged status of Jewish religion in the U.S.S.R. Here again, he has utterly neglected nearly all the major points I made.

Judaism and Jewish religious institutions are discriminated against in that they are deprived in whole or in part of the privileges accorded even by the officially atheist Soviet state to all the other major religions. I shall merely list these prerogatives; Jewish congregations are prohibited nationwide federations, religious publishing facilities and publications; no Hebrew Bible has been published since 1917, nor have any daily, Sabbath or holiday prayer books been published since 1917, nor have any daily, Sabbath or holiday prayer books been printed; there is a ban on the production of indispensable religious articles; the lone rabbinical seminary, shoddily housed in the Moscow synagogue, is arbitrarily and artificially restricted to four students; Jews are forbidden regular official contact (guaranteed by Soviet law), either through formal ties or delegation exchanges or religious pilgrimages, with coreligionists abroad. Even so hurried and sketchy a summary is sufficient to suggest the vast lineaments of the deprivations and discrimination to which hundreds of thousands of pious Soviet Jews are subjected—but Mr. Rozin has nothing to say about them.

He mentions the showplace Great Synagogue of Moscow—but he is somehow silent about the forcible closing down of dozens of synagogues in smaller cities which are off the beaten track of foreign tourists. Just in the past year synagogues were shut down in such cities as Lvov, Sverdlovsk, Zhitomir, Kazan, Grozny, Piatigorsk, Zhmerinka, Kalarash and Kaunas. About this Mr. Rozin is silent.

He talks about "numerous small prayer houses with an attendance of less than 100." This is most disingenuous. The "prayer houses" he refers to are not synagogues at all, but private homes where, deprived of a synagogue, Jews have taken to gathering for services. These *minyanim* (congregational quorums) are indeed numerous—but more important, it takes courage to attend them. For they have been pilloried in the press and harried and dispersed by the police all over the country. Among the most recent instances (there have been scores, probably hundreds in recent years) were the brutal disruption and dispersion of these private prayer meetings in Kolomea and Kharkov on the holiest day of the Jewish religious calendar —Yom Kippur of 1962. Mr. Rozin chooses to remain silent about this vicious harassment.

Is this treatment of synagogues and worshippers what he means by "a greater proportion of voluntary non-believers among Jews"? He does not, by the way, suggest any reason why this proportion should be greater for Jews than for Christians and Moslems. But even if it is so, it is surely not "voluntary," but rather better accounted for by the "special" position occupied by Judaism in the U.S.S.R.

Why No Matzoth?

Mr. Rozin plays fast and loose with the truth in discussing the ban on the public baking and sale of *matzoth,* the unleavened bread indispensable to the proper observance of the major Jewish holiday of Passover. He attributes this ban to the "Soviet adherence to the separation of Church and State"—a concept and a practice which he feels I do not understand. I understand it only too well—so much so that it puzzles me that there should exist a controlling governmental Council for the Affairs of Religious Cults in a country so dedicated to the principle of Separation.

As for *matzoth*, it should be pointed out that until two years ago they *were* baked and sold in state stores. Moreover, in a document submitted to the United Nations on July 11, 1956, the Soviet government stated: "By order of the U.S.S.R. Government, on days preceding particularly important holidays—such as Passover in the case of the Jews—the shops of the State trading organisations sell special types of bakery products, *matzoth* (unleavened bread) for Orthodox Jews, etc., to enable worshippers to perform the appropriate ritual." It would seem that, as regards *matzoth,* the principle of Separation was only discovered in the Soviet Union just in time for Passover 1962.

Mr. Rozin did not always resort to this pretext. A few months earlier, in a letter to *The Bulletin,* an Australian magazine, on January 12, 1963, he had another excuse. For both TMO and *The Bulletin*, however, he prefers to hide behind the authority of Rabbi Levin of Moscow. In the latter, he has the rabbi say: "A few words about *matzoth*. Until lately it was sold in state-run shops. However, last spring, a short while before Passover, the state bakery that made *matzoth* was closed down for repairs. That is why there was no *matzoth* in the shops." Not a word about Separation of Church and State; that principle was apparently found to be handy in the nick of time, in order to avoid the trouble of repairing the state bakery for Passover 1963.

Other Discriminations

As for discrimination against Jews in higher education, employment and government service, Mr. Rozin finds it "quite unnecessary to discuss this matter in greater detail." And I, in turn, have no space for it. "Whatever the facts," he adds, "I fail to see why Soviet authorities should be held responsible for the career preferences of individual Jewish students." Let me answer this question with another question: Has Soviet Jewish youth so drastically altered its character in the space of less than a generation that it has lost *all* interest in employment in the Foreign Service, in virtually all branches of the armed forces, etc.? Mr. Rozin is completely silent about the gross underrepresentation of Jews in all Soviet governmental bodies. He does tinker a bit with my figures that demonstrate the *declining proportion* of Jews in higher education, the sciences and the professions— but he has nothing to say about my explanation of this phenomenon.

Actually, it's not mine: It belongs to such Soviet leaders as Mr. Khrushchev, Mr. Pervukhin, Madame Furtseva and Mr. Ilychev, who, in interviews and statements to foreign journalists and delegations, stated flatly that Jews have had to make place for "our own intelligentsia" —as if their thousand-year residence on that soil did not make them fully as indigenous as the next fellow. It is this—and not, as Mr. Rozin falsely attributes to me, the Jews' own sense of alienation—that has led them *to be considered* an alien group.

Portraying the Jew

Mr. Rozin claims I have libeled the Soviet Union in talking about "popular" anti-Semitism.

He miscontrues. I did not "label whole regions of the country anti-Semitic." I wrote that the RSFSR, the Ukraine and Byelorussia are regions "where 'popular' anti-Semitism is still widespread and endemic"—which is a completely different affair. He claims I can refer to no newspaper and give no quotations in which the image of the Jew is portrayed in traditional anti-Semitic stereotypes, and he challenges me to name at least one Soviet newspaper which portrays the Jews as "money worshippers." There is space to cite only a few papers and quotations.

Leningradskaya Pravda (Leningrad, September 16, 1961): "From the pages of the protocol rises the loathsome portrait of the criminals, men without honor or conscience, whose idol was the 'Golden Calf.'" The men named were Kaplan, Shapiro, Oizerman, about whose identity as Jews a Soviet audience could have no doubt.

Zarya Vostoka (Tbilisi, Georgia, November 26, 1961): "They played and they cheated. Even the religious books of the Torah were used by several of them as hiding places for foreign currency. And all this was done in the name of one God—the Golden Calf." The men named were Kakiashvili, Khananashvili, Katzevshvili—unmistakably Jewish names in Georgia.

Minskaya Pravda (Minsk, April 4, 1961): "When it comes to the Golden Calf, they are ready for anything. Money! That is the God of the leaders of the Minsk Jewish religious community and their aides."

Pravda Ukrainy (Kiev, August 1, 1962): "Slaves of Gold" is the title of an article in which the villains are Greenberg, Katz, Goldenberg, Poisner, Kuris. Poisner is described in these terms: "Who is he, this man dried out by avarice, by the thirst for gain and profit? This is not simply a thief, not simply a crook. This is a predator, the evil one, the blood-thirsty one, the one prepared for anything at all only in order to have a few more golden coins. Gold! It blinded him, closed off the entire world."

And here is how the last remaining synagogue in Lvov, which was closed down forcibly last November, is described in a series of articles in the city's leading newspaper, *Lvovskaya Pravda:*

"Crooks and speculators of all stripes

gather in the synagogue which has been turned into a sort of black market." (February 16, 1962).

"Criminals and dishonest people feel perfectly good under the vaults of the synagogue." (October 26, 1962).

Had enough, Mr. Rozin? Now let me, in turn, issue a challenge to him. Let him cite me one single article in any Soviet newspaper in which a *non-Jew* is described as a "worshipper of the Golden Calf." If he cannot do so, of which I am certain, surely he will have to confess that one or another version of this style is the journalistic mode for anti-Semitic assaults.

Since the publication of my *Foreign Affairs* article, the figures of death sentence have risen steeply—but the proportion of Jews among them has remained curiously constant. Of some 145 death sentences reported in the Soviet press, 86 or 87 are Jews—just about 60 per cent. In view of the fact that the Jews constitute little more than one per cent of the total population, this can only mean that the Jews are being singled out for this barbarous treatment in a fantastic way. And the worst of it is that the Jews know it, their non-Jewish neighbors know it—and they all know that it is no "mere" accident.

Special Treatment

It is precisely this "special treatment" of the Jews in virtually all spheres of Soviet life against which Yevgeny Yevtushenko railed in his "Babi Yar." His very first line, protesting the absence of a monument to the scores of thousands of Jews slaughtered by the Nazis near Kiev, attests to the fact that Soviet authorities have been consistently silent about the Jewish holocaust. One press conference (in which Jews played an insignificant role), to which Mr. Rozin refers, is the swallow that does not make the spring. Let me just give the latest, most egregious example of what I mean Last April, the entire world commemorated the 20th anniversary of the heroic Warsaw Ghetto uprising. Every Jewish community, joined by its non-Jewish neighbors, observed it with great public attention and approbation Even the Jewish Communists throughout the United States held observances. And in Warsaw itself, the Polish government, and the Jewish community, undertook an international observance. Only Soviet Jewry was forced to remain silent, to abstain from sharing this solemn memory with its fellow Jews. And from one or two articles that appeared in the Soviet press, one could only derive with difficulty the grudging acknowledgement that this was a *Jewish* day of remembrance, of Jewish pain and Jewish triumph.

And again, it is no "mere" accident that Yevtushenko, and other young Soviet writers who feel as he does, is now the object of a vicious propaganda campaign himself—not least because of his daring expression of brotherhood with the Jews!

Mr. Rozin claims to speak *as* a Soviet Jew. But he surely does not speak *for* Soviet Jewry. He is surely aware of the truth of what I have written here and in *Foreign Affairs*. If he cares, his task is unenviably painful. If he does not care, what is there to say?

III.

types of tension and discrimination

introduction: some definitions

In Part I, a minority group in the United States was defined by the existence of discrimination against or deprivation of its members because of their affiliation with a distinguishable group and by a sense of belonging to the group on the part of the minority members themselves. In this part, the kinds of discrimination that minority groups in the United States face are examined; their attitudes and reactions toward their status are considered in Part IV.

A convenient way of classifying discrimination is to distinguish economic, political, legal, and social types. These categories are only abstractions, for in any actual case of discrimination, several types might be involved. For example, if a black should be kept out of a technical college because of his color, he would face economic handicaps because he could not get the training to secure the job for which he has the ability and interest; he would face social discrimination by being kept from contact with people of the same age, interest, and background; he would face legal discrimination because there would be a violation of the constitutional provision that equal public facilities must be available to all. The various minority groups meet these kinds of discrimination in different degrees. Jews face primarily social discrimination; whereas Catholics have faced primarily political discrimination. Blacks experience all four kinds in the South but mainly the economic and social varieties in the North. Some of the specific discriminations faced by minorities can be categorized only with difficulty under any one of the four rubrics; for example, the black in the South, in conversation with a white man, not so long ago was forced to punctuate his conversation at frequent intervals with the word "Sir." This custom is classified as social discrimination only because it creates barriers to the communication between the races. Despite such weaknesses, this fourfold classification has been found useful for detailing the innumerable instances of discrimination that individual members of minority groups face and for providing suggestive groupings for the analysis of the causes of prejudice (which are considered in Part V).

Economic discrimination, may be defined as any activity or lack of activity that prevents a member of a minority group from earning a living or getting other material benefits from society because of his membership in a minority group and not because of any defects in his training or ability. Economic discrimination thus includes the following:

1. A failure or refusal of employers to hire qualified minority members for job openings that they have available
2. A failure or refusal of employers to promote qualified minority members into higher-grade job openings
3. Barriers to union membership, to apprentice training programs controlled by unions, or to full participation in union benefits or activities
4. A refusal of landlords to sell or rent business property to minority members who wish to start bona fide businesses

5. A failure of banks to lend money to potential minority entrepreneurs who have adequate ability and security to start a business
6. A refusal of insurance companies to sell insurance to minority members covering all the various sorts of personal and property risks any businessman meets (or charging minority businessmen higher rates for these kinds of insurance)
7. A refusal of merchants or directors of nonprofit enterprises (such as hospitals) to provide equal services for minority group clients
8. A refusal to provide an adequate general or vocational education at the secondary or college levels, or segregation of minority members into inferior or overcrowded schools with inadequate access to materials of training
9. A refusal of state and local governments to provide minority members with public facilities (such as libraries, street paving, tax advice) of the same number and quality as are available to the majority group, so that minority members have to do without these facilities or pay for them out of their own pockets
10. A hindrance to the participation of minority group members in the organized or informal activities of their occupational group (such as professional organizations, businessmen's clubs, service clubs, or simply the informal get-togethers of businessmen where ideas, information, and economic opportunities are exchanged)
11. A hindrance of access to the markets or marketing facilities for manufactured products produced by minority group entrepreneurs

Each minority group in the United States experiences one or more of these examples of discrimination. The blacks experience all these forms of economic discrimination, in varying degrees in different parts of the country; at the other extreme, some of the nationality groups have only minor experiences of this type.

Legal discrimination includes both the biases contained in laws that create deprivations for certain minority groups and misapplications or violations of the law when directed against minority groups:

1. Laws that prohibit or restrict the immigration of people of a certain nationality or race regardless of their individual abilities and beliefs
2. Laws that provide for special treatment of members of minority groups (when the treatment is not intended to rectify an extralegal discrimination)
3. Partiality shown by public officials in applying the law without violating its letter
4. Deficiencies in providing minority groups with information and other services of the sort usually offered by government
5. Use of the power of executive orders by a president or governor to create unique hardships for minority groups
6. The taking over of legal powers by persons who have no official position to punish real or alleged criminals of minority group membership
7. Use of violence or other extralegal devices by law enforcement officials or other persons without being punished because the victim is a member of a minority group
8. Consistent failure to appoint law enforcement officials (including police and jury members) from among qualified minority group members
9. Race riots and other forms of intergroup violence, when directed against minority group members by the dominant group

In general, most legal discrimination in the United States takes the form of misapplication or violation of the law, rather than the passage of discriminatory laws. The Constitution explicitly forbids discrimination by government; thus prejudiced legislators are deterred, or the laws they enact are soon declared unconstitutional by the courts. The legal discriminations have been applied against minority groups in different degrees in different sections of the country. The southern states have been most prone to extralegal activity and misapplication of the laws. Again, blacks have, in general, experienced the greatest degree of legal discrimination; but during World War II, Japanese-Americans were faced with the greatest single deprivation of legal rights in American history. The legal status of religious minorities is given special attention in the United States Constitution, which guarantees religious freedom and explicitly limits the powers of government in its relationship to church activity. Some of the legal problems of religious minorities are not so much those of discrimination but of reactions to the application or misapplication of these constitutional provisions.

Political discrimination includes the following:

1. Restriction of the citizen's right to vote
2. The placing of barriers to the attainment of citizenship by minority group members
3. Unwillingness to nominate or vote for a candidate for public office because of his minority group membership
4. Campaigns against a candidate for public office on the basis of his minority group membership
5. Failure to appoint minority group members to appointive offices, such as judgeships, cabinet secretaryships, and ambassadorships

In the United States, members of the various Oriental groups were not allowed to become American citizens, regardless of ability or length of residence, until corrective statutes were passed in 1943 and 1951. In the South, many blacks are deprived of their right to vote and are prevented from running for political office or from receiving appointive posts. Throughout the country, there is still majority group sentiment against voting for Roman Catholics and Jews for high public offices, although the campaign and presidential career of John F. Kennedy did much to dispel that feeling.

Social discrimination refers to the barriers between people that prevent them from having the advantages of each other's company, that insult some by regarding them as inferior, and that deny some access to desirable places at which others assemble. Social discrimination against minority groups ranges from obvious physical exclusion to the most subtle remark to differentiate people and put subordinated members of minority groups "in their place." These are some specific categories:

1. Barriers against admission to places where people carry on their noneconomic activities, such as homes, hotels, restaurants, places of amusement, churches, schools, community centers
2. Barriers against the location of residence by members of a minority group in neighborhoods where persons of the majority group live
3. Barriers against membership in voluntary organizations that are otherwise open to "the general public," to "all who are interested," or to "those who have a certain skill or education"
4. Systematic derogation of minority group members in the behavior and language of majority group persons toward them, ranging from the use of epithets to the avoidance of physical contract with anything a minority person may have touched
5. Requirements that minority group members act in a servile manner when in the presence of majority group persons
6. Prohibitions or restrictions against intermarriage
7. The tendency of persons of the majority group to regard persons of the minority group as inferior and/or dangerous and to manifest this attitude in obvious or subtle ways

All racial minorities experience most kinds of social discrimination, and among the religious minorities, the Jews do also. In the case of blacks in the South, social discrimination is made the keystone of all other forms of discrimination. Social discrimination, because it is far more personal than the other forms, often has the greatest implications for the personality development of minority group members.

A.
ECONOMIC AND HOUSING DISCRIMINATION

17
employment, manpower training and the black worker

HERBERT HILL

The American economy is one of the wonders of the world, producing more wealth than any other society ever has. This is reflected in manufacturing plants, cities, utilities, transportation and communication facilities, and an unending stream of material products. In talking about minorities, there is a tendency to forget this because one of the main problems of most minorities is that they are left out of the economic mainstream. America's wealth also explains why most Americans are little concerned about those who are poor; when you are enmeshed in a rich environment, it is hard to believe that everybody is not.

The poor (and there are several ways to decide who fits into this category) are the old, the young in families where the wage earner is female, some young adults between sixteen and twenty-five years of age, and those who live in remote areas—such as Appalachia, Indian reservations, and impoverished rural areas of other kinds. Blacks, Indians, and Chicanos have more than their share of people in the poor categories.

Access to the economy also provides access to political power and social equality; minorities are well aware of this and complain that they are systematically excluded from economic opportunity. They are thus heavily represented in the poverty groups and underrepresented among the political and social elite.

The following article describes in detail the obstacles blacks face in the economic sphere. Mr. Hill is the national labor director for the National Association for the Advancement of Colored People.

The Report of the National Commission on Technology, Automation and Economic Progress notes that:

If non-whites continue to hold the same proportion of jobs in each occupation as in 1964 the non-white unemployment rate in 1975 will be more than five times that for the labor force as a whole.[1]

Reprinted from *The Journal of Negro Education* 38, no. 3 (Summer 1969), pp. 204-216. Reproduced by permission of the author and publisher.

The entire system of current occupational training operates to fulfill this dire prophecy. Indeed, one might conclude that it is designed to do so. The varieties of job training programs available to black youth, especially those financed with public funds, indicate that these programs function to perpetuate the highly undesirable pattern of Negro occupational distribution.

The status of the black worker in the American economy is now characterized by a growing crisis of unemployment and underemployment, by large-scale occupational dislocation as a result of technological change and by the emergence of a new generation of ghetto youth limited to a marginal economic existence.

For nonwhite teenagers the 1968 national unemployment rate was 25 percent compared with 11 percent for white teenagers. It is necessary to note that broad national statistical data obscure the full extent of Negro unemployment which can only be understood by examining information on specific major areas of urban Negro population concentration.[2]

In the black ghetto areas of Watts, East St. Louis, the Hough area of Cleveland, as well as in certain all-Negro census tracts in Philadelphia, Oakland, and elsewhere, the rate of male Negro unemployment and underemployment in many Negro ghetto areas now exceeds the general rate of unemployment for the entire nation during the Great Depression of the 1930's. The U.S. Riot commission Report concludes that ". . . in disadvantaged areas, employment conditions for Negroes are in a chronic state of crisis."

During 1968 and 1969, Negro workers continued to hold a disproportionate number of jobs in declining industries and the menial and unrewarding work available to most black workers permitted only a marginal subsistence for families living in the decaying slums of America's racial ghettos.

The U.S. Commission's Report sums up the data on Negro occupational concentration as follows:

. . . Even more important perhaps than unemployment is the related problem of the undesirable nature of many jobs open to Negroes. Negro workers are concentrated in the lowest skilled and the lowest-paying occupations. These jobs often involve substandard wages, great instability and uncertainty of tenure, extremely low status in the eyes of both employer and employees, little or no chance for meaningful advancement, and unpleasant or exhausting duties. Negro men in particular are more than twice as likely as whites to be in unskilled or service jobs which pay far less than most. . . .

If the traditional patterns of job discrimination are not rapidly eliminated, the continuing crisis of unemployment and poverty among Negroes threatens to plunge Negro communities into further alienation and despair.

Three basic factors may be isolated to explain the status of the black worker:

1. Current Training Programs Maintain Traditional Occupational Patterns. Only a very small number of those who need assistance participate in government-sponsored training programs. Those who do participate learn little or nothing that prepares them for entering into expanding sectors of the economy. Negro participation is concentrated in those programs that lead to low-paid, unskilled jobs. Negroes are generally barred from apprenticeship and other training programs where there are expanding job opportunities. Where training programs begin to open for blacks, it is in occupations that have already started to decline or will decline in the near future. Job training where the U.S. Government makes a direct contribution to employers is in almost every instance merely a subsidy to cut labor costs. Such training is invariably for low-paying, short-cycle, repetitive tasks. The prevocational training programs are based on the assumption that unemployed Negroes are unfit or unable to work. They are, in fact, not job training programs at all as they are not related to the requirements of the contemporary labor market. In many instances what is called job training is simply a custodial operation for black youth. These programs are not job-related and they do not lead to employment. It is very important to note that census data reveal that Negro high school graduates have a higher rate of unemployment than white high school drop-outs, and that the Negro who has attended college earns less than the white with only eight years of elementary school. Thus we are forced to assume that low education does not provide the total explanation for the economic status of the Negro. Even where blacks do participate in the educational process sharp rates of disparity in job status and income exist. At every level of educational experience, patterns of disparity between white and black wage earners remain intact. One is forced to the conclusion that the education system does not function for black workers.

2. Patterns of Housing Segregation and Job Opportunity.

The most significant expansion of new job opportunities during the past decade has been located outside the center cities. But 80 percent of all Negroes living in urban areas in 1960 were concentrated in central cities. During the same period there was a very significant movement of industry to suburban areas, where Negroes were denied housing. By 1970 less than 25 percent of the nation's white population will be living in the central city areas compared with almost 60 percent of the total Negro population. In every city experiencing a marked increase in Negro population, a parallel movement of heavy industry out of the city has taken place. Thus as black families come to the city in search of employment, jobs are rapidly leaving the city and are to be found in suburban areas where Negroes are unable to live, either because of discriminatory housing practices or because of the lack of available housing. The countermovement of blacks and jobs emerges as a major problem.

3. Barriers to Knowledge of Job Market Developments.

It is known that young white workers rely heavily on family and friends to learn of available jobs and training opportunities. Black workers, more than any other group in the labor force, are dependent upon state employment services for such information, but these institutions and other public agencies act as a barrier to exclude blacks from skilled-craft and other desirable jobs. (Litigation is currently pending in the Federal courts against several state employment services because of their discriminatory racial practices. Among the most important of these is the suit against the Ohio agency [*Jamar* v. *Ohio Bureau of Unemployment Compensation*] which charges that the state employment service refused to refer qualified Negro applicants to apprenticeship and other training programs on the same basis as whites.)

A number of studies describe the informal process by which young white workers

learn of apprenticeship and other vocational training opportunities through a parent, relative or neighbor and how such persons assist in achieving admission into such programs. In their analysis of the "Background and Career Choices of Tool and Die Makers," Swerdloff and Bluestone found that a significant number of tool and die makers attribute their occupational choice to the influence of family members and friends.[3] Schuster, in his study of apprentices, indicates that over 50 percent of his sample members were advised by their parents to become apprentices.[4] The same holds true of a study of apprentices in New York State which demonstrates that other role models are significant in addition to "relatives in the trade."[5] Lipset also found this factor in operation in his analysis of printing craftsmen.[6] The importance of the family unit role model in stimulating youth to become skilled craftsmen is clearly indicated by the fact that sons or nephews quite frequently do follow the same or a related trade as father, uncle, or other close relative. At times this appears to hold even in the face of objective opportunities to follow other careers, as indicated by Rogoff, Van Dusen, Schuster and Bendix and Lipset.[7] Despite Titles VI and VII of the Civil Rights Act of 1964 which prohibit discriminatory practices by the state employment services, many state employment referral systems are still highly discriminary. State employment services operate more than two thousand local offices, and in addition to providing job referral, counseling, and testing services, now also perform a major role in administering the several job training and manpower development programs sponsored by the Federal Government. For black workers in ghetto areas the racial practices of the United States Employment Service are a major barrier.

These three factors together with the general failure of government agencies to enforce the comprehensive body of civil rights laws and executive orders as they relate to employment and training programs combine to keep black workers outside of the "opportunity structure" of the labor force.[8] Some voluntary shifts in the private sector may be found but these are limited and not related to government-sponsored training programs. Taken as a whole, federally financed training programs have had little relevance for urban black workers.

THE "ETHNIC LOCK" IN APPRENTICESHIP

A major element in restricting training and employment opportunities for Negroes in desirable skilled occupations is what might be described as the "ethnic lock" on certain occupational categories. Dr. Kenneth Clark, writing in the HARYOU Report, *Youth in the Ghetto, A Study of the Consequences of Powerlessness,* states:

Through historical processes certain ethnic or religious minority groups come to predominance in certain kinds of jobs: the waterfront for the Italian, the police force for the Irish, the school system for Jews, and the personal services for Negroes. In addition, most skilled garment workers in New York are Jewish and of eastern European origin, or Italian. Many tool and die makers are of British and German extraction. The "ethnic lock" held by these groups over certain jobs means that employment opportunities in these fields, and the saliency of these fields as future occupations, are known and restricted primarily to members of these ethnic groups.

Most often labor unions are the decisive force in perpetuating the "ethnic lock" on occupations. This is done by preventing the entrance of black workers into union-controlled apprenticeship and other training programs and by discriminatory provisions in collective bargaining agreements. Two examples of how organized labor uses its power to maintain the "ethnic lock" are to be found by examining the racial practices of the International Ladies Garment Workers Union (AFL-CIO) and the craft unions in the building and construction trades.

The International Ladies Garment Workers' Union and the Amalgamated Clothing Workers Union have effectively prevented the use of the Federal funds for training purposes in the apparel industry, even though there are acute manpower shortages. In Newark (New Jersey), New York City, and elsewhere, action by the ILGWU has destroyed training programs involving unemployed Negro and Puerto Rican

ghetto youth. Evans and Novak, commenting on the restrictive practices of the ILGWU in their syndicated column in *The Washington Post* of January 2, 1969, wrote the following:

What makes this ban so strange is that the apparel industry is the last major unautomated industry with a capacity to hire workers in substantial numbers. It is thus peculiarly fitted for quick, relatively easy training programs to move the uneducated and unemployed poor—including ghetto blacks—into economic self-sufficiency.

As a result of demands by the International Ladies' Garment Workers' Union and the Amalgamated Clothing Workers of America (both AFL-CIO affiliates), Federal agencies refused to provide funds for manpower training programs in the apparel industry. A typical example of this development is the fate of the training program proposed by the United Community Corporation, the anti-poverty community action agency for Newark, New Jersey. This group operated under Title II, the Community Action Program of the Economic Opportunity Act of 1964. When representatives of the Newark agency requested an explanation for the refusal of the Office of Economic Opportunity to provide funds for an apparel trades job training program for 545 workers (200 of whom were welfare recipients), they were told by officials of the Department of Labor that the basis for the rejection was the refusal of the two unions to approve the job training program.

On August 22, 1963, the Department of Labor, which administers the Manpower Development and Training Act, received a fourteen-page statement of the "position of the International Ladies Garment Workers Union and the Amalgamated Clothing Workers of America, on the question of subsidized training programs in the apparel industry of the United States." In this document, signed by Lazare Teper, Research Director of the ILGWU, and Milton Fried, Research Director of the ACWA, the unions argued that

It is our considered judgement that the subsidized training of apparel workers under

the Manpower Development and Training Act is unnecessary. . . . On the basis of our many years of experience in the apparel industry we are convinced that such training of apparel workers is not only a waste of federal funds but sets in motion forces detrimental to the health and stability of our industry. (p. 5)

The report concludes:

These considerations apply to government financed training programs under the Area Redevelopment Act, as well as the Manpower Development and Training Act. We, therefore, respectfully urge that the Department of Labor as a matter of policy not sponsor or approve any training program for apparel workers under the Manpower Development Act. (p. 14)

Both the ILGWU and the ACWA have used their considerable political power to prevent in Newark and elsewhere the same kind of training programs that are operating with public funds in many other industries.

The union argument, that there is no need for training skilled workers, is directly contradicted by several studies as well as by the latest edition of the United States Department of Labor's *Occupational Outlook Handbook.*

It should be noted that several ILGWU contracts provide for a "learners" status of ten months and several union agreements require that a year shall pass before a new employee is entitled to the full rate of pay. The statement of the apparel labor unions is also contradicted by manpower studies of the industry. According to the "Occupational Training Need Survey, Research Series No. 18, September 1964, prepared and compiled by the State of New Jersey, Department of Labor and Industry, Division of Employment Security:

By 1965 there will be a shortage in three of the six semi-skilled occupations surveyed. These occupations are: machine presser in the garment, laundry, and cleaning and dyeing industries. By 1968 [in addition to those occupations expected to be in short supply in 1965]

there will be shortages of sewing machine operators and hand pressers in the garment, laundry, cleaning and dyeing industries.

These projections are extremely significant as they directly relate to the proposal submitted to the Office of Economic Opportunity for funding by the Newark anti-poverty council. Furthermore, Newark has been officially declared a depressed area with extremely high unemployment among Negroes. Recognizing the acute needs of the Negro community, the local anti-poverty agency was attempting to provide training for two hundred welfare recipients for existing job vacancies. Such job training programs, which will enable the long-term unemployed to leave the relief rolls by obtaining employment as a result of newly acquired skills, is the essence of any real "war against poverty."

The insistence of the two apparel unions that there is no necessity for training workers in the garment industry and their ability to prevent new opportunities under Federal training programs have a special implication for Negro workers. Negro applicants for jobs in the garment industry are often asked if they have had previous experience. Because they have been denied the opportunity to obtain such experience, they are either denied work or are employed only in menial and unskilled jobs. The ILGWU's restrictive practices are to a large degree responsible for the acute lack of mobility among Negro garment workers.[9]

The development of many large companies in this industry with modern production methods that require new skills has been evident for some time. But even though nonwhites constitute a potentially large source of skilled-labor recruitment for this industry, they have been effectively denied such opportunities mainly as a result of restrictive labor-union practices. (The *New York Times* of April 17, 1966, in a front-page story in its financial section, reported that "the shortage of skilled tailors . . . is forcing American manufacturers to import foreign workers for these jobs." On May 6, 1968, the *New York Times* quoted a spokesman for the garment industry who stated that: "Every factory has a crying need for skilled operators, pressers, and finishers.")

APPRENTICESHIP TRAINING IN
THE CONSTRUCTION INDUSTRY

Jobs in the nation's construction industry are of great importance to Negroes and members of other minority groups. In excess of $78 billion was spent for new construction during 1968 and public works accounted for almost a third, or $26 billion, of new construction.

Despite the vast amount of public funds spent for construction, and despite the growth of the building industry with its ability to provide hundreds of thousands of man-years of employment—together with the fact that acute labor shortages now exist in several skilled occupations—Negroes are permitted to receive what Roy Wilkins, executive director of the NAACP, calls "only the crumbs of expenditures for public construction."

The nation's construction industry is of unique importance to Negro wage earners for many reasons. Among these are the following:

1. It is a huge industry with vast growth potential. State and Federal social policies will in the future emphasize massive new urban development programs involving slum clearance, housing, schools and medical and other public facilities.

The Report of the National Advisory Commission on Civil Disorders (March 1968) proposed new social programs which, if even partially realized, would create thousands of new job opportunities in the construction industry. The estimate of the U.S. Department of Labor that the construction industry will require one million more workers by 1975 may be most conservative. (According to the *Engineering News Record* of October 18, 1968, acute labor shortages already exist in twelve building trades in thirty-one cities.)

2. The construction industry, in comparison with other large industries, is highly dependent on public funds. During 1968 public works represented approximately a third of all new construction. However, in the twenty-five major areas of Negro urban population concentration between 50 and 60 percent of new construction projects were financed by Federal, state and local agencies. Given the anticipated new programs, these proportions will be substantially increased.

3. Wages in the construction industry are among the highest in the nation. Wages for the craft occupations in the unionized building trades average about three times the general industrial wage. In 1968 in New York City construction, electrical workers earned $7.70 per hour, plumbers in several Ohio cities received in excess of $8.00 an hour. There is every indication that these wage levels will be increased during the next round of collective bargaining negotiations, as in Philadelphia where the Plumbers Union recently negotiated an agreement that provides for an annual minimum wage of $19,400. A disproportionately high percentage of employed Negroes work at jobs paying close to the Federal minimum wage. These are the working poor, who are limited to the lowest-paid menial work, and, although they are counted as employed, live in a permanent condition of poverty. The building and construction industry represents a major area of the economy which could provide mobility into higher-paying, more desirable occupations.

4. Jobs in the building trades are for men. In the highly important symbolic sense, as well as because of practical considerations, construction jobs are male jobs. These "manly" jobs with their high-status implications are especially important for Negro men, who are so frequently either denied employment or permitted to work only in low-paying, menial "dead end" jobs.

5. Jobs in the construction industry are highly visible and are of special significance to low-income Negro communities. Much of new construction, including urban renewal, model cities, highway and road building and public housing, is in, or very near, large Negro communities. Slum clearance programs are expected to provide employment to slum dwellers, especially as the model cities and other programs specifically require new job opportunities for members of minority groups living in the areas affected.

6. Finally, it should be noted that, throughout the nation, much of the test of what happens to major recommendations made in the Report of the National Advisory Commission on Civil Disorders will be decided in the construction industry and in the nation's housing and urban development programs. The

employment practices of the building and construction trades have unique social implications, especially for black workers, and if the recommendations of the Report have any meaning at all, it will be to a large extent revealed by the future status of black workers in the construction industry.[10]

The building trades unions permit only three thousand apprenticeship openings in the nationwide construction industry each year and maintain a ratio of one apprentice to eight journeymen. This is an arbitrary number based upon the restrictive anti-social practices of the craft unions. Recent findings by the Federal courts in several states and by the Equal Employment Opportunity Commission indicate that no alternation in the pattern of racial exclusion in the union-controlled construction industry has taken place. At best there has been a minimal strategic adjustment to the requirements of civil rights laws and to black protest, but the traditional pattern remains intact. (The response of the AFL-CIO building trades unions in Seattle, Washington, in the case of *Lewis and Murray* v. *Ironworkers Local 86* is typical of the current national pattern. On March 12, 1969, the Washington State Board Against Discrimination, after almost three years of investigations, hearings, and futile attempts at conciliation, found a ". . . history and record of deliberate, extensive and illegal discrimination practiced by Respondent Union. . . ." and ordered the admission of the Negro plaintiffs. The defendant union has refused to comply with the order of the State Commission and has laid the foundation for a series of appeals to state and Federal courts that will take a minimum of three years.)

A 1968 survey of 21 crafts in Detroit reveals that black workers constitute only 4 percent of those admitted to union membership in the construction trades, and most of these are concentrated in the "trowel trades" and carpenters union. Furthermore, Negroes constitute only 3 percent of those enrolled in union apprenticeship programs. These data clearly indicate that no significant change has occurred in the racial composition of the building trades in Detroit during the last decade. Other information reveals that the same

situation prevails in many other areas of Negro population concentration.[11]

Significantly, an ethnic survey made by the California Department of Industrial Relations released during February of 1969 reveals that the proportion of Negroes among apprentices throughout the State of California dropped 14 percent between 1965 and 1968 while the proportion of Mexican-Americans decreased 17 percent during the same period.

Periodically there appear announcements from the building trades unions or from spokesmen for the AFL-CIO proclaiming "new affirmative programs" that will, it is alleged, lead to the admission of untold numbers of black workers into union-controlled apprenticeship training programs in the building trades. An on-the-spot investigation made by the author during the week of April 21, 1968, of a much publicized program at public construction projects in Boston, revealed the reality of such "affirmative action." The Boston program consisted of a newly established four-week, on-the-job training course for laborers paying one-half less than the established union scale. At the end of the four-week period, the trainees were deemed "qualified laborers" and were replaced with another group of trainees.

However, the so-called "qualified laborers" are not given union membership, are not given access to the union-controlled hiring halls, are not given employment on public construction but in most instances are returned to the ranks of the ghetto unemployed. This is the reality of "affirmative action" programs, financed by Federal funds in Boston and many other cities throughout the country, and it explains why there are but fifty-eight black apprentices in twenty-six trades throughout the entire state of Massachusetts. (On July 17, 1969, after public hearings and investigation of the status of black workers in the construction industry in Boston, the Massachusetts State Advisory Committee to the United States Commission on Civil Rights concluded that: "Minority persons particularly those presently possessing construction or construction related skills, need new and more efficient entry routes to journeyman status and union membership. The existing Workers Defense League program is too limited and too restricted to service the needs of the minority community, and to redress the years of discriminatory exclusion.")

Vocational Education in Public School Systems

The term "vocational education" as used here refers to the Federally funded occupational training courses in the public school systems operating under state supervision. These programs have a special importance for the Negro community, as they are quite frequently the only form of job training accessible to large numbers of black youth. In 1961, prior to the passage of the Manpower Development and Training Act, President John F. Kennedy convened a Panel of Consultants on Vocational Education to evaluate the nation's vocational education system. In 1962 the Panel found that vocational education in the public schools was insensitive to major shifts in the nation's employment pattern.[12] This has long been true in Negro residential areas both in Northern as well as Southern states where Negro youths are "trained" for obsolete occupations or for jobs soon to be obsolete.

Only one-half to two-thirds of the technical training program graduates were finding training-related employment.[13] Rural schools were giving little attention to the occupational needs of students migrating to urban centers, despite the fact that his migration is one of the most important demographic changes in recent decades.[14]

Curriculums were not being developed for most of the newer occupational specialties. High school youth in large cities accounted for only 18 percent of the vocational education enrollment.[15] In 1966 the largest single category of vocational education in the public school was the nonemployment category of home economics, with 31.2 percent of the total vocational education enrollment.[16] Although the general employment trend is away from unskilled or low-skilled industrial jobs, 20.9 percent of the 1966 vocational education enrollees were receiving training in such industrial occupations.[17] Of the 20.4 percent of the enrollees in office occupations, 72.5 percent were training for typing, stenography and filing.[18] Only 6.9 percent of all enrollees were in training for "distributive" occupations which are primarily "white collar" jobs with advancement potential, and one-fifth of those enrollees were training for "general merchandise" occupations.[19]

Even after MDTA funds became available together with a mandate from the Vocational Education Act of 1963 emphasizing job training for persons with academic and social handicaps, the Federally aided vocational education system has not reorganized its applicant selection process. In a survey by the Advisory Council on Vocational Education, 75 percent of the local districts responding indicated that the student selection process had not changed in their schools.[20] The Advisory Council concluded that "it does not appear that existing student selection criteria were substantially altered as a result of program changes provided by the Vocational Education Act of 1963." The Advisory Council attributed the lack of changes to the inertia of vocational educators.[21]

Congressional enactments are based upon the demonstrably false assumption that those interests in control of vocational education programs can be persuaded to reorder priorities, and provide effective job training for black youth in both rural and urban communities, as well as for young disadvantaged white workers. The Vocational Education Amendments of 1968 provide increased appropriations to local institutions, with the provision that 15 percent of the funds are to be used exclusively to aid "the disadvantaged in 1970." (The Amendments establish a 25 percent allocation thereafter.)[22] There is no indication that the 1968 Amendments will succeed where the 1963 Act failed. The expenditure of greater funds within an unproductive and archaic structure has characterized the recent history of vocational education. Most of these programs have little or no relevance to the requirements of the contemporary labor market.

MANPOWER DEVELOPMENT AND TRAINING ACT PROGRAMS[23]

The Manpower Development and Training Act of 1962 together with later amendments established the most ambitious training program currently in operation.[24] Essentially the

Act provides three basic forms of training for employment: (1) institutional training, (2) on-the-job training, and (3) experimental and demonstration projects. The experimental and demonstration projects are used as testing laboratories to develop new types of training methods. (Since these are experimental they involve a very small number of workers and will not be discussed here.)

Institutional Training Programs

The Institutional Training Programs were devised to use the services of existing governmental institutions for the selection, training and placement of trainees. Selection and testing of applicants is handled by the State Employment Services, and the training function is usually performed by traditional training programs, operated by various agencies of the state governments and certain private interests. These are the same institutions which have traditionally "screened out" nonwhite, disadvantaged and undereducated applicants, or limited their participation to low-paying jobs or to employment in declining industries.

Congress unfortunately chose to channel MDTA funds through these institutions even though they have traditionally operated against the interest of black workers and other nonwhite groups. The record of these programs suggests that it is necessary to create new institutions to solve a series of complex problems which had not been dealt with previously.

It was the custom for the employment services, the vocational school system and the staff of the Bureau of Apprenticeship and Training to reject the black, the uneducated and the disadvantaged—that is, those potential workers who most need and are most qualified for job training assistance. In the first years of the MDTA program, this institutional "screening out" process remained unchanged. This practice was, in fact, given a Congressional mandate in the Act. A clause providing for the selection of trainees stated: "Before selecting a person for training, the Secretary shall determine that there is a reasonable expectation of employment in the occupation for which the person is to be trained."[25]

The "reasonable expectation of employ-

ment" requirement placed black applicants at a double disadvantage. It was the escape clause which the training institutions used to justify their rejection of the most uneducated and disadvantaged, and it also provided an excuse for placing those disadvantaged trainees which it did select into programs which led to unskilled, "dead end" jobs. Dr. Garth Mangum observed that the various state affiliates of the U.S. Employment Service

were conditioned to providing the best available applicants to fill employer job orders and thus were likely to "cream" those eligible for MDT. The concept of "outreach" to search out and bring in the disadvantaged awaited development by the Economic Opportunity Act's Community Action Agencies after 1964.[26]

The MDTA program has placed emphasis upon formal education through its institutional training. Enrollments in the institutional training program have risen from 32,000 in 1963 to 713,000 in 1968.[27] In each year since the Act's inception, only half of the institutional enrollees have found training-related employment.[28]

Negro participation in the institutional training program has grown from one-fifth in 1963 to 45.2 percent in 1968, for a total overall rate of 35.2 percent over six years.[29] However, the Negro participants who have completed MDTA institutional training have not enjoyed a success equal with that of their white counterparts. In 1965, the employment rate for those who had completed training courses was 74.6 percent for white trainees and 63.2 percent for Negro trainees.[30] The pattern continued in 1966. White trainees who had completed MDTA institutional courses had an unemployment rate of 14.0 percent, while Negro trainees were 24.3 percent unemployed.[31] Black workers were concentrated in the service category which comprised 14.2 percent of all trainees. In this category, training was available for housekeeper, cook, waiter/waitress, nurse's aid/orderly, psychiatric aid, and janitor.[32]

The amendments of 1966 to the Manpower Development and Training Act required

. . . the reorientation of MDTA programs in 1967 under which 65 percent of all training

slots were set aside for the most disadvantaged —those with combinations of problems such as lack of education, minority group status, long term unemployment, poverty, and being a teenager or an older worker.[33]

As a result of the 1966 amendments there was a substantial increase in the number of Negroes participating in MDTA-financed programs. However, black workers were concentrated in those programs which had little effect upon altering the existing racial pattern of occupational distribution. The number of participants in MDTA and other Federally financed training programs is quite small measured within the context of the magnitude of the problem. It should also be noted that most formal apprenticeship programs that are job-related, such as those in the metal crafts, the construction industry, and in the printing trades among many others, require more than the maximum two-year training period permitted under MDTA. The two-year limitation was written into the Act at the insistence of the craft unions.

The voluminous studies of the National Commission on Technology, Automation and Economic Progress, the Annual Manpower Reports of the President, and other sources demonstrate that unskilled and semi-skilled industrial jobs are declining but all available data indicate that MDTA-funded institutional programs continue to train people primarily for low-skilled, short-cycle, repetitive production jobs in industry. The result is that the institutional trainees, and particularly the black workers, concentrated at the lower end of the training spectrum, are not entering occupations which will provide higher-paying mobile employment opportunities. Because of the increasingly complex equipment being introduced into even the most menial and routine job operations, these trainees will find their limited training experience of little value on the job market. In some instances, the jobs were abolished by the time the trainees were ready for employment.

On-the-Job Training Programs

In addition to institutional training, the Manpower Development and Training Act pro-vides funds for on-the-job training programs. The on-the-job (OJT) programs seek to encourage employers to hire unqualified workers and train them for new skills while receiving normal wages. MDTA funds pay for the employer's expense in training workers but do not pay the trainees' salaries. Originally the Department of Labor assigned OJT administration to the Bureau of Apprenticeship and Training, which had strong ties with organized labor.[34]

Under the administration of the Bureau of Apprenticeship and Training, OJT programs failed to direct their efforts to reaching the culturally and economically disadvantaged. While Negro participants accounted for nearly one-third of the institutional trainees, their representation was substantially less in OJT programs. In the 1964-65 period, the percentage of Negro OJT trainees fell from 21.4 percent to 20.7 percent.[35]

Because of the commitment to the racial status quo by labor-union officials in control of the Bureau of Apprenticeship and Training, responsibility for administration of the OJT program was eventually transferred from BAT to the Bureau of Work and Training Program.[36]

Enrollments in on-the-job training programs have risen from 2,100 in 1963 to a high of 177,500 in 1966, with 140,000 in 1968.[37] Although Negro participation in the MDTA institutional programs has remained at a fairly constant one-third of institutional enrollees, the 1963-68 average for OJT programs has been 26.3 percent. In 1968 the proportion of Negro trainees rose substantially to 32.9 percent, up from 13.1 percent in 1963.[38]

Educationally handicapped trainees, among whom there is a large concentration of Negroes, have least benefitted by both the institutional and OJT programs, but OJT projects have proven themselves less receptive to the needs of the disadvantaged. Dr. Mangum has stated, "the enrollment of disadvantaged persons in OJT is inherently difficult. Not only is their proportion in OJT low, but there is no evidence of improvement."[39]

Experimental Programs

The administration of MDTA's institutional and OJT programs, after six years of operation, has proven itself incapable and, to a large degree, unwilling to concentrate its efforts toward training and retraining the hard-core unemployed and disadvantaged persons for work in the expanding employment sectors of the economy. Data also reveal that job training programs perpetuate occupational characteristics that limit many black workers to marginal employment at poverty or below-poverty levels.

In view of the fact that the consequence of current job training programs is to maintain and extend the patterns of Negro occupational concentration which lead to unemployment and underemployment, it is now necessary to proceed with a series of new assumptions and to develop new institutional approaches. Radical strategies must be designed to provide alternative routes to meaningful preparation for jobs in expanding sectors of the economy for large numbers of black workers. To do this it will be necessary to change the flow and distribution of power by creating new institutions controlled by Negro communities.

A significant example of this approach is to be found in the new consortium of black contractors in the building trades that are conducting their own apprenticeship training programs in conjunction with independent black-controlled unions in the construction industry.[40] These new training programs are successfully bypassing the archaic, discriminatory apprenticeship programs controlled by the AFL-CIO craft unions. Similar programs in other industries are now in formation. These new strategies create viable institutional means to alter the status of black labor in the economy. There will be an increasing utilization of such approaches as it has become clear that the nation's manpower training programs, especially those operating with public funds, are a major component of the web of urban racism that has catastrophic implications for Negro communities and for the entire society.

NOTES

[1] *Technology and the American Economy,* Report of the National Commission on Techonology, Automation and Economic Progress, Vol. 1 (Washington, D.C.: U.S. Government Printing Office, February 1966), p. 31.

[2] Published statistics on unemployment underestimate the problem for two reasons. First, they do not include the significant number of persons who have been driven out of the labor force as a result of long-term joblessness and who are no longer seeking employment. Second, in ghetto areas the undercount among Negro males in the primary working-age group is very high. It is generally estimated that population surveys miss between 13 and 15 percent of black workers as compared to about 2 percent of whites.

[3] Sol Swerdloff and Abraham Bluestone, "Background and Career Choice of Tool and Die Makers," *Monthly Labor Review* LXXVI (January 1953).

[4] Joseph H. Schuster, "Career Patterns of Former Apprentices," *Occupational Outlook Quarterly* III (May 1959). Washington, D.C.: U.S. Department of Labor, Bureau of Labor Statistics.

[5] Edward B. Van Dusen, *Apprenticeship in Western New York State,* N.Y. State School of Industrial and Labor Relations, Cornell University, Research Bulletin No. 2 (June 1949), p. 37.

[6] Seymour Martin Lipset, Martin Trow and James Coleman, *Union Democrarcy: The Inside Politics of the International Typographical Union* (New York: Free Press of Glencoe [Macmillan], 1956), pp. 322-323.

[7] See Natalie Rogoff, *Recent Trends in Occupational Mobility* (New York: Free Press of Glencoe [Macmillan], 1953), pp. 45-46; Richard Bendix, S. Lipset, and F. T. Malm, "Social Origins and Occupational Career Patterns," *Industrial and Labor Relations Review* VII (January 1954), 247-261; Schuster, *op. cit.,* p. 44.

[8] See Herbert Hill, *Testimony on Failure of Federal Contract Compliance,* Ad. Hoc. Committee Hearings on Contract Compliance, House of Representatives, Washington, D.C., December 5, 1968. Also, Hill, "Twenty Years of State Fair Employment Practice Commissions," *Buffalo Law Review* XIV (Fall 1964).

[9] For additional data on the ILGWU see Herbert Hill, "The Racial Practices of Organized Labor: The Contemporary Record," in Julius Jacobson (ed.), *The Negro Worker and the American Labor Movement* (New York: Doubleday, Anchor Books, 1968); also *Testimony, Congressional Record–House,* January 31, 1963, pp. 1496-1499.

[10] For additional data see Herbert Hill, "No End of Pledges: Continuing Discrimination in the Construction Unions," *Commonweal,* March 15, 1968.

[11] According to *Negroes in Apprenticeship* (Washington: U.S. Department of Labor, Manpower Administration: Manpower/Automation Research Monograph No. 6 (1967), p. 7, Negro participation on Federally

supported construction projects was 2.2 percent. The report significantly notes that "the 1960 census showed only 2,191 Negro apprentices in all trades throughout the country. That figure was one more than had been recorded in the 1950 census."

[12] A summary of the Report of the 1961-62 Panel of Consultants on Vocational Education is contained in the 1968 *General Report of the Advisory Council on Vocational Education,* U.S. Government Printing Office, p. 4.

[13] *Ibid.,* p. 4.

[14] *Ibid.*

[15] *Ibid.,* p. 6.

[16] 1968 *General Report of the Advisory Council on Vocational Education,* Table 4, p. 14.

[17] *Ibid.*

[18] *Ibid.,* and Table 33, p. 33.

[19] *Ibid.,* at Table 4, p. 14, and at p. 32. Other "distributive" occupations were real estate and management.

[20] *Ibid.,* at p. 110.

[21] *Ibid.,* at p. 110.

[22] 1969 *Manpower Report of the President,* p. 68.

[23] The U.S. Government through the Office of Economic Opportunity has also funded another series of so-called "training programs" mainly in ghetto areas. These are custodial operations for young persons below the age of twenty-one. Although a large number of black youth who urgently require genuine job-related training are enrolled, these programs contain no training component. Participants are engaged in low-paid work on municipal and county projects such as clearing vacant lots, weeding public parks, sweeping thoroughfares and in at least one instance working on a small poultry farm. At best they are a form of temporary subsistence to those who will remain in a permanent condition of poverty. At worst, they are a hoax as they promise jobs in a regular labor market.

[24] 42 U.S.C.A. S2571-4, S2581-7, S2601-2, S2611-20.

[25] 42 U.S.C.A. S2582 (e).

[26] Garth Mangum, *MDTA: Foundation of Federal Manpower Policy* (Baltimore: Johns Hopkins University Press, 1968), p. 51.

[27] 1969 *Manpower Report of the President,* Table F-2, p. 238.

[28] *Ibid.,* in 1968 out of 140,000 enrollees, only 63,500, or less than half, found training-related jobs.

[29] *Ibid.,* at Table F-3, p. 239.

[30] 1966 *Report of the Secretary of Labor on Manpower Research and Training Under the MDTA,* p. 19.

[31] *Ibid.,* p. 55.

[32] *Ibid.,* p. 177. For later data, see "Percent Distribution of Persons Enrolled in MDTA Institutional Training Programs, by Major Occupational Category and Selected Occupational Group, Fiscal Years 1967 and 1968," (U.S. Department of Labor, Manpower Administration, Office of Manpower Management and Data Systems, January 31, 1969).

[33] Department of Labor, *Manpower Report of the President* (Washington, D.C.: U.S. Government Printing Office, April 1968), p. 205.

[34] For a critical analysis of the racial practices of the Bureau of Apprenticeship Training, see *NAACP Labor Manual,* 1968 edition, p. 89; also Herbert Hill, *The Negro Wage-Earner and Apprenticeship Training Programs,* publication of the Department of Labor, NAACP, 1960.

[35] 1966 *Report of the Secretary of Labor,* p. 183.

[36] Dr. Mangum stated, "It was largely this continued failure to enroll a satisfactory proportion of the disadvantaged which led to the transfer of OJT authority from BAT to BWTP in 1967."

[37] 1969 *Manpower Report of the President,* Table F-2, p. 238.

[38] *Ibid.*

[39] Mangum, *op. cit.,* p. 92.

[40] For information on black-controlled union hiring halls in the construction industry see Herbert Hill, "Black Protest and the Struggle for Union Democracy," *Issues in Industrial Society,* New York State School of Industrial and Labor Relations, Cornell University, Ithaca, New York, Vol. 1, no. 1, (1969).

18
the 1968 housing act: new hope for negroes

WILLIAM R. MORRIS
The Housing and Urban Development Act, whose provisions Mr. Morris details in the following essay, has not had the beneficial effects he foresaw. Congress has not made sufficient appropriations to carry out the act, particularly the enforcement of open occupancy on a national level. There have been other obstacles: inflation has increased the cost of houses and raised the cost of borrowing money; red tape has delayed private and nonprofit builders from carrying through their projects. Even more important, nobody wants to build in the ghettos. Although buildings are dilapidated, the land is valuable, far more valuable than the same acreage would be in suburban areas. It is only profitable to build high-return apartment or office buildings on this land. The ordinary citizen or church group cannot put together enough land to protect a new building from the surrounding blighted areas unless there is a large-scale model city or urban renewal program. As a result, in most slum areas, bad housing has been torn down, but the new buildings do not provide low-cost housing for the former inhabitants.

The total number of low-cost housing units thus decreases; efforts to upgrade neighborhoods by enforcing building codes have often backfired. The landlords, who are either individuals who formerly lived in the area or large-scale holders (like insurance companies) waiting for the land values to inflate, find it cheaper either to raze all the houses or to walk away and leave them than to repair them. The rents would not cover the cost.

For reasons not entirely clear, low-cost, large-scale housing projects have been a dismal failure. Physically adequate when they open, such projects deteriorate rapidly both physically and socially. Experts feel this happens because the projects are not communities; they are collections of people, many in trouble, who do not know each other and who have no feeling of responsibility to one another. To think that people now living in housing projects would want to put their savings into owning part of them is foolish. It would take many well-trained professionals to convert a large-scale, disorganized housing project into a community. There is no provision for this, and even if there were, it is doubtful that there would be appropriations for such a purpose.

Blacks, who suffer most from poor housing, would improve their housing status by moving to the suburbs. There would undoubtedly be discrimination, and it would be necessary to organize through the NAACP, Urban League, and other groups to fight it under the open-occupancy provision of the housing act. Even if blacks were segregated by suburb, they would probably be better off. Land is cheaper; better housing could be bought there than for the same amount of

Reprinted from *The Crisis* 75, no. 9 (November 1968), pp. 313-317. Reproduced by permission of the author and publisher.

money spent in the city. Schools are newer; the environment, both physical and social, is healthier; jobs are increasing in the suburbs. But blacks have only recently moved into the cities and have become not only adjusted to but also fond of urban life. They resent having to fight discrimination and feel they might make great political sacrifices by moving out of the city. Fundamentally, the solutions to housing problems are tied up with the future of the cities, and until Americans as a people make firm decisions on where they want to live, housing programs will be erratic and unsatisfactory.

Mr. Morris is director of the housing program for the National Association for the Advancement of Colored People.

Hailed by President Johnson as "the most far-reaching and far-sighted housing legislation ever enacted," the Housing and Urban Development Act of 1968 envisions 26 million new or rehabilitated housing units over the next ten years, with 6,000,000 going to low-income families. Its aim is to rid the nation of all substandard housing. The first instalment of this three-year $5.3 billion package would enable 500,000 families to buy housing and provide another 700,000 new units of rental housing for low- and moderate-income families.

This new law, signed by the President on August 1, is highly significant in light of the Civil Rights Act of 1968 with its Title VIII fair-housing provision and the Supreme Court's ruling barring all discrimination in the sale and rental of housing. Thus a three-pronged attack upon bad housing, segregated housing and run-down neighborhoods is now possible—a development few considered attainable as recently as last year. It becomes more important than ever that all of our resources be mobilized to make these laws work for those in greatest need.

Reflective of the present mood of the 90th Congress is the slashing cut it made in the appropriation for the Department of Housing and Urban Development in September. For enforcement of the open-occupancy provision of the 1968 law, the Administration had requested $11.1 million to cover, primarily, employment of 850 enforcement personnel. Congress denied any funds for this purpose, prompting Secretary Robert C. Weaver to declare: "We simply cannot implement the fair housing law without more personnel. . . . Without manpower, the fair housing legislation is meaningless."

Funds for other aspects of the housing program were drastically reduced. For the Model Cities program Congress approved only $625 million, a little more than half the $1 billion requested. Similarly, funding for urban renewal was slashed from $1.4 billion to $750 million and for the rent supplement program from $65 million to $30 million.

These programs are all of prime importance to Negroes. The denial of funds for enforcement of fair-housing legislation and the abridgement of money for other housing programs provide a clear lesson for the American people, that is, the need to keep the pressure on Congress to see that it remains responsive to the needs of the people. This is the same Congress that earlier this year passed the fair-housing legislation and the Housing and Urban Development Act. The laws remain on the books, but to be implemented they have to be adequately funded.

The massive array of Federal housing programs contains revolutionary benefits for Negro Americans of low and moderate income. It could provide an improved quality of life for millions. Breathtaking in its scope, the bill begins with a recognition by the Congress that the national housing goals have not been fully realized for many lower-income families. It declared that the highest priority and emphasis should be given to meeting the urgent housing needs of these neglected families.

The year 1968 may well pinpoint in our history that white America began in earnest to eradicate the remaining vestiges of a dual racial society. Faced with mounting world criticism and domestic turmoil, the United States can and must move forward with affirmative action to implement the new laws and programs that are now available.

Vast social and economic returns to

black Americans can result from the 1968 Housing Act. The elimination of slums and blight, the development of a rewarding environment in communities and the relief of racial tensions are but a few of the many important benefits.

Statistics point up the pressing demand for improving the quality and quantity of housing in this country. Less than 1,000,000 dwelling units have been produced for low- and moderate-income families. At least 6,000,000 occupied units are currently substandard and unfit for continued use. Another 6,000,000 are classified as deteriorated. This represents almost one-fifth of our existing national housing supply. In 1967 the median sale price of new homes was $22,900 and only 11 per cent were sold for less than $15,000. Most new unsubsidized housing is beyond the reach of the one-fourth of the population with annual incomes of $4,000 to $7,000. The harshest impact obviously falls upon Negro families not only in urban ghettos but also in by-passed rural communities.

For Negroes the new law means that homeownership can now become a reality instead of a dream for nearly 500,000 families. It means that decent rental housing at greatly reduced rents can be provided for up to 700,000 families over the next three years. Rural families will benefit from improved housing; cities will be helped to rebuild ghetto areas; private enterprise and nonprofit groups will be used more extensively to combat slums and arrest urban blight.

Negroes can reap far greater benefits from the new program than any other disadvantaged group. Past practices, based upon white racism, which restricted Negroes to segregated areas with the worst housing, practically assure black communities of needed improvement. If the economic gap between white income and Negro income continues to widen, a greater percentage of Negroes will come under maximum-income limitations for subsidized programs.

New opportunities for training and jobs are required to be made available for residents in areas where housing is provided. The law also requires that contracts for work be awarded to business concerns residing in the areas of the covered new housing.

The poor and elderly will be assisted by a new provision that makes grants of up to $5,000 available to homeowners whose homes are taken by Federally assisted programs. This grant, when added to the price paid for homes being acquired will enable owners to secure a replacement home at today's cost. Rehabilitation grants of $1,500 have been upped to $3,000 and can now be obtained by low-income families outside urban renewal areas.

A key homeownership program known as Section 235 will enable families earning from $3,000 to $7,080 to buy homes for as little as $200 down and monthly payments equal to 20 per cent of monthly income. The government would pay all mortgage cost beyond 1 per cent—which includes taxes and fire insurance. Families can purchase homes up to $15,000 ($20,000 in high-cost areas). A family earning $3,600 could pay as little as $60 monthly for a $12,000 house.

Section 236, the new rental program, works much the same except that tenants pay 25 per cent of their income for rent. This program is expected to replace the Section 221 (d) (3) program within the next two years. The government subsidizes all but 1 per cent of mortgage charges. Mortgages may run for 40 years under the homeownership and rental programs, neither of which require community Workable Programs.

Home-improvement-loan limits are increased to $5,000 and seven years. Poor families can better afford major repairs to upgrade their housing.

A new credit-assistance program known as Section 237 provides credit and family counseling to help families with special problems qualify for homeownership. FHA will contract with local agencies and organizations to provide counseling. Negro groups can qualify for counseling buyers using this program.

Nonprofit sponsorship of sales and rental housing is given a boost with interest-free loans and technical assistance to groups needing help. Civic groups, churches, lodges and clubs will be encouraged to participate in local efforts to provide more housing.

New provisions are made by FHA to insure loans on homes in older, declining neighborhoods.

Section 221 (d) (3) housing may be converted from rentals to cooperative or condominium ownership.

In low-rent public housing rules are relaxed to permit tenants to purchase such units. New grants are made available to local authorities for tenant and social services. High-rise construction is now prohibited for families with children unless there is no alternative.

A new neighborhood redevelopment program permits a speed-up in urban renewal projects. Also, a majority of residential housing in renewal areas must be for lower- and moderate-income families.

For rural families the Farmers Home Administration may make loans with interest subsidies as low as 1 per cent to provide rental and cooperative housing. Grants to nonprofit groups can be made to assist self-help housing efforts.

A new life insurance program promises help to homeowners and business in riot-threatened areas.

Many other provisions contained in the bill are too numerous to identify in this article. Model Cities, urban renewal, increased mortgage limits for some FHA programs, and liberalized benefits are other programs of significant interest. It must also be noted that programs requiring the appropriation of funds must await Congressional action. All other authorizations are being placed into operation immediately.

It is no simple task to summarize adequately all of the benefits that the Act provides. Housing specialists admit they are not yet aware of all the implications of its clauses. The 300 pages of new and expanded existing programs contain benefits for families across the economic spectrum ranging from the low-income to the building of new communities and second homes for vacation use. Major emphasis is placed upon the production of 600,000 housing units per year over the next decade for low- and moderate-income families. A large share of this additional housing will be available to Negro families in urban and rural areas.

Because of its complexities there must first be launched widespread public education programs so that more elements of society will become familiar with the opportunities the law provides. Civil rights, social work, church and other groups will want to know how they can become active participants in using the nonprofit sponsor programs to build and rehabilitate sales and rental housing. Individuals seeking to purchase or rent housing need to be made aware of what the new programs offer, the eligibility requirements, and where and how to secure assistance. Lending institutions, builders, and tradesmen must also do their homework to become familiar with the changes and expansion in programs if their resources are to be more effectively utilized.

Where do we go from here and how do we get started? Meaningful economic benefits to Negroes themselves should receive top priority in any plans developed. The law specifies that area residents and area business be utilized to the maximum extent feasible. Large pools of trained specialists will be required in the planning and processing stage of development; contractors and sub-contractors will find vast new opportunities for participation; and last, but far from least, is the need that will be generated for trained management and maintenance specialists.

As of now it is recognized that technicians with these skills are in critical short supply. Educational institutions, government agencies, industry, and organizations such as the NAACP will need to launch training programs geared toward the large-scale production of housing. Technological and mangerial training opportunities must be made available to ghetto area residents. New careers in fields that inspire dignity, motivation, and higher levels of income will result from properly directed efforts.

It goes without saying that community organizations must be given greater support and recognition if they are to be an effective force in the decision-making process. Where is housing to be built? What kind of housing do we want in our neighborhood? Priorities, planning, and a host of other considerations will be placed before responsible groups that actually represent neighborhood residents. Negro organizations should move promptly to sponsor public education programs on the 1968 Housing Act. Officials from the Department of Housing and Urban Development, the Federal Housing Administration and the Farmers Home Administration should be called upon to address such meetings. New literature explaining the programs and how to use them must be made available for widespread distribution. Local mortgage firms, lending institutions, and real estate brokers are excellent sources that should be utilized by local groups seeking to understand the new law.

We cannot overlook the role of national organizations and their local affiliates. Informed leaders must be encouraged to re-examine their role and to undertake the sponsorship of sale and rental housing. They may contract with FHA to provide counseling and social services to lower-income families so that they may more easily qualify for all of the benefits that the law provides. Interest-free loans, training programs, and technical assistance are available to encourage locally oriented groups to help fill the need for better housing.

If we take an overall look at the Act and combine the legal tools contained in the fair-housing title, housing can be made available to Negro families in all areas of a community. Caution must be exercised to insure that the preservation of segregated living will not result. "Separate but equal" housing is a totally unacceptable approach and must be vigorously opposed. Whenever developments are located in already segregated areas there must be simultaneous activity to provide alternatives outside of the ghetto. Negroes must have the clear choice of selecting a place to live throughout the city and its suburban noose.

Our goal must continue to be the realization of a "single society"—a society based upon integrated living experiences—a society that will in all respects recognize and accept the concepts of equality. We now have the necessary legislative tools, the technical and financial resources, and the obvious need to do the job that cries to be done. Let us now get on with the business of accomplishment.

19
maximum feasible participation: the origins, implications and present status

LILLIAN B. RUBIN

If blacks and other racial minorities are confined to the cities and systematically excluded from the economic system, as the two previous readings try to describe, the result is poverty. It would seem that the simplest way to combat poverty is to provide jobs in the private economy or, if these are not available, to provide public jobs.

Instead, the assumption was made that minorities were either too uneducated, too un-trained in the techniques of modern industry, or too disorganized to hold jobs. They needed special training programs and special education and health programs to combat the effects of past poverty. By and large, the programs have not been well-enough funded to reach many peo-ple, nor have they been continued long enough to make a strong impact on the poorest, least-educated people. One aspect of these programs—maximum feasible participation of the poor in shaping and running poverty programs—has had the wholly unintended effect of training a community-leadership class. If the poverty programs have done little to help the hard-core poor, they have provided respectable, well-paid jobs for the upwardly mobile lower middle class, an unintended and probably unwanted consequence. It remains to be seen whether this new group will become the nucleus of political leadership in the future or whether they will continue their own movement upward into the middle class, abandoning the poor as other leaders have in the past.

Lillian Rubin is a staff member of the Department of Psychiatry at Cowell Hospital at the University of California, Berkeley. In her article, she examines the doctrine of maximum feasible participation and its results.

Recognizing the corrosive effects of poverty, men in all times have sought to assess the causes, fix the blame, and mitigate

First published as "Evaluating the War on Poverty," *The Annals of the American Academy of Political and Social Science* 385 (September 1969), pp. 14-29. Reproduced by permission of the author and publisher.

the consequences. The Economic Opportunity Act of 1964 (EOA) is part of recent American attempts to deal with this age-old problem. Since the passage of the act, the section that calls for the development of Community Action Programs (CAP's) and requires that these pro-grams be "developed, conducted, and adminis-tered with the maximum feasible participation of residents of the areas and members of the groups served"[1] has burst upon the public consciousness. Right-wing critics both in and out of Congress have branded community action programs as nothing less than a "blueprint for revolution." Mayors across the nation charged the federal government with financing an attack on city hall and undermining local influence and authority. Welfare agencies, responding to a threat to their jurisdiction and claim to professional expertise, simply asserted that involving the poor is not feasible. In city after city, attempts to implement community action programs met with a struggle over both the meaning of the clause and the extent and character of "participation" by the poor.

Despite the tumult and the shouting, no one seemed to know the origins, the legislative history, or the intent of the "maximum feasible participation" clause. What streams of thought were then current in American life that would have suggested such an approach? Was it the result of a changed view of the poor and their capabilities? Was there an awareness of the revolutionary implications to both the welfare and the political establishments in local communities, and ultimately to the nation as a whole? How was the notion of participation by the poor interpreted and implemented? These are some of the questions that guided this inquiry.

"MAXIMUM FEASIBLE PARTICIPATION"
The Origins

From the President's "Message on Poverty" on March 16, 1964, wherein he co.nmended the bill to the Congress, to its passage five months later, there was no public discussion of the participation clause. Although a great deal of debate centered on the general provisions of Title II, congressional committee hearings reveal that, with the exception of the statement by then Attorney General Robert F. Kennedy,[2] there is no mention of the clause by any other government official in several thousand pages of testimony. Even after Kennedy's testimony stressing the importance of participation in treating a community's ailments, not one congressman questioned his meaning or intent. The congressional debates are equally devoid of discussion about "maximum feasible participation."

In retrospect, it is indeed curious that this most controversial aspect of the bill was so little heeded. In the years to follow congressional hearings and debate on EOA were preoccupied largely with the controversy that had erupted over the mandate that the poor must participate in Community Action Programs.

Immediately after his declaration of war on poverty, President Johnson asked Sargent Shriver to direct a task force to draft the legislation to be submitted to Congress. Many people gathered in the little antipoverty office, representing interests both in and out of government—representatives of the Departments of Health, Education, and Welfare, Defense, Labor, Agriculture, and Commerce; of the President's Committee on Juvenile Delinquency and Youth Crime; and legal, community relations, poverty, and welfare experts.[3] Among them there is little consensus about the origins of the command that the poor must participate in CAP.

The clause . . . relating to participation of the poor was inserted with virtually no discussion in the task force and none at all on Capitol Hill. . . . I cannot say that I was aware of the implications of the clause. It just seemed to me like an idea that nobody could quarrel with.[4]

Its language was the result of countless hours of discussion among a dozen or so key people.[5]

It emerged from an evening drafting session which included Daniel P. Moynihan . . . , Harold Horowitz . . . , John Steadman . . . , and myself. None of us is quite sure who first thought of the phrase.[6] *The phrase "maximum feasible participation" entered into our discussions largely at the insistence of Dick Boone. . . . At one point after he had used it several times, I said, "You've used that phrase four or five times now." "Yes, I know," he replied. "How many more times do I have to use it before it becomes part of the program?" "Oh, a couple of times more," I told him. So he did, and it did become part of the program.*[7]

OEO officials even disagree on what would seem to be matters of fact.

Our General Counsel assures me that, although there is a positive legislative history of the phrase and its related intentions, *the section of the Act was adopted in its present form within the House and Senate Labor Committees while in Executive Session. No written record of their session was kept [emphasis added].*[8]

There is no explicit legislative history covering this particular phrase *in the Economic Opportunity Act. The legislation as introduced in 1964 contained this phrase. It was never challenged. Its full meaning and implementation were developed following the enactment and continues to be defined and implemented to this date [emphasis added].*[9]

Clearly, it is neither of great interest nor of great importance to know who thought of the words "maximum feasible participation" in that particular sequence. The story concerns us only insofar as it illustrates the degree of confusion and obscurity that surrounds the formulation and the meaning of the concept.

Perhaps it is true, as one observer suggests, that "the idea was in the air." If so, we can be sure that certain social forces put it there.

The History of an Idea

Although, obviously, the idea of "maximum feasible participation" had a social history before it became a legal reality, information is difficult or impossible to get. This analysis, therefore, is necessarily speculative.

By 1964 many ideas about how to combat poverty and its consequences had been tested. As early as the 1930's the area projects of Chicago, whose watchwords were self-help, local autonomy, and local responsibility, were mobilizing community resources to combat juvenile delinquency. Yet, one idea stands out as dominant in its influence—the concept of "community development," which, under the sponsorship of the United States government in the early 1950's, had been translated into successful action programs abroad.

The realignment of forces after World War II, the onset of the Cold War, and the restive demands of colonial nations for freedom and self-expression turned the attention of American foreign policy planners overseas. In

his inaugural address of 1949, President Truman proposed the Point Four Program to sponsor community development programs in underdeveloped nations throughout the world. These programs rested on the canons that indigenous leadership and resources could be discovered and developed in each community, and that such leaders would be able to articulate the needs, desires, and aspirations of the community.

Community organization specialists and others concerned with these problems have long found these ideas intriguing. The theme of the Seventh International Conference of Social Work in 1954 was self-help in a community action context. The American report to that Conference showed great sensitivity to the same questions which are now being debated with such heat.[10] How can indigenous leadership and resources be discovered and developed? How can external leadership and resources contribute to the development of self-help programs? How can people participate significantly in the development and execution of such programs? Nevertheless, the report noted, there were few such domestic programs, none with government sponsorship. Subsequent conferences continued to articulate interest in community development and to discuss the problems and feasibility "of involving the active participation of the people themselves at the local level."[11]

The lessons of our foreign-aid programs in Africa and Asia were not lost on the American Negro. The new African nations, freed from their colonial bonds, turned energetically to solving community problems, demonstrating their latent capabilities and resources. Their visibility on the world scene was high; they soon became the model for the American civil rights movement founded on the same demands of antipaternalism and individual dignity—on the insistence that a person has the right to help decide his own fate. Long before the passage of the antipoverty act, local groups in many places were operating their own preschool, tutoring, adult education, and retraining programs. It was precisely because the civil rights movement had already built organizations and mobilized community resources that "maximum feasible participation" was translated so quickly from abstraction to reality.[12] When the law was passed, the black leaders of the ghettos were ready to participate; indeed, they threw the full weight of their organized power into the demand that they be permitted to do so fully.

With the election of the late President Kennedy, Moynihan writes, American commitments to the developing nations

attained an extraordinary personification in the Peace Corps volunteer. . . . [T] he program was and is a great popular success, and the idea of doing something of the sort through Community Action Programs with the "underdeveloped peoples of the United States" came as a direct and obvious carry-over.[13]

Providing the added impulse was the growing recognition among many thoughtful observers that just as the paternalism of colonial powers had been a disabling factor in the development of colonial people, so the paternalism of existing welfare programs enfeebled and sapped the strength of the poor. For those who shared this view, participation was thought of as sociotherapy, a notion that says: Involve a man in succesful and significant social actions, give him a hand in decisions and institutions that affect his life, and he will soon develop psychological and social competence that will enable him to climb out of poverty.

This, then, is the development background of the concept that community action is a vehicle for community development. The civil rights movement and its demands, and the disillusion with the existing welfare programs in eliminating the poverty syndrome, furnished the thrust for translating the idea into action.

Some Precursors of CAP

The Chicago Experiments. The 1930's saw some of the earliest successful efforts in community action organization. Emphasizing the need for indigenous leadership, the Chicago Area Project of Clifford Shaw and his associates helped neighborhoods to organize into effective working units to combat delinquency. At the same time, Saul Alinsky helped to organize Chicago's Back of the Yards Neighborhood Council, which turned the stockyards area into one of the most desirable working-class neighborhoods in Chicago. Alinsky has since established the Industrial Areas Foundation, a non-profit institution dedicated to community development and community action. One of its most striking successes is The Woodlawn Organization (TWO) founded in 1960—a large, broadly representative organization in the black ghetto to the south of the University of Chicago campus. Unlike other community organizing efforts, Alinsky rejects the search for consensus and the alliance with the white liberals, seeking instead to organize ghetto residents into an effective power bloc.[14] In training community leaders to use the politics of conflict and confrontation, the task, he says, is "to rub raw the sores of discontent"—a job he does with obvious relish. With the advent of the civil rights movement and the ferment in urban black communities, his methods have gained national attention, and his services have been widely sought.

Although the debate and controversy over Alinsky and his methods is heated, and consensus about his effectiveness is lacking, there is little argument about his impact on those whose job it is to deal with the problems of poverty. The very existence of the controversy gives testimony to that. Abrasive, forceful, impolite, and irreverent, he has forced the professionals to continue to re-evaluate their doctrines and their dogma. Moynihan goes so far as to lump the rest of the programs to be discussed below under the rubric "The Alinsky Concept."[15]

The Ford Foundation. Throughout the 1950's, the Ford Foundation was showing increasing concern for the problems of American cities. Beginning in 1960, the Foundation instituted the Great Cities School Improvement Program in ten cities. Grants totalling $3.2 million were made for a series of educational experiments focused on the needs of culturally disadvantaged children. These exploratory programs led the Foundation to a conviction that a more coordinated attack on all aspects of deprivation was necessary. By late 1961, the Community Development Program (more commonly known as the Gray Areas Projects) was born with a three-year $2-million grant to the city of Oakland to mount an integrated effort to ameliorate slum conditions and to bring slum residents into the mainstream of American life. Soon after, New Haven, Boston, Philadelphia, and North Carolina received grants.

Two articles of faith of the Foundation's philosophy were that effective community action needed participation of the groups involved and that indigenous leadership was necessary to provide communication between the planners and the community. Both were considered essential to ensure that projects met the felt needs of the community, and to faciliate the continuity of any programs undertaken. The manner in which affected groups would participate, however, was never clarified; each program developed its own definitions locally. Sometimes participation meant that some members of the target area sat on the agency's policy board; more often, it meant that a few indigenous leaders were hired by the community organization agency.

New Haven was soon displayed as the model of how an antipoverty program can work. The city organized Community Progress, Inc., a non-profit corporation with a small board, which was highly ballyhooed as broadly representative of the community. Three of its members were to be appointed by the Mayor, and one each by the Redevelopment Agency, the Board of Education, the Community Council, the United Fund, the Citizens' Action Commission, and Yale University—a board representative of everyone but the residents of the target areas.

In Philadelphia, the Council for Community Advancement, set up by the Ford grant, had scarcely begun organizing when it was met with a wave of protest from black militants demanding recognition. The planning staff, wrote its executive director some time later, "had to learn to plan *with* the community and not *for* the community."[16] Therefore, its prospectus recommended the expansion of a center in North Philadelphia (that city's black ghetto) so that "if the citizenry should want to 'Go Fight City Hall,' *they should have an effective mechanism to speak for them at a local level* [emphasis added]."[17] In telling this story, Charles Silberman comments with some acerbity: "The notion that the citizens conceivably

might want to speak for themselves obviously never occurred to the academicians, government officials, and civic leaders who drew up the document."[18]

PRESIDENT'S COMMITTEE ON JUVENILE DELINQUENCY AND YOUTH CRIME.

Finally, with the appointment of the President's Committee on Juvenile Delinquency and Youth Crime on May 11, 1961, the late President Kennedy took a major step toward moving the federal government into domestic community development and action programs. The supporting legislation, known as the Juvenile Delinquency and Youth Offenses Control Act of 1961, authorized $10 million for each of three fiscal years through June 30, 1964, for demonstration and training projects in the most effective ways of using total resources to combat juvenile delinquency in local communities. Grants were made to sixteen cities to develop delinquency prevention programs and to carry them out within limited target areas.

Leonard Cottrell, chairman of the Grant Review Panel of the Committee, had long been concerned with the issue of "competence." By 1961 his thinking had enlarged to encompass the concept of "community competence." Accordingly, he laid great stress on programs that encouraged the development of competence—on the "necessity for upgrading the capabilities of the inarticulate and disadvantaged to become more articulate and more capable of participating effectively in the setting of goals and implementing those goals in the life of the community."[19]

The most widely heralded and the most controversial of these programs were Harlem Youth Opportunities Unlimited (HARYOU) and Mobilization for Youth (MFY),[20] both in New York City. Describing the activities and dimensions of HARYOU to a congressional committee, Robert Kennedy said:

In central Harlem, youth of the area were involved throughout the development of the program. This project will employ, to work with other people, 2,000 young people who live in central Harlem. It will employ mothers, who are receiving welfare payments, as teachers and assistants in preschool nurseries. Youth and adults who live in Harlem will sit on the five neighborhood governing boards.[21]

MFY also spurned the traditional rehabilitation and support programs. Its goal: to uproot poverty by engaging the total local community in self-help, assisting residents to teach and to help one another instead of relying on professional social workers. Although the agency itself took no position, MFY workers counseled and advised on issues of concern to the area, stimulating community awareness of available remedies. Lawyers and community action workers helped to organize a rent strike; supported the civil rights boycott of the New York City schools in February 1964; and acted to protect citizens from capricious police and welfare decisions. Militant social action was to be the vehicle through which the community would learn to help itself—a policy that soon put the organization into direct conflict with the political and welfare establishments of the city who moved quickly to decimate it.

Responding to a question about the relationship of these ideas and programs to the participation clause in the antipoverty act, Mr. Cottrell writes:

When the Economic Opportunities Act was formulated, the section on Community Development was formulated by people who worked on the President's Committee staff, and who carried some of my ideas into the wording of the Act.

Most observers agree.[22]

The Intent

From the preceding analysis, it is clear that by the time the task force on poverty began to work, several blueprints for action were in existence. Furthermore, many of the people who had drawn those blueprints were now called upon to bring their experience to bear on the broader problems of poverty. What their intentions were when they called for "maximum feasible participation" is still unsettled; indeed, it probably will remain so forever.

Daniel Moynihan and Nathan Glazer

have variously described CAP as "an effort to change the poor who are produced by the system,"[23] and "the art of using government funds for . . . controlled revolution."[24] There is some truth in both views. Some of the drafters may have understood and advocated its revolutionary implications; most would probably agree with the observer who writes: "None of us in the CAP program really predicted that the concept would become such a controversial issue."[25] Had their intention been to foment "controlled revolution," surely the controversy would have been foreseeable.

In fact, it is this very lack of foresight about the implications of "maximum feasible participation"—the apparent inability to foretell the nature of the response—that is so puzzling. By 1964, the profound relationship between poverty and race was widely recognized and understood. The civil rights movement had developed organization and leadership in urban ghettos; an ethos of rising expectations and militant demands had replaced the passivity of earlier times. Yet, the men who framed the act seem to have missed the point.

One can only speculate that despite their disaffection with the welfare system, despite their sympathetic concern for civil rights, these men were themselves bound by the power of American preconceptions. Still powerful are notions that the poor are really lazy, irresponsible, apathetic, satisfied with their lot; that the Negro—that special case of poverty—is poor because black men know less, need less, are less. A lifetime spent in an atmosphere dominated by racism and the casework emphasis of modern rehabilitation philosophy infects even the most sophisticated and sympathetic. It is difficult indeed to penetrate the stereotype fully—to envision and comprehend a poor man grasping abstract concepts of participation, a black man asserting his manhood. The comments of one task force member are illustrative.

I had never really conceived that it [participation] would mean control by the poor of the community action organization itself. . . . I expected that the poor would be represented on the community action organization but that such representation would be some-

*thing in the order of 15 to 25% of the board.
. . . Moreover, I don't think it ever occurred
to me, or to many others, that the representatives of the poor must necessarily be poor
themselves.*[26]

Many men with diverse backgrounds and
commitments came together to draft the anti-
poverty bill. There were, no doubt, some shared
understandings, orientations, and experiences,
and a common goal—to alleviate the distress of
poverty. One can reasonably suggest that they
were responding to the demands of the civil
rights movement and to their own convictions
about the failure of welfare colonialism. But
what, if anything, they as a body actually intended when they insisted on participation by
the poor remains unclear.

The Problem of Definition
and Implementation
Almost immediately after the passage of
the act, the problem of defining participation
emerged. With no legislative history to serve as
a guide, the debate rose quickly to a deafening
roar. Did participation mean that the poor people would work in the programs, or that they
would share the policy-making role? Some
opted for the former as the central meaning of
participation; others for the latter. Those who
spoke for the poor wanted both. Four years
later, after several congressional attempts at
clarification, the debate continues.

Hiring the Poor to Work With the Poor.
Most clearly articulated by Frank Riessman
and his associates,[27] the idea of employing the
poor in subprofessional jobs calls for aggressive
recruitment of those whose main qualification
is that they are part of the "culture of poverty"
—people who might serve their communities
in a variety of ways, as mental-health aides,
mothers' aides, recreation aides, research aides,
parent-education aides, and many more.
The essential value of the indigenous
nonprofessional is his capability for acting as
a bridge between the middle-class professional
and his client. "This ability . . . is not based on
things they have been taught, but on what they
are."[28] Ideally, the nonprofessional aide is able
to interpret community life and values to the

professionals, helping them to establish better
rapport with their clientele, and to serve as
interpreter of the professionals to the community. By communicating the needs and values
of the community to the agency, it is hoped
that he will be instrumental in reshaping agency
programs, procedures, and values.
The logic of this argument would not
seem to lend itself readily to controversy. Yet,
professionals in welfare agencies see a threat
to their professionalism in these concepts and
have offered stubborn resistance. An OEO-
sponsored program evaluation revealed in 1966
that "while the personal relationships between
the professionals and their aides was reported
as good, there is no evidence of significant
change in policies or values of the professionals
or of the institutions employing them."[29] Complicating the picture is the fact, pointed out by
Riessman, that one of the greatest problems of
the nonprofessional is "role ambiguity or lack
of role identity: he doesn't know who he is or
who he is becoming. . . . He is a highly marginal person."[30] Thus, although the evidence is
not conclusive and the reasons are not clearly
understood, the failure of the subprofessionals
to constitute a force for change seems to be
related both to the attitude of their professional superiors and to the fact that these nonprofessional workers often are distant from
and do not identify with the troubled members of the poor community whom they must
represent.
The program has been only slightly more
successful in providing employment opportunities. By the end of fiscal 1967 only 41,000
poor people were working in CAP programs[31]
—a pitifully small number when measured
against the millions of unemployed and underemployed poor.[32]
Current information about the socio-
demographic characteristics of these nonprofessional workers is unavailable from OEO;[33]
but the 1966 study already cited showed that
while the total employed labor force in nine
cities sampled was 89 percent white, nonprofessional aides were 79 percent black. Further
findings indicate that the majority of the nonprofessional aides were not hard-core poor;
only 47 percent were actually unemployed at
the time of accepting a job with CAP. Except

for race, they were not significantly different from the bulk of the employed work force.[34] These data suggest that there is a considerable amount of "creaming"—selection of those who are the most acceptable and offer the most likelihood of success. We observe here one of the universal attributes of the welfare bureaucracy—the tendency to concentrate efforts on those who are most likely to assure the institution a favorable image and an impressive record. Harold Wilensky notes this principle in operation:

> There are strong resistances built into the antipoverty agencies and programs themselves. Just as vocational training until 1963 reached only the already literate, the already work-oriented youngster, so the Job Corps program avoids seriously delinquent or disturbed youth. . . . Especially in new programs and in areas of controversy, welfare administrators, afraid of recalcitrant clientele and anxious to minimize risk of failure, concentrate on salvaging the almost saved.[35]

Yet, if the program is to be more than a vehicle that facilitates the upward movement of those already most mobile, we must face these and other tough questions. How do we recruit more effectively to attract the indigent unemployed? What shall be the selection process? Clearly, ordinary tests and measures that aid personnel selections are inadequate to a population with low educational levels and verbal skills. What training procedures can we devise to ensure that we tap the capabilities of the worker adequately? What placement procedures must we use to assure that workers and jobs are matched for compatibility with capabilities and temperament? Do the jobs in community action programs offer "new careers," providing opportunity for learning and holding out the promise of advancement? Or, are they both the beginning and the end of the line?[36] As we confront these questions and attempt their solution, we must be prepared to risk an initial reduction in efficiency, increased costs, and the political pressures of the attendant unfavorable publicity.

Planning and Policy-making. The notion that the poor should be actively and effectively involved in policy-making led to even more serious controversy and raised critical questions. How many poor people must serve on a Community Action Agency (CAA) board to guarantee effective representation? How shall they be selected? Who shall select them? The controversy quickly organized around "how many." At stake was a fundamental problem: Is it possible for the poor—inarticulate, uneducated, suffering from feelings of low esteem, unaccustomed to the rules and procedures of organization—to make an effective contribution on councils heavily weighted with representatives of powerful organizational interests?

For two years OEO's post hoc interpretations offered little clarity. Sargent Shriver made public statements insisting that flexibility was the keystone of CAP programs, that each community would decide how many poor people on the board were "feasible." Privately, however, he sent memoranda to OEO regional directors proposing that representatives of the poor should number approximately one-third of the CAP governing body.

In cities like San Francisco, Los Angeles, Rochester, and Syracuse the issue was settled only after long, bitter, and costly struggles. Most often the poor neighborhoods had to settle for one-third. In San Francisco, however, the target areas won a majority of the seats on the Economic Opportunity Council, the city-wide CAA, as well as a majority on the area boards. But the victory has carried a price. The boards have been rent by seemingly endless quarrels, born, in part, from a basic lack of understanding of the difference between policy-making and administrative functions and from a fear that to give up any part of decision-making is to let slip the reins of control. Consequently, critics insist that until poor people gain the requisite skills and experience, experts must run the programs. But if we adopt that stance, how will the poor ever acquire the experience? Perhaps we must endure this period of transition while poor communities develop leadership and create community resources with which to help themselves.

The issue in the numbers game was clear —power. With billions of dollars to be spent, he who controls the purse strings may also control the votes, and will surely influence the programs—a serious threat to both the political establishment and the welfare bureaucracy. Experience with militant social action programs like MFY and HARYOU had already frightened these groups who have so much to lose from an organization of the poor dedicated to social and institutional change. If the representation mandate were implemented with vigor and poor people controlled the policy councils, they would acquire experience in community affairs. There might emerge from such experience a political consciousness and political organizations not beholden to incumbent officeholders and party leaders—a new and coherent force in the cities. Out of the most elementary instincts of self-preservation, this is the last thing which incumbents wish to see in their jurisdictions.

Meanwhile, the strident charges and countercharges escalated. The Republicans feared (not entirely without justification) that CAP was a national Democratic party plot to replace its fading urban, ethnic political base with the organized, urban poor equally beholden to Democratic politicians. The Democrats, they charged, were making a political pork barrel of CAP. On the other hand, local Democratic officials, fearing a challenge to their control of city hall and the county courthouse, complained vociferously that CAP was disruptive of the urban status quo—that the federal government was financing an attack on city hall. All the critics agreed in their insistence that the poor were being used and duped by the political troublemakers. From whatever the source, and whatever the reason, the result seemed to be one vast, shrill cry demanding the end of CAP.

With the Economic Opportunity Amendments of 1966 Congress tried to end the arguments about the number of the poor to be included on CAA boards by stipulating that the poor must comprise at least one-third of the board membership. Still the wrangling continued. Finally, the 1967 amendments further specified the composition of a CAA board. It can have no more than fifty-one members—a minimum of one-third poverty area representatives; a maximum of one-third public officials or their appointed representatives; and the remainder representatives of business, industry, labor, welfare, education, or other major groups and interests in the community. Al-though this provision has often been interpreted ominously by participation advocates, in effect, Congress has simply articulated publicly the rule of thumb for CAA participation with which the OEO had been working privately. And by providing a maximum of one-third from the public sector and a minimum of one-third from the poor community, the law need have no effect on existing relations. For example, The San Francisco Economic Opportunity Council now has a fifty-one member board, twenty-six of whom are representatives of the five target areas in the city.

As this is being written, however, the Mayor appointed seventeen city officials to the board, including himself and three members of the city's Board of Supervisors—an action that brings questions about effective participation sharply to mind. Even on councils where they are not greatly outnumbered, will an alliance between public officials and the representatives of the other major community interests still the voices of the poor and block their will? Can poor people compete successfully against the organizational skills of politicians, businessmen, and bureaucrats?

The 1966 amendments also tried to deal with the problems and controversies that had, by then, developed around the selection of representatives of the poor.[37] The new law requires that these representatives are to be selected democratically by the residents in the poverty areas, that representatives of the poor must live in the geographic area which they represent, and that special emphasis is to be given to the participation of those who are poor. These provisions have helped to eliminate the spectacle of programs that technically meet the numerical requirements, but in which the representatives of the poor are, in Alinsky's apt phrase, "poverty specimens hand-picked by the prevailing political powers."[38]

The preoccupation with numbers and the process of selection, however, has diverted attention from equally important questions about the quality of representation. Not only must we ask how many representatives and how they will be chosen, but also to what extent they will be responsible to a constituency. Is the choice made from among those who have demonstrated some qualities of leadership and are, therefore, already somewhat removed from the mainstream of community problems? Once having been selected as representatives or leaders of the poor, how can co-optation into the established power structures be avoided? Given a taste of success, can a representative of the poor remain unseduced by the offerings of the world to which he has just been admitted?

In the final analysis, the pressure against CAP was too strong to be resisted. While Congress was clarifying and specifying the meaning of participation, it was at the same time earmarking ever-larger proportions of CAP funds to what are called in the trade "canned" programs—those, like Head Start, Follow Through, Upward Bound, Legal Services, and Comprehensive Health Services, which are initiated and controlled by Washington—and cutting back on the politically troublesome activities of the local agencies. Thus, in fiscal 1967, the OEO had $66 million less for versatile and flexible community action activities than in fiscal 1966.[39] And, although the 1967 amendments have eliminated congressional earmarking of funds, Congress carefully specified the kind of programs that would qualify for assistance and enumerated eight (all national in scope) that must take precedence in funding.[40] The guide for funding priorities distributed by national OEO to regional and local offices clearly reflects congressional sentiments. OEO officials advise that while the total CAP appropriation increased from $864 million in 1968 to $931 million in 1969, each year has seen a decrease in funds for versatile, locally initiated programs.[41]

Further circumscribing the creative potential of CAP, the 1967 amendments provide that no more than 15 percent of community action appropriations may be allocated to research and pilot programs, and that one-third of that amount must be devoted to a program to stem the rural-to-urban migration.

Finally, to the anguished cries of the Republican minority—their worst fears that CAP is a Democratic party plot to retain control of the urban areas about to be realized— the administration-backed Green Amendment was included in the 1967 EOA. This requires that community action agencies must become instrumentalities of state or local governments.

As of June 30, 1968, the private, non-profit agency can exist as the CAA only if it is so designated by the state or local government, or when appointed by the OEO director, in the event that the state or local government fails to establish a CAA. Representative Charles Goodell (R-NY) promptly dubbed it "the bosses and boll weevil amendment," charging that henceforth CAP's would be dominated by a northern city hall or a southern county courthouse. The sudden surge of support for CAP from local Democratic politicians who had earlier been hostile suggests that Mr. Goodell's fears may not be unfounded.

At this writing, however, it is still too early to determine the effect of the Green Amendment on CAP.[42] Much will depend on the political eomplexion and persuasion of the various local and state officials, and on what the nature of the struggle has been between the existing CAA and the politicians. Just as in the past, the picture will probably be mixed, and the range and freedom of local agencies will vary. In those communities where CAA's have established a strong constituency and can count on support, it is unlikely that local politicians will infringe on their jurisdictions.[43] On the other hand, where political hostilities are intense, placing the CAA's under the control of local officials may lead to their demise through a spinning off of programs at the local level, with different agencies picking up the various programs.

Regardless of which path local politicians may choose, the heat of the controversy has long since made OEO officials less than enthusiastic about this troublesome problem-child. And the very existence of the amendment may well be enough to make CAA's move ever more cautiously. In any case, the Republican victory in November may pose the greatest threat yet to CAP since it could portend some fundamental changes in the administration of antipoverty programs. A major objective of Republican critics has been to disassemble the OEO and to disperse its programs throughout the appropriate federal departments—a goal that may be more readily attainable with a sympathetic President. CAP could easily fail to survive such a reorganization in any viable form.

SUMMARY AND CONCLUSIONS

To summarize, this analysis argues that the idea of "maximum feasible participation" by the poor has its roots in the community development programs sponsored by the United States in underdeveloped nations; that the burgeoning, militant civil rights movement gave impetus to translating these conceptions to the domestic scene; and that there was disquietude with existing welfare policy and patterns of paternalism that debilitate rather than rehabilitate. Together these forces resulted in several precursors of CAP—demonstration projects emphasizing the need for citizen participation. The notions of participation that these programs were exploring were incorporated into the antipoverty act by much the same people who had designed the programs already in existence. This, then, is the confluence of ideas and forces in American life which suggested such an approach to the problem of poverty.

Although it is also argued that there was no unitary intention in the task force, it can be said with some certainty that many of its members were motivated by a concern about what Richard Boone calls

the increasing constrictions imposed by professionalism in social work and public education [and a] dehumanizing helping system which demanded that the individual adjust to community institutions rather than trying to change those institutions to meet the needs of the poor. It was a concern about a system of referral from nowhere to nowhere.[44]

While these considerations were not explicitly articulated in relation to a changed view of the poor and their capabilities, they did call the whole welfare system into question, and offered a program of community action as a substitute or a supplement. This suggests that these men believed that, given the tools and the chance, poor people would use them well —a judgment about the capabilities of the poor which, it turns out, seems to be well ahead of its time.[45]

Yet, the revolutionary implications of what they were proposing escaped the framers of the act. Richard Boone writes:

The full ramification of the idea dictating the involvement of the poor was probably not considered at the time. . . . Even now the implications seem staggering. The government was preparing to let those at the bottom of the society have a say in the administration of a major piece of antipoverty legislation designed to coordinate federal antipoverty efforts.[46]

It seems never to have occurred to them that the poor would take it so seriously. Considering the time—1964; considering the men—sophisticated, urbane intellectuals who were keenly attuned to the civil rights movement; considering the militancy of that movement—the extent to which ghetto communities in northern cities had already demonstrated a capacity for action; this is indeed anomalous. The answer, I suggest, lies in the preconceptions about poverty, race, and welfare that grip American thought and distort our vision.

Finally, the dimensions of the struggle over defining and implementing the participation clause are highlighted, the discussion focusing on the two major aspects—policy-making and jobs. While both threatened some already-existing interests, the most profound controversy settled around the policy-making component. Although their motives may have differed, welfare agencies and politicians made massive efforts to retain their doctrine, dogma, and power, while the leaders of the poor did, indeed, use federal funds to try to force institutional change.

In conclusion, I would suggest that the idea has had a profound impact on the society in general, and on communities of the poor in particular. Although fearful politicians may ultimately emasculate CAP, I must agree with Leonard Cottrell who says: "The seed has been planted, and the idea will not die out."[47]

Despite its limitations in practice, the concept of "new careers" for the poor has taken root; tens of thousands of people are now working in city and neighborhood organizations in self-respecting jobs in which one major asset is their background of poverty and their knowledge of their communities' problems. With the Scheuer-Nelson Amendment, Con-

gress gave further encouragement and legitimacy to the notion.

Most significant: for the first time, poor
people have been told by legislative mandate
that they are capable of taking a hand in their
affairs. They have been called upon to speak
in their own behalf, to assess their needs, and
to join in the design and implementation of
programs to meet those needs. The response
has been overwhelming at times. In communities all over America militant groups have
organized independently to allevaite their distress. Small victories are won—a tenants' council in San Francisco's Hunter Point forces
the Housing Authority to paint the buildings;
a rent strike in New York wins some rodent
control; another compels landlords to supply
more adequate heating; a coalition of organizations defeats a San Francisco urban renewal
plan that threatens home and community
without offering satisfactory alternatives. And
each victory generates confidence in self—a
necessary precondition to action—and confidence in the efficacy of organization to correct
the gnawing grievances that plague their lives.
Finally, four years after "maximum feasible

participation" was written into law, we witness
the Ocean Hill-Brownsville struggle in New
York City, where demands for local determination and control so terrified the city's educational bureaucracy; and we see the rise of black
militant groups like the Black Panthers, whose
goals include local autonomy and control of
all ghetto institutions including police functions.

As the struggle has grown, the dilemmas
inherent in notions about participation become
increasingly apparent. For the bureaucracy,
participation has often served to ensure that
its programs will function smoothly and meet
with minimal resistance. For the poor, however, who have few effective political resources,
participation is steadily being reinterpreted to
mean control. "Maximum feasible participation" has, indeed, captured the imagination of
the leaders of the poor with the force of an
idea whose time has come. It has helped to
validate and legitimate the aspirations of the
poor and the minorities in America for self-
determination. The problem is no longer
whether, nor even when, it should be implemented; rather, it is how.

NOTES

[1] 78 *Statues at Large,* vol. 508, sec. 202(a)

[2] U.S., Congress, House, Committee on Education and Labor, Subcommittee on the War on Poverty
Program, *Hearings on Economic Opportunity Act of 1964,* 88th Cong., 2d sess., 1964, Part I, March 17-20,
April 7-14; Part 2, April 15-21; Part 3, April 22-28 (Washington, D.C.: Government Printing Office, 1964),
pp. 301-339; U.S., Congress, Senate, Committee on Labor and Public Welfare, Select Committee on Poverty,
Hearings on Economic Opportunity Act of 1964, 88th Cong., 2nd sess., June 17, 18, 23, and 25, 1964 (Wash-
ington, D.C.: Government Printing Office, 1964), pp. 207-212.

[3] Interestingly enough, according to Moynihan, there was not one Negro "involved in any significant
way at any significant stage in planning the Economic Opportunity Act of 1964." See "The Professors and
the Poor," 46 *Commentary* (August 1968), p. 23.

[4] Personal communication, James L. Sundquist, December 14, 1966.

[5] Personal communication, Hyman Bookbinder, December 6, 1966.

[6] Personal communication, Frank Mankiewicz, January 9, 1967.

[7] Adam Yarmolinsky. "The Origin of Maximum Feasible Participation," *Social Science Forum* (Fall-
Winter 1966-1967), p. 19.

[8] Personal communication, Theodore M. Berry, December 9, 1966.

[9] Bookbinder, *loc. cit.*

[10] "Promoting Social Welfare Through Self-Help and Co-operation in the United States," United States
Committee Report on the Theme of the Seventh International Conference of Social Work, Toronto, Canada,
1954.

[11] "Rural and Urban Community Development," 2 *International Social Work* (April 1959), p. 15; and
"Mobilizing Resources for Social Needs," Statement by the Pre-Conference Working Party to the Ninth International Conference of Social Work, *ibid.,* pp. 1-9.

[12] John H. Wheeler, "Civil Rights Groups—Their Impact Upon the War on Poverty," 31 *Law and Contemporary Problems* (Winter 1966), pp. 152-158; and Richard W. Boone, "The Poor and the War on Poverty,"
mimeographed.

[13] Daniel P. Moynihan, "What is Community Action?," *The Public Interest* (Fall 1966), p. 6.

[14] In Rochester, the Alinsky organization (FIGHT) insisted that a white person must be sponsored by a black member of the organization before being permitted to join. See James Ridgeway, "Saul Alinksy in Smugtown," 152 *New Republic* (June 26, 1965), pp. 15-16; and Charles E. Silberman, *Crisis in Black and White* (New York: Vintage Books, 1964), pp. 308-355, for an uncritical but illuminating account of Alinsky's philosophy and organizing methods.

[15] Moynihan, "What is Community Action?," p. 5.

[16] *American Community Development: Preliminary Reports by Directors of Projects Assisted by the Ford Foundation in Four Cities and a State,* Twenty-Ninth Annual National Conference, National Association of Housing and Redevelopment Officials, Denver, October 1, 1963. (New York: Office of Reports, Ford Foundation, 1964), p. 26.

[17] Quoted in Silberman, p. 353.

[18] *Ibid.,* p. 353.

[19] Personal communication, January 10, 1967. See also Leonard S. Cottrell, Jr., "Social Planning, the Competent Community, and Mental Health," November 1964, xeroxed.

[20] MFY antedated HARYOU and was supported by funds from the President's Committee on Juvenile Delinquency and Youth Crime, the National Institute of Mental Health, the Ford Foundation, and New York City.

[21] U.S., Congress, House, Committee on Education and Labor, *Hearings on Economic Opportunity Act of 1964,* p. 305.

[22] Personal communications from Sanford L. Kravitz, December 7, 1966; Robert Morris, November 21, 1966; James N. Adler, December 5, 1966; and Bookbinder, *loc. cit.* Also, Boone, "The Poor and the War on Poverty," and Daniel P. Moynihan, "Three Problems in Combating Poverty," in *Poverty in America,* ed. Margaret S. Gordon (San Francisco: Chandler, 1965), pp. 41-53; and Yarmolinsky, "The Origin of Maximum Feasible Participation."

[23] Moynihan, *ibid.,* p. 47.

[24] Nathan Glazer, "A Sociologist's View of Poverty," in Gordon, ed., *Poverty in America,* p. 24.

[25] Kravitz, *loc. cit.*

[26] Adler, *loc. cit.*

[27] Frank Riessman, "Anti-Poverty Programs and the Role of the Poor," in Gordon, ed., *Poverty in America,* pp. 403-412; Frank Riessman, "The New Anti-Poverty Ideology and the Negro," prepared for the White House Conference on Civil Rights, November 17-18, 1965, mimeographed; Frank Riessman, "Suggestions for Community Action Programs," June 1966, mimeographed; Arthur Pearl and Frank Riessman, *New Careers for the Poor* (New York: Free Press, 1965); Robert Reiff and Frank Riessman, *The Indigenous Nonprofessional: A Strategy of Change in Community Action and Community Mental Health Programs,* National Institute of Labor, Education, Mental Health Program Reports, no. 3, November 1964; Frank Riessman and Emanuel Hallowitz, "The Role of the Indigenous Nonprofessional in a Community Mental Health Neighborhood Service Center Program," prepared for the American Orthopsychiatry Association Meeting, San Francisco, California, April 1966, mimeographed; Martin Rein and Frank Riessman, "A Strategy for Anti-poverty Community Action Programs," 11 *Social Work* (April 1966), pp. 3-12; Frank Riessman, "Issues in Training the New Nonprofessional," 2 *Poverty and Human Resources Abstracts* (September-October 1967), pp. 5-17.

[28] Reiff and Riessman, *ibid.,* p. 8.

[29] Oscar Ornati, "Program Evaluation and the Definition of Poverty," Paper prepared for the Industrial Relations Research Association Meetings, San Francisco, December 27-29, 1966, p. 10.

[30] Riessman, "Issues in Training . . . ," p. 8.

[31] U.S. Office of Economic Opportunity, *Third Annual Report,* p. 13. These figures represent only those employed by CAP. It should be noted that Riessman estimates the total number of indigenous subprofessionals employed in various antipoverty efforts to be well over 100,000. Riessman, "Issues in Training . . . ," p. 5.

[32] Perhaps it ought to be said that this is due not so much to any inadequacy in the program as to the tragic funding limitations of the antipoverty skirmish.

[33] At this writing, OEO officials in Washington and the Western Region are in the process of gathering this information for transmittal to Congress after the opening of the next session. Among the difficulties in collecting national statistics is that they are dependent on local agency reports which are often very slow and seldom based on categories—or data gathering and recording procedures—that are comparable from one agency to another.

[34] Ornati, "Program Evaluation and the Definition of Poverty," pp. 10, 15.

[35] Harold L. Wilensky and Charles N. Lebeaux, *Industrial Society and Social Welfare* (New York: Free Press, 1965), p. xxxvii.

[36] Congress tried to meet this problem with the Scheuer-Nelson Subprofessional Career Amendment to the EOA of 1966, which appropriated $73 million to employ and train subprofessional aides, and requires that the jobs for which training is given provide for at least some career advancement.

[37] Originally, OEO encouraged and financed target-area elections. But by mid-1966, the results were so disappointing, the turnouts so dismal, and the congressional howl so loud that financing was discontinued. In Philadelphia, 2.7 percent of the voters turned out; Los Angeles, 0.7 percent; Boston, 2.4 percent; Chester, Pennsylvania, 6 percent; Cleveland, 4.2 percent; Kansas City, Missouri, 5 percent; Huntsville, Alabama, 15.6 percent.

[38] Saul D. Alinsky, "The War on Poverty—Political Pornography," 21 *Journal of Social Issues* (Janaury 1965), pp. 41-47.

[39] *The 23rd Annual Congressional Quartlery Almanc,* 90th Cong., 1st sess., 1967 (Washington, D.C.: Congressional Quarterly Service, 1968), p. 1077.

[40] These eight programs are: Head Start, Upward Bound, Legal Services, Comprehensive Health Services, Follow Through, Emergency Food and Medical Services, Family Planning, and Senior Opportunities and Services.

[41] CAP Budget Office, Western Region, and OEO Information Center, Washington, D.C. These officials also point out that, given rising costs, the annual increases in appropriations permit nothing more than the refunding of existing programs.

[42] An OEO survey of the effects of the Green Amendment shows that of 790 local governments reporting, as of August 30, 1968 (of 1,018 CAA's across the nation), about 97 percent, or 768, plan to continue to operate with existing CAA's. It is important to notice, however, that the survey does not report how many of those 768 responses came from communities where the CAA is already under the control of the local government. U.S. Office of Economic Opportunity, *A News Summary of the War on Poverty,* September 23, 1968.

[43] Yet even in San Francisco, where the CAA has developed a sizable constituency, the Mayor recently exercised his control option by designating the City Controller as the financial officer of the Economic Opportunity Council, in effect ousting the agency-appointed financial director.

[44] Boone, "The Poor and the War on Poverty," pp. 5-6.

[45] The "welfare backlash" implicit in the recent presidential elections, which saw about 9.9 million votes cast for George Wallace, suggests that general attitudes toward the poor are still influenced by the individualist ethic of America, by the myth that every boy can grow up to be President. Much sentiment still views the poor man as a victim of his own deficiencies. Complicating the matter is the fact that, in the cities, the poor are usually black. Insistence that their condition is due to their own failings comports with prevailing racist attitudes and obviates the need to reappraise those beliefs.

[46] Boone, "The Poor and the War on Poverty," p. 7.

[47] Cottrell, "Social Planning, the Competent Community, and Mental Health."

B.
LEGAL DISCRIMINATION AND TENSION

20
the police and the
community

THE NATIONAL ADVISORY COMMISSION ON CIVIL DISORDERS
A policeman's lot is not a happy one; it probably never has been. Policeman, like teachers
and preachers, are expected to keep other people moral and law-abiding. Today, however, the
police are subject to pressures from many sources. Minority groups feel that the police represent
the oppressive larger society, and they direct their hostility to the police not only as a result of
police activity but as a symbol of oppression. The courts and groups concerned with civil liber-
ties have increasingly restricted the activities of the police, activities they have always engaged
in even though they are clearly unconstitutional. Crime has been rising (for reasons having noth-
ing to do with the police per se), exposing policemen to more physical danger and increasing the
"law and order" cry from aspiring politicians and citizens who feel threatened. As with many
jobs, the educational requirements to be a policeman have been rising; those with only a high
school education and the relatively low salary that accompanies it feel insecure in their jobs and
resentful of the younger, better-trained officers. Finally, policeman have been and still are being
recruited largely from ethnic groups that have been in hostile competition with blacks, Mexi-
cans, and Puerto Ricans in the past. The result of the interplay of all these factors is that the
police themselves feel like an oppressed minority, but an oppressed minority trained to exercise
authority and to back it up with force. The result is disastrous.
There are certainly no short-term solutions, but there may be some long-term ones. For
one thing, as the general educational level rises, the educational level of the police will rise, too.
If blacks do increase their economic level, they will move out of the ghetto. This would help
matters. Because the ghetto is always in the most undesirable area of the city, it is also the place
where vice (prostitution, drugs, gambling) is, too. Some people think that it is blacks who
bring the vice. Not so. The vice has always been there, and the juvenile members of the succes-
sive immigrant groups who lived in the ghetto before blacks moved in were, like young blacks
today, exposed to vice and crime. Where vice and crime are, there is the policeman, and he may
be excused if he cannot distinguish the law-abiding from the lawbreaking in a hostile and dis-
organized area. Even if blacks do not move out of the inner city, if they move out of the ghetto
into lower-middle-class areas, their relationship with the police will improve.
America might follow the English example and put the policeman back on foot. The Eng-
lish have found that the efficiency of putting policemen into cars does not compensate for the
knowledge and good will that the foot policeman generates on a neighborhood beat. It certainly
does not look as if it will come about soon, but the disarming of the ordinary policeman and

Reprinted from *Report of the National Advisory Commission on Civil Disorders* (New York: E. P.
Dutton & Co., Inc., 1968), Chapter 11, pp. 299-310.

strict gun control (again, as in England) would calm the situation down. Recruiting members of the minority groups into the police has long been advocated as a measure for healing relations between the police and minority communities. An article in the New York Times *(January 25, 1971) reported that except for the District of Columbia, this campaign had failed. Blacks and other minorities often cannot pass the required civil service tests; they may often have juvenile arrest records that disqualify them; they may not want to become identified with the police. The same article reported that Washington, with 75 percent of its residents black, has 25 percent blacks on its police force; Chicago, with a third of the city black, has 16.5 percent blacks on its police force. New York has 5 percent of its police force black; Detroit has 12 percent. Berkeley is considering zoning the city so that black policemen police only black communities and white policeman are assigned to white communities.*

The article that follows describes in some detail police practices that cause resentment and hostility and recommends some practical changes. It is from the Report of the National Advisory Commission on Civil Disorders, *which was appointed by President Johnson in 1967 following widespread urban riots in the preceding two years.*

INTRODUCTION

We have cited deep hostility between police and ghetto communities as a primary cause of the disorders surveyed by the Commission. In Newark, in Detroit, in Watts, in Harlem—in practically every city that has experienced racial disruption since the summer of 1964—abrasive relationships between police and Negroes and other minority groups have been a major source of grievance, tension and, ultimately, disorder.

In a fundamental sense, however, it is wrong to define the problem solely as hostility to police. In many ways the policeman only symbolizes much deeper problems.

The policeman in the ghetto is a symbol not only of law, but of the entire system of law enforcement and criminal justice.

As such, he becomes the tangible target for grievances against shortcomings throughout that system: against assembly-line justice in teeming lower courts; against wide disparities in sentences; against antiquated corrections facilities; against the basic inequities imposed by the system on the poor—to whom, for example, the option of bail means only jail.

The policeman in the ghetto is a symbol of increasingly bitter social debate over law enforcement.

One side, disturbed and perplexed by sharp rises in crime and urban violence, exerts extreme pressure on police for tougher law enforcement. Another group, inflamed against

police as agents of repression, tends toward defiance of what it regards as order maintained at the expense of justice.

The policeman in the ghetto is a symbol, finally, of a society from which many ghetto Negroes are increasingly alienated.

At the same time, police responsibilities in the ghetto have grown as other institutions of social control have lost much of their authority: the schools, because so many are segregated, old, and inferior; religion, which has become irrelevant to those who lost faith as they lost hope; career aspirations, which for many young Negroes are totally lacking; the family, because its bonds are so often snapped. It is the policeman who must fill this institutional vacuum, and is then resented for the presence this effort demands.

Alone, the policeman in the ghetto cannot solve these problems. His role is already one of the most difficult in our society. He must deal daily with a range of problems and people that test his patience, ingenuity, character, and courage in ways that few of us are ever tested. Without positive leadership, goals, operational guidance, and public support, the individual policeman can only feel victimized. Nor are these problems the responsibility only of police administrators; they are deep enough to tax the courage, intelligence, and leadership of mayors, city officials, and community leaders. As Dr. Kenneth B. Clark told the Commission:

This society knows . . . that if human beings are confined in ghetto compounds of our cities, and are subjected to criminally inferior education, pervasive economic and job discrimination, committed to houses unfit for human habitation, subjected to unspeakable conditions of municipal service, such as sanitation, that such human beings are not likely to be responsive to appeals to be lawful, to be respectful, to be concerned with property of others.

And yet, precisely because the policeman in the ghetto is a symbol—precisely because he symbolizes so much—it is of critical importance that the police and society take every possible step to allay grievances that flow from a sense of injustice and increased tension and turmoil.

In this work, the police bear a major responsibility for making needed changes. In the first instance, they have the prime responsibility for safeguarding the minimum goal of any civilized society—security of life and property. To do so, they are given society's maximum power—discretion in the use of force. Second, it is axiomatic that effective law enforcement requires the support of the community. Such support will not be present when a substantial segment of the community feels threatened by the police and regards the police as an occupying force.

At the same time, public officials also have a clear duty to help the police make any necessary changes to minimize so far as possible the risk of further disorders.

We see five basic problem areas;

The need for change in police operations in the ghetto to ensure proper individual conduct and to eliminate abrasive practices
The need for more adequate police protection of ghetto residents to eliminate the present high sense of insecurity to person and property
The need for effective mechanisms through which the citizen can have his grievances handled
The need to develop community support for law enforcement

Our discussion of each of these problem areas is followed by specific recommendations which relate directly to more effective law enforcement and to the prevention and control of civil disorders.[1]

1. POLICE CONDUCT AND PATROL PRACTICES

In an earlier era third-degree interrogations were widespread, indiscriminate arrests on suspicion were generally accepted, and "alley justice" dispensed with the nightstick was common. Yet there were few riots, and the riots which did occur generally did not arise from a police incident.

Today, many disturbances studied by the Commission began with a police incident. But these incidents were not for the most part, the crude acts of an earlier time. They were routine, proper police actions such as stopping a motorist or raiding an illegal business. Indeed, many of the serious disturbances took place in cities whose police are among the best-led, best-organized, best-trained and most professional in the country.

Yet some activities of even the most professional police department may heighten tension and enhance the potential for civil disorder. An increase in complaints of police misconduct, for example, may in fact be a reflection of professionalism; the department may simply be using law enforcement methods which increase the total volume of police contacts with the public. The number of charges of police misconduct may be greater simply because the volume of police-citizen contacts is higher.

Here we examine two aspects of police activities that have great tension-creating potential. Our objective is to provide recommendations to assist city and police officials in developing practices which can allay rather than contribute to tension.

Police Conduct

Negroes firmly believe that police brutality and harassment occur repeatedly in Negro neighborhoods. This belief is unquestionably one of the major reasons for intense Negro resentment against the police.

The extent of this belief is suggested by attitude surveys. In 1964, a *New York Times* study of Harlem showed that 43 percent of those questioned believed in the existence of police "brutality."[2] In 1965, a nationwide Gallup Poll found that 35 percent of Negro men believe there was police brutality in their areas; 7 percent of white men thought so. In 1966, a survey conducted for the Senate Subcommittee on Executive Reorganization found that 60 percent of Watts Negroes aged 15 to 19 believed there was some police brutality. Half said they had witnessed such conduct. A University of California at Los Angeles study of the Watts area found that 79 percent of the Negro males believed police lack respect for or use insulting language to Negroes and 74 percent believed police use unnecessary force in making arrests. In 1967, an Urban League study in Detroit found that 82 percent believed there was some form of police brutality.

The true extent of excessive and unjustified use of force is difficult to determine. One survey done for the Crime Commission suggests that when police-citizen contacts are systematically observed, the vast majority are handled without antagonism or incident. Of 5,339 police-citizen contacts observed in slum precincts in three large cities, in the opinion of the observer, only 20—about three-tenths of 1 percent—involved excessive or unnecessary force. And although almost all of those subjected to such force were poor, more than half were white. Verbal discourtesy was more common—15 percent of all such contacts began with a "brusque or nasty command" on the part of the officer. Again, however, the objects of such commands were more likely to be white than Negro.

Such "observer" surveys may not fully reflect the normal pattern of police conduct. The Crime Commission Task Force concluded that although the study gave "no basis for stating the extent to which police officers used force, it did confirm that such conduct still exists in the cities where observations were made."

Physical abuse is only one source of aggravation in the ghetto. In nearly every city surveyed, the Commission heard complaints of harassment of interracial couples, dispersal of social street gatherings, and the stopping of Negroes on foot or in cars without obvious basis. These, together with contemptuous and degrading verbal abuse, have great impact in the ghetto. As one Commission witness said, these strip the Negro of the one thing that he may have left—his dignity, "the question of being a man."

Some conduct—breaking up of street groups, indiscriminate stops and searches—is frequently directed at youths, creating special tensions in the ghetto where the average age is generally under 21. Ghetto youths, often without work and with homes that may be nearly uninhabitable, particularly in the summer, commonly spend much time on the street. Characteristically, they are not only hostile to police, but eager to demonstrate their own masculinity and courage. The police, therefore, are often subject to taunts and provocations, testing their self-control and, probably, for some, reinforcing their hostility to Negroes in general. Because youths commit a large and increasing proportion of crime, police are under growing pressure from their supervisors—and from the community—to deal with them forcefully. "Harassment of youths" may therefore be viewed by some police departments—and even members of the Negro community—as a proper crime prevention technique.

In a number of cities the Commission heard complaints of abuse from Negro adults of all social and economic classes. Particular resentment is aroused by harassing Negro men in the company of white women—often their light-skinned Negro wives.

"Harassment" or discourtesy may not be the result of malicious or discriminatory intent of police officers. Many officers simply fail to understand the effects of their actions because of their limited knowledge of the Negro community. Calling a Negro teenager by his first name may arouse resentment because many whites still refuse to extend to adult Negroes the courtesy of the title, "Mister." A patrolman may take the arm of a person he is leading to the police car. Negroes are more likely to resent this than whites because the action implies that they are on the verge of flight and may degrade them in the eyes of friends or onlookers.

In assessing the impact of police misconduct we emphasize that the improper acts of a relatively few officers may create severe tensions between the department and the entire Negro community. Whatever the actual extent of such conduct, we concur in the Crime Commission's conclusion that: ". . . all such behavior is obviously and totally reprehensible, and when it is directed against minority-group citizens it is particlarly likely to lead, for quite obvious reasons, to bitterness in the community."

Police Patrol Practices

Although police administrators may take steps to attempt to eliminate misconduct by individual police officers, many departments have adopted patrol practices which in the words of one commentator, have ". . . replaced harassment by individual patrolmen with harassment by entire departments."

These practices, sometimes known as "aggressive preventive patrol," take a number of forms, but invariably they involve a large number of police-citizen contacts initiated by police rather than in response to a call for help or service. One such practice utilizes a roving task force which moves into high-crime districts without prior notice, and conducts intensive, often indiscriminate, street stops and searches. A number of persons who might legitimately be described as suspicious are stopped. But so also are persons whom the beat patrolman would know are respected members of the community. Such task forces are often deliberately moved from place to place making it impossible for its members to know the people with whom they come in contact.

In some cities aggressive patrol is not limited to special task forces. The beat patrolman himself is expected to participate and to file a minimum number of stop-and-frisk or field interrogation reports for each tour of duty. This pressure to produce, or a lack of familiarity with the neighborhood and its people, may lead to widespread use of these techniques without adequate differentiation between genuinely suspicious behavior, and behavior which is suspicious to a particular officer merely because it is unfamiliar.

Police administrators, pressed by public concern about crime, have instituted such patrol practices often without weighing their tension-creating effects and the resulting relationship to civil disorder.

Motorization of police is another aspect of patrol that has affected law enforcement in the ghetto. The patrolman comes to see the city through a windshield and hear about it over a police radio. To him, the area increasingly comes to consist only of lawbreakers. To the ghetto resident, the policeman comes increasingly to be only an enforcer.

Loss of contact between the police officer and the community he serves adversely affects law enforcement. If an officer has never met, does not know, and cannot understand the language and habits of the people in the area he patrols, he cannot do an effective police job. His ability to detect truly suspicious behavior is impaired. He deprives himself of important sources of information. He fails to know those persons with an "equity" in the community—homeowners, small businessmen, professional men, persons who are anxious to support proper law enforcement—and thus sacrifices the contributions they can make to maintaining community order.

Recommendations

Police misconduct—whether described as brutality, harassment, verbal abuse, or discourtesy—cannot be tolerated even if it is infrequent. It contributes directly to the risk of civil disorder. It is inconsistent with the basic responsibility and function of a police force in a democracy. Police departments must have rules prohibiting such misconduct and enforce them vigorously. Police commanders must be aware of what takes place in the field, and take firm steps to correct abuses. We consider this matter further in the section on policy guidelines.

Elimination of misconduct also requires care in selecting police for ghetto areas, for there the police responsibility is particularly sensitive, demanding and often dangerous. The highest caliber of personnel is required if police are to overcome feelings within the ghetto community of inadequate protection and unfair, discriminatory treatment. Despite this need, data from Commission investigators and from the Crime Commission disclose that often a department's worst, not its best, are assigned to minority group neighborhoods. As Professor Albert Reiss, Director of the Center for Research on Social Organization, University of Michigan, testified before the Commission: ". . . I think we confront in modern urban police departments in large cities much of what we encounter in our schools, in these cities. The slum police precinct is like the slum school. It gets, with few exceptions, the worst in the system." Referring to extensive studies in one city, Professor Reiss concluded:

In predominantly Negro precincts, over three-fourths of the white policemen expressed prejudice or highly prejudiced attitudes toward Negroes. Only one percent of the officers expressed attitudes which could be described as sympathetic toward Negroes. Indeed, close to one-half of all the police officers in predominantly Negro high crime rate areas showed extreme prejudice against Negroes. What do I mean by extreme racial prejudice? I mean that they describe Negroes in terms that are not people terms. They describe them in terms of the animal kingdom. . . .

Although some prejudice was displayed in only 8 percent of police-citizen encounters: "The cost of such prejudiced behavior I suggest is much higher than my statistics suggest. Over a period of time, a substantial proportion of citizens, particularly in high crime rate areas, may experience at least one encounter with a police officer where prejudice is shown."

To ensure assignment of well-qualified police to ghetto areas, the Commission recommends:

Officers with bad reputations among residents in minority areas should be immediately reassigned to other areas. This will serve the interests of both the police and the community. Screening procedures should be developed to ensure that officers with superior ability, sensitivity and the common sense necessary for enlightened law enforcement are assigned to minority group areas. We believe that, with proper training in ghetto problems and conditions, and with proper standards for recruitment of new officers, in the long run, most

policemen can meet these standards. Incentives, such as bonuses or credits for promotion should be developed wherever necessary to attract outstanding officers for ghetto positions.

The recommendations we have proposed are designed to help ensure proper police conduct in minority areas. Yet there is another facet of the problem: Negro perceptions of police misconduct. Even if those perceptions are exaggerated, they do exist. If outstanding officers are assigned to ghetto areas, if acts of misconduct, however infrequent, result in proper—and visible—disciplinary action, and if these corrective practices are made part of known policy, we believe the community will soon learn to reject unfounded claims of misconduct.

Problems stemming from police patrol cannot, perhaps, be so easily resolved. But there are two considerations which can help to allay such problems. The first consideration relates to law enforcement philosophy behind the use of techniques like aggressive patrol. Many police officials believe strongly that there are law enforcement gains from such techniques. However, these techniques can also have law enforcement liabilities. Their employment therefore should not be merely automatic, but the product of a deliberate balancing of pluses and minuses by command personnel.

We know that advice of this sort is easier to give than to act on. The factors involved are difficult to weigh. Gains cannot be measured solely in the number of arrests. Losses in police protection cannot be accepted solely because of some vague gain in diminished community tension. The kind of thorough, objective assessment of patrol practices and search for innovation we need will require the best efforts of research and development units within police departments, augmented if necessary by outside research assistance.

The second consideration concerning patrol is execution. There is more crime in the ghetto than in other areas. If the aggressive patrol clearly relates to the control of crime, the residents of the ghetto are likely to endorse the practice. What may arouse hostility is not the fact of aggressive patrol but its indiscriminate use so that it comes to be regarded not as crime control but as a new method of racial harassment. All patrol practices must be carefully reviewed to ensure they are properly carried out by individual officers.

New patrol practices must be designed to increase the patrolman's knowledge of the ghetto. They will require getting the patrolman out of the car and into the neighborhood and keeping him on the same beat long enough to get to know the people and understand the conditions. They will require training the patrolman to convince him of the desirability of such patrol There must be continuing administrative supervision. In practice as well as theory, all aspects of patrol must be lawful and conform to policy guidelines. Unless carried out with courtesy and with some understanding of the community, even the most enlightened patrol practices may degenerate into what residents will come to regard as harassment. Finally, this concept of patrol should be publicly explained so that ghetto residents understand it and know what to expect.

NOTES

[1] In performing this task we wish to acknowledge our indebtedness to and reliance upon the extensive work done by the President's Commission on Law Enforcement and Administration of Justice (the "Crime Commission"). The reports, studies, surveys and analyses of the Crime Commission have contributed to many of our conclusions and recommendations.

[2] The "brutality" referred to in this and other surveys is often not precisely defined, and covers conduct ranging from use of insulting language to excessive and unjustified use of force.

21
the evacuation of the japanese americans and its aftermath

THE JAPANESE AMERICAN CITIZENS LEAGUE

The history of the Japanese-American minority in the United States is peculiar in several respects. Until the end of World War II, people born in Japan, as well as in other Asian countries, were denied the right to become naturalized citizens. The Japanese were concentrated on the West Coast, and the prohibition of naturalization enabled the western states to discriminate against Asians by making laws against aliens. Aliens, for example, were not permitted to buy or own farmland, a grave discrimination against the Japanese, who are expert farmers. After they had turned a fallow piece of land into a highly productive farm, the white owners could, and often did, evict them.

Shortly after Japan attacked Pearl Harbor, in December, 1941, the Japanese were evacuated from the West Coast and placed in concentration camps, allegedly out of fear of sabotage. Not a single case of sabotage occurred, either before or after the evacuation. The evacuees included not only the Japanese-born (Issei), who were prevented by law from becoming citizens, but also American-born citizens of Japanese ancestry (Nisei) and even the children of Nisei (Sansei), although there were not many of these in the population. It is impossible to view the arbitrary evacuation of law-abiding American citizens, against whom no evidence of wrongdoing was ever adduced, as any different from the exile of Russian political prisoners to Siberia. Most non-Japanese Americans do not know about the relocation centers or have conveniently repressed this knowledge because it was an action in violation of every tenet of American government, law, and justice. Probably every citizen of Japan and of other Asian countries knows about it, however, and this action, along with the dropping of atomic bombs on Japan, explains some of the profound distrust Asians exhibit toward Americans.

The end of the story is considerably happier than the beginning. Despite their arbitrary and unjust treatment, the Nisei have never wavered in their loyalty to the United States. During the last part of World War II, they volunteered and fought bravely for the United States. With the help of some of the churches and welfare agencies, the government made every effort to help Japanese Americans reestablish themselves. Today, although many Japanese Americans have returned to the West Coast, many others have settled in other parts of the United States. They

Statement of the Japanese American Citizens League for the Jonas Subcommittee on Claims, Committee on the Judiciary, House of Representatives, West Coast Hearings, San Francisco and Los Angeles, California, August 30-31 and September 1-3, 1954, on H.R. 7435, Evacuation Claims Amendment. Mimeographed.

have been warmly welcomed and have met with relatively little discrimination. Their isolation from American life, which their concentration in one geographic area before the war encouraged, has broken down. Most Japanese Americans are middle class. Their strong family structure and interest in obtaining good educations have protected them from social disorganization.

Evacuation cost the Japanese Americans dearly, and Congress has made some effort to reimburse them for the loss of their life savings that resulted from the arbitrary action of the army and the federal government. The following article is a portion of a statement made by Mike M. Masaoka, Washington representative of the Japanese American Citizens League (JACL), before a congressional subcommittee charged with investigating the payment of Japanese-American claims.

EVACUATION SUMMARY

Twelve years ago, the arbitrary mass evacuation of 110,000 persons of Japanese ancestry from the west coast took place because of alleged "military necessity."

In that summary movement, 110,000 persons of Japanese ancestry, two-thirds of whom were United States citizens, were evicted from their homes and associations and herded into ten inland camps called War Relocation Centers.

Because of the very nature of that unprecedented action and the "temper of the times" on the Pacific Coast, property losses were inevitable. Some lost everything they had; many lost most of what they had. Every evacuee suffered substantial and irreparable property losses.

The United States Supreme Court, late in 1944, in a six to three opinion, upheld the right of the military in wartime to take such precautionary action with a group who had "an affinity with the enemy."

After the end of hostilities, and in 1948, the Congress of the United States enacted legislation authorizing "the Attorney General to adjudicate certain claims resulting from evacuation of certain persons of Japanese ancestry under military orders," Public Law 886, 80th Congress.

REASONS FOR CONGRESSIONAL APPROVAL

The Report of the Committee on the Judiciary, issued in 1947 in connection with this legislation, sums up the reasons for the enactment of this Act.

. . . The Committee was impressed with the fact that, despite the hardships visited upon this unfortunate racial group brought about by the then prevailing military necessity, there was recorded during the war not one act of sabotage or espionage attributable to those who were the victims of the forced relocation. Moreover, statistics were produced to indicate that the percentage of enlistments in the armed forces of this country by those of Japanese ancestry of eligible age exceeded the nationwide percentage. The valiant exploits of the Four Hundred and Forty-Second Regimental Combat Team, composed entirely of Japanese Americans and the most decorated combat team in the war, are well known. It was further adduced that the Japanese Americans who were relocated proved themselves to be, almost without exception, loyal to the traditions of this country, and exhibited a commendable discipline throughout the period of their exile. . . .

The Committee considered the argument that the victims of the relocation were no more casualties of the war than were many millions of other Americans who lost their lives or their homes or occupations during the war. However, this argument was not considered tenable, since in the instant case the loss was inflicted upon a special racial group by a voluntary act of the Government without precedent in the history of this country. Not to redress these loyal Americans in some measure for the wrongs inflicted upon them would provide ample material for attacks by the followers of foreign ideologies on the American way of life, and to redress them would be simple justice.

Under authority of this statute, the Department of Justice established a Japanese Claims Section within first their Claims and now their Civil Division, and invited the evacuees to file their claims.

23,924 CLAIMS TIMELY FILED

Within the 18 months' statutory deadline, 23,924 claims were timely filed with the Government. The total amount claimed was $129,996,589.80. In this connection, it is interesting to note that in 1942, at the time of the evacuation, the Federal Reserve Board estimated the losses suffered by the evacuees in the neighborhood of 400 million dollars.

The adjudicative program moved so slowly in the initial stages that, at one time in 1950, it was estimated that a hundred years would pass before the program would be completed. Moreover, because of the lack of administrative funds, only two field offices—one in Los Angeles and the other in San Francisco —were established. This meant that practically all of the claims adjudicated in the early stages of the program were limited to those filed in California.

ADJUDICATION RECORD

In calendar year 1950, the Department of Justice adjudicated only 211 claims, of which 73 were dismissals. For the 137 claims allowed, payment of $62,595.16 was authorized. The original amount claimed by these evacuees was $141,373.83.

In the previous calendar year (1949), during which claims were being filed pursuant to the law, only 21 claims were adjudicated, one of which was dismissed. Out of the total of $13,543.99 originally claimed, $6,882.20 was paid in awards. . . .

1954 FISCAL YEAR END STATUS

At the end of fiscal year 1954 (June 30, 1954), we estimate (in round numbers) as follows:

1. Claims compromised and settled: 19,750
   Amount awarded: $23,000,000
   Amount originally claimed: $63,700,000
2. Claims adjudicated: 590
   Amount awarded: $700,000
   Amount originally claimed: $1,700,000
3. Claims dismissed: 975
   Amount originally claimed: $3,300,000

(Since an earlier report, a number of claims previously dismissed were reinstated.)

This adds up to a total of 21,315 claims that have been adjudicated and compromised, with 975 of the adjudications resulting in dismissals. This means that 20,340 claims have been awarded either by adjudications or by compromise settlements.

In terms of dollars (round numbers), $23,700,000 have been awarded. The total amount originally claimed, including those dismissed, was $68,730,000.

3,000 CLAIMS LEFT

Less than 3,000 claims remain to be processed, but they are the substantially larger ones, in that these remaining claims were filed for approximately $65,000,000, or about the same total originally requested by all of the claims thus far disposed of by compromise, adjudication, and dismissal. . . . The major objective of H. R. 7435 is to speed up the final determination of the remaining 3,000 claims.

The Japanese American Citizens League (JACL) is the only national organization representing persons of Japanese ancestry in the United States of America. Most, but not all, of our members are American citizens of Japanese ancestry. At the present time, we have more than 85 chapters with members in more than 32 states and the District of Columbia and the Territory of Hawaii. Our members and supporters number more than 20,000. . . .

The motivation of our organization during our entire history, from 1930 to the present, is expressed in our twin national slogans: "For Better Americans In A Greater America" and "Security Through Unity."

WORLD WAR II

After Japan attacked Pearl Harbor, the leadership of the Japanese population on the continental mainland of the United States fell to the JACL more or less by default because we were the only organization of American citizens of Japanese ancestry functioning at that time either on a local or regional basis.

In order to appreciate the resulting situation, it is necessary to understand the makeup of the Japanese communities, particularly those in California, Oregon, Washington, and Arizona—the areas in which the evacuation took place.

Because the Japanese are among the latest of the immigrant groups to seek new opportunities in this country, for all intents and purposes there are only two generations to consider. The first generation or immigrant parent group is called the Issei. Their average age at the time of evacuation was about 55 years. All of them were subjects of Japan, since none of them could become naturalized citizens under our federal statutes until the Immigration and Nationality Act of 1952 was enacted. The second generation, called the Nisei, are American citizens by virtue of having been born in this country. Their average age at the time of evacuation was about 19 years.

Of the approximately 127,000 persons of Japanese ancestry in the United States in 1940, two-thirds were Nisei or United States citizens; 110,000 resided on the west coast in 1941.

Since the Nisei group was so young at that time, practically all of the business, agricultural, civic, and religious leaders were Issei. This accounts for the fact that most of the larger claims are those belonging to this group.

After December 7, 1941, all of the Issei were automatically classified as "enemy aliens" since, through no fault of their own, they were subjects and nationals of enemy Japan. Many of the Issei leaders were interned by the Federal Bureau of Investigation (FBI) as a precautionary measure. All of them were later released or paroled.

Executive Order No. 9066

For about six weeks after the outbreak of war, the public and government treatment of the Japanese gave no indication that such drastic action as mass evacuation was contemplated. Thus, when the President issued Executive Order No. 9066 on February 19, 1942, the officials of the JACL as well as most of the friends of the Japanese on the west coast were surprised and caught completely unawares. This Executive Order authorized the Secretary of War, or any military commander designated by the Secretary, to establish "military areas"

and to exclude therefrom "any or all persons."

Since this is not the appropriate time, nor place, we shall not raise the question again here of the necessity or the constitutionality of that arbitrary racist action which was taken at a time when our courts were functioning and in the absence of martial law. We would, however, like to outline our part in the evacuation program to indicate our concern for the basic Evacuation Claims Act of 1948, the compromise settlement authorization for smaller claims amendment of 1951, and the pending legislation in the nature of another amendment to expedite the determination of the remaining claims.

JACL Policy

Once evacuation became an established government policy—sanctioned by the President, ordered by the military, and approved in a sense by the Congress which passed implementing legislation—although we steadfastly refused to concede either to its legality or need, the JACL decided that it was our patriotic duty as Americans to abide by this wartime decision and to urge the Japanese, aliens and citizens alike, in the areas concerned to cooperate in their own removal to the best of their respective abilities. We appreciated the great economic losses, the sacrifices, and the suffering that such a mass movement entailed, but we felt we had no alternative. We were in no position, even if we had wanted to do so, to challenge the Army in this matter—for it was wartime and we, by the accident of birth and the hysteria of the moment, were identified with the Japanese enemy.

Needless to say, this was a most difficult decision to make, for all of us were, and are, American citizens who believe in certain basic human and civil rights. Nevertheless, once JACL's policy was agreed upon, we did everything possible to cooperate with the various military and government agencies concerned.

One of our first recommendations was to the effect that as far as possible every protection ought to be given to the property of the evacuees. We even went so far as to suggest a special government custodian similar to the one appointed during World War I to handle the property of certain German aliens. But this suggestion, like so many others, was never accepted.

While practically all of the evacuees acquiesced in our recommendation that they cooperate in their own evacuation, frankly speaking, it was not a popular alternative. Our own organizational membership, for example, dropped from its all-time pre-evacuation high of 20,000 to less than 2,000. And there were many who, in the idleness of the camps, charged the JACL with having "sold them down the river."

In spite of the ill will that our decision evoked, the fact that the JACL as the one functioning responsible organization urged cooperation is credited with the generally cooperative attitude assumed by almost every evacuee, an attitude that bordered on submissiveness and that probably could have been matched by no other racial or minority group in the United States. This significant role of the JACL in the evacuation is attested to by Dr. Milton S. Eisenhower, the President's younger brother, who was the first director of the War Relocation Authority (WRA), in hearings before the House Appropriations Committee in 1942.

Even after the evacuation itself was an accomplished fact and the 110,000 Japanese had been removed from the west coast and placed in so-called relocation centers without trial or hearing, the JACL continued to stress Americanism in its program.

From the very beginning, JACL urged that high school and college students be allowed to leave the centers in order to complete their education in normal communities. The next step was to recommend that Nisei, and finally the Issei, be permitted to find employment and housing in areas outside the Western Defense Command in order that they might not only enjoy normal lives but might also contribute to the war effort at a time when manpower was short.

When Selective Service adopted a policy of reclassifying Japanese Americans so that they could not be called up for service and when the Army itself refused to accept Nisei volunteers, the JACL carried its fight to Washington. After several months of representations, in which we were supported by many Ameri-

cans of good will, the Army relented to the point of first using qualified Nisei in its intelligence work against the Japanese enemy and then agreeing to the formation of a special Japanese American Combat Team.

Once the Army agreed to use Japanese American troops on a voluntary basis, we carried on extensive campaigns within the barbed-wire confines of the camps to urge all eligible Nisei to volunteer for either military intelligence against the Japanese enemy or for what eventually became the 442nd Regimental Combat Team. Our aggressive campaign aroused the antagonism of the bitter and resentful element in the camps, with the result that many of our leaders were beaten up. Our then national president, for example, was mobbed so badly that he was hospitalized for a month.

In spite of threats and intimidation by the disgruntled and the disillusioned, as the records show, several thousand Japanese Americans whose loyalty had been questioned by their own government volunteered to fight, and if necessary to die, for our country. This, we submit, was a demonstration of real faith in America and the American way seldom, if ever, surpassed.

Nisei War Record

General Charles A. Willoughby, intelligence officer for General MacArthur, General Bonner Fellers, psychological warfare officer for General MacArthur, and the late General Joseph E. Stillwell all have testified to the great and gallant work of the Nisei in combat intelligence against the Japanese enemy in the Pacific. Colonel Sidney F. Mashbir, chief of the Allied Translator-Interpreter Service, devotes considerable space to the contributions of the Nisei who saved thousands of American casualties and millions of dollars in material, in addition to shortening the Pacific war by months, in his recently published book *I Was An American Spy*.

The record of the 442nd Regimental Combat Team, featured in the MGM motion picture "Go For Broke," is too well known to need repeating here. Suffice it to say that this Combat Team, serving in Italy and France, is generally recognized as the most decorated military unit in American history for its size and length of service.

Many of the Issei, though technically subjects of Japan, taught in military language schools sponsored by the Army and the Navy; served as interpreters, translators, and documentarians of captured Japanese documents; drew the maps by which Japan was bombed into submission; and even engaged in counterintelligence work with the Office of Strategic Services. As nationals of Japan because they could not become naturalized citizens, had Japan won the war or if they had been captured by the enemy, they would have been shot for treason or subjected to brutal treatment that is worse than death.

JUSTIFICATION

Because of this unprecedented record of service and devotion, JACL feels most justified in seeking corrective and remedial legislation for these evacuated people.

Since the initial stages of evacuation, the JACL has been on record that some kind of indemnification or compensation for evacuation losses should be provided for these loyal evacuees who proved their allegiance under the most difficult of circumstances.

From time to time, especially after the Exclusion Orders were lifted early in 1945 and evacuees allowed to return to their former homes, questions were raised as to whether the evacuees should seek restitution or indemnification as individuals or await possible government action to this end.

There were many who felt that either the military establishment or the federal government should be sued in the courts; there were others who believed that private bills for individual relief should be introduced into Congress; and there were still others who hoped for general remedial legislation.

In view of the many oral promises made by various government officials that they would recommend appropriate group legislation for general compensation, the JACL counseled the evacuees to wait for the enactment of a public law as the most effective and reasonable method of resolving this matter. And the JACL assumed the leadership in the drive for corrective legislation. This, perhaps, accounts

for the rather startling fact that neither litigation was instituted in the courts nor thousands of private bills dropped into the congressional hopper prior to consideration of legislation leading up to the passage of the basic statute in 1948.

Throughout the entire evacuation process, the JACL has maintained a consistent program—to do nothing that would hamper, jeopardize, or compromise America's war effort, but rather to aid in every way possible the achieving of victory. Our faith has been, and is, that American democracy, once the facts are in, will correct its mistakes and its abuses; that the American people, in the long run, tend to be honest, fair, and just. Once the hysteria and confusion of war were removed, we were confident that the Congress, representing the American people, would not let us down.

EVACUATION CLAIMS LAW

The 80th Congress justified our faith and confidence by enacting what we designate now as the Japanese American Evacuation Claims Act, Public Law 886, the Act of July 2, 1948.

When administrative difficulties threatened to nullify that law, the 82nd Congress amended the basic statute to authorize the compromise settlement of smaller claims under $2,500 by enacting Public Law 116, the Act of August 17, 1951.

Now, this Congress and more particularly this subcommittee have before it another amendment proposed to expedite the final determination of the remaining claims in order that this program, at long last, may be completed.

This, then, explains the interest and concern of the JACL in the instant bill. From the beginning of the evacuation program more than 12 years ago, JACL has been more intimately connected with the problems incidental thereto than any other organization. In a real sense, JACL feels that it has a primary obligation to the remaining evacuees to see that this amendment becomes law in order that their faith, and ours, in the integrity of the American way will not be destroyed. . . .

Although some of these adverse adjudications were clearly within the language of the "barred items," JACL takes exception to many, especially in the light that the Evacuation Claims Law was an act of grace on the part of the Congress and was intended to be remedial legislation, not an adversary proceeding.

NONCOMPENSABLE ITEMS

In the case of Mary Sogawa, for one, the Attorney General held that the extraordinary and unusual expenses incurred in preparing for evacuation are not compensable. If there had been no evacuation, Mary Sogawa would not have purchased, for example, three suitcases and a trunk. In addition, the Attorney General ruled in this same case that the transportation charges she incurred in returning from Chicago, where she resettled from a WRA camp, to Los Angeles, her pre-evacuation home, was also not a compensable item. Had there been no evacuation, Mary Sogawa would never have gone to Chicago; she would have remained in her native city. Because there was an evacuation, she was relocated to Chicago and it was only natural for her to expect that the government would compensate her for railroad fare back to her former place of residence.

Because almost every claim includes some items for pre-evacuation and post-evacuation expenses, this adverse adjudication affects every claim whether it was compromised or adjudicated. And yet, were it not for the fact of evacuation, these evacuation preparation and return expenses would never have been incurred. We hold that this ruling is outrageous.

INTERNEE LOSSES

In another adjudication to which we take exception, the claim for property of an internee whose family was later evacuated was disallowed. We admit that internment by the FBI of an alien Japanese residing in the "free zone" does not entitle that alien Japanese to evacuation claims. For, as with German and Italian aliens who were also interned, his family and friends could have carried on his business and taken care of his property during his period of internment.

But, the alien Japanese living on the west coast was in an entirely different situation. When he was interned, his business and his property were taken over by his family. A few months later, however, his family was evacuated and his property lost. Therefore, it seems quite clear to us that such property losses as were suffered are the direct and reasonable consequence of the evacuation, and not of internment.

Moreover, when he was released or paroled, as all of them were, this alien Japanese who formerly resided on the west coast could not return to his old home but had to go to a WRA camp or another territory outside the Western Defense Command because he was excluded from that area on account of his racial ancestry.

Samples of other adverse adjudications include (1) out-of-state fees of colleges and universities, (2) self-evident low rentals, and (3) so-called management costs.

Extra Tuition

As for increased tuition paid to colleges and universities as out-of-state students, it should be pointed out that, were it not for evacuation, these same students in all probability would have gone to colleges and universities in their own states. Since, in most cases, they would have lived at home or with friends, they would not have had to pay extra for board and room either, except that they were evacuated.

Low Rentals

In many instances that we know of, evacuees requested non-Japanese friends to occupy their homes and premises at ridiculously low rentals in the hope that these friends would keep the house or property in good repair, including furniture and fixtures, as the case may be. They did this to protect their property against loss and deterioration. And, in a sense, because they took these extra precautions, the government now proposes to penalize them for their special pains. If they had not taken such steps to protect their property, their evacuation losses would have been considerably more than the difference between "fair rental value" and the low rents they charged.

Mangement Costs

Then, there are the so-called "management" expenses of businessmen and farmers. In order that their properties might be kept in good repair or cultivation, that their businesses or operations might be continued even though they themselves were evacuated, a number of prudent evacuees deliberately hired or retained high-priced experts to manage their properties during their enforced absence, not only paying them exorbitant salaries but also promising them as much as half or more of all sales and profits. If these "conservatory" steps had not been taken, without doubt their property losses would have been considerably higher than they were.

By holding such expenses as noncompensable, the Attorney General is penalizing those who tried to prevent losses and to protect their property and favoring those who simply took no action but abandoned their property. By so doing, he has established a bad precedent for future emergencies when government action is necessitated for any reason: the premium has been placed on "junking everything," not on trying to protect and conserve value.

There are, of course, several other adverse adjudications which, on their face, also seem inequitable and unjust to us. Remedial legislation such as this Act should not be tortured and twisted to deprive the unfortunate of every conceivable item claimed. Rather, justice would be better served if the Attorney General had adopted a liberal, generous attitude instead of an adversary, legalistic one.

Low Valuations

In addition to being unduly harsh in the matter of determining eligibility, the Department of Justice has been parsimonious in its determinations of valuations for the compensable items.

In the field of agriculture, to illustrate, it was an accepted fact that the Japanese grew more per acre and received a better price per unit than the average farmer. Nevertheless, the Attorney General accepted certain averages developed by the Department of Agriculture and used these as yardsticks in determining the value of all crops, etc. This, we submit, is manifestly unfair.

In any program of this nature, when human elements are involved, we admit that emotional factors often cloud our better judgment. But we hold that when a particular formula or interpretation is obviously in error, it should be changed.

COMMENDATIONS

At the same time, JACL desires to pay public and deserved tribute to Assistant Attorneys General Holmes Baldridge and Warren Burger who have supervised this program in their respective capacities as Assistant Attorneys General in charge of the Claims and now the Civil Division, and especially to Enoch E. Ellison chief of the Japanese Claims Section, and his staff generally, both in the Washington Office and in the field offices, for their courteous and cooperative attitudes in administering what is without doubt one of the more difficult programs of these times.

22
a critical reexamination of the social and political characteristics of riot cities

BRYAN T. DOWNES

Gunnar Myrdal, in An American Dilemma, *talked about "the convenience of ignorance," by which he meant that Americans chose not to know how badly blacks fared in the United States because then they did not have to face up to the failure of the American belief in equality. This ignorance was rudely shattered by the explosion of riots in almost all American cities where there were substantial numbers of blacks. There had been riots before, but in widely scattered areas and with long periods of time intervening. The riots of the 1960s differed in another way from earlier riots. There had been hand-to-hand fights between armed bands of blacks and whites; there had been heavy casualties, heavier among blacks than among whites; and these clashes had often been followed by improved race relations. The 1960 riots involved very few whites (except those that came into the ghettos after the riots to loot); casualties were few; the riots were against property. Houses and stores were burned down. The particular targets were stores the blacks felt had cheated them, but once fires got under way, whole blocks were destroyed. Investigations of the causes of the riots have all indicated that the riots were spontaneous outbursts of frustration and hatred; except for isolated incidents, they were not in any way organized.*

There is still debate in the black community about the effects of the riots. Some feel that large parts of the ghetto housing and services were destroyed and have not and never will be rebuilt, a high price to be paid by a community whose resources are very low. Others feel that only riots or something similarly violent and widespread could penetrate American apathy and that the long-term effects of the riots in stirring consciences and prodding the government to action were worth it.

The following selection seeks to isolate the causal situations that produced riots by means of a detailed examination of the characteristics of the major cities in which riots occurred.

Mr. Downes is an associate professor of political science at Michigan State University.

Reprinted from *Social Science Quarterly* 51, No. 2 (September 1970), pp. 349-360. Reproduced by permission of the author and publisher.

From 1963 through 1968 many United States cities experienced collective racial violence which has been described as black-dominated and property-orientated[2]. Since late 1968, a new pattern or type of violence—black-dominated but person-oriented—has emerged.[3] Taking the form of a more systematic attack on "whitey" in the role of policeman, fireman or ghetto merchant, this form of violence could lead to greater harassment and suppression of blacks in the United States by a numerically larger and more politically powerful white population.[4]

Although the form may change from time to time, confrontations between blacks and whites probably will continue to occur in our nation's cities and on college and university campuses, as leaders of the black community press their demands through direct action. However, expectations are beginning to out-distance the concrete accomplishments of programs designed to bring about black equality.[5] In addition, blacks are becoming increasingly disillusioned with the ability of existing political institutions and the willingness of political leaders to undertake innovative political change. Although Congress has begun to respond to black demands, the pace has been too slow for many militant black leaders. Programs have been forthcoming but the allocation of funds for these programs has been limited.[6] The scarcity of resources even in a nation as rich as ours is underlined, for we have found it difficult to fight wars abroad and at the same time adequately cope with the problems of the poor and disadvantaged in our own society.

WHY BLACKS REVOLT: THE SEARCH FOR ULTIMATE CAUSES

Social scientists have increasingly turned their attention to the problem of explaining the occurrence and/or severity of the collective racial violence we have witnessed since 1963. The search, however, has frequently been for a single determinant of these violent events. Although this orientation is understandable, since simplicity is one of the aims in theory construction, it is nevertheless regretable due to the empirical inadequacy of such theories.[7] For example, a number of "folk theories" have been developed which hold that collective racial violence is largely the result of: (1) a conspiracy of communists or outside agitators; (2) the recent migration of ghetto residents; (3) criminal elements and riff-raff in the ghetto; (4) teenage rebellion; (5) grievances of the dispossessed and hard-core poor; and (6) police brutality.[8] While these explanations may prove psychologically satisfying to certain segments of our population they have largely been disproved empirically. Other social scientists, using more sophisticated approaches and methodology, have focused their attention on rapid and dynamic change, objective deprivation, relative deprivation, rising expectations, frustration-aggression, societal strain, unresponsive institutions, and so on, as possible determinants of collective racial violence.[9]

In an earlier article, I examined some of the social and political characteristics of those cities which had experienced racial violence since 1964, as well as the impact of these contextual and political factors on the intensity or severity of these violent events.[10] One could view that article as a preliminary "test" of the "objective deprivation thesis," which holds that urban racial violence is largely attributable to poor living, working, learning, and recreational conditions within a city plus the low socioeconomic status of its residents, particularly its black minority. In this article, we turn once again to the notion of objective deprivation and reexamine what impact the quality of life in cities has on the occurrence and severity of urban riots. We will also critically discuss two research reports which have appeared since my original study.[11] Although the research of both Wanderer and Ford and Moore raises questions about some of the findings in my preliminary article, both studies suffer from a number of serious methodological problems which make it extremely difficult to compare their findings with either my initial results or those which I report here.

EXPANDING OUR DATA BASE ON COLLECTIVE RACIAL VIOLENCE

The time period covered in our earlier study was January 1, 1964 to May 31, 1968. During those 54 months, we found that 239

TABLE 1. Yearly Breakdown of Hostile Outbursts

Data on hostile outbursts	1963	1964	1965	1966	1967	1968	Total
Number of cities having outbursts	8	16	20	44	71	106	265[a]
Number of outbursts	12	16	23	53	82	155	341[b]
Total number of days of hostilities	16	42	31	92	236	286	703
Total number arrested	780	2,000	10,245	2,216	16,471	21,697	53,409
Total number wounded	88	580	1,206	467	3,348	2,770	8,459
Total number killed	1	9	43	9	85	75	221

[a]Many of the same cities had more than one incident each year, which is why this figure is so high. Of the 676 cities which had 25,000 or more persons in 1960, 149 (22 per cent) had experienced one or more hostile outbursts since 1963. In these 149 cities, 283 incidents of collective racial violence occurred, with an additional 58 incidents taking place in cities under 25,000 persons.
[b]Smaller (less violent) incidents are underreported.

incidents of collective racial violence occurred. We have since expanded this time period to include outbursts taking place in 1963 and during the last six months of 1968. Both 1963 and 1968 are important years to include, for it was in 1963 that black-dominated, property-oriented outbursts first occurred and it was in 1968 that such violent events reached their peak and began to decline. According to our sources of information, in 1963, 12 incidents of collective racial violence occurred and an additional ninety took place in the last half of 1968 (see Table 1). During the total 72-month period, we found that 341 hostile outbursts had taken place. Table 1 presents a yearly breakdown of some of the information collected on these violent events.[12]

Although our data still suffer from the same problems discussed in the preliminary study[13] and therefore should be looked upon as approximate and subject to some change as more complete information becomes available, our effort still represents the most comprehensive set of data available to social scientists on collective racial violence taking place in the 1960's. Both the Wanderer and Ford-Moore studies, for example, restrict their attention to shorter time periods. Wanderer examines only those incidents occurring from April 1 to September 8, 1967 (five months) and Ford-Moore only collective racial violence taking place from 1965 through September 8, 1967 (31 months). In addition, both relied on the same source for their information on racial violence,

the Permanent Subcommittee on Investigations of the Committee on Governmental Operations of the U.S. Senate.[14] This Subcommittee collected very complete data on the occurrence and severity of major riots from the various cities in which these violent events took place, but a comparison of any data with those of the Subcommittee indicated that they tend to underreport smaller, less violent incidents to an even greater extent than the *New York Times,* the primary souce of our data. It would be unwise, therefore, to view the riots studied by Wanderer or Ford-Moore as a total universe of events. Consequently their findings, particularly those of Wanderer, may not be very generalizable and are not fully comparable to those which I reported previously nor to those set forth in this article.

SELECTING AN APPROPRIATE UNIT OF ANALYSIS

We turn now to the question of the unit of analysis employed in each of these studies. Race riots take place in cities, usually in an area commonly referred to as the black ghetto. However, very little valid and hence comparable information exists on these areas and the people living in them. This, coupled with our interest in examining whether the quality of life in the cities has any impact on the occurrence and severity of collective racial violence, led us to select the city as our empirical and theoretical unit of analysis.

Alford had previously collected a comprehensive set of data on cities from the 1960 Census and the 1963 *Municipal Yearbook* and was kind enough to let us use his information in our study.[15] This provided the basic data on our independent variables. However, Alford collected data only on cities of 25,000 or more persons, of which there were 676 in 1960. Of these 676 cities, 149 or 22 per cent had experienced one or more incidents of collective racial violence since 1963. In our preliminary study, 129 cities had experienced such violent events. In the 149 cities, 283 riots occurred, while an additional 58 took place in cities under 25,000 persons.

In a footnote, Wanderer indicates that of the 137 cities contacted by the Senate Subcommittee, 128 responded and provided information on racial violence for the years 1965-1967.[16] Wanderer focused on riots as his empirical unit of analysis, instead of adopting the city as I did. That is, each time a riot occurred, the city in which it took place was included even if it had previously been incorporated into his analysis. Thus contextual data on certain cities are included more than once.[17]

Ford-Moore on the other hand, adopt the metropolitan area as their unit of analysis.[18] They collect census information on 135 metropolitan areas and in turn relate this to the occurrence and severity of urban riots, making it extremely difficult to compare their findings with those based upon research adopting the city as the primary unit of analysis. For example, my concern is with examining the impact that objective deprivation within cities has on racial violence, while Ford-Moore examine whether objective deprivation within metropolitan areas affects the occurrence and severity of urban riots. These seem to be two different empirical questions.

A REEXAMINATION OF THE CHARACTERISTICS OF RIOT AND NON-RIOT CITIES

We began this analysis, as we did our preliminary one, by dividing cities over 25,000 persons into two groups, those which had no incidents of the collective racial violence and those which did. We then ran some of the Al-

ford data against this dichotomous (nominal) dependent variable. In this portion of the study we selected various independent variables which would enable us to present a balanced descriptive characterization of cities in which these violent events took place, as well as "test" various hypotheses incorporating some of the objective environmental conditions thought to underlie racial violence in the United States.

When tables incorporating percentage distributions of these data were compared with those in the preliminary study almost no differences were found in the nature and strength of the relationships even though the data base has been expanded somewhat. To indicate more precisely the association between independent variables and the occurrence of riots, Goodman-Kruskal gammas and their statistical significance are reported in Table 2.

Not unexpectedly, we found that those cities in which outbursts occurred tend to have very distinctive social and to a lesser extent political structural characteristics. Incidents of collective racial violence were not randomly distributed among the 676 cities in the United States which had 25,000 or more persons in 1960; this in itself is a significant finding given the number of cities (149) in which one or more outbursts have taken place. For example, cities experiencing these violent events tend to be our largest, least rapidly growing, most densely populated central cities, whose citizens have less education, lower incomes, and higher unemployment rates than those in municipalities in which no incidents of racial violence have taken place. They also tend to have higher proportions of nonwhites and nonwhite populations that have increased, sometimes quite substantially, since 1950. Those factors which correlated most highly with the occurrence of collective racial violence include total population, population decline, density, per cent nonwhite, change in per cent nonwhite, low educational levels, lack of sound housing units, lack of home ownership and metropolitan status.

Except for the negative relationship between home ownership and the occurrence of hostile outbursts, these findings differ quite markedly from those presented by either Wan-

TABLE 2. Relationships Between the Contextual and Political Characteristics of Cities and the Occurrence of Collective Racial Violence

Contextual and political characteristics of cities of 25,000 or more persons, 1960[a]	OCCURRENCE OF COLLECTIVE RACIAL VIOLENCE	
	Hypothesized direction	Actual sign and gamma coefficient[b]
1960 population	+	+0.70
Population growth, 1950-1960	−	−0.41
Population per square mile, 1960	+	+0.36
Deaths per 1,000, 1959	+	+0.18
Per cent nonwhite, 1960	+	+0.74
Change in per cent nonwhite, 1950-1960	+	+0.54
Per cent persons 25 years and over who have completed 4 years of high school or more, 1960	−	−0.36
Median family income, 1960	−	−0.26
Per cent of labor force unemployed, 1960	+	+0.30
Per cent housing units sound, with plumbing facilities, 1960	−	−0.35
Per cent occupied housing units owner occupied, 1960	−	−0.49
Metropolitan status, 1963[c]	−	−0.38
Economic base, 1963[d]	−	−0.18
Per cent employed in white-collar occupations, 1960	−	−0.18
Form of government, 1963	+	−0.18
Type of election, 1963	−	+0.32
Number of councilmen, 1963	+	+0.30
Term of office, 1963	+	+0.21
Per capita general expenditure, 1963	+	+0.28
Per capita sanitation expenditure, 1963	+	+0.22
Per capita debt outstanding end of year in $10 units, 1963	+	+0.23

[a]Some of these variables and their hypothesized relationships with riots are discussed more fully in the original article.
[b]All of these correlations are significant at the 0.05 level.
[c]Three types of cities are distinguished by metropolitan status. Each city is identified as a central city, a suburb, or independent.
[d]Seven types of cities are distinguished through the use of data on employment in the city from the 1959 census of business and manufactures: manufacturing industrial, diversified manufacturing, diversified retail, retail trade, wholesale trade, service, government and transportation, resort or retirement and education.

derer or Ford-Moore. Of the four comparable independent variables examined by Wanderer— per cent increase in nonwhites, racial composition, home ownership, and population density—none were related to the occurrence of racial violence.[19] In the Ford-Moore study only lack of home ownership among blacks was significantly related to the occurrence of hostile outbursts.[20] Of the other independent variables examined by Ford-Moore, the effect of low educational levels was not clear and per cent Negro was not related to the occurrence of collective racial violence. However, income of nonwhites, contrary to their initial expectation, was positively related to the occurrence of these violent events.

A REEXAMINATION OF THE CHARAC-
TERISTICS OF CITIES EXPERIENCING
MORE VIOLENT OUTBURSTS

In the second phase of our data analysis, we were primarily concerned with explaining the intensity or severity of incidents of collective racial violence. What impact do the factors examined in the first phase of the analysis have on the intensity of these violent events? Do the same factors which were related to the occurrence of collective racial violence also influence their severity?

In measuring the intensity of violence in our preliminary study, the following index was used as an ordinal scale:

(0) No violence
(1) Low intensity of violence (rock and bottle throwing, window breaking, fighting)
(2) Medium intensity of violence (the above plus some looting and arson)
(3) High intensity of violence (above plus much looting and arson)
(4) Very high intensity of violence (the above plus widespread looting and arson, sniping)

We originally anchored this index with cities in which no racial violence occurred, a procedure we have since rejected.[21] When these cities are dropped from the analysis, as they have been in Table 3, the size of both the gamma and product-moment correlations decrease and in several instances signs change. This raises a very interesting methodological question: when attempting to explain the intensity or severity of incidents of racial violence, should the analysis be restricted to only those cities in which such violent events took place or should all cities being studied, in this case 676 cities, be included?

It appears that both Wanderer and Ford-Moore anchored their measures of the severity of violence with cities or metropolitan areas in which no racial violence took place.[22] However, because they have so few cities or metropolitan areas in this category it probably does not affect their results very much. But when 527 cities anchor such an index or scale, as

they did in our preliminary study, they have a definite impact.

We would argue that when an attempt is being made to explain the intensity of violence of hostile outbursts, only cities in which such events took place should be included in the analysis. This appears to be a more theoretically defensible position than the one taken in our preliminary study, that is, violence has to occur in a city before its intensity can be explained.

In their article, Ford-Moore note that in our preliminary study we used a rather "crude" measure of association (Goodman-Kruskal gamma) when the relationship between various city characteristics and the intensity or severity of incidents of collective racial violence was examined. As a result, in Table 3 we have included a second and hopefully "less crude" measure of association.[23] We have also indicated whether or not the various relationships are statistically significant.

The product-moment correlations are generally lower than the gamma's. We have, therefore, based our interpretation of this analysis on the lower coefficients. Although these are some statistically significant relationships, most of the correlations are not particularly strong, except for that between total population in 1960 and riot intensity. In addition, when the effects of other significantly related variables were partialled out total population still tends to be consistently related to riot intensity. On the other hand, most other correlation coefficients decreased in size and were no longer significant when total population was controlled.[24] Examination of these data arrayed in tabular form, however, does indicate that the various relationships tend to be most accentuated in those cities which experienced the most intensely violent outbursts.

Turning to the other two studies, in his analysis, Wanderer found no relationship between any of his four comparable independent variables and riot severity.[25] While Ford-Moore found home ownership and home ownership differentials between blacks and whites in metropolitan areas to be negatively correlated with riot severity, none of their other inde-

TABLE 3. Relationships Between the Contextual and Political Characteristics of Cities and the Intensity or Severity of Collective Racial Violence

Contextual and political characteristics of cities of 25,000 or more persons[a]	Hypothesized direction	INTENSITY OR SEVERITY OF COLLECTIVE RACIAL VIOLENCE		
		Actual sign and gamma coefficient[b] (original analysis)[c]	Actual sign and gamma coefficient[b] (modified original analysis)[a]	Actual sign and product-moment coefficient[b] (current analysis)[a]
Population, 1960	+	+0.75	+0.62	+0.57
Population growth, 1950-1960	−	−0.39	−0.33	−0.27
Population per square mile, 1960	+	+0.43	+0.38	+0.28
Death per 1,000, 1959	+	+0.36	+0.33	+0.24
Per cent nonwhite, 1960	+	+0.70	+0.12	+0.15
Change in per cent nonwhite, 1950-1960	+	+0.65	+0.45	+0.25
Median age of city, 1960	+	+0.31	+0.24	+0.20
Per cent persons 25 years old and over who have completed 4 years of high school or more, 1960	−	−0.41	−0.20	−0.15
Median family income, 1960	−	−0.14	+0.06*	+0.03*
Per cent of labor force unemployed, 1960	+	+0.30	+0.16	+0.14
Per cent housing units sound, with plumbing facilities, 1960	−	−0.26	−0.02*	−0.00*
Employment residence ratio, 1960	+	+0.37	−0.13*	−0.09*
Per cent housing units owner occupied, 1960	−	−0.47	−0.20	−0.14
Manufacturing ratio, 1960	+	+0.12	+0.06	+0.05*
Per cent employed in white-collar operations, 1960	−	−0.15	−0.06*	−0.06*
Form of government, 1963	+	−0.21	−0.27	−0.08
Type of election, 1963	−	+0.21	+0.07*	+0.05*
Number of councilmen, 1963	+	+0.32	+0.35	+0.35
Term of office, 1963	+	+0.17	+0.02*	+0.10*
Per capita general expenditure, 1963	+	+0.41	+0.33	+0.30
Per capita sanitation expenditure, 1963	+	+0.29	+0.20	+0.20
Per capita debt outstanding end of year in $10 units, 1963	+	+0.31	+0.32	+0.25

[a]Some of these variables and hypotheses are explained more fully in the original article.
[b]Correlations followed by an * are not significant at the 0.05 level. All other correlations are significant at the 0.05 level.
[c]No-violence cities included in analysis.
[a]No-violence cities excluded from analysis.

pendent variables showed any consistent relationship to the severity of racial violence.[26] The one exception to this which they did not explain was the positive correlation between Negro income levels and riot severity. If one turns to the literature on revolution, this is not an unexplainable relationship: the poor only revolt when their lot in life begins to improve.

CONCLUSION

One of the very real problems illustrated by these studies is the general lack of agreement on the meaning and hence measurement of objective deprivation. Before we go much further with this type of analysis a critical look should be taken at the key concepts being used in this research.[27] What is meant by objective deprivation? There seems to be little agreement among Wanderer, Ford-Moore, and myself.[28] If some general agreement could be reached on the meaning of this concept, then attention could be devoted to developing more adequate and valid measures of objective deprivation. Once this has been done, further analyses could be undertaken.

Similarly, what is it about the objective characteristics of a city and/or its population that gives rise to incidents of collective racial violence? Why do these events occur? Why do our nation's largest cities have the most severe outbursts of racial violence? These questions cannot be answered by this analysis. Indeed, they may never be answered in a very satisfactory manner unless greater attention is devoted to clarifying and specifying the exact nature of the theory underlying this research.

However, at least regarding the occurrence of hostile outbursts our data generally support the following argument which we set forth in the initial article:

Indeed, one might hypothesize that collective racial violence is likely to occur in a municipality when a certain threshold in some of these conditions is reached—that is, when environmental conditions within a particular city reach a particularly "explosive point."[29] It is not so much that these conditions "cause" hostile outbursts to occur. However, they do represent conditions or strains which can further the spread of hostile beliefs and attitudes among individuals in the black community.

When these generalized hostile beliefs and attitudes are channeled into specific fears, antagonisms, and hopes by a precipitating factor blacks are ready to be mobilized for participation in these violent events.[30] Whether or not they are mobilized is dependent on a number of factors, such as the control capability of authorities, the intensity with which hostile attitudes are held by blacks, the nature of the precipitating event, and so on.

However, to ignore the use of violence as a political resource by relatively powerless groups attempting to gain a more viable bargaining position vis-à-vis political authorities, as well as its other objectives or purposes, is to seriously neglect the political implications of these particular events.[31]

Furthermore, today's hostile outbursts represent a serious attack on existing institutions, as well as an effort to secure a response from public officials.[32] In fact, attacks on political agents and institutions have been the major characteristics distinguishing current racial violence from other social upheavals.[33] Such events, therefore, should not be viewed as pathological, exceptional, spasmodic, or purposeless. In many respects current racial violence represents, "to paraphrase von Clausewitz, the conduct of politics by other means, particularly when normal channels for accommodating public complaints have become inadequate for the task."[34]

Perhaps, then, we might learn more about the basic "causes" and hence "cures" for urban racial violence, if we devote greater attention to examining institutional impediments to change, that is institutional racism.[35] We cannot afford to be content with "explanations" of black protest (particularly urban racial violence, which is apolitical) that reduce the causes of racial confrontation to the level of psychological and personal factors or objective conditions.[36] For too long, weighty theses have been advanced which trace the anger of black citizens to the pathology and/or conditions of the ghetto rather than to the institutional arrangements which sustain the ghetto. Thus, "what American society faces is a political crisis, a crisis brought about because the promises and practices of political democracy have never been extended below some fixed social line established by racial and economic conditions."[37]

NOTES

[1] Selected portions of this article have been drawn from "Black Protest and Urban Racial Violence: Confrontation Politics," in James A. Riedel, ed., *State and Local Politics* (Waltham: Blaisdell, forthcoming, 1970). The author gratefully acknowledges the support of the department of political science at Michigan State University. I would also like to thank two of my colleagues, Timothy M. Hennessey and Elizabeth Powell, for their constructive comments on this article.

[2] These distinctions were first brought to my attention by Louis H. Masotti. See Louis H. Masotti, Jeffrey K. Hadden, Kenneth F. Seminatore, and Jerome R. Corsi, *A Time to Burn?* (Chicago: Rand McNally, 1969).

[3] *Ibid.* See also Civil Violence Research Center, Case Western Reserve University, *Shoot-Out in Cleveland* (New York: Bantam Books, 1969). For a somewhat different position on these violent events see Terry Ann Knopf, "Sniping—A New Pattern of Violence?" *Transaction* 6 (July-August 1969) pp. 22-29.

[4] See Mildred A. Schwartz, *Trends in White Attitudes Toward Negroes* (Chicago: National Opinion Research Center, 1967); and the attitudinal studies reported in *Supplemental Studies for the National Advisory Commission on Civil Disorders* (Washington, D.C.: U.S. Government Printing Office, July 1968). See also Paul B. Sheatsley, "American Attitudes on Race and Civil Rights," A Model Lecture prepared for the U.S. Information Agency (Chicago: National Opinion Research Center, September 1965).

[5] Harlan Hahn, "Political Objective of Ghetto Violence," A paper presented at the 1969 Annual Meeting of the American Political Science Association, New York, September 1969.

[6] For a discussion of the immensity of the problem of bringing about black equality see Michael Harrington, *The Other America: Poverty in the United States* (New York: Macmillan, 1962); and Kenneth B. Clark, *Dark Ghetto, Dilemmas of Social Power* (New York: Harper & Row, 1965). For a discussion of one attempt at resolution see John C. Donovan, *The Politics of Poverty* (New York: Pegasus Press, 1967); and Kenneth Clark and Jeannette Hopkins, *A Relevant War Against Poverty: A Study of Community Action Programs and Observable Social Change* (New York: Harper & Row, 1968).

[7] For a discussion of this problem see Bryan T. Downes and Timothy M. Hennessey, "Theory and Concept Formation in the Comparative Study of Urban Politics: Problems of Process and Change," A paper presented at the 1969 Annual Meeting of the American Political Science Association, New York, September 1969, pp. 20-22.

[8] Peter A. Jupsha, "On Theories of Urban Violence," *Urban Affairs Quarterly* 4 (March 1969), pp. 273-296.

[9] *Ibid.*

[10] Bryan T. Downes, "Social and Political Characteristics of Riot Cities: A Comparative Study," *Social Science Quarterly* 49 (December 1968), pp. 504-520.

[11] Jules J. Wanderer, "An Index of Riot Severity and Some Correlates," *American Journal of Sociology* 74 (March 1969), pp. 500-505; and William Ford and John Moore, "Additional Evidence on the Social Characteristics of Riot Cities," *Social Science Quarterly* this issue, pp. 339-348.

[12] We relied upon the same basic sources for our information on these violent events—the Congressional Quarterly special report entitled *Urban Problems and Civil Disorder*, and the *New York Times*.

[13] See the discussion of these problems in Downes, "Social and Political Characteristics," p. 506.

[14] Wanderer, "An Index," p. 500; and Ford and Moore, "Additional Evidence," footnote 7.

[15] These sources are cited in the original article.

[16] Wanderer, "An Index," p. 500.

[17] *Ibid.*, p. 501.

[18] Ford and Moore, "Additional Evidence," footnote 11.

[19] Wanderer, "An Index," pp. 501-503.

[20] Ford and Moore, "Additional Evidence," Tables 2 and 3.

[21] In our original article, the no-violence category which anchored this index or nominal scale was not indicated at the bottom of Table 6.

[22] For example, see Wanderer, "An Index," pp. 500-501. This Guttman scale is also discussed in Jules J. Wanderer, "1967 Riots: A Test of the Congruity of Events," *Social Problems* 16 (Fall 1968) pp. 193-198.

[23] This is the Pearson product-moment correlation coefficient.

[24] Further statistical analysis using multiple regression now seems appropriate in order to sort out the relative impact of the various independent variables on both the occurrence and intensity of collective racial

violence. However, most of the variance in our dependent variable will still be left unexplained by these contextual factors. Thus we still appear to be some distance from an adequate explanation for these events.

[25]Wanderer, "An Index," pp. 501-503. As I have previously pointed out, methodological differences are largely responsible for the divergence in the findings of these three studies.

[26]Ford and Moore, "Additional Evidence," Tables 2 and 3.

[27]For a discussion of the need for clear concise concepts informing one's research and the problems which arise when such concepts are unclear and/or ambiguous see: Downes and Hennessey "Theory and Concept Formation," part 1.

[28]For example, my notion of objective deprivation appears quite broad when compared to that used by either Wanderer or Ford-Moore. Does this concept refer to objective attributes of cities, individuals, or both?

[29]Downes, "Social and Political Characteristics of Riot Cities," pp. 519-520.

[30]*Ibid.,* p. 520.

[31]Hahn, "The Political Objectives," p. 6.

[32]*Ibid.*

[33]*Ibid.,* p. 3.

[34]*Ibid.,* p. 4. See also H. L. Nieburg, "Violence, Law, and the Informal Polity," *The Journal of Conflict Resolution* 13 (June 1969), p. 192; and H. L. Nieburg, "Uses of Violence," *The Journal of Conflict Resolution* 7 (March 1963), pp. 43-54.

[35]For a discussion of institutional impediments to change see Paul Jacobs, *Prelude to Riot: A View of Urban American From the Bottom* (New York: Random House, 1966); Louis L. Knowles and Kenneth Prewitt, eds., *Institutional Racism in America* (Englewood Cliffs: Prentice Hall, 1969); Jerome Skolnick, *The Politics of Protest* (New York: Ballantine Books, 1969); and Urban American, Inc. and the Urban Coalition, *One Year Later* (New York: Praeger, 1969).

[36]Knowles and Prewitt, eds., *Institutional Racism in America,* p. 13.

[37]*Ibid.,* p. 78.

C.
POLITICAL DISCRIMINATION

23
the second reconstruction: black political strength in the south

JOE R. FEAGIN and HARLAN HAHN

The first Reconstruction was the period between 1867 and 1876 in the former Confederate States when Congress tried to help the freed slaves enter into the mainstream of political and economic life. Immediately after the Civil War, the victorious North took no action, assuming that white and black southerners would come to some accommodation; instead, the southern legislatures passed a peries of laws that forbade blacks to move from their jobs, to vote, or to exercise the rights of free citizens in any way. Slavery was reestablished in fact, if not in name. It was after two years of this that Congress acted. They disenfranchised those who had been active in the Confederacy, enfranchised all others, passed a civil rights act, and sent down federal troops to protect the former slaves from their former masters.

As a result, blacks began to enter the political life of the South. Many served in state offices, although they never dominated the political life of the states, as is sometimes alleged; and from 1870 until 1901, there were twenty-two blacks who served in Congress. In 1876, the federal troops were withdrawn from the South; and from then on, blacks were steadily excluded from all aspects of political life, including voting. Only recently, with the passing of the federal Voting Rights Act of 1965 and concerted registration drives, have blacks again been participating in political life.

Although blacks are not a majority in any southern state (as of 1970, Mississippi had the largest percentage of blacks, with 36.8 percent; South Carolina had 30.5 percent; Louisiana, 29.9 percent; and Alabama, 26.4 percent), some counties and some small towns have a black majority. Voting means a great change in these counties and towns; it means control of police violence and access to public services. In the state legislatures, blacks have been able to articulate black needs and push for legislation of benefit to poor black constituents. Blacks have not yet realized their full voting potential, but when they do, it is likely to mean the end of the southern one-party system, already in decline, and a far more democratic political life in the South.

Reprinted from *Social Science Quarterly* 51, no. 1 (June 1970), pp. 42-56. Reproduced by permission of the authors and publisher.

The authors of the following selection trace in detail the recent history of black political life in the South. Mr. Feagin is a sociologist at the University of Texas, and Mr. Hahn is a political scientist at the University of California, Riverside.

In December, 1968, an unusual meeting was convened in Atlanta, attended by half of the nearly 400 black candidates elected to political offices in the South. This first major conference of black elected officials in the twentieth century constituted a striking symbol of the changes that have occurred in southern politics. Even five years earlier, such a meeting would have drawn—at most—a few dozen officeholders. The rapid increase in the number of elected officials reflects the dramatic resurgence of black participation in southern politics, but black citizens still face some imposing obstacles in their efforts to establish an effective political movement.

In general, minority groups must satisfy special requirements that are not imposed upon the majority to achieve their political goals. Minority voters frequently have been denied the opportunity to acquire the political training necessary to promote their interests and demands. As a result, minorities may lack the political skills, knowledge, and resources available to the majority. A complete list of the conditions that minority groups must fulfill in order to maximize their political effectiveness, therefore, would be long and complicated. Although this study will not attempt to fully catalogue those requirements, such criteria as the acquisition of political experience, the development of seasoned political leaders, the protection of legal safeguards, and a willingness to engage in a gradual rather than a swift capture of political influence might be included among them.

In addition, some especially fundamental requirements have been imposed on minority voters by the majoritarian principles of a democratic political system. A partial list of those requirements might include the following: (1) a large number of minority voters; (2) higher voter registration and turnout, (3) nearly maximal cohesion or unanimity in the choice of candidates; and (4) a divided vote among majority electors. Gains for minority voters on each of these criteria should increase their probability of securing political advantage. Although these considerations may form necessary conditions for the growth of political effectiveness, they are not totally sufficient conditions. Intervening factors may prevent minorities from achieving significant political power even if they have satisfied these requirements. Moreover, gains in electoral strength may not be translated into the public policy decisions sought by minority groups.[1] Nonetheless, these four criteria seem to constitute the necessary requirements for the attainment of political influence by minority voters.

The political activity of black citizens in the South has been a critical test of the ability of minority groups to accomplish their objectives in a democratic society. For centuries black political participation was suppressed by law or custom. As a result many observers were essentially pessimistic about the potential impact of black voters on southern politics. Although V. O. Key noted that politics in the South traditionally had been based on demagogic appeals to "the frightening specter of mass registration and block voting by Negroes," he concluded that the deeply entrenched fears and habits of black residents "made predictions of immediate mass voting improbable."[2] More recently, Wilson has argued, "even if discriminatory practices were ended, however, the low socioenomic status of the Negro would result in relatively low registration and voter turnout figures."[3] Since most studies of black political mobilization were made prior to the passage of the Voting Rights Act of 1965,[4] however, few have examined the effects of black voting under the conditions of legal equality enjoyed by white voters.

The purpose of this study, therefore, will be to analyze the growth of black political strength in the South and to examine its effectiveness in relation to the requirements that usually must be satisfied by minority groups seeking to maximize their political influence.

THE SIZE OF THE BLACK VOTE

One of the most important features of any political minority is the relative size of the group. In general, the larger the number and proportion of minority voters, the greater is their probability of exerting political influence. In the South the potential strength of black voters has been affected by two opposing trends: the persistent northward migration of black residents and the expanding opportunities for black political participants established by federal legislation. Simultaneously, the white population has not experienced a migration of similar proportions, and the increasing black political activity has apparently stimulated corresponding action among white voters. The recent growth of both black and white voter registration in the 11 states of the Old Confederacy is revealed in Table 1.

Between 1963 and 1967 the percentage of black adults registered to vote grew in all southern states. In addition, there was an important increase in the critical ratio of the proportion of blacks registered to the proportion of whites registered in all states except Tennessee. From 1963-1964 to 1967 the proportion of adult black Southerners that were registered to vote increased from slightly more than one-third to more than one-half. In 1963-1964 the proportion of blacks registered was about half the proportion of whites registered; but by 1967 the black-to-white ratio had jumped to 0.74.

However, white Southerners did not remain dormant in the face of rapid gains in black voter registration. The proportion of white adults registered also increased between 1963-1964 and 1967 in every southern state except North Carolina and Texas. In 1967 the percentage of the white adult population registered to vote in the South as a whole still exceeded the proportion of black citizens registered by 20 per cent. Only in Texas was a larger proportion of blacks registered than of whites.

Changes in both black and white voter registration rates between 1967 and 1968

provide a crude measure of the stability of emerging trends in southern politics. While the proportion of white Southerners registered rose by 1 per cent, the percentage of black Southerners registered climbed by 5 per cent. But the 1968 black-to-white ratio revealed relative losses for black voters in Florida, Mississippi, Texas, and Virginia, while black residents continued to gain vis-à-vis whites in Alabama, Arkansas, Louisiana, North Carolina, South Carolina, and Tennessee. Between 1967 and 1968 the percentage of registered black adults increased in seven states, declined in two states, and remained relatively unchanged in two other states. On the other hand, the proportions of whites registered grew in five states, decreased in four states, and remained constant in two other states. Although black citizens have continued to make greater registration gains than whites in many southern states, white increases have outdistanced black progress in other states.

Just how remarkable these recent gains in black voters are can be graphically illustrated by reference to the historical background. Table 2 reproduces data on the growth of black voter registration since 1940. In 1940 the number of black voters was quite small, about 250,000, or 5 per cent, of the black adult population. The proportion of black adults registered rose gradually until 1964, growing from 5 per cent to 38 per cent in that period. Between 1964 and 1968, however, the percentage of registered black Southerners almost doubled, and their numbers grew by more than one million. By mid-1968 approximately 17 per cent of *all* registered voters in the South were black citizens, a figure only somewhat below the percentage of black adults in the southern population (approximately one-fifth).

There is some evidence that the greatest gains in black voter registration have occurred in so-called "Black Belt" counties that contain large black populations, but that previously had a low percentage of registered black voters. An investigation in Alabama, for example, found that counties with a large black population had a higher percentage of registered black voters in 1966 than counties con-

TABLE 1. Black and White Voter Registration in the South Before and After 1965 Voting Rights Act

	Pre-act per cent of VAP[a] registered (1963-1964)	Black/white ratio (1963-1964)	Post-act per cent of VAP registered (1967)	Black/white ratio (1967)	Post-act per cent registered (1968)	Black/white ratio (1968)	Post-act registration (1968)
Alabama	Black, 19	0.28	52	0.58	57	0.69	273,000
	White, 69		90		83		1,117,000
Arkansas	Black, 40	0.61	63	0.88	68	0.91	130,000
	White, 66		72		75		640,000
Florida	Black, 51	0.68	64	0.79	62	0.74	292,000
	White, 75		81		84		2,195,000
Georgia	Black, 27	0.43	53	0.66	56	0.66	344,000
	White, 63		80		85		1,524,000
Louisiana	Black, 32	0.40	59	0.63	59	0.67	305,000
	White, 81		93		88		1,133,000
Mississippi	Black, 7	0.10	60	0.65	59	0.64	251,000
	White, 70		92		92		691,000
N. Carolina	Black, 47	0.48	51	0.61	55	0.70	305,000
	White, 97		83		79		1,579,000
S. Carolina	Black, 37	0.49	51	0.62	51	0.77	189,000
	White, 76		82		66		587,000
Tennessee	Black, 70	0.96	72	0.89	73	0.90	228,000
	White, 73		81		81		1,448,000
Texas	Black, 53[b]	Less than 1.00[c]	62	1.17	83	1.15	540,000
	White,		53		72		3,532,000
Virginia	Black, 38	0.62	56	0.89	58	0.87	255,000
	White, 61		63		67		1,256,000
Total	Black, 36	0.49	57	0.74	62	0.79	3,112,000
	White, 73		77		78		15,702,000

SOURCE: Calculated from tables in U.S. Commission on Civil Rights, *Political Participation* (Washington, D.C.: U.S. Government Printing, 1968), pp. 12-13, 222-223; and Voter Education Project, Southern Regional Council, *Voter Registration in the South* (Atlanta, Georgia: 1968), p. 2. The registration percentages are crude estimates, since the VAP figures are not for the same year as the registration figures.

[a] VAP - voting-age population in 1960.
[b] Figures not available by race.
[c] Estimated.

TABLE 2. Black Voter Registration in the South: 1940-1968

Year	Estimated number of registrants	Percentage of voting-age population
1940	250,000	5
1947	595,000	12
1952	1,008,614	20
1956	1,238,038	25
1960	1,414,052	28
1964	1,907,279	38
1968	3,112,000	62

SOURCE: These figures were taken from the following: Voter Education Project, Southern Regional Council, *Voter Registration in the South* (Atlanta, Georgia: 1968); D. R. Matthews and J. W. Protho, *Negroes and the New Southern Politics* (Chicago: Harcourt, Brace and World, 1966), p. 18. These should be construed as crude estimates, since voting-age population figures are not always for the same year as the registration statistics.

taining relatively few black residents. Variables such as nonwhite socioeconomic status, as well as rates of poverty, tenancy, and agricultural employment, that had been negatively correlated with black voter registration in 1960 were positively related to black registration in 1966.[5] Changes in black political mobilization in the South, therefore, have contradicted the old aphorism that "the more Negroes, the fewer are registered."[6] Furthermore, this trend has enabled black voters to take advantage of the structure of American Federalism that often has enabled relatively small groups in the electorate to command decisive majorities within specific localities and to use their local victories as a basis for gaining influence within larger political jurisdictions or organizations. While black citizens may never be able to attract the support of most southern voters, they already have scored some major successes at the county or municipal level.

Although black voters may never achieve an absolute majority in the South, their electoral gains have been sufficient to confound earlier pessimism about black political participation. Perhaps the nearly total disenfranchisement of black Southerners was necessary to prevent them from acquiring political influence. As the number of black voters has expanded, southern politicians probably have experienced growing temptations to seek their favor. The acquisition of a clear majority has

never been a prerequisite for the attainment of political objectives; relatively large minorities have had a broad variety of tactics available to them for securing major concessions and gains without resorting to the ultimate test of voting power. The relative size of the black electorate in the South seems to be approaching the critical level at which it can no longer be safely ignored.

LEGAL PROTECTION OF VOTING RIGHTS

The most striking gains in black voter registration have occurred since the passage of the federal Voting Rights Act of 1965. This measure suspended a variety of malevolent voter registration tests in the South and provided for the creation of a corps of federal examiners who have been sent to at least 58 counties in five southern states—Alabama, Georgia, Louisiana, Mississippi, and South Carolina—to accelerate the registration of black voters.[7]

As Table 3 demonstrates, in the years 1963-1964, before the passage of the Voting Rights Act, the proportion of the nonwhite voting-age population registered was higher in the "non-examiner" counties in four of the five states than in the counties that were later visited by federal examiners. After the Voting Rights Act and the actions of federal examiners, the total proportion of black adults registered in the "examiner" counties exceeded

TABLE 3. Nonwhite Voter Registration, by State, for Examiner and Non-examiner Counties in Five Southern States: 1963-1964 and 1967

	POST-ACT NUMBER REGISTERED TO VOTE		PRE-ACT PERCENTAGE OF VAP[a] REGISTERED (1963-1964)		POST-ACT PERCENTAGE OF VAP REGISTERED (1967)	
	Examiner counties	Non-examiner counties	Examiner counties	Non-examiner counties	Examiner counties	Non-examiner counties
Alabama	127,416	121,016	15	23	59	45
Georgia	6,013	316,483	10	28	63	53
Louisiana	50,413	252,735	9	37	54	60
Mississippi	94,674	86,559	8	5	71	50
South Carolina	9,377	180,640	17	38	72	51
Total	287,893	957,433	12	30	62	53

SOURCE: U.S. Commission on Civil Rights, *Political Participation* (Washington, D.C.: U.S. Government Printing Office, 1968), pp. 222-224.

[a]VAP - voting-age population as of 1960 Census. These figures reflect the estimates of official and unofficial sources and vary in reliability.

that of the "non-examiner" counties. Even in Mississippi, where in 1963-1964 the proportion of black adults registered in "examiner" counties had been slightly larger than the figure for "non-examiner" counties, by 1967 the percentage of black adults registered had grown to more than two-thirds in the areas visited by federal examiners, while increasing to only one-half in the other counties. The close association between black voter registration and the activities of the federal examiners has demonstrated that the protection of legal rights is a necessary prerequisite to the exercise of significant political influence. Black voter registration in the South, however, has not expanded without determined white efforts to end or reverse this trend. The U.S. Civil Rights Commission devoted more than half of its 1968 report to the documentation of white efforts to prevent black political activity.[8] This resistance not only has indicated the importance that white Southerners attach to recent black political accomplishments, but it also has underscored the significance of legal guarantees in promoting political participation.

Private civil rights organizations, in particular southern-based groups such as the Voter Education Project of the Southern Regional Council, also have played a major role in black voter registration. A report of the Voter Education Project compared registration statistics in three important Deep South states—Alabama, Mississippi, and South Carolina—for counties that had both federal examiners and a private voter registration project, counties with only one of those activities, and counties that did not have either type of voter registration activity.[9] In Alabama, for example, the ranking from highest to lowest percentage of black adults registered to vote was: (1) counties with both efforts, 70 per cent registered; (2) counties visited only by federal examiners, 64 per cent registered; (3) counties with only a Voter Education project, 58 per cent; and (4) counties with neither effort, 45 per cent. Similar patterns were found in South Carolina and Mississippi. Although voter registration has increased throughout the South, the activities of federal examiners and private civil rights organi-

zations have contributed significantly to this trend, particularly in counties of the Deep South that have strongly resisted black political activity.

BLACK ELECTED OFFICIALS

In 1968 the states with the largest proportions of registered black voters in the electorate were Mississippi, 27 per cent; South Carolina, 24 per cent; Louisiana, 21 per cent; and Alabama 20 per cent. As Table 4 indicates, three of these states—Mississippi, Louisiana, and Alabama—also led the list of southern states in the number of black candidates elected to public office. Forty-four per cent of all the elective offices held by black Southerners were won in those states. Ironically, the five states—Alabama, Louisiana, Mississippi, Arkansas, and Georgia—that cast their electoral votes for George Wallace in 1968 accounted for nearly two-thirds of the black elected officials in the South. While white voters were venting their frustrations in the national election, black citizens were making significant inroads into the foundations of local political power.

Although the number of southern black elected officials increased dramatically from 72 in 1965[10] to 473 in mid-1969[11] they have been disproportionately represented in a limited number of local offices. The largest number of elected black officeholders, for example, were municipal officials; but 93 per cent of these positions were on city councils. In addition, 83 per cent of the black law enforcement officials were justices of the peace or constables. Two-thirds of the black county officials were serving on county governing boards. And only five of the thirty black legislators in the South were in state senates. The gradual erosion rather than the immediate capitulation of white political domination apparently has been a primary objective of many black political leaders in the South. By focusing their attention on public offices at the grass-roots level, black candidates have sought to gain initial political experience and to establish the basis for an enduring role in southern politics.

In addition, black candidates have begun to make increasingly serious attempts to cap-

TABLE 4. Elective Offices Held by Black Southerners: January 1969

	Alabama	Arkansas	Florida	Georgia	Louisiana	Mississippi	N. Carolina	S. Carolina	Tennessee	Texas	Virginia	N	Per cent
City offices	31	14	16	6	14	8	11	16	8	10	18	152	39
Law enforcement offices	28	3	1	0	18	16	1	4	8	0	2	81	21
School board offices	5	33	0	3	9	6	4	2	1	8	0	71	18
County offices	3	0	1	6	11	20	1	4	5	0	3	54	14
State legislative offices	0	0	1	14	1	1	1	0	8	3	1	30	8
Total N	67	50	19	29	53	51	18	26	30	21	24	388	100
Per cent	17	13	5	7	14	13	5	7	8	5	6	–	100

SOURCE: Voter Education Project, Southern Regional Council, *Black Elected Officials in the Southern States* (Atlanta, Georgia: 1969), p. iii. In Tennessee one man is both a "city official" and a "state legislator" and is counted twice in the table.

ture southern Congressional seats. In 1962 two black residents qualified as candidates for Congress from Mississippi.[12] After the 1964 elections the Mississippi Freedom Democratic party unsuccessfully challenged the regular Mississippi Congressional delegation and elected alternate representatives in three districts.[13] In 1968 at least ten black Southerners ran for Congress, including six candidates in Alabama, four of whom belonged to the new National Democratic party of Alabama. They polled from 8 to 24 per cent of the total vote cast in those districts, altogether about 60,000 votes. Black candidates also competed with whites in three Virginia Congressional districts, where they garnered from 14 to 28 per cent of the votes cast.[14]

The most widely heralded 1968 election was held in the third Congressional district of Mississippi, which illustrated the strength of black voter turnout.[15] Although he eventually lost the run-off election, civil rights leader Charles Evers won 29 per cent of the total vote in the primary, while his nearest white opponent secured only 25 per cent.[16] In the primary an estimated 45 per cent of the black registered voters in the district actually cast their ballots, while 65 per cent of the white registrants voted.[17] In the run-off election, however, the black turnout figures jumped to 60 per cent, compared to 68 per cent for white. By demonstrating that black voters were a force to be reckoned with, the election had a major effect on the district, solidifying previously competitive black political groups into a unified, efficient campaign and forcing white candidates to modify their positions.

An important indication of the national significance of black voting strength in the South has been evident in the growing number of black Southerners selected as delegates to national party conventions. In 1968 approximately 106 black delegates were chosen to participate in the Republican and Democratic conventions, 88 per cent of whom were Democrats.[18] Each of the eleven southern delegations to the Democratic convention contained at least a few voting black delegates, while only three southern delegations (Georgia, Arkansas, Tennessee) to the Republican meeting included black party members as full delegates.

In addition to unseating the regular delegations from Georgia and Mississippi, the 1968 Democratic national convention placed the name of a black man, Reverend Channing Phillips, into nomination as candidate for President, a step taken by a major political party for the first time in American history; and he received 67½ delegate votes.[19] Subsequently, another black Southerner, Representative Julian Bond, was nominated for Vice President and polled 48½ votes before withdrawing from the race.

The growth of black voting strength has compelled both major political parties to grant increasing recognition and attention to the interests of minority citizens in the South. Historically most political organizations have been reluctant to repudiate the support of a sizeable bloc of voters, even when parties have failed to endorse their demands. By allowing the limited participation of minorities in partisan activities, each party has attempted to prevent those voters from threatening its political position or joining the opposition. But the entrance of black voters into party organizations has offered them a new opportunity to project their own policy preferences into party platforms. Regular processes of intraparty accommodation, therefore, have provided black citizens with an important means of securing political influence.

BLACK VOTING COHESION

Perhaps the most critical test of the political effectiveness of any minority group has been its ability to maintain electoral cohesion. A divided vote has diluted the strength of minorities and reduced their probability of gaining political influence. As Table 5 indicates, however, the 1968 presidential election yielded an impressive unanimity of choice among black voters in southern cities with widely different features and various levels of political organization. For example, in Houston, the largest southern metropolis, Humphrey polled 98 per cent of the vote in the city's predominantly black precincts. This lop-sided plurality also appeared in black precincts in such medium-sized cities as Tallahassee and Chattanooga, where Humphrey's proportion of the vote was also about 98 per cent. Throughout the South Vice President

TABLE 5. Black Support for the Democratic Presidential Candidate in 1968: Selected Southern Cities

City	Number of precincts	Per cent for Humphrey
Large cities		
Houston, Tex.	41	98
Memphis, Tenn.	2	97
Fort Worth, Tex.	6	98
Norfolk, Va.	1	95
Atlanta, Ga.	17	98
Dallas, Tex.	5	97
Medium-sized cities		
Richmond, Va.	22	92
Charlotte, N.C.	4	96
St. Petersburg, Fla.	1	91
Nashville, Tenn.	7	97
Chattanooga, Tenn.	2	98
Tallahassee, Fla.	2	97
Baton Rouge, La.	8	96

SOURCE: *Election Analysis: 1968 and the Black American Voter* (Washington, D.C.: Republican National Committee, 1969); *Tallahassee Democrat*, November 6, 1968; *San Antonio News*, November 6, 1968; *Houston Chronicle*, November 6, 1968; *Memphis Commercial*, November 6, 1968; *Memphis Commercial Appeal*, November 7, 1968; *Fort Worth Star-Telegram*, November 6, 1968; *Richmond Times-Dispatch*, November 7, 1968; *Chattanooga Post*, November 6, 1968; *Charlotte Observer*, November 6-7, 1968; *Nashville Tennessean*, November 6, 1968; *Norfolk Virginian-Post*, November 6, 1968; *St. Petersburg Times*, November 6, 1968. Several other southern newspapers which we examined reported "near-unanimous" votes for Humphrey in black precincts but gave no specific figures.

Hubert Humphrey received approximately 95 per cent of the black vote, a margin that even exceeded his support among black voters in other parts of the country.[20]

Black voters also have displayed unusual sophistication in casting their ballots in state elections. In 1966 for example, 91 per cent of the black voters in Virginia supported a moderate Democrat, William Spong, in one senatorial contest; but they gave less than 20 per cent of their votes to the conservative Democrat Harry Byrd, Jr., for the other Virginia Senate seat.[21] Similarly, in Alabama, Senator John Sparkman was supported by an estimated 71 per cent of the black voters, while the Democratic candidate for Governor, Lurleen Wallace, was able to gain only one-third of the black vote against a Republican segregationist.[22] In a few southern states local Democrats with favorable civil rights records even have outpolled national party candidates. In his 1968 bid for the U.S. Senate, for example, former Governor Leroy Collins ran ahead of the Democratic presidential candidate by from 1 to 4 per cent in several black precincts in Florida cities.[23]

Black support for Vice President Humphrey in 1968, however, represented a significant increase over the estimated 71 per cent of the southern black vote given John F. Kennedy in 1960, which provided Kennedy with a winning margin in four southern states.[24] Although the black vote was probably decisive in 1964 for President Johnson in four southern states,[25] both the 1964 and the 1968 elections were uniquely affected by candidates with a special sectional appeal, Goldwater and Wallace, whom southern white voters could support unequivocally and around whom they could rally. Nominees with such a sectional appeal, therefore, may have prevented the democratic presidential candidates from reaping the benefits of the normal divisions in the white electorate and the unified black vote.

In the first presidential election after the passage of the Voting Rights Act, Texas was the only southern state won by Hubert Humphrey with the aid of black votes. However,

Humphrey did receive approximately two million black votes across the South. This tremendous vote for the Democratic party belies the argument that political mobilization in the South "might be much lower if the candidate supported by Negroes had no chance of winning—as would be the case if he did not have the backing of a substantial block of white voters."[26] Nor did the election results indicate that "the southern Negro voter is not as firmly committed as the northern Negro voter to the Democratic Party."[27] Unanimity has seldom, if ever, been achieved in political campaigns; but the votes cast by black citizens in the South have closely approximated that standard in an effort to enhance their effectiveness.

SUMMARY AND DISCUSSION

Developments in southern politics since the passage of federal civil rights legislation in the early and mid-1960's have required some important revisions of earlier conclusions about black political activity in the South. In contrast to the fears expressed by many observers, black voter registration since 1960, and especially since 1964, has increased dramatically. Since minority voters in the South have emerged in sufficient numbers to affect the outcome of major elections, the foundation apparently has been established for the use of the black vote as a "veto," a "balance of power," or a component part of a coalition with other segments of the electorate.

However, since the growth of black voting strength has been closely related to the activities of federal examiners and private civil rights organizations, the possible expiration of the Voting Rights Act sanctions in 1970 has been a source of serious concern to black citizens. Vernon Jordan, former Director of the Voter Education Project, has recently commented on the potential seriousness of the situation:

Once Southern states are freed from the bonds of the Voting Rights Act, it is highly likely that they will want to do something about their 740,000 new black voters, whose presence on the voting lists is profoundly af-

fecting Southern politics. It is highly likely that these states will require that all voters re-register. A number of localities in the South . . . already have procedures requiring re-registration. As black leaders . . . have pointed out, re-registration can be a considerable burden for Negroes who were fearful and reluctant about going to the courthouse in the first place.[28]

The ability of black citizens to produce additional changes in southern politics, therefore, may depend upon both the continuation and the intensity of future support provided by the federal government.

Black political activity in the South already has yielded some significant gains. A relatively large, and rapidly growing, number of black candidates have been elected to local political offices, and black citizens have begun to occupy important positions in local political party organizations. By serving as a foundation for political experience and ambition, those offices have formed a natural basis from which black politicians might launch campaigns for higher public offices or for significant modifications in national party platforms.

Black voters in the South also have fulfilled perhaps the most important requirement for the political effectiveness of minority blocs by maintaining a high degree of cohesion in their voting behavior. In the 1968 presidential election, for example, black Southerners approached a level of unity and agreement seldom achieved by other minority groups in American politics.[29] As growing Republican strength produces sharp divisions within the white electorate, this disciplined and cohesive bloc of black voters probably will gain increasing importance not only in determining the outcome of elections but also in shaping the nature of Democratic party candidates and platforms.

While the unusual circumstances of major elections held since the passage of the Voting Rights Act probably have obscured the potential impact of black voting strength, the growth of black political participation already has produced some major changes in southern politics. Black voters have satisfied many of the conditions required of minority groups to maximize their political effectiveness. Although black political activity will require continuous public and private support, the growth of black voting strength in the South has displayed many of the characteristics of a broadly based and potentially enduring political movement.

NOTES

[1] William R. Keech, *The Impact of Negro Voting: The Role of the Vote in the Quest for Equality* (Chicago: Rand McNally, 1968).

[2] V. O. Key, Jr., *Southern Politics in State and Nation* (New York: Alfred A. Knopf, 1949), pp. 646-647.

[3] James Q. Wilson, "The Negro in American Politics: The Present," in John P. Davis, ed., *The American Negro Reference Book* (Englewood Cliffs, N.J.: Prentice Hall, 1966), p. 434.

[4] John H. Fenton and Kenneth N. Vines, "Negro Registration in Louisiana," *American Political Science Review* 51 (September 1967), pp. 704-713; Harry Holloway, "Negro Political Strategy: Coalition or Independent Power Politics?" *Social Science Quarterly* 49 (December 1968), pp. 534-547; Everett Carll Ladd, Jr., *Negro Political Leadership in the South* (Ithaca, N.Y.: Cornell University Press, 1966); Donald R. Matthews and James W. Prothro, *Negroes and the New Southern Politics* (New York: Harcourt, Brace and World, 1966); Hugh Douglas Price, "The Negro and Florida Politics, 1944-1945," *Journal of Politics* 17 (May 1955), pp. 198-200; Hugh Douglas Price, *The Negro and Southern Politics* (New York: New York University Press, 1957); James Q. Wilson, *Negro Politics: The Search for Leadership* (Glencoe, Ill.: The Free Press, 1960).

[5] Johnnie Daniel, "Negro Political Behavior and Community Political and Socioeconomic Structural Factors," *Social Forces* 47 (March 1969), pp. 274-280.

[6] Wilson, "The Negro in American Politics: The Present," p. 436.

[7] U.S. Commission on Civil Rights, *Political Participation* (Washington, D.C.: U.S. Government Printing Office, 1968), p. 12. The terms "black" and "nonwhite" will be used interchangeably to refer to the nonwhite data in this paper, since over 95 per cent of the nonwhites in the South are black Americans.

[8] *Ibid.*, pp. 19-31. The report documented the following evasive tactics: (1) changing from district to county-wide elections to dilute the black vote; (2) the consolidation of adjoining counties to increase the proportion of white voters in legislative districts; (3) abolishing elective offices contested by black candidates; (4) extending the terms of incumbent officials; (5) imposing additional filing fees and requirements for elective office; (6) withholding the information necessary for contesting a public office; (7) delaying the certification of nominating petitions; (8) efforts to postpone or prevent the seating of duly elected black officials; (9) the exclusion of black voters from crucial political meetings and conventions; (10) the harassment of black voters by election officials; (11) the omission of registered black voters from voting lists; (12) the failure to assist illiterate voters; (13) the disqualification of ballots cast by black voters for implausible technical reasons; (14) racially separate polling facilities; (15) the discriminatory location of polling places; (16) interference with black poll watchers; (17) vote fraud; (18) threats of physical violence and intimidations; and (19) economic reprisals for voting. On the important role of federal observers in deterring discriminatory election practices, see *ibid.*, p. 158.

[9] Voter Education Project data are taken from a Civil Rights Commission summary of the results in *ibid.*, p. 155. Technically, federal examiners do not "register" voters, but they examine voting qualifications and place the names of qualified persons on the list of eligible voters.

[10] Voter Education Project, *Black Elected Officials in the Southern States* (Atlanta: Southern Regional Council, 1969), p. i.

[11] Willadeane Clayton, "Black Elected Officials in South Now Total 473," *V.E.P. News* 3 (July 1969), p. 1.

[12] *Congressional Quarterly Weekly Report,* May 4, 1962, p. 811.

[13] *Congressional Quarterly Weekly Report,* January 1, 1965, p. 4.

[14] *Congressional Quarterly Weekly Report,* November 15, 1968, p. 3058.

[15] Further data on black voter turnout, respectable by southern standards, can be found in a recent Civil Rights Commission report. U.S. Commission on Civil Rights, *Political Participation,* pp. 14-15.

[16] *Congressional Quarterly Weekly Report,* March 15, 1968, p. 555.

[17] In 1969 Evers won the race for mayor, against a white opponent in the Mississippi town of Fayette, where black votes substantially outnumber white votes. Jack Nelson, "Evers' Victory Raises Hope of Black, White," *Los Angeles Times,* May 15, 1969, pt. 1, p. 5.

[18] *V.E.P. News* 2 (July 1968), pp. 1-3. Only half were "regular" delegates; the rest were alternates.

[19] *V.E.P. News* 2 (August 1968), p. 2.

[20]*Congressional Quarterly Weekly Report,* November 19, 1968, p. 3218.

[21]William Brink and Louis Harris, *Black and White* (New York: Simon and Schuster, 1966), p. 76

[22]*Ibid.,* p. 77

[23] *Tallahassee Democrat,* November 6, 1968, p. 18; *St. Petersburg Times,* November 6, 1968, p. 3-b. Southern black voters have also shown they can abandon the Democratic party in a highly disciplined manner in order to punish opponents of civil rights. In the 1968 election the Richmond, Virginia, Crusade for Voters asked voters to split their tickets. While the Democratic presidential candidate received 92 per cent of the votes cast in the black precincts, the Crusade-endorsed Republican candidate for Congress also obtained 77 per cent of the black votes in those same precincts. James E. Davis, "Democratic Loyalty Cut Negro Vote for Hansen in Richmond about 20%," *Richmond Times-Dispatch,* November 7, 1968, p. C4.

[24]Brink and Harris, *Black and White,* p. 75; *Congressional Quarterly Weekly Report,* November 11, 1960, p. 1846. It has been estimated that 60 per cent of Negro voters went for the Democratic candidate in 1956. *Congressional Quarterly Weekly Report,* March 30, 1962, p. 506.

[25]Brink and Harris, *Black and White,* p. 75; *Congressional Quarterly Weekly Report,* November 13, 1964, pp. 2674-2675.

[26]James Q. Wilson, "The Negro in Politics," *Daedalus* 94 (Fall 1965), p. 958.

[27]Wilson, "The Negro in American Politics: The Present," p. 441.

[28]*V.E.P. News* 3 (March 1969), p. 5.

[29]For statistics on voting by blacks and other minority groups in earlier elections, see Lucy S. Dawidowicz and Leon J. Goldstein, *Politics in a Pluralist Democracy: Studies of Voting in the 1960 Election* (New York: Institute of Human Relations Press, 1963).

24
red guard on grant avenue

STANFORD M. LYMAN

For a very long period, China has had a large population, many of whom emigrated. Chinese first came to the West Coast of the United States in the early nineteenth century as laborers in a period of acute labor shortage. At first, they were welcomed and admired as hard workers, thrifty and law-abiding. When, however, they came into competition with European immigrants in a period of declining need for labor, they met great hostility. The first laws excluding immigrants on the basis of nationality were passed against the Chinese in 1882; legal immigration of Chinese was not reestablished until 1943.

Anti-Chinese hostility and the interruption of immigration had a strong effect on the development of the Chinese community. In order to protect the community from discrimina-tory practices by the police, by the courts, or in economic matters, the Chinese drew upon a tradition of community and family self-help and self-control. Chinese children, for example, did not exhibit a pattern of juvenile delinquency, as the children of other immigrants did. They were restrained by enormous internal controls but also by a self-segregated community organi-zation that did its own disciplining. Family members and groups of families organized them-selves for mutual economic protection and in order to negotiate with the larger society as a group.

Most Chinese on the United States mainland live either on the West Coast or in New York City; a third live in Hawaii. Their history in Hawaii has been entirely different. The Chinese were the first laborers hired to work on the plantations, but very shortly afterward they began to move into the larger economy as entrepreneurs. The racism of the mainland was lacking, and the Chinese intermarried with other groups on the islands. Today they are an assimilated and important part of Hawaii's economic political, and educational life.

The article that follows examines both the changes that are occurring among Chinese communities on the United States mainland and the reasons for these changes. Mr. Lyman teaches sociology at the University of Nevada.

Visitors to San Francisco's historic Portsmouth Square on 7 May 1969 were startled to see the flag of the People's

Reprinted from *Trans-action* 7, no. 6 (April 1970), pp. 21-34. Copyright © April 1970 by Trans-action, Inc., New Brunswick, New Jersey. Reproduced by permission of the author and publisher.

Republic of China flying over the plaza. The occasion had begun as a rally to commemorate the 50th anniversary of the May 4 movement in Peking, when Chinese students demonstrated to protest the ignominious treaties forced on a moribund Chinese Empire by Occidental imperialists. Now a half century later in San Francisco, a group of disaffected Chinatown youth took over the rally from its sponsors to protest against the community's poverty and neglect and to criticize its anachronistic and conservative power elite.

Calling themselves the Red Guards, the youths asserted their right to armed self-defense against the city police and called for the release of all Asians in city, state and federal prisons on the ground that they had had unfair trials. On a more immediate and practical level, the Red Guards announced plans for a remarkably unradical petition campaign to prevent the Chinese Playground from being converted into a garage and for a breakfast program to aid needy children in the Chinatown ghetto. If the platform of the Red Guards sounded vaguely familiar, a spokesman for the group made it plain: "The Black Panthers are the most revolutionary group in the country and we are patterned after them."

To most San Franciscans the rise of youthful rebellion in the Chinese quarter of the city must come as a surprise. For the past three decades Chinese-Americans have been stereotyped in the mass media as quiet, docile and filial, a people who are as unlikely to espouse radicalism as they are to permit delinquency among their juveniles. In the last few years, however, evidence has mounted to suggest a discrepancy between this somewhat saccharine imagery and reality. Not only is there an unmistakable increase in delinquent activity among Chinese young people, there is a growing restlessness among them as well. Chinatown's younger generation feels a gnawing frustration over hidebound local institutions, the powerlessness of youth and their own bleak prospects for the future. The politics as well as the "crimes" of Chinatown are coming to resemble those of the larger society, with alienation, race consciousness and restive rebelliousness animating a new generation's social and organizational energies.

A basic cause for the emergence of youthful rebellion among the Chinese is the increase in the youthful population itself. There are simply more Chinese youth in the ghetto now than there ever have been before, a fact that can be attributed to an increasing birth rate among the indigenous population and a sudden rise in immigration from Hong Kong and other Asian centers of Chinese settlement.

By 1890, eight years after a wave of sinophobia had prompted Congress to block any further immigration of Chinese to this country, there were approximately 102,620 residents here. The vast majority were laborers or small merchants lured here by the promise of the "Gold Mountain" in California and work on the railroads. But a more significant fact is that the vast majority were also men. Before the turn of the century there were about 27 men for every woman among the Chinese in America. What this meant for white perceptions of these newcomers is probably familiar enough. Forced into ghettos, their women and children left behind to care for and honor their parents, these men joined together in clan associations and secret societies to provide them with some sense of familiarity and solidarity; and they turned as well to the typical pleasures of lonely men—prostitutes, stupefaction (through opium) and gambling. Just as typically, in a society known for its hostile racial stereotypes, the Chinese came to be identified with these "vices" in the minds of many white Americans and to be regarded as bestial, immoral and dangerous. But the alarming imbalance in the sex ratio also meant that the Chinese communities in America were almost incapable of producing a second generation of American-born Chinese. It wasn't until 1950 that the American-born made up more than half the total Chinese population, and even this growth only came about through the small trickle of illegal entries made by Chinese women prior to 1943 and the much larger number who entered since that date, thanks to gradual but important relaxations of the immigration laws.

The most radical of these relaxations came with the Immigration Act of 1965 which repealed the entire system of quotas based on national origins and substituted an entry procedure based on skills and the reuniting of families. Under this law, according to District Immigration Director C. W. Fullilove, there will be approximately 1,200 Chinese entering San Francisco every year with the intention of staying there.

Although not all of them will do so, this new influx of Chinese makes up a significant proportion of San Francisco's burgeoning Chinese population, and many of them fall between what Fullilove calls "the problem ages" for Chinese youth, 16 to 19.

THE GOLD MOUNTAIN

Of course, sheer numbers alone do not account for the rise of rebelliousness among young Chinese in San Francisco. A more significant factor is that conditions of life in Chinatown are by no means pleasant, productive or promising. We must distinguish, however, from among the Chinese those who have escaped the ghetto, those who are American-born but who still inhabit Chinatown and the foreign-born youth who reluctantly find themselves imprisoned within a ghetto even less of their own making than it is of the other's. Among those who have escaped there are, first, the scholars, scientists, intellectuals and professionals—many of whom hail from regions other than southeastern China, the original home of the bulk of America's Chinese immigrants—who have found work and residence within the larger society. Enclosed in university, corporation, professional or government communities, these Chinese do not for the most part feel themselves to be a part of Chinatown; they go there only occasionally for a banquet or for a brief sense of their ethnic origins. A second group much larger than the first, although actually quite small in relation to the total number of Chinese, consists of those American-born Chinese who have successfully completed high school and college and gone on to enter the professions—most frequently pharmacy and engineering—the American middle class and, when they can evade or circumvent the still-prevalent discrimination in housing, the finer neighborhoods or the suburbs. This "gold Bourgeoisie"—to paraphrase E. Franklin Frazier—is also estranged from Chinatown. Proud of his own achievements, wary of any attempt to thrust him back into a confining ghetto existence and alternately angered, embarrassed or shamed by the presence of alienated, hostile and rebellious youth in Chinatown, the middle-class American Chinese holds tenaciously to his newly achieved material and social success.

Nevertheless, middle-class native-born Chinese are discovering that the American dream is not an unmixed blessing. The "Gold Mountain" of American bourgeois promise seems somehow less glittering now that its actual pinnacle has been reached. Chinese, like other descendants of immigrants in America, are discovering that the gold is alloyed more heavily than they had supposed with brass; but, like their second- and third-generation peers among the Jews and Japanese, they are not quite sure what to do about it. The price of success has been very great—not the least payments being the abandonment of language, culture and much of their ethnic identity. Among some there is a new search for cultural roots in Chinese history, a strong desire to recover the ancient arts and a renewed interest in speaking Chinese—at least at home. Others emphasize, perhaps with too much protestation, their happiness within the American middle class and carry on a conspicuous consumption of leisure to prove it. Finally, a few recognize their Chinatown roots and return there with a desire to aid somehow in the advancement of the Chinese ghetto-dwellers. Sometimes their offers of help are rejected with curses by the objects of their solicitude, but in any event the growing number of restive Chinatowners constitutes another challenge to the comfort of bourgeois Chinese.

In its most primordial sense the visible contrast between the style of life of the impoverished ghetto-dweller and that of the middle-class professional promotes guilt and shame. Somehow it seems wrong that one's ethnic compatriots should suffer while one enjoys the benefits of success. Yet middle-class Chinese are quite ready to attribute their success to their own diligence, proverbial habits of thrift and hard work and to their conscious avoidance of delinquent or other kinds of unruly behavior. Naturally, then, some middle-class Chinese are equally quick to charge the angry Chinatown youth with indolence, impropriety and impiety. But even as they preach the old virtues as a sure cure for the young people's personal and social ailments, some perceive that there is more to these problems than can be solved by the careful nurturing of Confucian or Protestant ethics. They see more clearly than the Americanized and less-alienated Chinese of the fifties that poverty, cultural deprivation and discrimination are truly obdurate barriers to the advancement of the ghetto-dwellers of today. Moreover, there is an even more profound problem. Like other alienated youthful minorities, the youth of Chinatown appear to reject just that dream which inspired and activated the now bourgeois Chinese. For the middle-class Chinese, then, the peak of the "Gold Mountain" seems to have been reached just when those still down below started to shout up that the arduous climb isn't worth the effort.

SOCIAL BANDITS AND PRIMITIVE REBELS

Among Chinatown's rebellious groups there are two distinguishable types of youth—those who are American-born but have dropped out of school and form part of the under- or unemployed proletariat of the Chinese community; and those recently arrived immigrant youth who, speaking little or no English and having little to offer in the way of salable skills, find themselves unable to enter the city's occupational and social mainstream. Both native- and foreign-born Chinese are included among the ranks of the quasi-criminal and quasi-political gangs that are accused of contributing to the mounting incidence of delinquency in the Chinese quarter. Culture, language and background have divided the native from the foreign-born Chinese in the past, and it is only recently that there is any sign of a common recognition between the two groups.

It is traditional to focus on Chinatown gangs as an unfortunate form of juvenile delinquency among a people otherwise noted for their social quiescence and honesty. A more fruitful approach however would adopt the perspective taken by E. J. Hobsbawm in his discussion of social bandits and primitive rebels. According to Hobsbawm, who has studied these phenomena in Europe, social banditry

is a form of pre-ideological rebellion which arises among essentially agrarian, unskilled and unlettered peoples who are at great cultural distance from the official and oppressive power structure. It is led by those who enjoy a certain amount of local notoriety or awe. Often enough social banditry remains at a stage of petty criminality which is of concern, if at all, only to the local police. At a more refined stage, however, predatory gangs are formed which confine their criminal activities to attacks on strangers and officials and share any loot with local community members who, though not a party to the attacks, identify with and protect the robbers.

It is important to note that bandit gangs may adopt a populist or a conservative style. The former is symbolized by Robin Hood, who robbed the rich to feed the poor and attacked civic or state officialdom as intruders in the community's traditional way of life. In the conservative style, bandit gangs are co-opted as toughs and thugs to defend local satrapies and powerful petty interests. Social banditry may exist side by side with ideologically rebellious or revolutionary elements but is usually untouched by them except for particular reasons of strategy or tactics. Essentially, it is separated from ideological politics by its deep involvement with local ethnic rather than cosmopolitan class interests. However, it is not impossible for class and ethnic interests to merge and for the liberation of local groups to become enmeshed within the revolutionary aims of a radically politicized sector of a modern party state.

From the perspective of "primitive rebellion," Chinatown's gangs take on a greater significance for the understanding of loosely structured pluralistic societies like the United States. Gangs in Chinatown are by no means a new phenomenon, but their activities in the past describes mainly the early stages of social banditry. For the most part Chinatown's traditional social banditry has been of a particularly conservative type, identified with the recruitment of young toughs, thugs, and bullies into the small criminal arm of Chinatown's secret societies. They formed the "flying squads" of mercenaries who "protected" brothels, guarded gambling establishments and enforced secret society monopolies over other vice institutions of Chinatown. From their numbers came assassins and strong-arm men who fought in the so-called tong wars that characterized Chinatown's internecine struggles of a half century ago and which still occasionally threaten to erupt today. But this form of social banditry was an exclusive and private affair of Chinatown. Insofar as Chinatown's violent altercations were circumscribed not only by the invisible wall around the ghetto but also by the limited interests of the contending parties for women, wealth and power, the community was isolated by its internal conflicts. Whether manifested in fearful acquiescence or active participation, the ghetto's residents were bound together in a deadly kind of "antagonistic cooperation."

Since 1943 a progressive cycle of rebellion among Chinatown's youth has metamorphosed from crime to politics, from individual acts of aggression to collective acts of rebellion and from nonideological modes of hostility to the beginnings of a movement of ideological proportions. From 1943 until 1949 juvenile crime in Chinatown was largely the activity of a small number of native-born boys about 15 years of age, hurt by unemployment, difficulties in home life or inadequate income. Their crimes were typical of the most individualized and inarticulate forms of primitive rebellion. Burglary, auto theft, robberies, larcenies, holdups and assault and battery constituted 103 of the 184 offenses for which Chinese male juveniles were referred to San Francisco's juvenile court in those years. There were also gangs of native-born youth, apparently sponsored by or under the protection of secret societies, who occasionally assaulted and robbed strangers in Chinatown, not a few of whom, incidentally were Japanese-Americans recently returned from wartime internment camps and also organized into clubs, cliques and gangs.

Petty criminal gangs emerged more frequently among both the native- and foreign-born youth in Chinatown from 1958 to 1964. In some cases these gangs were composed of young men sponsored in their criminal activities by secret societies. An example was the "cat" burglary ring broken up by police in

1958 and discovered to be a branch of the Hop Sing Tong. Three years later, two gangs, the "Lums" and the "Rabble Rousers," were reported to be engaged in auto thefts, extortion, street fights and petty larcenies. In January 1964 members of a San Francisco Chinatown gang were charged with the $10,000 burglary of a fish market in suburban Mountain View. A year later, the police broke up the "Bugs," a youthful criminal gang whose members dressed entirely in black, with bouffant hair styles and raised-heel boots, and who, in committing 48 burglaries, made off with $7,500 in cash and $3,000 in merchandise in a period of six months. The "Bugs"—who capitalized on an otherwise-stigmatizing aspect of their existence, their short stature—reemerged a year later despite an attempt by Chinatown's leaders to quell juvenile gangs by bringing in street workers from San Francisco's Youth for Service to channel the gang toward constructive activities. By the mid-1960s Chinatown's burglary gangs had begun to branch out and were working areas of the city outside the Chinese quarter.

The present stage of a more politicized rebellion may be dated from the emergence in May 1967 of Leway, Incorporated. In its history up to August 1969, the Leways experienced almost precisely the pattern of problems and response that typically give rise first to nonideological rebellion and then, under certain conditions, to the development of revolutionary ideology. Leway (standing for "legitimate way") began as a public-spirited self-help group among American-born Chinese teen-agers. Aged 17 to 22, these young men organized to unite Chinatown's youth, to combat juvenile delinquency and to improve conditions in the poverty-stricken Chinese ghetto through helping youths to help themselves. In its first months it gained the support of such Chinatown luminaries as Lim P. Lee, now San Francisco's postmaster and a former probation officer, and other prominent citizens. Through raffles, loans and gifts, these youths, many of whom could be classed as delinquents, raised $2,000 to rent a pool hall near the Chinatown-Filipino border area. And, with the help of the Chinese YMCA and Youth for Service, they outfitted it with five pool tables, seven pinball machines, some chairs and a television set. "This is a hangout for hoods," said its president, Denny Lai, to reporter Ken Wong. "Most of us cats are misfits, outcasts with a rap sheet. What we're trying to do is to keep the hoods off the streets, give them something to do instead of raising hell."

Leway was a local indigenous group seeking to employ its own methods and style to solve its own members' problems. And it was precisely this that caused its downfall. Police refused to believe in methods that eschewed official surveillance, sporadic shakedowns and the not always occasional beating of a youth "resisting arrest." Leway tried a dialogue with the police, but it broke down over the rights of the latter to enter, search and seize members at Leway's headquarters, a tiny piece of "territory" which the young Chinese had hoped to preserve from alien and hostile intrusion. Leway claimed it wanted only to be left alone by this official arm of a society which they saw as already hostile. "We are not trying to bother them [the police] . . . and we won't go out of our way to work with them either."

In addition to continuous harassment by white police, Leway failed to establish its legitimacy in Chinatown itself. The Chinese Chamber of Commerce refused it official recognition, and as a result Leway could not gain access to the local Economic Opportunity Council to obtain much-needed jobs for Chinatown youth. The Tsung Tsin Association, which owned the building where Leway had its headquarters, threatened to raise the rent or lease the premises to another renter. Finally, whether rightly or not, the members of Leway, together with other Chinatown youth groups, were blamed for the increasing violence in Chinatown. Throughout 1968-69 reports of violent assault on tourists and rival gangs were coming out of Chinatown. Police stepped up their intrusive surveillance and other heavy-handed tactics. Chinese youth charged them with brutality, but the police replied that they were only using proper procedures in the line of a now more hazardous duty. In late summer 1969 the combination of police harassment, rent hikes, Leway's failure to secure jobs for its chronically unemployed members

and its general inability to establish itself as a legitimate way of getting Chinatown youth "straightened out" took its final toll. Leway House closed its doors. Dreams of establishing on-the-job training for the unskilled, new business ventures for the unemployed, a pleasant soda fountain for Leway adolescents and an education and recreation program for Chinatown teen-agers—all this was smashed. The bitterness stung deep in the hearts of Chinatown young people. "Leway stood for legitimate ways," a 15-year-old youth told reporter Bill Moore. "Helluva lot of good it did them." The closing of Leway destroyed many Chinatown young people's faith in the official culture and its public representatives.

The stage was set for the next phase in the development of rebellion. Out of the shambles of Leway came the Red Guards, composed of the so-called radical elements of the former organization. But now Leway's search for legitimacy has been turned on its head. The Red Guards flout the little red book *Quotations from Chairman Mao Tse-tung* as their credo, make nonnegotiable demands on the power structure of Chinatown and the metropolis and openly espouse a program of disruption, rebellion and occasionally, it seems, revolution.

Leway had been modeled after other San Francisco youthful gang reform groups, but the Red Guards have adopted the organizational form, rhetorical style and political mood of the Black Panthers. A few years ago this would have seemed highly improbable. In the 1960s there were frequent bloody clashes between gangs of Chinese and Negroes, and interracial incidents at Samuel Gompers School—a kind of incarceration unit for black and Oriental incorrigibles—had not encouraged friendly relations among the two groups. Nevertheless it was just these contacts, combined with a growing awareness of Panther tactics and successes, and some not-too-secret proselytization by Panther leaders among the disaffected Leway members, that brought the young Chinese to adopt the black militant style. Whatever prejudices Chinese might harbor against Negroes, Black Panther rhetoric seemed perfectly to describe their own situation. After all, Leway had tried to be good, to play the game according to the white man's rules, and all it had gotten for its pains were a heap of abuse and a few cracked skulls. Now it was time to be realistic—"to stop jiving" and "to tell it like it is." Police were "pigs"; white men were "honkies"; officially developed reform programs were attempts to "shine" on credulous Chinese youth; and the goal to be attained was not integration, not material success, but power. "We're an organization made up mainly of street people and we're tired of asking the government for reforms," said Alex Hing, a 23-year-old Chinese who is the minister of information of the Red Guards. "We're going to attain power, so we don't have to beg any more."

URBAN POPULISM

The Red Guards are a populist group among Chinatown's "primitive" rebels. They stand against not one but two power structures in their opposition to oppression and poverty—that of old Chinatown and that of the larger metropolis. Ideologically they are located somewhere between the inarticulate rumblings of rustic rebels and the full-scale ideology of unregenerate revolutionaries. They cry out for vengeance against the vague but powerful complex of Chinese and white elites that oppress them. They dream of a world in which they will have sufficient power to curb their exploiters' excesses; meanwhile they do the best they can to right local wrongs and to ingratiate themselves with the mass of their Chinatown compatriots. The free breakfasts for indigent youngsters, a copy of the Panthers' program, attracts popular support among Chinatown's poor at the same time that it shames Chinatown's elites for allowing the community's children to go hungry. The demand for the release of all imprisoned Asians seems to place the Red Guards squarely on the side of all those "little people" of Chinatown who feel themselves victimized by an alien and oppressive police system. However, their ethnic consciousness usually supersedes and sometimes clashes with their alleged attachment to a class-oriented ideology, as it did when the Red Guards accepted an invitation to guard a meeting of the Chinese Garment Contractors' Association against a

threatened assault by Teamsters seeking to organize Chinatown's heavily exploited dressmakers. But it is precisely their parochial dedication to a sense of Chinese ethnicity that endears them to the less hardy of young Chinatowners who secretly share their dilemmas and dreams, as well as limits their political effectiveness.

Populist rebellion is not the only form of social politics in Chinatown. A conservative type of rebelliousness is illustrated in the evolution of the Hwa Ching and the Junior Hwa Ching. Hwa Ching emerged in 1967 as a loose association of mostly Hong Kong-born youth in Chinatown. Estimates of its size vary from 25 to 300, and this fact alone testifies to its low degree of cohesiveness and the sense of drift that characterizes its members. Until very recently Hwa Ching was represented in most public discussions by a "spokesman" (its looseness of organization prevented any greater clarification of title), George Woo, a former photographer who took on the task of bridging the communication gap between the largely Chinese-speaking youths and the officials of the metropolis. The aims of this association are difficult to ascertain exactly, partly because there was little agreement among its members and partly because spokesman Woo usually tended to a violently polemical speaking style in order to call attention to the situation of Chinatown's immigrants. Hwa Ching had less of a perfected program than a set of practical problems. Hong Kong youth were insufficiently educated and skilled to obtain any jobs other than Chinatown's dreary positions of waiter, busboy and sweated laborer; unequipped linguistically to enter the metropolis and, in the beginning, unwilling to accept confinement in a congested, poverty-stricken and despotically ruled ghetto.

Hwa Ching seemed to form itself around El Piccolo, an espresso coffeehouse opened in Chinatown in 1967 and operated by Dick and Alice Barkley. Alice Barkley, herself a Hong Kong-born Chinese, turned the coffeehouse into a haven for foreign-born Chinese youth. There they could meet in peace and with freedom to discuss, argue, complain and occasionally plan some joint activity. Reaction to their clubby fraternization at El Piccolo was mixed.

Traditional Chinatowners accused the Bark-
leys of offering asylum to raffish criminal elements; a newly aroused college and university
group of Chinese-Americans praised the establishment of a place for impoverished immigrants to congregate; and most San Franciscans
didn't even know the Hwa Ching existed.

Early in 1968 Hwa Ching approached
the Human Relations Commission, the Economic Development Council and the Chinese
business elite to ask for their aid in establishing an educational program for alleviating the
misery of Chinatown's immigrant youth. Their
approach was unusually frank and plainly
practical. They proposed the establishment of
a comprehensive two-year educational program to provide Chinatown's young immigrants with a high school diploma and vocational training in auto repair, business machine
operation, construction, sheet metal, electrical installation and plumbing. They closed
with a statement that was unfortunately taken
as a warning and a threat. "We've been hearing too many promises. The rise and fall of
our hopes is tragic and ominous."

This first bid for help was unsuccessful.
In late February, however, the Hwa Ching
tried again and spoke to the Chinatown Advisory Board of the Human Relations Commission. This time Hwa Ching, represented by
the fiery George Woo, was more modest in its
request for a comprehensive program, but
more militant in its presentation. Hwa Ching
wanted $4,322 to build a clubhouse, but al-
though Woo reiterated the same arguments as
other Hwa Chings had presented in January,
the tone was different. Describing his constituents, Woo said, "There is a hard core of delinquents in Chinatown who came from China.
Their problems are the problems of all poor
with the addition that they don't speak English." Then he added that "they're talking
about getting guns and rioting. . . . I'm not
threatening riots. The situation already exists,
but if people in Chinatown don't feel threatened they won't do anything about it." The
mention of guns and the warning of possible
riots were too much for John Yehall Chin, a
prominent Chinese businessman, principal of
Saint Mary's Chinese Language School and
member of the Human Relations Commis-

sion's Chinatown Advisory Board. In reply to
the Hwa Ching's request he advised the commission, and indirectly the youths, "They
have not shown that they are sorry or that
they will change their ways. They have threatened the community. If you give in to this
group, you are only going to have another
hundred immigrants come in and have a whole
new series of threats and demands. Although
the commission expressed its interest, Hwa
Ching's demand was rejected.

They tried again. In March the Hwa
Ching's president, Stan Wong, presented the
immigrant youths' case before the Chinese
Six Companies, the oligarchy that controls
Chinatown. Speaking in Cantonese, Wong
repudiated the threat of riots made at the February meeting. "We made no threats," he said.
"They were made by nonmembers. We need
to help ourselves. We look to the future and
are mindful of the immigrant youths who will
be coming here later. We hope they do not
have to go through what we've been through."
Later he answered a question about possible
Communist affiliation: "Hwa Ching is not in-
volved with any political ideology." Although
Commissioner Chin pointed out that the Hwa
Ching had mended its ways, the Six Compan-
ies refused them help. Meanwhile the Human
Relations Commission, under the direction of
Chin, organized an Establishment-controlled
Citizens for Youth in Chinatown. The Hwa
Ching felt utterly rejected.

In their bitterness and anger, however,
the Hwa Ching did not turn to populist revolt,
as had the Leways. Instead they fragmented
even more. Their loose coalition at El Piccolo
ended when that establishment closed its
doors in August 1968. The Hwa Ching had
never in fact professed an ideology. What
seemed to be one was more a product of the
fervid imaginations of alarmed whites and of
the fiery invective of George Woo than it was
any coherent line of political or revolutionary
thought. The Hwa Ching's practical needs
were too immediate, their literacy in English
too low and their limited but practical political experience in Hong Kong and Chinatown
too real for them to accept an organization
that used Mao's red book and which therefore
ran for them the risks of political persecution

and possible deportation. As Tom Tom, a 23-year-old immigrant who had been one of the earliest members of Hwa Ching, explained to a reporter, the immigrant youth were independent of the Leway and all other Chinatown groups, affected none of the hippie-Che-Raoul-Panther styles and wanted little more than jobs, girls and to be left alone. The Hwa Ching found themselves oppressed by their supposed allies nearly as much as by their condition. Leway boys and other American-born Chinese called them "Chinabugs" and attacked them in gang rumbles; Negroes picked on the diminutive Chinese until they learned to retaliate in numbers and with tactics; college students sought to tutor and to evangelize them with secular and sometimes political ideas but succeeded mostly in making them feel inferior and frightened by a kind of politics they abhorred.

By the middle of 1969 the Hwa Ching had split into three factions. One returned to the streets to fight, burglarize and assault all those available symbols and representatives of the seemingly monolithic power structure that had scorned them; two other factions apparently accepted cooptation into Chinatown's two most powerful though age-ridden secret societies—the Suey Sing and Hop Sing Tongs. There their anger could find outlet at the same time that their strength could be utilized for traditional aims. The secret societies could pay for the immigrant youths' basic needs and with the same expenditure buy the muscle to keep control of their own interests and institutions. And since the Tongs were part of the complex congeries of associations that make up Chinatown's power elite, it is not surprising that leaders of this same elite gave tacit approval to the Tongs' recruitment of what had appeared in early 1968 to be a serious threat to the old order. Unlike the Leway, which could not join the old order and may have been too Americanized to accept secret society patronage, the immigrant youth find in it a perhaps temporary expedient in their dilemma. Not being politicized, they can more readily join in the protection of old Chinatown. They have resumed a posture typical of earlier youthful generations' response to anger and poverty in China-

town. They form the conservative wing of Chinatown's complex structure of conflict and rebellion.

In other areas and times of primitive rebellion, conservative and populist factions often fought each other as much as their professed enemies. Similarly, in Chinatown the young toughs who have become paid guards of the secret societies' and, occasionally, the Six Companies' meetings are not infrequently arrayed against the Leway-Red Guard gangs. And in this sense young Chinatown recapitulates a structure of conflict that characterized that of its earlier generations. Conservative-populist conflicts isolate the contending parties from outside groups and larger issues. The violent fights and smouldering feuds appear to noncomprehending outsiders to be exclusively Chinese in their nature and content. And this intramural conflict in turn circumscribes Chinatown and once again cuts it off from the metropolis.

OUTSIDE IDEOLOGIES

However, connections to the larger society of San Francisco in particular and the United States in general do exist. For the youth the most important one is the Intercollegiate Chinese for Social Action (ICSA). This group was formed at San Francisco State College from among the more socially concerned and politically aware Chinese-American students. For a while it managed the special program by which Chinese students from the ghetto were recruited to the college. But the long Third World strike at San Francisco State College in 1968-69 radicalized its members and propelled them into even greater contact with the Chinatown community. They became actively oriented toward conditions about which they had been only vaguely aware before. ICSA asserted aloud and with emphasis what had been but an open secret for decades—Chinatown was a racial ghetto—poverty-stricken, disease-ridden, overcrowded, underdeveloped and with a population growing in Malthusian proportions. To the remedy of all these defects they dedicated themselves and established offices not only in the college but in Chinatown itself. ICSA provides tutoring services to Chinatown's less-educated youth and urges that San Francisco State College establish even more programs for community rehabilitation. The community-oriented Chinese college youth do not openly attack Leway or the Red Guards but remain in communication with them as well as with the erstwhile Hwa Ching. But, observes George Woo, now as an ICSA member, "We can also see the pitfalls in using too much of the blarney, as the Red Guards did. As a result, they alienated immigrant youths and the whole community in three months' time." By keeping open contacts among the native- and the foreign-born, among Hwa Ching and Leway-Red Guards, among status-conscious diploma-bearers and socially stigmatized delinquents and among the legitimated and the lowly, ICSA may yet be able to blunt the deadly edge of conflict and build a durable community for Chinatown.

What this means specifically is by no means clear even to the ICSA members themselves. "I'm still trying to figure out what I am supposed to be as a Chinese-American," complained a 21-year-old college student, echoing the inner nagging question of most of his compatriots. And George Woo replied, "I know how you feel. I don't identify with China either and I certainly don't identify with the petty American middle-class values of my aunts and uncles." ICSA emphasizes a two-way learning process between the lettered and the dropouts and calls for the formulation of a new ethic to replace the Confucian-Protestant ethos of Chinese America. As ICSA leader Mason Wong has said, "Our generation here will no longer accept the old and still-prevalent Confucian doctrine of success coming only from hard work and humility." What that ethic will be is not yet known. However, the Chinese must still contend with the traditional social order that is Chinatown's Establishment.

THE OLD ORDER

Anyone at all conversant with San Francisco's Chinatown will have heard of the Chinese Six Companies. In a vague sense he might know about some of its activities, be able to point out its headquarters and note that it is a benevolent, protective and repre-

sentational body of Chinese who enjoy unofficial but influential standing at City Hall. Beyond this he might know very little but the familiar litany that the Chinese take care of themselves, contribute little, if at all, to the welfare rolls or to the city's alarming rate of juvenile delinquency and, that while the Chinese were perhaps at one time a troublesome minority, they are now safely ensconced in their own quarter of the city where they enjoy a modicum of freedom to practice peculiar cultural expressions derived from a China that is no more. To him the Six Companies is one aspect of that cultural freedom.

Like many stereotypes that arise in racist societies, this one too contains some kernels of truth. The Chinese in San Francisco, like the Chinese in Calcutta, Singapore, Bangkok, Saigon, Manila and indeed in almost every large city to which Chinese have migrated, enjoy a measure of home rule that far exceeds that of any other minority group in the metropolis. During the colonial period in Southeast Asia, the British and Dutch formalized their practices of indirect rule into a specified system of titles. "Kapitan China" was the Dutch designation for the uniformed and bemedalled Chinese who represented his people in the colonial councils at Batavia, and the "Captain China" system prevailed in British Malaya and other colonies as well. For the colonial powers indirect rule was an expedient way of maintaining sufficient control over restless and hostile native peoples in a precariously pluralistic society in order to extract their labor and the colony's natural resources without having to contend with all their tribal and customary ways and woes. For the subject peoples it meant that they could freely organize their lives in accordance with traditional practices, so long as they didn't interfere with the rather limited interests of the imperial powers. Outside the colonial area, Chinese immigrant elites also managed to establish a kind of cultural extraterritoriality and to achieve an added legitimation to their traditional control over their fellow migrants by winning unofficial but practically useful recognition from white civic elites. In Vancouver and in New York City the Chinese Benevolent Association has obtained such prerogatives; in San Francisco it is the Chinese Six Companies.

But to understand Chinatown's power structure fully, it is necessary to analyze the several kinds of traditional associations from which it is composed. First there are clan associations, or "family associations" as Occidental journalists and sociologists usually term them. Clan associations derive from the lineage communities so prevalent in Kwangtung and ideally unite all persons descended from a common male ancestor. Overseas, however, the more manageable lineage unit was replaced by a kinship network wider than that which originally enclosed only a compact village. The clan association includes all who bear the same surname. In the early days of Chinese immigration, the clan associations became a special kind of immigrant aid society providing the newcomer with food, shelter, employment, protection and advice. Furthermore, the clan leaders reminded the immigrant of his obligations to parents and family in the home village and, in the absence of the village elders, assumed a role in loco parentis, settling disputes, arbitrating disagreements and in general containing intraclan differences within the kinship fold. Some clan associations exercised a monopoly over a trade or profession in Chinatown and effectively resisted encroachments on these monopolies by ambitious Chinese upstarts from other clans. Until the recent arrival of large numbers of immigrants from Hong Kong, the clan associations had been declining in power and authority as a result of the aging of their members and the acculturation of the American-born Chinese. However, even this new lifeblood is less acquiescent than the former sojourner members. Chinatown clan associations are now challenged to provide something more than a paltry benevolence in exchange for their petty despotism.

In addition to clans, however, there developed among overseas Chinese a functionally similar but structurally different type of association. The hui kuan united all those who spoke a common dialect, hailed from the same district in China or belonged to the same tribal or ethnic group. (It is a mistake to suppose, as many Occidentals do, that the peoples of China are culturally homogeneous. In the tiny area around Canton from which most of America's immigrants have come, there are numerous dialects which, while they have a common script, are almost mutually unintelligible when spoken.) In many ways the hui kuan were similar to those immigrant aid and benevolent societies established by Germans, Irish, Jews and other Europeans in America. In San Francisco and other cities in which Chinese dwelt, the hui kuan, like the clan association, maintained a headquarters and served as caravansary, hostelry, credit association and employment agency. In all these matters it exercised authoritarian control, and since most of the Chinese in America were debtors, directly or indirectly, to their hui kuan, its officers were not infrequently suspected of taking an excessive interest or a corrupt profit from their charges. The hui kuan, again similar to the clan, conducted arbitration and mediation hearings between disputing members, managed and collected the debts of its members and in addition charged them various fees for its services. An aging membership and the flight of the American-born bourgeoisie tended to undermine hui kuan authority, but the old businesses in Chinatown still affiliate with them and accept their mediation and arbitration services. They are especially important in the ownership and control of Chinatown property which they administer in a traditional way quite different from real estate management in the Occidental parts of the city.

The third major type of association in Chinatown is the secret society. Like the clan and the hui kuan, the secret society originated in China where for centuries it served as a principal agency for popular protest, violent rebellion and social banditry. The overseas migrants from Kwangtung included not a few members of the Triad Society, the most famous of China's clandestine associations. In nearly every significant overseas community of Chinese they established chapters of, or models based on, that order. In the United States secret societies among the Chinese were set up by the early immigrants in the cities and also in those outlying areas where clans and hui kuan could not form a

solid base. Inside Chinatown the secret societies soon took over control of gambling and
prostitution, and it is with these activities
rather than with their political or charitable
activities that they are most often associated
in the minds of non-Chinese in America. Clans,
hui kuan and the several chapters of secret
societies often fell out with one another over
their competition for women, wealth and
power inside Chinatown, and these so-called
tong wars raged intermittently until a Chinatown Peace Association established a still-
perilous peace between the warring factions
in the 1920s. The charitable works of secret
societies were confined for the most part to
giving mutual aid to their own members, the
establishment of headquarters and hostelries
and in recent years the building of clubhouses
where their aged bachelor members might
find hospitable fraternity. The political activities of the secret societies have consisted in
their intermittent interest in the fortunes of
China's several regimes, but they have not
shown any particular interest in upsetting the
national politics of the United States. Meanwhile the secret societies' most successful
source of revenue in Chinatown—the control
over gambling and prostitution—diminished
as the Chinese bachelors aged and died and
the American-born declined interest in these
activities. The recruitment of the newly arrived and disaffected immigrant youth from
Chinatown has undoubtedly done much to rejuvenate these societies, but it remains to be
seen whether this will lengthen their lives as
institutions in America or change their function in accordance with new interests and
current developments.

At the top of the community power
structure of Chinatown is the Chinese Benevolent Association, commonly known as the
Chinese Six Companies. It was formed in the
late 1850s as a confederation of hui kuan—
later it incorporated clans, guilds and, reluctantly, secret societies—in order to provide
community-wide governance, to promote
intracommunity harmony and to present at
least the appearance of a common Chinese
front to white society. Until the 1870s it
functioned as an agency of international
diplomacy and consular activity as well, since

the Chinese Empire did not provide a specific
overseas office for those duties. The Six Companies has been the principal spokesman for
the Chinese to white America. It has protested against the anti-Chinese legislation,
helped fight discriminatory laws in the courts,
petitioned federal, state and local governments
in behalf of the Chinese and generally provided
Chinatown with a modest respectability in
the face of sinophobic stereotypy. One of its
more recent efforts in defense of Chinese in
America was a protest against Secretary of
Transportation John Volpe's omission of the
role that Chinese played in the building of
the Transcontinental Railroad when he spoke
at the centenary celebration of its completion.

Gradually the Six Companies estab-
lished its legitimacy as rightful representatives
of the Chinese in San Francisco. Composed
of merchants and traders, the leaders of the
Six Companies seemed to inspire assurance
among civic leaders that the Chinese were not
a threat to the city's economic base. Moreover, the anti-Chinese movement in America
was largely a movement of small farmers and
laborers against what they described as the
unfair competition of Chinese laborers. Once
labor agitation had succeeded in driving the
Chinese workers out of the city's industries
and into the confines of Chinatown—a mission
largely accomplished by 1910—civic function-
aries were quite prepared to negotiate with
the Six Companies whatever agreements
might have to be reached between the ghetto
and the metropolis. For its part the Six Companies, although it protested against the excesses of ghettoization, must have realized
the gain to be made in its own power by having the great majority of Chinese housed and
employed in Chinatown. The final establishment of Chinatown as an unofficial but real
quarter of the city consolidated and enhanced
the power of the Six Companies over its
denizens.

In effect the Six Companies' authority
over Chinese in San Francisco was—until the
advent of the American-born and the rise of
intracommunity rebellion—an institutionalized version of the kind of control over
Negroes in America exercised by Booker T.
Washington and his "Tuskegee Machine"

from 1890 until 1915. The slow growth of a second generation prevented an effective counteraction to its powers by an acculturated group demanding a new politics. To be sure, Chinatown's Six Companies had its W. E. B. DuBoises—men who opposed the despotic benevolence it exercised, the containment of Chinese in the ghetto that it tacitly espoused and the corruption in its offices. But they were too few in number to be effective, too readily co-opted into the controlled violence of Chinatown's secret societies or too easily frightened into silence by threats of financial loss, deportation or conviction of trumped-up crimes in the white man's courts, where Chinese interpreters could be bought and perjured witnesses were easily obtainable. When the American-born generation did reach maturity, many of its members went to college, entered the professions and departed from Chinatown. This caused the Six Companies some loss in its Chinese constituency, but, since the Chinese-American bourgeoise did not challenge the authority of the Six Companies, the loss did not undermine its control over Chinatown.

LEGITIMATE AND ILLEGITIMATE REBELLION

Today, in addition to the "illegitimate" rebellion of youth in Chinatown, there is a "legitimate" counteraction of adults against the community-wide authority of the Six Companies. This loyal opposition includes several intra-Chinatown associations composed of "respectable" members of the American-born and, occasionally, a foreign-born Chinese leader who opposes the associational oligarchy. Until 1956 the only significant organization among the American-born Chinese was the Chinese-American Citizens' Alliance, a group so small that in its early days, more than a half century ago, it was little more than a name promising assimilation. Since the mid-1950s, however, a new association has arisen—the Chinese-American Democratic Club (CADC). This organization of politically minded and socially conscious Chinese-Americans heralds a shift from communal-oriented traditionalism to civic-minded cosmopolitanism in Chinatown. Still another

organization outside the domination of the Six Companies is the Concerned Chinese for Action and Change, a loose and informal association of middle-class Chinese-Americans who live outside the ghetto but who can be counted on to mass for support of more liberal social action in Chinatown. Third, the Chinatown-North Beach Area Youth Council, a product of the Economic Development Agency in Chinatown, seeks to link up the respectable middle-class Chinatowners with its less-respectable youth groups. Finally, there is one aging Chinese, J. K. Choy, who almost alone has opposed the old order in Chinatown without effective reprisal. A Columbia-educated banker and a professed disciple of Fabianism, Choy has exposed the poverty and neglect hidden beneath the tinseled glitter of Chinatown's neon-lit ghetto. He organized a reading room and English classes for immigrants in the offices next to the branch bank which he oversees as general manager. When in October 1966 he advised the women employed in Chinatown's sweatshops to organize for better wages, shorter hours and improved conditions and offered a devastating criticism of the ghetto's poverty program, rumors were started in the community which resulted in a three-day run on the bank. Unlike the old Chinese boycotts, which were used so effectively in the early days of the economically isolated Chinatown, this attempt to destroy a Chinatown reformer failed because the bank was protected by its connections to the larger banking system of the state. The failure to silence Choy by traditional methods is a measure of the ghetto's growing interdependence with the nation and a testimony to the decreasing power of traditional sanctions available to intracommunity elites.

In Chinatown the arena of battle between the new opposition and the old order has been for seats on the poverty board organized under the community action program of the Economic Opportunity Act of 1964. In April 1969, after three years of internecine in-fighting, the liberal opposition—largely composed of the members of the CADC—was finally able to depose the Six Companies' man on the board, Chairman

Dapien Liang, and to replace him with a chairman more to its liking. The Six Companies charged that the poverty board was dominated by "left-wing militants" but was unable to secure its complete control over Chinatown's poverty program. However, the Chinatown program is budgeted so far only to the beginning of 1970. If the program is scrapped, the arena of conflict and opposition in Chinatown may shift on to some other plane.

Another challenge to the old order has been hurled recently by ICSA. In August 1969 a news reporter interviewed Foo Hum, tea merchant, mogul in the Chinese Six Companies and representative on the Chinatown antipoverty board, concerning Chinatown's social problems. In addition to denying that the community's problems were either exclusive or very grave, Hum refuted the assertion that they were atrributable to newly arrived immigrants. Then he launched into an attack on the native-born youth, especially the Red Guards and the ICSA and was quoted in the press as saying, "The Red Guards and the Intercollegiate Chinese for Social Action—theirs are Communist activities. They should not be blamed on the new immigrants." ICSA promptly filed a slander suit against Hum for $100,000 general damages and $10,000 punitive damages. Hum, backed by a Six Companies legal defense fund of $10,000, refused to settle out of court to an offer made by Mason Wong, ICSA president, that the suit be dropped in return for Hum's writing a letter of apology and publishing it in all local papers, paying all legal fees that have arisen thus far and donating a token gift of money to ICSA.

The crust of Chinatown's cake of customary control may be beginning to crumble. The old order must contend not only with the mounting opposition of the community's respectable, professional and American-born younger and middle-aged adults, but also with the militant organization of Chinatown's disaffected youth. In addition, one cannot count on the new immigrants to bow to Chinatown's traditional power elite in the future as they have in the past.

It is by no means clear, however, what the outcome of this continuing power struggle will be. Chinatown's more liberal-minded leaders may defeat themselves by their ambiguous support of both progressive policies and a new racial consciousness. The former may call for a need to push for the introduction of unionization and other characteristic features of white America into Chinatown's anachronistic institutions. But the new ethnic consciousness, a consciousness that in its extreme forms opposes both the old order of transplanted Cathay and the middle-class ways of white America, may forbid cooperation with those institutions—progressive or not—that are dominated by Caucasians. It is in this possible paralysis that Chinatown's old order coalesces with its new rebels. Both seem to oppose the imposition of the metropolis upon the ghetto, but for quite different reasons. For the old elites any greater intrusion might undermine their exclusive and "extraterritorial" power; for the new rebels any intrusion might wrest away their newly discovered desire for ethnic self-determination. It would not be impossible for Chinatown's garment workers, as well as the community's other unprotected and impoverished denizens, to be caught helplessly in the vice of this excruciating cultural conflict.

DISCRIMINATION AND NATIONAL OPPRESSION

Beyond the problems of the ghetto itself—some of which are typical of all poor ethnic enclaves in American cities, some of which are peculiarly Chinese—loom the attitude and action of the larger society. Chinatown's myth of social propriety, communal self-help, familial solidarity and a low crime rate was a carefully nurtured mystique, prepared to counteract the vicious stereotype of coolie laborers, immoral practices, murderous tong wars and inscrutable cunning that characterized the American white man's perspective. As a pervasive mystique coloring most reports of Chinatown for the past three decades, it has succeeded up to a point in its original purpose—to substitute a favorable stereotype for an unfavorable one. It had other latent functions as well, not the least of which was to protect the community's social and political structure from excessive scrutiny and destruction. So long as Chinatown could "contain" its problems, circumscribe its para-governmental institutions with bourgeois or innocuously exotic descriptions and control its members, the community was safe, and the city adopted a relaxed attitude toward its own cosmopolitan character.

But Chinatown's safety rests also on America's foreign relations with China. The repeal of the exclusion laws in 1943 was a gesture of reconciliation toward the country's wartime ally in the war against Japan, just as the incarceration of the Japanese -Americans during that same war was a hostile move against those Americans who had the misfortune to be physically identifiable with America's enemy. Aware of the dangerously changeable character of America's friendliness toward her racially visible peoples, Chinatown has presented a picture of cultural identity with nineteenth-century Cathay and of moral sympathy for the Nationalist regime in Taiwan. This is not a false picture, for the political identity of the aged aliens is of very low intensity, but if it must be linked to old China it is most probably to the Republic founded by Sun Yat-sen and continued under Chiang Kai-shek. The American-born Chinese are not "Zionists" to any degree and therefore feel themselves to be Americans politically and socially and do not identify with either China. Even the Red Guard's rhetorical usage of Mao's book is more a symbol of an American rebellion than the substance of Communist affiliation. And the new immigrants have shown a profound disinterest in associating even with the symbols of Maoism.

Nevertheless, the fires of fear and prejudice are still kindled in America. Not only are acts of prejudice and discrimination still visited upon Chinese-Americans in everyday life, at least one agency of the government itself is still not wholly satisfied with the loyalty of Chinese in America. On 17 April 1969 J. Edgar Hoover testified before a subcommittee of the House Committee on Appropriations that "the blatant, belligerent and illogical statements made by Red China's spokesmen during the past year leave no doubt that the United States is Communist China's No. 1

enemy." Hoover went on to warn the subcommittee of Communist Chinese intelligence activity "overt and covert, to obtain needed material, particularly in the scientific field." After hinting darkly that a Chinese-American who served a 60-day sentence in prison for making a false customs declaration about electronic parts being sent to Hong Kong might have been an agent of a Communist country, Hoover asserted, "We are being confronted with a growing amount of work in being alert for Chinese Americans and others in this country who would assist Red China in supplying needed material or promoting Red Chinese propaganda." "For one thing," he continued, "Red China has been flooding the country with its propaganda and there are over 300,000 Chinese in the United States, some of whom could be susceptible to recruitment either through ethnic ties or hostage situations because of relatives in Communist China." Hoover went on to say that "up to 20,000 Chinese immigrants can come into the United States each year and this provides a means to send illegal agents into our Nation." Hoover concluded his testimony on this point by asserting that "there are active Chinese Communist sympathizers in the Western Hemisphere in a position to aid in operations against the United States." Thus the Chinese in America were reminded that perhaps all their efforts at convincing white America that they were a peaceable, law-abiding, family-minded and docile people who contributed much and asked little in return had gone for naught. In time of crisis they too might suffer the same fate that overtook the highly acculturated Japanese-Americans a quarter century before—wholesale incarceration. When Hoover's remarks are coupled with the widespread report in 1966 that China's atomic bomb was "fathered" by Dr. Tsien Hwue-shen, an American-educated Chinese who was persecuted here for five years during the McCarthy era and then allowed to return to the country of his birth and citizenship, and with the fact that under Title II of the Emergency Detention Act of 1950 any person or group who is deemed to be a "threat to the internal security of the United States" may be incarcerated in the same detention camps in which the American Japanese were imprisoned, the safety of the Chinese in America from official persecution is by no means assured. The Chinese, of course, protested against Hoover's remarks, and one San Francisco paper labeled his testimony an irresponsible slur on "a large and substantial segment of American citizens." Meanwhile, Japanese-American, Chinese-American and several other kinds of organizations have joined together to attempt to get Congress to repeal the infamous Title II.

Race prejudice, as Herbert Blumer has reminded us, is a sense of group position. It arises out of the belief, supported and legitimated by various elites, that a racial group is both inferior and threatening. Such a belief may lie dormant beneath the facade of a long-term racial accommodation, made benign by a minority group's tacit agreement to live behind the invisible, but no less real for that, wall of a ghetto. Then when circumstances seem to call for new meanings and different explanations, the allegedly evil picture and supposedly threatening posture may be resuscitated to account for political difficulties or social problems that seem to defy explanation.

History, however, does not simply repeat itself. There is a new Chinatown and new sorts of Chinese in America. The old order holds its power precariously in the ghetto, and the new liberals and the now vocal radicals bid fair to supplant them and try new solutions to the old problems. Finally, the Japanese experience of 1942 may not be repeated either because the United States has learned that lesson too well or because too many Americans would not let it happen again.

25

the meanings of black power: a comparison of white and black interpretations of a political slogan

JOEL D. ABERBACH and JACK L. WALKER

It has been said in other places in these introductory notes, and it is probably worth saying again, that white culture contains a great fear of being overwhelmed by a flood of blacks; this despite the fact that blacks constitute only a little over 11 percent of the population. Nothing has aroused this feeling more than the slogan "black power." It seems to have been uttered rather casually by Stokely Carmichael, an oratorical flourish to a speech, rather than a well-thought-out political concept. But the term caught on, first with black militants, then with whites.

Stokely Carmichael and the political scientist Charles Hamilton later wrote a book called Black Power *and in it tried to analyze what the words meant. To them, black power is not a very complicated, bloodthirsty concept; it is a call to unity in the black community to the end of controlling the community's destiny. To many blacks in the streets, black power can be translated: "Whitey, get off our backs!" As the authors of the following essay point out, however, the meaning of the term reflects not so much what is in the term itself, as defined by its author, as the generalized attitude of an individual of one race toward another race.*

This selection is a careful study of what a selected group of whites and blacks from Detroit felt the term means. Much can be learned about both the black and white communities by looking at their reactions to these two little words.

Both Mr. Aberbach and Mr. Walker are political scientists at the University of Michigan.

1. INTRODUCTION

Angry protests against racial discrimination were a prominent part of American public life during the 1960's. The decade opened with the sit-ins and freedom rides, continued through Birmingham, Selma, and the march on Washington, and closed with protests in hundreds of American cities, often punctuated by rioting and violence. During this troubled decade the rhetoric of protest became increasingly demanding, blanket

Reprinted from *The American Political Science Review* 64, no. 2 (June 1970), pp. 367-388. Reproduced by permission of the authors and publisher.

charges of pervasive white racism and hostility were more common, and some blacks began to actively discourage whites from participating either in protest demonstrations or civil rights organizations. Nothing better symbolized the changing mood and style of black protest in America than recent changes in the movement's dominant symbols. Demonstrators who once shouted "freedom" as their rallying cry now were shouting "black power" —a much more provocative, challenging slogan.

The larger and more diverse a political movement's constituency, the more vague and imprecise its unifying symbols and rallying cries are likely to be. A slogan like black power has no sharply defined meaning; it may excite many different emotions and may motivate individuals to express their loyalty or take action for almost contradictory reasons. As soon as Adam Clayton Powell and Stokely Carmichael began to use the phrase in 1966 it set off an acrimonious debate among black leaders over its true meaning. Initially it was a blunt and threatening battle cry meant to symbolize a break with the past tactics of the civil rights movement. As Stokely Carmichael put it in one of his early speeches:

The only way we gonna stop the white men from whippin' us is to take over.

We've been saying freedom for six years and we ain't got nothing. What we gonna start saying now is black power, . . . from now on when they ask you what you want, you know to tell them: black power, black power, black power![1]

Speeches of this kind not only were a challenge to the white community; they also were attacks on the currently established black civil rights leaders, especially those who had employed more accommodating appeals or had used conventional political and legal channels to carry on their struggle. Carmichael's speeches brought a swift, negative response from Roy Wilkins:

No matter how endlessly they try to explain it, the term black power means anti-white power. . . . It has to mean going it alone. It has to mean separatism. Now separatism . . .

offers a disadvantaged minority little except a chance to shrivel and die. . . . It is a reverse Mississippi, a reverse Hitler, a reverse Ku Klux Klan. . . . We of the NAACP will have none of this. We have fought it too long.[2]

Although not so adamant and uncompromising as Wilkins, Martin Luther King expressed the doubts of many moderate leaders when he said:

It's absolutely necessary for the Negro to gain power, but the term "black power" is unfortunate because it tends to give the impression of black nationalism. . . . We must never seek power exclusively for the Negro, but the sharing of power with the white people. Any other course is exchanging one form of tyranny for another. Black supremacy would be equally evil as white supremacy. My problem with SNCC is not their militancy. I think you can be militantly nonviolent. It's what I see as a pattern of violence emerging and their use of the cry "black power" which whether they mean it or not, falls on the ear as racism in reverse.[3]

This disagreement over the implications of the black power slogan was caused partly by a clash of personalities and ambitions, but it was also the result of fundamental differences over the proper role of a black minority in a society dominated by white men. Should the ultimate goal be complete assimilation and the development of an essentially "color blind" society, or should blacks strive to build a cohesive, autonomous community, unified along racial lines, which would be in a stronger position to demand concession and basic social changes from the whites? For American Negroes, who bear the brutal legacy of slavery and are cut off from their African heritage, this is a terribly difficult choice. As James Baldwin said when he compared himself with the lonely, poverty-stricken African students he met in Paris:

The African . . . has endured privation, injustice, medieval cruelty; but the African has not yet endured the utter alienation of himself from his people and his past. His mother

did not sing "Sometimes I Feel Like A Moth-
erless Child," and he has not, all his life long,
ached for acceptance in a culture which pro-
nounced straight hair and white skin the
only acceptable beauty.[4]

The slogan black power raises all the agonizing dilemmas of personal and national identity
which have plagued black Americans since the
end of slavery; the current dispute over its
meaning is echoed in the speeches of Frederick Douglass, Booker T. Washington, W. E. B.
Du Bois, and Marcus Garvey.

Those, like Harold Cruse,[5] interested
in a comprehensive social theory to guide
black development in the United States are
not particularly impressed with the term black
power because: it is open to just as many
diverse and conflicting interpretations as the
former abstractions Justice and Liberation.
While it tries to give more clarity to what
forms freedom will assume in America as the
end product of a new program, the black
power dialogue does not close the conceptual
gap between shadow and substance any more
than it plots a course for the program dynamic.[6]

Cruse hopes for the development of a
synthetic political ideology in the classic sense
which brings together economic, cultural and
political factors; black power, at this point in
time, is a label for a series of ideas which fall
far short of this goal.

Whatever interpretation may be given it,
black power is a provocative slogan which
causes excitement and elicits strong responses
from people. Even though, as Charles Hamilton says, "in this highly charged atmosphere
it is virtually impossible to come up with a
single definition satisfactory to all,"[7] the
definition an individual selects may tell us a
great deal about how he defines himself politically in a society torn by racial strife. His definition is a way for him to bring together his
views on leaders and events in the environment. If he agrees with Stokely Carmichael
and Charles Hamilton, he sees black power as
"a call for black people in this country to
unite, to recognize their heritage, to build a
sense of community."[8] He may also see it as
a call for anything from "premeditated acts

of violence to destroy the political and economic institutions of this country" to "the
use of pressure-group tactics in the accepted
tradition of the American political process."[9]

We know that community leaders have
strong reactions to the black power slogan, but
little is known of its impact on ordinary citizens, both black and white. As we shall demon-
onstrate, for the white citizen the slogan usually provokes images of black domination or
contemporary unrest which he cannot understand or tolerate. For the black citizen, it is
more likely to raise subtle issues of tactics and
emphasis in the racial struggle. In this essay we
will examine how blacks and whites in a large
urban center define black power, why they
define it as they do, and whether their view of
the slogan is part of a coherent set of interpretations and evaluations, a racial ideology,
which they used to define the role of blacks
as political and social actors in our society.

2. THE DATA

Our analysis is based on data gathered
in a survey of Detroit, Michigan, completed
in the fall of 1967. A total of 855 respondents
were interviewed (394 whites and 461 blacks).
In all cases whites were interviewed by whites,
blacks by blacks. The total N came from a
community random sample of 539 (344
whites and 195 blacks) and a special random
supplement of 316 (50 whites and 266 blacks)
drawn from the areas where rioting took place
in July, 1967.[10] Since there are few meaningful differences between the distributions or
the relationships of interest in the random and
riot-supplement samples, we have employed
the total N in the analysis so that a larger
number of cases are available when controls
are instituted.

3. A PROFILE OF COMMUNITY OPINION

Since there is such confusion and uncertainty over the meaning of black power
among the writers, spokesmen and political
leaders of both races, we might wonder if the
slogan has had any impact at all on average
citizens. The first questions we must ask are
simply: do our respondents recognize the
term, have they formed an elaborate reaction
to it, and if so, what meaning do they give it?

TABLE 1. Black Power Interpretations, by Race

Question: "What do the words 'black power' mean to you?"

Interpretation	Blacks (%)	Whites (%)
Unfavorable		
Blacks rule whites	8.5	38.6
Racism	3.9	7.3
Trouble, rioting, civil disorder	4.1	11.9
"Nothing"	22.3	5.3
Negative, imprecise comments (ridicule, obscenity, abhorrence)	6.5	11.7
Other[a]	4.3	5.9
	49.6	80.7
Favorable		
Fair share for black people	19.6	5.1
Racial (black) unity	22.6	5.6
	42.2	10.7
Don't know, can't say	8.2	8.6
Total	100	100
(Number)	(461)	(394)

[a]"Other responses were scattered and inconsistent, although generally negative. They include references to black power as communism, radicalism, a return to segregation and a sophisticated failure to define the concept because of a perception that it has contradictory meanings. The latter answer was given by 1 black and 5 white respondents.

Because of the lack of consensus among community leaders about the precise meaning of black power or even agreement on a common framework for discussing the slogan, we were reluctant to use a close-ended question to capture our respondents' interpretations of the term. In order to avoid the danger of biasing responses or eliciting a random choice we used a simple, open-ended question: "What do the words 'black power' mean to you?" This has the advantage of permitting people to speak with a minimum of clues, but it also has disadvantages which we recognized. Respondents may not have given the term a great deal of thought and their answers may be unreliable indicators of their opinion (or lack of opinion). Use of the vernacular at times inhibited interpretation of the answers.[11] It was sometimes difficult to judge whether a respondent was sympathetic or unsympathetic to black power as he interpreted it. For example, a small number of Negro respondents (N=3) could only define black power as "rebellion." We can guess their feelings about this word

from the context of the interview, but this carries us a step away from their answers.

Fortunately, the answers were generally quite comprehensible and when we asked the same open-ended question of a subsample of the original respondents one year later (1968) we received answers consistent with their first response from a majority of the people.[12] In addition, in 1968 we supplemented the question on the meaning of black power with a close-ended item: "Do you approve or disapprove of 'black power'?" This provided a means of checking the criteria we developed in 1967 from the open-ended question for deciding whether respondents had a favorable or unfavorable view of the black power slogan. The correlation between our scoring as favorable or unfavorable of the 1968 respondents' interpretations of black power on the open-ended question and their own assessment, on the close-ended question, of their position was (Gamma) 0.99 for blacks and 0.97 for whites.[13]

Table 1 presents a simple profile of Detroit community responses to our question on black power. As noted above, since there were no appreciable differences for either race in the interpretations given by respondents in the riot or non-riot areas, we have included all our respondents in the analysis.[14]

Interpretations indicating a favorable or unfavorable attitude toward black power are marked off for the convenience of the reader. As we go through the various categories the reasons for our designations will be explained in detail.

Almost 40 percent of the whites believe black power means black rule over whites, while only 9 percent of the black respondents hold this view. This attitude of the whites is clearly not a function of a rational projection that the increasing black population in the city of Detroit (now about 40 percent) will soon elect a black mayor, but is an almost hysterical response to the symbolism of the slogan. White people in this category usually refer to blacks taking over the entire country or even the world.[15]

[White, male, 47, 12 grades] Nasty word! That the blacks won't be satisfied until they get complete control of our country by force if necessary.

[White, male, 24, 12 grades plus] Black take-over. Take over the world because that is what they want to do and they will. There's no doubt about it. Why should they care? I'm working and supporting their kids. In time they'll take over—look at how many there are in Congress. It's there—when they get to voting age, we'll be discriminated upon.

[White, female, 28, 12 grades plus] The colored are going to take over and be our leaders and we're to be their servants. Yes, that's exactly what it means.

[White, female, 28, 12 grades] They want the situation reversed. They want to rule everything.

[White, male, 32, 11 grades] The Negro wants to enslave the white man like he was enslaved 100 years ago. They want to take everything

away from us. There will be no middle class, no advancement. He is saying, "If I can't have it neither can you." Everything will be taken away from us. We'll all be poor.

[White, female, 40, 12 grades] I don't like the sound of it. Sounds like something coming to take over you.

Most of our black respondents do not interpret black power in this way. Blacks who were coded in this category were usually also hostile to black power. For example:

[Black, male, 28, 12 grades plus] It means dominating black rule—to dominate, to rule over like Hitlerism.

[Black, female, 38, 11 grades plus] It means something I don't like. It means like white power is now—taking over completely.

[Black, male, 29, no answer on education] It means to me that Negroes are trying to take over and don't know how.

A few others gave this answer because they have very vague ideas about the concept:

[Black, female, 50, 9 grades] Sounds like they want to take over control.

There were only seven people in this group of 37 blacks who saw black domination over whites as the definition of black power and whose answers could possibly be interpreted as approval of this goal.

A small number of whites and blacks simply defined black power as racism or race hatred. The comments of blacks holding this view were especially scathing:

[Black, female, 57, 11 grades] It's like the Ku Klux Klan and I don't like it.

[Black, female, 38, 12 grades] It means something very detrimental to the race as a whole. This is the same tactic the whites use in discriminating.

The black power definitions of about 12 percent of the white population and 4 percent of the blacks sampled were directly influenced by the violence of the 1967 Detroit disorders. Terms like "trouble" and "rioting" were commonly used by these individuals, especially blacks in the riot areas and whites outside of it. Clearly, however, the vast majority of black people sampled do not see black power as a synonym for violence and destruction, racism or even black rule over whites, while 57.2 percent of the whites do.

Two views of black power predominate among our black respondents. One represents a poorly articulated negativism or opposition to the term and the other a positive or approving interpretation of the concept and its meaning. Roughly 23 percent of the black respondents indicated that the term meant "nothing" to them. This category was coded separately from the "don't know," "can't say," and "no answer" responses because the work "nothing" is generally used as a term of derision, especially in the black community. Some examples of extended responses give the proper flavor:

[Black, female, 39, 10 grades] Nothing! [Interviewer probe] Not a damn thing. [Further probe] Well, it's just a word used by people from the hate school so it don't mean nothing to me.

[Black, male, 52, 12 grades plus] It means nothin'! [Probe] A word coined by some nut. [Further probe] There is only one power and that is God.

[Black, female, 60, 5 grades] It doesn't mean nothing. [Probe] Biggest joke in the 20th century.

It is, of course, possible that some people use "nothin'" as a synonym for "I don't know." We have two major pieces of evidence which indicate that this is not so for the major proportion of blacks giving the response: (1) while direct expressions of ignorance ("I don't know," "can't say," etc.) are a function of educational level, "nothing" is used in the same proportion by blacks no matter what their academic accomplishments; (2) blacks use the expression more than four times as often as whites (22 percent to 5 percent) in trying to

express what black power means to them; and (3) almost 90 percent of the respondents who interpreted black power in this way in 1968 also expressed disapproval of the term on our close-ended question.[16]

There are other individuals who give less ambiguous, clearly negative interpretations of the term. A small proportion of our respondents (1.3 percent of the blacks and 0.7 percent of the whites) found profanity indispensable as the sole expression of their definition. Others (5.2 percent of the blacks and 11.0 percent of the whites) were slightly more articulate in their condemnation, although their definitions were still imprecise. Often, especially for the whites, they reflect a general abhorrence of power in any form:

[White, female, 52, 12 grades] I hate the expression because I don't like power. It's very domineering and possessive and [they] have only themselves in mind.

[White, male, 54, 4 grades] No more than the words white power mean. They should cut that word out.

[Black, female, 37, 9 grades] Black power and white power means the same to me which is no good. Man should be treated as a man.

[White, female, 55, 12 grades] Disaster! You know what you can do with your black power.

[White, female, 53, 12 grades] Scare! Why should there be black power any more than white power? Don't blacks agree that all races are equal?

The last remaining major category of answers clearly distinguishes the black from the white community in its views of black power. In their statements 42.2 percent of our black respondents as compared to 10.7 percent of the whites emphasized a "fair share for black people" or "black unity." We coded all those answers which stressed blacks getting their share of the honors and fruits of production in society, exercising equal rights, bettering their living conditions or gaining greater political power into our "fair share" categories. Definitions stressing black unity or racial pride were coded separately.[17] Since only 7 blacks and 2 whites mentioned racial pride specifically, we will refer in the text to "black unity" or "racial unity" only. We felt that a definition of black power in terms of black people gaining political power in areas where blacks are in the majority fell under our fair share concept, but there were only two statements of this type. This definition may be implicit in the statements made (or in some of our black unity interpretations), but virtually all references are to justice and equity rather than exclusive control of geographical area.

Fair share answers were given by almost 20 percent of our black respondents. People whose responses fall into this category see the black power slogan as another statement of traditional Negro goals of freedom, equality and opportunity. Respondents often take pains to reject notions of blacks taking advantage of others:

[Black, female, 47, 12 grades plus] That we should have blacks represent us in government—not take over, but represent us.

[Black, male, 40, 9 grades plus] Negroes getting the same opportunities as whites when qualified.

[Black, male, 24, 12 grades] Negroes should get more power to do the same things which whites do.

[Black, female, 52, 12 grades plus] Give us an equal chance.

[Black, male, 39, 12 grades] Equal rights to any human being.

[Black, female, 54, 7 grades] That America is going to have a new power structure so black people can have a share.

[Black, male, 55, 12 grades] It means equal opportunities for both races. What's good for one is good for the other.

About 23 percent of our black respondents gave "black unity" responses.[18] These were more militant in tone than the fair share definitions, sometimes extremely nationalistic, but always (as in the fair share answers) concerned with bettering the situation of the black man and not putting down the white man. In fact, the data suggest to us that blacks who are most favorably disposed toward black power simply do not see the political world as one where blacks can gain something only at the expense of whites and vice versa. As we have seen, however, large numbers of whites do see things this way. For them, one group or the other must tend to "take over."

The major difference between the "fair share" and "black unity" groups is that the former places heavy stress on blacks as equal participants in the total society, while the latter emphasizes black togetherness and achievement without the same attention to the traditional symbols of Negro advancement. We know from extended answers to our black power question and others that individuals giving black unity responses want equality and a just share of America's goods, but "thinking black" and speaking militantly and with pride are given primacy when talking about black power.[19] It is not that they are against white people; they are simply for black people and deeply committed to the idea of black people working together:

[Black, male, 35, 9 grades] People getting together to accomplish things for the group.

[Black, male, 36, 12 grades plus] Negroes have never been together on anything. Now with the new movement we gain strength.

[Black, male, 24, 12 grades] We people getting together, agreeing on issues and attempting to reach a common goal.

[Black, male, 28, 12 grades] Sounds frightening, but really is what whites, Jews, Arabs and people the world over do—divided we fall united we stand.

[Black, female, 41, 12 grades] Togetherness among Negroes, but it means you can get along with others.

[Black, female, 37, 10 grades] It means being true to yourself and recognize yourself as a black American who can accomplish good things in life.

[Black, female, 57, 10 grades] The white man separated us when he brought us here and we been that way ever since. We are just trying to do what everybody has—stick together.

As we have noted, the number of whites giving either the fair share or black unity response is small—just over 10 percent of the white sample. To most whites, even those who think of themselves as liberals, the concept of black power is forbidding. The 1967 riot is certainly one factor that might account for this, but we found little evidence of it. Only 5 whites in the entire sample (1 percent) gave answers like the following:

[White, female, 23, college] It's gotten [away] from the original meaning. Means violence to me now.

In addition, as we shall see, even whites who have very sympathetic views about the causes of the disturbances can hardly be described as favorable to black power. The negative presentations of black power in the mass media may be responsible, but Detroit Negroes are also attentive to the same media and their views are quite different. The evidence presented in Table 1 points strongly toward a simple conclusion—the overwhelming majority of whites are frightened and bewildered by the words black power. Some of this seems rooted in abhorrence of stark words like power, but the term black power is obviously intolerable. The words conjure up racial stereotypes and suspicions deeply ingrained in the minds of white Americans. The slogan presents an unmistakable challenge to the country's prevailing racial customs and social norms; for precisely this reason it seems exciting and attractive to many blacks.

In summary, the vast majority of white people are hostile to the notion of black power. The most common interpretation is that it symbolizes a black desire to take over the country, or somehow deprive the white man. Blacks, on the other hand, are almost

evenly divided in their interpretations with 42.2 percent clearly favorable to black power and 49.6 percent defining it in an unfavorable way. Those blacks who are favorable to black power see it as another call for a fair share for blacks or as a rallying cry for black unity, while those who are negatively inclined tend to see it as empty and meaningless (our "nothing" category, for example). Blacks certainly do not interpret the term the way the whites do. They do not see it as meaning racism, a general black takeover, or violence, and those few blacks who do define the term in this way are negative about such meanings. It is evident that "black power" is a potent slogan which arouses contradictory feelings in large numbers of people. Interpretations of the term may differ, but the slogan clearly stimulates intense feelings and may be exciting enough to move to purposeful action.

Although these data invite many different forms of analysis, we have decided that an attempt to understand the sources of favorable reactions to the black power slogan is of primary importance. We have, accordingly, conducted a detailed investigation of factors which predispose an individual to give a "fair share" or "black unity" response to our question on the meaning of black power. In the case of blacks, we are confident that all such definitions indicate a favorable attitude and for whites we know that they usually represent a positive attitude and always indicate at least a grudging respect or admiration. Certainly, as indicated above, we will miss a few black people who are favorable to black power if we follow this procedure, but the number is very small. In most cases, in order to keep the tables and text from becoming inordinately complex, we will combine the fair share and black unity categories and speak of individuals favorably interpreting black power, but where differences between respondents giving these two answers are of great importance we will consider them separately.

4. THE APPEAL OF BLACK POWER: SOCIAL CHANGE, SOCIALIZATION AND DEPRIVATION

Many social scientists in recent years have been struggling to understand the increasing militancy within the black community and the concurrent rise in popularity of slogans like black power. To date, most systematic social science research in this area has centered on the "conventional militancy" of the early 1960's[20] or the backgrounds and attitudes of rioters and those who sympathize with them.[21] The civil disturbances of the mid-1960's were clearly watersheds in American racial history, but most scholars concentrating on the riots would agree that there is more to the current upheaval in the black community—symbolized by the slogan black power—than violence. Recent calls for racial pride, black unity and black self-esteem, and programs to promote these ends, are meant to reach members of the community and help them to become a constructive force in their own behalf.

This section is devoted to a discussion of the factors which predispose an individual to interpret black power favorably. The major emphasis in our analysis will be on our black respondents, but at times we will compare them to whites in order to highlight certain points. The relative lack of support for black power among white respondents prevents a more elaborate analysis of their views in this section stressing favorable versus unfavorable interpretations of the term.

It is probably best to begin by laying to rest the so-called "riffraff" theory, which has been the favorite target of many riot researchers, as a possible explanation for the appeal of the black power slogan. The riffraff theory, drawn from the report of the McCone Commission on the Watts riots of 1964,[22] holds that urban unrest is a product of a deprived underclass of recent unassimilated migrants to the cities. We will discuss the issue of migration below, but neither education (Gamma = -0.02)[23] nor income (Gamma = -0.06) nor occupation (Gamma = -0.00) is a very potent predictor of favorable interpretations of black power for blacks. For whites, on the other hand, education (Gamma = 0.32), income (Gamma = 0.23) and occupation (Gamma = 0.48) are associated with positive views of black power, but here it is the upper-status elements who interpret the slogan favorably.[24] It is clear that any notion that black power appeals strictly to the less-privileged in the black community is without foundation.

Some scholars, and many journalists and politicians, have adopted the clash between generations as a principal explanation of the growing popularity of the black power slogan.[25] The riots in Detroit and Los Angeles are seen as only one manifestation of a worldwide revolt of youth against the established order. The young are said to be more impatient and less willing to accept marginal gains than their elders.

When we divided our respondents according to age, however, we did not find great differences over the interpretation of black power within either racial group, although age was a better predictor for whites (Gamma = -0.26) than for blacks (Gamma = -0.11). Among blacks, 51 percent of those in their twenties gave the racial unity or fair share interpretations, but almost the same percentage of thirty-, forty- and fifty-year-olds gave similar responses. Approval of black power drops off among sixty- and seventy-year-old blacks, but they constitute a small percentage of our sample. As noted above, age is a better predictor for whites with individuals forty and older somewhat less likely to offer an approving interpretation of black power than those under forty.

A. Social Change and Socialization: Breaking the Traditional Mold

One might assume after examining this relationship that the much discussed "generation gap" is not very wide, especially in the black community. But that conclusion would be unwarranted. Differences among blacks exist, not between youth and age, but between those who grew up in Michigan and those who were born and grew up in the South. Blacks who were born in Michigan are much more likely to give the racial unity or fair share interpretation of black power than those born in the South (Gamma = 0.33).[26] When we related age and attitudes toward black power with regional background controlled (Table 2), we found that the background factors clearly predominated. Those in our sample who were born in Michigan are much younger, on the average, than the rest of our respondents (78 percent are under 40 years old and 98 percent are under 50), but definitions of black power are almost invari-

TABLE 2. Percentages of Black Respondents Favorably Interpreting Black Power,[a] According to Their Ages and Regions of Birth

Present age (in ten's)	Southern born (arrived in Michigan after age 21)		Southern born (arrived in Michigan before age 21)		Born in Michigan	
10's		[b]	33%	(6)	67%	(12)
20's	39%	(13)	46	(26)	59	(41)
30's	21	(19)	44	(45)	58	(24)
40's	52	(25)	64	(31)	55	(20)
50's	35	(20)	63	(19)		[b]
60's	17	(12)	33	(12)		[b]
70's	33	(12)		[b]		[b]
	(Gamma = −0.02)		(Gamma = 0.15)		(Gamma = −0.12)	

[a]For economy of presentation and because of the complexity of our black power code, we display only the percentages of respondents favorably interpreting black power, that is, those who gave fair share or black unity interpretations of black power.
[b]Percentages are not displayed if N is less than 5.

able for this group between age categories. There is also very little variance between age categories for those who were born in the South and came to Michigan after they were 21 years old, although, of course, there is much less approval for black power in this group. In both cases, it is regional background and not age which is the most powerful explanatory factor. Further confirmation of this conclusion comes when we examine those respondents who were born in the South, but arrived in Michigan before they were 21.

Within this group we find that the percentage of those voicing approval of black power actually increases along with age from the teens to the fifties, and then decreases again for the small number who are in their sixties. It might be thought that regional differences mask a more fundamental difference between blacks who were born in cities and those raised in rural areas. This is not the case. Thirty-nine percent of Southern-born Negroes who grew up on farms and in small towns favored black power; the percentage giving fair share or black unity interpretations is only 4.3 percent higher (43.3 percent) for respondents raised in the large Southern towns and cities (Gamma = 0.03).

This evidence leads us to conclude that, for all but the very old, it is primarily the experience of life in Michigan and not the respondent's age which helps determine his reaction to black power.[27] A great migration began during World War II which brought thousands of black workers to the auto plants and foundries of Detroit. Their children are coming of age in the 1960's. It is not their youth, however, which leads them to see black power as a call for racial unity or a fair share for their race; it is their experience with the culture of the urban North. It seems that the further one is from life in the South, and the sooner one experiences life in a city like Detroit, the more likely one is to approve of black power.

Life in the Northern city brings to bear on a black person forces which lead him to reject the traditional, subservient attitudes of Southern Negroes, particularly if these forces represent his major socializing experience. Away from the parochial, oppressive atmosphere of the South, he is born into or slowly appropriates the more cosmopolitan, secularized culture of the North. The new life in the promised lands of Detroit, New York and Chicago is exciting and disillusioning at the same time. It brings new hopes and the promise of a better life, and disappointments when achievements do not live up to expectations.

The Southern migrant arrived in the "promised land" to find bigotry, filth, and more sophisticated forms of degradation. With time, he grasps sufficient information about the urban paradise. Traditional attitudes of

TABLE 3. Percentages of Black Respondents Favorably Interpreting Black Power, by Church Affiliation, with Birthplace Controlled

| | PLACE OF BIRTH | |
Affiliation	South	Michigan
Church member	33% (143)	39% (58)
Non-member	48 (107)	67 (33)
	(Gamma = −0.32)	(Gamma = −0.52)

deference and political passivity fade as a militant social and political stance gains approval in the community.[28] This is the atmosphere for the emerging popularity of fair share and racial unity interpretations of slogans like black power.

Just as the trip North represented an attempt to find deliverance, so the Negro church was another traditional avenue of entry into the "promised land." Most blacks who break with the church are more likely to define black power in fair share or unity terms.[29] This relationship holds even with region controlled (Table 3). In fact, membership and place of birth exert an independent effect. Michigan-born church members are about mid-way between Southern-born church members and Southern non-members in their approval of black power. Retention of a church affiliation acts as a brake on the effects of being raised in the Northern urban environment. It represents a strong tie to the traditional Negro culture.[30]

Another aspect of traditional Negro culture is the unique measure of esteem granted the federal government and its personnel. Through the years the federal government, for all its shortcomings, has been the black man's special friend in an otherwise hostile environment. It won him his freedom, gave him the best treatment he received in his worst days in the South, provided relief in the Depression and in the difficult periods which have followed, and has done the most to secure his rights and protect him during his struggle for equality.[31] In addition, it has been the symbol of his intense identification with and "faith in the American Dream."[32] Evaluation of local government in the North has been less positive, but still higher than

evaluation of local government in the South.

Systematic research on political trust is rather recent, but what does exist indicates that blacks have always had at least the same distribution as whites on answers to political trust questions focused on the federal government.[33] In fact, when one takes into account the extraordinary amount of interpersonal distrust present in the black community,[34] the level of trust in the federal government has always been remarkable. Our data indicate that this pattern is now breaking down, at least in cities like Detroit. Using the Standard University of Michigan Survey Research Center political trust questions, we found blacks less trusting of both the federal and Detroit governments than whites.[35] These differences in levels of political trust are not a function of education, income or other non-racial status discrepancies.

Let us assume that the black power slogan strikes a most responsive chord in the minds of black people who want to break their traditional ties with paternalistic friends and allies. For them, expressing distrust of government, especially the federal government, is in fact a rejection of dependency—an assertion of self-worth and non-utopian thinking about the realities in the United States.[36] As we can see in Table 4, expressions of political trust and approval of black power are indeed inversely related. The higher a person's score on the various trust indices, the less likely he is to favorably interpret black power. This relationship is especially strong for trust in the federal government which has traditionally been granted unique esteem in the black community.

When we consider all three indicators of traditionalism together—place of socializa-

TABLE 4. Gamma Correlations for Blacks Between Measures of Political Trust and Favorable Interpretations of Black Power

	Trust Detroit government[a]	Trust federal government[b]	General (combined) measure of political trust[c]
Black power interpretation[d]	−0.22	−0.52	−0.39

[a]The "trust Detroit government" measure is a simple additive index of answers to the following questions:
1. How much do you think we can trust the government in Detroit to do what is right: just about always, most of the time, some of the time, or almost never?
2. How much do you feel having elections makes the government in Detroit pay attention to what the people think: a good deal, some, or not very much?

[b]The "trust federal government" measure is a simple additive index of answers to the following questions:
1. How much do you think you can trust the government in Washington to do what is right: just about always, most of the time, some of the time, or almost never?
2. Would you say that the government in Washington is pretty much run for the benefit of a few big interests or that it is run for the benefit of all the people?
3. How much do you feel that having elections makes the government in Washington pay attention to what the people think: a good deal, some, or not very much?

[c]The "general political trust" measure runs from 0 to 4 and equally weights the "trust Detroit government" and "trust federal government" answers.

[d]A negative coefficient indicates that the higher a person's score on the various trust indices (high score equals high trust), the less likely he is to favorably interpret black power.

TABLE 5. Percentages of Black Respondents Favorably Interpreting Black Power, According to Church Affiliation, Place of Birth, and Levels of Trust in Government

Level of trust in government[a]	PLACE OF BIRTH: SOUTH		PLACE OF BIRTH: MICHIGAN	
	Church member	Non-member	Church member	Non-member
High (2-4)	20% (76)	29% (65)	38% (16)	58% (26)
Low (0-1)	55 (40)	66 (73)	44 (16)	77 (31)

[a]The general political trust measure was employed in this table.

tion, church affiliation and level of political trust—we see that each is important in its own right (Table 5). The combined explanatory power of these variables is substantial. Only 20 percent of the Southern-born church members who exhibit high levels of trust give approving interpretations of black power compared to 77 percent of the Northern-born non-members who are distrustful of government. Michigan-born church members are a particularly interesting group for further study in that church membership significantly depresses the effects of political trust. Our future research will emphasize the impact of socialization into the secular political culture of Northern black communities, with special attention to the development of more refined indicators which will help us to understand better this acculturation process.

B. Deprivation: Dissatisfaction and Discrimination

We asked our respondents to tell us about "the life you would most like to lead, the most perfect life as you can see it." Once they had described this kind of life they were shown a picture of a ladder with ten rungs and asked to imagine that their ideal lives were at the top of the ladder, on rung number ten. They were then asked to rank, in comparison with their ideal, their present lives, their lives five years ago, and what they ex-

TABLE 6. Correlations (Gamma) for Blacks Between Ladder Positions on the Self-anchoring Scales, Experiences of Discrimination, and Approval of Black Power, by Level of Education.

Scales	Zero order	Low education[a]	High education[a]
Present life[b]	-0.27	-0.34	0.06
Future life[b]	-0.40	-0.47	-0.05
Reported experiences of discrimination[c]	0.30	0.34	0.20

[a]Respondents in the low-education group (N = 322) include all those who have completed high school (but had no additional training), while those in high-education group (N = 122) have, at minimum, gone beyond high school to either specialized training or college. We chose education as a status indicator and dichotomized the sample so as to preserve the maximum number of cases for the analysis.

[b]The ladders were trichotomized as follows: 1-3 = 0; 4-7 = 1; 8-10 = 2. Therefore, a negative coefficient means that the higher a person's score on the ladder, the less likely he is to give a fair share or racial unity interpretation of black power.

[c]This is a simple additive index of reports of personal experiences of discrimination in Detroit in obtaining housing, in the schools, from a landlord, or in obtaining, holding or advancing on a job.

pected their lives to be five years in the future.[37] Answers are therefore based on standards meaningful to the individual, with no simple objective indicator of achievement such as education, income or occupation serving as a substitute for his subjectively defined goals.[38]

This question revealed a great deal of current dissatisfaction in the black community, but also substantial optimism about the future. When asked to rank their lives five years ago only 13 percent of our black respondents put themselves in the top four categories (7, 8, 9 and 10); when asked to rank their present lives 23 percent placed themselves within the top four ranks; but 64 percent chose the top four categories to describe their lives as they expected them to be five years in the future.

As Table 6 indicates, both current dissatisfaction and, to a greater extent, pessimism about the future are strongly related to approval of black power in the zero-order case. When we control for level of education group, the same general trend holds true for reports of experiences of discrimination. However, the differences are less pronounced. Experience of discrimination is a more powerful predictor of fair share or racial unity interpretations of black power for the lower than the upper education group, but it still has a

noticeable effect for the upper education group.[39]

These data fit a general pattern which we have discussed in detail elsewhere.[40] For lower-education blacks, approval of black power is strongly influenced by dissatisfaction with one's current lot and pessimism about the future as well as by reported experiences of discrimination. For blacks with higher levels of educational attainment, however, personal dissatisfaction with present achievements or prospects for the future do not help us to understand favorable interpretations of black power. Even reported personal experiences of discrimination are only moderately related to approval of the slogan. The views on black power of this higher-education group are more strongly influenced by their identification with others in the community—their feelings for the group.

Upper-status blacks who have broken free from traditional moorings become a part of a black political community which includes persons from all social classes. The responses of these upper-status blacks to questions about the interpretation of significant events and the evaluation of leaders are most strongly affected by their sense of empathy and identification with their racial community than by their feelings of achievement or even their personal expectations about the future.

Black power by	Low education	High education
Church membership	-0.38	-0.42
Place of birth	.31	.34
Political trust	-0.39	-0.37

They share a set of beliefs and a mood of protest about racial issues with those lower-status segments of the black community who have also assimilated the secular culture typical of the urban North.[41]

The major difference between the two groups is that dissatisfaction with one's current lot and prospects for the future interact with church membership, region of socialization and political trust in determining interpretations of black power for the lower-education group, but not for the upper education group.

5. THE BLACK POWER IDEOLOGY

So far our attention has been concentrated on the demographic and attitudinal correlates of approval of black power. Some scholars have argued that interpretations of this kind of slogan stem from a more comprehensive belief system, a "riot ideology," which is said to be developing within the black community.[42] We found that knowledge of the black power slogan has diffused widely through the black community of Detroit. There are many different interpretations of the slogan, but only about 8 percent of the population were unable to respond when asked about its meaning. The question remains whether an individual's reaction to black power, be it positive or negative, is related in any logical way to his attitudes about other issues of racial policy, his interpretation of significant events, and his choice of leaders or representatives. In order to investigate this question, we turned to our data in search of evidence of a coherent or constrained belief system on racial matters within Detroit's black community; something we might justifiably call a racial ideology.

Anyone acquainted with recent research on public opinion might doubt the existence of a set of ideas resembling a racial ideology among any but a small activist fringe in the black community. Public attitudes about political leaders or questions of public policy are usually fragmentary and contradictory. Citizens readily express opinions about public issues, but these beliefs seldom hang together in a coherent system; knowing an individual's position on one issue does not allow one to predict his positions on other, related issues. The classical liberal or conservative ideologies may often be employed by political activists or leaders as a guide to policy making, but most citizens seem to use as a guide some form of group identification or other considerations of self-interest when formulating their attitudes toward political questions.[43]

Converse argues that the degree of constraint in a belief system is determined most directly by the amount of information the individual has acquired about the issues involved. Levels of information, in turn, are usually affected by the relative centrality or importance of the issues to the individual. The more deeply concerned the individual becomes about a subject, the more likely he is to seek information about it, and, as time passes, to form consistent or comprehensive beliefs about the issues involved. Converse, of course, has dealt most often with liberalism and conservatism in their American incarnations. Comprehensive belief systems of this sort generally "rest upon the kinds of broad or abstract contextual information about currents of ideas, people, or society that educated people come to take for granted as initial ingredients of thought."[44] This form of contextual or background information is usually accumulated after extensive, formal education, a factor which seems to be a prerequisite to ideological thinking, in most cases. Since only a small minority of the public possesses this important educational prerequisite, ideological thinking is said to be rare.

Since our respondents share the educational limitations of average Americans, and do not have any special access to political information, we would not expect them to be capable of broadly ideological thinking. As Converse suggests at several points, however, it would be unwarranted to infer from this fact that average citizens are incapable of consistent thinking about all areas of public affairs. Even without a grasp of classical liberalism or conservatism and with a minimum of formal education, respondents might have consistent belief systems concerning subjects which they found to be of inescapable personal importance, and which also involved the social groupings with which they most strongly identify.

Bearing in mind the possibility that considerable structure might be uncovered in the social and political thought of our respondents if the proper issues could be identified, we asked open-ended questions at several points in our interview about topics we thought might be salient for our respondents. Using these methods we discovered clear indications that a coherent belief system dealing with racial matters has developed within Detroit's black community. This belief system seems well organized and serves as a guide for most of our respondents in formulating their answers to our questions about racial problems. The high degree of constraint existing among the elements of this belief system is displayed in Table 7 where we present a matrix of correlations of answers by our black respondents to five questions concerning racial issues.[45] The coefficients appearing below the diagonal are for all those with a high school education, or less, while above the diagonal are findings for those who have, at minimum, progressed beyond high school to either specialized training or college. The relatively high correlations in this table make us feel justified in referring to this set of opinions as a racial ideology.

One of the most significant aspects of Table 7 is the attitudinal consistency existing among those with lower educational achievements. A careful examination of the table shows that the two educational groups display almost the same levels of constraint. Associa-

tions among the upper education group are slightly higher, as earlier research on ideology might lead one to expect, but only by 0.02, on the average. Further, as we shall establish, respondents in our sample are not only capable of consistency, but display, as well, an impressive amount of knowledge about these questions, and demonstrate the capacity to make several subtle distinctions among leaders and political symbols.

The results of Table 7 are even more significant in view of the fact that three of the five items in the matrix were completely open-ended questions. We have already discussed our open question on the meaning of black power and the way in which we constructed our code and identified favorable and unfavorable responses. The question on the word used by the respondents to describe the riot was also open-ended. At the beginning of each interview respondents were asked what word they would use to describe the events "that occurred in Detroit between July 23rd and July 28th" of 1967, and that word was used by the interviewers throughout the interview. Although some responses were quite unorthodox (one young woman called it a "steal-in" and an older woman called it "God's vengeance on man"), we found it possible to code most of the answers into four categories: revolt, riot, disturbance, and lawlessness, which roughly form a dimension from an understanding of the events as an expression of political demands, to a belief that they were an anomic, lawless outburst. We also asked our respondents, without supplying any cues, to name "the single national or local leader who best expresses your views on relations between the races." The list of leaders mentioned were then arranged according to their publicly stated views on black power. This arrangement was made on the basis of our knowledge of these leaders and their public statements.[46]

Open questions require respondents to formulate their own answers, a formidable challenge to those with limited powers of expression. Some error may be introduced by interviewers when recording answers to open questions, and once they have been recorded, they must be coded. It is extremely difficult,

TABLE 7. Correlations (Gamma) Among Responses to Racial Issues by Black Respondents, by Education[a]

Low education (N = 322)	HIGH EDUCATION (N = 122)				
	1. Approval of black power	2. Word to describe riot	3. Sympathy for the rioters	4. Reasons for the riot	5. Leader who represents you
1. Approval of black power[b]		0.34	0.46	0.32	0.29
2. Word to describe riot[b]	0.36		0.40	0.58	0.22
3. Sympathy for the rioters[b]	0.45	0.30		0.62	0.49
4. Reasons for the riot[b]	0.64	0.37	0.48		0.41
5. Leader who represents you[b]	0.41	0.29	0.32	0.35	

[a]Respondents in the low-education group include all individuals who have completed high school (but had no additional training), while those in the high-education group have, at minimum, gone beyond high school. Correlations for the high-education group are recorded above the diagonal, and those for the low-education group are below the diagonal.

[b]The following items make up this table:

1. "What do the words 'black power' mean to you?" For this table only the signs on the black power code are reversed so that all coefficients are positive.
2. "What would you call the events that occurred in Detroit between July 23 and July 28? What word would you use?" Open-ended question coded as follows: (1) insurrection; (2) riot; (3) disturbance; (4) lawlessness.
3. "Do you sympathize with the people who took part in the [respondent's term for the event]?" (1) yes; (2) somewhat; (3) no.
4. "Which of the following comes closest to explaining why the [respondent's term for the event] took place: (1) people were being treated badly; (2) criminals did it; (3) people wanted to take things?"
5. "What single national or local leader best expresses your views on relations between the races?" Open-ended question coded as follows: (1) militant black leaders; (2) other black leaders, excluding Martin Luther King; (3) Martin Luther King; (4) white leaders, excluding Robert F. Kennedy. A militant is defined here as someone who unequivocally endorsed black power before the time of our interviewing (September, 1967). Persons identifying Robert F. Kennedy were not considered in the calculation of coefficients for this question because of the special nature of his partisans. See below (footnotes to Table 11) for a discussion of this.

both to construct comprehensive codes for responses of this kind, and to complete the coding process without introducing even further error. In view of all these difficulties, the relatively strong associations we have found among the items in Table 7 are strong evidence of the existence of a racial ideology. We believe that the success of these techniques and the high degree of consistency in our respondents' opinions was due to their intense interest and concern with racial issues. It would seem that the relative salience of an issue for an individual, or his interest in a subject, is more important than his educational level or his ability to manipulate abstractions in determining the coherence of his beliefs.[47]

Our findings confirm the proposition that where issues of sufficient personal importance are concerned, even the poorly educated are capable of developing relatively sophisticated, inter-related, ideological belief systems.

A. Black Power Ideology and Integration

Some of our respondents may not have an advanced understanding of the justifications for their views, but we are certain that the questions in our matrix require a choice among legitimate alternatives; they are not being translated by our black respondents into simple tests of racial loyalty. An inspection of our questions will show that we are not ask-

TABLE 8. Percentages of Respondents Favorably Interpreting Black Power, by Race, According to Attitudes Toward Integration

Forms of race relations preferred	PERCENT FAVORABLY INTERPRETING BLACK POWER	
	Whites	Blacks
Integration	25% (96)	46% (364)
Something in between	8 (197)	46 (54)
Separation	5 (65)	a
	(Gamma = −0.57)	(Gamma = 0.01)

[a] N is less than 5.

ing merely if they are sympathetic or unsympathetic toward the aspirations of blacks in America. Our respondents are being called upon to identify and evaluate political leaders as representatives, interpret the causes of the Detroit riot, and define the meaning of a controversial political slogan. One can be closely identified with his racial group and greatly concerned for its welfare, and yet be either positive or passionately negative about black power, the riot, or many black political leaders. Our black respondents are prevented from employing some simple form of racial chauvinism as a guide for answering our questions because of the necessity of choosing sides in fundamental disputes over the role of blacks in American society which have traditionally divided their racial community.

Some symbols and ideas, of course, seem to be accepted by virtually all members of the black community. Had questions concerning these topics been included in our matrix we would not have such strong evidence of a racial ideology, because our responses could then be interpreted as mere expressions of support for the black community. This would have been true, for example, of any questions dealing directly with racial integration. In order to find how both racial groups felt about this issue, each of our respondents was asked whether he favored "racial integration, total separation of the races, or something in between." In response to this question, 27 percent of our white respondents endorsed integration, 17 percent favored total separation, and 54 percent chose "something

in between." Even the most sympathetic whites overwhelmingly disapprove of black power, but as we can see in Table 8, approving interpretations of black power came most often from those whites who endorsed integration. The relationship was matched by a separate finding that whites who reported having friends among blacks were somewhat more approving of black power, although blacks who reported having white friends did not differ appreciably from others in their interpretations of the slogan. All of the aversion of whites toward black power cannot be attributed to an aversion toward blacks; some of it grows out of a fear and dislike of the general use of power to achieve social ends, and an unease of resentment of all forms of protest. Nevertheless, it is our impression that when most whites are asked about symbols like black power and integration, they are less likely to respond directly to the complicated issues being raised, but are tempted to translate the questions into the much simpler issue of whether they are favorable or unfavorable toward black people.[48]

When our black respondents were asked the same question about racial integration, 86 percent endorsed integration, while only 1 percent chose separation. Years of struggle against institutionalized segregation and great efforts by opinion leaders in both racial communities for almost a century have made integration a potent, positive symbol for blacks. Asking for an endorsement of this idea is almost akin to asking for an expression of loyalty to the black community. Since we

TABLE 9. Percentages of Black Respondents Favorably Interpreting Black Power, According to When They Believe Integration Will Occur

Time for integration	FAVORABLE INTERPRETATIONS OF BLACK POWER				
	Fair share	+	Black unity	=	Total
Near future	18%		16%		34% (140)
Distant future	22		33		55 (206)

recognized the emotional connotation of these terms we substituted the word "separation" for "segregation" in our questions, but even in this form the positive attraction of integration proved overwhelming. The consensus on the desirability of integration includes most black writers and intellectual leaders as well as the average citizens. Debate over the idea has remained sharp and vigorous, but it has primarily concerned the question of whether integration ultimately should result in virtual assimilation, or in some form of social pluralism.[49]

In view of the special status of integration as a symbol within the black community, it is not surprising that we should find conclusive evidence that approval for black power among blacks does not imply approval of racial separation. In Table 8 there are no appreciable differences in approval for black power between black respondents who endorse integration and those who do not.

The racial ideology we have identified, even though not merely an expression of racial loyalty, may still have social rather than purely intellectual origins. An individual's status or the role he plays in the economy may prompt him to adopt the beliefs of the leaders of his social group because he is convinced that this is a way to advance his own interests. This form of intellectual emulation would be most likely among those, like many of our respondents, who have little education or experience with abstract thinking, and also have a strong sense of group identification. Several beliefs may be appropriated by an individual under these circumstances which may appear to him as natural collections of

interdependent ideas, even if he does not have the intellectual capacity to make a similar synthesis of his own. In other words, he may know that several different elements of his belief system naturally go together, and he may also know that certain kinds of responses are considered appropriate for certain kinds of questions, without having any notion of why.[50]

Our respondents' racial ideologies may have originated through this process of social diffusion and group mobilization, but we find enough subtlety in the responses to conclude that many individuals have developed a surprisingly elaborate understanding of the applicability and meaning of the beliefs they hold. For example, although virtual unanimity exists within the black community about the desirability of integration as an ultimate goal, there is considerable disagreement over how soon it might occur. As we can see in Table 9, those who believe that realization of the goal is in the distant future are more likely to approve of black power than those who believe it will soon appear. In analyzing our data we have found that the perception of obstacles to racial progress, or the actual experience of some form of discrimination, is related to approval of black power. Table 9 demonstrates that the more pessimistic respondents are also more likely to interpret black power as an appeal for racial unity rather than a call for a fair share or an equal opportunity. There is evidence in this table, and in others we shall present, that the capacity for subtle shifts of emphasis and interpretation is not merely confined to the community's activist minority, but instead is widely diffused among a large segment of Detroit's black population.

TABLE 10. Percentages of Respondents Favorably Interpreting Black Power, by Race, According to Word They Use to Describe the Riot

Word used to describe riot	PERCENT FAVORABLY INTERPRETING BLACK POWER	
	Whites	Blacks
a. Total sample		
Revolt	32%　(28)	62%　(51)
Riot	10　(212)	50　(194)
Disturbance	0　(19)	33　(42)
Lawlessness	8　(25)	27　(33)

	INTERPRETATION OF BLACK POWER		
	Fair share　+	Racial unity　=	Total
b. Black respondents only			
Revolt	25%	37%	62%　(51)
Riot	23	27	50　(194)
Disturbance	19	14	33　(42)
Lawlessness	21	6	27　(33)

B. Black Power Ideology and the Detroit Riot

The Detroit riot of July, 1967 caused fear and anxiety among almost all the citizens of the city, both black and white. Immediate reactions to the event ranged from those who believed it was a sign that the Negro citizens of the city were rising up in revolt against discrimination and injustice to those who saw it as an uncivilized expression of lawlessness and hooliganism. If, as we have suggested, responses to black power are a part of an individual's basic orientation toward race relations, there should be a strong relationship between his response to this slogan and his evaluation of the causes and consequences of the riot.

In Table 10 we can see that in both races those who use the word "revolt" to describe the events were much more likely to express approval for black power. In Table 10b where the black respondents are divided according to whether they gave racial unity or fair share responses we find that racial unity interpretations clearly predominate among those who see the riot as a protest against injustice. This is another demonstration of the shift in emphasis that occurs among those who are most aware and resentful of discrimination and inequality. The more convinced our black respondents are of the existence of injustice, the more they begin to interpret black power as a call for racial solidarity.

C. Black Power Ideology and the Choice of Leaders

Our respondents were asked to name "the single national or local leader who best expresses your views on relations between the races." This question, like the one on black power, was completely open-ended. Table 11 displays the relationship for Negroes between the selection of various leaders and fair share or black unity interpretations of black power.

The list of leaders is arranged so that the percentage totals of respondents favoring black power are in descending order. The table seems to us to indicate the validity of our measure since respondents identifying with militant black leaders are the most favorably disposed toward black power while those choosing white leaders are least positive. In

TABLE 11. Percentage of Black Respondents Favorably Interpreting Black Power, According to Their Selection of a Leader Best Representing Their Views on Race Relations

	BLACK POWER INTERPRETATION		
Leader best representing respondent[a]	Fair share (%) +	Racial unity (%) =	Total (%)
Militant black leaders (N = 59)	26	50	76
Robert F. Kennedy (N = 17)	12	47	59
Other black leaders, excluding Martin Luther King (N = 107)	17	34	51
"No one" (N = 20)	10	30	40
Martin Luther King (N = 150)	28	10	38
White leaders, excluding Robert F. Kennedy (N = 30)	11	13	24

[a]Question: "What single national or local leader best expresses your views on relations between races?" N's in parentheses are the bases for the calculation of percentages, i.e., persons giving don't know or no answer responses to the black power question were not used in the table. Total N's for the categories on leadership are given in the explanations of the leader classifications below:

A militant black leader (N = 61) is defined here as someone who unequivocally endorsed black power before the time of our interviewing (September, 1967). They include: Muhammed Ali (N = 3); H. Rap Brown (N = 9); Stokely Carmichael (N = 15); State Senator James Del Rio (N = 13); Dick Gregory (N = 6); Floyd McKissick (N = 3); Adam Clayton Powell (N = 8); and Rev. Albert Cleage (N = 4). Del Rio and Cleage are local figures.

Robert F. Kennedy (N = 21).

Other black leaders, excluding Martin Luther King (N = 111), mentioned were: Senator Edward Brooke (N = 16); Ralph Bunche (N = 3); U.S. Representative John Conyers (N = 31); U.S. Representative Charles Diggs (N = 17); Detroit Common Councilman Nicholas Hood (N = 10); Detroit Urban League Head Francis Kornegay (N = 1); Judge Thurgood Marshall (N = 4); Carl Rowan (N = 1); Roy Wilkins (N = 17); State Senator Coleman Young (N = 1); Whitney Young (N = 5). Hood, Kornegay and C. Young are local figures.

"No one" (N = 21).

Martin Luther King (N = 165).

White leaders, excluding Robert F. Kennedy (N = 33), mentioned were: Senator Dirksen (N = 1); President Eisenhower (N = 1); TV commentator Lou Gordon (N = 1); Vice President Humphrey (N = 1); President Johnson (N = 14); President Kennedy (N = 9); Walter Reuther (N = 3); Governor Romney (N = 3). Gordon is a local figure.

The total N = 412. Of the remaining 49 individuals in our black sample, 27 could not answer the question and 22 mentioned their minister (no name given), coach or assorted persons (including themselves) we could not categorize with confidence on a leadership spectrum.

addition, the assumptions that were made earlier about the meaning of the "black take-over" and "nothing" responses also seem warranted as individuals who identify with the least militant leaders most often give responses of this kind.

There are some more subtle differences revealed in this table. Negroes who felt best represented by black leaders other than the late Martin Luther King favored racial unity over fair share definitions of black power by a ratio of two to one. Dr. King's partisans, however, heavily emphasized fair share definitions. In addition, the likelihood of a favorable defi-

nition of black power is a direct function of the type of black leader selected. As a general rule, the more militant the leader who represents the respondent, the greater the chance of a positive orientation toward black power.

Over 75 percent of our Negro respondents chose a black leader who best represented their views, but there were white leaders selected as well and instances where the interviewee could make no selection. The number of respondents who could not name a leader is small and we have divided them into two groups. "No one" is a category for individuals who decisively stated that they had no representative. This tiny group was often cynical about black power (and everything else) with over one-third saying that black power meant "nothing" to them. When they did define the slogan, however, black unity was the dominant theme. Another small group (N = 25) simply could not think of any person who represented them and they were also unlikely to answer the question about black power (i.e., they were coded in the don't know or no answer category on black power). These individuals were not visibly cynical about racial leaders or approaches; they were simply uninformed.

Thirty-one respondents identified with white leaders other than the late Senator Robert F. Kennedy. They were generally negative about black power, showing no meaningful preference for either positive interpretation. Over 50 percent of the black respondents who selected Senator Kennedy, however, gave favorable definitions of black power and they were disposed towards racial unity definitions of the term by a ratio of four to one. While the number of people who named Senator Kennedy is small, his importance as a link with the more militant elements in the black community should not be underestimated. The severing of this connection between the white and black worlds is a major tragedy. In the next phase of our research we will explore the impact of the deaths of both Kennedy and King on the beliefs of their followers.

D. Black Power Ideology: An Overview

Black power has no direct, generally accepted meaning, but the slogan still provokes strong responses from both blacks and whites. The power of all effective political slogans lies in "the emotional charges or valences they carry, the very elements that make cognitions dissonant or consonant," and in "their associative meanings, the very ambiguities that permit them, like Rorschach ink blots, to suggest to each person just what he wants to see in them."[51] In their efforts to shape a fundamental meaning for black power, our black respondents have fallen back upon fundamental sets of beliefs which have

spread through all sectors of their most profound implications, but the beliefs are consistently organized in the minds of our respondents primarily because they are securely focused on the issue of racial injustice in America, a problem faced by most blacks in one form or another virtually every day of their lives.

When Converse speaks of ideological thinking, of course, he usually refers to "belief systems that have relatively wide ranges and that allow some centrality to political objects."[52] The racial ideology we have identified has a much narrower range. Given the limitations of our data, we cannot be sure that individuals holding a consistent racial ideology would also have consistent opinions about federal aid to education, or governmental measures designed to ensure full employment. Those with a racial ideology might be able to think in coherent ways only about questions of public policy which bear some relationship to the status of blacks in American society, but not about the general relationship between government and private business, or about America's relations with foreign countries.

The ideology of black power is not a wide-ranging, highly elaborated, political world view. Nevertheless, the tone and quality of American political life in the latter 1960's was profoundly altered by the development of this belief system and its exceptionally wide diffusion among black Americans. In its radical form, as it is developing among our more disillusioned black respondents, the belief system includes doubts about the possibilities of realizing the goal of integration in the near future, sympathetic explanations of the July, 1967 disturbances in Detroit and a revolutionary label for them, selection of a militant leader as a spokesman, skepticism about improvements in the quality of life in the future, and a definition of black power which stresses the need for greater racial solidarity. This system of beliefs doesn't arm many of our respondents with concrete programs of social and economic reform, but in spite of its limited scope, its existence is of great potential significance. Its impressively wide diffusion is a striking indication of the growing mobilization and increasing sense of group identification within the black community.

6. SUMMARY AND CONCLUSIONS

Black power is a potent, meaningful slogan for most of our respondents. Some react with fear, others with cynicism, many with warm approval or strong disapproval, but in most cases reactions are intense and interpretations of the idea's meaning are related to an individual's basic orientation toward social and political problems. Whites have an overwhelmingly negative reaction to black power. The slogan is seen by most whites as an illegitimate, revengeful challenge. Among blacks, however, about 42 percent of our sample see the term either as a call for equal treatment and fair share for Negroes, or as an appeal for racial solidarity in the struggle against discrimination.

The partisans of black power among Negroes are somewhat younger than the rest of the black community but neither their age nor other standard demographic factors, such as income, occupation, and education, are very helpful in explaining the distributions we have found. Sharp divisions exist within the Detroit black community, but they are not merely the result of a clash between young and old; instead, they represent a clash between those who have appropriated the cosmopolitan, secularized culture typical of the North and those whose social outlook and political attitudes are rooted in the paternalistic culture of the South. Approval for black power, as our analysis has shown, comes most often from those who were born or grew up in Detroit, are not members of churches, and have begun to doubt the trustworthiness of government in both Detroit and Washington.

Black power is the rallying cry of a generation of blacks whose fathers fled from the South to seek a new life in the "promised lands" of Detroit, New York, or Chicago. The move from the grinding poverty and overt oppression of the South to the cities of the North was seen as a great step forward by the original pioneers. But most of their children cannot be satisfied by these changes. In the words of Claude Brown: "The children of these disillusioned colored pioneers inherited the total lot of their parents—the disappoint-

ments, the anger. To add to their misery, they had little hope of deliverance. For where does one run to when he's already in the promised land?"[53]

This modern generation finds little compensation or hope in the evangelical, "old-time religion" of their parents, nor do they share the traditional faith of Southern Negroes in the ultimate benevolence of white men. Many are distrustful of government, unimpressed with most of the civic notables and established political leaders of both the black and white communities, and increasingly pessimistic about their chances to achieve a satisfactory life in this country. They have not surrendered the ultimate aim of social equality and racial integration, but they have begun to doubt that the goal will be reached in the foreseeable future.

We encountered few racist, anti-white interpretations of black power among our black respondents and most of those came from respondents who were not sympathetic to black power. There was chauvinism and some glorification of blackness, especially among those who interpret black power as a call for racial unity or solidarity, but most were pro-black rather than anti-white. Black unity definitions of black power are not disguised appeals for separation from American society; at least, not at the present moment. If insufficient progress toward racial accommodation is made in the future and tensions continue to mount, separationist sentiments might begin to spread within the black community. Today, we find, instead, a deep concern with the rights of and desires for respect within the American black community. These feelings are most eloquently expressed in the interpretation of black power given by one of our young respondents:

[Black, male, 19, 12 grades] It means mostly equality. You know, to have power to go up to a person, you know, no matter what his skin color is and be accepted on the same level, you know, and it doesn't necessarily have to mean that you gotta take over everything and be a revolutionary and all this; just as long as people are going to respect you, you know, for what you are as a person and not, you know, what your skin color has to do with the thing.

Restraining ties with the traditional culture of the South are being steadily eroded as the percentage of blacks who were born and grew up in the North increases, the influence of the church wanes, and faith in the benevolence of paternalistic friends and allies weakens. The children born in Detroit since World War II are coming of age politically in the midst of a social revolution. Events as diverse as the Detroit riot, the dominance of black athletes in every major American spectator sport, the collapse of colonial empires in Asia and Africa, the total integration of American armed forces, and the murders of Martin Luther King and Robert Kennedy are all accelerating the break with traditional modes of thought and accommodation. The reservoir of potential supporters for black power is bound to grow.

The social revolution now in progress has resulted in a more unified, more highly mobilized black political community. Franklin Frazier's accommodating, apolitical "black bourgeoisie"[54] is rapidly disappearing as the sense of empathy and racial identification among the black middle class grows stronger. This developing racial community is profoundly restless and is searching for new forms of political expression and participation. The result of this search is likely to be increased activity of all kinds, both conventional and unconventional. Our data indicate a willingness to participate in political campaigns and elections on the part of even the most militant advocates of black power. Their involvement in this activity, however, would not preclude their taking part in other, more flamboyant, forms of protest.

No single dominant tactical stance is likely to evolve among blacks; questions about the feasibility and utility of tactics are major sources of disagreement within the black community. Most of our black respondents for example, believe the Detroit riots of 1967 were an understandable reaction to social injustice, and there is some sympathy for the individuals who actually did the rioting, but there is almost no approval of the sniping and fire bombing that took place. Extreme violence of this kind is presently thought of as a legitimate or useful expression of grievances by only a tiny minority of blacks in Detroit,

TABLE 12. Percentages of Black Respondents Favorably Interpreting Black Power, According to Their Willingness to Take Part in a Riot

Would you riot[a]	Percent favorably interpreting black power
No	35% (262)
Yes	57 (60)
Maybe	69 (93)

[a]Question: "Can you imagine any situation in which you would take part in a _____ [respondent's term for the events of July, 1967]?"

but many others express considerable ambivalence about the utility of violent protests. For example, when we asked our black respondents, "Can you imagine any situation in which you would take part in a —— [Respondent's term for the events of July, 1967]?" a majority said no, but, as we can see in Table 12, respondents who expressed ambivalence were even more supportive of black power than those who said they definitely would participate. This undecided group is a substantial proportion of our sample, they have made the sharpest break with traditional forms of social thought, they are the most sympathetic toward the black power ideology, and they are wavering.

The outcome of this search by blacks for acceptable modes of political expression will depend primarily on the behavior of whites, both those who control all the public and private institutions that matter, and the average citizens who must adjust to changes in prevailing customs. If Detroit's future is to be peaceful, ways must be found to pull down the barriers to equal opportunity which now exist, and there must be radical improvement in the prospects for personal advancement of the city's black population. Although success in these efforts depends in large measure, on the flexibility and compassion of the whites, it also depends on the capacity of many public and private governmental institutions to mobilize the resources necessary to create a decent, livable, urban environment.

Some of the most important decisions about Detroit's future will not be made in the city, but in Washington, in suburban city halls, or in the state capitol in Lansing; the policies adopted by labor unions, businesses and manufacturers in the city will probably be more important than anything done by the officials of city government. This complex, decentralized system of social choice, with its elaborate checks and balances and its many barriers to radical change, will be faced during the next decade with an insistent challenge from a new generation of black Americans. To successfully meet their demands large efforts will have to be made toward the creation of a truly inter-racial society. Depending on the extent and success of these efforts, this new black generation could either become a persuasive and creative new influence within the democratic system, or a force bent on the violent disruption of American urban life.

NOTES

[1] William J. Brink and Louis Harris, *Black and White* (New York: Simon and Schuster, 1966), p. 50.

[2] *New York Times,* July 6, 1966, p. 14.

[3] *Ibid.,* July 6, 1966, p. 15; and July 9, 1966, p. 8.

[4] James Baldwin, *Notes of a Native Son* (Boston: Little, Brown, 1955), p. 122.

[5] Cruse, for example, in his provocative series of essays, *The Crisis of the Negro Intellectual* (New York: William Morrow, 1967), p. 557, says that "the radical wing of the Negro movement in America sorely needs a social theory based on the living ingredients of Afro-American history. Without such a theory all talk of Black Power is meaningless."

[6] *Ibid.,* p. 545.

[7] Charles Hamilton, "An Advocate of Black Power Defines It," *New York Times Magazine,* April 14, 1968, pp. 22-23, 79-83, reprinted in full in Robert L. Scott and Wayne Brockriede, eds., *The Rhetoric of Black Power* (New York: Harper & Row, 1969), pp. 178-194. This statement is found on p. 179.

[8] Stokely Carmichael and Charles V. Hamilton, *Black Power: The Politics of Liberation in America* (New York: Vintage Books, 1967), p. 44.

[9] Hamilton, op. cit., p. 179. For a view of the concept from a broader perspective see Locksley Edmondson, "The Internationalization of Black Power: Historical and Contemporary Perspectives," *Mawazo* (December, 1968), pp. 16-30.

[10] Riot areas were defined by a location map of fires considered riot-related by the Detroit Fire Department.

[11] See our discussion below of "nothing" as a response.

[12] The correlation between interpretations of black power on the open-ended question in 1967 and interpretations in 1968 is (Gamma) 0.54 for blacks and 0.78 for whites. We will be gathering data from the same respondents once again in September, 1970, and will report our findings in detail after the third round is completed.

[13] We will present our codings below. A more conservative coefficient for demonstrating the relationship between interpretations of black power on the open-ended question and approval or disapproval on the close-ended question would be Kendall's tau-beta. See Leo A. Goodman and William H. Kruskal, "Measures of Association for Cross Classification," *Journal of the American Statistical Association* (December, 1954). The tau-beta correlations are 0.86 for blacks and 0.60 for whites. The lower coefficient in the white case reflects the relatively large percentage of whites who give favorable interpretations of black power but disapprove of the slogan. This will be discussed in more detail in the text.

[14] For the blacks, the riot-area respondents gave a greater emphasis to black unity as opposed to fair share interpretations of black power, but the differences are not great. Non-riot area respondents actually were slightly more favorable to black power if we consider unity and fair share responses as indicators of positive feelings.

[15] The quotes presented here are typical examples of black power definitions coded in each category. Respondents are identified by race, sex, age and educational attainment for the benefit of the reader. In cases where the respondent has some specialized training, he is coded with a "plus" after his grade level.

[16] All of the few whites who interpreted black power as "nothing" in 1968 were negative about the slogan.

[17]In a few cases (N = 20) respondents stressed black unity in order to achieve a fair share. We are considering first mentions here and in our analysis, but will probe this in detail when we have more time.

[18]We will combine black unity definitions with the few racial pride references for purposes of analysis.

[19]See footnote 17. About 20 percent of the black respondents mentioning racial unity saw it as a means of achieving equality. For example:

[Black, male, 42, 12 grades] Negroes getting together and forcing whites to realize our importance—our worth to the United States. Gaining respect and equality. The more articulate members of the black unity group are concerned with ends as well as means. See Carmichael and Hamilton, *op. cit.*, pp. 46-47.

[20]The best example of work in this area is Gary T. Marx, *Protest and Prejudice: A Study of Belief in the Black Community* (New York: Harper & Row, 1967). Marx defined "conventional militancy" by the standards of civil rights activists and organizations at the time of his study (1964). All were (pp. 40-41) "urgently aware of the extensiveness of discrimination faced by the American black man. All called for an end to discrimination and segregation and demanded the admission of the Negro to the economic and political mainstream of American life. And they wanted these changes quickly—"Freedom Now." In pursuit of this end, participation in peaceful demonstrations was encouraged."

[21]Riot research is widespread. See, especially, David O. Sears and John B. McConahay, "Riot Participation," and Raymond J. Murphy and James M. Watson, "The Structure of Discontent: Grievance and Support for the Los Angeles Riot," *Los Angeles Riot Study* (Los Angeles: Institute of Government and Public Affairs, University of California, 1967); Nathan S. Caplan and Jeffery M. Paige, "A Study of Ghetto Rioters," *Scientific American* (August, 1968), pp. 15-21, also reported in the *Report of the National Advisory Commission on Civil Disorders* (The U.S. Riot Commission Report) (Washington: U.S. Government Printing Office, 1968); *Supplemental Studies for the National Advisory Commission on Civil Disorders* (Washington: U.S. Government Printing Office, 1968), especially Angus Campbell and Howard Schuman, *Racial Attitudes in Fifteen American Cities,* Chapters 5-6, and Robert M. Fogelson and Robert B. Hill, *Who Riots: A Study of Participation in the 1967 Riots*; and Louis H. Masotti and Don R. Bowen, eds., *Riots and Rebellion: Civil Violence in the Urban Community* (Beverly Hills: Sage Publications, 1968). Studies which emphasize aggregate data can be found in Ted R. Gurr and Hugh D. Davis, eds., *The History of Violence in America* (New York: Bantam Books, 1969).

[22]*Violence in the City—An End or a Beginning? A Report by the Governor's Commission on the Los Angeles Riots* (Los Angeles: McCone Commission Report, 1965).

[23]In the calculations which follow, unless otherwise noted, the black power variable is dichotomized with a favorable interpretation ("fair share" or "racial unity") scored one and unfavorable interpretations scored zero. Respondents with "don't know" or "no answer" responses were not used in the analysis. In this association, for example, those with low educational achievement were slightly less likely to approve of black power (give the "fair share" or "racial unity" interpretations) than those with substantial educational achievement.

[24]We do not think that this is simply because their higher level of education makes them more aware of the content of the actual debate over black power. Relative youth, education, and support of integration are all intertwined and each of these factors is related to a favorable interpretation of black power.

[25]See Jerome H. Skolnick, *The Politics of Protest* (New York: Simon and Schuster, 1969), p. 162, and the U.S. Riot Commission Report, op. cit., especially p. 93, where "a new mood among Negroes, particularly among the young" is described. "Self-esteem and enhanced racial pride are replacing apathy and submission in "the system." Moreover, Negro youth, who make up over half of the ghetto population, share the growing sense of alienation felt by many white youth in our country. Thus, their role in recent civil disorders reflects not only a shared sense of deprivation and victimization by white society but also the rising incidence of disruptive conduct by a segment of American youth throughout the society."

[26]We have defined the South as the 11 states of the Confederacy (N = 255) and the border states of Kentucky, Maryland, Oklahoma, and West Virginia (N = 49). Blacks born in border states were actually less likely to interpret black power in fair share or black unity terms than those born in the former states of the Confederacy, although the differences are small. One hundred and seven of our black respondents were born in Michigan (coded one). This accounts for only 412 respondents. Of those remaining, 43 were born in the United States, but outside of Michigan and the South, 1 in Canada, 1 in the West Indies and 1 in Puerto Rico. We lack information on 3 individuals. The 43 respondents born in the U.S., but not in Michigan or in the South, come from a wide variety of places. They are more favorably disposed toward black power than the Southerners but less so than the Michigan-born.

[27]Other bodies of data and our own show that almost all riot participants are young and that age does have an impact on favorable attitudes toward violence, especially for young men. This is not surprising in light of the physical attributes helpful to a participant in a disturbance and the bravado of the young. However, age is unrelated to more general notions of whether riots helped or hurt the black cause (Murphy and Watson, op. cit., p. 82) as well as to attitudes toward black power. It is clear that age is an important variable in the study of our recent strife, but by itself does not explain contemporary militance or even sympathy for those who participate in civil disturbances.

[28]See Samuel P. Huntington, Political Order in Changing Societies (New Haven: Yale University Press,

1968), pp. 280-283, for a discussion of the potential for "political radicalism" of second-generation slum dwellers. Claude Brown makes the same points in the graphic foreword to his autobiography, *Manchild in the Promised Land* (New York: Macmillan, 1965). We will make some distinctions between the effects of dissatisfaction on lower- and upper-status groups in the section on deprivation below.

[29] The sample was divided into church (coded one), non-members (coded zero) and members of groups, usually action groups, connected with a church (not included in the analysis). People in the latter category (N = 25) chose to emphasize their group above their church affiliation in answering our open-ended question on membership in "church or church-connected groups." They were about as likely as the non-members to approve of black power and should be the subject of intense study because of their pivotal position in the black community.

For a detailed discussion of the similar influence of religion on conventional militancy among blacks, including consideration of denomination and religiosity, see Gary T. Marx, "Religion: Opiate or Inspiration of Civil Rights Militancy Among Negroes," *American Sociological Review* (1967), pp. 64-72.

[30] The impact of region as a variable will surely diminish over time as the effects of national black leadership and the messages of the media and relatives are diffused throughout the nation. However, church affiliation is likely to remain important.

[31] For example, see William Brink and Louis Harris, *The Negro Revolution in America* (New York: Simon and Schuster, 1964), pp. 131 and 232-233, on black attitudes toward various political institutions and figures.

[32] See Louis E. Lomax, *The Negro Revolt* (New York: Harper & Row, 1962), p. 250; and also Gunnar Myrdal, *An American Dilemma* (New York: Harper & Row, 1944), pp. 3-5, 880 and 1007, on blacks as "exaggerated Americans."

[33] Donald E. Stokes, "Popular Evaluations of Government: An Empirical Assessment," in Harlan Cleveland and Harold D. Lasswell, eds., *Ethics and Bigness* (New York: Harper & Row, 1962), pp. 61-73; and Joel D. Aberbach, *Alienation and Race* (unpublished Ph.D. dissertation, Yale University, 1967), pp. 119-126.

[34] Lee Rainwater's "Crucible of Identity—The Negro Lower-Class Family," in *Daedalus* (1966), especially pp. 204-205 and 215, is very insightful on this point, but this distrust is not confined to lower-class ghetto dwellers. See Aberbach, op. cit., pp. 104-114, for a detailed discussion.

[35] For a detailed discussion of our findings and a critique of the existing literature on political trust see Joel D. Aberbach and Jack L. Walker, "Political Trust and Racial Ideology," a paper delivered at the 1969 Annual Meeting of the American Political Science Association, especially pp. 2-7. A revised version will appear in this review (December, 1970).

[36] Political trust has complex roots. See *ibid.*, pp. 7-13, for an analysis of its origins.

[37] This is the famous Cantril Self-Anchoring Scale which indicated the discrepancy between an individual's definition of the "best possible life" for him and his past, present, or future situation. See Hadley C. Cantril, *The Pattern of Human Concerns* (New Brunswick: Rutgers University Press, 1965). Our respondents were given the following set of questions:

"Now could you briefly tell me what would be the best possible life for you? In other words, how would you describe the life you would most like to lead, the most perfect life as you see it?" [Show R card with a ladder.]

"Now suppose that the top of the ladder represents the best possible life for you, the one you just described, and the bottom represents the worst possible life for you."

"Present Life" A. Where on the ladder do you feel you personally stand at the present time?"

"Past Life" B. Where on the ladder would you say you stood five years ago?"

"Future Life" C. Where on the ladder do you think you will be five years from now?"

[38] In the black community sample, for example, level of education is correlated (Gamma) 0.06 with scores on the past-life ladder, 0.09 with scores on present life on the ladder and 0.29 with the future-life ladder. Education is, therefore, only important as a predictor of assessments of future prospects and even here other factors are obviously at work. Income and occupation work much the same way. It is clear that people's evaluations of their achievements vary more within than between objectively defined status groupings.

[39] Reported experiences of discrimination are unrelated to education (Gamma = −0.01).

[40] Aberbach and Walker, op. cit. (1969), especially pp. 11-16.

[41] The correlations (Gamma) between church membership, place of birth and approval of black power are actually slightly higher in the upper education than in the lower-education group:

[42] T. M. Tomlinson, "The Development of a Riot Ideology Among Urban Negroes," *American Behavioral Scientist* (1968), pp. 27-31.

[43] The best single statement is Philip E. Converse, "The Nature of Belief Systems in Mass Publics," in David E. Apter, ed., *Ideology and Discontent* (New York: Free Press, 1964), pp. 206-262. For a brief review of this literature see Lester W. Mibrath, *Political Participation* (Chicago: Rand McNally, 1965); and Herbert McClosky, "Consensus and Ideology in American Politics," this review (1964), pp. 361-382. For some

recent work see Robert Axelrod, "The Structure of Public Opinion on Policy Issues," *Public Opinion Quarterly* (1967), pp. 49-60; and Norman R. Luttbeg, "The Structure of Beliefs Among Leaders and the Public," *Public Opinion Quarterly* (1968), pp. 398-410.

[44]Converse, op. cit., p. 255.

[45]To judge the relative strength of these relationships, see a similar matrix for a national cross-section sample in Converse, op. cit., p. 228.

[46]The two remaining questions in the matrix were close-ended and provided respondents with a set of alternative answers from which to choose. See the footnotes of Table 7 for their exact wording.

[47]See Converse, op. cit.; and Roy T. Bowles and James T. Richardson, "Sources of Consistency of Political Opinion," *American Journal of Sociology* (1969), who argue on p. 683, that "interest in politics is a more powerful predictor of both ideological conceptualization and consistency of opinion than is ability to use abstract ideas."

[48]The issue of the nature of racial ideology among whites will be explored in Joel D. Aberbach and Jack L. Walker, *Race and the Urban Political Community* (Boston: Little, Brown, forthcoming).

[49]Strong advocates of black power are almost uniformly in favor of social pluralism and reject cultural assimilation as resting on the demeaning "assumption that there is nothing of value in the black community" (Carmichael and Hamilton, op. cit., p. 53). However, they do not endorse separatism holding that black power is "ultimately not separatist or isolationist" (Hamilton, op. cit., p. 193). The basic idea is that after the black man develops "a sense of pride and self-respect . . . if integration comes, it will deal with people who are psychologically and mentally healthy, with people who have a sense of their history and of themselves as whole human beings" (Hamilton, op. cit., p. 182). Detailed discussion on the meanings of assimilation can be found in Milton M. Gordon, *Assimilation in American Life* (New York: Oxford University Press, 1964).

[50]Converse discusses this possibility in a section called "Social Sources of Constraint," Converse, op. cit., pp. 211-213. For other treatments of the origins of ideology, see William H. Form and Joan Rytina, "Ideological Beliefs on the Distribution of Power in the United States," *American Sociological Review* (1969), pp. 19-30; Samuel H. Barnes, "Ideology and the Organization of Conflict," *Journal of Politics* (1966), pp. 513-530; Richard M. Merelman, "The Development of Political Ideology: A Framework for the Analysis of Political Socialization," this review (1969), pp. 750-767; Everett C. Ladd, Jr., *Ideology in America* (Ithaca: Cornell University Press, 1969), pp. 341-350; and Robert E. Lane, *Political Ideology* (New York: Free Press, 1962), pp. 213-439.

[51]Robert E. Lane, *Political Thinking and Consciousness* (Chicago: Markham, 1969) p. 316.

[52]Converse, op. cit., pp. 208-209.

[53]Claude Brown, op. cit., p. 8.

[54]E. Franklin Frazier, *Black Bourgeoisie* (New York: Free Press, 1957).

IV.
group identification and minority adjustment

A. GROUP IDENTIFICATION AND THE MINORITY COMMUNITY
B. MINORITY ADJUSTMENT AND MALADJUSTMENT

introduction: some definitions

One of the major determinants of a minority group is that its members *consider themselves* to be a minority group. This feeling involves one or both of the following attitudes: (1) The members feel that they are the objects of prejudice and discrimination and that they need to combine in order to protest and to feel safe and comfortable; (2) the members feel that they have inherited cultural values the expression of which requires that they continue to associate with each other. The former attitude creates a sense of group identification; the latter creates a community.

The term *group identification* is used here in a positive sense. It involves not only a recognition that because of one's ancestry one is a member of a racial or religious group and a recognition that the majority group defines one as belonging to that racial or religious group; it also involves a positive desire to identify oneself as a member of the group and a feeling of pleasure when one does so. Since group morale can be defined as the ability of members of a group to hold together in the face of adversity and to act together in a concerted way to achieve the group's goals, group identification is closely related to group morale.

The majority group considers the members of the minority group to be alike, even if they are not; and it is not uncommon for members of the minority group to express their feelings of kinship by emphasizing those common traits that the majority group holds to be characteristic of them. The members of the group have common experiences that are important to them, and therefore they have common understandings. When the minority group emphasizes its minority characteristics and gives great weight to its common understandings, it may be said to have high morale or high group identification; it is proud of its minority status and is opposing the majority group. But a minority group may have low morale. It may be so downtrodden and so ashamed of its subordinate status that the only shared experience the members of the group think they have is that of being discriminated against by the majority group.

Group identification is promoted by means of a number of techniques and institutions. Protest organizations and, frequently, newspapers and magazines of the group are established especially for the purpose of maintaining group identification. Other community institutions that tend to be segregated from the general body of American life provide a means whereby the members of the group may associated with each other away from those who are not members. Churches in particular offer such an opportunity. Some minorities, such as the French Canadians, center almost their entire group existence around the church. Other institutions grow up around the church or around the area of residence: schools, recreational associations, social clubs, community houses, community welfare organizations, youth groups. These institutions help stimulate group identification largely because when members of the group gather together, they frequently begin to talk about their common problems and relate instances of injustice. Even when the members do not deliberately talk about their minority problem, it slips into their conversation in examples, allusions, and jokes. Thus, they are unconsciously as well as consciously drawn closer to their group which has shared a number of common experiences.

Some of the institutions have programs intended to promote group identification. Such efforts are most generally characteristic of the minority press. It gains its readership by providing news that is specifically directed at minority experience. In the case of the nationality minorities, the newspaper provides a means of maintaining the ancestral language. It also reports injustices to members of the group in any part of the country or the world and shows how minority opposition is being organized to meet injustice. Although the churches are primarily oriented toward the discussion of religious values, they tend, when they do discuss current social problems, to choose those faced by the minority group. Not infrequently, a religious or nationality minority may establish a school in connection with a church. Such a school may be a parochial school that takes the place of the public school, an after-school language class where the language of a nationality group is taught, or a part-time religious school where the faith of the religious minority is transmitted to the young.

Even some of the community functions that are carried on in conjunction with those of the larger American society tend to develop group identification in the minority. Business, for example, can be a means for developing pride in the group. In several minority groups, deliberate efforts are made to promote a campaign to buy from members of one's own group. Even where this policy does not operate on the deliberate level, it operates on the informal one. Businesses owned by members of some minority groups tend to hire members of the same group as workers and thus provide another basis of association. In the realm of politics, there is frequently special support for the minority group member who is running for office. A number of studies have shown that certain minority groups attach themselves to certain political parties. More important, some of these minority groups have shown themselves capable of shifting their vote radically in one direction or the other for a party or a candidate who indicates an attitude for or against the minority's interest.

On a less formal level, there are other bases of group identification. The use of a foreign tongue has already been mentioned, but it should be recognized that even where the English language is used, there will be certain words, allusions, and topics that are unique to the minority group and are generally understood only by those who have had the group's experiences. A conversation in English among members of one minority group in which special terms are used is different from a conversation between a member of a minority group and an outsider in which the general English language must be employed. Not only the form of speech but also its content is determined by minority group experience, and this promotes group identification. Even though competition may be intense among the members of the minority group and a great deal of jealousy may be expressed, there is, nevertheless, when comparison is made with the outgroup, a sense of pride expressed toward those members of the minority group who have achieved unusually high status and prestige. Feelings of antagonism and resentment against the dominant group will be expressed in conversation. Some of it takes a humorous form, and it is likely that every minority group has its own jokes that disparage the dominant group. These are mechanisms of defense that unite the minority group and keep it protesting against the subordination to which the dominant community subjects it. The protest language occurs not only in private conversation but also in public speeches and in writing. Thus, every instance of discrimination, if it is talked about and written about, provides a further basis of group identification. Every group activity, even if conducted by only a small proportion of the total membership of the minority group, and even if conducted in an out-of-the-way place (since reports of it are widely disseminated), is a basis for the development of stronger cohesion and group identification.

Insofar as there are class differences in the minority group (and there are in all groups that have been in the United States for more than a few years), these serve to provide a basis of differentiation that works against the total minority group identification. Sometimes, the enforced segregation of the minority group provides a basis of privilege for some of its members; for example, where minority members are concentrated in a certain school or in a certain residential area, they are obliged to take advantage of the professional services of those, necessarily members of their own group, who can or do live or work in those areas. To use the phrase of an outstanding black sociologist, E. Franklin Frazier, there are certain "advantages to the disadvantages."

Sometimes a minority group is not a single cultural group. The dominant group may define it as a single group, but the group itself may be beset by cleavages among its members because of divergent backgrounds or interests. An example of ethnic differences within a minority group can be seen in the distinctions among Spanish, German, and eastern European Jews. There are similar differences among full-blooded blacks, mulattoes, and West Indian blacks and between northern Italians and southern Italians or Sicilians. Other cleavages develop on the basis of a difference between generations or religious beliefs. First- and second-generation Japanese-Americans in the United States are divided in many ways. Jews are divided as to religion among Orthodox, Conservative, Reform, and nonadherent Jews. Such cleavages are very important within the minority group, even if the outside world does not see them. As with any group of people, a minority will be split along ideological lines. There are ideological differences about how to strengthen the position of the group: some favor an aggressive approach; whereas others are conciliatory. As in politics, where there will be radicals, liberals, and conservatives, members align themselves differently on general issues, provided the issues involved do not concern the minority group directly.

One of the most important sources of minority group cleavage and low group identification is the phenomenon of *group self-hatred,* which affects various members of the minority group in different degrees and is more prevalent in some minorities than in others. It expresses itself in hatred of the group, of its culture, and even of oneself because one is a member of the group. Group self-hatred may be thought of as the opposite of group identification. It manifests itself in all the expressions of prejudice that characterize the prejudiced members of the majority group. It also appears in a desire to escape all identification with the minority group: one passes, tries to pass, or becomes an emotional advocate of passing into the dominant group. A distinction should be made, however, between the person who advocates assimilation because of a rational belief that it is the best solution to the minority problem and the person who advocates assimilation primarily because he personally would like to escape being a member of the minority group. Among Jews, the latter type has been defined as a Jew who will associate only with those Jews who will not associate with other Jews. Because of his physical features, the black usually finds it more difficult to assimilate, and therefore his group self-hatred takes somewhat different forms.

There are ups and downs through time in the level of group identification for each minority group, depending on the state of these influencing forces. In general, the level of group identification among blacks has been rising since about 1900, at first slowly and then with increasing speed. By 1936, the northern blacks were able to shift their voting behavior to a marked degree in response to their group interests as affected by the policies of the two major parties. By 1942, they were able to exert sufficient collective pressure to get President Roosevelt to issue an executive order establishing the Fair Employment Practices Commission (FEPC). In the post-World

War II years, group identification grew to the extent that few blacks could publicly support any form of segregation, which many had done in the past. By the 1960s, blacks in both North and South were organizing mass demonstrations in protest against discrimination. This culminated in the huge but orderly March on Washington in July, 1963. In 1964, some of the demonstrations took violent form, despite the efforts of most national civil rights leaders. It seems evident that group identification has become so powerful among blacks that only those leaders who urge their followers to greater extremes of protest and self-sacrifice can be successful. It is doubtful whether the level of group identification can subside rapidly, even if blacks achieve most of their long-standing aims of complete equality of treatment and opportunity. Group pressures on the individual are now so strong that only the gradual emergence of diversified individual interests can counterbalance the power of the long-developing, discrimination-fed, and thus bitter group interests. Strong group identification among blacks is likely to remain and manifest itself in various forms of opposition to the dominant white society long after the conditions that gave rise to it have disappeared.

Apart from the existence of group identification and group self-hatred, the minority community differs from the general American community in only limited ways. Except for members who have arrived in the United States recently (a small number because of the immigration restrictions) and those who have been isolated for a long while (such as the Hispanos, French Canadians, and a small proportion of the northern European groups who live in rural areas), the major patterns in the United States are those that have been developed through the centuries by the conglomeration of people now known as Americans. Each racial, religious, and nationality group has contributed its own culture to the growing stream; and out of common experiences, new patterns have also developed. The process by which immigrant groups have contributed their unique cultures and by which they themselves have absorbed the newly developing culture is known as *assimilation.* The popular term for the result of this process is the *melting pot.* As the preceding chapters have shown, assimilation has progressed more rapidly in urban than in rural areas, and it is in the cities that most of the minority groups live, with some noteworthy exceptions. It should not be thought, however, that assimilation is making all Americans alike; Americans are still differentiated by class, region, neighborhood, occupation, and interest, as well as other variables.

Although the general culture patterns dominate the behavior of the minority as well as the majority groups, there are some important reasons for the preservation by minorities of deviant characteristics. There is, for one thing, the desire to retain from ancestral traditions some of the desirable features not available in the American culture. To a certain extent, the tenacity of religion has such a basis. Other foreign ways, ranging from food habits to rules for bringing up children, may be found similarly desirable and worth retaining. But even highly desirable patterns cannot be sequestered. In the free and mobile civilization that predominates in the United States, members of other groups tend to recognize the advantages of many foreign culture patterns and gradually to absorb them. Latin American music and Jewish cooking are almost as popular with the dominant group in the United States as they are with those who first brought them to this country. Religions tend to be more limited in their acceptance, but even in this respect, large numbers of people change their religion because some other system of beliefs is found to be more acceptable.

A second explanation for the retaining of ancestral culture patterns lies in the discrimination that tends to isolate minority groups from the American mainstream. Their members often cannot learn what the general patterns are. Also, because they are rejected by outsiders, they tend to retain what is uniquely theirs, becoming defensive about their traditions and thereby holding on to them more tenaciously. In fact, group pride or race pride tends to develop to the extent that the products of the minority's own culture are thought of as being always superior, and no recognition is given to the values of the majority. This pride is one of the characteristics of highly intensive group identification.

It is to be noted that pressures from the outside world create a certain need to retain old ways in unmodified form. For example, the older Jewish Orthodox religion and the Catholic religion formerly were more flexible than they are today. They were able to change to meet new needs when there was no threat to their religious beliefs. But when popular religious ideas entered a period of rapid change at the same time that the religious-group members were becoming more personally insecure because of discrimination, the religions themselves tended to become more inflexible. Jewish orthodoxy has never in its long history been as rigid as it has during the last hundred years. Pope Pius XII (1939-1958) warned Catholics, especially priests, not to deviate from the literal interpretation of the dogmas and doctrines of the church, even in order to attract new members to the faith. (On the other hand, Pope John XXIII and Pope Paul VI have encouraged somewhat more flexibility since 1958.) Orthodoxy thereby becomes one security in a world that is insecure because of intergroup conflict and discrimination.

Discrimination limits the cultural characteristics of minority groups in still another way: It creates for the minority certain problems that require special adjustments. Special culture patterns develop to meet these needs. In the black community, for example, the greater employability of the female compared with the male has created a relatively high proportion of female-headed families (28 percent of all black families). Dangers to the entire Chinese community arising from violations of the law by a few members result in the development of special law enforcement authorities in Chinatowns.

Sometimes the problems created by discrimination cannot be compensated for by cultural adjustment. One of the first products of discrimination is poverty, which is in itself a social problem and which tends to create other social problems. It tends to be a contributing factor to personal, family, and community disorganization. Sometimes foreign culture patterns are retained in an attempt to avoid the social problems stimulated by poverty. For example, religious activities are encouraged for Jewish children partly in order to keep them from becoming delinquents. For other minority groups, the high incidence of certain social problems becomes part of the group's cultural pattern. Minority groups collectively have a higher incidence of most social pathologies than the dominant group does. However, each minority group tends to have a higher incidence of some kinds of social problems than it does of others. For example, the black groups are highly afflicted with family disorganization and crime; whereas the Jewish groups have low rates in these problems but a high degree of mental disorder and suicide. The manifestation of one social problem rather than another is a result of the special history and culture of the group, including the history of discrimination that the group meets in the United States.

The minority community is thus to be distinguished in terms of group identification, group self-hatred, assimilation, the retention of desirable cultural values, isolation from the general stream of American culture, and social pathology.

26
catholic church professionals

JOSEPH H. FICHTER

Because so much attention has been focused on the physical concentration of minority groups, it is possible to forget that a community can be physically dispersed and cut across class lines. The Catholic community, for example, is held together only by common beliefs and a feeling of mutual solidarity.

The Catholic church is in the throes of the greatest change since the Reformation. How these changes affect the professional in the church is the subject of the following essay. Reflected in it are the changes in the society that are requiring adjustments on the part of the professionals. How changing attitudes and roles of professionals are received by and affect the laity can only be speculated on, but it may well be that to the extent that new professional activities meet the needs of the lay Catholic, to that extent the Catholic community will be strengthened and solidified in the long run.

Dr. Fichter is Stillman Professor of Roman Catholic Studies at the Harvard University Divinity School.

It is a commonplace now to remark that organized religion in America is experiencing a time of change and challenge and that the challenge is most acute where the change is most sudden. This seems to be the case dramatically in the Roman Catholic church, which held the line of ecclesiastical tradition and theological conservatism, more or less successfully, between the Council of Trent and the Second Vatican Council. Adaptations that could have been reasonably and gradually introduced during these four centuries suddenly exploded in the last four years.

All American Catholics are affected by these adaptations in some ways, but the people most affected are at the core of the system—

the full-time professionals who officially maintain the organization, represent its formal ideology, and perform its central functions. These are the clergy, the religious Brothers and Sisters, who peaked numerically at over a quarter million (253,167) in 1966, the year after the Second Vatican Council closed. Approximately one-quarter of these people are ordained clergymen, seven out of ten are religious Sisters, and the remainder are religious Brothers. Our intent here is to explore what is happening to these church professionals during this post-Council period of challenge and change.

MANPOWER SHRINKAGE

The official *Catholic Directory*[1] for 1969 records a total of 238,872, which is a decrease of 5.6 percent between 1966 and 1969, a period during which the American Catholic population is estimated to have in-

Reprinted from "The Sixties: Radical Change in American Religion," *The Annals of the American Academy of Political and Social Science* 387 (January, 1970), pp. 78-85. Reproduced by permission of the author and publisher.

creased by 3.5 percent. During this short time, the ratio of ecclesiastical personnel to the Catholic population has changed from one in 183 Catholics in 1966 to one in 200 Catholics in 1969. For the first time since the *Catholic Directory* has been publishing national statistics, the parallel growth rates have ended; the Catholic population increases steadily while the statistics on church personnel show an annual decrease.

This shrinkage of personnel cannot be explained by an increase in mortality rates. It cannot be explained by retirement because these people remain in the statistics even when they are too old or too sick to perform their work. The general explanation has to be that an increasing number of people are leaving this profession, and proportionately fewer are entering it, than ever before. After an unprecedented growth during the 1950's, there occurred what has been called the "crisis in vocations" that was already perceptible in the early 1960's.

The numerical decline has been most noticeable among the religious women. There were 14,254 fewer American Sisters in 1969 than in the peak year of 1966, and this is a proportional decline of 7.8 percent over the period. The great majority of American Sisters teach in Catholic schools where the "shortage" has been most publicized. The number of Catholic elementary schools (both parochial and private) also peaked in 1966 at 10,962, but declined to 10,406 in 1969. Despite a growing child population during the same period, there were 574,034 fewer pupils in these elementary schools in 1969 than there had been in 1966.

Although many former Sisters have told their story for publication, the growing number of former priests has probably gained more public attention.[2] According to the *Catholic Directory,* the largest number (59,892) of American priests on record was in 1967. Since then the number still officially on the record has declined to 59,620. These rough statistics mean that the number of young men entering the priesthood through ordination has not kept up with the number who die or leave the priesthood. Fewer men are being ordained because there are fewer seminarians preparing for ordination. Between 1965 and 1969, the seminary population has declined by 31 percent.[3]

Any profession is in trouble when the input of personnel does not equal the exodus (by both death and resignation), and this becomes more acute as the population that is served by the profession expands. The diocesan priesthood, which is mainly responsible for maintaining the parishes, has, up to now, kept a balanced input and exodus, but it is portentous that seminarians preparing for the diocesan priesthood have declined by 27 percent since 1965. The recorded imbalance in clergy has been among priests of the religious orders, who do most of the specialized work of the church, and whose numbers declined by 3.7 percent. More worrisome is the fact that the seminarians of religious orders have decreased by 35 percent since 1965.[4]

THE PAROCHIAL MINISTRY

The distinction between the parochial ministry and the other specialized apostolates of the church gives an indication of the effect that the manpower shrinkage may have on the operation of the Catholic church in America. As in every large organized religion, the local congregation is the place where the largest number of lay people practice their religion. Other ministries may be abandoned, but new parishes are established every year. Catholic officials are reluctant to close parishes, even those in the inner city where the number of parishioners has drastically dwindled. There are now 18,146 parishes in the United States, an increase of 381 parishes since 1966. But there are 500 fewer parochial schools than there were in 1966.

It is at the parish level that the lay people recognize changes in traditional patterns of the ministry, and it may be that many of them have been ill-prepared to accept innovations and adaptations. The liturgy is now mainly in the English language; folk-song Masses are promoted for and by the young people; Masses are celebrated in the evening; laymen participate from the sanctuary; and in some places, the Sunday obligation can be fulfilled on Saturday. On weekdays, the liturgy is often celebrated in private homes for families and neighbors. Parish priests report that more people now receive Holy Communion, but fewer go to confession.

The younger clergy have been, by and large, enthusiastic about these forms of liturgical renewal, and they tend now to give brief informal homilies instead of the traditional sermon. The thrust for change has gone beyond this into what has been called the "underground" church, or into "floating" parishes, which do not observe the restrictions of territorial boundaries. How widespread this movement is, is not known, or whether it can even be called a movement, but it represents a grass-roots approach that does not wait for episcopal initiative or directions from the diocesan chancery office. In many instances, it is broadly ecumenical, inviting non-Catholics to participate in the liturgy.

The priest-parishioner relationship is changing in other ways, partly to relieve the clergyman of his so-called "secular" roles, and partly to involve the laity in the operation of the parish. It is common practice for Protestant congregations to have a board of deacons, or vestrymen. This arrangement was the pattern among Catholics in some countries (like French Canada and Germany), but not in the United States, until it was recommended in the aftermath of Vatican II. There is now wide experimentation with parish councils. The leaders, with whom the priests now share the processes of planning, development, and decision-making, are elected from the laity.

COLLEGIALITY

What is happening in this respect at the parish level is an extension of the central concept of collegiality—widely discussed at the Second Vatican Council—which concerns the general relationship between authority and obedience in the church. The Pope would seek consultation and share policy-formation, if not ultimate decisions, with the bishops, the bishops with their priests, the priests with the laity, and the religious superiors with the membership of the order. In political terms, this implies a shift in the power centers, from the Vatican Curia to the Episcopal Synod, from the diocesan chancery to the clergy senate. It does not mean popular democracy, but, to the extent that collegiality is seriously implemented (and there are those who now sense a backlash to prevent it), it would tend to move

the Catholic church from a strongly authoritarian structure to a semblance of representative or participatory democracy.

At the diocesan level, collegiality is structured into priests' senates, which were recommended by the Second Vatican Council and which have been officially accepted by most American bishops. In some places where there is no senate, and in a few where a senate exists, the priests have established voluntary associations with the intention of working with the bishop on the problems of the diocese. The prime movers in both senates and associations have been the diocesan priests, with only minimal participation by priests in the religious orders. The National Federation of Priests Councils is a voluntary, and at best quasi-official, federation of both senates and associations, with a permanent office, quarterly meetings of a board of directors, and an annual convention of delegates.

In the wake of this trend to ecclesiastical collegiality, there has evolved an informal network of organizations that might be politely called "pressure groups." One of the more publicized has been the National Association for Pastoral Renewal which seems to focus mainly on the removal of obligatory celibacy for Catholic priests. A priest in California attempted to establish a kind of labor union for lower-echelon priests; and a monsignor in New York countered with a plan for a managerial organization of pastors and diocesan administrators. There are relatively few Negro priests in America, but they have organized loosely in a Black Clergy Caucus. Some countervailing groups, with the intention to preserve church traditions and stem the tide of change, also exist.

The practice of collegiality has proceeded further in the religious orders than it has elsewhere in the church. A kind of women's liberation movement, although it was not called that, had its seeds in the Sister Formation program of the 1950's. The Sisters have taken the call to *aggiornamento* seriously, and have evolved plans for personal and organizational renewal that do not always find favor with some of the prelates. Impatience with the pace of change has been expressed by the Black Sisters Caucus, and, more recently, by the organization of a National Coalition of American Sisters.

THE TASK FORCE

In all these efforts for collegial, cooperative, and consensual reform, a profound change
in the life-style of the church professional is
implied. This is not simply a matter of less-
familial nomenclature (the titles of Father,
Sister, Brother), or of less-traditional garb (the
wearing of civilian clothes), or of a more relaxed daily horarium. Deeper than these external adaptations is the willingness among the
church professionals to promote and accept a
sense of personal responsibility and self-direc-
tion. These changes lift institutionalized
restrictions that had long been felt to be a
barrier to initiative, maturity, and creativity.[5]

Beyond these personal patterns, there is
a collective development that has both structural and functional implications. This is a
switch of emphasis from the large, secondary
association—the diocese for secular priests or
the province for members of religious orders—
to the small primary group—the task force in
the form of the Christian koinonia. There is
still some confusion among those who prefer
what they call a person-orientation rather than
a task-orientation, but the general notion is
that professional functions can be best performed in small teams made up of people who
share common interests and who can find self-
fulfillment in such face-to-face relationships.

Religious Sisters who formerly lived in
large communities of thirty or more members—
as in high schools, colleges, and hospitals—are
now regrouping to rent apartments where three
to five can live together. Diocesan priests are
experimenting with the team concept in the
inner-city areas where the traditional forms of
parish activities seem to have become dysfunctional. Young priests who are doing graduate
work no longer find lodging in the nearest
rectory, and seminarians who are attending
universities often live now in small autonomous
groups. This arrangement provides mutual support in their main common function and removes the impersonality and coldness of the
larger houses in which they previously resided.

The emphasis on the primary group, or
small task force, carries overtones of an anti-
institutional bias. In this bias, the institution
represents both bigness and repression. The
bigness is objectionable because it is said to be
bureaucratic, aloof, impersonal, cold, and ma-
chinelike. The church professional feels that
his identity lies in an IBM card in the chancery
office or in the Provincial's file cabinet. The
oppressiveness of the large institution is often
manifested in the formal regulations that become sacred and obligatory simply because
they have existed for a long time.

The anti-institutional bias among the
younger clergy and religious is often accompanied by, or sometimes confused with, criticism of church leadership. Many feel that their
bishops and other religious superiors not only
are aloof from them, but are also failing to
implement the promises of the *aggiornamento*.
The American episcopate has been, traditionally, most loyal to the Holy See and, unlike
the bishops of some countries, seems reluctant
to take the initiative in American church reform. The Provincials of large religious orders,
both of women and of men, have been much
more progressive and creative than the bishops.

From the functional point of view, an
odd dilemma exists in this situation. The
church professional is acting on the assumption that institutional rigidity has been relaxed
but that the bishops are unwilling to relax their
authoritarian posture. The formation of task
forces has proceeded on the assumption that
collegial relations would be introduced at all
levels of the church. It is difficult to see how
the professionals can function well until this
dilemma disappears.

PERSONALISM AND PROFESSIONALISM

The obverse of the anti-institutional bias
is the propersonal bias. The perennial problem
in any large-scale organization is the constant
search for balance between the institutional
patterns and purposes, on the one hand, and
the personal needs and performance of the
individual on the other. Some are leaving the
service of the church in a search for self-fulfillment, and they are finding that institutional
demands are also exacting in other types of
employment, as well as in marriage. Many who
leave the church have already had the benefit
of specialized professional training.

Dissatisfaction with the role of "general
practitioner" is much more common among

diocesan parochial priests than it is among the members of religious orders who are in the specialized ministries of the church. It is obvious that the transition to a nonchurch occupation is smoother for the person who already has professional credentials, as social worker, scientist, teacher, nurse, or other specialist. We have no research data to test this hypothesis, but if it is true that the professionally trained person is more likely than the general practitioner to leave the ecclesiastical ministry, it would seem self-defeating on the part of church officials to encourage such professional training.[6] Yet, this was an important goal of the Sister Formation movement, largely inspired in the early 1950's by Pope Pius XII, who urged that full professional training be given to religious Sisters preparing for teaching and hospital work.

Professionalism and personalism are cumulative and mutually influential. Self-confidence and self-fulfillment are likely to characterize the church functionary who knows that he is competently performing a professional function that serves the needs of people. Men and women in the religious orders have been required by their specialized ministries to "keep up" with their extraecclesiastical professional peers. A more recent development is the increasing numbers of diocesan priests who are doing graduate studies and working for professional degrees.

The church professional who finds satisfaction in his work may be dissatisfied with the authoritarian structure in which he works. The professional does not expect to be treated like a job-holder or a general practitioner, or like an IBM card in the files of ecclesiastical authorities. Furthermore, the church vocation is described as one which, ideally, calls for warm human relations, personal devotion, and mutual love and respect throughout the system. This is where we come full circle with the question of collegial relations within the church. The need for improved management in dioceses and religious orders is not merely a matter of humanizing the managers themselves, or of satisfying needs of church personnel. It is more urgently a matter of the proper utilization of manpower in the church so that these trained professionals will not go else-where to make the most of their expertise in the service of God's people.

RELIGIOUS ORDERS

The trained professionals who have done most of the specialized nonparochial work of the church have been the members of religious orders. Schools, colleges, hospitals, and social welfare agencies have been largely staffed by these people, and they have had a notably higher rate of resignation from the active ministry than has been the case with diocesan priests. This poses both a structural and a functional problem for the church. There are those who argue that the whole concept of religious life is outmoded, others who say that the only genuinely priestly work is that of the sacristy and the sanctuary, and still others who hold that this priestly work is, at best, only a part-time occupation.[7]

Historically, the religious orders have always been the spearhead of renewal and reform in the church. They have traditionally expected a total commitment of their members; they have also traditionally made a corporate commitment to the service of the church and the needs of society. Except for some cenobitic groups that "flee the world," these religious orders have been the most dedicated and zealous reformers of both the church and the world. The great charismatic leaders like Benedict, Dominic, Francis of Assisi, and Ignatius Loyola introduced different kinds of organizations because the pragmatic function that each envisioned was different.

Profound changes are now occurring in the lives of religious men and women: new groups are forming; old orders are reforming; new directions are opening up; and new interpretations are being made of the vows of poverty, chastity, and obedience so that they may become more meaningful in an affluent, sensate, and democratic society. The question of the *aggiornamento* is not whether these religious orders will survive or whether the modern church needs their services. Rather, the question is how they can be systematically reorganized so that their members can be both socially effective and personally fulfilled.

The so-called religious revival after the

Second World War was accompanied by a continuous expansion of the religious orders and by what is now seen as an overextension of their programs of service. With the shrinkage of personnel, there is now a program of retrenchment. This has already been seen in the closing of parochial elementary schools. At the second level, religious orders are handing over some of their high schools to diocesan control or to private Catholic corporations. In some instances, the religious orders are withdrawing from administrative control of—and from financial responsibility for—the colleges, hospitals, and other service agencies that they have been operating.

The internal affairs of the religious orders are being carefully re-examined, first, to understand why there is so much discontent among the membership, and, second, to reorganize the functional purpose of each group. In an urban, industrial society of large-scale organizations, many of these religious orders are also large-scale. They are also subject to the same complaints of impersonality, bureaucracy, coldness, alienation, and inflexibility. The sacred rule, formerly covering the minutiae of daily living, is being updated to fit the mood of this culture and this era. The stumbling block for many now seems to be the promise and practice of celibacy.

CELIBACY

Religious brotherhoods and sisterhoods are, by definition, unisex organizations. It would require a radical change of the whole community life of these orders to permit marriage among the members, and no one is seriously suggesting this change. What is happening is that people are leaving the celibate communities, and many are making the personal change from the celibate life to the married life, and are thus lost to the ranks of church personnel. There are other reasons for the exodus from the religious orders, but much evidence points to celibacy as one of the crucial factors.

The priesthood, both diocesan and religious, is being numerically and functionally affected by the problems of institutionalized celibacy. Discussion of this question about

and among the Catholic clergy has been given an inordinate amount of attention since the Second Vatican Council.[8] In the Latin rite of the Western church it has been taken for granted among the laity, and among seminarians, that celibacy is a fixed condition for ordination to the priesthood. All the institutional—if not personal—arguments were in its favor, especially that the unmarried priest could give himself wholeheartedly to his work without the distractions and burdens of family life. Celibacy was enveloped in a sacred aura that tended to make marriage a second-rate state of life.

Whatever may be said about the sacred and traditional values of clerical celibacy, the empirical fact is that more than two-thirds of the men leaving the priesthood get married (with or without a dispensation from their ordination vows). An indefinite number of these former priests say they would like to remain in the active ministry, or return to it, if they could do so as married men. Their cause is supported by the National Association for Pastoral Renewal, and especially by an offshoot from this group calling itself Priests for a Free Ministry, who are willing to support themselves by their present occupation and also to function as part-time priests.

The proposal for a part-time priesthood can be related to Ivan Illich's conviction that there are already too many clergymen in the Catholic church and to the further conviction that the priest is essentially nothing more than a leader of worship services and a builder of the cultic community. If this closely honed version of the sacerdotal function is acceptable, the church can focus exclusively on its parishes; the manpower shrinkage becomes a nonproblem; and the married tentmakers among the clergy can supply all the needed services to the people of God.

Fanciful proposals of this kind set episcopal teeth on edge. The Pope and his closest advisors are adamantly opposed to married priests in the Latin rite, although the Pope has personally ordained married men to the diaconate. This concession was considered dangerous by some of the delegates to the Second Vatican Council, who thought it would be an open door to the married priesthood. Meanwhile pressure is growing, especially among the younger clergy, that they be given the option for either marriage or celibacy. The acceptance of a married clergy in the Catholic church will set off a chain reaction of other changes involving finances, relationships with authority, relationships between celibate and non-celibate priests, problems of promotion, and new modes of seminary training.

PROFESSIONAL PREPARATION

Everything we have said up to now is descriptive of a new and different Catholic church in America, for which future full-time personnel must now be trained. The decline in seminarians, more notable in the religious orders than in the dioceses, has been more than matched by the decline in the numbers of young women who aspire to the Sisterhoods. Seminaries and houses of study are closing in many parts of the country, and their properties are now in the real estate market. In those areas where there is mutual access between Catholic seminaries and Protestant divinity schools, a kind of academic consortium allows cross-registration for students.[9] Training places have also moved from rural isolation so that

seminarians, and student Sisters and Brothers, are getting more of their schooling at open colleges and universities.

It must not be thought that the necessity for retrenchment alone brought about these changes. The Second Vatican Council gave serious attention to the training of church personnel and provided the motivation for renewal. Some of the younger priests remark that they were trained according to pre-Vatican ideals which did not prepare them for the post-Vatican church. Others say that their seminary gave them up-to-date training which is being thwarted in dioceses and religious provinces that persist in out-of-date practices. This means that progressive change has been uneven, both at the training level and in the places where the training is to be put into professional practice.

The youthful and decimated generation of trainees will unquestionably add a new dimension to the whole ecclesiastical profession of the future. They are no less spiritual, zealous, and commited than their predecessors were. They appear to be adaptive to sudden change and to accept the challenge of a more professional approach to the work of the new church.

NOTES

[1] Published annually by P. J. Kenedy and Sons, New York, who are the first to admit that it is difficult to "keep up" with church statistics. For example, the names of men who have left the priesthood, especially diocesan priests, are kept in the *Directory* until their resignation can be officially verified.

[2] There have been many popular and personal accounts by and about former priests and former Sisters, and there has been much speculation concerning "why they leave," but there has been no systematic, large-scale phenomenon.

[3] It appears that "new" seminarians now enter training at the college level rather than in the preparatory seminaries. For a refinement of statistics, see *Catholic Priesthood Training Centers* (Washington, D.C.: Center for Applied Research in the Apostolate, 1969).

[4] *Ibid.*

[5] Many dioceses and religious orders are conducting self-surveys, with open and democratic discussions in which consensus is sought in all aspects of reorganization. In some instances, contracts are made with business management firms, or university research teams, to lend sophisticated expertise to the survey.

[6] Many other factors must be considered. See Joseph H. Fichter, *Religion as an Occupation* (Notre Dame, Ind.: University of Notre Dame Press, 1961); and Joseph H. Fichter, *America's Forgotten Priests* (New York: Harper & Row, 1968).

[7] See the views of Ivan Illich, "The Vanishing Clergyman," *The Critic* (June-July 1967), pp. 18-27, and some views to the contrary in Joseph H. Fichter, "The Myth of the Hyphenated Clergy," *The Critic* (December 1968-January 1969), pp. 16-24.

[8] For a many-faceted treatment of this subject, see George H. Frein, ed., *Celibacy: The Necessary Option* (New York: Herder and Herder, 1968).

[9] See the excellent work by Walter D. Wagoner, *The Seminary: Protestant and Catholic* (New York: Sheed and Ward, 1966).

27
jewish intermarriage in the united states

ERICH ROSENTHAL

Jews have always maintained strong barriers against intermarriage, probably not because they consciously thought about the danger this would pose to the continued existence of the group but in reaction to prejudice directed against Jews. Whatever the reason, Jewish communities did not feel threatened by outgroup marriage until recently. American Jews frequently live in neighborhoods where they are in the majority, but the young people of marriageable age go to high schools and colleges where they meet unprejudiced non-Jewish boys and girls; and as might be expected, marriage frequently follows. The Jewish community has very few tactics at its disposal to prevent outgroup marriages; their successful assimilation has destroyed both their differences from and their distrust of the gentiles. They have invested heavily in community centers and youth programs designed specifically to bring young Jewish boys and girls together during adolescence. Parents of young children have returned to the synagogue and revived old customs in the home, hoping to build loyalty to the group in their children. Should the rate of outmarriage continue to rise, the Jewish group and its culture will disappear in the United States, a very uncomfortable situation for many Jews, and not only those who are devoutly religious. Ironically, intermarriage signals the end of anti-Semitism.

Dr. Rosenthal is professor of sociology at Queens College.

How widespread is intermarriage among Jews in the United States?

Most people have thought it to be negligible since the postwar American-Jewish renascence. Dr. Erich Rosenthal's new report shatters that belief.

It shows that more than 13% of Jews in a large American city intermarry, and that the figure is bound to rise. For, according to the study, intermarriage is greater for every generation born in the United States and rises even more sharply among the college-educated. A whopping two-thirds of all Jewish youngsters now go to college.

Reprinted from *Council Woman* (November 1963), pp. 6-7. Published by the National Council of Jewish Women, New York.

In the large city, where the overall intermarriage rate was 13.1%, the rate for native-born Jewish men of native parentage was 17.9%, jumping to 37% for those who had attended college. In an area of smaller Jewish communities the intermarriage rate was 42.2%.

These figures mark the first time such a study has been done in 40 years—thus covering a whole new generation. They come from two sets of statistics never before interpreted. One is a survey of the Jewish community of Greater Washington, D.C., compiled at American University in 1956. The other is data collected between 1953 and 1959 by the state of Iowa, one of only two states in the union to gather information about the religion of brides and grooms. (The other is Indiana, which started collecting such data only in 1959.)

Since five-sixths of American Jews live in large cities, the figures for Washington are the most telling. They show that intermarriage increases sharply with each succeeding generation. Intermarriage among foreign-born Jewish men was 1.4%, among the native born of foreign parentage 10.2%, and among the native born of native parentage 17.9%. There can be no further doubt, says Dr. Rosenthal, that the loosening of ties with the old culture and the increasing assimilation into the American mainstream makes for more intermarriage.

The statistics also show, he adds, that the theory of the "return of the third generation" to the traditional community has no basis in fact.

Are the Washington figures inordinately high because of the unique character of the city with its high number of professional and white-collar workers? No, says Dr. Rosenthal. This was indicated by another set of figures, which showed the city of origin of the persons covered by the Washington survey. Although Greater Washington natives had the highest intermarriage rate—14.9%—former residents of larger cities—mainly New York, Baltimore, Philadelphia, Boston and Chicago—had an 11.7% rate.

Both the Washington and Iowa statistics show that the larger the city and its Jewish community, the lower tends to be the rate of intermarriage. This seems to reflect the greater availability of social contact with other Jews.

Jewish men, says the study, have a much higher intermarriage rate than Jewish women. In Washington, the rate of Jewish men was 9.4%, for Jewish women, only 4.5%. Dr. Rosenthal feels that this reflects the fact that men have more social freedom and, perhaps, that Jewish women have more group loyalty.

What effect does the higher rate of male intermarriage have on Jewish women's chances of finding a husband? Since their intermarriage rate is low, are many Jewish women remaining spinsters? Or are they actually intermarrying too, but no longer even identifying themselves as Jews? The figures are not yet in. However, says Dr. Rosenthal, at least some rabbis seem to feel that the group loyalty of Jewish women is also breaking down.

Among second-generation Jews the country of origin of the parents also has an effect on the tendency to intermarry. Those whose parents came from Central and Western Europe had a much higher intermarriage rate (22%) than those whose ancestry was Russian (10.1%), Polish (1.5%) or of other Eastern European origin (5.8%).

Secular education, particularly college education, which tends to uproot the Jewish youth from his home community, was found to have an important effect upon intermarriage. In all generations (foreign born, native born of foreign parentage and native born of native parentage), college education produced increased intermarriage. Among the native born of native parentage, the 17.9% intermarriage rate more than doubled—to 37%—for those who had attended college.

At this point, however, another interesting factor appears. The intermarriage rate dropped sharply—to 14.9%—for third- and later-generation persons who had gone to graduate school. This was also true—though the figures were not so extreme—for the second-generation group, though not for the foreign born.

The reason, Dr. Rosenthal thinks, is not so much that graduate education produces greater group loyalty, as that Jews who take postgraduate studies are more likely to be studying for a traditional "Jewish profession," such as medicine.

The tendency for a group to concentrate in certain occupations and professions—as the Jews have for many historical reasons—notes Dr. Rosenthal, makes for "in-marriage" rather than intermarriage. This is natural because colleagues would tend to have the same outlook and aspirations, and would tend to mingle socially.

The statistics on occupation and intermarriage seem to bear this out. Third- and later-generation professional men had a 19.6% intermarriage rate, one not too different from the average for their group. This was in sharp contrast to the intermarriage rate for "managers, officials and proprietors," which was 34.9%.

The high figure for this group, Dr. Rosenthal feels is mainly attributable to the "officials," many of whom were government employees. A further breakdown shows that the "proprietors," or self-employed business-men—another typical Jewish occupation—had a very negligible rate of intermarriage.

For the present-day Jewish parent who wishes to discourage intermarriage among his children, perhaps the most interesting of all the statistics are those on the effects of religious education. Dr. Rosenthal found that although such education has not lessened inter-marriage among the foreign born and second generation (although the reasons aren't clear, second-generation men with religious school-ing tended to intermarry more) there was a de-cided effect on the third and later generations. Of the native-born men of native parentage who had some religious education, 16.4% inter-married; of those with no religious education, 30.3% married non-Jews.

What happens to the religious affiliation of Jewish people who intermarry? The study seems to show that if they themselves are not lost to the Jewish community, most of their children are. It was found that well over 70% of the intermarried couples raised their chil-dren as non-Jews. Intermarried families in which the wife was Jewish were even less in-clined to raise their children as Jews.

Taken as a whole, Dr. Rosenthal says, the new statistics add up to a glum prospect for hopes for a growing Jewish community in the United States—particularly since other studies he has done show that Jews also tend to have fewer children than most Americans.

It has always been a bedrock belief in Judaism that intermarriage is a threat both to the Jewish identification of the individual and to the survival of a constantly embattled reli-gion and culture. Now, in the accepting and agnostic American environment, the barriers are ever more surmountable. What may the Jewish community expect for the future? What can it plan for? Dr. Rosenthal's study provides the facts—and the challenge.

28
the black muslims

C. ERIC LINCOLN

Some organizations within the black community, such as the Urban League and the National Association for the Advancement of Colored People (NAACP), consider themselves pressure groups; they use the law and political activity to force or shame the white community into giving justice to the black community; they are focused on black-white relations.

The Black Muslims are the prototype of another set of organizations within the black community. They are more aware of the hostility and dominance of the white community and much more concerned with the psychological damage political, economic, and social inferiority has produced in the black community. Their first aim is to put the blame for the conditions in the black community squarely where it belongs: on the white community. Their second aim is to increase the morale of the black community so that blacks will no longer be afraid to defend themselves. Thirdly, they try to organize the black community for self-improvement. They are often segregationist because they feel that the white community will not grant equality and that its overwhelming strength destroys the morale of the black community.

Predecessor to the Black Muslims was the ill-fated but influential Garvey movement of World War I and the early twenties. Established by a West Indian black, Marcus Garvey, the movement glorified blackness, encouraged large-scale economic ventures, and urged Afro-Americans to turn their backs on the United States and go back to Africa.

The Black Panthers are a recent organization similar to the Muslims in aims, although their leaders are younger, better educated and less willing to face a segregated existence. The future of the Black Panthers is very much in doubt; their leadership has been destroyed partly by their own reckless activities, partly by a systematic attack by the police in a number of large cities.

The Black Muslims, in contrast, have been remarkably stable. They are now almost forty years old. At one time, a young and brilliant leader, Malcolm Little, better known by his Muslim name of Malcolm X, challenged the leadership of the Muslim movement. If he had not been murdered, he might have taken the Muslim group toward a less segregationist, more internationalist stance, but the group then might not have endured so well.

Groups that emphasize blackness and self-defense scare the community; white police, particularly, feel threatened by them. In part, the emphasis on blackness touches deep fears of being overwhelmed by a black flood; in part, the police feel that their rightful authority is challenged, as they did when Black Panthers patrolled streets with the announced intention of preventing the police from harassing black citizens. What seems harassment to the blacks seems normal to the police, although the courts have recently sided with the blacks in restraining the police from time-hallowed practices used to control the black community.

Abridged from "The Black Muslims as a Protest Movement," in Arnold M. Rose (ed.), *Assuring Freedom to the Free.* Reprinted by permission of the Wayne State University Press. Copyright © 1964 by Arnold M. Rose.

Although the Muslims are small because they make severe demands on their membership, and although the Panthers are unlikely to survive, it is safe to say that until blacks achieve equality in the society, similar organizations will continue to arise. They are devices for obtaining both physical control of the community and psychological balance.

Professor Lincoln teaches at Union Theological Seminary in New York. In the following article, he discusses the significance of the Black Muslim movement.

The social movement called the "Black Muslims" is symptomatic of the anxiety and unrest which characterizes the contemporary world situation. It is not an isolated phenomenon; for it has its counterparts in Asia, in Africa, in South America, in Europe, and wherever the peoples of the world are striving for a realignment of power and position. Such conditions of social anxiety generally follow in the wake of major disturbances in the power equilibrium, or in anticipation of such disturbances. Wars ("hot" or "cold"), major political changes, in short, whatever is perceived as a threat to the continued existence of the group, or the values without which existence would be interpreted (by the group) as meaningless, contributes to a condition of anxiety which may well be reflected in various forms of conflict—of which the protest movement is one. . . .

The Black Muslims are a symbol and a product of social conflict. They represent a point at the extreme edge of a spectrum of protest organizations and movements which involves, directly or indirectly, probably every Negro in America. The spectrum of protest begins on the near side with the conservative churches, then shades progressively into the relatively more militant congregations, the Urban League, the NAACP, the SCLC, the SNCC, CORE, and finally the unknown number of black nationalist organizations of which the Black Muslim movement is the largest and the best known. The organizations mentioned do not exhaust the roster of protest by any means. Some of the protest movements have sizable memberships in spite of their amorphous character. Some have no more than ten or twelve members. Some do not even have names.

But almost every church, every social club, sorority, or fraternity, every business or civic association doubles as a protest organization. The effort is total, or very nearly total.

In some cities the protest membership is quite fluid, with individuals moving freely from group to group within a defined range as they become more activist-oriented, or perhaps less certain of the final efficacy of the action groups. The wide range of affiliative possibilities is both functional and dysfunctional to the protest interests. Because there are many organizations, there is greater opportunity for a wider variety of personal expression than was possible when the Urban League and the NAACP had the field to themselves. However, the supply of leadership material has not kept pace with the proliferation of movements and organizations. The most effective leadership remains concentrated in a few organizations, while the energies and enthusiasms of a good number of the lesser-known protest groups are dissipated for want of planning and direction. Theirs is an inarticulate protest—unknown and ineffective.

The Black Muslims are among the best organized and most articulate of the protest movements. In terms of their immediate internal objectives, they have a highly effective leadership, some of which has been recruited from the Christian churches and retrained by Elijah Muhammad to serve the cause of Black Islam. Their newspapers and magazines are superior in layout and technical quality to much of the Negro press; and their financial support of the movement is probably higher in proportion to income than that of any similar group. Yet, the Black Muslims are not generally acceptable to the spirit of protest which has won universal respect and frequent admiration for some other members of the Negro's spectrum of protest. To understand why this is so, it will be fruitful to offer some analysis of the circumstances out of which the movement was born, the character of its membership, and the nature of its goals.

The psychological heritage of the Black Muslim movement, in common with that of all other Negro protest organizations, is at least as old as the institution of slavery in America. Protest has been a distinctive although frequently a subdued thread widely distributed across the whole fabric of white-black relations throughout the history of white and Negro contact in America. The successive roles of masters and bondsmen, masters and slaves, white men and freedmen, majority and minority groups have been successive arrangements of hegemony and subordination in which the Negro's role *vis-à-vis* that of the white man has not changed. From time to time, especially since the Second World War, there have been varying degrees of adjustment *within the system of arrangements,* but the power relationship has remained constant. Hence, the capacity of Negroes to affect decisions relating to themselves and the system of values they hold to be important is not appreciable.

Even the Negro's limited capacity to affect decisions and produce change depends primarily upon the conscience and the convenience of the white man, rather than upon any existing corpus of power possessed by Negroes. Indeed, it is unlikely that the Negro will ever have a dependable share in the control of the decision-making apparatus of his country until he either controls a significant segment of the economy, or a much larger percentage of the vote than he does at present. His inordinate dependence upon "protest" derives precisely from his failure to achieve the more dependable protection for his interests that comes from sharing the white man's power rather than appealing to the white man's conscience.

A protest movement is an aggressive expression of a subordinated group. It is the organization of the resources of the subordinated group to resist the coercive power of the dominant group, or to challenge the morality of the justice of the expression of that power. The Negro did not wait until he was delivered in America to begin his protestation of the white man's concept of the black man's "place" in the caste system to be established here. Available records show that no fewer than fifty-five slave revolts occurred at sea between 1700 and 1845. During the height of the slave period—the two hundred years from

1664 to 1864, there are recorded accounts of at least 109 slave insurrections which occurred within the continental United States. Since it was customary to suppress all news and information concerning revolts lest they become infectious, it is reasonable to assume that the reported cases were of some magnitude, that very many cases were not reported, and that some cases which were reported have not yet been made available to research.

Protest was not limited to armed insurrection. The rate of infanticide was high. Suicide became a problem of such magnitude as to require the slave owners to devise "the strongest arguments possible," (supported by religious and social taboos) to reduce the rate of self-destruction. Sabotage of livestock, machinery, and agricultural produce was not unknown. "Taking" (from the white man, as distinct from "stealing" from each other) was routine. Running away was a form of protest so common as to have been considered a disease. Southern physicians described its symptoms in the journals of the period and gave it the name monomania—"a disease [it was said] to which the Negro is peculiarly subject."

As slavery became increasingly profitable, the slavocracy became concerned to offer a moral justification for its peculiar institution. At the same time, it sought to inculcate the illiterate slaves (as it sought later to indoctrinate the freedmen and their abolitionist friends) with an image of the Negro shrewdly designed to discourage protest and to encourage resignation and accommodation. This was the "Myth of the Magnolias," so called because it was usually accompanied by a fantasy of banjo-strumming darkies lounging peacefully under the sweet-scented magnolias behind the big house—happy and contented in their station, and forever loyal to the kind-hearted master and his arrangements for their mutual felicities. The Magnolia Myth explained the Negro's condition in terms of "his *natural docility,* his *instinctive servility,* and his *inherent imbecility.*" It alleged that the Negro's "docile nature" led to his willing acceptance of his condition of bondage, and that his "instinctive servility" made him an ideal slave—a being equipped psychologically to submit his will completely to that of another; who sensed his own inferiority, and who willed that his body be at the complete disposal of the more sophisticated will of his master. His alleged "imbecility" derived, it was urged, from an inherent incapacity to be creative, or to learn at a level beyond the simple abilities of a child. This was a principal intent of the Magnolia Myth—to perpetuate an image of the Negro as being inherently intellectually inferior, and therefore incapable of mastering the complex requirements of adult citizenship and self-determination. The Negro was a child who could never grow up. He would never be "ready." This was the image he was required to accept of himself. This was the image the world was asked to accept.

The historians, the novelists, the politicians, and a varied assortment of other myth-makers have done America a great disservice. Each repetition of the myth makes it more difficult, for those segments of the white majority who believe it, to understand the behavior of Negroes; and each repetition of the myth increases the determination of the Negro minority to belie it. Both science and history have discredited the Magnolia Myth, but the protest movements provide the most dramatic refutation. There are, for example, no docile Muslims. There are no servile students participating in the sit-ins. And considering its success before our highest tribunal, it is hard to believe that the legal staff of the NAACP is a council of imbeciles.

The Magnolia Myth with local modifications remains a pervasive influence in our society. Our information media have done little to refute it. The editors of the texts we use to educate our children have done even less. It has remained then to the Negro to destroy the myth himself. The Black Muslims have gone a step further and have created for themselves a countermyth, *the myth of black supremacy*.

The Black Muslim movement had its beginning in the black ghetto of Detroit. The time was 1930. It was the first year of the Great Depression—a time of hunger, confusion, disillusionment, despair, and discontent. It was a period of widespread fear and anxiety. Between 1900 and 1930 two-and-a-quarter-mil-lion Negroes left the farms and plantations of the South. Most of them emigrated to selected urban areas of the North—New York, Philadelphia, Chicago, and Detroit being among the most popular destinations. The Negro population of Detroit, for example, increased 611 per cent during the ten years of 1910 to 1920. During the same period, the total Negro population in the North increased from a mere 75,000 to 300,000, an increase of 400 per cent.

Floods, crop failures, boll weevils, and the revival of the Ku Klux Klan all served to hasten the Negro's departure from the South. One hundred Negroes were lynched during the first year of the twentieth century. By the outbreak of the First World War in 1914, the number stood at 1,100. When the war was over, the practice was resumed—28 Negroes being burned alive between 1918 and 1921. Scores of others were hanged, dragged behind automobiles, shot, drowned, or hacked to death.

The Negroes who left the South were temporarily welcomed in the North, although the congenialities of the North have always been of a most impersonal sort. Many industries sent agents into the South to lure the Negroes north with promises of good jobs. But the Negro was soon to find that it was his labor, not his presence, that was wanted. It was a common practice for the agents to purchase tickets for whole families and to move them *en masse* for resettlement in the great industrial cities. The war had drained away the white manpower needed to build the ships, work the steel, pack the meat, and man the machines; and it had also cut off the normal supply of immigrant labor from Europe.

After the war was over the Negro's welcome wore thin. It became increasingly hard for Negroes to get jobs except as strike-breakers. Soon there were not enough jobs to go around, and thousands of Negroes were fired and replaced with white men. There was not enough housing, and most Negroes were crowded into the black ghettos in the most deteriorated part of the inner city. Landlords and law-enforcement agencies alike were unsympathetic. But still the Negroes came out of the South. Few had skills; many were illiterate.

All were filled with hope for something better than what they had left. Soon there was hunger and crime and delinquency—and trouble with the police. The bright promise of the North had failed. Hope turned to desperation. In desperation is the onset of anxiety.

It is an interesting historical phenomenon that when a people reach the precipice of despair, there is so often waiting in the wings a savior—a messiah to snatch them back from the edge of the abyss. So it was that in Detroit there appeared in the black ghetto a mysterious Mullah who called himself W. D. Farad Muhammad. He had come, he told the handful of Negroes who gathered to hear him, from the holy city of Mecca. His mission, as he described it, was "to wake the 'Dead Nation in the West'; to teach [them] the truth about the white man, and to prepare [them] for the Armageddon." . . .

The fame of the Prophet spread and he soon established in Detroit the first of the Temples of Islam. As his following increased he grew more bold in his attacks upon the habits and the cultural symbols the Negroes had always taken for granted. In the first place, he taught his followers that they were not "Negroes," but "Black Men." The word "Negro" was alleged to be an invention of the white man designed to identify his victims better and to separate them from their Asian and African brothers. Further, the so-called Negro was not an American, but an "Asiatic," for his forefathers had been stolen from the Afro-Asian continent by the white slavemasters who came in the name of Jesus. Christianity, the Prophet taught, was a white man's religion, a contrivance designed for the enslavement of nonwhite peoples. Wherever Christianity has gone, he declared, men have lost their liberty and their freedom. Islam was declared to be "the natural religion of the Black Man." Only in Islam could the so-called Negroes find freedom, justice, and equality.

Little by little the Prophet began to enlighten these disillusioned migrants from the South about their true history and their place in the future. Black Man was the "Original Man," he taught. On the continent of Afro-Asia black civilizations flourished "long before the white man stood up on his hind legs and crept out of the caves of Europe." Further, the white man was pictured as "a devil by nature." He is, the Prophet taught, the physical embodiment of the principle of evil, and he is incapable of doing good. Further, said Farad, "the white man is the eternal adversary of the one true God whose right and proper name is Allah."

By "tricknology" the blue-eyed devils had enslaved the Black Man, the chosen people of Allah. The devils had taken away the slaves' native language (which was Arabic), and forced them to speak a foreign tongue. The white devils had taken away their names (i.e. their identity), and given them European names (which are to be hated as badges of slavery). Above all, the cruel slavemasters took away their natural religion (which is Islam) and made them worship a blue-eyed Jesus with blond hair, telling them that this was their God.

The so-called Negroes, although unknown to themselves, comprised "The Nation of Islam in the West." They had been brainwashed and given a false image of themselves by their white teachers, especially the Christian preachers who lulled them into submission by promising them a home "over Jordan" when they would no longer hew the wood and draw the water for the white man's comfort.

"The wheel must turn," the Prophet insisted. The Nation of Islam had a manifest destiny. The Armageddon must come. It would come as soon as the Black Man in America learned who he himself was, and accepted the truth about the white man, which the Prophet had been sent to declare.

Not all of Farad's energies were spent in attacking the white man. He taught his followers cleanliness and thrift. He persuaded them to give up liquor and such "unclean" foods as pork, cornbread, peas, possums, and catfish, bidding them to separate themselves from the habits they acquired in slavery. He established a school where homemaking, Negro history, Arabic, and other subjects of interest to the Muslims were taught. He demanded that his followers be clean at all times, bathing at least once each day. He taught them to give an honest day's work for an honest day's pay. He taught them to be respectful of others, and above all, to respect themselves. They must obey "all constituted authority," but they must require an eye for an eye and a tooth for a tooth. The *lex talionis* was the law of survival.

The Prophet's first appearance in Detroit is dated as July 4, 1930, and no one remembers seeing him after June 30, 1934. There are many legends, but no authentic information on where he came from, or where he went. But four years of preaching left a legacy of good and evil for eight thousand Negroes who had come to call themselves Muslims. . . .

The Prophet had not left himself without a witness. Very early in his brief ministry in Detroit he had attracted the admiration and the loyalty of a young Negro from the town of Sandersville, Georgia. Elijah Poole, son of a Baptist minister, was already embittered by the harshness of race relations in the South when he left Georgia and migrated to Detroit with his family in the early 1920's. In Detroit, his disillusionment with the "promised land" was almost immediate, for he soon discovered that the limitations which prescribed his place in the North differed only in degree from the familiar pattern of circumscription in the South. For a time, better jobs were available in the North, but Poole was soon to discover that job security operated on a racial basis. Housing was more strictly segregated than in the South, and living conditions in the black ghetto were often worse than they had been in the sharecropper's cabin. The lynchings in the South had their counterparts in the race riots of the North. There seemed to exist a universal conspiracy to make life in America as untenable as possible for Negroes. . . .

Farad had the explanation of the white man's cruelty as well as the key to his power. Eventually, Farad entrusted his mantle and his mission to Elijah. He made Poole First Minister of Islam and put the Muslim school, the training of ministers, and the highly secret FOI (the Fruit of Islam, the leadership training corps "for the coming Armageddon") under his direction. Later, Poole was sent to Chicago to found Temple No. 2, the present headquarters of the movement.

In recognition of Poole's dedicated lea-

dership, Farad relieved him of his "slavename" (i.e., "Poole") and honored him with the Muslim name "Muhammad." Thereafter Farad's public appearances were progressively less frequent until the day of his final disappearance.

Under Elijah Muhammad, the new "Messenger of Islam," the movement spread from the initial temple in Detroit to almost every major city in the country where there is a sizable Negro population. In most of these cities there is a temple; in others, where the movement is less strong, there are missions. Where there are no missions there are likely to be representatives of the movement who are in contact with the Muslim leadership in nearby cities.

The black ghetto is the principal source of Muslim recruitment. There, in the dirty streets and crowded tenements where life is cheap and hope is minimal, where isolation from the common values of society and from the common privileges of citizenship is most acute, the voice of the Messenger does not fall upon deaf ears. So often, his is the only message directed to the pimps, the prostitutes, the con men, the prisoners, the ex-cons, the alcoholics, the addicts, the unemployed, whom the responsible society has forgotten. It is a voice challenging them to recover their self-respect, urging them to repudiate the white man's religion and the white man's culture, daring them to believe in black supremacy, offering them a Black God and a Black Nation, promising them that the day will come when "we will be masters . . . and we are going to treat the white man the way he should be treated," demanding of them that "if anyone comes to take advantage of you, *lay down your life!* and the Black Man will be respected all over the Planet Earth."

"Never be the aggressor," the voice proclaims, "never look for trouble. But if any man molests you, may Allah bless you."

"We must take things into our own hands," the Messenger insists. "We must return to the Mosaic law of an eye for an eye and a tooth for a tooth. What does it matter if 10 million of us die? There will be 7 million of us left and they will enjoy justice and freedom."

Such is the challenge of Elijah Muhammad who is hailed by his ministers as "the most fearless black man in America." His followers are, with few exceptions, from America's most underprivileged class. They are denizens of the black ghetto. To them, the voice of Elijah Muhammad is a voice raised against injustice—real or imagined. Muhammad is a paladin who has taken up the cudgel against the "devil" responsible for all of their miseries and their failures. The resentments and the hostilities that breed in the ghetto are finally brought to focus upon a single object—*the white man*. Outside the black ghetto there are Muslim units in many of the state and federal prisons acros the country. Here the movement finds its prison audiences to be ready made and highly receptive, for the racial character of the law-enforcement agencies, the courts, and the custodial personnel is a key factor in sharpening the Negro prisoner's resentments and his sense of persecution. . . .

In a recent issue of the official Muslim newspaper, *Mr. Muhammad Speaks*, the Muslims stated their protest in the form of the following ten propositions:

1. *We want freedom. We want a full and complete freedom.*
2. *We want justice. Equal justice under the law. We want justice applied equally to all, regardless of creed or class or color.*
3. *We want equality of opportunity. We want equal membership in society with the best in civilized society.*
4. *We want our people in America whose parents or grandparents were descendants from slaves, to be allowed to establish a separate state or territory of their own. . . .*
5. *We want freedom for all Believers of Islam now held in federal prisons. We want freedom for all black men and women now under death sentence in innumerable prisons in the North as well as the South.*

    We want every black man and woman to have the freedom to accept or reject being separated from the slave master's children and establish a land of their own. . . .
6. *We want an immediate end to the police brutality and mob attacks against the so-called Negro throughout the United States.*
7. *As long as we are not allowed to establish a state or territory of our own, we demand not only equal justice under the laws of the United States, but equal employment opportunities—NOW! . . .*
8. *We want the government of the United States to exempt our people from ALL taxation as long as we are deprived of equal justice under the laws of the land.*
9. *We want equal education—but separate schools up to 16 for boys and 18 for girls on the condition that the girls be sent to women's colleges and universities. We want all black children educated, taught without hindrance or suppression.*
10. *We believe that intermarriage or race mixing should be prohibited. We want the religion of Islam taught without hindrance or suppression.*

    These are some of the things that we, the Muslims, want for our people in North America.

Some of the proposals of the Muslims are obviously unrealistic, and we need not discuss them here. Other tests and demands of the Black Muslims as stated in the foregoing propositions do not seem unreasonable. I do not know any Americans who do not "want freedom," for example. Justice under the law, equality of opportunity, and freedom of worship are all "approved values" in our society, and they find their sanctions in the American creed. Further, they are objectives which are implicit in the programs of all other movements within the Negro spectrum of protest. What, then, are the factors which qualify the Muslim protest movement and make it unacceptable to the general American public?

The fundamental differences between the attitudes, the behavior, and the goals of the Black Muslims as compared to other Negro protest organizations may be explained in terms of their differing degrees of dissociation deriving from the unusual anxiety and frustration incident to their status in the American social arrangement. Negroes, as a caste, are *all* outside the assimilative process, and they exhibit from time to time the frustrations which are the corollaries of their marginality. However, the dissociation of the Muslim membership from the larger society, and even from the general Negro subgroup (which ordinarily seeks to identify itself with the American mainstream), may be considered extreme. In reacting to the unique pressures of their day-to-day experiences as low-caste Negroes in a white-oriented society, the Muslims have abandoned the fundamental principles of the American creed and have substituted in its place a new system of values perceived as more consistent with the realities of their circumstances.

It is meaningless to label the Muslims as "un-American," for the American creed is not a legal or constitutional document against which the political loyalty of a group may be measured. The American creed is a common set of beliefs and values in which all Americans have normally found consensus. It is a body of ideals, a social philosophy which affirms the basic dignity of every individual and the existence of certain inalienable rights without reference to race, creed, or color. The roots of the American creed are deep in the equalitarian doctrines of the eighteenth-century Enlightenment, Protestant Christianity, and English law. For most of us, it has been the cultural matrix within which all discordant sociopolitical attitudes converge, and from which derives the great diversity of social and political interpretations which makes democracy possible in a society of widely variant populations.

The Black Muslims, by the nature of certain of their goals and institutions, have excepted themselves from the aegis of the American creed. The Black Muslims repudiate American citizenship in favor of a somewhat dubious membership in a mystical "Asiatic" confraternity, and they are violently opposed to Christianity, the principles of which are fundamental to our understanding of the democratic ideal. Not only do they resist assimilation and avoid interracial participation in the life of the community, but the Muslim creed assigns all nonblacks to the subhuman status of "devils" (and promises to treat them as such); the sustaining philosophy is one of black supremacy nurtured by a careful inculcation of hatred for the white man and his characteristic institutions. By their own choice the

Black Muslims exclude themselves from the body of principles and the system of values within the framework of which Americans have customarily sought to negotiate their grievances.

Other groups advocate white supremacy, resist the assimilation of Negroes and others, and practice hatred rather than love, yet they retain an idealistic loyalty to the principles of the American creed. The point is that although the creed is violated constantly in practice, it remains an *ideal* to which all give their asseveration—in which all believe, and from which we continue to derive our laws and our moral values in spite of our failures to honor them completely.

The Black Muslim movement does not conceive itself to be in violation of the principles and values of the American creed. Rather, the movement views itself as having substituted new principles, new values, and a new creed based on a radically different interpretation of history from that expressed in the American creed. Muhammad promises a new order based on the primacy of a nation of Black Men with a manifest destiny under a Black God. His is a nation radically different from those now shaping the existing American society. In spite of the fact that the Black Muslim movement shares at some points the immediate goals of the lesser Negro protest movements, its oppugnance to traditional values limits its general acceptability as a protest organization. The action impact of the movement on the general Negro community has been negligible considering the fact that most of America's twenty million black citizens live under conditions considerably more iniquitous than those which at other times and places have been productive of the gravest social consequences. This is not to suggest that Negroes are not aware of the movement. They are. And there are important pockets of sympathy among Negroes for the Muslims as a class more oppressed than other Negro classes, and a certain covert admiration for their militant, nonaccommodative stance against the traditional aggressions of the white man.

Nevertheless, the depth of the Negro's commitment *as a class* to the democratic procedures implicit in the American creed has operated successfully to contain the Muslim movement—eliminating it as a serious threat to racial peace or national security. But the Black Muslims remain a somber symbol of the social callousness that is possible even in an equalitarian democracy. Such movements do not "just happen." The Muslims are the most insistent symptoms of the failure of this society to meet effectively the minimum needs of one-tenth of its population to find a meaningful level of participation in the significant social values most Americans take for granted.

The Muslims represent that segment of the Negro subgroup who, being most deprived of traditional incentives, have finally turned to search for alternatives outside the commonly accepted value structure. They are the products of social anxiety—people who are repeatedly frustrated in their attempts to make satisfactory adjustments in a society unaware of their existence except as the faceless subjects of statistical data. As Negroes, their future was unpromising. As Muslims, theirs is a creed of futility. As Americans, the responsibility for what they are, or what they will become, is our own.

29
comparative life-styles of anglos and mexican-americans

T. ALLEN CAINE

It has become increasingly clear that ethnic groups which have recently immigrated to the United States, far from amalgamating either with Old Americans or with each other, persist as separate entities for long periods. It is not clear whether ethnic groups are loyal to their original cultures because they reject American ways or because their economic situation, which in turn depends upon recency of immigration, makes Old American cultural patterns either unknown to them or too expensive for them.

Mr. Caine has offered another explanation: Ethnic groups at first lose their cultures rather rapidly, but revive them as a protection against the alienation of lower-class urban American life or when their economic position is threatened by other groups.

The essay that follows is an attempt to find out to what extent ethnicity is maintained and in what areas by comparing a Mexican-American group with an Anglo group living in the same neighborhood.

Mr. Caine is an assistant professor of sociology at St. Mary's College, Winona, Minnesota.

Elsewhere in the thesis from which this paper is taken, the Mexican-Americans and the Anglos in the sample were compared on basic socio-economic indicators. It was found that the Anglos were somewhat more socio-economically mobile than the Mexicans and had had over-all better job experiences, although job experiences for the two groups have overlapped considerably. This does not, of course, mean that the ethnic divisions are comparable but merely that in their life careers they have had comparable experiences. It was shown in addition that length of residence in the com-

Abridged from "Social Life in a Mexican-American Community: Social Class or Ethnic Grouping," master's thesis, University of Minnesota, 1971.

munity, age, and marital status do not vary substantially by ethnic classification. However, occupational mobility, amount of education, geographical mobility, length of residence in the state of Minnesota, and number of children do vary, the Mexicans having experienced less of all characteristics except geographical mobility and children. It is evident that the Mexicans have experienced somewhat greater hardship than the Anglos have.

These similarities and differences are very much related to the culture and life-styles of the respondents. As has been argued, the life-style and culture of an ethnic group is not so much related to its ethnicity as it is to its members' life situation. And its life situation is a generalized condition which varies according to social-class position and the community opportunity structure. Even though ethnic identity may be strong, unless one ethnic group is able to usurp the benefits of society for itself and thus effectively raise its eth-class position above another group, attributes of ethnic groups must necessarily be the same to the extent that they share the same characteristics. This is because all persons will be brought together in the same kind of associational, recreational, occupational, and general cultural milieu with relatively equal opportunity to have a piece of the American pie.

The task now is to examine the two ethnic divisions in terms of their cultural and lifestyle content. In the present chapter the two groups will be compared for differences which might be attributed to ethnicity on those items which other studies have suggested as indicators of ethnically derived differences. It will be shown that groups are responding to the same class-community structure and that when differences occur they are usually in a direction which would lead us to conclude that the Mexicans are less "Mexican" than are the Anglos.

If Mexicans are in fact unacculturated, we would expect the responses of the Mexican sample to lie somewhere between those of the Anglo sample and descriptions of Mexican culture and life-style. If, on the other hand, the Mexicans are acculturated, we would expect Mexican and Anglo responses to be quite similar to each other.

For the purpose of clearly juxtaposing Mexican culture against American, a distillation of Mexican characteristics is presented. According to Penalosa, a review of the literature by Mexican social scientists reveals the following characteristics to be aspects of Mexican culture and life-style.[1] The Mexican family is based essentially on male-female relations as defined by rigid sex roles. Mexican culture grants to the male biological, social, and intellectual superiority over the female. The female, because she is devalued, turns to her sisters and to her children for her emotional gratification in life. Performing essentially a mothering and housekeeping function, her place is quite clearly in the home. For her to take a job is to threaten the male because

TABLE 1. "Planning only makes a person unhappy since your plans usually don't work out anyhow."

Agree	Mexicans		Anglos	
Agree	29	(62%)	20	(61%)
Disagree	18	(38%)	13	(39%)
Total	47	(100%)	33	(100%)

she gains for herself a certain amount of self-sufficiency. The male carries out his family obligations pretty much as he sees fit. Women, in turn, often have children because of their need to continue in the role of a self-denying mother. Children are raised to emulate parents of the same sex. The husband is estranged from religion and probably from other organizations as well. Isolated from organizational activity and separated by sex-based role divisions from his family, for the Mexican male the peer group becomes all important.

As will be seen, this is not a very good description of the Mexican-American respondents in the sample. And for that matter, when deviations occur between the two ethnic divisions in the tabulations, the direction of the difference will be away from Penalosa's description.

FATALISM AND NONMANIPULATION

The previous chapter has stressed the uncertainty of life in this lower-class community. The uncertainty experienced in such communities has been linked by some to fatalism and a nonmanipulative view of the world.[2] These are characteristics which have also been identified as Mexican. That such attitudes do exist in this sample was borne out by the responses to several questions taken from the f-scale.

One of the more interesting questions taken from the f-scale is as follows. "Planning only makes a person unhappy since your plans usually don't work out anyhow." As can be seen from Table 1, Mexicans and Anglos do not disagree much on this question.

A similar response set was found when another f-scale question "The secret of happiness is not expecting too much and being content with what comes your way" (Table 2).

TABLE 2. "The secret of happiness is not expecting too much and being content with what comes your way."

	Mexicans		Anglos	
Don't know	1	(2%)	0	(0%)
Agree	36	(77%)	28	(85%)
Disagree	10	(21%)	5	(15%)
Total	47	(100%)	33	(100%)

TABLE 3. "Nowadays, with world conditions the way they are, the wise person lives for today and lets tomorrow take care of itself."

	Mexicans		Anglos	
Don't know	2	(4%)	0	(0%)
Agree	22	(47%)	23	(70%)
Disagree	23	(49%)	10	(30%)
Total	47	(100%)	33	(100%)

TABLE 4. "When a person is born, the success he is going to have is *not* already in the cards."

	Mexicans		Anglos	
Don't know	3	(6%)	1	(3%)
Agree	39	(83%)	32	(98%)
Disagree	5	(11%)	0	(0%)
Total	47	(100%)	33	(101%)

TABLE 5. "The best job to have is one where you are part of a group working together, even if you don't get much individual credit."

	Mexicans		Anglos	
Don't know	3	(6%)	2	(6%)
Agree	31	(66%)	25	(76%)
Disagree	13	(28%)	6	(18%)
Total	47	(100%)	33	(100%)

"Nowadays, with world conditions the way they are, the wise person lives for today and lets tomorrow take care of itself," again elicited a different similar set of responses. The Anglos proved on this question to be substantially more fatalistic than the Mexicans (Table 3).

There was a different, and yet very American, response to the question "When a person is born, the success he is going to have is not already in the cards, each makes his own fate" (Table 4).

Such views of the world have been said to be the result of peer-group pressures. On the basis of an f-scale question tapping this aspect of other-directedness, this would seem to be true. The question "The best job to have is one where you are part of a group working together, even if you don't get much individual credit" elicited the following responses (Table 5).

Further substantiation of these findings concerning fatalism and nonmanipulation came from responses to other questions in the interview. When respondents were asked if they thought that strict punishment was best for their children, thirty-four percent of the sample representing thirty-one percent of the Mexicans and thirty-nine percent of the Anglos said that it didn't matter because the kids would do what they wanted anyway. The same kind of orientation was found in aspirations for children. When asked what they wanted their children to be like when they grew up, sixty-six percent of the sample representing sixty percent of the Mexicans and seventy-six percent of the Anglos said they wanted their children "to be good." And when asked how certain they were that their children would be like they wanted them to be, seventy-eight percent of the sample representing seventy-four percent of the Mexicans and eighty-five percent of the Anglos admitted that they were only somewhat certain or didn't expect it at all.

We might conclude, then, that insofar as fatalism and nonmanipulation are concerned, there is little difference between the two ethnic divisions. On both the f-scale questions representing American clique forms and those questions which deal with the life situations of the respondents there is considerable unanimity of response. To the extent that differences do occur, it is the Anglos more than the Mexicans who conform to "Mexicanness."

These responses all indicate an inability on the part of these mothers to cope with their desires to live the kinds of lives they want to live as well as to have their children grow up to live good lives. They are expressive of an insecure world in which the desired rewards are only a television knob away but always seem to remain as elusive in reality as T.V. imagery. That this is so can be seen in additional information gleaned from the interviews. Even though a majority of the respondents did present a world view emphasizing an inability to deal with life's problems including a rejection of planning, most persons indicated that their behavior is not congruent with their presumed ethos. That is, although a majority indicated as an example that they did not believe in planning, a majority of this group did indicate at one or another place elsewhere in the interview that they do a great deal of planning. Family affairs such as recreation and budgeting are often carefully planned. The immediate tomorrow is not left for itself by any means, although the distant future often is. It would seem to be correct to suggest on the basis of the interviews that it is the distant future, the fulfillment of hopes for one's own future happiness and security as well as one's children's future, which disturbs the respondents. They wish as much as anyone to fulfill the American dream of success, the prosperous family living in a comfortable house, with new furniture, a nice car, a color television set, and a happy, harmonious, and successful family. It is the failure to achieve this goal, this measure of success, to which they are really resigned.

HUSBAND-WIFE RELATIONSHIPS

If the fatalism of the respondents is futuristic, it may well be that this has something to do with the quality of male-female relationships in the community. Rainwater has shown that husband and wife relationships affect greatly the ability to manipulate ongoing events.[3] His specific example is the relationship of husbands and wives to the effectiveness of contraceptive techniques. This idea would

seem to suggest an insight into male-female relationships and world view in this particular community.

Descriptions of both the lower-class family and the Mexican family have sometimes held that the father is an authoritarian figure, aloof from the goings-on of the household, and somewhat distant emotionally from his wife. Because I did not interview husbands, there is a lack of certainty as to what extent there is husband-wife agreement on the responses to my questions. Moreover, there is no way to ascertain to what extent the wife is submissive and the husband dominating in interaction. Regardless, the data provide an interesting perspective on a relationship of sex roles to fatalism. Whatever the uncertainty of the distant future, husbands in general do provide more role support than might have been expected and husbands and wives share more in family-care activities than might have been anticipated.

The respondents were asked "How important is it for the ideal marriage that the husband wear the pants in the family?" This is a question which has been found to differentiate the unacculturated from the acculturated in one study. In my sample, the relationship of responses to ethnicity was the reverse of what it should be according to the traditional perspective of Mexicans. Anglos show a small but persistently greater tendency within each response category to grant authority to the male (Table 6).

The women were probed to obtain some indication as to what extent actual role behavior was congruent with the preferred dominance-submission patterns. As far as could be determined, there is no substantial difference between the two ethnic divisions (Table 7). It is reasonable to assume, however, that in the families which share authority, the male tends to be dominant. At any rate, there is no tendency here toward the kind of family Penalosa's survey of the Mexican literature suggested.

The women were also questioned on role divisions within household work tasks. The severity of male-female task-role separation has been questioned in several recent studies of the

TABLE 6. "How important is it for the ideal marriage that the husband wear the pants in the family?"

	Mexicans	Anglos
"Very important."	7 (15%)	6 (18%)
"He should be the head of family."	9 (19%)	8 (24%)
"He should be head but wife should share in decisions."	6 (13%)	6 (18%)
"Should be 50-50."	17 (36%)	13 (39%)
"Husband shouldn't be the boss."	5 (11%)	0 (0%)
Derided husband or idea without answering question	3 (6%)	0 (0%)
Total	47 (100%)	33 (99%)

TABLE 7. Decision Making in Families With Male Head of Household

	Mexicans	Anglos
Husband makes most decisions	11 (31%)	7 (25%)
Husband and wife share in decisions	23 (64%)	20 (71%)
Wife makes the decisions	2 (6%)	1 (3%)
Total	36 (101%)	28 (99%)

TABLE 8. "What kinds of things should a man do around the house?"

	Mexicans	Anglos
Nothing at all	11 (23%)	2 (6%)
Fix things, do yard work, and house chores if wife is ill	16 (34%)	20 (61%)
Help out with house chores occasionally	5 (11%)	6 (18%)
Take regular part of house chores	15 (32%)	5 (15%)
Total	47 (100%)	33 (100%)

Anglo working class but remains a supposed cultural trait of Mexican-Americans. The respondents were asked "What kinds of things should a man do around the house?" The results are shown in Table 8.

Child rearing can be considered a part of the household tasks. It is held that the father is the proper purveyor of family justice within the working-class home although the mother is often the actual mentor of justice. In one case, this is said to be a class trait, in another it is said to be a Mexican trait. When mothers were asked "Who should discipline the children in the family?," a different response than might have been anticipated was found. Exactly two-thirds of both the Mexicans and the Anglos say that both parents should be responsible for disciplining children (Table 9). Again, the mothers were probed for actual behavior. The number of Mexican mothers who alone disci-

pline their children seems to be largely a function of the number of Mexican husbands who hold late-shift jobs (Table 10).

Women were also asked "Do you think a wife should know all about her husband's income and spending?" This is a question which probes role distance in male-female relationships generally (Table 11). Again, the Anglos, given the prior description of Mexican culture, appear to be slightly more Mexican than do the Mexican-Americans.

No direct probe was made of this response set to determine what extent actual behavior corresponds to preferred behavior. However, the incidental statements made by the respondents and recorded by the interviewers show that ninety-three percent of each ethnic group does in fact know their husbands' income. But, it appears that actual family planning in financial areas pretty much corresponds

TABLE 9. "Who should discipline the children in the family?"

	Mexicans		Anglos	
Mother should	3	(6%)	0	(0%)
Father should	9	(19%)	7	(21%)
Father usually	4	(9%)	4	(12%)
Both parents	31	(66%)	22	(67%)
Total	47	(100%)	33	(100%)

TABLE 10. Actual Family Disciplinarian in Families Having Male Head of Household

	Mexicans		Anglos	
Mother	13	(34%)	5	(16%)
Father	3	(8%)	2	(6%)
Both parents	22	(58%)	25	(78%)
Total	38	(100%)	32	(100%)

TABLE 11. "Do you think that a wife should know all about her husband's income and spending?"

	Mexicans		Anglos	
"Yes. They should plan together."	21	(45%)	6	(18%)
"Yes. So a woman can do the budgeting."	7	(15%)	12	(36%)
"Yes. So the wife can get her portion."	10	(21%)	3	(9%)
"Yes. If she is interested."	5	(11%)	4	(12%)
"No. Not if provided for."	4	(9%)	8	(24%)
Total	47	(101%)	33	(99%)

to the responses to the preceding question.

Although the responses to these questions are within the tradition of working-class literature, they are clearly outside of the tradition of Mexican studies. Moreover, they are suggestive of a greater egalitarianism in the family than might have been expected on the basis of either body of literature. These findings might very well be related to the way in which the respondents perceive males as biogenic and psychogenic entities. It will be remembered that Penalosa found in his survey of Mexican literature that it was generally concluded that the rigid sexual divisions are based upon the attributing to the male of biological, social, and intellectual superiority. In this light, the variation in responses to the following question is very interesting.

The respondents were asked "Do you think it is difficult for men to understand women?" A total of fifty-two percent of the Mexicans and sixty-three percent of the Anglos responded with statements which either flatly agreed with the question, granted inherent sexual differences, granted social superiority to the male as in "Yes, my husband says so," or acknowledged a distinct maleness as in "Men don't care to!" In contrast, twenty-two

percent of the Mexicans and nine percent of the Anglos flatly rejected the notion. Twenty percent of the Mexicans and eighteen percent of the Anglos said that "each person is different." And seven percent of the Mexicans and nine percent of the Anglos said that it is difficult for men to understand women because they "live in different worlds." A total then of forty-eight percent of the Mexicans and thirty-six percent of the Anglos rejected the notion of inherent differences between the sexes. Again, the Anglos prove to be a bit more Mexican than the Mexicans (Table 12).

PARENTS AND CHILDREN

The picture drawn often of both Mexican and Anglo working-class families is one in which the relationships between husband and wife are fairly rigidly defined, and also those between parents and children. That is to say, these families are held to be adult-centered. Just as there is a certain amount of deviation from this picture in terms of husband-wife relationships, the nature of parent-child relationships is a bit more complicated also.

One question asked of the mothers concerns strictness in child discipline. There was,

TABLE 12. "Do you think it is difficult for men to understand women?"

	Mexicans		Anglos	
"Yes. Men and women are different."	17	(36%)	17	(52%)
"Yes. Men don't care to."	5	(11%)	3	(9%)
"Yes. My husband says so."	2	(4%)	1	(3%)
"Yes. Because they live in different worlds."	3	(7%)	3	(9%)
"No. Each person is different."	9	(19%)	6	(18%)
"No."	10	(21%)	3	(9%)
"Don't know."	1	(2%)	0	(0%)
Total	47	(100%)	33	(100%)

TABLE 13. "Do you believe that strict parents raise the best children?"

	Mexicans		Anglos	
Yes.	16	(34%)	10	(30%)
"No. Kids need freedom."	15	(31%)	10	(30%)
"No. They will do it anyway."	14	(30%)	13	(39%)
Don't know	2	(4%)	0	(0%)
Total	47	(100%)	33	(99%)

TABLE 14. "Do you agree with the idea that children should be seen but not heard?"

	Mexicans		Anglos	
"Yes. Agree very much."	12	(26%)	5	(15%)
"Yes. But children should be able to say what's on their mind."	12	(26%)	12	(36%)
"No. Kids should be free to talk."	17	(36%)	14	(42%)
"No. Not at all."	6	(13%)	2	(6%)
Total	47	(101%)	33	(99%)

however, no substantial ethnic difference in the responses to the question "Do you believe that strict parents raise the best children?" (Table 13). The question "Do you agree with the idea that children should be seen but not heard?" received a response dissimilar to the previous question but again there was complete congruence between the two ethnic groups (Table 14).

Some differences between the ethnic divisions did appear in response to another question, "Do you think that it is important that children talk over their feelings about family matters with you?" (Table 15). The differences which occur here are not attributable to ethnicity, however, but rather to the respondents' positions within the community, explored in a later chapter. The differences between the ethnic division which appeared in

the above question disappeared when the respondents were probed for actual behavior (Table 16). Again there seem to be no substantive differences between the ethnic divisions.

So far, then, there appears to be a considerable amount of congruence between Mexicans and Anglos in this community. There seems to be a similar range of attitudes and behavior within each group as far as male-female relationships and the place of the child in the home are concerned. Likewise, a family configuration emphasizing greater equality in familial relations seems to be emerging. The picture, however, is far from complete at this point.

To draw a clearer picture of the family in this neighborhood, questions which relate to husband-wife interaction in nontask areas were asked. The working-class wife as well as

TABLE 15. "Do you think that it is important that your children talk over their feelings about family matters with you?"

	Mexicans	Anglos
"Yes. So we know what they are doing."	19 (41%)	14 (42%)
"Yes. It gives a family a sense of feeling."	7 (13%)	5 (15%)
"Yes. Helps kids with problems."	13 (28%)	4 (12%)
"Yes. I don't know everything, kids can give advice."	1 (2%)	1 (3%)
"Yes. Everyone should be a part of family decisions."	1 (2%)	3 (9%)
"Maybe"; "guess so"; "hadn't thought about it."	2 (4%)	1 (3%)
"O.K.—can talk way out of it if I disagree."	0 (0%)	2 (6%)
"No. Many things aren't their business."	5 (11%)	3 (9%)
Total	47 (101%)	33 (99%)

TABLE 16. Parents' Actual Tolerance of Children in Family Matters

	Mexicans	Anglos
Allow children to solve problems	14 (30%)	10 (30%)
Children too young to have a say	6 (13%)	2 (6%)
Encourage children to raise problems	4 (9%)	5 (15%)
Allow children to take part in family planning	23 (48%)	16 (48%)
Total	47 (100%)	33 (99%)

TABLE 17. "How important is it that a man and wife go places together?"

	Mexicans	Anglos
"Important, should enjoy the same things."	17 (36%)	12 (36%)
"Good. Helps keep family together."	7 (15%)	12 (36%)
"More important for wife to go out."	10 (21%)	6 (18%)
"Important, except for those things which are just woman's."	2 (4%)	0 (0%)
Don't know	2 (4%)	1 (3%)
"It's more important to take care of the kids."	1 (2%)	0 (0%)
"Wife shouldn't have to go out with husband."	2 (4%)	1 (3%)
"It's not important."	2 (4%)	0 (0%)
Total	47 (99%)	33 (99%)

the Mexican wife is thought of as a person who turns to her female relatives and neighbors for advice, affective support, and sociability. This is partly because of strong sex-based peer-group activity and because stereotypic attitudes held by males and females toward each sex block understanding between marital partners.

Responses to questions asking about non-task relationships did not always yield a great deal of information, save the "yes," "no," and "sometimes" responses favored by some investigators. It was almost as if the husband-wife relationship was so matter of fact, that respondents could not understand what was being asked of them. The interviewers perhaps stood to the respondent in much the same fashion that a magazine reporter does to a company president when he asks "What is it like to be president of a large company?" Of course, unlike the company president, the respondents had not developed pat responses.

Some insight is gained into the ideal husband-wife relationship by the responses to the question "How important is it that a man and wife go places together?" (Table 17).

The above set of responses is rather interesting in that it is one of the few instances

TABLE 18. "Who do you like to talk to?"

	Mexicans		Anglos	
Nobody	2	(4%)	3	(9%)
Husband	6	(13%)	4	(12%)
Friends	19	(40%)	7	(21%)
Kinfolk	11	(23%)	8	(24%)
Married daughter	1	(2%)	0	(0%)
Minister	0	(0%)	1	(3%)
Anybody	44	(9%)	4	(12%)
Just mother	3	(6%)	6	(18%)
Don't know	1	(2%)	0	(0%)
Total	47	(99%)	33	(99%)

in which the Mexican-American respondents appear to be more Mexican than the Anglos in terms of Penalosa's summation of Mexican literature. Actually, as later will become evident, the Mexican respondents seem to be reflecting their immediate life situations rather than their cultural preferences as are also the Anglos. The Anglos' response indicating that it is important for a husband and wife to go out together because it helps to keep the family together came largely from respondents who are not very well off financially, even as compared to the rest of the community. A rereading of the interviews leads me to believe that their responses reflect the same husband-wife tensions which led the poorer Mexicans to emphasize the importance of a wife getting out on her own sometimes. Both groups were reflecting their problems in managing a family rather than what they actually would like.

A differential response was also found when the respondents were asked "Who do you like to talk to?" (Table 18). The responses, whatever the ethnic variation, would appear to suggest the presence of a strong female peer-group orientation. Or, if not that, a strong home-centeredness. A look at the respondent's actual activity outside of the home clarifies the preceding responses considerably and will leave a somewhat different impression.

Most of the women frequently participate in coffee klatsches. About ten percent of each ethnic group do not do so regularly. The others vary considerably in their regularity. A majority of each group do so on a daily basis,

although their companions might number but one. By such a measure, the female peer-group, in keeping with the questions concerning who the respondents like to talk to and how important it is for a husband and wife to get out together, would seem to be fairly strong. However, a look at the wife's activity in other things besides neighborly activity presents us with a different picture.

The respondents were asked to list the kinds of things they did outside the home. Activities they mentioned included such things as women's clubs, visiting, and going to shows, zoos, parks, museums, lectures, and bingo games. Also mentioned were picnics, fishing and hunting, swimming, boating, camping, dancing, night-clubbing, and dining out.

The frequency with which different kinds of activity were mentioned showed considerable variation by ethnicity. Upon first examination of the data, about the only similarity between the ethnic groups which showed up was the frequency of activity outside of the home (Table 19). When the specific activities are examined, ethnic differences do occur (Table 20).

The only differences which are clearly related to ethnicity are in the number of Mexicans and Anglos who attend nightclubs or dine out and the number who attend dances. However, the only real difference between the two groups seems to be related to whether your night out on the town is at an ethnic dance or a nightclub where one also dances. In reality, about thirty percent of each group are going dancing.

Other differences in reported activities are not so clear. The differences between the number of Mexicans and the number of Anglos reporting that they go bowling and to the movies may appear to be related more to an attempt on the part of Anglos to find some activity they could report. Differences here almost disappeared when the respondents were later asked how many times a month they engaged in such activities, the excess proportion of Anglos rarely or never getting out for movies or bowling.

Differences in the percentage of Mexicans and Anglos reporting field and water activities such as hunting, fishing, boating, and

TABLE 19. Frequency of Recreational (Nonorganizational) Activities Outside of the Home

	Mexicans	Anglos
Several times a week	10 (21%)	6 (18%)
Once or twice a week	10 (21%)	7 (21%)
Two or three times a month	13 (28%)	12 (36%)
Once a month	2 (4%)	4 (12%)
Never or seldom	12 (26%)	4 (12%)
Total	47 (100%)	33 (99%)

TABLE 20. Proportion of Respondents Engaged in Recreational Activities With Any Frequency[a]

	Mexicans	Anglos
Dining and/or nightclubs	7 (15%)	10 (30%)
Dancing	15 (32%)	5 (15%)
Bowling	3 (6%)	6 (18%)
Movies	16 (34%)	17 (50%)
Zoos and parks	36 (17%)	3 (9%)
Picnics	7 (15%)	7 (21%)
Hunting and fishing	3 (6%)	5 (15%)
Swimming and boating	5 (11%)	7 (21%)
Camping	1 (2%)	3 (9%)
Museums and libraries	3 (6%)	1 (3%)
Clubs	2 (4%)	1 (3%)
Visiting	17 (36%)	10 (30%)

[a]Totals are not included because respondents often answered to more than one category.

TABLE 21. Frequency of Respondents' Recreational Activity With Husband

	Mexicans	Anglos
Several times a week	7 (15%)	0 (0%)
Once or twice a week	7 (15%)	2 (6%)
Two or three times a month	0 (0%)	3 (9%)
Once a month	0 (0%)	5 (15%)
Occasionally	5 (11%)	6 (18%)
Never	28 (59%)	17 (52%)
Total	47 (100%)	33 (100%)

swimming largely reflect occupational levels. Most women reporting such activities are married to husbands who have skilled and white-collar jobs. There are proportionately about twice as many Anglos in these jobs as Mexicans.

Somewhat more informative than what recreational activities the respondents participate in is the frequency of activity and who the respondents do things with. These responses show a much greater amount of husband-wife activity than might have been anticipated from some of the preceding responses as well as from the idea of the sex-graded community structure.

Fifteen percent of the Mexicans and none of the Anglos reported that they do things outside of the home with their husbands several times a week (Table 21).

In general, there is a fair amount of husband and wife nontask-oriented activity. When the figures are combined, about sixty percent

TABLE 22. Frequency of Respondents' Recreational Activity With Husband and Children

	Mexicans	Anglos
Once or more a week	6 (13%)	3 (9%)
One to three times a month	4 (9%)	8 (24%)
Occasionally	6 (13%)	3 (9%)
Never	31 (66%)	19 (58%)
Total	47 (101%)	33 (100%)

TABLE 23. Proportion of Respondents Who Participate With Specified Companions Other Than Husband or Husband and Children in Recreational Activity Outside of the Home Once a Month or More[a]

Recreate with	Mexicans	Anglos
Alone	1 (2%)	2 (6%)
Friends	8 (17%)	2 (6%)
Relatives	4 (9%)	1 (3%)
Children	5 (11%)	1 (3%)
Husband and friends	0 (0%)	6 (18%)
Husband and relatives	3 (6%)	3 (9%)
Husband, relatives, and friends	5 (11%)	5 (11%)
Mother only	0 (0%)	1 (3%)

[a]Totals are not included because respondents often answered to more than one category.

TABLE 24. Proportion of Respondents Engaging in Home-Centered Activities With Any Frequency[a]

	WITH RELATIVES		WITH FRIENDS	
	Mexicans	Anglos	Mexicans	Anglos
Holidays	26 (56%)	17 (52%)	3 (6%)	0 (0%)
Sunday dinner	16 (33%)	10 (30%)	2 (4%)	2 (6%)
Birthdays	9 (19%)	6 (18%)	1 (2%)	0 (0%)
Talk and TV	28 (60%)	20 (60%)	32 (68%)	19 (58%)
Partying	9 (19%)	8 (24%)	11 (23%)	9 (27%)

[a]Totals are not included because respondents often answered to more than one category.

of each group gets out on a once-a-month or more regular basis with either husband or with the husband and children (Table 22). There is considerably more activity with the husband in recreational activities outside of the home than with other possible companions.

That the husband is indeed the most important recreational companion can be seen in Table 23 which tabulates the number of persons who never get out with various companions. No more than nineteen percent of either ethnic group ever participate in recreational activity with any given companion or combi-

nation of companions other than the husband or the husband and children. In general, activity levels are low.

Although the husband is the most important recreational partner, it is also interesting to note that the respondents who are most active with their husbands are also the women who are most active with other companions.

The bulk of recreational activity in this community takes place within the home, among kin and the age- rather than sex-based peer group (Table 24).

Home-centered activities reported by the

TABLE 25. Proportion of Husbands and Wives Attending Organization Meetings and Activities At Least Once a Month or Every Time Organization Meetings Held If Less Than Once a Month

Attender	Mexicans		Anglos	
No one	29	(63%)	16	(49%)
Wife	0	(0%)	4	(12%)
Husband	6	(13%)	5	(15%)
Wife and husband	12	(25%)	8	(24%)
Total	47	(101%)	33	(100%)

TABLE 26. Organizational Activity Adjusted for Union-Membership Bias

Attender	Mexicans		Anglos	
No one	30	(64%)	19	(58%)
Wife	1	(2%)	8	(24%)
Husband	5	(11%)	2	(6%)
Wife and husband	11	(23%)	4	(12%)
Total	47	(100%)	33	(100%)

respondents include Sunday dinner, holiday get-togethers, birthday celebrations, card-playing and watching television, and partying with card-playing and liquor.

Sunday dinner with relatives or friends is one home-centered activity which showed similar ethnic patterns. Holidays spent with friends and relatives in home-centered activities show similar patterns. Birthdays, like holidays and Sunday dinners, are celebrated mainly with much less frequency. A common home-centered activity is getting together to talk and watch television. Whereas a majority of each ethnic group do not get together with friends. or kinfolk for Sunday dinners, holidays, or birthdays, a majority of the community's families do get together for talk and television. Similar results were found in the frequency with which people get together with their friends for talk and television. Some persons get together coinstantaneously with friends and relatives for talk and T.V., of course. The number who do so is not as great as might have been expected on the basis of peer-group-oriented conceptualizations of the lower class. Only eight percent of the Mexicans but twenty-one percent of the Anglos get together with kin and friends. The difference here between the two ethnic groups is not as large as it appears. Most of the Anglos get together in kin-friend gatherings for talk and television only occasionally. And, the over-all differences appear to reflect the number of Mexicans who do not have relatives living in the area as a consequence of their migrant careers. Drinking and card-playing is a less common activity than getting together for palaver. Home-centered

activities are clearly a primary source of recreation for lower-Westsiders, Only two percent of the Mexicans and three percent of the Anglos do not participate in any of the activities I have called "home-centered." In each case, these persons represent the most poverty stricken of the community.

ORGANIZATIONAL ACTIVITY

Lower-Westsiders are fairly active in formal organizations as well. They are much more active than might have been expected on the basis of the literature. Lack of organizational activity has been identified as a Mexican characteristic as well as a lower-class characteristic. Taking the sample as a whole, no family members are active in organizations in forty-nine percent of the Anglo families and in sixty-three percent of the Mexican families. In none of the Mexican families, but in twelve percent of the Anglo families, only the wife is active. In thirteen percent of the Mexican families and fifteen percent of the Anglo families, only the husband is active. And, in about twenty-five percent of the families in each ethnic group, both the husband and wife are active (Table 25).

A certain amount of Anglo activity, however, is derived from union membership. More Anglos than Mexicans belong to unions as a consequence of differential employment. If organizational activity is adjusted by dropping union activity from the tabulations, the variation between the two groups is modified substantially (Table 26). Regardless of the adjusted statistics, it remains that proportionately less Mexicans than Anglos belong to formal organizations. However, Mexicans do proportionately belong to more organizations within the community than do Anglos as the adjustment for noncommunity-located unions

TABLE 27. Average Monthly Attendance, According to Ethnicity in Various Organization Types: Attenders and Average Monthly Attendance

| | Mexicans | | | | | | Anglos | | | | | |
| | WIVES | | | HUSBANDS | | | WIVES | | | HUSBANDS | | |
Organization type	No.	%	xf	No.	%	xf	No.	%	xf	No.	%	xf
Community improvement	8	17	4.0	7	15	4.1	3	9	1.3	2	6	4.5
P.T.A.	9	19	1.4	8	17	1.5	9	27	1.1	2	6	1.5
Fraternal club	0	0	0.0	3	6	1.0	0	0	0.0	3	9	1.3
Union	0	0	0.0	3	6	1.0	0	0	0.0	7	21	1.0
Church groups	0	0	0.0	3	6	2.0	2	6	3.0	1	3	4.0
Sports clubs	0	0	0.0	5	11	4.4	0	0	0.0	1	3	3.0
Ethnic groups	0	0	0.0	4	9	1.5	0	0	0.0	1	3	1.0

TABLE 28. Church Membership

	Mexicans		Anglos	
None	2	(4%)	2	(6%)
St. Guadelupe	43	(91%)	17	(52%)
St. Matthew	0	(0%)	2	(6%)
St. Michael	0	(0%)	2	(6%)
Unknown Catholic	1	(2%)	1	(3%)
Jehovah's Witnesses	1	(2%)	0	(0%)
Lutheran churches	0	(0%)	5	(15%)
Baptist churches	0	(0%)	3	(9%)
Mormon	0	(0%)	1	(3%)
Total	47	(99%)	33	(100%)

shows. Mexicans also belong to more organizations than do Anglos. Mexican respondents listed a total of fifty-nine organization memberships whereas Anglos listed forty-four memberships. This is an average of 0.8 organizations per Mexican family and 0.79 organizations per Anglo family. Or, of those families who have organizational memberships, Mexicans averaged two memberships as compared to 1.7 for Anglo families.

A general idea of organizational involvement can be gotten from Table 27 which tabulates wife and husband organizational attendance by ethnic groups in different kinds of activity. As can be seen from the table, a larger percentage of Mexicans than Anglos participate in community-improvement types of organizations, although the average attendance is about the same. More Anglo women and less Anglo men attend Parents and Teachers Association meetings than do Mexican women and men although again, average attendance is about the same. A similar number of men participate in fraternal orders with about the same attendance for each ethnic group. Considerably more Anglo men participate in union activity although again, average attendance is about the same. There is little difference in church-related group activity except that no Mexican women belong to such groups. Considerably more Mexican men than Anglos belong to sports clubs. And, slightly more Mexican men than Anglo men belong to Mexican ethnic groups. Attendance is impossible to define for these groups as most belong to the local brown beret group which is loosely organized.

The one organizational form which most all of the respondents belong to is the church (Table 28). Not only do most of the respondents belong to churches, but church attendance is fairly high (Table 29).

Although attitudes toward the church will be pursued in the next chapter, a brief description here will be informative. The respondents were asked "Do you think that a family benefits by going to church together?" The responses are reported in Table 30.

There is little variation between the two ethnic divisions in culture and life-style on the basis of the criteria so far reviewed. This is despite the fact that almost all of the Mexican-

TABLE 29. Frequency of Church Attendance

	Mexicans	Anglos
Never	5 (11%)	5 (15%)
Occasionally	5 (11%)	5 (15%)
Once or twice a month	16 (34%)	8 (24%)
Weekly	20 (43%)	15 (45%)
Two or more times a week	1 (2%)	0 (0%)
Total	47 (101%)	33 (99%)

TABLE 30. "Do you think a family benefits by going to church together?"

	Mexicans	Anglos
"No. It's an individual thing."	5 (11%)	8 (24%)
"Yes. It looks good."	7 (15%)	3 (9%)
"It brings the family together."	17 (36%)	10 (30%)
"It's good training for the children."	7 (15%)	6 (18%)
"It's good recreation."	4 (8%)	0 (0%)
"It's O.K."; don't know	7 (15%)	6 (18%)
Total	47 (100%)	33 (99%)

TABLE 31. Languages Spoken

	Mexicans	Anglos
English only	8 (16%)	29 (88%)
Spanish only	4 (9%)	0 (0%)
English and Spanish	35 (75%)	3 (9%)
English and French	0 (0%)	1 (3%)
Total	47 (100%)	33 (100%)

Americans in the sample are no more than one generation removed from Mexican communities in the Southwest or from Mexico. This is also despite the fact that the Mexican-Americans in the community do possess ethnic attributes such as language and food customs which set them apart from the rest of the community.

ETHNIC CHARACTERISTICS

Only sixteen percent of the Mexican respondents speak no Spanish at all. Nine percent of the Mexican respondents speak only Spanish. The remaining seventy-five percent of the Mexican respondents are bi-lingual (Table 31). Thirty-six percent use Spanish as their everyday language. Nine percent speak Spanish only with their husbands. Thirteen percent use the language only with their parents. Seventeen percent use Spanish only with non-English speakers, usually elderly people. And two percent reported they rarely use Spanish anymore.

Among the Anglo respondents, only nine percent reported acquaintance with a second language. Of these, three percent reported swearing in a European tongue. And six percent reported using Spanish. The Spanish-speaking Anglos only use Spanish in conversation with elderly persons of Mexican descent.

As might be expected in a working-class community, relatively few of the respondents reported reading in a non-English language. However, only nineteen percent of the Mexican respondents reported that they are unable to read Spanish. Thirteen percent of the Mexican-Americans exchange letters written in Spanish with relatives in the Southwest and in Mexico. Another seventeen percent read magazines and newspapers written in Spanish and published in Mexico. None of the Anglos reporting acquaintance with a non-English tongue could read that language.

The respondents also reported eating a fair amount of ethnic foods (Table 32). Some of the comments made by Anglos who eat Mexican foods are interesting. One Anglo

TABLE 32. Proportion of Respondents
Eating Mexican Foods

	Mexicans	Anglos
Never	1 (2%)	23 (70%)
Rarely	3 (6%)	5 (15%)
Monthly	7 (15%)	2 (6%)
Once or twice a week	7 (15%)	2 (6%)
Several times a week	10 (21%)	0 (0%)
Every day	19 (40%)	1 (3%)
Total	47 (99%)	33 (100%)

TABLE 33. "How many of your friends are
Mexican?"

	Mexicans	Anglos
None	6 (13%)	14 (42%)
One	3 (6%)	9 (27%)
Two	5 (11%)	3 (9%)
Three	7 (15%)	5 (15%)
Four	4 (9%)	2 (6%)
Five	22 (47%)	0 (0%)
Total	47 (101%)	33 (99%)

TABLE 34. "It is not wise to marry someone
whose skin is a different color
than your own."

	Mexicans	Anglos
Don't know	3 (6%)	0 (0%)
Agree	12 (26%)	9 (27%)
Disagree	32 (68%)	24 (73%)
Total	47 (100%)	33 (100%)

married to a Mexican said, "He eats my food, why shouldn't I?" Another, "You live in different neighborhoods and they have different nationalities. You get to learn their foods and cook them too." Several Anglo wives who do not cook any Mexican foods at all wished, as did several Mexican mothers who do not usually prepare Mexican foods, that their families would eat such because it is cheaper.

Few comments were made by Mexicans on eating Mexican food. Most who did commented on how they wished their families would eat more. Said one, "I wish they would eat more, but all they want is hamburgers."

Just as traits such as an ethnic language and ethnic foods are present in the community, traits often suggested to evidence the presence of an ethnic culture, so too is there a tendency to limit social interaction to members of one's own ethnic group, as revealed in Table 33. These responses indicate a fair amount of ethnic closure. In fact, there is actually more closure than the above table would suggest. Many of the Mexicans who reported having one or more Anglo friends just previously have reported they only had two or three friends, both of whom were Mexican-Americans. Similarly, a number of Anglos who reported having several Mexican friends had also reported that they only had a few friends and that they were Anglo. In each case, the respondents seemed to be trying to demonstrate that they are not prejudiced, a sensitive issue in the community. In reality, a solid majority of each ethnic group does not associate voluntarily with members of the other ethnic group.

The responses indicate more than ethnic closure, but also an awareness of ethnicity. The respondents were asked what nationalities are represented by their non-Mexican friends. Forty-seven percent of the Mexicans and forty-two percent of the Anglos have no Mexican friends. Thirty-eight percent of the Mexicans and fifteen percent of the Anglos classified their non-Mexican friends using such terms as "white," "Anglo," "American," and "whatever you call them" which meant Anglo. "White" was the most common term used. Fifteen percent of the Mexican and eighty-five percent of the Anglos listed the ethnic derivation of their non-Mexican friends. The number of nationalities listed varied considerably, ranging from one to eight.

The variation in Mexican and Anglo responses to the question concerning the nationality of non-Mexican friends is a response to the way in which ethnic divisions are drawn in the community. As shown in the tabulation of ethnic traits, on the lower-Westside, it is only the Mexicans who have retained the physical and verbal evidence of their national origins. Anglos displaying ethnic characteristics in fact usually possess Mexican traits such as food or

TABLE 35. "People coming to America have always lived in neighborhoods with others from their native country or from their parents' native country. Do you think this has been a good or bad thing?"

	Mexicans	Anglos
Don't know	15 (32%)	11 (33%)
"It's bad."	1 (2%)	0 (0%)
"Creates prejudice," etc.	2 (4%)	2 (6%)
"People get clannish."	4 (9%)	9 (27%)
"Nothing wrong with it."	8 (17%)	7 (21%)
"Keeps up culture," etc.	8 (17%)	2 (6%)
"Good. People can get help."	13 (28%)	1 (3%)
"Can keep out funny people."	2 (4%)	1 (3%)
Total	53 (113%)	33 (99%)

language. Moreover, of course, it is also the Mexican group which is largely physically differentiated from the rest of the community. Thus, the use of the terms "white" as contrasted to "Mexican." Both Mexicans and Anglos differentiate the two groups according to white and Mexican.

Differentiation within each group is not very much a part of the reality structure of the other group. Mexican-Americans differentiate according to Mexican and Indian, for example. Only rarely, however, have I heard an Anglo refer to a Mexican-American as Indian, and on investigation, the Anglos were discovered to be using the term only because Mexican friends did so and they had no understanding as to why the term is used. Indian, of course, is used by the Mexican-Americans to distinguish persons of mestizo (mixed) ancestry from persons of Indian ancestry. Some Mexicans then do worry about in-group differentiation but none of the Anglos are concerned about distinctions within the Mexican group.

In the same way, eighty-five percent of the Anglos could differentiate their non-Mexican friends on the basis of national origins, but only fifteen percent of the Mexicans could do so. The national origins of Anglos had no bearing on the Mexican community, but it was important apparently to the Anglos.

Although the respondents tended uniformly to use terms such as "white" as contrasted to "Mexican," there was an effort on the part of many to assert a nonracial quality

to their relationship with persons other than their own ethnic division. When asked "It is not wise to marry someone whose skin is a different color than your own," twenty-six percent of the Mexicans and twenty-seven percent of the Anglos agreed that this is indeed a true statement. However, sixty-eight percent of the Mexicans and seventy-three percent of the Anglos disagreed with the idea. As can be seen by Table 34, the only difference between the two groups is that the Mexicans disagreed more emphatically than did the Anglos. The greater emphasis on the part of the Mexicans seems to be an attempt to assert their equality with Anglos. In the same vein, most of the Anglos seemed to disagree with the question only insofar as they would "legitimize" a marriage of an Anglo to a Mexican. Most Anglos and Mexicans qualified their disagreement in one way or another, indicating that the statement was not true as regards Mexicans but either explicitly or implicitly suggested that this did not extend to blacks.

Along these lines, an ambiguous question concerning ethnic communities was also asked to attain insight into ethnic closure. The question was "People coming to America have always lived in neighborhoods with others from their native country, or from their parents' native country. Do you think this has been a good or a bad thing?" There was a substantial amount of variation between the two ethnic groups in response to this question (Table 35).

Thus, we have what would seem to be a typical ethnic community. It is comprised not only of the ethnic group which gives it its ethnic tones, but also of persons mainly of European descent who are ethnic only to the extent of identifying themselves and their friends in terms of national origins. In this case, the community seems to be divided pretty much according to "white" and "Mexican." The Mexican group possesses those cultural artifacts which identify it as Mexican, possesses some kind of a Mexican identity, and seeks a certain amount of closure from other ethnic groups. But even so, the cultural and life-style characteristics of the Mexican group are not according to the established criteria different from those of the Anglo community. The Mexicans in fact seem to be very acculturated. The possession of Mexican traits such as language does not seem to imply, as commonly thought, the presence of an unacculturated group.

NOTES

[1] Fernando Penalosa, "Mexican Family Roles," *Journal of Marriage and the Family* vol. 30 (November 1968), pp. 680-89.

[2] Lee Rainwater, *And the Poor Get Children* (Chicago, 1960), pp. 56-8.

[3] *Ibid.*, p. 58.

B.
MINORITY ADJUSTMENT AND MALADJUSTMENT

30
puerto rican americans

HÉCTOR I. VÁZQUEZ

Chapter 9 discussed the Puerto Ricans in Puerto Rico. Here is a description of the Puerto Rican community in New York City. Puerto Ricans face many problems; like former immigrants from Europe, they come from rural backgrounds, are unskilled, and speak a foreign language. This hinders their getting jobs and creates obstacles to learning for the children who are attending English-speaking schools. The city is also more difficult to live in now than it was when European immigration was at its peak. It is larger, faster-paced; there are fewer unskilled jobs; public facilities such as schools, community centers, and parks are more run down.

The New York public school system has experimented with teaching primary classes in Spanish and English as a second language, which, of course, is for Puerto Rican students. There are Spanish newspapers, and there has been a movement to permit those literate in Spanish only to vote. Welfare and other public agencies such as the police have begun to employ Spanish speakers; nevertheless, language barriers operate against Puerto Ricans both in school and in obtaining employment.

Unlike the former immigrants from Europe, Puerto Ricans are colored, having a mixed African, Indian, and Caucasian ancestry. Some look like Europeans; some, like Afro-Americans. Color differences in Puerto Rico are of little importance, but when dark-skinned Puerto Ricans come to the mainland, they are classed as blacks and are similarly discriminated against. Sometimes relations between Puerto Ricans and Afro-Americans are friendly, sometimes not. Puerto Ricans have followed Afro-American techniques of defense. Where they are concentrated, as in New York City, they have voted as a bloc in order to win political offices for their members. They have organized to get control of Model Cities and other antipoverty community programs. This has at times brought them into conflict with Afro-Americans. In imitation of the Black Panthers, young Puerto Ricans have an organization called the Young Lords; they wear uniforms, submit to discipline, and think of themselves as protectors of the community, particularly against police harassment.

It should not be forgotten that many Puerto Ricans have overcome the handicaps any immigrant faces and become absorbed in the economic life of the society. Many others return to Puerto Rico, and some go back and forth frequently. The mainland lures with its economic promises and repels with its racism. Should Puerto Rico opt for independence, Puerto Ricans living on the mainland would have to make a difficult decision.

Mr. Vazquez is executive director of the Puerto Rican Forum, Inc., of New York City.

Reprinted from *The Journal of Negro Education* 38, no. 3 (Summer 1969), pp. 247-256. Reproduced by permission of the author and publisher.

All recent reports indicate that Puerto Rican children have the lowest record of achievement of any identifiable group within the New York City public school system. The problem has been widely recognized and many new programs have been introduced to remedy the situation. The consensus of opinion is, however, that there has been no significant change in school performance and that there are even signs that the situation is deteriorating further.

The implications of such failure are alarming since one out of every four children in the public schools in New York is now Puerto Rican and all indications are that this sector of the school population will continue to grow. Furthermore, current political unrest, particularly in the low-income areas, centered as it is around the question of educational achievement, is manifesting itself in a growing dissatisfaction on the part of the Puerto Rican community with an educational system that has proved itself incapable of meeting the educational needs of their children. In this respect, the educational fate of the Puerto Rican is closely tied to that of the black American and the Mexican-American. With both groups, the present system has failed. But the solutions cannot be the same. There are unique cultural and linguistic differences at the base of the Puerto Rican educational dilemma which call for different objectives, methods and programs. The failure to recognize these differences has resulted to a large extent in the so-called "Puerto Rican problem" in the schools.

The present study will summarize briefly the background of the problem, the school situation, community involvement and will conclude with some specific recommendations. Emphasis will be on New York City not only because most studies have focused on this area but because the situation does not vary significantly in other cities.

First a word about available data. Most studies are based on the 1960 census figures, and the interim period of rapid change in population and distribution is not reflected. Grouped with Negro or "nonwhite" figures, the Puerto Rican tends to fade statistically as Herbert Bienstock has noted.[1] Moreover, interpreted from the point of view of previously established criteria and/or collected by individuals who have an imperfect knowledge of the human factors involved, such data often merely obscure the picture and lead to programs which are in the long run ineffectual.

BACKGROUND OF THE PROBLEM

The Puerto Rican problem in the schools is part of a more complex totality that reflects migration trends, employment opportunities, housing and family stability. The counterpart is the situation on the island itself which cannot be overlooked.

The 1960 census reports the Puerto Rican population in the United States as 855,724. Recent estimates indicate, however, an increase based on school enrollment figures of 730,618, bringing the total to 1,586,342.[2]

Although New York City has traditionally represented the stopping-off place for newly arrived migrants, the present trend is toward greater dispersal. Margolis estimates that the rate of increase has soared since the 1960 census with increases of 208 per cent in Chicago, 73 per cent in Philadelphia, 88 per cent in Hoboken and 118 per cent in Newark. Other cities, including Rochester, Cleveland and Jersey City report similar increases in school enrollments.

In New York City, public school enrollment figures for 1967, last available data, were 244,458 or 22.1 per cent of the total enrollment. These figures are now higher and represent, together with the Negro pupil enrollment, 55 per cent of the public school population.

The parents of these children are young, low-skill, low-wage migrants who have come in search of better job opportunities. It is estimated that Puerto Ricans are the youngest age group in New York City. The median age of Puerto Ricans in New York City was reported to be 21.7 years in 1964 in comparison to 26.5 years for nonwhites and 38.4 years for whites.[3] The additional factors of early marriages and high birth rates suggest a predominance of Puerto Rican children in the public schools of the city within the foreseeable future.

More than half of these young migrants, two-thirds under age 24, have no previous work experience and more than one out of every four has worked as a farm laborer or semi-skilled worker. This pattern carries over into New York City where the occupational distribution is 65 per cent blue-collar workers (50% in low-wage factory production). This compares with 40 per cent for nonwhites and 32 per cent for whites in similar jobs. White-collar employment figures are 19 per cent for Puerto Ricans, 30 per cent for nonwhites and 58 per cent for whites. The situation is further aggravated by the substantial loss of factory jobs in New York City in recent years.

The effect of this work pattern on education and income is perpetual poverty. In 1960 less then 1 per cent of the total Puerto Rican population had completed four or more years of college; 87 per cent of all Puerto Ricans over the age of 25 had not finished high school.

In the same year, 34 per cent of all Puerto Rican families in New York City had incomes of less than $3,000, compared with 27 per cent for nonwhites and 12 per cent for whites. More than half (54%) of all Puerto Rican families had incomes of less than $4,000, in contrast to 19 per cent for white families.

In 1964 the Population Health Survey reported an average income of $6,708 for white families in New York City, $4,833 for nonwhite families and $3,900 for Puerto Rican families.

The Puerto Rican's lack of education and training is also reflected in unemployment rate percentages: 9.7 per cent for Puerto Rican males in comparison to 6.8 per cent for nonwhites and 4.4 per cent for all races combined.

The new concept of subemployment presents a more accurate picture of the Puerto Rican: 33.1 per cent for Puerto Ricans as a whole, 37 per cent in East Harlem, a predominantly Puerto Rican area, in comparison to 28.6 per cent for Harlem and 27.6 per cent for Bedford-Stuyvesant, areas of Negro concentration.

Puerto Rican families live in the oldest residential structures in New York City: 40.1 per cent lived in deteriorating and dilapidated structures in comparison to 33 per cent nonwhites and 11 per cent whites. The United States Census Bureau defines "dilapidated" as housing that "does not provide safe and adequate shelter."

Given family size, Puerto Ricans are crowded for living space to a degree not found among nonwhites and whites. Thirty eight per cent of Puerto Rican households were in units of 1.01 or more persons per room in comparison to 22.1 per cent for nonwhites and 8.7 per cent for other white households.

The housing situation has deteriorated further since 1960. New construction is forcing the Puerto Rican family out of its inadequate yet available housing and is being replaced by so-called "middle-income housing" that the average householder cannot afford. For example, between 1946 and 1965, corresponding to the greatest influx of Puerto Ricans to New York City, 203,600 units were demolished. (It is assumed they were substandard). During the same period the New York Housing Authority built only 97,200 units and public housing is the only hope for decent shelter for most Puerto Ricans. This represents a net loss of 106,400 low-rent units. In comparison, the same period witnessed the construction of 478,000 full tax-paying units (and, therefore, probably upper middle income or luxury), 83,600 public-assisted private housing units and 26,000 New York City Housing Authority no-cash subsidy project units were built—a total of 588,300 housing units in categories most Puerto Ricans cannot afford.[4]

Moreover, statistics do not reflect the serious human problems which uprooting through relocation produce.

It is, therefore, not surprising that Puerto Rican families have the highest mobility rate in New York City. The Population Health Survey reports that 71.6 per cent had moved at least once from 1960 to 1965 in comparison to 59.7 per cent for nonwhites and 41.1 per cent for white families. (The white-family percentage reflects in part the exodus to the suburbs.) According to this report mobility was higher for in-migrants, families of 6 or more persons, younger children, female heads and younger family heads—categories that are typical of Puerto Rican families.[5]

THE SCHOOL SITUATION

The physical and psychological hardships inherent to the family life represented by the above data need not be labored. In short, Puerto Rican children reach school burdened by many ills which the schools are neither prepared nor willing to face. Instead of a haven for learning, schools simply compound the problems.

A survey conducted by the United Bronx Parents[6] and published in 1968 reveals the failure of the New York City Board of Education to deal effectively with the Puerto Rican child and its reluctance to make equitable distribution of funds and professional resources. The survey compared the "top" 12 and the "bottom" 12 elementary schools in the borough of the Bronx, the area of highest Puerto Rican concentration in the city. The following categories were compared.

1. The Metropolitan Reading Achievement Test Scores of May 1966. All the "top" schools scored above the norm (5.8 in May and 5.7 in April) for the fifth grade. In contrast, all of the "bottom" schools were more than one year below the norm.

2. Ethnic Distribution. All of the 12 "bottom" schools were located in the southern and eastern poverty areas of the Bronx where Negroes and Puerto Ricans live.

3. Physical Plant. Whereas only 8 per cent of the "top" schools occupied buildings fifty years and older, 42 per cent of the "bottom" schools did. Buildings under twenty years of age were occupied by 25 per cent of the "top" schools and 8 per cent of the "bottom" schools. Ninety-two per cent of the "bottom" schools occupied physical plants thirty years and older in comparison to 66 per cent of the "top" schools.

4. Plant Utilization. No "top" school was classified "very crowded" or "jammed" (25% "uncomfortable") in comparison to 82 per cent for the "bottom" schools.

5. Short Time and Double Sessions. No "top" school was on short time or double session and the first grade had a full five-hour day in contrast to 92 per cent for the "bottom" schools.

6. Average Class Size. Despite the Board of Education's policy of extra teachers and reduced class size for deprived areas no real difference in class size was found.

7. Pupil Population or Registers. According to planners these should range between 800 and 1,200 pupils. Seventy-five per cent of the "top" schools had 1,000 or less pupils in comparison to 25 per cent for the "bottom" schools and 58 per cent of the "bottom" schools had 1,400 or more pupils.

8. Teaching Staff. In the "top" schools 67 per cent of the teachers were licensed, 83 per cent experienced and earned salaries of $10,000 or more and 59 per cent were tenured. In the "bottom" schools only 17 per cent were licensed, 17 per cent experienced, 17 per cent earned over $10,000 (67% earned less) and 26 per cent were tenured.

9. Per Pupil Expenditure. Although according to the Mayor's Expense Budget Message of April, 1967, Special Service Schools (predominantly Negro and Puerto Rican) were to receive additional per pupil allowances of between $150 and $200 in addition to the $750 per pupil allotment to regular elementary schools, in practice such monies were not made available. On the whole, schools in the "top" group received an average of $670 per pupil whereas the "bottom" group, comprised totally of Special Service Schools, received only $519. Among the latter, schools with a majority of Puerto Rican pupils were receiving less than predominantly Negro schools. Schools with 60-80 per cent white population were receiving proportionately the most money per child.

The current practice is to budget about $9,000 per teacher for a given school, assigning a teacher at a salary of $6,500 and returning the remaining $2,500 to the Board of Education headquarters. This excess is then alloted to white neighborhood schools which, in turn, hire a teacher at $11,000. Moreover, since state funds are allotted on an attendance basis, it is obvious that ghetto schools receive less funds.

10. Achievement. In the "top" schools 56 per cent of the pupils received a junior high school diploma in comparison to 30 per cent for the "bottom" junior high schools. Of the graduates, 88 per cent from the "top" schools went to an academic high school, 9 per cent to a vocational high school, 9 per cent to private or parochial schools.

The pattern carries over into the high schools. Graduates from the "top" schools attend the special and academically superior high schools whereas Negro and Puerto Rican children end up in the "other" high schools. The results are that over 50 per cent of the "special school" graduates receive an academic diploma etc. (92% for the Bronx High School of Science and 65.4% for the High School of Music and Art) and less than 3 per cent of the pupils from the "bottom" schools. (2.9% for Morris High School and 1.8% for Benjamin Franklin High School, predominantly Puerto Rican schools).

Furthermore, all the vocational high schools in the Bronx are located in the ghetto area while only one academic high school (Morris) has been established in the same area.

It is, therefore, not surprising that college enrollment figures for Puerto Ricans are the lowest for any ethnic group in the city. The 1967 Ethnic Census of the City University of New York[7] reveals that 81.8 per cent of the university enrollment is white, 10.2 per cent Negro and 2.9 per cent Puerto Rican. Of the 1,923, or 2.9 per cent, Puerto Rican students, 1,562 were in the nonmatriculate category.

Data comparing the ethnic distribution of matriculated and nonmatriculated students at the City University reveal the following per cents: matriculated—white, 87.1; Negro, 5.8; Puerto Rican, 2.4; nonmatriculated—white, 71.4; Negro, 18.9; Puerto Rican, 3.8. A greater proportion of Negro and Puerto Rican students are enrolled as nonmatriculants. Moreover, Negro and Puerto Rican students make up 20 per cent and 5 per cent respectively of enrollments in the community colleges compared to 6 per cent and 5 per cent in the senior colleges.

The report emphasizes the fact that low minority enrollment may be attributed to the fact that at the critical "choice points," where the student's decision will determine whether he will qualify as a candidate for college, minority group students are more likely to "make choices, or to have choices made for them," which decrease their ability to meet regular admissions requirements. As indicated by the United Bronx Parents survey, Negro and Puerto Rican students are more likely to enroll in vocational high schools, leave prior to completion of the senior year, and, if they do stay, receive a "general" diploma. A 1963 study by Frank M. Dordasco[8] reports that in this year only 3.7 per cent Negro students and 1.6 per cent Puerto Rican students earned an academic diploma in the New York City schools (21,000 were awarded). The City University Ethnic Census estimates on this basis that in June 1967 approximately 720 Negro students and 310 Puerto Ricans earned an academic diploma of 19,495 awarded. This estimate of 5.3 per cent contrasts sharply with the fact that these two groups comprise 38 per cent of the total high school population.

COMMUNITY INVOLVEMENT

The Puerto Rican community has long suffered from a lack of cohesive organization. As migrants arrived, hundreds of "home-town" clubs were organized but the function of these clubs has remained largely social. Several factors may account for this lack of organization: namely, dispersal of population, high mobility, lack of political sophistication and the stultifying effects of economic demands in an alien environment. In this respect, Puerto Ricans differ significantly from former immigrants who found solidarity in ethnic clubs. Moreover, the Puerto Rican has been inhibited in organizing by the attitude that he is not here to stay; his "commuter" status has contributed to a feeling of instability which is not conducive to community concern and participation. And, unlike other groups, he has arrived at a time when traditional political structures are breaking down. The old political-boss system, despite its corruption, favored immigrant organizations by allowing them to barter favors for votes.[9] Three factors have contributed to the emergence of more politically and socially oriented groups within the last decade. These are: the enactment of anti-poverty legislation with its emphasis on community organization and participation, the Negro struggle for civil rights and the political controversy over the decentralization of public schools.

The emergence of these organizations, several devoted to education, has led to the convocation of several widely publicized conferences. These conferences have focused on the overall problems of the Puerto Rican community and have evidenced the awakening of strong leadership, a well-informed and articulate youth and a general awareness of what the problems are and the formulation of specific recommendations in terms of the Puerto Rican ethos by the Puerto Ricans themselves. Chief among these were the Mayor's Conference of 1967, the ASPIRA Conference on Education of 1968, and the Puerto Rican Forum's 1968 Conference on Economic Development and the Puerto Rican New Yorker.

Joseph Fitzpatrick has called the Mayor's Conference of 1967 "a turning point in the experience of Puerto Ricans in New York City. There were numerous indications of organizational and political sophistication, and an obvious spirit of unity."[10] Conference participants recommended the implementation of bilingual programs, courses in Puerto Rican culture, literature and history, community participation, the hiring of Puerto Rican paraprofessionals to assist in the schools and representation on the Board of Education.

Fitzpatrick also notes that the most significant factor about the conference was the fact that strong community opposition forced the planners to convene the conference on the mainland (it was formerly celebrated in San Juan) and to replace participants by locally based and representative groups and leaders.

An evaluation of the situation of Puerto Rican children in the public schools prepared in advance of the ASPIRA Conference by

Richard J. Margolis was significantly entitled *The Losers.*[11] The report, commissioned by ASPIRA, aimed at surveying the current scene, particularly beyond the New York City area. The writer visited seven cities—Bridgeport, Chicago, Philadelphia, Newark, Patterson and New York. Teachers, administrators, children and parents were interviewed. The situation, Margolis concludes, does not vary from city to city. Puerto Rican children, in the words of the writer, "tend to learn less, lose heart more and drop out sooner." He also found that "the longer a Puerto Rican child attends public school, the less he learns." In comparing the fate of Negro and Puerto Rican children in the schools, Margolis found that, although they both share many humiliations, the Puerto Rican child has additional burdens. These are his status as a stranger, his imperfect grasp of English which often causes him to be labeled "slow" and his confusion about race and culture. Quoting from the Coleman Report, *Equality of Educational Opportunity,* Margolis notes that the Puerto Rican child is further hampered by the attitude that he has no control over his life and destiny. The cause of much of this Margolis attributes to the treatment received at school by teachers who do not understand the children linguistically or culturally and are, thus, unable to communicate positively with them. The result, he states, is a general exodus out of the schools. And although dropout rates are not available, there is a shocking discrepancy between elementary and high school enrollments.

School boards in New York City and elsewhere have confronted the problem with a long list of reports, special programs, teacher orientation, etc., but there is general agreement on the failure of such programs. Margolis labels them "random activity that creates the illusion of progress." Fitzpatrick evaluates the situation with a quotation from a recent article by Edmund W. Gordon and Adelaide Jablonsky:

Compensatory education models have been widely and enthusiastically accepted. However, when one looks at their impact on academic performance in the target population, it is obvious that compensatory educa-

tion as presently practiced is either insufficient or irrelevant to the needs of disadvantaged young people.

Fitzpatrick goes on to explain that "little methodologically sound, substantial and up-to-date data on the Puerto Rican child are either available in the field of education or, if available, integrated into effective compensatory educational programs," and laments the lack of attention given to specifically Puerto Rican problems in available literature and proposals on compensatory education.[12]

A new trend is becoming evident, however, which is pressing toward a true cultural pluralism rather than the older ideal of Americanization. Legal recognition of Spanish as the language of native-born Americans was finally achieved in 1965 through the change in the New York State voter registration laws requiring an English literacy test. And the Bilingual Education Act, passed by Congress in January 1968, has specified the legal right of Puerto Ricans to have their children educated bilingually.

Moreover, recent research on the "culturally deprived" or "disadvantaged" child has led to new interpretations of these terms which are most encouraging for the education of the Puerto Rican youngster. Fitzpatrick notes that Frank Reissman in his book *The Culturally Deprived Child*

urged recognition of the positive values and cultures of various ethnic and racial groups comprising the lower socio-economic levels of our society . . . a use of existing cultural contributions of the various ethnic and racial groups involved and a relating of these to other, wider cultural pursuits. . . . Programs should be designed not only in relation to the problems, handicaps, and poor conditions of the deprived person's life, but also in relation to the strengths and positive aspects of the way of life of the poor, their different but impressive styles of art, language, expression, their imaginativeness and initiative in finding ways to cope with their difficult situation; the values which they cherish but which they express in quite different ways from those of the more affluent teachers and citizens.[13]

Gerald Lesser's ideas on the disadvantaged are not dissimilar:

The strategy in this case must not be that of giving equal opportunity to all in order to equalize the development of all as was advocated in the Coleman report but that of giving equal opportunity to all ethnic groups in order to maximize their development—even if this means the continuation of ethnic differences among the groups.[14]

And at the Congressional hearings on the issue of bilingual education, Joshua Fishman promoted bilingualism as a value in itself.[15]

One of the dominant themes at the ASPIRA Conference was the question of bilingual education. On this issue, most conference participants seemed to agree. Several studies support this community demand for bilingual education as the most effective means of improving learning among Puerto Rican school children. In 1950 Anastasi and DeJesus found that Puerto Rican preschool children were superior to white and Negro children in New York City in early linguistic development. In 1952 Cruz DeJesus in a master's thesis at Fordham University replicated these findings and also proved that Puerto Rican children were essentially normal in intellectual development. In 1953 Anastasi and Cordova concluded from a study that inferior performance on school I.Q. tests by Puerto Rican children resulted from the use of English only in the tests.[16]

The other dominant theme at the ASPIRA Conference was the need for Puerto Rican political powers. Fitzpatrick, himself a participant, has concluded:

If the Puerto Ricans are to overcome the serious disadvantages which they suffer, especially in education, they must become a political voice, an interest group pressuring for their own rights, and interests. Formation of a political bloc is dependent upon two factors: first, the establishment of a common identity and secondly, an issue about which to rally forces. Language is one possible characteristic which could fulfill these two requirements.[17]

Margolis voices the same sentiments in his report: "No school system, no matter how humane its intentions, is likely to come up with a comprehensive program aimed at saving Puerto Rican children unless the community suggests one and presses for its enactment."[18]

On the issue of decentralization, the opinion of the Puerto Rican community has been neither clear nor consistent, in the words of Fitzpatrick. Decentralization has been supported by Antonia Pantoja, founder of the Puerto Rican Forum, Inc., and member of the Bundy panel; Héctor I. Vázquez and Ana Conigliaro, Puerto Rican members of the Board of Education; ASPIRA; the Puerto Rican Educators Association; the United Bronx Parents, a predominantly Puerto Rican organization; and other representative groups. Hermán Badillo, a native Puerto Rican and Bronx Borough President accepts decentralization, but has expressed reservations as to how far it should be carried out. The Kings County Puerto Rican Leadership Conference, attended by a thousand leaders of the Puerto Rican and Spanish-speaking community in Brooklyn demanded greater representation in exchange for support of decentralization plans.

The Puerto Rican community, therefore, does not oppose the educational ideal of decentralization but tends to fear the political reality of community control. Since Puerto Ricans are dispersed throughout the city and must share community leadership with the more powerful Negro groups in some areas, or with the mainland whites in others, these doubts are not entirely unfounded. In the resolution of this problem may lie the future development of the Puerto Rican community in New York because, as it has so often been repeated, the struggle for decentralization is essentially a struggle for political power as well as educational reform.

RECOMMENDATIONS

As voiced by a majority of the participants at the first national conference on "Meeting the Special Educational Needs of Urban Puerto Rican Youth" (May 14 and 15, 1968), sponsored by ASPIRA, the major recommendations were: (1) to increase and upgrade Puerto Rican and bilingual educational personnel and administrators; (2) to improve school-community relations; (3) to make curriculum relevant; (4) to increase Puerto Rican political power and community action; (5) to strengthen adult education; (6) to prepare youth for post-secondary education; (7) to act on the national level.

In these recommendations are condensed the desires and aspirations of Puerto Rican Americans to improve their lot.

As witnessed by its commitment to educational reform, the Puerto Rican community has come a long way in its endeavor to formulate and implement programs and policies to remedy its specific needs. Whether it will gain the public support to translate these plans into action, will depend in no small degree on its ability to persist and organize.

NOTES

[1] Herbert Bienstock, *Labor Force Experience of the Puerto Rican Worker* (Washington, D.C.: U.S. Department of Labor, Bureau of Labor Statistics, 341 Ninth Avenue, N.Y.C., May 20, 1968).

[2] Richard J. Margolis, *The Losers: A Report on Puerto Ricans and the Public Schools,* ASPIRA, Inc., 296 Fifth Avenue, New York, New York 10001.

[3] Bienstock, *op. cit.,* p. 4 and pp. 6-8 (employment), p. 8 (education), p. 9 (incomes), p. 10 (unemployment and subemployment).

[4] The Puerto Rican Forum, Inc., *1964 Report of Poverty Conditions in the New York Puerto Rican Community.* Published by Puerto Rican Forum, Inc., New York, New York 10001, pp. 59-67.

[5] Population Health Survey, Research Memorandum, Center for Social Research, Graduate Study, The City University of New York City, 1965, p. 8.

[6] "Distribution of Educational Resources Among the Bronx Public Schools." A survey conducted by the United Bronx Parents, unpublished, 1968.

[7] Report of the Fall 1967 Undergraduate Ethnic Census. The City University of New York.

[8] Frank M. Cordasco, "The Puerto Rican Child in the American School." *Congressional Record,* Reprint 3:195 (October 19, 1955).

[9] Nathan Glazer and Daniel P. Moynihan, *Beyond the Melting Pot* (Cambridge: The M.I.T. Press, 1963).

[10] Joseph P. Fitzpatrick, "Educational Experience of the Puerto Rican Community in New York City: A Review Paper." Unpublished study commissioned by the Puerto Rican Institute for School and Community Interaction of the Puerto Rican Forum, Inc., 1969, p. 67.

[11] Margolis, *op. cit.*

[12] Fitzpatrick, *op. cit.*, pp. 25-26.

[13] *Ibid.*, pp. 27-28.

[14] *Ibid.*, p. 32.

[15] *Ibid.*, p. 49.

[16] *Ibid.*, pp. 52-53.

[17] *Ibid.*, p. 56.

[18] Margolis, *op. cit.*, p. 4.

31
ethnicity, poverty and selected attitudes: a test of the "culture of poverty" hypothesis

LOLA M. IRELAN, OLIVER C. MOLES, ROBERT M. O'SHEA

It is well known and documented in a variety of ways in this book that blacks, Chicanos, Indians, and some ethnic groups do not do as well in society as other groups. There are a large number of explanations. Since biological explanations are no longer intellectually respectable, it has been fashionable to depend on cultural explanations. Groups are "culturally deprived" or suffering from the "culture of poverty" or unable to master middle-class standards and values. It should be pointed out that all these explanations put the blame for failure to achieve education and prosperity on the minority groups. The alternate explanation—discrimination—puts the blame on the majority groups, so it is not a very popular explanation.

The following selection attempts to see whether the very poor, regardless of their ethnicity, do have the values associated with the "culture of poverty." It should be read in conjunction with the Caine article (Chapter 29) on the similarity of attitudes between lower-middle-class Anglos and Mexican-Americans. It may be that the student will be willing then to throw away the jargon and consider the nature and effects of discrimination.

Lola M. Irelan and Oliver C. Moles work for the U.S. Department of Health, Education, and Welfare; and the third author, Robert M. O'Shea, teaches at the State University of New York at Buffalo.

The phrase "culture of poverty" has become current before the reality of its referent has been established. It has been used as a summarily descriptive term, as an explanation of behavior, and as a basis for programs both of exhortation and of action. Frequently it appears as a shorthand term referring to the variety of ways in which economic deprivation can influence ideas and actions with a single society.

Reprinted from *Social Forces* 47, no. 4 (June 1969), pp. 405-413. Reproduced by permission of the authors and publisher.

Precisely used, the basic concept "culture" refers to a systematic, integrated pattern for living. A culture is such by its distinctness from other cultures. This, indeed, is the quality specifically assigned the culture of poverty by careful users of the concept. In 1958, Walter Miller described a lower-class cultural system: "a long established, distinctively patterned tradition with an integrity of its own." Subsequently, Oscar Lewis further suggested that there is a culture of poverty which

transcends national boundaries and regional and rural-urban differences within nations.

Wherever it occurs, its practitioners exhibit remarkable similarity in the structure of their families, in interpersonal relations, in spending habits, in their value systems, and in their orientation in time.[2]

Thus carefully phrased, the concept invites testing which it has not yet received. Lewis and others are engaged in observing, listing, and describing the apparently common characteristics of the poor in various countries. If this effort is followed by systematic measurement of the extent of cultural similarities between groups of poor people, the utility of the culture of poverty concept will have been tested.

Both the Miller and Lewis statements imply, at the least, the simple hypothesis that very poor people from groups characterized by different major cultures are markedly similar to each other in certain attitudes, values, and patterns of behavior.

It has been possible to take a first step in the testing of this hypothesis by analyzing data originally collected for another purpose. Measures of several attitudes held by people on two levels of poverty from three different ethnic backgrounds have been tested for significant differences. This paper reports the findings.

DATA

Data used were collected in California during 1964 in the course of research into characteristics associated with receipt and nonreceipt of public assistance funds by economically deprived families.[3] Respondents were the male heads of 1,156 intact families, each of whom could be classified as either Spanish-speaking American, Negro-American, or Anglo-American. The three ethnic groups were represented in approximately equal numbers (440, 316, and 400, respectively). Approximately half of each group were selected from recipients of Aid to Families of Dependent Children with Unemployed Parents (AFDC-UP). The rest were drawn from contacts, in the same counties, of various social service agencies. None of these latter families were receiving public assistance at the time of the interview. Each consisted of at least a father, mother, and one minor child. Two primarily rural and two primarily urban counties were represented. Respondents were distributed about equally among the four counties.

All respondents were poor. Median reported income was $3,306 annually, and median family size was 6.8 persons. An income scale matching the AFDC-UP payment levels for families of different sizes was used to select the nonrecipient families (e.g., $2,492 for 4 persons), but in order to reach the quota in urban areas some were included whose income was as much as 30 percent above these figures. Thus nonrecipients as a whole had slightly higher incomes. A large majority of the men reported either unskilled or semi-skilled occupations. In general respondents' families were without savings, insurance, or pension coverage. Seventy-six percent were in debt for an average amount of $1,572.[5]

HYPOTHESIS

The general hypothesis stated above was operationalized as a null hypothesis specifying 8 value orientations: No significant difference will be found between Anglo-American poor, Spanish-speaking American poor, and Negro-American poor in the extent to which they:

1. feel themselves to be dependent people
2. behave dependently
3. give precedence to family of orientation over family of procreation
4. appear to value child autonomy
5. consider parents responsible for the behavior of their children
6. have fatalistic attitudes
7. express feelings of social alienation
8. value the securing or holding of a job

The relevance of these items to the culture of poverty concept will be discussed below.

ANALYSIS PROCEDURES

The data are additive summaries of responses to attitude items (3- and 5-point scales) in several attitude domains. As such, they meet the requirements of the Kruskal-Wallis nonparametric one-way analysis of variance by ranks.[6] A probability level of 0.05 was specified as significant and sufficient to reject the stated null hypothesis.

TABLE 1. Kruskal-Wallis One-Way Analysis of Variance Tests, Ethnicity, Poverty and Attitudes

	H VALUE[a]		SIGNIFICANCE LEVEL	
Attitude measured	Public assistance recipients	Nonrecipients	Public assistance recipients	Nonrecipients
1. Dependent feelings	20.85	54.58	0.001	0.001
2. Dependent behavior	45.42	24.57	0.001	0.001
3. Primacy of family of orientation	28.60	11.92	0.001	0.01
4. Child autonomy	28.15	16.84	0.001	0.001
5. Responsibility for child behavior	8.55	27.42	0.02	0.001
6. Fatalism	4.33	24.45	NS	0.001
7. Social alienation	19.84	47.10	0.001	0.001
8. Job value	6.03	2.16	0.05	NS

[a]H designates the basic measure produced by the Kruskal-Wallis test.

To utilize the full possibilities of the data, responses of men who had received public assistance were tabulated and tested separately from those of men with no such experience. The hypothesis was thus tested on two levels of poverty.[7]

RESULTS

Results of the 16 applications of the Kruskal-Wallis tests are summarized in Table 1. In 14 cases, differences among the three ethnic groups were found to be significant at the 0.05 level or better. Eleven were significant at the 0.001 level. In 2 applications nonsignificant differences were found. Considerable doubt is thus cast upon the validity of the culture of poverty concept. The results will now be discussed in more detail.

DEPENDENCY

Lewis has stated in several publications that dependency is a notable characteristic of the culture of poverty.[8] Two sets of dependency questions, measuring dependent feelings and dependent behavior, were included in the questionnaire of the original study.[9] Both "acceptable" and "unacceptable" dependency questions were included but it was decided to use only the unacceptable items. They could be expected to separate more and less dependent persons more clearly (Table 2).

The reliability of differences which emerge here is quite high. For both recipients and nonrecipients of public assistance, ethnicity is significant at the 0.001 level as a trait associated with the extent of dependent feeling and dependent behavior. In both cases average scores indicate that Spanish-speaking respondents were most dependent, and that Anglos and Negroes were similar in their lesser dependency.

FAMILY-RELATED ATTITUDES

Lewis believes that poverty has a strong effect upon family organization, behavior, and attitudes. Repeated emphasis is placed by him on the detachment which characterizes husband-wife relations, the mother-centeredness of families, the lack of protective and cherishing attitudes toward children, and, withal, the strong verbal emphasis upon family solidarity.[10] It is logical, then, to use measures of a man's attachment to his own parents contrasted with ties to his wife and children, attitudes toward autonomy of children, and beliefs about responsibility for children's behavior to test this aspect of the culture of poverty hypothesis.[11]

The lack of agreement on items relating to these areas is documented in Table 3. The statistical significance of ethnicity as a determinant was, in all instances, well under the 5 percent level. Ethnic variations again are similar to those for the dependency area. Spanish-speaking men stand out among both assistance recipients and nonrecipients for the greater

TABLE 2. Dependency Feelings and Behavior Among Low-Income Anglo, Spanish-speaking, and Negro Recipients and Nonrecipients of Public Assistance

| | Percent of Persons Agreeing with Item Among | | | | | |
| | PUBLIC ASSISTANCE RECIPIENTS | | | NONRECIPIENTS | | |
	Anglo (N = 210)	Spanish-speaking (N = 212)	Negro (N = 165)	Anglo (N = 189)	Spanish-speaking (N = 227)	Negro (N = 151)
Dependency feelings items						
I secretly wish I were a child again.	34.0	39.9	23.2	19.7	41.4	17.3
I feel a person must "play politics" to get promotions or increases in pay and jobs.	25.4	30.6	33.1	22.3	41.3	39.7
I feel out of sorts if I have to be by myself for any length of time.	33.7	43.7	30.5	20.2	39.2	27.2
Average score for all items[a]	4.3	5.4	4.1	3.0	5.3	3.7
Dependency behavior items						
I feel afraid of being alone or not being wanted.	31.6	32.2	27.3	25.5	35.4	23.8
I do a great many things just to avoid criticism.	40.0	52.6	56.1	38.3	51.3	50.7
Because I want to be liked, I tend to be apologetic and won't stand up for what I know are my real feelings.	26.3	39.6	31.1	20.1	44.2	24.5
Average score for all items[b]	4.6	5.6	4.8	3.9	5.5	4.4

[a]Based on each person's total score derived by combining all responses. Average scores may range from 1 to 13. All items were 5-point scales with "strongly disagree" and "strongly agree" as the extreme low and high point responses.
[b]Total number of respondents on which percentages were based are approximately the same for all tables. For some percentages numbers are slightly smaller because of missing data.

TABLE 3. Family-related Attitudes Among Low-Income Anglo, Spanish-speaking, and Negro Recipients and Nonrecipients of Public Assistance

| | *Percent of Persons Agreeing with Item Among* | | | | | |
| | PUBLIC ASSISTANCE RECIPIENTS | | | NONRECIPIENTS | | |
	Anglo	Spanish-speaking	Negro	Anglo	Spanish-speaking	Negro
Items on primacy of family of orientation						
The responsibilities of taking care of his wife and children should not keep a husband from spending plenty of time with his own parents.	35.9	57.5	50.9	40.5	50.4	47.7
There is no excusing a wife who tries to come between a man and his parents.	45.4	50.0	47.8	47.8	57.3	41.6
A man should be careful that his marriage doesn't result in his losing interest and close contact with his own mother and father.	48.5	67.6	67.5	55.1	73.8	71.5
Average score for all items[a]	6.2	7.7	7.1	6.5	7.4	6.8
Items on child autonomy						
If children plan their own work and do it without the direction of parents they are more willing to help, and they do more.	65.9	54.3	77.0	67.6	46.9	67.3
Parents should keep out of children's activities as much as possible so that children can learn to do things on their own.	41.9	47.1	58.5	44.1	44.9	57.0
Managing their own affairs without interference develops responsible children.	59.2	50.2	68.3	53.5	49.8	57.0
Average score for all items	7.0	6.3	8.0	6.8	6.0	6.8
Items on responsibility for child behavior						
No matter what the parents try to do, there are children who don't change at all in the way they behave. (Percent disagree)	23.1	23.9	16.0	26.7	18.6	19.9
When neighbors or teachers complain about the behavior of a child this shows that the parents haven't done a good job.	47.1	58.2	50.3	38.4	66.8	40.4
Problems in children come out of trouble inside the family.	77.0	73.6	69.9	71.3	79.7	59.7
Average score for all items	6.2	6.5	5.8	6.1	6.7	5.4

[a]Average scores may range from 1 to 13. All items were 5-point scales with "strongly disagree" and "strongly agree" as the extreme low and high point responses.

importance they attach to their parents (the family of orientation), the lesser concern they have for children's development of autonomy, and their more common belief that parents are responsible for children's behavior. Negro men stand second in relative attachment to parents. They also tend most often to view the child as autonomous and, perhaps consequently, to believe least often that parents are responsible for children's behavior.

FATALISM

The fatalistic outlook of the poor, their resignation to an uncontrolled future in the face of which they feel helpless and for which, therefore, they see no point in planning—these are repeatedly pointed out as traits of the poverty culture.[12] The questionnaire included four items related to an orientation of fatalism. Distribution of agreement and disagreement with each item is recorded in Table 4. Treated as a simple additive scale, these questions elicited no significant differences among Anglos, Spanish-speaking Americans, and Negroes who had received public assistance. Conversely, an ethnic difference significant at the 0.001 level was demonstrated for the respondents who had not received assistance. The relationship of fatalism and ethnicity is not a consistent one. Considered individually, there is only one item, "the wise person lives for today and lets tomorrow take care of itself," on which the assistance recipients agreed more highly than their nonassisted ethnic counterparts. Even that agreement was less than a majority of each group. A second item, "Saving for a rainy day," showed almost nobody disagreeing. It thus contributes little variation to the total scores. The remaining two items are a mixture of directional differences. Finally, when the average scores of the groups are compared, they are consistently lower for Anglo and nonrecipients, the economically better-off poor respondents. It would seem that, indeed, the more extremely deprived (public assistance recipients) do resemble each other closely in the extent of their fatalism— but only the Spanish-speaking among them show more fatalism than do the less-extremely deprived.

SOCIAL ALIENATION

Social alienation and cynicism are nominated by Lewis as outstanding characteristics of the culture of poverty.[13] Four attitude items from the original questionnaire allow measurement of this theme.[14] They are displayed in Table 4. On both levels of poverty— that at which self-sufficiency has been maintained and the more extreme level at which public help has been necessary—ethnic groups remain reliably distinct from each other. Ethnically associated variety in responses appears to be greater among nonrecipients.

VALUE OF WORK

The evaluation of work has not been specifically mentioned as a point of divergence between poverty's culture and the larger ones which surround it. It is implied, though, in suggestions that (1) the culture of poverty is most likely to manifest itself in a society which prizes thrift and upward mobility,[15] and that (2) a prominent characteristic of a particular poverty culture is its antipathy to the larger culture's values.[16]

In the data which were analyzed, five items tested the men's willingness to take jobs which would make certain demands upon them. If poverty induces attitudes similarly at variance with an achievement-oriented society's evaluation of work, it should also produce similar responses when people are asked to choose between work and certain other values.

Table 5 lists the items analyzed and variations in response to them. Public assistance recipients are ethnically distinct from each other in reported attitudes. Nonrecipients are not, in terms of statistical significance. Again, as with fatalistic attitudes, there is a suggestion that extent of deprivation among Negroes makes some difference in orientation. Two points are of special note about these findings. First is the high level of preference for taking and keeping jobs when such alternate values as friendship, easy work, familiar routines, and level of responsibility are considered. Second is the even higher degree of preference among public assistance recipients. Far from being content with living on welfare money and

TABLE 4. Fatalism and Alienation Among Low-Income Anglo, Spanish-speaking, and Negro Recipients and Nonrecipients of Public Assistance

Percent of Persons Agreeing with Item Among

	PUBLIC ASSISTANCE RECIPIENTS			NONRECIPIENTS		
	Anglo	Spanish-speaking	Negro	Anglo	Spanish-speaking	Negro
Fatalism items						
Planning only makes a person unhappy, since your plans hardly ever work out anyway.	55.0	69.2	66.7	50.0	70.5	56.0
It is always a good idea to put away some of your money for "a rainy day." (Percent disagree)	2.4	0.5	—	2.6	1.3	1.3
When a man is born, the success he is going to have is not already in the cards; each makes his own fate. (Percent disagree)	5.3	7.2	9.1	10.3	11.1	7.3
Nowadays, with world conditions the way they are, the wise persons lives for today and lets tomorrow take care of itself.	38.3	48.6	44.8	24.5	46.3	37.7
Average score for all items[a]	5.0	5.6	5.6	4.3	5.5	4.8
Alienation items						
In general, lots of things are going down hill. Lots of people have less chance than was true in the past.	54.1	53.8	51.5	33.5	49.8	37.1
Nobody cares whether you attend church or not except the clergy (ministers).	49.0	66.8	57.3	46.6	62.5	42.0
Cheating on income tax is nobody's business but the government's.	40.9	57.3	48.5	33.3	66.1	39.1
People who go out of their way to help a personal friend are usually disappointed.	47.4	56.0	74.8	39.9	57.3	59.7
Average score of all items	8.3	10.0	9.6	7.0	9.7	7.6

[a]Total scores may range from 1 to 17. All items were 5-point scales with "strongly disagree" and "strongly agree" on the extreme low and high point responses.

TABLE 5. Occupational Values Among Low-Income Anglo, Spanish-speaking, and Negro Recipients and Nonrecipients of Public Assistance

Percent of Persons Giving Positive Replies Among

	PUBLIC ASSISTANCE RECIPIENTS			NONRECIPIENTS		
	Anglo	Spanish-speaking	Negro	Anglo	Spanish-speaking	Negro
Would you take or stay in a job if it would require you to move around the country a lot?	36.8	40.6	46.1	31.7	42.9	44.7
Would you take or stay in a job if it would require you to leave your friends?	87.6	89.6	93.3	83.6	87.1	85.3
Would you take or stay in a job if it would mean you'd have to learn a new routine?	90.4	92.5	93.3	85.6	91.1	90.7
Would you take or stay in a job if it would mean you'd have to work harder than you are now (or harder than most)?	81.3	73.6	80.0	77.7	63.6	74.8
Would you take or stay in a job if it would mean you'd have to take on more responsibility?	84.2	80.1	87.8	87.6	76.9	83.4
Average score for all items[a]	8.1	7.9	8.4	7.9	7.8	8.0

[a]Total scores may range from 1 to 11. All items were 5-point scales with "would be less likely" and "wouldn't matter" as the extreme low and high point responses.

being unwilling to apply themselves, as they are often pictured, a large majority of men receiving AFDC-UP gave support to every job question but one. That single exception asked about willingness "to move around the country a lot," a condition very disruptive to established social and family relationships.

DISCUSSION

To recapitulate: It was found that, in 14 out of 16 tests, ethnic groups differed significantly from each other. Average scores for 8 of these 16 comparisons show differences of 10 percent or more between any two of the three ethnic groups. For example, in Table 2 each point in the range of average scores from 1 to 13 represents about an 8 percent difference. Therefore, a difference of 1 3/10 points in Table 2 scores represents about a 10 percent difference, and 3 of the 4 comparisons there are at least that large. In total, half of the tabulated average score comparisons indicate at least moderate divergence. There is much less similarity of viewpoint than the culture of poverty concept implies. Its tenability, as it has heretofore been used, is questionable. The null hypothesis stated at the beginning of this paper must be rejected.

It is striking to note that the Spanish-speaking have demonstrated most strongly the traits associated with the culture of poverty concept. In a slight majority of the comparisons Negroes were second, although their average scores tend to look more like those of the Anglos than of the Spanish-speaking. Taken together, these findings suggest that a systematic consideration of ethnic groups other than the Spanish-speaking might have led Lewis to different conclusions about the existence, scope, and intensity of the culture of poverty.

Besides ethnic variations, there are some consistent differences between assistance-recipient and nonrecipient men of the same ethnic groups. In particular, expressions of dependency feelings and behavior, fatalism, and alienation are higher among Anglo and Negro recipients than among their nonrecipient counterparts. These values are central to the culture of poverty concept and, while no significance tests are offered, the size and consistency of the differences warrant comment. The fact that there is little difference among the Spanish-speaking again suggests that the culture of poverty concept, largely developed through experience with persons of Latin American origin, may have limited general utility and should be re-examined.

It would seem more profitable to examine the impact of poverty, welfare dependency, and related phenomena on values and attitudes in the context of the particular cultures of interest. Perhaps, for some societies and ethnic groups, optimism and the belief in one's own efficacy are diminished by poverty but not necessarily reduced to a common level with the poor of all cultures. However, the evidence from the Spanish-speaking men warns against a too-general application of this idea since many of their attitudes were not noticeably altered by receipt of public assistance. Perhaps the language handicap in an English-speaking society was enough to make them fatalistic and dependent. Or are these attitudes general Latin cultural values?

There is no doubt that prolonged economic deprivation, wherever it occurs, influences many aspects of total life outlook as well as specific attitudes. The limited analysis reported here does, however, raise serious doubt that poverty overrides basic cultural orientations as an attitude and value determinant.

Conclusive evidence can, of course, come only from larger-scale, cross-societal studies. Such studies would need to include a wider variety of attitude areas, as well as family-life patterns and other behaviors. Other deprived ethnic and nationality groups should be included. Each should be similarly disadvantaged economically in a society where others are much more favored. A control group of higher-status persons should be included for each ethnic category. With such a design it would be possible to tell whether any similarities reflect a culture common to the poor or one more broadly based in individual societies.

NOTES

[1] Walter Miller, "Lower Class Culture as a Generating Milieu of Gang Delinquency," *Journal of Social Issues* 14 (July 1958), p. 5.

[2] Oscar Lewis, "The Culture of Poverty," *Scientific American* (October 1966), p. 19.

[3] Sponsored cooperatively by the Welfare Administration of U.S. Department of Health, Education, and Welfare (CRD Grant No. 207) and the California State Department of Social Welfare. Principal investigators were Robert C. Stone, San Francisco State College, and Frederic T. Schlamp, California State Department of Social Welfare. We are grateful to these investigators for making their data available to us.

[4] The proportion of respondents from rural and urban counties did, however, differ among ethnic groups. The rural counties contained 65 percent of the Spanish-speaking and 62 percent of the Anglos, but only 16 percent of the Negroes. This was not an important variable for the present analysis, since Lewis' theory specifically posits no differences between the poverty culture of rural and urban groups.

[5] For a detailed report of the design and findings of the study, see Robert C. Stone and Frederick T. Schlamp, "Characteristics Associated with Receipt or Non-receipt of Financial Aid from Welfare Agencies" *Welfare in Review* 3 (July 1963) pp. 1-11; and Robert C. Stone and Frederick T. Schlamp, *Family Life Styles Below the Poverty Line*, unpublished report to the State [California] Social Welfare Board from the Institute for Social Science Research, San Francisco State College, 1966.

[6] The Kruskal-Wallis one-way analysis of variance by ranks is a test for deciding whether K independent samples (in this case poor Anglo-Americans, Spanish-speaking Americans, and Negro-Americans) are from different populations. It requires at least ordinal measurement and assumes underlying continuous distribution of the variable being studies. Compared with the F-test under comparable conditions, the Kruskal-Wallis test has asympototic efficiency of $\frac{3}{\pi}$ = 95.5 percent. A brief discussion of it is found in Sidney Siegel, *Nonparametric Statistics* (New York: McGraw-Hill Book Co., 1956), pp. 184-194.

[7] Lewis has suggested that receipt of public assistance serves to perpetuate the culture of poverty. See Oscar Lewis, *La Vida* (New York: Random House, 1965), pp. xlv, xlvi; his unpublished report to the Social Security and Welfare Administration, *The Culture of Poverty in Puerto Rico and in New York* (Cooperative Research Grant No. 127), p. 8; and Lewis, 1966, *op. cit.*, p. 21.

[8] Oscar Lewis, "The Culture of Poverty," in TePaske and Fisher (eds.) *Explosive Forces in Latin America* (Columbus: Ohio State University Press, 1964), p. 154; Lewis, 1965, *op. cit.*, p. xlvii; and Lewis, 1966, *op. cit.*, p. 23.

[9] These scales were drawn from Arthur Lamphere, "The Relationship between Dependency Factors and Goal Setting in Duodenal Ulcer Patients," unpublished Ph.D. dissertation, University of Washington, 1953. Items were originally selected on the basis of judgment by clinical psychologists.

[10] Lewis, 1964, *op. cit.*, p. 153; Lewis, 1965, *op. cit.*, p. xlvii; and Lewis, 1966, *op. cit.*, p. 23.

[11] Primacy of family of orientation and attitudes toward child autonomy were measured by items taken from the Parental Attitude Research Instrument developed by Earl Schaefer and Richard Bell, "Development of a Parental Attitude Research Instrument," *Child Development* (September 1958). Beliefs about responsibility for child behavior were assessed by applying the scale reported by Gildea, Glidewell, and Kantor in "Maternal Attitudes and General Adjustment in School Children," in John C. Glidewell (ed.) *Parental Attitudes and Child Behavior* (Springfield, Illinois: Charles C. Thomas, 1961).

[12] Lewis, 1964, *op. cit.*, p. 153; Lewis, 1963, *op. cit.*, p. xlviii; and Lewis, 1966, *op. cit.*, p. 23.

[13] Lewis, 1964, *op. cit.*, p. 154; Lewis, 1965, *op. cit.*, p. xlvi; and Lewis, 1966, *op. cit.*, p. 23.

[14] The tetrachoric intercorrelations of these items are all positive, but fairly low.

[15] Lewis, 1965, *op. cit.*, p. xliii, xliv; and Lewis, 1966, *op. cit.*, p. 21.

[16] Lewis, 1964, *op. cit.*, p. 154; Lewis, 1965, *op. cit.*, p. xlvi; and Lewis, 1966, *op. cit.*, p. 23.

32
jewish student activism

JACK NUSAN PORTER

Jewish students, like other students, are disenchanted with the world as they find it; and they blame their parents for its condition. Ideological generation splits are no new thing to Judaism; the second generation of American immigrants broke with their parents, if not physically, certainly in values and life-styles. Many left Judaism entirely, many in all-but-nominal ways. Not until this first American-born generation had children did they begin to raise questions about their Jewish identity.

This is the group that has succeeded economically, has been the mainstay of liberal politics, and whose children are now reevaluating traditional Jewish values to fit into the modern scene.

The Jewish community is small, and Jewish parents are concerned about and influenced by their children. Jewish students are a larger proportion of students than the Jews are of the population; therefore, what goes on among the small group of radical students described below will have greater repercussions than their number would indicate.

Mr. Porter is assistant professor of sociology at the State University of New York at Cortland.

All action has been speeded up during this past decade. Social upheaval has occurred at an unprecedented level. In fact, it is both fascinating and frightening to note what changes can take place in simply one year. For example, in the winter 1969 issue of *Judaism,* two articulate Jewish intellectuals, Milton Himmelfarb and Prof. Leonard Fein, both wrote articles despairing of the role and identity of Jewish students and disparaging the role and duties of the Jewish "establishment." They were right on target as to the failings of the latter, but as for the former, neither of them foresaw the changes that were to take place among Jewish college students. As a graduate student myself at an "elite"

Midwestern university, I have seen a transformation take place.

Fein, however, did delineate the dilemmas confronting Jewish identity and he is correct—there are serious conflicts between being a Jew and being an intellectual; between being a Jew and being a student; between being a Jew and being a pants' manufacturer's son; and yes, between being a Jew and being a radical.

Fein furthermore, is correct in his view that the Jewish "establishment" is patronizing and self-serving in its dealings with Jewish young people. It is true, as he stated, that

we have tended not to take the kinds of problems that students have very seriously . . . we have tried to convert the student to a Judaism organized in forms which have little to do with his position and with his understanding. Nei-

Reprinted from *Jewish Currents* (May 1970), pp. 28-34. Reproduced by permission of the author and publisher.

ther defense nor fund-raising are the sorts of things to inspire a student. . . .

These statements point out the serious gap in communication and education between our generations. How does one bridge the gap? Unfortunately, both Fein and Himmelfarb offer very few concrete solutions. Himmelfarb, for example, feels that increased proselytism and intermarriage will turn the trick. This, as he says, will be "furiously controversial" and will "shake up" both synagogue and community center. Himmelfarb is, sadly, off base and, moreover, he badly misgauges the temper of the present Jewish youth culture. As for Fein, he is more cautious in his proposals and I respect him for this, but he, too, like many social scientists, is a poor prophet. However, Fein did put his finger on an important topic —the need for "Jewish identity projects," serious introspection into the Jewish student psyche. One needs fewer symposia, and more innovative, imaginative and, yes, *radical* programs.

The gist of my argument is simply that both Fein, Himmelfarb and nearly every other Jewish commentator failed to predict the militant mood of many of today's Jewish college students, especially among a growing radical vanguard that will directly influence modern Jewish institutions. Only "repression," which is unlikely among libertarian Jews, or apathy, which is a distinct possibility, on the part of the over-40 (I upped the age) generation will "kill" this movement. I am even optimistic enough to predict that the movement will succeed despite these obstacles and disabilities.

What really happened this past year—1969? Stated simply, the following occurred: What the parents forgot, the children wanted to remember! If the second generation was interested in "making it," financially and socially, and wanted their Judaism reduced to a sparseness that would be parallel to their lifestyle, the third generation (and even fourth) wants to reconstitute Judaism with vigor and pride. This has occurred not only because Judaism is "in" today, even campy; no, it goes even deeper. There is a sincere desire on the students' part not only re-educate themselves, but to go two steps further—to re-educate their elders and to re-educate the gentile. In doing so, they hope to transform the Jewish community.

The rise of such activism stems directly out of the swirl of social movements that envelop our society. The Jew is a product of his age and reflects its madness, its idealism and its love of freedom.

The following are posited as "theories" as to why Jewish activism arose in the latter half of this decade:

a. The spread of racial and ethnic chauvinism
b. The Israeli-Arab Six-Day War and its influence
c. The impact of the New Left and general student unrest
d. Anti-Zionist and Anti-Semitic postures in the New Left
e. The abhorrence of middle-class, middle-brow Jewishness (not Judaism, if the distincition can be understood)

Let's take these issues one by one.

Racial pride and ethnic pride, whether it be among blacks, Indians, Mexicans or Puerto Ricans, have influenced and laid the foundation for Jewish "nationalism," Jewish pride and the cries of Jewish "power." The rise of the Jewish Student Movement at Northwestern University (one of the first), the Jewish Liberation Project in New York, the Jewish Radical Union in Berkeley, and similar groups at UCLA, CCNY, University of Chicago, University of Illinois and Columbia among others is a manifestation of today's "new" radical Jew. Other radical and/or socialist organizations that should be included are Habonim, Students for Israel, Havurah, the Jews for Urban Justice and the representatives of the University Service department of the Jewish Agency. Even the names of their journals and newspapers give notice of their ideals: *The Jewish Radical, Jewish Liberation Journal, Flame, Other Stand, Ha-Orah (The Light), Jewish Urban Guerilla, Response, Echo* and the *Jewish Peace Fellowship Newsletter.*

The list is extensive and growing; it is what sociologists can rightly label a *movement.* It has already had an exhilarating effect upon the American Jewish community. Yet as I have emphasized, it has its roots in the drive for freedom among oppressed groups in this country and, particularly, in the new racial pride of black people. The reasoning goes as follows: when blacks began to look to their collective past, to their historical roots, and to their culture, they implicitly asked each American to seek and understand his own roots, his own culture and his own past. Afro-Americans directed white and brown people to do this so that the latter could better comprehend the black man's own search for manhood and dignity in "Babylon."

Therefore, one sees militant Indians "on the warpath"; Mexicans organizing behind Cesar Chavez; and Puerto Ricans organizing into radical groups. Whether these movements will lead to further divisiveness and hatred is not the point for now—what is essential is that it is happening to Jews. And some may ask— why not?

Such stirrings have brought fear and apprehension. Some have labeled it a "revolution"—yet it is a revolution of values, a dramatic return to the cultural pluralism that is essentially America. The "beef stew analogy" of Leonard Fein is apt here. We are all individual components composing a very "sloppy, messy, but tasty dish" called the U.S.A. The present Jewish radical is a product of this cultural pluralism.

The Israeli-Arab Six-Day War in June, 1967 shocked many people, and they were not all Arabs either. This war also awakened an entire generation to the possibility that Israel could be destroyed. One must remember that the present Jewish college student population (age 18-24) has *never* known what it was like *not* to have the presence of a Jewish State, and they had begun simply to take it for granted. To them, unlike their elders who had suffered through Auschwitz, Babi Yar and finally the creation of a Jewish homeland, Israel had "always" existed. They needed a jolt, and they received it in the early dawn of June 5, 1967.

Hundreds wished to emigrate, make *aliyah*; thousands attended rallies and donated money, and waited for Israel to survive. This "jolt" carried over into the school year in the fall of 1967 and into 1968. It was like tinderwood waiting for a spark to touch it off into an acclamation of pro-Jewish and pro-Zionist sentiment. The Six-Day War then was a catalyst for the latent feelings of Jewish pride and identity that were bubbling beneath the surface. These feelings developed slowly, but were nurtured by the violence and tumult of the years between 1967-1970.

One parenthetical influence of Israel and its militancy: fear of violence among Diaspora Jews. For years the Jew was portrayed as a pathetic, frightened proprietor. While this is still relatively true, a significant portion of young Jews have conquered their fear of bloodshed, of the gun and the rock. One has only to mention that a *third* of the SDS Weathermen arrested in their confrontation with police were *Jewish,* and of these there were a disproportionate number of Jewish *women.* The resort to violence is a manifestation of the violent climate in America, yet it is an acclamation of the gun-toting Jew represented by Warsaw Ghetto fighters and Israeli paratroopers. I am not so bold as to compare Jewish partisans to Jewish Weathermen, for the comparison is unfair to the memory of the former, yet this acquiescence to violence by the "new" Jew is obviously not a historical quirk. The Dayan image of cool unruffled force is a two-edged sword. It provokes both fear and adulation. For Jews these are ambivalent feelings, yet conquering the fear of violence is a healthy sign. Jewish radical groups arose to meet this challenge. What exactly happened between the years 1967 to now in 1970?

These years found America with more bloodshed, riot, rebellion, and revolt than any in this century. The cries of Black Power sprang up in 1967 when Stokely Carmichael crusaded in the South and the consequences of this movement surfaced at the August, 1967 Conference on New Politics in Chicago. This convention of leftist groups in America cleared the air between black and white radicals, and Jews at the conference had to make a painful decision and a more painful rerouting of their position. This event is a landmark in the history of U.S. radicalism. (See Jack Weinman's fine article in *Jewish Currents,* Dec., 1967).

What occurred to Jews was the following: one, they were no longer welcome in the Black Power Movement. If they wished to do "something," they would *now* have to do it among their *own people* (i.e., among whites). Two, they knew that they would face (at least in the form of verbal abuse) anti-Zionist, anti-Israel and even anti-Semitic rhetoric from black and white radicals. What was to occur was common in the Jewish tradition: the struggle between the universalism of radical/socialist thought and the particularism of one's Judaism and concern for Jews. However, it is more subtle. Radical Jews began to feel the "pinch" of their more liberal, more conservative, and more reactionary coreligionists, who had come under attack as avaricious ghetto slumlords and merchants by militant black and white radicals (including Jews).

Thus, many young Jewish activists were caught in a bind between one's professed ideals of freedom for all and one's concern for one's fellow Jews, especially those who were not "living up" to the noble and prophetic vision of Judaism. Student unrest, led mainly by SDS, had begun to increase rapidly during this period. There were arrests, marches, broken windows and busted heads. Students, many of them Jews, began to understand what it was like to be "niggers"—to feel oppression, fear and hatred.

White radicals began to relate to the new emerging black struggle, that of the Newark rebellion of 1967, Detroit in 1968, the killing of Martin Luther King, the exile of Black Panther leader Eldridge Cleaver, the jailing of other Black Panthers, the gun-toting of Cornell black students. The mood was increasingly militant. Jews felt that they too had to respond to this newly articulated violence. The goal was to develop a militancy that would appeal to young Jews as well as be a forum for Jewish radicals in their confrontation with the sterility of the Jewish "establishment" and the ignorance and/or naiveté of the black and the SDSer.

The irrationality of this era, at times, led radical groups to take stands and present ideological positions that are neither correct nor productive, i.e., the status of Israel as an imperialist nation. As the *Jewish Radical* stated in an editorial (Jan., 1969):

> . . . *One of the reasons that so many of us came together to start this paper was a growing concern with our radical communities' increasingly anti-Israel posture. As radicals we find this inappropriate, at best. We believe that the easy acceptance of empty metaphors and lack of desire to make meaningful distinctions between vague analogies concerning the Middle East does irreparable damage to the morality of the movement.*

However, for the sake of revolutionary solidarity and Third World rhetoric, black and white radicals have taken anti-Israel and anti-Semitic stances. Jewish student movements have arisen to meet this challenge, to correct and refute these ideologies, and to seek a *rapprochement* with such revolutionaries. Furthermore, when "real" anti-Semitism might raise its head, Jewish radical groups can easily mobilize into defense groups to neutralize such action. For the time being, Jewish radicals will take what is *good* from blacks and SDSers, but will reject what is *bad,* i.e., any invalid anti-Israel or anti-Jewish positions.

Unlike liberal Jews, radical Jews are not afraid of using militant tactics, nor will they "throw the baby out with the bath water." They will condemn Jewish slumlords, but will support Black Power demands of, let us say, more jobs, better housing, community control of schools, police, and political structures. They will denounce the New Left's biased account of Zionism, yet will seek a homeland for the Arab Palestinians. The will denounce the Jewish establishment, yet will work within the Jewish structure to change it.

SDS's *New Left Notes,* the Weathermen's *Fire,* the Black Muslims' *Muhammed Speaks,* the Black Panther paper, plus the house organs of Progressive Labor, the Young Socialist Alliance, Youth Against War and Fascism, and others—all contain biased and unbalanced accounts of Jews and Israel. These statements must be met vigorously with a more balanced picture. However, the goals and ideals of the Black Panther Party, SDS, or the Black Muslims, those goals that are within the prophetic vision of Judaism, must be supported by radical Jewish groups, and indeed they are, to the astonishment and trepidation of many Jewish liberals in Hadassah, B'nai B'rith and the Jewish Welfare Boards.

The final theory (or theoretical perspective) explaining why Jewish students are forming activist groups on campus is their distaste for their elders' life-styles. Though there are many fine Jewish parents who attempt an imaginative and provocative left-liberal lifestyle, there are far too many of the type found in a Philip Roth novella, Brenda Patemkin's parents in *Goodbye, Columbus*. This is manifested as a revolt against the ostentatiousness of a Miami Beach or a Grossingers; the traumatic vulgarity of a Jewish wedding or bar mitzvah; the single-minded pursuit of materialism of a parent that, in one generation, has moved from a Newark to a Scarsdale or from a Rogers Park to a Skokie.

The available alternatives for a young Jewish person coming out of this environment are few; to join a commune in Haight-Ashbury; to be in the streets with a rock in one's hand ready for the "pigs," or simply to get a degree, a wife, a job, a career, a split-level and a mahjong game, and move right back into that sterile suburb. However, an alternative to all of this is to become a Jewish radical. Happily, this is being done today.

These then are five theories that can explain the drive toward Jewish activism. There are others, but these are the major ones. However, what has passed is only intellectual exercise.

Let me conclude this article with what Jews call *tachlis,* which can be defined as the Protestant ethic of putting ideas into action. In short, what does a Jewish activist do? what does a Jewish activist movement do?

First, like all good radicals, one must first *talk,* and then talk some more. A dialogue with the Jewish community must begin, goals must be articulated, for this is a new phenomenon, a new movement. Let me speak then about the Jewish Student Movement in Chica-

go since I know it best. Unlike many "establishment" Jewish groups, what such movements *idealize* and what they *do* are identical. The following are the goals of the JSM (in the form of our program):

1. We first recognize that we have not been educated properly as Jews. Our lack of education has weakened our identity, and because action must be based on knowledge, we therefore must re-educate ourselves.

2. We will continue to work for humane, just, and right causes, and we will identify as Jews with other movements striving to improve society, because 4,000 years of prophetic tradition demand that we do so.

3. We recognize and actively support the integral role that the State of Israel plays in the life of the Jewish people. In addition, we will not identify with or join with any groups that argue for the destruction of the State of Israel.

4. We feel that we can help ourselves and our Jewish brothers all over the world by building a strong, united American Jewish community.

5. We welcome the support of non-Jews in our struggle if they concur with our goals and means.

6. Similar movements are now arising on other campuses. We must establish and maintain close contact with them to achieve our common aims.

These then are the goals of a typical Jewish activist group. It is similar to many such groups throughout the country. But what do we do? Sartre is correct: our actions determine our life.

Here is a recent sampling: a picketing of the French consulate in the winter of 1968 protesting de Gaulle's anti-Israel policies; a vigil and a protest on campus to mourn the hanging murder of nine Jews by the Iraqi government; a continuing local struggle over our university's consistent policy of scheduling school registration and orientation on Jewish holidays; this led to the first "Jewish sit-in" in the 1960's in the dean's office in the spring of 1969 over a Jewish issue, not an SDS one (the struggle continues since the administration has done nothing); and last, an involvement in the controversy in Chicago between exploitive Jewish contract-housing sellers/realtors and their black victims.

Our re-education process is undertaken by weekly seminars given by *our* members to *our* members. We educate ourselves. We have the task of destroying the myths upon which we have been brought up. We, like the blacks, need a new look at our history and image. Furthermore, armed with facts and vigor, we have sent student speakers to Jewish fraternities, sororities, temples, men's clubs, luncheons, and even mah-jong socials, and we have left our audiences impressed.

A dialogue began. Such events are occurring elsewhere and are garnering a great deal of publicity. One need only see the coverage in *Newsweek* Dec. 8, 1969 for a description of the confrontation in Boston between Jewish activists and the leaders of the national welfare funds.

We are now preparing for an even more difficult decade, the 1970's, and Jewish radicalism must meet the challenge. As we enter this new decade, we, the products of our age, must dare to struggle for a new self, a new manhood, a new Jew. We have joined with our Jewish brothers in movements elsewhere in a solidarity that will bring grace and strength to Jews in America.

Hippies may be "dead," yet people have become hip; SDS may be "dying," yet people have become radicalized; God may be "dead," yet people have faith; Judaism may be "dying," yet young Jews have begun to rejuvenate it, as young Jews have begun to vitalize secular Jewishness too.

33
ethnic-group cohesion

J. T. BORHEK

This article should be read in conjunction with Nathan Glazer's essay (Chapter 46). Mr. Borhek's research shows that education breaks down ethnic-group boundaries more effectively than anything else, although they are maintained to some extent by physical isolation. Mr. Glazer indicates that the culture of some ethnic groups operates to prevent their using educational institutions, and thus, if Mr. Borhek is right, retards assimilation. In one way or another this entire book addresses itself to the problem of which is most desirable: assimilation or cultural pluralism. As with all value questions, the individual (in this case, the student) must make up his own mind.

Mr. Borhek teaches sociology at the University of Arizona.

This study develops a model to explain variation in two measures of the breakdown of the structural and cultural boundaries of a large and, as yet, basically unassimilated white ethnic minority group.[1]

The structure and persistence of ethnic communities have been the subject of much attention by sociologists, and there is a large and well-known literature in the area. In this literature, there is a remarkable lack of system in language which mirrors a plethora of concepts related to the problem of the viability of group structure and culture. What in some studies is called a high (or low) state of assimilation is called, in other studies, a low (or high) state of cohesiveness, solidarity, group morale, acculturation, or integration.

The problem of the viability of group structure and culture is complex for more than just semantic reasons. At base the problem is the simple and familiar one of the use of a single term to denote quite discrete phenomena, coupled with the use of numerous terms to denote a single phenomenon—hence the tendency noted by Gross and Martin (1957)

Reprinted from the *American Journal of Sociology* 76, no. 1 (July 1970), pp. 33-45. Reproduced by permission of the author and publisher.

for nominal and operational definitions not to square with each other.

In this study I refer to the problem of maintenance of the integrity of group boundaries as the problem of cohesion, and to the process by which the boundaries of ethnic groups are broken down as one of assimilation. Assimilationism, then, is a set of attitudes favorable to assimilation and hence inimical to cohesion.

There are essentially two general models of the process by which ethnic and other groups first lose cohesiveness and finally their entire identity, although these have been elaborated into many subtypes by various authors.[2]

1. A Model Based Upon Attitudes Favorable Or Unfavorable to the Group. Cartwright and Zander (1960), among others, define cohesiveness as: "the attractiveness of a group for its members." For this model, appearance of attitudes unfavorable to the group is a sign of decreasing cohesiveness, and high consensus on group norms is a sign of high cohesiveness. Factors which lead members to dispute the basic tenets of group belief are regarded as sources of lowered cohesion (Rose 1949,

1952, 1965, pp. 674-704; Park 1924; Gordon 1964).

2. A Model Based Upon Involvement and Interaction. It is assumed that the penetration of outside institutions by group members and the consequent formation of intimate personal relations outside the group weaken group structure. It is assumed that persons with intimate personal relations outside the group are less committed and more likely to defect. Factors which lead members to form close ties with persons outside the group are regarded as sources of lowered cohesion (Cartwright and Zander 1960; Seashore 1954; Pepitone and Kleiner 1957; Gordon 1964). Because sociometric models of this type have been used rather indiscriminately, it should be pointed out that they assume that the member has a good deal of choice in the persons with whom he forms primary relations. In the case of many types of natural groups—for instance, ethnic groups—this may not be true. There may be constraints of many kinds placed upon the member. Used by themselves, sociometric models are probably not altogether adequate for groups in which membership is not voluntary and which may put restraints upon the range of a member's outside associations.

There are many studies of ethnic minority communities and immigrants. Recent studies have tended to focus on the assimilation of the immigrant into the new society (Campisi 1948; Eisenstadt 1951, 1952a, 1952b; Jones 1950; Taft 1961; Richardson 1961). The older, Chicago-style studies focused on the minority community itself, and all were at least secondarily concerned with the problem of the maintenance of a viable group (Bogardus 1943; Brown and Roucek 1945; Finkelstein 1949; Hughes 1943; Kosa 1957; Miyamoto 1939; Park and Burgess 1924; Poll 1962; Warner and Srole 1945; Thomas and Nishimoto 1952; Young 1931; Young 1932). This literature suggests that increasing social differentiation leads to a decrease in ethnic-community cohesiveness. Increasing differentiation in status, in the number of types of positions members occupy, in the division of labor, in residential-area type, and in religious affiliation all lead to

decreases in consensus on aspirations and norms and eventually to the dissolution of the group. This literature consists, for the most part, of case studies, and case studies seem to have as an inherent trait that they lead researchers to conclude that a large number of variables acting independently contribute in an additive manner to the observed effect. My original hypotheses were derived from this literature and were quite simple: any index of increasing or increased social differentiation should be associated with primary relations outside the group and with lack of enthusiasm for ethnic culture, and any variation in the two types of cohesion I was able to explain would be explained by a fairly large number of variables acting independently and in sum.

THE STUDY

The study was carried out over a three-year period from 1963 to 1966 and is a stratified, systematic sample survey of adult Ukrainian-Canadians chosen from voting registration lists in the province of Alberta. In Canada, the best source of samples of adults is the comprehensive voting registration list. Ukrainians were identified by name from the voting registration lists by a panel of judges. Interviewing proved that errors in name identification were no more than 10 percent. Most Ukrainian names end with the syllable "uk" and are therefore easy to recognize. Errors of identification occurred in the cases in which Ukrainians share names with other Slavs. The sample of 809 was stratified to produce a rough balance in terms of age and sex, urban and rural residence.[3]

Ukrainian-Canadians are not a new immigrant group of the type studied by Eisenstadt (1951) or by Taft (1961) and Richardson (1961), but an "old" immigrant group now beginning its fourth generation in a society which is officially pluralistic. The respondents live in a province which is ethnically heterogeneous and in which it would be difficult to specify the characteristics of the mass culture into which they might be absorbed were some kind of melting-pot model applicable. As Vallee, Schwartz, and Darknell (1957) and Porter (1965) have pointed out, however, there are some serious objections to the application of this model to Canada.

The respondents were drawn from three small towns and a city of 400,000.[4] Two of the three small towns are predominantly Ukrainian in population; the city and one small town are ethnically heterogeneous. In addition to Ukrainians, there are German, Dutch, and Italian minorities of substantial size and high definition. The melting pot may occur in the future despite the official pluralism of Canada, but the present reality is a mosaic with clear social boundaries between Jew and Gentile, German and Italian, Ukrainian and Dutchman, "Frenchman" and "Englishman." In addition to restriction of interaction and pressures against intermarriage between members of different ethnic communities, there is a certain amount of residential segregation in Edmonton. Although the term "ghetto" is not applicable, areas of the city do have reputations for being German, Italian, Ukrainian, or Jewish; and a check of the voting registration list does show heavy concentrations of ethnically identifiable names. It would be a serious error to draw a parallel between the white ethnic structures of Canada and the United States and to equate the Ukrainian-Canadian community with, let us say, the Polish-American community (see Porter 1965, pp. 68 ff.). The Ukrainian community in Canada is essentially unassimilated. Ukrainian culture flourishes in the new country. Ukrainian is heard on the streets and in the pubs of all western cities and is almost the exclusive language of many small towns. The prairies are dotted with the domed churches and double-barred crosses of the Eastern churches, and the Dionysian wedding customs of the eastern European peasantry persist and form almost the entire social life of many small Alberta towns. Ethnic restaurants and groceries are present and are treated in a sense quite different from that implied by a self-conscious "return" to ethnic identity (see Herberg 1960). Ethnic fraternal and cultural associations exist and are very active. Extremely acidic political and religious conflicts still persist between first- and second- generation Ukrainian-Canadians who are leftist or rightist vis-à-vis the Ukraine.

Ukrainian immigrants to Canada have been predominantly either farmers or unskilled laborers; very few have been skilled laborers or professionals. The vast majority of these immigrants settled in the prairie provinces. Now in its fourth generation, the Ukrainian community has penetrated all levels of the stratification system, but Ukrainians are proportionately slightly underrepresented in all categories of white-collar, business, and professional work and heavily overrepresented among farmers and farm workers (Hobart 1968, p. 135; Dominion Bureau of Statistics 1961).

We are dealing with an established ethnic group which has maintained cultural and structural autonomy, and we are concerned with the sources of pressures toward breaking down this autonomy which emanate from within the group.

DEPENDENT VARIABLES
Assimilationism

Models of group cohesion which are based upon consensus concerning the worth of the group are relatively easy to apply through the use of attitude devices. The respondent's enthusiasm for Ukrainian culture, or the lack of such enthusiasm, was measured by a simple three-item device. In each question the respondent was offered a pair of alternatives, one pole of which implied a willingness to abandon ethnic norms and the other, unwillingness. The items were limited to simple alternatives because interviews were conducted in both English and Ukrainian and items of this type present no difficulties in translation.

1. Some of our customs should no longer be practiced because they delay acceptance of Ukrainians into Canadian society. Do you agree or disagree?
2. Do you think that intermarriage between Ukrainians and non-Ukrainians should be discouraged?
3. How do you feel about Ukrainians changing their names to English names? Do you feel it is:
   a. never justified

b. justified if the person's success in his work depends on it
c. up to the individual

A respondent who answered "agree" to question 1 or "disagree" to question 2, or who agreed with part b or c of question 3, will hereafter be called an Assimilationist, and we will call the device Assimilationism. Assimilationism is not a scale. We are identifying as Assimilationists anyone who responded in an assimilationist direction on any of the three questions. Slightly over 35 percent of the respondents are Assimilationists.

Ingroup Choice

Models of group cohesion based upon involvement of members with each other or with outsiders assume that intimate ties outside the group indicate lowered cohesion. These models may be operationalized with one of the sociometric questions. In this case we asked the respondents: "Think of your three best friends; how many are Ukrainians?" If the respondent's three best friends were all Ukrainians, he will be described as having had high Ingroup Choice. If the respondent named one or more non-Ukrainians among the three, he will be described as having had low Ingroup Choice. About 30 percent of the sample have low Ingroup Choice.

INDEPENDENT VARIABLES

The literature generally suggests that a large number of variables indicative of social differentiation should be associated with the two models of cohesion, each contributing independently to a total effect. The populations studied derive from a rural, farm base, wtih low levels of education. Any variable describing movement away from this type of population toward a relatively more educated urban population of heterogeneous occupational status should be associated with assimilationist attitudes and primary relations outside group boundaries. This is not, in fact, the case. Either the Ukrainian population does not conform to the pattern observed in other studies or social differentiation does not directly lead to loss of cohesion. The model which develops to explain variation in the two

dependent variables is quite different from a simple additive model and includes only four variables: occupational status, farm or non-farm labor (hereafter called workplace), residence in an ethnically heterogeneous or homogeneous community (hereafter called residential site), and years of formal education. Furthermore, as will be shown, these variables do not function as would be expected on the basis of previous literature.[5]

A fairly wide range of variables has no independent effect on either dependent variable. Apparent relationships between various indicators of both intra- and intergenerational social mobility and the dependent variables are a product of maldistributions of occupational status and education. Geographical mobility and changing from a traditional to a nontraditional church are unrelated to either Ingroup Choice or Assimilationism. Peculiarly, even generation, which would seem to be an indirect indicator of widely variant cultural experiences, is negligibly related to either dependent variable once residential site and education are controlled. Apparent relationships between urban or rural residence and the two dependent variables seem to be a result of the operation of residential site.[6] Only four variables seem to be independently related to the dependent variables.

Occupational Status

High occupational status describes respondents who held white-collar jobs if they were nonfarm laborers, or farmed five-eighths of a section (400 acres) or more if they were farmers. Low occupational status refers to respondents who held skilled, semiskilled, or unskilled jobs if they were nonfarm laborers, or farmed less than five-eighths of a section if they were farmers. Our decision to classify farmers as having higher or lower status on the basis of the number of acres farmed is an arbitrary one. All the farmer respondents listed themselves as "general farmers" but devoted a large percentage of their acreage to grains. Farmer stratification in the northern Great Plains areas is exceedingly complex and involves a number of purely noneconomic variables. It is "better," for instance, to farm wheat for profit than to run grain through pigs, although the latter is more profitable and infinitely safer. Although we have only very indirect evidence, we suspect that prairie farmers acquiesce in the romantic myth of being wheat farmers in good years but are rational enough to hedge their bets with other crops such as oil grains for the normally bad years. Although a wide spectrum of information was available, it seemed that the number of acres farmed was the best single indicator of a large number of other status variables.

Residential Sites

The sample was drawn from a middle-sized city and three small towns in its hinterland. Two of the small towns come close to being ethnically homogeneous—they are Ukrainian towns in the most important sense —one could probably survive better without English than without Ukrainian. The larger city and the smallest of the towns are ethnically heterogeneous. The distinction made in this analysis is between residence in a homogeneous community and residence in a heterogeneous community. Residential site seems to account for almost all of the observed relationships between "urban" and "rural" residence and the two dependent variables.

Workplace

We distinguish between farm and non-farm labor. This distinction is between respondents who make their living from farming or from other sources regardless of residence on farms, in the small towns, or in the city. This variable was discovered accidentally but seems to operate independently although at relatively low power.

Education

Education refers to formal years of schooling. The sample includes both native- and foreign-born respondents, and every attempt was made to equate European with Canadian schooling. Nevertheless, a number of respondents were dropped from the analysis at this point because their education in Europe simply could not be equated with anything in the Canadian system. High education describes respondents who had some high school or more. Low education describes

those who had less. The distinction between high and low was made to maximize cell size rather than for theoretical reasons. A more detailed breakdown of education strengthens rather than weakens the association between education and the two dependent variables which is described in the following text.

PROCEDURES

The analysis of data proceeds by multivariate analysis of dichotomous attributes according to the model developed by Coleman (Coleman 1964, esp. pp. 193-213).[7] This procedure is analogous to multiple regression but was designed for dichotomous attributes and is a vast improvement over the always tricky, frustrating, and uncertain process of visual inspection of a highly detailed percentage table involving two, three, or four independent variables. This technique permits analysis of departures from multivariate additive effects by providing both observed and expected cell frequencies; that is, it identifies interaction effects. Departures from additivity manifest themselves in discrepancies between observed and expected frequencies. Because the relationships between three of the four independent variables and the two dependent variables are not simple additive relationships, detailed percentage tables will be presented for illustration. The amount of variation explained is based on weighted estimates due to the small size of many of the cells in the total tables (Coleman 1964, pp. 203-4). This procedure seems superior to visual inspection for a number of reasons, not the least of which is that in measuring effects it provides a precise summary statement of results.

It is, of course, true that any classification or categorization of data destroys something—if only the rawness of the data. All the variables used in this analysis could have been presented in three or more categories. However, if this had been done, we would be back to trying to understand a very complex percentage table with many small cells, and the more powerful Coleman procedure would have had to be abandoned. It was decided to dichotomize all the variables and trade the loss of detail for more powerful analytic tech-

TABLE 1. Four Variables on Assimilationism

	HIGH OCCUPATIONAL STATUS		LOW OCCUPATIONAL STATUS	
	% high assimilationism	Total N	% high assimilationism	Total N
Heterogeneous[a]–farm[b]				
High education	40	15	24	25
Low education	0	2	6	18
Homogeneous–farm				
High education	49	45	42	97
Low education	20	5	16	31
Heterogeneous–nonfarm				
High education	37	72	26	154
Low education	0	6	11	88
Homogeneous–nonfarm				
High education	65	60	53	47
Low education	0	4	21	33

[a]Residential.
[b]Workplace.

TABLE 2. Four Variables on Ingroup Choice

	HIGH OCCUPATIONAL STATUS		LOW OCCUPATIONAL STATUS	
	% low ingroup choice	Total N	% low ingroup choice	Total N
Heterogeneous[a]–farm[b]				
High education	35	23	27	15
Low education	0	2	12	17
Homogeneous–farm				
High education	20	46	19	99
Low education	40	5	7	28
Heterogeneous–nonfarm				
High education	54	72	40	52
Low education	0	6	13	83
Homogeneous–nonfarm				
High education	35	60	15	47
Low education	20	5	18	33

[a]Residential site.
[b]Workplace.

niques. Dichotomization is a conservative adaptation in the case of these data. It does not mask any peculiarities in the relationships but tends to show them as less powerful than they would appear with more categories of each variable.

Table 1 is a total percentage table for Assimilationism and the independent variables. Table 2 is a total table for Ingroup Choice and the independent variables. Table 3 presents data for the analysis of dichotomous attributes.

TABLE 3. Effects of Four Variables on Assimilationism and Ingroup Choice

Variable	Effect on assimilationism	z	Effect on ingroup choice	z
Occupational status	0.054	2.39	0.033	1.29
Workplace	0.058	1.62	0.058	1.67
Residential site	0.181	5.03	0.098	2.88
Education	0.329	8.73	0.254	8.93
% of variation explained	62.314	–	44.392	–

ANALYSIS OF DATA
Occupational Status

When education, workplace, and residential site are controlled, occupational status explains a little over 5 percent of the variation in Assimilationism. This general finding is somewhat misleading, however, because there is a fairly marked relationship between high occupational status and high Assimilationism among the highly educated. Among the less-educated, however, high or low occupational status is unrelated to Assimilationism.

Occupational status explains only a little over 3 percent of the variation in Ingroup Choice, but again the relationship is one in which high occupational status is associated with low Ingroup Choice among the highly educated; among the less-educated there is no relationship between occupational status and having primary relations outside the group.

Generally, occupational status is a variable which operates only in the presence of high education but explains more than a negligible amount of the variation in the two dependent variables.

Workplace

Nonfarm labor explains 6 percent of the variation in both Assimilationism and Ingroup Choice with the other variables controlled. Workplace is not a powerful predictor of Assimilationism but seems strongest among respondents with high education living in ethnically homogeneous areas—nonfarm labor being associated with high Assimilationism when the other variables are controlled. Workplace predicts Ingroup Choice best among the highly educated—nonfarm labor being associated with low Ingroup Choice.

Residential Site

With the other variables controlled, residential site explains 18 percent of the variation in Assimilationism and 10 percent of the variation in Ingroup Choice. Living in an ethnically homogeneous area is associated with Assimilationist attitudes, and living in an ethnically heterogeneous area is associated with having non-Assimilationist attitudes. The relationship is most pronounced among the respondents with high education. There is nothing in previous literature on ethnic communities which would lead one to expect this; yet residential site explains a substantial amount of the variation in Assimilationism. The "city as melting pot" is a theory as old as interethnic contact and implies that cultural breakdown occurs in interethnic or cross-cultural contact. These data suggest the opposite, or at least suggest that the process is not as simple as it has been presumed to be. An explanation for this finding which suggests itself immediately is that in a homogeneous community little or no anti-Ukrainian prejudice is encountered and ethnic identity is something of which one can make light. In a heterogeneous community one is faced by other ethnic groups, encounters prejudice, and consequently must take ethnic identity much more seriously. A partial test of the proposition that encountering prejudice leads to non-Assimilationism was inconclusive. Despite the failure of this test, one is strongly tempted to see this relationship in cognitive dissonance terms.

This finding also bears a resemblance to something which anthropological students of the diffusion of culture have observed; the purest case of a culture type usually appears at some distance from the center of the culture area. Day (1968) observes, for example, that Catholic fertility is higher in countries in which Catholics are a minority than in countries in which they are a majority. He concludes that the pronatalism of the church increases natality only in situations in which Catholics define themselves as a numerically and politically important minority of the population. Something like esprit de corps is involved. The temptation to apply this kind of model to my finding is strong for two reasons. First, we are dealing with a culture of Canada, not a culture of the Ukraine. Second, the center of this culture is in the small towns on the edge of the bush where the first immigrants settled. Canadian-Ukrainian culture has diffused from the small towns to the city rather than the other way around, as has typically been the case in America. The respondents who live in heterogeneous areas must define themselves as a significant minority but a minority nevertheless.

Residential site explains 10 percent of the variation in Ingroup Choice. Respondents living in ethnically heterogeneous areas are more likely to have low Ingroup Choice, as one would expect. The effects of homogeneity and heterogeneity of residential site on the two measures of group cohesion are in the opposite direction. Thus, although cultural breakdown seems to be inhibited by residence in an ethnically heterogeneous area, structural breakdown is facilitated. The two are obviously independent in some important respects.

Education

With other variables controlled, education explains 33 percent of the variation in Assimilationism and 25 percent of the variation in Ingroup Choice. The relationship is entirely consistent and strongly positive under all conditions. The single variable, then, which best predicts both dependent variables is formal education. Whereas occupational status and workplace are weak and residential site is moderate, education is strongly related to the dependent variables. This is altogether consistent with the findings by many other sources that higher formal education is associated with lower prejudice, chauvinism, and

tendency to stereotype. We would be inclined to speculate that what education does in this case is to tear people loose from an ethnic culture rather than to indoctrinate them in some mass culture. As previously cited (Vallee, Schwartz, and Darknell 1957), there does not seem to be a mass culture to which they might become assimilated.

SUMMARY

Gordon (1964) suggests that there are two general types of processes in which the boundaries of ethnic groups break down—one cultural, one structural. Literatures on large and small groups also tend to be concerned with only two main types of cohesion, although semantic problems sometimes obscure this. This analysis has been concerned with explaining variation in two measures of ethnic-group cohesion which conform to the two general models of group cohesion.

The general model suggested by the literature on ethnic cohesion consists of a large number of variables related to the differentiation of the ethnic community and contributing independently to a total effect. My findings do not lend support to this model. Rather, I find a small number of variables related to high Assimilationism and low Ingroup Choice, and only two of these are powerful. I would like to emphasize two main points: (1) the single, most powerful predictor of both measures of cohesion is formal education, which alone accounts for 25 percent of the variation in Ingroup Choice and 33 percent of the variation in Assimilationism; (2) it is among the more highly educated that the other variables are most important. Among the less-educated respondents, the effects of workplace, occupational status, and residential site are much muted. The model which these data suggest, then, is a sequential one. Education is a variable which prepares a community for the other effects of social differentiation—it is apparently a necessary precondition for the operation of other variables.[8] Only in the presence of higher formal education do other aspects of social differentiation lead to decreasing ethnic loyalties and involvement. The obvious implication of this is that, at least for this group, increasing affluence will not, by itself, lead to the destruction of the Ukrainian community but increasing education eventually will. However, there is a countertendency which must be noted. The second most important source of Assimilationist attitudes in this population is residence in an ethnically homogeneous community, which, essentially, means isolation from other cultural groups. This isolation is based upon the original settlement patterns of the group in question and is breaking down. Residence in an ethnically heterogeneous community will characterize a greater percentage of this population in the future, and residence in such a community seems to induce non-Assimilationism, although it also induces low Ingroup Choice. These two processes, education and deisolation, seem to pull in opposite directions. The net result will probably be a slow rate of defection from Ukrainian culture and social organization, but at a slower rate than one would expect from simply looking at the relationship between formal education and Assimilationism. There seems to be, therefore, a high probability of an economically diversified ethnic community which maintains considerable cohesiveness in both senses and which will be worn down only very slowly.

In general, this research suggests that the theory of ethnic-group loss of cohesion which develops from the older literature is in part mistaken. It is not simply social differentiation manifested in a number of ways, acting independently and contributing to a total effect, but one powerful variable which makes possible the operation of others. A number of possibilities for further testing of this proposition exist in the countries which still have large, important, and unassimilated immigrant ethnic minority communities.

NOTES

[1] I am indebted to Lylian Klimek of the University of Alberta for bibliographic assistance with this paper and to the Ukrainian Canadian Research Foundation and the Department of Citizenship and Immigration for funding the original study. This report is done from data gathered for Hobart et al. (1968), but it does not duplicate any part of that work. I am also indebted to a number of people for assistance, but especially to Richard F. Curtis and Jerry L. L. Miller of the University of Arizona.

[2] Gordon (1964, pp. 60-63) describes seven types of assimilation, but all fall into either one or the other of the two general types described in this text. He makes "structural assimilation" (see my no. 2 below) the "keystone" of assimilation (p. 81).

[3] No attempt was made to locate Ukrainian women who had married outside the group. One attempt to study persons who had changed their names was a failure.

[4] Edmonton, Lamont, Willingdon, and Thorhild, Alberta.

[5] These variables taken together explain 64 percent of the variation in Assimilationism and 46 percent of the variation in Ingroup Choice. This is equivalent to multiple r's of approximately 0.8 or 0.7, respectively (see Table 3).

[6] Apparent relationships between age and sex and the dependent variables are entirely a product of the maldistribution of education in this sample.

[7] This analysis would not have been possible without the work of Miller (1968). I am deeply indebted to Jerry L. L. Miller and Richard F. Curtis for assistance.

[8] In contrast with my findings, nationalist sentiment seems to have been strongest among the intelligentsia in European nationalist movements of the eighteenth and nineteenth centuries (see Snyder 1964 for bibliography). It may be that education acts in the same way but in the opposite ideological direction when nationalism is vigorously on the wax.

REFERENCES

Bogardus, Emory S., 1943. *The Mexican in the United States.* Los Angeles: University of Southern California Press.

Brown, F. J., and J. S. Roucek, eds. 1945. *One America.* Englewood Cliffs, N.J.: Prentice-Hall.

Campisi, P. J. 1948. "Ethnic Family Patterns: The Italian Family in the United States." *American Journal of Sociology* 53 (May): 443-49.

Day, Lincoln H. 1968. "Natality and Ethnocentrism: Some Relationships Suggested by an Analysis of Catholic-Protestant Differentials." *Population Studies* 22 (March): 27-50.

Dominion Bureau of Statistics. 1961. Census of Canada. Ottawa: Queen's Printers.

Eisenstadt, S. N. 1951. "The Place of Elites and Primary Groups in the Absorption of New Immigrants in Israel." *American Journal of Sociology* 57 (November): 222-31.

———. 1952a. "The Process of Absorption of New Immigrants in Israel." *Human Relations* 5 (August): 223-46.

———. 1952b. "Institutionalization of Immigrant Behaviors." *Human Relations* 5 (November): 313-95.

Finkelstein, L. 1949. *The Jews, Their History, Culture and Religion.* New York: Harper.

Gordon, Milton M. 1964. *Assimilation in American Life.* New York: Oxford University Press.

Gross, N., and W. Martin. 1957. "On Group Cohesiveness." *American Journal of Sociology* 57 (May): 549-54.

Herberg, Will. 1960. *Protestant, Catholic, Jew.* Garden City, N.Y.: Anchor.

Hobart, C. W., W. E. Kalbach, J. T. Borhek, and A. P. Jacoby. 1968. "Persistence and Change: Alberta Ukrainians." Mimeographed. Toronto: Ukrainian Canadian Research Foundation.

Hughes, E. C. 1943. *French Canada in Transition.* Chicago: University of Chicago Press.

Jones, F. 1956. "A Sociological Perspective on Immigrant Adjustment." *Social Forces* 35 (March): 39-47.

Kosa, John. 1957. *Land of Choice: The Hungarians in Canada.* Toronto: University of Toronto Press.

Miller, Jerry L. L. 1968. "A Fortran Program: Multiple Regression with Dichotomous Data." *Behavioral Science* 13 (March): 165.

Miyamota, S. Frank. 1939. *Social Solidarity Among the Japanese in Seattle.* Seattle: University of Washington Press.

Park, Robert F., and Ernest Burgess. 1924. *Introduction to the Science of Sociology.* Chicago: University of Chicago Press.

Pepitone, A., and R. Kleiner. 1957. "The Effects of Threat and Frustration on Group Cohesiveness." *Journal of Abnormal and Social Psychology* 54 (March): 192-99.

Poll, Solomon. 1962. *The Hasidic Community of Williamsburg.* New York: Free Press.

Porter, John. 1965. *The Vertical Mosaic.* Toronto: University of Toronto Press.

Richardson, A. 1961. "The Assimilation of British Immigrants in a West Australian Community." *Research Group for European Migration Problems Bulletin* 9:1-52.

Rose, A. M. 1949. *The Negro's Morale.* Minneapolis: University of Minnesota Press.

———. 1952. *Union Solidarity.* Minneapolis: University of Minnesota Press.

———. 1965. *Sociology.* New York: Knopf.

Seashore, Stanley E. 1954. *Group Cohesiveness in the Industrial Work Group.* Ann Arbor: Survey Research Center, University of Michigan.

Snyder, Louis L. 1964. *The Dynamics of Nationalism.* Princeton, N.J.: Van Nostrand.

Taft, R. 1961. "The Assimilation of Dutch Male Immigrants in a Western Australian Community." *Human Relations* 14 (August): 265-81.

Thomas, D. S., and R. S. Nishimoto. 1946. *The Salvage.* Berkeley: University of California Press.

Vallee, F., M. Schwartz, and F. Darknell. 1957. "Ethnic Assimilation and Differentiation in Canada." *Canadian Journal of Economics and Political Science* 23 (November): 540-49.

Warner, W. Lloyd, and Leo Srole. 1945. *The Social Systems of American Ethnic Groups.* New Haven, Conn.: Yale University Press.

Young, Charles H. 1931. *The Ukrainian Canadian: A Study in Assimilation.* Toronto: Nelson.

Young, Pauline V. 1932. *The Pilgrims of Russian-Town.* Chicago: University of Chicago Press.

34
ghetto and gown: the birth of black studies

ROGER A. FISCHER

The obstacles Dr. Fischer saw in 1969 in the establishment of black studies have not materialized. Almost every major college and university now has a black studies program; they are not training grounds for revolutionaries (in the immediate, violent sense); they are under black control; most of their students are black; and they are at least as academically respectable as departments of journalism or public administration, and sometimes much more so.

In his article, Dr. Fischer also indicates why these programs have been successful. They fill, in part at least, the agonizing, gnawing need of young, articulate blacks for pride in their culture and for at least an exploration into new ways to help the entire black community. Although on any campus there are black students who eschew the black studies program, most black students, even though they may be taking most of their courses outside the program, gather in the offices, know the teachers, and know their fellow black students. Thus mutual support and solidarity among black students is a secondary effect of black studies programs.

A careful reading of the following article will demonstrate the range of needs and interests that have sparked black studies programs. Dr. Fischer is an associate professor of history at Southwest Missouri State College.

Unlike most academic programs, black studies was not born in a faculty senate chamber or in a dean's conference room, or even on a college campus. It all began more than a decade ago at those Southern lunch counters and deserted bus stops where black people finally rose in rebellion against nearly three and a half centuries of second-class citizenship.

Northern college campuses soon became hotbeds of sympathy for the "movement" and in the process discovered embarrassing inconsistencies between their libertarian beliefs and their lily-white student bodies. All too often, black enrollment was limited to a star basketball player or two and a few local Negroes who

Reprinted from *Current History* 57, no. 339 (November 1969), pp. 290-294, 299-300. Reproduced by permission of the author and Current History, Inc., Philadelphia.

showed up for classes, then obligingly disappeared when it was time for social activities. Finally, while the state universities of Mississippi and Alabama made their stand for segregation by massive resistance and redneck rhetoric "in the schoolhouse door," many of the better Northern schools began to fulfill a commitment to racial equality by earnestly recruiting black students without regard to their prowess at broken field running or the zone defense.

These young black men and women undoubtedly went to college with naively high expectations. If Negroes since Booker T. Washington have regarded higher education as the key to opportunity, surely the prestigious Northern universities were the path to the promised land. Negro students were looking for the American dream, but found instead the bitter disillusionment of hopeless alienation. Some whites literally smothered them with paternalism. As one proud black man remembered his two years at Yale, he had been "the chosen one on whom all the benefits of a guilt complex could be bestowed—a kind of little tan Orphan Annie befriended by a great white Daddy Warbucks." Other whites tried to destroy racial differences by ignoring them. An eminent historian rhapsodized in his introduction to a study of slavery, "Negroes are, after all, only white men with black skins, nothing more, nothing less." In short, the white university unwittingly tried to transform its black students into what Lerone Bennett, Jr., has described as "Orwellian non-persons" by failing to come to terms with their blackness.

The identity crisis of the black students was compounded by the Anglo-Saxon orientation of their studies. American literature courses meandered from Michael Wigglesworth to J. D. Salinger without acknowledging the poems of Lawrence Dunbar or the novels of James Baldwin. Music professors blandly attributed the origins of jazz to Paul Whiteman. Few dramatic courses interrupted their readings of the hallowed classics to pay any attention to Lorraine Hansberry's brilliant *Raisin in the Sun*. All too often, the only Negroes encountered in studies of American culture were little Topsy, Uncle Remus and those docile darkies of *Green Pastures*, Sambo stereotypes created by white writers for white readers.

United States history courses ignored the African heritage so completely that it seemed to Lerone Bennett as if "black Americans appear suddenly by a process of spontaneous generation." Negroes merited attention in American history surveys only when they were making trouble or when white agitators were doing so on their behalf. Ten Jeffersonians arrested under the Alien and Sedition decrees often received as much time as and more sympathy than four million enslaved blacks. Instructors spent weeks discussing the white immigrant ghettos of the nineteenth century, then ignored Harlem, Hough and Watts altogether.

Stripped of their identities as black people and forced into a curriculum that denied

their heritage by an unconscious conspiracy of silence, black students found themselves completely, irreconcilably alienated within the ivy-covered confines of the white universities. Integration seemed to lead only to invisibility and those tempted to try it were haunted by fears that they might become, as Dartmouth's F. Woody Lee put it, "little more in the eyes of many whites than a genteel nigger—a showcase coon." Rebellion seemed the only answer, and black students eagerly embraced the heady new doctrines of black consciousness. From Malcolm X they discovered the brotherhood of all blacks and the essential dignity of the black identity. From Stokely Carmichael and H. Rap Brown they learned how to transform Malcolm's teachings into the political activism of Black Power. And so they rebelled, in part against the racism of the white university system, but primarily against their own false prophets who had deluded them with hair straighteners and colored country clubs and Urban League brotherhood week banquets.

The wave of campus confrontations that began at the Berkeley campus of the University of California five years ago was essentially a white phenomenon, but it provided watchful black militants with an excellent practical education in the tactics of disruption. From such white radicals as Mario Savio, they learned that a great university could be literally immobilized by boycotts, sit-ins, and the "liberation" of administration buildings. They discovered the awesome secret of student power, that the university was pathetically vulnerable to the pressures that could be brought to bear upon it by a relatively small cadre of well-organized, deeply dedicated student revolutionaries. Blacks began to organize, and soon groups known by such titles as the United Black Students, the Association of African and Afro-American Students, the Onyx Society, the Soul Students Advisory Council, and the Black Students Union appeared on campus after campus.

The names may have differed, but the common goal of these organizations was the "de-honkification" of the universities. To achieve that result, these black student unions issued a series of demands, among them the

hiring of more black professors and the enrollment of more black students through recruiting, scholarships and relaxed admissions
standards. Specific demands varied greatly,
including moratoriums on failing grades,
blanket subsidies for minority students, and a
school holiday on the birthday of Malcolm X.
But one demand was virtually universal and
led nearly every list of priorities. It called for
the creation of programs in black studies.

The idea was wholeheartedly embraced
by many beleaguered administrations and
faculties. Universities where tranquillity still
reigned joined in the rush to establish black
studies programs to head off future trouble.
Everybody, it seemed, favored black studies
in the abstract. The problems began on many
campuses when the militants and the Establishment sat down together to iron out specific details and discovered that neither group
had the slightest notion what the other really
meant by "black studies." For the past two
years, the development of black studies as an
academic discipline has been stalled by this
communications barrier. Unless one faction
capitulates completely or both can agree on a
common definition, black studies may be
bogged down indefinitely.

Academic traditionalists, including most
scholars and nearly all administrators, think of
black studies as the body of subject matter
relating to the Negro experience in Africa and
the New World. Within their frame of reference, a curriculum in black studies would consist of such courses as African and American
Negro history, tribal anthropology, the politics and sociology of ethnic minorities and
Negro music, art, literature and theater. They
would most probably be grouped together in
an interdisciplinary "area studies" program,
with supervision divided among a coordinating
committee, the participating departments and
the administration. These courses would be
taught by professors, white or black, with the
proper academic credentials, and would be
open to all eligible students. In defining black
studies in this manner, traditionalists are
merely following hallowed academic practices.
Courses have always been organized into disciplines by the nature of their subject matter.
Control has invariably rested within the chain

of command which comprises the administrative hierarchy. Possession or pursuit of the
doctorate, not skin color, has long been the
yardstick of serious scholarly intent.

These criteria, however important they
may be to the maintenance of academic excel-
lence, are regarded by many militant Negroes
as irrelevant, possibly dangerous, obstacles to
their pursuit of a black studies program as
they envision it. They have not yet developed
a common blueprint for the operational
mechanics of a black studies program tailored
to their tastes, although an ambitious project
in that direction was begun this summer by
Vincent Harding at the Institute for the Black
World in Atlanta. Most militants see black
studies not as a labyrinth of curriculum committees and degree requirements, but as a col-
legiate training ground with a single over-riding
purpose, the advancement of the black revolution in every facet of American life.

As Cornell's Harry Edwards has noted,
"The time is gone for black cats to flee to
Baldwin Hills and eat pickles and hors
d'oeuvres and watch the riots on color TV."
According to Nathan Hare, recently deposed
black studies director at San Francisco State
College, "black today is revolutionary and
nationalistic. A black studies program which is
not revolutionary and nationalistic is, accordingly, quite profoundly irrelevant." In keeping
with the activist definition, a meaningful black
studies program must train black students to
organize the urban ghettos and the black-belt
South, to utilize the tactics of civil disobedience against racial discrimination, and to guide
their brothers and sisters who never got to college toward greater social, economic and political opportunities.

Embittered by the oppressions of the
past and impatient to undertake the reconstruction of the future, these black militants
hold very little reverence for traditional academic niceties. Lectures on such esoteric
topics as "the social dynamics of a fifteenth-
century West African agricultural village" or
"Camille Thierry, free Negro poet in Paris"
may indeed warm the cockles of the scholastic
heart, but they seem rather pointless to those
whose daily lives have been endless struggles
against ghetto rodents or "white only" rest

rooms. Even topics much more pertinent to current realities have been dismissed by many activists as meaningless. Commenting on Edward Greenberg's course on "The Politics of Race" in the black studies program at Stanford University, one Negro student complained, "Greenberg tells us the blacks haven't gotten anyplace politically. . . . Hell, we know that. What I want to know is where we can go from here, and how."

Complaining about the Establishment's concepts on curriculum, Cornell's Bill Osby lamented, "They will simply let us study black history and wear dashikis while we get ready to work for Xerox or IBM." Black ideas on curriculum vary widely. Nathan Hare favors a "comprehensive, integrated body of interdisciplinary courses" emphasizing the "black perspective," including economics, science and mathematics. "Black mathematics," as Hare envisions it, "would not be saturated with middle-class referents such as stocks and bonds" and a course in "black biochemistry" might study such topics as rat control. Other black studies architects advocate more limited programs based upon the black experience in social sciences and the arts. Many activists demand a curriculum which reflects their revolutionary ideology. They favor such courses as San Francisco State's "Sociology of Black Oppression," in which instructor Jerry Varnado wrote out the formula for napalm so that his students could "pour it on a piece of meat or on the police or somebody and see exactly how it works."

If many black militants find conventional ideas on curriculum annoyingly irrelevant, they regard the traditional "power structure" of the university as the ultimate enemy. If absolute sovereignty over black studies rests with the deans and the trustees, Negroes fear that these programs will most probably be systematically emasculated of any productive value they might otherwise engender. Overwhelmingly white, middle-class, middle-aged and politically "safe," college administrators and trustees have come to personify the hated white Establishment to many campus blacks. This suspicion has led to demands for "autonomy," or black control over black studies programs.

Proposals on how autonomous status can be attained are varied, including such ambitious schemes as totally separate colleges for black studies within the university system, with independent governing boards and budgets. Most often, however, proponents of autonomy advocate separate departments of black studies with black student power over curriculum and the hiring and firing of faculty. This dispute has been a volatile one, for militants and administrators know well that the nature and philosophy of any academic program is largely determined by those who possess the ultimate control over it.

The most explosive issue of all has been the question of white participation in black studies. Directly related to the bitter integrationist-separatist controversy now ripping apart the delicate unity of the "movement" itself, black militant demands for the exclusion of white professors and students have alienated many Negroes and virtually all of the white academic community. Separatists argue that no white scholar, however illustrious his learned degrees and publications, can truly understand the black experience. As Johnie Scott, a Stanford University senior from Watts, expressed it, "No white man can talk about Rap Brown or Stokely Carmichael."

Separatists object to the presence of white students in black studies courses for a variety of reasons. Some of the more paranoid blacks have expressed the fear that whites would take advantage of the knowledge they gained to keep on exploiting the blacks. Others feel that the presence of whites retards open discussion. A black student at Oakland's Merritt College, urging a lone white to leave a class in black philosophy, pointed out, "So long as this white boy is in this class, we're going to be talking elliptically, all around and over the subject, but no one is really going to be saying anything."

A few schools have apparently surrendered to the new apartheid. At Merritt College, black instructors reportedly prevent white students from attending some of the 15 courses in their black studies program. Officials at other schools have allegedly ignored incidents in which whites have been ejected from classes by black student vigilantes.

Antioch College gained nationwide notoriety this past year by summarily excluding white students from its black studies institute, a policy which the United States Office of Education regarded as a violation of Title VI of the Civil Rights Act. Faced with the loss of federal funds, Antioch administrators defended their actions by arguing that admission to the program was based not on race but on its "relevance" to the needs and experiences of the students, a subterfuge hauntingly reminiscent of the "grandfather clause" of another generation.

The Antioch situation is by no means commonplace, for nearly all college administrations have opposed institutional color lines and most Negroes reject separatism emphatically. As integrationist Negro spokesman Roy Wilkins has pointed out, "We have suffered too many heartaches and shed too much blood in fighting the evil of racial segregation to return in 1969 to the lonely and dispiriting confines of its demeaning prison." Negro psychologist Kenneth Clark has stated that to encourage separatism "is to reinforce the Negro's inability to compete with the whites for the real power of the real world." Even Nathan Hare, an outspoken black militant, has remarked, "We think that separatism is often a pretext to evade acting in a revolutionary fashion now."

Even so, the Antioch controversy symbolizes too well the current dilemma of black studies. If it is ever going to develop into a meaningful academic discipline, traditionalists and black militants must somehow reach understandings on such basic issues as curriculum, control and interracial participation. Accommodation will probably be difficult to achieve, for the rhetoric of revolution is seldom conducive to the realities of compromise. If confrontation is allowed to escalate beyond the point where reasonable debate remains possible, black studies will be the inevitable victim. The militants have been successful with the strategy of limited disruption, but they lack the power to immobilize most universities completely and even the most timorous trustees and administrators unquestionably have their breaking points. Every indication points to a rising tide of social reaction, to a

climate in which repression would be welcomed by regents, legislators and a public which remembers too vividly the guns of Cornell. If reaction and repression ever become the order of the day, black studies will surely die the death of a sacrificial lamb.

It is most unlikely that many colleges will permit the militants to define the curriculum in terms of the philosophy of black revolution. To grant any ideology such privileged status would be a gross violation of the traditional concept of the university as a laissez-faire marketplace for the free exchange of ideas. Moreover, if most regents, administrators and legislators were given to promoting special treatment for any political philosophy, it most assuredly would not be Black Power. Few members of the Establishment would look fondly upon a black mathematics course in which, as Nathan Hare has suggested, the instructor might ask, "If you loot one store and burn two, how many do you have left?" It seems equally unlikely that black autonomy will be taken very seriously by most college administrations. Most regents and administrators believe that their surrender of control would lead to out-and-out anarchy. Few of them, needless to say, are anarchists.

The militants must also abandon the notion that white students and professors should be excluded from participation in black studies programs. This latter-day apartheid is legally questionable and morally indefensible. Moreover, separatism could well prove suicidal to the black studies program. If "white racism" is the greatest single obstacle to black aspirations, as the Kerner Commission has alleged, then white students would be the most logical beneficiaries of black studies. At the very least, their presence in the classes would add the element of interracial dialogue. Black studies programs also need qualified white professors, for such programs will need all of the academic talent they can muster to survive their infancy and justify their existence as a discipline.

White scholars have contributed substantially to black studies in the past. It would be impossible, for example, to imagine a course on slavery which neglected the writings of Kenneth Stampp, Stanley Elkins and Eugene Genovese or a study of segregation which ignored the works of Gunnar Myrdal, John Dollard and C. Vann Woodward. It would be tragic if the Myrdals and Woodwards of the future were forced to detour into other disciplines because black studies discouraged them with signs saying, in effect, "No Irish Need Apply."

Compromise should not come, however, completely on traditionalist terms. The proposals of the black militants may be impractical and in some cases academically unsound, but they convey an urgency and an immediacy so often missing in the Ivory Tower. Autonomy may be unrealistic, but black students certainly deserve a meaningful voice in determining the faculty and curriculum of black studies programs. Above all, the courses must attempt to meet contemporary needs. As the Stanford student pointed out, "What I want to know is where we can go from here, and how." Nathan Hare's concept of a black science course to study rat control is excellent and should be expanded into other areas.

Black economics should study welfare survival in the ghetto and the feasibility of boycotting merchants guilty of discriminatory hiring practices. Black political science must teach its students to organize the ghetto and the bottomlands, to elect black officials and apply maximum pressure on white politicians. The possibilities are virtually endless.

If honest compromise is possible, the Establishment must remain rigid in defense of its academic integrity, but it must also allow enormous flexibility to avoid smothering promising innovations. It must remember that a university which buries its problems in the name of tranquillity has already abandoned its place in a free society. Black militants must realize that the failure of black studies might mean a return to the silent racism of college life as it was a decade ago. Compromise will undoubtedly demand twice the wisdom of Solomon and three times the patience of Job, but it must be achieved. The alternatives are frightening.

V. race and the causes of prejudice

A. RACE: SCIENTIFIC AND POPULAR DEFINITIONS
B. THE CAUSES OF PREJUDICE

introduction: some definitions

The causes of intergroup tension and conflict in American society are manifold. Most of those who have given close attention to the subject and who are not apologists for one theory of social behavior or another are aware that no single factor is the determining cause of prejudice or its manifestations in discrimination. The phenomena to be explained are manifested in such diverse ways and the influences on them are sometimes so complicated and subtle that all the factors involved are not yet known. The following analysis is therefore tentative and consists of a number of hypotheses for further testing. In each case, there is a good deal of evidence in support of the proposition given, but in no case is there adequate proof. Thus, although the following theories are not enitrely satisfactory, they are far more acceptable than the popular attempts at explanation that are known to be wrong.

The sources of intergroup discrimination and prejudice may be considered in five categories: power conflict, ideological conflict, racism, social structure, and individual psychology. These categories are more or less mutually exclusive for theoretical purposes only; in any concrete situation, several causes are likely to be operating at once and in such an integrated manner that it is difficult to disentangle their effects. Each problem of intergroup relations has its own relatively unique historical-cultural context, and the sociologist's effort to draw some generalizations from the "seamless web" of social facts is based on theoretical conceptualizations and arbitrary distinctions, which, however artificial, are necessary for understanding and scientific prediction. Furthermore, in attempting to explain the nature and causes of intergroup conflict, several levels of explanation that have a concurrent validity must be used, even though they are different. For example, intergroup antagonism can be explained in terms of historical development, contemporary social forces, and mechanisms of individual psychology. These all operate simultaneously to "cause" a given complex of intergroup relations.

In considering the causes of intergroup conflict, their connections with the general theories of sociology and psychology and with specific researches which analyze their impact in concrete situations will be mentioned. Because of limitations of space, this will be done briefly. Most theories in the social sciences have not been presented in systematic fashion, and most researches fail to meet all the accepted scientific requirements; hence there are further restrictions on the presentation of a theoretical framework and a research buttress for statements made here.

Power conflict may be defined as a struggle for control of scarce values. These may be economic, in which case, one group seeks domination over another in order to take its wealth or labor at less than its recognized value. The minority group may be enslaved or simply underpaid. Karl Marx is the best-known writer to explain intergroup antagonism in terms of power conflict over economic values. He observed that the English and Irish proletariats were split into hostile camps, hating one another as competitors and so coming to feel a national and religious antipathy toward one another. Believing that such conflicts are spurious in view of a basically common interest among all members of the proletariat, he also held that the antipathies were artificially nurtured by the bourgeois class.[1]

Other scarce values for which groups struggle and for which one group seeks domination over another include prestige, symbolic expressions of ascendancy, and sexual access. John Dollard has emphasized conflict over these values in his study of black-white relations in the southern United States.[2] When there is a power conflict, the dominant group practically never seeks to exterminate the minority group; it seeks only its wealth, its labor, its according of prestige and ascendancy, or its women for sexual purposes; in other respects, it leaves the minority group alone. It threatens violence to get these things, however—which distinguishes conflict from mere competition. Power conflict is rational in the sense that it involves a weighing of costs against the values gained. Slavery in ancient Greece and Rome and in the Moslem world today may be taken as examples of power conflict between groups. The relationship between the ancient Roman conquerors and their conquered peoples involved more than economic exploitation; but in many areas, in fact, the only gains to the Romans were those of prestige and ascendancy. This situation also obtains in some parts of some modern empires, for example, Mussolini's conquest of Ethiopia in the late 1930s. Piracy as it has existed down through the ages in many parts of the world involved only power conflict. Power conflict was the main factor in the struggles between the American colonists and the Indians and blacks until about 1810.

Ideological conflict may be defined as struggle for the supremacy or maintenance of a given way of life or belief system. Perhaps the term *cultural* would be more adequate than ideological except that that term has been used in so many diverse ways that it would not aid communication. In ideological conflict, groups oppose two distinct sets of values, each of which is believed to be the only right, good, and even necessary one. Historically, most ideological group conflicts have been between organized religions. In recent centuries, they have been less religious and metaphysical and more political and economic in the specific content of the values contested.

Conflict over political and economic ideologies is to be sharply distinguished from conflict for the possession of scarce political and economic values. Whereas the aim of the power type of conflict is to assume possession of the scarce values, the aim of ideological conflict is to annihilate or convert those who do not accept what the group considers to be true or necessary values; or if victory is out of the question, the aim is to avoid annihilation or conversion. Whereas the former is selfishly motivated, the latter is selfless and even self-sacrificing. In religious conflict, the true values are supposed to emanate from a supernatural source, and the motivation to impose these values on nonbelievers is considered to be service to this supernatural power. A group that denies the true God is insulting to this highest good and therefore must be destroyed or converted.

Groups engaged in ideological conflict that is not religious have substituted for God such forces as history or the true happiness of mankind. If history is believed to decree that the bourgeoisie must disappear, then the bourgeoisie must be annihilated or converted to a proletarian way of life; or if utopia does not have a class of employers, then present employers must be convinced that they should not continue to perform their current role. Ideologies that are the source of ideological conflict invariably are absolutistic. The values and forces of God, history, or utopia are in some way transcendent over all others.

The third major type of motivation for intergroup conflict that has been noted is *racist*.

It rests on the desire to maintain what is believed to be biological purity and caste separation. Whereas the goal of power conflict is the seizure of scarce values and the goal of ideological conflict is annihilation or conversion of nonbelievers, the goal of racist conflict is complete separation; and the strongest demands are for the avoidance of personal contact. One group, members of which consider themselves to be a biological unit or race, takes steps to segregate the other groups in the society from all spheres of life where they may come in contact with the active group. The segregation is, where possible, on the basis of physical distance without interference with economic exploitation; otherwise, it is on the basis of symbolic separation. It is also possible for nondominant numerical minorities to have racist motives and to initiate conflict. In such cases, the nondominant numerical minorities generally segregate themselves to keep their biological condition uncontaminated, and conflicts set in when outgroups find the self-segregating activities of the minorities a nuisance obstructing the maintenance of the functions of the society. Groups with racist beliefs regard themselves as biologically superior, and any publicity given to that belief encourages bad relations.

Racist conflict is almost entirely a modern development, since knowledge and interest about the biological composition of a population only began at the end of the eighteenth century. However, there are certain weak parallels in the "chosen people" concept of the ancient Hebrews, in the ancient Greeks' concept of their distinctiveness from barbarians, and in the tendency of many societies to regard their members as the only "true people," to be distinguished from "semianimals." But the main and true examples of racist conflict come from the United States, Germany, and South Africa in the nineteenth and twentieth centuries.

The ideology of racism consists of the following elements:

1. The various races were offshoots of the evolutionary tree at different stages of development, so that the black race is lowest, not far above the apes, and the white race is highest. This theory of *polygenesis* is no longer held by biological scientists. The present theory of *monogenesis* is that man—the species Homo sapiens—evolved only once and then divided into races after migration to different parts of the globe. However, no scientific biologists ever held that the races of men were distinct species (i.e., as far apart as horse and ponies, for example), which seems to be the popular theory.

2. Culture is a product solely of biological capacity. Each race produces the artifacts and institutions of which it is capable, and a lower race is not capable of carrying on the cultural life of a higher race.

3. The offspring of a mixed racial union would at best be midway, in biological capacity, between his two parents; and sometimes an anomaly would be created that might even be inferior in certain respects to his lower parent.

4. Amalgamation of two races would therefore result in the rapid deterioration of the culture of the higher race. Specifically, if the white race of North America should intermarry with any lower race, its great achievements in art and literature could no longer be maintained and appreciated, and its institutions of government (democracy and federalism), economy (free enterprise), religion (Christianity), and family (monogamy) would disappear. "Savage life," such as was believed to be characteristic of central African culture, would replace these. Thus, in order to maintain the good things of Western culture, the races must be kept biologically separated.

This ideology of racism provided a most effective rationalization for keeping both slavery and democracy: The blacks were not capable of having democracy and the rest of Western culture but could experience some of its benefits by serving the white race. The analogy was the superiority of the domesticated animal over the wild animal. The black was "all right in his place," but if he aspired to equality or intermarriage, he was dangerous and had to be beaten back. ("Dogs are fine animals, but if they should seek to be equal to us or to marry our daughters, they would have to be exterminated.") Democracy and the rest of Western culture can *only* be maintained by slavery.

Racism transformed the relationships between blacks and whites. Slavery (or its post-Civil War equivalent of systematic discrimination) was no longer regarded as a mere economic arrangement but rather as the basis of a way of life. Any efforts by blacks to improve themselves outside the status of slaves had to be immediately repressed. Any effort to eliminate slavery had to be fought with every resource. All the other institutions of society had to be mobilized to maintain slavery (or its later equivalent). For example, the family had to be based on the sexual "purity" of the white woman (since white men had extramarital relations with black women and offspring of mixed unions had to be outside the family); the economy must never allow black workers to enter the same occupations as white workers (this inhibited the South from industrializing); the government must never allow blacks to vote or hold public office; education for the black must be limited to agriculture and handicrafts; literature and art had the task of explaining and glorifying these racist requirements. A new social system had to be developed to carry out all the implied requirements of racism; sociologists usually call this the *caste system* because its forms and manifestations (although not its causes) are almost identical with the caste system that developed much earlier in Hindu society. Specifically, the caste system took off from the last element of the racist ideology and had the following provisions:

1. Systematic separation of the races, called segregation or Jim Crow. If facilities have to be provided for blacks, they must be separate from those for whites, so that there can be no social equality and no opportunity for black men and white women ever to see each other as potential mates.

2. Black men and white women must never have sex relations, and the frequent relations between white men and black women must be illicit and the children classed as blacks.

3. When whites and blacks have to come together, usually for economic reasons, a rigid and pervasive series of customs must formalize and limit their contacts so that they will never become equalitarian. Sociologists have called this "the etiquette of race relations,"[3] since there are hundreds of rules specifying proper behavior. But it should be understood that this is not etiquette in the usual sense, since the rules often require impoliteness rather than politeness. In general, the rules of interpersonal relations require a continuing demonstration that the black is inferior to the white man: Blacks and whites must not shake hands when they meet; the white man must start the conversation (although the black can hint that he wants to talk); the black must address the white person as "Mr.," "Mrs.," or "Miss," but he must never be addressed by these titles himself. (Blacks are addressed by their first name, or called "uncle," "aunty," "darky," "nigger," or in some cases, for politeness' sake, may be called by their last name or by such titles as "doctor," "professor," or "preacher.") The topic of conversation must be limited to specific job matters or to personal niceties (e.g., inquiries after one's health); it must never stray over to larger matters of politics or economics or to personal matters such as white husband-wife relationships. Blacks should never look into the eyes of white people when they talk but should keep their eyes on the ground or shifting, and their physical posture in front of white people should be humble and self-demeaning. There are hundreds of such rules, although they differ slightly from one area to another.

4. Blacks must not have the same occupations as white people. The major exception has been in agriculture, but outside of this, blacks could only be servants, in one capacity or another, and white people were generally not allowed to be servants. Blacks could be entertainers, provided they did not perform alongside whites, because entertainment could be con-

sidered a type of service. Of course, blacks could serve other blacks in all sorts of occupations (including the liberal professions), but this was strictly to prevent blacks from coming into contact with whites in these capacities. The main occupational significance of the caste system is that blacks could not work in manufacturing, commerce, or transportation except in such servant capacities as janitor, elevator operator, or porter.

5. Blacks must not be allowed to vote or to hold political office.

6. Blacks must not be allowed to have legal rights vis-à-vis whites. This means that whites could commit crimes against blacks without fear of punishment (for over 50 years—1890 to 1945—there was not a single case in any of the eight deep southern states in which a white who committed a crime against a black was punished by law in any way). It also means that blacks who commit crimes against whites were punished severely by the southern courts. Blacks who commit crimes against other blacks are regarded as children and punished lightly or not at all if some white man asks that they not be punished.

7. Violations of the caste rules must also be punished, usually not by the courts, since most of the rules were not in law, but by individual or group act. The most severe punishment is meted out for sex relations between white women and black men. The men are immediately killed (by a lynching mob or by group-appointed individuals), and the women are exiled (unless they are declared to be innocent and the relationship forced on them). Severe punishment is also usually inflicted on those blacks who "pass" or attempt to "pass" as whites. Such blacks either are killed, are severely beaten, or have their property destroyed. Still, few "passing" blacks are detected because many more blacks appear to be whites than the whites know about; the passers do so in communities (usually cities) where they are virtually unknown; and the black community has seldom been known to betray a passer no matter what the resentment there might be against him as an individual.

The most important thing about the caste system, as outlined above, is that it transformed the whole culture of the southern states. It made its mark on every institution, whether of whites or blacks; and it created suspicion, antagonism, and violence in the relations between the races. It permeated the conversation, the thought, and the literature of the South. This caste system developed gradually during the nineteenth century; in fact, it did not take complete form until several decades after the end of slavery, around the 1890s. It remained in almost complete form until about 1940, after which parts of it began to crumble. Today, it is much modified; and from the rate of change since 1940, it may be predicted that the caste system is doomed to disappear despite the efforts of a vigorous minority of white southerners to keep it alive. Racism, the ideology which underlies caste, is still very strong and is more closely linked with other aspects of American culture (like the belief in biological determinism) than is caste, which has always seemed to most to be at least a little un-American.

Certain other aspects of racism must be pointed out. It is a complex of deep-seated feelings and attitudes that manifest themselves in behavior both consciously and unconsciously. The specific manifestations vary from culture to culture, but since the ideology is based on a conception that men belong to different races, each with its own distinctive biological potentiality, there is always a manifestation of the belief that men can be ranked in terms of biological worth and that this cannot be changed by any amount of learning or new environment. One racist society will define people as belonging to different races that another racist society will not; there is little relationship between a scientist's categorization by race, which is based on biologically inherited physical traits, and the racist's categorization by race, which may be based on religion, language, nationality, or anything else. Racism in the United States, which first developed in connection with blacks, quickly got transferred not only to Indians and Asiatics but also to the Irish, Italians, Poles, Jews, Catholics, Hispanos, Mennonites, and dozens of other groups. Racism, once it exists within a culture, has a tendency to be directed toward ever-different groups of people. The history of the United States from 1820 to 1940 exemplifies the spread of racism from one group to another. So does the history of South Africa, now probably the most violently racist nation in the world, which developed racism first in connection with white-native relations, then transferred many of the attitudes to Indian and southern European migrants.

Racism also has a tendency to spread rapidly from person to person within a given society. Thus, racism began in the southern states and spread very rapidly to the North, although only a few aspects of the caste system came along with it. Racism does not require an object to exist. There are areas in certain northern states that have never seen a black but in which there are well-developed racist attitudes toward blacks. There are few Turks in the United States, and those few probably would not be identified as Turks, but for a long while there were strong racist attitudes with regard to Turks.

Since racism purports to base itself on unchanging biological differences and includes a belief that people have an instinct to hold themselves aloof from those of different races, racists believe that their ideology has always existed and is, in a real sense, natural and timeless. They honestly believe that the group relationships they practice have always existed. Racists are surprised and unbelieving when they learn that racism began in the nineteenth century, that most people in the world are not racist, and that racism can be eliminated very rapidly if certain institutional changes occur in a society.

Certain *social structural* factors have been found to be associated with prejudice and discrimination against minorities. In a comparative study of forty societies, it was found that absolute monarchies showed the greatest harshness toward minorities, especially in regard to personal violence and economic exploitation.[4] The same study showed personal violence toward minorities to be associated with feudal economies, low respect for law, and well-defined class systems. Cultural traditions of prejudice and discrimination, although they should not be considered as causes in their own right, have carried on patterns of harshness toward minorities even when the causes that gave rise to them have disappeared.

Deliberate propaganda may originate antagonism toward minorities or accentuate an antagonism that already exists. There was very little anti-Japanese feeling in the United States until the Hearst and other newspapers took up an anti-Japanese theme, apparently as a means of building circulation.[5] There was little anti-Semitism in the United States until the White Russian émigrés after World War I brought the czar's propaganda to the United States and persuaded Henry Ford of its authenticity, so that he had it disseminated at his own expense.[6] Shortly after Ford stopped this propaganda, the German government's agents in the United States (in the 1930s) used many new forms of anti-Semitic propaganda, and they were successful in creating widespread anti-Semitism.[7] The German government's purpose was to create sympathy for its own anti-Semitic policy and divide Americans so that they would be less likely to resist Germany when it declared war on France and England. Some propaganda is not deliberate but is effective nevertheless. A study by L. L. Thurstone[8] demonstrated that certain American entertainment movies, notably the Fu Manchu films, were perpetuating anti-Chinese sentiment in the United States; and the United States government discouraged Hollywood from producing such films when it sought to build friendly attitudes toward China during the 1930s.

In recent years, there have been many studies of *psychological factors in prejudice.* They fall into diverse theoretical frameworks. Two older hypotheses concerning prejudice, stemming respectively from the instinct school and the original behaviorist school, have been discarded by contemporary psychologists. Some of the instinctivists posited a natural "dislike of differences," but this was soon seen as far from universal, and its object was held to be social variation just as often as racial or ethnic differences. Some of the early behaviorists held that unpleasant experiences with members of minority groups resulted in negative conditioning that could be called prejudice. Although this no doubt occurs, it is far from general, and studies have found that prejudice may be just as strong where members of the minority are few or even nonexistent as it is where they are numerous and hence available as conditioned stimuli.[9]

The contemporary neo-behaviorist school is inclined to explain prejudice in terms of the theory of frustration-aggression, which has a similarity to the Freudian theory of displacement. Studies[10] have shown that when people are prevented from doing the things they want to do, they are likely to react by hitting at something or trying to make someone else unhappy. Thus, frustration stimulates aggression. Now, if a person cannot hit back at the thing that makes him unhappy, he finds a substitute. When a group of people, perhaps a whole country, feels frustrated, its substitute for the object of aggression must be something widely available and yet weak. Minority groups serve that function and become scapegoats for the feelings of frustration of a whole nation. People may feel frustrated by bad economic conditions, unemployment, low wages—conditions that many southerners, especially, have been subject to for a long time. Or they may feel frustrated by failure to become a leading nation of the world, as Germans did after losing World War I. A people in this condition is ripe for a scapegoat or substitute object of aggression. It is frequently a seeker after political power who may name the object, since such a person can thereby gain leadership and also divert attention from his own deficiencies as a political leader.

Frustration may help to explain the force behind prejudice, but it does not explain why certain minority groups are chosen to be scapegoats. To explain this choice, psychologists and sociologists have offered another theory—the symbolic theory—based on the important fact that one thing can stand for something else in the unconscious mind. One often finds oneself liking something (certain houses or scenes, for example) without knowing why. If these feelings could be traced to their origin, the newly seen object would be found to remind one of something important and desirable. There does not have to be any real connection at all. The unconscious mind is always making connections, so that one thing will substitute for another. The question is: Why are certain minority groups disliked by so many people? Obviously, they must be symbolically connected with something very important to, and in this case hated by, many people. Among the things that are important to many people are an interesting life, money, opportunities for advancement, a belief in being kind and just to others, family life and sexual satisfaction, good health, and so forth. Concerning all these, people have mixed attitudes, at once liking them and also disliking them. People might be a little afraid of some of them, might wish to rebel against them, but they cannot say so. It is not proper or even desirable from a personal standpoint to dislike these values and goals. So the dislike becomes unconscious and can be expressed only through a substitute. Minority groups become symbolic substitutes for useful and important values in the culture with which they have deep psychological and historical connections. People cannot publicly admit dislike or fear or say that they would like to revolt against these things, so they express the attitude against their substitutes, which are frequently minority groups. Analyses by Samuel, McLean, Halsey, Rose, and Smith[11] advocate this theory.

A more characteristic psychoanalytic explanation of prejudice is the hypothesis of the authoritarian personality. Some mental disorders can be traced to inadequacies in personality development, and prejudice may be regarded under this theory as the result of a particular kind of development. Most of the studies in support of this view take the form of comparing groups of prejudiced and unprejudiced persons on a number of questions about personality characteristics and personality development. The items where significant differences appear are then integrated into a clinical picture of the prejudiced personality. Using this approach, Frenkel-Brunswick and her colleagues, for example, have discovered the typical anti-Semite to be a compulsive conformist, exhibiting anxiety at the appearance of any social deviation. He appears to be a person with no insight into himself, who projects his own undesired traits onto other people. He has a tendency toward stereotyped thinking and is unimaginative. He has unconscious inferiority problems centering on a feeling of sexual inadequacy. He expresses strong parental and religious devotion but manifests unconscious hatred of parents and social values. He exhibits aversion to emotionalism but unconsciously has feelings of inferiority toward it. He is prone to aggressive fantasies. Such a personality development is a product of rigid and repressive childhood training. It expresses itself in many ways, but prominent among them is prejudice against minority groups.

Obviously, not all prejudiced people have authoritarian personalities; if they did, most white southerners and a large proportion of northerners would have to be thought of as authoritarian (and they do not fit the definition except for their prejudice). And it is apparent that some authoritarian personality types are not particularly race-prejudiced (for example, the late Senator Joseph McCarthy and his immediate aides). But the concept of authoritarian personality aids in the understanding of an especially virulent form of race prejudice often found among lower-middle-class people.

Still another Freudian concept used to explain prejudice is that of projection, which refers to the tendency of people, under some circumstances, to attribute to others motives which they sense in themselves but which they would not wish to acknowledge openly. Fascists whose aim is world dominance accuse the Jews of plotting to seize control of all countries. White southerners who hunger for an unbounded sex life accuse the blacks of being naturally immoral and "animallike." People who are fearful because of the many uncertainties of modern existence are likely to persecute all the people they can, and that includes the minorities because the latter are weak. In David Petegorsky's words, the fearful "persecute so that they may project upon others the fear that is gnawing at their own hearts. By creating in others terrors greater than they themselves experience, men seek to build up for themselves an illusion of security and safety."[12]

In addition the various psychological theories of prejudice, one other social factor may prove helpful in the explanation of prejudice because it seems to activate some of the psychological mechanisms. This is the condition of the mass society that is partially characteristic of modern Western culture.[13] It is a state of society in which individuals have diminished communications with each other and in which most communication is one-way from certain central sources through the mass media. It is created by urbanization, relatively rapid mobility, and the development of mass media that do not allow for two-way communication. Under these conditions, members of a society cannot get together to develop new meanings and values to cope with the changed situation. The consequence of the mass society for the individual is a pervasive feeling that one does not understand, or participate in the control of, the forces that shape the society. Also contributing to this sense of social alienation is the weakening of traditional cultural values under conditions of rapid change, so that the traditional ways of regarding social forces are inadequate. Consequently, there is a tendency to consider these forces as mysterious and to attribute their control to uncomprehended powers such as Wall Street, labor bosses, international bankers, and Jews. Jews and Catholics receive the brunt of antagonism stimulated in this way, but the general anxiety characteristic of the mass society may find its outlet in violence and prejudice directed to any minority group.

The mass society has a special set of relationships to the psychological mechanisms already considered. Many of the frustrations of modern life are associated with its characteristics. The relatively rapid movements of the individual, both in terms of the groups with which he is associated and in terms of his economic employment, create problems for him as well as satisfy his wants. The movements are not always voluntary but are frequently the function of impersonal economic and political forces (depressions and wars, for example) and of the rapid turnover of social groups when communication and interests are segmentalized. Even when the movements are voluntary, it seldom happens that only the desired goals are achieved, unattended by some losses and disappointments. Among the detriments resulting from almost any movement is a loss of friends and acquaintances and, consequently, a further weakening in the possibilities for communication. Thus, rapid movement, whether it be physical or simply a change in group affiliation, is bound to create frustration; and rapid movement is a characteristic of a mass society.

There are several ways in which a decrease or segmentalization of communication is frustrating. First, there is the loss of affection and the decrease in a sense of security in interpersonal relationships. In a society in which group affiliations are generally rapidly changing (on the job, in the neighborhood and voluntary associations, and even in the family through divorce), the possibilities for the transmission of affection are reduced. Second, there is less ability to handle new problems, which arise at an increasing rate in a changing society. One of the first impulses a person has when a new problem arises is to talk it over with other people. The person who faces or sees the new problem seeks reassurance as well as ideas for coping with the difficulty. If the same new problem faces a large number of people, the development of a collective adjustment may be necessary or at least considered desirable. Insofar as communication is decreased, segmentalized, or made impersonal, these satisfactions become weakened or nonexistent. Of course, during times of collective catastrophe, the desire for communication is so great that it can be established with astonishing rapidity outside the ordinary rules. Bombs falling on a city will quickly make most people friendly toward each other, and even a minor accident on a public vehicle will establish social contact between the bodies that were only physically packed together a few minutes before. But it may be questioned whether this talking to strangers during times of crisis or stress is as satisfying as talking to friends, whose honesty, intelligence, and personality characteristics have already been gauged.

Now that some of the frustrating effects of economic and political insecurity and of competitive striving for wealth or prestige have been noted and some of the studies that try to tie these frustrations directly to race prejudice have been examined, a correlation can be established between the general economic status of a minority group and the average class position of the members of the majority group most antagonistic to it.[14] For example, there is a relatively greater concentration of anti-Semitism in the upper- and middle-income brackets than there is of antiblack prejudice, which finds its relative concentration in the lower-income brackets. Thus, competition seems to be a factor. A study by C. I. Hovland and R. R. Sears has demonstrated that lynchings in the South regularly increased when the price of cotton fell.[15]

Although the major concern here is to ascertain the specific character of the frustrations of modern society, the question of whether there are more or less of them in other societies may be raised. Preliterate and even medieval Western peoples were undoubtedly afflicted with greater hazards to life and well-being than Western man is today, except for the fearful possibilities of the atomic era. That famine and disease created great anxiety there can be no doubt. Certain natural phenomena (such as eclipses and freak storms) when interpreted in terms of superstitious beliefs, presented threats to felt security; whereas few would be concerned with such things in Western culture today. However, most other cultures had a more integrated and definite set of values, including a cosmology and metaphysics as well as ethics, which nearly everyone accepted without question. These explained catastrophes and also told people how to act in regard to them. In some cultures, where catastrophes were regarded as manifestations of the deity's will, they could even be regarded as having an ultimately benign purpose. These are among the major reasons why contemporary observers of the remains of preliterate cultures and of Oriental cultures regard them as fatalistic, even in the face of disaster. It seems likely that hazards to life and well-being are less frustrating when people are fatalistic. In modern mass society, where few persons accept any philosophy or value system unreservedly, there is less fatalism and more anxiety concerning catastrophes and new problems. This situation would seem to be more productive of psychological frustration.

Insofar as displacement is a mechanism involved in race prejudice and intergroup antagonism, it also is affected by the conditions of the modern mass society. An integrated and completely accepted philosophy and value system would channelize the direction of displacement. The displacement of hostile impulses might be directed toward minority groups or outgroups, but it might not, depending on the specific cultural definitions. In a mass society, where traditional philosophies and value systems are much less able to direct displacement, hostile attitudes are likely to be displaced onto weaker groups, which become minorities by definition. In preliterate societies, hostility was displaced onto lambs or goats, and this displacement often occurred on ceremonial occasions. In modern society, hostility is more regularly displaced onto minority groups, without benefit of ceremony.

The breakdown of complete communication within the community would seem to contribute to the displacement of hostility toward minority groups. Where people are in regular communication with each other, they are less likely to pick each other for displacing hostility in any regular fashion. It is to be noted that in medieval society, it was the persons estranged from the rest of the community by virtue of feeblemindedness, psychosis, or belief in their own supernatural powers who were regarded as witches or other allies of the devil and, therefore, as proper objects for the displacement of aggression. In both medieval and preliterate societies, there was a good deal of hostility against outgroups, such as people in the next town or country, and these, too, were cut off from communication. In modern mass society, there are all sorts of estrangements and barriers to communication within the community, and thus any group can become a minority group chosen for the displacement of hostility.

Most of what has been said about the direction of displacement could also be said about the direction of projection. Furthermore, insofar as the motive force behind projection is divided conscience, it is more likely to occur in a mass society than in any other kind of society. Where there is a single value system and the pressures of society on the individual are solely in terms of this one system, the individual is not likely to contain within himself differing conceptions of how to think and act. But when he does have such differing conceptions, resulting from contact with a variety of value systems and incomplete indoctrination in any one of them, he may have an internal conflict over what is right. This may be one type of occasion when he needs to eliminate the vanquished desires and thought to avoid conscious guilt, and projection is a mechanism for such elimination. This hypothesis, like the others presented, needs testing by comparison of cultures. One fact is clear from history: In a mass society, political leaders are partially able to divert criticism from themselves by projecting their faults on scapegoats.

The mechanism of unconscious symbolism operates largely through projection, and it also comes into use when there is ambivalence of attitude. If an object is both liked and disliked and is also considered so important that the individual feels the need to take a conscious stand for or against it, the rejected features of the object may be projected onto something else with which it is culturally associated, and the stand opposed to the one consciously taken toward the object is taken toward its substitute. This may result in either love or hate toward the substitute, or symbol. Ambivalence, which is the basis of all unconscious symbolism, is to a considerable extent the product of a society containing diverse value systems and inadequate communication to reduce conflicts of attitudes. American society offers its members all sorts of mental conflicts and does not provide adequate means of resolving them. Hence, there is extensive use of this kind of symbolism. The direction of repressed attitudes onto minority groups in a mass society has already been discussed. This shows up most clearly in the case of unconscious symbolisms. Of all the things blacks might stand for, the thing they are chosen to stand for by prejudiced persons is uninhibited and passionate sexuality. Of all the things Jews might stand for, they are chosen to stand as symbols of urbanism, rational capitalism, radicalism, and pacifism. Although blacks and Jews do have a cultural connection with these things, the things are important objects of culture toward which there are ambivalent attitudes. Thus, it is to ambivalence that the use of the symbolism mechanism must be traced as a source of race prejudice.

The personality type shown in the several researches by psychologists to be high in prejudice—the type called the authoritarian personality by the California group—is hypothesized to be the product of rigid, overdemanding, nonaffectionate childhood experience. The pattern of child rearing is largely a function of a specific culture, as the culture and personality school of anthropology has demonstrated.[16] But within any given culture, there are variations in child-rearing practices, and the culture itself may show trends away from or toward a more permissive and affectionate attitude toward children. The question is whether any of these variations and changes are associated with the characteristics of the mass society. To a considerable extent, parents and other adults who manifest affection and permissiveness toward children are those who are themselves secure and not highly frustrated. It has already been seen that insecurity and frustration are partly a function of mass society. Further, the general attitude toward children is partly a result of attitudes toward alternative uses of wealth and time. Especially in an urban civilization, children are expensive to raise, and many a prospective parent weighs the advantages of having children against the advantages of conspicuous consumption, to the frustration of the child. Any given value system places a high premium on children; else the culture would cease to exist. But when values weaken, attitudes toward children may deteriorate. These are among the factors in the mass society that contribute toward the development of children into authoritarian personalities.

NOTES

[1] American writers who have attempted to explain intergroup relations in Marxist terms include Carey McWilliams, *A Mask for Privilege* (Boston: Little, Brown, 1948); and Oliver C. Cox, *Caste, Class, and Race: A Study in Social Dynamics* (New York: Doubleday, 1948).

[2] *Caste and Class in a Southern Town* (New Haven: Yale University Press, 1937).

[3] See Bertram Doyle, *The Etiquette of Race Relations in the South* (Chicago: University of Chicago Press, 1937).

[4] Arnold M. Rose, "The Comparative Study of Intergroup Conflict," *Sociological Quarterly* 1 (January, 1960): 57-66, which comprises Chapter 11 of this volume.

[5] Carey McWilliams, *Prejudice: Japanese-Americans, Symbol of Racial Intolerance* (Boston: Little, Brown, 1944).

[6] Oscar and Mary F. Handlin, *Danger in Discord* (New York: Anti-Defamation League of B'nai B'rith, 1948).

[7] Donald S. Strong, *Organized Anti-Semitism in the United States* (Washington, D.C.: American Council on Public Affairs, 1941).

[8] "The Influence of Motion Pictures on Children's Attitudes," *Journal of Social Psychology* 2 (1931): 291-305.

[9] Eugene Hartley, *Problems in Prejudice* (New York: King's Crown Press, 1946).

[10] For example, John Dollard et al., *Frustration and Aggression* (New Haven: Yale University Press, 1939).

[11] Maurice Samuel, *The Great Hatred* (New York: Knopf, 1940); Helen V. McLean, "Psychodynamic Factors in Racial Relations," *Annals of the American Academy of Political and Social Science* 244 (March 1946): 159-166; Margaret Halsey, *Color Blind* (New York: Simon and Schuster, 1946); Arnold M. Rose, "Anti-Semitism's Root in City Hatred," *Commentary* 6 (October 1948): 374-378; Lillian Smith, *Killers of the Dream* (New York: Norton, 1949).

[12] David W. Petegorsky, "The Strategy of Hatred," *Antioch Review* I (September 1941): 377.

[13] Arnold M. Rose, *Theory and Method in the Social Sciences* (Minneapolis: University of Minnesota Press, 1954), chap. 2. For some political implications of mass society, see Hannah Arendt, *The Origins of Totalitarianism* (New York: Harcourt, Brace, 1951); Franz L. Neumann, *Behemoth* (New York: Oxford University Press, 1942); William Kornhauser, *The Politics of Mass Society* (New York: Free Press, 1959).

[14] Frank K. Westie, "Negro-White Status Differentials and Social Distance," *American Sociological Review* 17 (October 1952): 550-558. See also E. L. Horowitz, "Race Attitudes," in *Characteristics of the American Negro,* ed. O. Klineberg (New York: Harper & Row, 1944), part IV.

[15] C. I. Hovland and R. R. Sears, "Minor Studies of Aggression: Correlation of Lynching with Economic Indices," *Journal of Psychology* 9 (1940): 301-310. This particular correlation no longer holds because the changing culture has all but wiped out lynching.

[16] For example, Abram Kardiner, *The Psychological Frontiers of Society* (New York: Columbia University Press, 1945); Ralph Linton, *The Cultural Background of Personality* (New York: Appleton-Century-Crofts, 1945); Ruth Benedict, *The Chrysanthemum and the Sword* (Boston: Houghton Mifflin, 1946).

35
the study of race

SHERWOOD L. WASHBURN

In this paper, originally his presidential address to the American Anthropological Association, Professor Washburn criticizes not only popular concepts of race but also outmoded ideas of raciation often found in anthropological texts. In particular, he insists that the formation of races has occurred by adaptation to particular historical situations, resulting in great racial variation rather than in the four or five races known to the layman.

Professor Washburn concludes that how one classifies races depends on the purpose of the classification. This point of view is surely new to most people, who think of races as fixed entities about whose characteristics there can be no doubt. In this selection are highly original discussions of the capacity of man to learn, intelligence testing and race, and the new conditions that modern industry and technology impose on the future development of races.

Professor Washburn is a physical anthropologist specializing in the study of the structure of the face.

I INTRODUCTION

The races of man are the result of human evolution, of the evolution of our species. The races are open parts of the species, and the species is a closed system. If we look, then, upon long-term human evolution, our first problem must be the species and the things which have caused the evolution of all mankind, not the races, which are the results of local forces and which are minor in terms of the evolution of the whole species. (A contrary view has recently been expressed by Prof. Carleton S. Coon in *The Origin of Races.* I think that great antiquity of human races is supported neither by the record nor by evolutionary theory.)

The evolution of races is due, according to modern genetics, to mutation, selection, migration, and genetic drift. It is easy to shift from this statement of genetic theory to complications of hemoglobin, blood groups, or other technical information. But the point I want to stress is that the primary implication of genetics for anthropology is that it affirms the relation of culture and biology in a far firmer and more important way than ever in our history before. Selection is for reproductive success, and in man reproductive success is primarily determined by the social system and by culture. Effective behavior is the question, not something else.

Drift depends on the size of population, and population size, again is dependent upon culture, not upon genetic factors as such. Obviously, migration depends on clothes, transportation, economy, and warfare and is reflected in the archeological record. Even mutation rates are now affected by technology.

Genetic theory forces the consideration of culture as the major factor in the evolution of man. It thus reaffirms the fundamental belief of anthropologists that we must study man both as a biological and as a social organism. This is no longer a question of something that might be desirable; it must be done if genetic theory is correct.

We have, then, on the one hand the his-

Reprinted from *American Anthropologist* 65, no. 3, part 1 (June 1963), pp. 521-531. Reproduced by permission of the author.

tory of genetic systems, and on the other hand the history of cultural systems, and finally, the interrelation between these two. There is no evolution in the traditional anthropological sense. What Franz Boas referred to as evolution was orthogenesis—which receives no support from modern genetic theory. What the geneticist sees as evolution is far closer to what Boas called history than to what he called evolution, and some anthropologists are still fighting a nineteenth-century battle in their presentation of evolution. We have, then, the history of cultural systems, which you may call history; and the history of genetic systems, which you may call evolution if you want to, but if you use this word remember that it means selection, migration, drift—it is real history that you are talking about and not some mystic force which constrains mankind to evolve according to some orthogenetic principle.

There is, then, no possibility of studying human raciation, the process of race formation, without studying human culture. Archeology is as important in the study of the origin of races as is genetics; all we can do is reconstruct as best we can the long-term past, and this is going to be very difficult.

THE PROBLEM OF CLASSIFICATION

Now let me contrast this point of view with the one which has been common in much of anthropology. In the first place, anthropology's main subject, the subject of race, disregarded to an amazing degree the evolution of the human species. Anthropologists were so concerned with the subdivisions within our species and with minor detailed differences between small parts of the species that the physical anthropologists largely forgot that mankind is a species and that the important thing is the evolution of this whole group, not the minor differences between its parts.

If we look back to the time when I was educated, races were regarded as types. We were taught to go to a population and divide it into a series of types and to re-create history out of this artificial arrangement. This kind of anthropology is still alive, amazingly, and in full force in some countries; relics of it are still alive in our teaching today.

Genetics shows us that typology must be completely removed from our thinking if we are to progress. For example, let us take the case of the Bushmen. The Bushmen have been described as the result of a mixture between Negro and Mongoloid. Such a statement could only be put in the literature without any possible consideration of migration routes, of numbers of people, of cultures, of any way that such a mixing could actually take place. The fact is that the Bushmen had a substantial record in South Africa and in East Africa and there is no evidence that they ever were anywhere else except in these areas. In other words, they are a race which belongs exactly where they are.

If we are concerned with history let us consider, on the one hand, the ancestors of these Bushmen 15,000 years ago and the area available to them, to their way of life, and, on the other hand, the ancestors of Europeans at the same time in the area available to them, with their way of life. We will find that the area available to the Bushmen was at least twice that available to the Europeans. The Bushmen were living in a land of optimum game; the Europeans were living close to an ice sheet. There were perhaps from three to five times as many Bushmen ancestors as there were European ancestors only 15,000 years ago.

If one were to name a major race, or a primary race, the Bushmen have a far better claim in terms of the archeological record than the Europeans. During the time of glacial advance more than half of the Old World available to man for life was in Africa. The numbers and distributions that we think of as normal and the races whose last results we see today are relics of an earlier and far different time in human history.

There are no three primary races, no three major groups. The idea of three primary races stems from nineteenth-century typology; it is totally misleading to put the black-skinned people of the world together—to put the Australian in the same grouping with the inhabitants of Africa. And there are certainly at least three independent origins of the small, dark people, the Pygmies, and probably more than that. There is no single Pygmy race.

If we look to real history we will always find more than three races, because there are more than three major areas in which the raciation of our species was taking place.

If we attempt to preserve the notion of three races, we make pseudo-typological problems. Take for example, again, the problem of the aboriginal Australian. If we have only three races, either they must be put with the people of Africa, with which they have nothing in common, or they must be accounted for by mixture, and in books appearing even as late as 1950, a part of the aboriginal Australian population is described as European, and listed with the Europeans, and the residue is listed with the Africans and left there.

The concept of race is fundamentally changed if we actually look for selection, migration, and study people as they are (who they are, where they are, how many they are); and the majority of anthropological textbooks need substantial revision along these lines.

Since races are open systems which are intergrading, the number of races will depend on the purpose of the classification. This is, I think, a tremendously important point. It is significant that as I was reviewing classifications in preparing this paper, I found that almost none of them mentioned any purpose for which people were being classified. Race isn't very important biologically. If we are classifying races in order to understand human history, there aren't many human races, and there is very substantial agreement as to what they are. There are from six to nine races, and this difference in number is very largely a matter of definition. These races occupied the major separate geographical areas in the Old World.

If one has no purpose for classification, the number of races can be multiplied almost indefinitely, and it seems to me that the erratically varying number of races is a source of confusion to student, to layman, and to specialist. I think we should require people who propose a classification of races to state in the first place why they wish to divide the human species and to give in detail the important reasons for subdividing our whole species. If important reasons for such classification are given, I think you will find that the number of races is always exceedingly small.

THE INFLUENCE OF MIGRATION

If we consider these six or nine geographical races and the factors which produced them, I think the first thing we want to stress is migration.

All through human history, where we have any evidence of that history, people have migrated. In a recent issue of *American Anthropologist* there is a suggestion that it took 400,000 years for a gene that mutated in China to reach Europe. We know, historically, that Alexander the Great went from Greece into Northern India. We know that Mongol tribes migrated from Asia into Europe. Only a person seeking to believe that the races are very separate could possibly believe such a figure as that cited.

Migration has always been important in human history and there is no such thing as human populations which are completely separated from other human populations. And migration necessarily brings in new genes, necessarily reduces the differences between the races. For raciation to take place, then, there must be other factors operating which create difference. Under certain circumstances, in very small populations, differences may be created by genetic drift, or because the founders are for chance reasons very different from other members of the species.

However, the primary factor in the creation of racial differences in the long term is selection. This means that the origin of races must depend on adaptation and that the differences between the races which we see must in times past have been adaptive. I stress the question of time here, because it is perfectly logical to maintain that in time past a shovel-shaped incisor, for example, was more efficient than an incisor of other forms and that selection would have been for this, and at the same time to assert that today this dental difference is of absolutely no social importance. It is important to make this point because people generally take the view that something is always adaptive or never adaptive, and this is a fundamental oversimplification of the facts.

Adaptation is always within a given situation. There is no such thing as a gene which has a particular adaptive value; it has this value only under set circumstances. For example, the sickle-cell gene, if Allison and others are right, protects against malaria. This is adaptive if there is malaria, but if there is not malaria it is not adaptive. The adaptive value of the gene, then, is dependent on the state of medicine and has no absolute value. The same is true of the other characteristics associated with race.

I would like to go over some of the suggestions which have been made about the adaptive values of various structures in human beings, because I think these need to be looked at again.

I have stressed that the concept of race which comes from population genetics is compatible with what anthropologists have thought. I think that this concept represents great progress. But when I read the descriptions of the importance of adaptive characteristics, I am not sure that there has been any progress since the nineteenth century.

In this connection I should like to speak for a moment on the notion that the Mongoloids are a race which are adapted to live in the cold, that these are arctic-adapted people.

In the first place, in marked contrast to animals which are adapted to live in the arctic, large numbers of Mongoloids are living in the hot, moist tropics. Altogether unlike animal adaptation, then, the people who are supposed to be adapted to the cold aren't living under cold conditions, and I think we should stress this. For thousands of years the majority of this group have not been living under the conditions which are supposed to have produced them. They are presumed, as an arctic-adapted group following various laws, to have short extremities, flat noses, and to be stocky in build. They are, we might say, as stocky as the Scotch, as flat-nosed as the Norwegians, and as blonde as the Eskimos. Actually, there is no correlation, that is, none that has been well worked out, to support the notion that any of these racial groups is cold-adapted.

A few more words on this lack of correlation. If one follows the form of the nose, in Europe, as one moves north, narrow noses are correlated with cold climate; in Eastern Asia low noses are correlated with cold climate. In neither case is there the slightest evidence that the difference in the form of the nose has anything whatsoever to do with warming the air that comes into the face. Further, if we look at these differences expressed in this way, we see that they are posed in terms of nineteenth-century notions of what a face is all about.

Let us look at it differently. The nose is the center of a face. Most of a face is concerned with teeth, and bones, and muscles that have to do with chewing. The Mongoloid face is primarily the result of large masseter (chewing) muscles and the bones from which these muscles arise. This is a complex structural pattern related to the teeth, and a superficially very similar pattern may be seen in the Bushman, whose facial form can hardly be attributed to adaptation to cold.

The face of the Neanderthal man has recently been described also as cold-adapted, though it does not have the characteristics of the Mongoloid face. We are told that the blood supply to the Neanderthal face was greatly increased because the infraorbital foramen was large, bringing more blood to the front of the face. In actual fact, most of the blood to our face does not go through that artery. The artery that carries most of the blood to the face comes along the outside, and even our arteries are far too large to go through the mental or infraorbital foramen of Neanderthal man. This kind of statement, as well as the statement that the maxillary sinus warmed the air and that the function of a large orbit was to keep the eyes from freezing, seems to me an extraordinary retrogression to the worst kind of evolutionary speculation—speculation that antedates genetics and reveals a lack of any kind of reasonable understanding of the structure of the human face.

The point I wish to stress is that those who have spoken of the cold-adaptation of the Mongoloid face and of the Neanderthal face do not know the structure of the human face.

The adaptive value of skin color has been repeatedly claimed, but recently Blum has indicated that the situation is more complicated than it appeared. In the first place, he points out the melanin in the skin doesn't do what anthropologists have said it has done. The part of the skin which mainly stops ultraviolet light, the short-wave length light, is a thickened *stratum corneum,* rather than melanin.

Again, the chimpanzee and the gorilla live in precisely the same climatic conditions in Uganda, but the gorilla has one of the blackest, most deeply pigmented skins of the primates and the chimpanzee has a very light skin. It simply is not true that skin color closely parallels climate. The point here is that racial classification tells us very little. The classification poses problems; it does not solve them.

In scientific method, as I see it, one looks at relevant data and when these data are laid out, as in, say, the classification of races, one may then find a correlation which is helpful. But after that, one has to do an experiment; one has to do something that shows that the correlation has validity. And it's no use continuing to correlate nose form or skin color with climate. The crude correlations were made many years ago, and to advance the study of race requires new methods and more sophisticated analyses.

When I was a student, there were naive racial interpretations based on the metrical data. When these became unacceptable politically the same people used naive constitutional correlations to reach the same conclusions of social importance. Today we have naive concepts of adaptation, taking the place of the earlier interpretations, and a recrudescence of the racial thinking.

All along the line there have been valid problems in race, valid problems in constitution, and valid problems in adaptation. What I am protesting against strongly is the notion that one can simply take a factor, such as a high cheekbone, think that it might be related to climate, and then jump to this conclusion without any kind of connecting link between the two elements—without any kind of experimental verification of the sort of material that is being dealt with. If we took really seriously this notion that a flat face with large maxillary sinuses, deep orbits, and big brow ridges is cold-adapted, it is clear that the most cold-adapted animal in the primates is the gorilla.

Race, then, is a useful concept only if one is concerned with the kind of anatomical, genetic, and structural differences which were in time past important in the origin of races. Race in human thinking is a very minor concept. It is entirely worth while to have a small number of specialists, such as myself, who are concerned with the origin of gonial angles, the

form of the nose, the origin of dental patterns, changes in blood-group frequencies, and so on. But this is a very minor, specialized kind of knowledge.

If classification is to have a purpose, we may look backward to the explanation of the differences between people—structural, anatomical, physiological differences—and then the concept of race is useful, but it is useful under no other circumstances, as far as I can see.

When the meaning of skin color and structure is fully understood, it will help us to understand the origin of races, but this is not the same thing as understanding the origin of our species. It will help in the understanding of why color was important in time long past, but it will have no meaning to modern technical society.

THE INFLUENCE OF CULTURE

I turn now to a brief statement on the influence of culture upon race. Beginning with agriculture and continuing at an ever-increasing rate, human customs have been interposed between the organism and the environment. The increase of our species from perhaps as few as five million before agriculture to three billion today is the result of new technology, not of biological evolution. The conditions under which the races evolved are mainly gone, and there are new causes of mutation, new kinds of selection, and vast migration. Today the numbers and distribution of the peoples of the world are due primarily to culture. Some people think the new conditions are so different that it is better no longer to use the word race or the word evolution, but I personally think this confuses more than it clarifies.

All this does not mean that evolution has stopped, because the new conditions will change gene frequencies, but the conditions which produced the old races are gone. In this crowded world of civilization and science, the claim has been made repeatedly that one or another of the races is superior to the others. Obviously, this argument cannot be based on the past; because something was useful in times past and was selected for under conditions which are now gone, does not mean that it will be useful in the present or in the future.

The essential point at issue is whether the abilities of large populations are so different that their capacity to participate in modern technical culture is affected. Remember in the first place that no race has evolved to fit the selective pressures of the modern world. Technical civilization is new and the races are old. Remember also that all the species of *Homo* have been adapting to the human way of life for many thousands of years. Tools even antedate our genus, and our human biological adaptation is the result of culture. Man and his capacity for culture have evolved together, as Dr. Theodosius Dobzhansky has pointed out. All men are adapted to learn language—any language; to perform skillful tasks—a fabulous variety of tasks; to cooperate; to enjoy art; to practice religion, philosophy, and science.

Our species only survives in culture, and, in a profound sense, we are the product of the new selection pressures that came with culture.

Infinitely more is known about the language and culture of all the groups of mankind than is known about the biology of racial differences. We know that the members of every racial group have learned a vast variety of languages and ways of life. The interaction of genes and custom over the millennia has produced a species whose populations can learn to live in an amazing variety of complex cultural ways.

Racism is based on a profound misunderstanding of culture, of learning, and of the biology of the human species. The study of cultures should give a profound respect for the biology of man's capacity to learn. Much of the earlier discussion of racial inferiority centered on the discussion of intelligence; or, to put the matter more accurately, usually on that small part of biological intelligence which is measured by the IQ. In the earlier days of intelligence testing, there was a widespread belief that the tests revealed something which was genetically fixed within a rather narrow range. The whole climate of opinion that fostered this point of view has changed. At that time animals were regarded as primarily instinctive in their behavior, and the genes were supposed to exert their effects in an almost mechanical way, regardless of the environment. All this intellectual climate has changed. Learning has proved to be far more important in the behavior of many animal species, and the action of the complexes of genes is now known to be affected by the environment, as is, to a great degree, the performance that results from them. For example, Harlow has shown that monkeys learn to learn. Monkeys, in other words, become test wise. They become skillful in the solution of tests—so monkeys in Dr. Harlow's laboratories are spoken of as naive or as experienced in the use of tests. To suppose that humans cannot learn to take tests is to suppose that humans are rather less intelligent than monkeys.

Krech and Rosenzweig have shown that rats raised in an enriched environment are much more intelligent and efficient as maze-solvers than rats that have been given no opportunity to learn and to practice before the testing. To suppose that man would not learn through education to take tests more efficiently is to suppose that our learning capacities are rather less than those of rats.

The human is born with less than a third of the adult brain capacity, and there is tremendous growth of the cortex after birth. There is possibly no mammalian species in which the environment has a longer and more direct effect on the central nervous system than man. We should expect, then, that test results are going to be more affected by the environment of man than in the case of any other animal. Deprivation studies of monkeys and chimpanzees and clinical investigations of man show that the lack of a normal interpersonal environment may be devastating to the developing individual.

INTELLIGENCE TESTING

Today one approaches the study of intelligence expecting to find that environment is important. The intellectual background is very different from that of the '20's. The general results on testing may be briefly summarized as follows:

The average IQ of large groups is raised by education. I believe the most important data on this are the comparisons of the soldiers of World War I and of World War II. More than

80 per cent of the soldiers tested in World War II were above the mean of those tested in World War I. This means a wholesale massive improvement, judged by these tests, in the sons of the people who fought in World War I.

In the states where the least educational effort is made, the IQ is the lowest. In fact, as one looks at the review in Anastasi's book it is exceedingly difficult to see why anyone ever thought that the IQ measured innate intelligence, and not the genetic constitution as modified in the family, in the schools, and by the general intellectual environment.

I would suggest that if the intelligence quotients of Negroes and Whites in this country are compared, the same rules be used for these comparisons as would be used for comparisons of the data between two groups of Whites. This may not seem a very extreme thing to suggest, but if you look at the literature, you will find that when two groups of Whites differ in their IQ's, the explanation of the difference is immediately sought in schooling, environment, economic positions of parents, and so on, but that when Negroes and Whites differ in precisely the same way the difference is said to be genetic.

Let me give you but one example of this. Otto Klineberg showed years ago in excellent studies that the mean test scores of many Northern Negro groups were higher than those of certain groups of Southern Whites. When these findings were published, it was immediately suggested that there had been a differential migration and the more intelligent Negroes had moved to the North. But the mean of Northern Whites' test results is above that of Southern Whites. Are we to believe that the intelligent Whites also moved to the North?

There is no way of telling what the IQ would be if equal opportunity were given to all racial and social groups. The group which is sociologically classifed as Negro in the United States, about one-third of whose genes are of European origin, might well test ahead of the Whites. I am sometimes surprised to hear it stated that if Negroes were given an equal opportunity, their IQ would be the same as the Whites'. If one looks at the degree of social

discrimination against Negroes and their lack of education, and also takes into account the tremendous amount of overlapping between the observed IQ's of both, one can make an equally good case that, given a comparable chance to that of the Whites, their IQ's would test out ahead. Of course, it would be absolutely unimportant in a democratic society if this were to be true, because the vast majority of individuals of both groups would be of comparable intelligence, whatever the mean of these intelligence tests would show.

We can generalize this point. All kinds of human performance—whether social, athletic, intellectual—are built on genetic and environmental elements. The level of all kinds of performance can be increased by improving the environmental situation so that every genetic constitution may be developed to its full capacity. Any kind of social discrimination against groups of people, whether these are races, castes, or classes, reduces the achievements of our species, of mankind.

THE COST OF DISCRIMINATION

The cost of discrimination is reflected in length of life. The Founding Fathers were wise to join life, liberty, and the pursuit of happiness, because these are intimately linked in the social and cultural system. Just as the restriction of social and economic opportunity reduces intelligence so it reduces length of life.

In 1900 the life expectancy of White males in the United States was 48 years, and in that same year the expectancy of a Negro male was 32 years; that is a difference of 50 per cent, or 16 years. By 1940 the difference had been reduced to ten years, and by 1958 to six. As the life expectancy of the Whites increased from 48 to 62 to 67 years, that of the Negroes increased from 32 to 52 to 61 years. They died of the same causes, but they died at different rates.

Discrimination, by denying equal social opportunity to the Negro, made his progress lag approximately 20 years behind that of the White. Somebody said to me, "Well, 61, 67, that's only six years." But it depends on whose six years it is. There are about 19 million people in this country sociologically classified as Negroes. If they die according to the death rate given above, approximately 100 million years of life will be lost owing to discrimination.

In 1958 the death rate for Negroes in the first year of life was 52 per thousand and for Whites 26. Thousands of Negro infants died unnecessarily. The social conscience is an extraordinary thing. A lynching stirs the whole community to action, yet only a single life is lost. Discrimination, through denying education, medical care, and economic progress, kills at a far higher rate. A ghetto of hatred kills more surely than a concentration camp, because it kills by accepted custom, and it kills every day in the year.

A few years ago in South Africa, the expectation of life for a Black man was 40 years; but it was 60 at the same time for a White man. At that same time a White woman could expect 25 more years of life than a Black woman. Among the Blacks the women lived no longer than the men. People speak of the greater longevity of women, but this is only because of modern medicine. High birth rates, high infant mortality, high maternal mortality —these are the hallmarks of the history of mankind.

Of course there are biological differences between male and female, but whether a woman is allowed to vote, or the rate that she must die in childbirth, these are a matter of medical knowledge and of custom. Biological difference only expresses itself through the social system.

Who may live longer in the future— Whites or Negroes? There's no way of telling. Who may live longer in the future—males or females? There is no way of telling. These things are dependent on the progress in medical science and on the degree to which this progress is made available to all races and to both sexes.

When environment is important, the only way genetic difference may be determined is by equalizing the environment. If you believe in mankind, then you will want mankind to live on in an enriched environment. No one can tell what may be the ultimate length of life, but we do know that many people could live much longer if given a chance.

Whether we consider intelligence, or length of life, or happiness the genetic potential of a population is only realized in a social system. It is that system which gives life or death to its members, and in so doing changes the gene frequencies. We know of no society which has begun to realize the genetic potential of its members. We are the primitives living by antiquated customs in the midst of scientific progress. Races are products of the past. They are relics of times and conditions which have long ceased to exist.

Racism is equally a relic supported by no phase of modern science. We may not know how to interpret the form of the Mongoloid face, or why Rh° is of high incidence in Africa, but we do know the benefits of education and of economic progress. We know the price of discrimination is death, frustration, and hatred. We know that the roots of happiness lie in the biology of the whole species and that the potential of the species can only be realized in a culture, in a social system. It is knowledge and the social system which give life or take it away, and in so doing change the gene frequencies and continue the million-year-old interaction of culture and biology. Human biology finds its realization in a culturally determined way of life, and the infinite variety of genetic combinations can only express themselves efficiently in a free and open society.

36
race, diet, and intelligence

JOSEPHINE SCHUYLER

As Josephine Schuyler points out, the question of whether intelligence is related to race is unanswerable (at least in the present state of genetic knowledge). Sociologist are, however, beginning to learn something about environmental factors that depress intelligence, and these at least can be controlled. The following article talks about the effects of diet on children and adults. More recent research shows that a lack of protein in the mother carrying a child and in children under two years of age can (and probably does) cause irreparable damage to the central nervous system. At a later age, lack of protein hinders growth and health, but when the nervous system is developing—and among humans, it continues to develop after birth—protein deficiency can permanently damage the intelligence. It is no accident then that the poor of all times and places seem less intelligent than the well-to-do.

Intelligence is a very elusive thing to define, and to define it by the results of a culturally biased reading and writing test is ridiculous. It is only recently and in a few societies that reading and writing skills have been important to society. Today, probably three-quarters of the people in the world cannot read, and considering all the people who have lived in the 5,000 years since writing was invented, the proportion of people who have ever been able to read and write is about one-hundreth of one percent; man not only survived but also produced scores of great civilizations.

Nevertheless, today, reading and writing skills are important in industrial societies; it is important to stop talking about a narrowly defined intelligence and instead to find out how to improve the skills the society is interested in. Recent research shows that verbal fluency is much enhanced by verbally fluent mothers and early linguistic stimulation of the child. Improving the linguistic environment of the child is not as simple as adding protein to the diet. Day-care centers and nursery schools can do some of this, but the research findings show that it is the pre-two-year-old who needs the stimulation. Experiments are being conducted in which mothers are being trained to stimulate their children verbally. In general, it is suggested that the environment be controlled in those ways that are known to be relevant to general intelligence as well as verbal skills, since it is known environment has an effect, and the specific ways in which it operates are beginning to be learned.

Mrs. Schuyler, a free-lance writer, died recently in New York City.

Reprinted from *The Crisis,* 76, no. 5 (May 1969), pp. 207-210. Reproduced by permission of the publisher and Mr. George Schuyler.

The proverbial storm in a teacup has now been transferred to the gene. Dr. Arthur R. Jensen of the University of California at Berkeley has recently stated in the *Harvard Educational Review* that intelligence is largely determined by heredity and cannot be altered significantly by improving environment. This controversy of genetics versus environment has been raging since before the Russian Revolution. Far-reaching social programs are dependent upon the answer.

Dr. Jensen states in sum:

That Negroes average 15 points below whites on I.Q. tests.

That children from Negro professional families average 2.6 points below the whites on the lowest income level. And that American Indian children who are more disadvantaged economically than American Negro children still rate higher on almost every level of the I.Q. test. And further that I.Q.'s below 75 occur 13 times more frequently among Negroes in the higher income bracket than among upper-class whites. That a Negro slum neighborhood which had only 5 per cent of the city's children provided one-third of the city's retardates.

On the other hand he found:

That in rote learning the Negro and white children did about equally well, though their I.Q.'s differed by as many as 15 or 20 points. That Negro infants did better between the ages of 9 and 12 months in muscular coordination and other aspects than did white babies. In some sections Negro infants up to 6 months of age scored 8 points above white norms.

Dr. Jensen concludes that research clearly shows differing patterns of intellectual skills among races and that discrepancies in performance cannot be completely or directly attributed to discrimination or inequalities in education. Therefore, he concludes that big programs of "compensatory" education costing the taxpayers millions of dollars annually are doomed to failure.

The main difference between the intelligence of white and colored children appears to lie in the area of abstract reasoning, called "cognitive" learning.

The statistics presented by Dr. Jensen are too confused to justify such definite conclusions. After World War I, this same argument was waged with the statistics of the U.S. Army Intelligence scores where the Negro soldiers rated below whites in general but if they came from the North they scored above white soldiers born and reared in the South.

All during the Twenties and Thirties learned treatises were written at Columbia University "proving" that Negro children in the South rated below the white children there on all I.Q. tests. And if elsewhere they equaled white children their rate of "growth" started petering off at puberty.

Then a number of Negro youngsters appeared on the educational scene with extremely high I.Q.'s—among them a Chicago lad, J. Ernest Wilkins, Jr., who entered college at 12, and my daughter Philippa Schuyler, whose I.Q. tests were made by Columbia, New York University and Fordham and rate above 180 points. The performances of these two young people never leveled off but continued to mount. Such instances may be put down as "the exception which proved the rule." Nevertheless, the publicity about them and others whose names I have now forgotten did have a salutary effect on theorizing about Negro and white intellectual differences.

Now, more than a generation later, a great mass of Negro youth has suddenly become a football of power for opportunists of both groups to kick around and capitalize on by massive programs which they intend to "guide" at $30,000 a year or make the subject of learned papers which enable the author to pose as an authority in educational research.

The fact is, no really scientific studies have yet been made and possibly cannot be made because when you try to measure white, American Indian and American Negro intelligence it is first necessary to define what you mean by these terms. We know what constitutes some (not all) whites: that is, they are of unmixed European ancestry; and we know what some American Indians are (many are intermixed with Negroes); but WHAT is an American Negro? According to the late Melville J. Herskovits (formerly of Northwestern

University and the foremost authority on this subject), at least 80 per cent of American Negroes are of mixed genetic ancestry, including Caucasian, American Indian and African; so that the Bantu strain which gives him the status of a "race" is but one-third of his genetic makeup. He is, therefore, not a "race" but a sociological phenomenon.

The number of "white" persons in the United States with some African ancestry, while not precisely known, has been variously estimated at from 5,000,000 to 20,000,000 by sociologists, anthropologists and journalists.

A race, even at its "purest" (which is hard to find even among Bushmen and Eskimos), is a vague concept and originally arose as a semantic convenience and a political instrument. Every civilized group has been intermixed by invading conquerors beyond counting since man began. The West African Bantu that made up the bulk of slaves brought to the New World was already greatly intermixed with the Arab slavers who had pushed their way deep into the African continent long before European slavers arrived in the Fifteenth Century. But the "one-drop" theory was as profitable to the white slaveholder as it is now to the black militant, several hundred years and many mixtures later.

To have accredited scientists soberly weighing genetic differences among Americans, based on what was a phantom in the first place, is the height of absurdity. But it is profitable, so it will continue.

An equally vague area in this attempt to measure "racial" differences among Americans lies in the concept of environment. Where do genetics end and where does the environment begin? Most people assume that when a baby is born, its environment begins. But what of the environment of the fetus in the womb? The development of the fetus has been dependent on this environment which in turn depends on the mother's habits of nutrition and general well-being, including the air she breathes and the stress she endures, as well as the drugs she takes. (Drug addicts give birth to babies who are addicts.)

But it is not only narcotics which affect unborn infants but a thousand other drugs.

Poor mothers are more the victims of improper medication than others. The placenta has been found to attract the accumulation of poisons. Who can determine whether a genetical inferiority has produced a retardate or the environment of the fetus produced by the nutritional deficiencies and general inadequacies surrounding the mother. Then after birth the infant is the victim of the food habits of its home. If Negro mothers even from the upper level persist in serving the most "traditional" food then the child suffers. And its performance in the classroom is lowered. Some of the most revered food is the worst. To mention some favorites: cornbread, grits, pork, flapjacks, rice (polished), fried chicken and the like.

Dr. Weston A. Price, a dental surgeon from the Crile Laboratories in Cleveland, wrote an impressive book in the late 1930's called *Nutrition and Physical Degeneration,* with a foreword by Professor Ernest Hooton of Harvard University, then the leading American anthropologist. In this book Dr. Price presented extensive research results gathered in a field trip around the world which he made to evaluate the relation between health, intelligence and nutrition. He found no superiority of lighter-skinned people to those of darker hue. But he did find definite inferiority between those subjected to modern, refined diets and those living in areas remote from civilization who did not eat store-bought food. I corresponded with these scientists about the American diet which both condemned. Dr. Price was able to raise the I.Q. of a group of students at Ohio State University by 20 points just by improving their diet. (Just this would be enough to wipe out the difference between the I.Q.'s of white and colored children.) Dr. Price and Professor Hooton are both dead and the new men on the scene do not even seem to know of their thoroughly documented findings.

In the December, 1942, issue of *The Crisis* I wrote an article entitled "Nutrition and Racial Superiority," in which was stated:

Of all Americans, Negroes most need to know about food. They have the worst health, the highest death rate and the worst eating habits in the country. Naturally, this is not due to any racial propensity toward malnutrition, it is mainly because so large a percentage of Negroes live in or have lived in the South where evils are usually exaggerated and fear of change predominates. When colored folk move away, unfortunately, they carry their food habits with them. Pork and cornbread remain favorites. Although the government warns the public to always cook its pork well done, it does not explain in detail why. Nor does it tell you that most hotdogs, hamburgers and sausages have large admixtures of pork that may not be well cooked, so you still might get trichinosis. This is a dreaded disease. Its symptoms are similar to rheumatism. There is no cure.

Now, 27 years later, the only thing that has changed is that more and more Americans are incapacitated by pork worms masquerading as arthritis. Today, almost everyone has heard that refined rice and flour are unhealthful. Yet how many people put this knowledge in practice? According to an authority, Ruth Winter, in *Poisons in Your Food* (Crown, 1969): "The bread you put in your mouth daily is literally embalmed . . . and the dessert you eat may be colored with a cancer-causing agent."

People with Southern-based menus eat far too much bread. The eating habits of the average colored American family could easily explain the difference in the I.Q. tests of their children and the average American white child outside the South. The higher I.Q. rate of Indian children even on reservations is due to fresh game and fish they may have combined with better air and less drugs.

Instead of spending millions on enriching a school program, that money spent on enriching school lunches would do far more good. Even the milk is now contaminated with pesticides, according to Dr. Robert Cook of Illinois State University, though this could be improved by adding charcoal to the food of dairy animals. The soft-drink field is the worst of all; especially the new "low-caloried beverages." This is but a small part of the dreadful overall picture of American nutrition which affects the poor most of all. It is not a matter of starvation, but malnutrition due to ignorance on the part of the consumer and license on the part of the food industry.

The place to start improving the intelligence of the youth of American is in the wombs of their mothers

37
happenings on the way back to the forum: social science, IQ, and race differences revisited

MARTIN DEUTSCH

It is regrettable that in 1972 there is still serious discussion of whether poor performance in school or on intelligence tests is due to genetic factors. In 1897, Charles Cooley wrote an article ("Genius, Fame and the Comparison of Races," Annals of the American Academy of Political and Social Science *[May 1897], pp. 317-358) that established the proposition most biological and social scientists now agree with: Large amounts of observed differences in intellectual performance can be explained by environmental factors, and until these are controlled, the effect of the genetic factors cannot be determined. Almost seventy-five years of research have not overthrown these conclusions.*

It is, however, interesting to know why, of all the learned articles published in obscure scientific journals, the article by Arthur R. Jensen should have hit the front pages. The answer is obvious. People would like to believe that blacks are biologically inferior. This lets everybody off the hook. Whites can go on discriminating, only now they need not have guilty consciences. Racism, as a systematic ideology, when it originated, relied on nineteenth-century biology, which is now known to have been incorrect. If racism can be based on psychological testing, it would be possible to retain both the cake of racism and the eating thereof, intellectual respectability.

For those who have to be convinced that there is no scientific respectability in racism, Martin Deutsch's article is included in this book, complete with his formidable array of references.

Martin Deutsch is professor of early childhood education at the New York University School of Education and director of the Institute for Developmental Studies.

Reprinted from Martin Deutsch, "Happenings on the Way Back to the Forum: Social Science, IQ, and Race Differences Revisited," *Harvard Educational Review* 39 (Summer 1969), pp. 523-557. Copyright © 1969 by President and Fellows of Harvard College. Reproduced by permission.

The publication in the Winter issue of this journal of the long article by Arthur Jensen ("How much can we boost IQ and scholastic achievement?") has resulted in a torrent of commentary, rebuttals, and related articles.

Because of the publication lag in professional journals, most of this response appeared in the popular press and in general media such as *The Saturday Review, The New Republic,* and *U.S. News and World Report.* With the possible exception of the articles which appeared in the Spring issue of HER—and which were written before the publication and attendant publicity of the Jensen article—there has been no discussion to date which puts the Jensen argument and the commentaries it has provoked into a full psychological and social science perspective.

The conclusion is inescapable that the central thesis of the Jensen piece is a wholly antidemocratic eugenic position, and this is dealt with at length later on in this discussion in an assessment of Jensen's concept of two ability groups (his Level I and Level II). Thus, this relatively brief article will deal broadly with some of the specific issues raised, the arguments advanced, and the implications drawn, rather than focusing on a point-by-point discussion and refutation of errors.

I should like to make it clear at the outset, however, that in Jensen's article I found many erroneous statements, misinterpretations, and misunderstandings of the nature of intelligence, intelligence tests, genetic determination of traits, education in general, and compensatory education in particular. A colleague reports coming across 17 such errors in a casual perusal. For example, on pages 86-87, a 68% gets transposed into an 86%; on page 87 a study (Dustman & Beck, 1965) is reported with a 0.80 heritability factor in EEG patterns, but what is omitted is the fact that the subjects were identical twins. Perhaps so large a number of errors would not be remarkable were it not for the fact that Jensen's previous work has contained so few, and, more malignant, all the errors referred to are in the same direction; maximizing differences between blacks and whites and maximizing the possibility that such differences are attributable to hereditary factors.

In addition, in many of his citations of the literature, Jensen gives only part of the data or interpretation, or leaves out a piece of information which is crucial to his own interpretation. He also tends to use selective and sometimes inappropriate sources.

The Nelson and Dean study (1959) cited by Jensen on page 87, for example, relies on an analysis of brain wave patterns of newborn infants. Since the science of electroencephalography has yet to develop a stable picture of normative patterns in infancy, such findings are, at best, highly tentative. Interpretations from the Nelson and Dean study are further qualified by the fact that the statement about African newborns is based on only eight subjects and that the authors themselves caution the reader to treat the results with "reserve" (p. 781).

An example of Jensen's use of sources unsuited to a scholarly publication is his citation of a 1968 study from *Medical World News,* which he uses to suggest a link between an aspect of brain waves and IQ. The *Medical World News* consists of popularized abstracts, not scientific papers. Another example is his use of the *U.S. News and World Report* as the source for Armed Forces Qualification Test data. The figures presented in a popular publication may be correct, but an article in such a magazine cannot possibly include the subanalyses and collateral data which determine the meaning of the central test scores, to say nothing of the environmental and historical conditions which initially differentiated the populations.

Before continuing with this critique, I should like to add a personal note. I have known Arthur Jensen and respected his work for many years. He was a coeditor with Irwin Katz and me of a SPSSI-sponsored volume (*Social class, race, and psychological development*) in which the orientation was diametrically opposed to his currently stated position. His own chapter in that book, "Social class and verbal learning," is a model of clear and careful exposition of his own and others' work in this complex field (and, incidentally, is quite divergent in orientation and conclusion from his HER article). I am publishing this critique because I believe the impact of Jensen's article was destructive; that it has had negative implications for the struggle against racism and for improvement of the educational system. The conclusions he draws are, I believe, unwarranted by the existing data, and reflect a consistent bias toward a racist hypothesis.

I have a special responsibility to contribute to the correction of the conclusions and their foundations for two major reasons: (1) my current position as President of the Society for the Psychological Study of Social Issues, an organization dedicated to careful evaluation and interpretation of socially relevant data, in the interests of the best utilization of social science information and understanding for the betterment of man and his society;[1] and (2) my own heavy involvement in scientific and professional work related to the issues Jensen raises—the role of environment in behavior and intelligence, stimulation of intellectual development, and general compensatory and intervention efforts —which has consistently led me to quite opposite conclusions from Jensen's about the processes involved in the acquisition of knowledge, the functional dynamics of intelligence, and the severe limitations of a psychometric approach to the description of intellectual performance in human populations.

At the same time that I deplore the nature, conclusions, and effects of Jensen's article, I support the right of free inquiry into all issues, popular or unpopular. Arthur Jensen has been a consistently careful and dedicated behavioral scientist who has made substantial contributions to the study of children's learning, and especially to verbal learning. In fact, it is hard for one who has followed and read his previous work to believe that he wrote the HER article. One must deplore and reject the many *ad hominem* criticisms to which he has been subjected. There are enough issues raised and arguments presented in his article to provide concrete bases for disagreement and the presentation of an alternative point of view. In the critique which follows I have attempted always to remain on an *ad verbum* level.

AN INVITATION TO MISUNDERSTANDING

Jensen's article takes the basic position that intelligence test differences between groups—most particularly between black and white groups—are reflections of differences in genetic endowment. Since the average scores of blacks are rather consistently below the average white scores, his conclusion is that these presumed genetic differences operate to make blacks inherently less competent. Contrary to the impression given by the mass media, Jensen offers no new data to support this position, but only a reorganization of existing old data. (It is important to remember that the data are mostly psychometric and not experimental or genetic.) He does add some of his own work on associative versus conceptual learning, on the basis of which he concludes that black children are more capable of concrete learning than of learning by abstraction. The policy implications he derives from this conclusion involve different curricula for black children and different expectations of their eventual intellectual level. Jensen includes numerous caveats with respect to not assuming a certain level on the part of any given individual on the basis of the known group differences, but he does not include any suggestions as to how one can identify a potential conceptual thinker in early childhood other than by his skin color.

In our present rather explosive social climate in the United States, it is not surprising that the publication of this argument and these views by a respected professor of education with extensive experimental productivity has been met by a storm of emotions and rhetoric.

In general, the published popular commentaries on the article have accepted most or all of Jensen's assertions regarding intelligence, many of his statements about the measurement of intelligence, most of his genetic discussion, and with only a few demurrers, his verdict on compensatory education. Thus, James Cass in *The Saturday Review* states, "An impressive study of the nature of intelligence, its sources, and its implications for school and society was published last month in the Winter issue of the *Harvard Educational Review.* . . ." While Cass goes on to indicate that, "Dr. Jensen has presented his case, but the jury of his professional peers is still out," nevertheless the impression is created that the article is a fair and lucid discussion of the issues. In fact, however, the article falls into serious contradictions in a number of places, and completely lacks a sophisticated understanding of the magnificent complexity of environment-organism interactions.

An important consequence of Jensen's article has been to focus attention on the role of social scientists in interpreting behavior. The article has also highlighted the implications of such interpretations for formulating social and educational policy. The responsibility thus assumed by social scientists is a grave one. The Society for the Psychological Study of Social Issues (SPSSI) released a statement about the issues and arguments advanced by Jensen which dealt in part with this matter.

The statement concluded with the assertion that the Council of the Society

. . . reaffirms its long-held position of support for open inquiry on all aspects of human behavior. We are concerned with establishing high standards of scientific inquiry and of scientific responsibility. Included in these standards must be careful interpretation of research findings, with rigorous attention to alternative explanations. In no area of science are these principles more important than in the study of human behavior, where a variety of social factors may have large and far-reaching effects. When research has bearing on social issues and public policy, the scientist must examine the competing explanations for his findings and must exercise the greatest care in his interpretation. Only in this way can he minimize the possibility that others will overgeneralize or misunderstand the social implications of his work.

One major aim of the present article is to evaluate Jensen's report in the context of the foregoing consideration: it is my belief that, among other major weaknesses, Jensen's article did not demonstrate sufficient cognizance of these principles, and that the implications he draws, and most particularly the practical suggestions he makes, go far beyond what is warranted by the data he presents—or by our present state of knowledge in these areas.

One of the most forthright statements in this area was made by a geneticist, Dobzhansky. In the context of affirming the rights of scientists to free inquiry and free expression of views he stated: "The opinions uttered by scientists are, however, prone to be utilized by politicians and propagandists for purposes of their own. Is a scientist accountable for misuses of his discoveries and utterances? He ought to be articulate enough at least to disown such misuses (1968, p. 129)."

In exploring the implications of research on racial difference, Chicago historian Mark Haller notes: "We should not be so naive as to believe that findings on racial differences will have no policy implications in the major domestic issue that now faces the United States (1968, p. 224 f.)."

LOSING SIGHT OF THE INDIVIDUAL

While Jensen repeatedly indicates that decisions about individuals should not be based on conclusions drawn from group data, the educational implications of his thesis prevent the drawing of this distinction between groups and individuals. Having developed the notion that white and black children tend to differ in their learning abilities according to particular parameters, which he designates Level I (associative, or rote learning) and Level II (conceptual), he then advocates differential teaching for the two groups. Despite his statement that, "The reality of individual differences . . . need not mean educational rewards for some children and frustration and defeat for others (p. 117)," it is hard to understand how differential teaching for children, grouped early in life on the basis of type of learning ability (Level I and Level II), can lead to flexibility of cognitive types of teaching procedures. Further, it would be doubtful that a child taught consistently by associative, rote techniques would be able to shift to a situation in which instruction was carried out by conceptual methods. This is a critical point for occupational and status advancement, inasmuch as the greater rewards in an advanced technological society go with the more conceptual work. To assume that rote-learning and conceptual-learning groups could be maintained without status attributions and implications as simply a part of "diversity rather than uniformity of approaches and aims (p. 117)," would imply a highly naive view of the social milieu.

Jensen seems to equate his Level I and Level II with different learning styles, or patterns of ability, almost as cognitive styles, even while he designates them hierarchically as I and II, with the latter subsuming advanced cognitive and conceptual abilities. If they were only styles, then there would be little reason to assume that even the child who learned scholastic skills by Level I methods (Jensen believes that Level I children can learn all the basic scholastic skills) could not perhaps go on to use those skills conceptually to solve other and more complex problems. If Jensen is referring to cognitive style, then it is likely that there are more than two styles; consequently it would be necessary to develop many different educational strategies to meet the needs of individual children. It would seem that the style notion is introduced only to make more palatable the lengthy prior argument of a dichotomy in learning ability (higher and lower) which demands differential educational organization amounting to segregation on the basis of presumed genetic inheritance.

Jensen completely neglects the failure of the school system or the larger society to achieve mass success in teaching even the basic scholastic skills. His lengthy critique assumes that potential or actual inputs are received by the child and that they get through the complex maze of environmental disorientation, scholastic chaos, and inadequately prepared teachers to a receptive organism. In essence, he fails to acknowledge the role of the school environment, the complexities of the educational system, and of the interpersonal dysfunctioning that typically characterizes the relationship of the school administration to the teaching staff, the teaching staff to the children, and inversely, of the children to their teachers. At an early age, children, often with considerable intuition and great intelligence, learn not to cope with the school situation, not to attend, not to take it seriously. In other words they find it intellectually non-stimulating, non-motivating, and in circumstances where children and teachers come from different social-class and caste backgrounds, children are likely to find the interaction as

well as the instruction threatening to their ego structures and personal identities. This is true for normative circumstances; it is most objective and descriptive of ghetto situations.

As I pointed out several years ago:

. . . middle-class people who work and teach across social-class lines often are unable to be aware of the negative aspects of the middle-class background because of its apparent superiority over the less advantageous background provided by lower-class life. We really have no external criterion for evaluating the characteristics of a milieu in terms of how well it is designed to foster development; as a result, we might actually be measuring one area of social failure with the yardstick of social catastrophe. (Deutsch, 1967, pp. 40-41)

With the paucity of funds available for so-called compensatory education, we have never really had a national compensatory effort. We simply must face the grim truth that while we have had social destruction and urban decay, our overall thrust as an organized society has placed our major resources in the arena of war rather than in the area of improving general social organization, teacher training, equipment, school structures, and meaningful administrative and community participation. It would be more possible to supply both educational systems and children with relevant reading materials and the new technological aids, as well as with better-trained teachers, and pre- and paraprofessionals if our priorities were reoriented toward social evolution. All these constitute requirements if any real effort is to be made toward the enhancement of the intellectual growth of the child. Until such an effort is made, it is simply not possible to arrive at a verdict as to the efficacy of education, to say nothing of the efficacy of compensatory programs.

SUCCESSFUL ENVIRONMENTAL INTERVENTION

As part of his general discounting of the effects of compensatory education programs for disadvantaged children, Jensen attributes the positive results obtained by our Institute for Developmental Studies demonstration program to the selection of samples not representative of a truly disadvantaged population (p. 98 f). He points out, correctly, that the experimental sample is composed of children whose parents volunteered them for the program. (Indeed, can one ever operate a program for four-year-olds living at home unless their parents agree to it?) He hypothesizes that, "Parents who seek out a nursery school or volunteer their children for an experimental preschool are more apt to have provided their children with a somewhat better environment than would be typical for a randomly selected group of disadvantaged children (p. 98)." He fortifies his assumption that it is the self-selection that makes the difference in the Institute program by noting some data on the program indicating that the experimental (E) group and the self-selection control (Css) group did not differ significantly on Stanford-Binet IQ at the end of the kindergarten year.

Several points, both general and specific, need to be made about this reasoning and the data Jensen used. First, because we were concerned that self-selection would result in an atypical sample, we formed the Css group. This was done by selecting a larger group of four-year-olds than could be included in the experimental program and then randomly assigning them to experimental and control groups. However, at the time these groups became eligible for kindergarten, a second control group (Ck) was selected, consisting of children coming to school for the first time in the kindergarten year. On the necessarily gross social-class categorization measures, the groups do not differ from each other.

Lest the term "self-selection" give rise to a misunderstanding about how the groups were constituted, it should be made clear that the situation was not one in which there was simply formal announcement that applications would be considered. Rather, doors were knocked on in central ghetto areas; school, church, and social groups were contacted: posters were placed in various community shops and facilities. While intangibles in home atmosphere necessarily could not be measured, care was taken to ensure inclusion only of children whose families could be classified at the bottom of the socioeconomic class (SES)

ladder, as measured on the IDS 10-point SES scale and subsequently trichotomized Index (see *The disadvantaged child,* especially chapters 15 and 17).

The data Jensen referred to arise only from the second group, or wave, which was in the Institute's experimental program. It is interesting to note that Jensen failed to use the first-wave data, which demonstrated significant differentiation in favor of the experimental group. Later analyses indicate that results on that second wave showed significant differences in favor of the experimental group. (There was an error in the report of these data in a nonscientific, popular publication by Powledge, cited by Jensen.) We have recently completed an analysis in which results of four waves of experimental and control groups were examined. These are reported in Table 1.

These data refer to several waves or groups and reflect a much more substantial N. They indicate that though the E and Css groups do not differ significantly at the time of pretest they do differ significantly at the end of the nursery year and at the end of the kindergarten year. Thus, the program has an effect independent of the self-selection variable. In addition, the Css and Ck groups do not differ significantly, either before or after the kindergarten year. Since the Ck group is randomly selected from entering kindergarteners in the same schools in which the experimental classes are located, it appears that the factor of self-selection for the experimental program did not produce a group of subjects atypical of the disadvantaged population in the neighborhood of the school. Therefore, Jensen's argument that the E and Css samples are not representative does not hold.

Other test results (Lorge-Thorndike, Illinois Test of Psycholinguistic Abilities) on these samples confirm the positive findings with respect to the effects of a longitudinal enrichment program. On the data from the Illinois Test of Psycholingusitic Abilities (ITPA), for example, differences between E and Css groups were greater in the third grade than at the time of earlier testing. Data analyses reveal significant differences in favor of the experimental children on the ITPA total score, and on six of the nine subtests. On the other

TABLE 1. Analysis of IQ Data for Four Waves of Experimental, Self-selected Control, and Kindergarten Control Groups in the IDS Experimental Compensatory Education Program

					Time of Test				
		PRE-PREKINDERGARTEN			POST-PREKINDERGARTEN			POST-KINDERGARTEN	
Group	N[a]	Stanford-Binet	Peabody picture vocab.	N	Stanford-Binet	Peabody picture vocab.	N	Stanford-Binet	Peabody picture vocab.
E	274	92.31	68.14	260	99.17	81.93	184	100.49	88.14
Css	129	91.37	65.50	142[b]	92.08	72.38	98	93.17	80.82
Ck	–	–	–	180	90.95	72.39	177	92.50	81.22

[a]N's differ because of attrition. A special analysis indicated that there was no relationship between attrition and IQ score, indicating that attrition was not selective in terms of IQ score.

[b]Increase in N's is because only half of the first-wave group was pretested to control for possible effect of pretest on posttest. (There was no effect.)

three subtests, the experimental group scored higher, but the differences were not statistically significant (C. P. Deutsch & C. Silfen, 1969). Analysis of results from recent testing (Spring, 1969) with six subtests of the revised longer ITPA is confirming these earlier findings. It appears from the subtest pattern that intervention specifically may help to counteract initial deficiencies in the auditory and vocal modalities, thereby enhancing development of verbal association and communication. In addition, recent data from the Metropolitan Reading Test indicate that reading scores of experimental children are at, or above, national grade average at the end of third grade, and are significantly different from control group scores.

It would appear, at least from the results of the Institute's program, that Jensen has prematurely classified compensatory education as a failure. The findings briefly reported here clearly demonstrate that continuous and carefully planned intervention procedures can have a substantially positive influence on the performance of disadvantaged children and avoid the cumulative failure all too frequently found. The Institute program and data have been used for illustration, as I am most familiar with them. However, there are other effective compensatory programs which have been reported elsewhere. Some of these are discussed explicitly in the recent report by the American Institutes for Research (1969).

LONG-TERM PROGRAMS ARE NEEDED

No doubt one factor that led Jensen to an erroneous conclusion is that focused compensatory education for disadvantaged children is a quite recent development, and early reports of results necessarily came from shorter and usually more hastily conceived and poorly handled programs, on both federal and local levels. It should come as no surprise that children born into poverty and all it implies cannot be rescued in an isolated summer or even by a year of a nonstimulating school program. When one considers the magnitude of the problem, especially when deprivation is confounded by the effects of discrimination suffered by many minority groups, it is hardly surprising that programs such as summer Head Start generally failed to have any lasting influence on the lives of disadvantaged children. However, the above data from the Institute's program, and those from other long-term efforts, indicate that long-range enrichment with specially trained teachers, careful planning and supervision, and adequate funding can produce positive effects on IQ scores, on specific language skills, and on school achievement measures. Even though it is not yet possible to tell what the longer-term effects will be (e.g., on high school performance and on adult occupational status), the current results are encouraging indeed, and are more than sufficient to reject the blanket conclusion that compensatory education has failed (if one assumes that it has ever really been attempted). On the contrary, what is strongly indicated is the establishment of more long-range, continuing programs for children from the slums. Careful evaluation of results of varying programs will yield information as to the best operative procedures and should lead to more efficient and more effective compensatory education, even in the context of an increasingly dysfunctional and irrelevant school system.

Unfortunately, Jensen apparently has a somewhat idealized view of the school system. He says, "The interesting fact is that, despite all the criticisms that can easily be leveled at the educational system, the traditional forms of instruction have actually worked quite well for the majority of children (p. 7)." This makes Jensen one of the few professional observers who would defend the current school system and the opportunities it offers for both specific skill development and more broadly defined intellectual growth. He takes the position that the curriculum is organized in a way that demands and fosters abstraction, problem solving, and concept formation. In actuality, schools are oriented far more to associative or rote learning, as can be seen in workbooks and sample lesson plans, as well as in the overstructured, noncreative, nonresponsive classes that typify most of America's schools. For the black ghetto child, Kozol's *Death at an Early Age* is a much more accurate rendering of the objective school experience. In Lewinian terms, one might say that the black ghetto child's life space and opportunity for independent behavior are rather harshly restricted, and in actuality often reflect a behavioral rendition of the desolate landscape of the moon.

Jensen doubts that IQ can be much affected by environmental effects in utero. Such a position appears unwarranted, in view of lines of evidence from sources other than the previously discussed reports of positive effects of some compensatory education programs.

Some of the most interesting work on the modifiability of intellectual abilities comes from studies of children in Israeli kibbutzim. Smilansky (1964) reported some of the early data which were also discussed in a 1964 conference. (For a report of the proceedings of the conference, see Hess, Davis & Bloom, 1965). Particularly dramatic are data showing changes in the IQs of Oriental children after four or more intensive years in the kibbutz nursery. Bloom (1969) refers to findings that under these conditions the IQ levels of Oriental children rose from a mean of 85 to a mean of 115. The direction of change, although not its magnitude, is consistent with the early reports of Klineberg (1935) and the later study by Lee (1951) which demonstrated an increase in the mean IQ of southern Negroes who migrated to the North. Both lines of data indicate the role of environment in modifying IQs, with the differential magnitude of change undoubtedly attributable to the very different levels of fostering conditions in kibbutzim and in northern American cities.

The work of Feuerstein (1968) with retarded children in Israel casts further doubt on Jensen's view that environment has little effect after the child is born. Feuerstein has shown that, with adequate stimulation, many children who initially show a low level of functioning (comparable to Jensen's Level I) can reach a much higher level of functioning (similar to Jensen's Level II). Considering Jensen's statement that he had found ". . . no studies that demonstrated gains in relatively non-cultural or non-verbal tests like Cattell's Culture Fair Tests and Raven's Progressive Matrices (p. 101)," it is pertinent to note that one of Feuerstein's measures on which gains were noted was the Raven. The magnitude of gains reported by Feuerstein and others is so substantial that a question must be raised as to the even elementary adequacy of our own current intervention models. In this area it would appear that Jensen has inverted his periscope and is looking at the wrong answers, as well as at the wrong questions.

EXTRAPOLATIONS, CONTRADICTIONS, AND MISINTERPRETATIONS

Jensen relies very heavily (especially on pp. 84-87) upon the Coleman report (1966) to indicate that situational-environmental factors are not of essential importance to school achievement. He refers to two studies—the only two he characterizes as "methodologically adequate"—of father absence. Both studies, he says, indicate that the father factor does not contribute independently to variance in intelligence or scholastic achievement. It seems somewhat incredible that one of the two studies he finds "methodologically adequate" is the Coleman report, inasmuch as this is one of the most massively criticized reports issued in recent years, with the bulk of the criticism centered on its methodological inadequacies (e.g., Jencks, 1968).

One problem in the Coleman report comes from the fact that there was a substantial differential response rate to the questionnaires on which it is based. In numerous categories there was a return of less than 50%. In addition, the data suffer from a great unevenness, as they were gathered by means of questionnaires filled out by school administrators, teachers, and others of varying levels of involvement, understanding, and sophistication. Most of the questionnaires were sent and returned by mail, which further added to the differential return and validity. In a limited number of instances, the data were gathered by untrained interviewers working with a questionnaire that was unfamiliar to them and which demanded that they ask probing questions as to reading material in the home, cultural amenities, preschool education, parents' education, child's self-concept, and so on. It is not my purpose here to discredit the Coleman report, but only to delineate the controversy which has surrounded it, and to which Jensen gives us no clue. It is almost impossible to make valid generalizations from the Coleman report which was hastily conducted and included numerous methodological difficulties. Any social scientist who chooses to use these data in support of his position must at least acknowledge the methodological problems and the limited scope of these data. In his use of the Coleman data, however, Jensen demonstrates an absence of understanding of these limitations.

Jensen makes another fundamental error in equating social class across caste lines, as if black middle-class experience were identical with white middle-class experience. Actually, it may take as much as two or three generations of real middle-class status before a black man will be able to have the kind of socializing advantages that most white people in our society enjoy today. This means that it is impossible to verify or validate most of the studies that have been done in this area except to look at them as interesting operations in terms of the first encounters of social scientists with the complexity of the human experience and human organization.

In an important review of the literature comparing the performance of Negroes and whites, Dreger and Miller (1960) state that it is not enough to equate ethnic groups in terms of social class and economic variables; that there is a caste as well as a class difference; that Negroes with earnings equal to or better than whites will still typically be prevented from living the same kind of life. This conclusion is stated in the context of Dreger and Miller's explicit statement that they take no sides in the so-called traditional heredity-environment controversy.

Citing both Coleman (1966) and Kuttner (1967), Jensen claims that American Indians are considerably more disadvantaged than black Americans or other minority groups (p. 85). The Kuttner data did not come from the Coleman study, and therefore may or may not be using comparable samples with respect to income and unemployment statistics. What these data basically indicate is a greater degree of structured environmental deprivation within the Indian community than within the ghetto. Jensen says ". . . the American Indian ability and achievement test scores average about half a standard deviation higher than the scores of Negroes (p. 85)" and that ". . . differences were in favor of the Indian children on each of the four tests used by Coleman: non-verbal intelligence, verbal intelligence, reading comprehension and math achievement (p. 85 f)." Then Jensen submits, "If the environmental factors assessed by Coleman are the major determinants of Negro-white differences that many social scientists have claimed they are, it is hard to see why such factors should act in reverse fashion in determining differences between Negroes and Indians . . . (p. 86)." Such a question simply ignores the problem of measuring the salient or operative variables within any disadvantageous situation and relating them to criterion measures. What is implied by the question is that all disadvantage is essentially the same, and exists only in differing quantities. Actually, of course, it is impossible to avoid recognizing that there are qualitative differences between environments, and that these are probably highly relevant to any discussion of environment-behavior relationships. For example, in superficially comparing Indians and Negroes, Jensen completely ignores the special conditions of American Indians: their history, their current social organization, and their schooling.[2]

Perhaps more important than Jensen's oversimplification of the Coleman data, or his ignoring evidence of success through compensatory education, is his attempt to generalize from the classic heritability studies. They are, after all, studies of Caucasian children, especially separated twins or siblings, whose environmental variation is not thought by scholars to be representative of the general population. To say it bluntly, Jensen (and the rest of us) have no idea what the proper estimates of V_H, V_E, and so forth are for black people, and we have only very tentative guesses as to what they are for Londoners and northern midwest Americans. The estimates of heritability, upon which Jensen's entire argument depends, are only accurate if each possible genotypic child is placed randomly in each conceivable environment. To approximate such a study, researchers must at least include black children and a representative range of environments.

If we take into consideration a number of factors discussed on different pages of the article, we find that Jensen destroys his own main argument. He explicitly states that the median IQ difference between Negro and white samples is 15 to 20 points. If we add the 8 or 10 points attributable to the test situation, the few points which Jensen concedes can be gained in compensatory education, and the additional 5 points which he is willing to attribute to poor environments, we find that all statistically significant differences have been obliterated. Jensen thereby leaves himself with no argument.

It is this kind of conflicting and contradictory reporting that makes it very difficult to take the Jensen article seriously in either scientific or logical terms It is tragic, therefore, that its conclusion have been so widely disseminated by the mass media.

Another example of Jensen's misinterpretation of his own data is to be found on page 83. In his analysis of his own table on the prevalence of retarded children by race and SES, Jensen says, "If environmental factors were mainly responsible for producing such differences, one should expect a lesser Negro-white discrepancy at the upper SES levels." In examining the table, if we look at percentage differences between Negroes and whites at each SES level, we find a difference of 2.6% at the highest SES level and 35.1% at the lowest SES level. This analysis, based on Jensen's own data, supports the environmental hypothesis. However, he goes on to discuss the issue as though the table demonstrated the reverse; he is consistent with his bias but not with his data.

Hefner (1969) criticizes the logic of Jensen's statement on page 83: "Since in no category of socioeconomic status (SES) are a majority of children found to be retarded in the technical sense of having an IQ below 75, it would be hard to claim that the degree of environmental deprivation typically associated with lower-class status could be responsible for this degree of mental retardation (p. 4)." Hefner suggests that the statement would be equally logical if other phrases, such as "found to be undernourished," or "found to have only one leg," were substituted for that on retardation. Even apart from this all-purpose statement, however, is the fact that differential prevalence of IQs below 75 and the probability that very low IQs are associated with neurobiological deficits (by no means necessarily genetically determined) may have nothing at all to do with observed test score differences in the IQ range above 75.[3]

On page 62 f., Jensen discusses the Wheeler (1942) data and appears to say that a decline in IQ was observed in a longitudinal study. Again, I quote Hefner,

. . . but in fact there is only a 1930 and a 1940 cross section. Thus, when he says that the "decline in IQ from age 6 to 16 was about the same in 1940 (from 103 to 80) as in 1930 (from 95 to 74)," what he really means is that separate samples from the group which averaged 95 in 1930 at age 6, averaged 80 in 1940 at age 16—after some years of state and Federal intervention to improve the environment of the area. There is no group that "declined" from 103 to 80, or from 95 to 74. (p. 4)

In another seeming contradiction (p. 100), Jensen states that he would put little confidence in a single test score, and especially if it were a child's first test score; he adds his limited confidence in the result if the child is from a poor background and of a different race from the examiner. On page 108, Jensen points out that educators should de-emphasize IQ scores as a means of assessing gains and use mainly direct tests of the skills the instructional program was intended to teach. Despite this cautious view of IQ tests, however, Jensen give us 100 pages of interpretation of IQ test results in terms of race, genetic determination, teaching methods, and general environmental influences.

As evidence for his conclusion that middle-class white children do better than lower-class black children on conceptual (Level II) tasks, Jensen relies heavily on a study by Glasman (1968). Jensen describes the results as indicating that middle-class children do better on recall of objects, which can be clustered into meaningful categories, than do lower-class children. He relates this to a previous finding of his own that SES differences are not apparent in free recall of unrelated objects. However, he does not indicate if the two samples

were comparable; he does not even give the age(s) of his sample. The critical importance of age is clear from the report of the Glasman study, which found no SES differences between recall on categorized and uncategorized lists in kindergarteners, while differences were present for fourth- and fifth-grade children. Thus, while Jensen reports the Glasman study as a kind of extension of his own earlier work, and as support for his Level I-Level II differentiation, the age-related differences would have to be compared for the two studies before any conclusions could be meaningful.

In trying to explain his own observed finding that Level I tasks correlate with IQ among middle-class children but not among lower-class children, Jensen postulates a scatter diagram of correlations within class groups. He says,

Since large representative samples of the entire school population have not been studied so far, the exact form of the correlation scatter diagram has not yet been well established, but the schematic portrayal of Figure 18 is what could be most reasonably hypothesized on the basis of several lines of evidence now available. (p. 113)

Since he does not specify the "several lines of evidence now available," what he has apparently done is to construct two diagrams that would reflect his findings without destroying his conclusions. There is, thus, no apparently valid relationship between the stated finding of high Level I task/IQ correlations among middle-class children, and low correlations for lower-class children, and his later statement that "Level I ability is distributed about the same in all social class groups, while Level II ability is distributed differently in lower and middle SES groups (p. 114)" might have the effect of making the already tired reader ignore the inconsistency of the two statements.[4]

Jensen's postulation of Levels I and II—separate associative and conceptual intellective processes—cannot be seriously considered from a theoretical point of view. If one were to draw on current intellective and behavioral theories, there would be a basis for a theory of intelligence founded on a total interpenetration of cognitive and associative levels. I would postulate further a third level, which would subsume the other two and include as well the organism's own personal experiences and history; its deprivations and reward systems. These systems embody as well an internalized responsive network that creates a self-reinforcing organismic individuality, which would constitute the psychobehavioral level of the self-fulfilling prophecy. (A fuller discussion of this construct is included in a paper to be published in the winter issue of *The Journal of Social Issues.*)

THE EUGENIC TAUTOLOGY

In evaluating Jensen's dual cognitive typology of intellectual performance, it is necessary to read carefully his discussion on page 114. He says:

That learning is necessary for Level II no one doubts, but certain neural structures must also be available for Level II abilities to develop, and these are conceived of as being different from the neural structures underlying Level I. The genetic factors involved in each of these types of ability are presumed to have become differentially distributed in the population as a function of social class, since Level II has been most important for scholastic performance under the traditional methods of instruction.

This is perhaps the clearest statement of the position which is fundamental to Jensen's total argument. It is quite similar to Shockley's request to the National Academy of Sciences (1966) in which he suggested that the Academy undertake a major investigation of the possible genetic determinants of racial differences in intelligence. In the Academy's most recent rejection of Shockley's proposal (in which Shockley cited Jensen's HER article) Dr. Frederick Seitz, the President of the National Academy of Sciences, was quoted as saying, "It is essentially impossible to do good research in this field as long as there are such great social inequities." Dr. Seitz based his position on the Academy's policy statement (*NAS News Report,* November, 1967), which

holds that it is not clear, despite the tests which have been done, whether differences in intelligence between the black and white populations are genetic or environmental and that there is no scientific basis for supposing them to be either one or the other. Subsequently, in an even stronger statement clarifying the Academy's view, Seitz said, "There is a strong feeling within the Academy that social inequities make it impossible to do reasonable scientific research in this area. . . . In addition, the conduct of such research at the present would tend to heighten current social tensions to a very destructive degree (1969, p. 652)."

Jensen's later discussion of his dual cognitive typology of intellectual performance (Levels I and II) is not consistent with his earlier apparent characterization of levels of abilities as "styles." In the statement on page 114, Jensen assumes that there are different neural structures characterizing Levels I and II and that there are important genetic factors involved in determining these structures. This is a restatement of the old Galtonian eugenic point of view, which essentially hypothesizes high positive correlations among social-class, intelligence, and neural factors. The social implications of this are enormous, obvious, and totally antidemocratic, and would tend to create a permanent caste society in which those of lower caste (mostly black) would be forever doomed by their hypothesized neural structures to remain in an inferior position, with all that it implies for future occupational attainment and the antecedent educational opportunities.

The impossibility of linking genetic factors with racial factors, social factors, and intelligence is described by Fried (1968):

Absolutely no study yet done on a so-called racial sample of human population adequately links intelligence, potential ability, educability or even achievement to a specifiable set of genetic coordinates associated with any aggregate larger than a family line or perhaps lineage. (p. 124)

Scott (1968) further points out: "the range of human adaptation is so great that it is doubtful whether population differences on any behavioral test of complex performance ever can be assigned to any definite genetic basis (p. 65)."

I think it is of primary importance in this discussion that we recognize that there is no built-in correlation between IQ test measurements and the nature of intelligence. They are quite different, and, unfortunately, Jensen's article continually translates one into the other. In spite of disclaimers, he constantly uses the terms interchangeably, and the general reader comes out with the impression that an IQ score and intelligence are synonymous.

What Chein pointed out in 1945 is still true: "No psychologist has ever observed intelligence; many have observed intelligent behavior. This observation should be the starting point of any theory of intelligence, but such has, unfortunately, not generally been the case (p. 111)."

With respect to intelligence testing, it would seem that we are deluding ourselves if we believe that such tests truly indicate something about capacity or about general learning ability, or that they even reflect a child's current cognitive skills, to say nothing of predicting his potential skills, especially if facilitating stimuli are given, such as Black (1968), Feuerstein (1968), Caldwell and Richmond (1968), Deutsch (1967), and others have demonstrated.

IQ IS NOT A MEASURE OF CAPACITY

Standard intelligence tests measure essentially what children have learned, not how well they might learn something new. Intelligence tests have been constructed within a certain kind of society and a certain kind of cultural milieu, basically white middle-class America. During a period of dynamic social change, tests have remained static and have become increasingly irrelevant for understanding the nature and evolution of an organism's intellectual behavior.

Chein, later in his important article on the nature of intelligence, states:

*Psychologists who are keenly aware of the fallacy of reification with respect to other concepts and even those who have in their dis-*cussions of intelligence, often enough, verbalized the danger of hypostatizing entities where none exist have, nonetheless, tended to ascend the ladder of abstraction so rapidly that they have often left the fundamental observation far behind. (1945, p. 111)*

Arthur Jensen has committed this error in his rapid ascent from tests results to heritability formulas for "intelligence."

Early in the paper, Jensen introduces the concept of g, which designates the theory of intelligence proposed by Spearman (1923). It refers to the notion that all intellectual activity partakes of a common, general (g) factor. Jensen's subsequent discussion of intelligence and intelligence tests, including his definition of Levels I and II, is based on the g theory: he defines tests in terms of how much g loading they have, and describes his Level II intellectual functions as g.

However, g represents only one theory of intelligence, among many others. It is by no means a universally accepted concept among psychologists and others who work in this area. Yet from Jensen's paper, the general reader would never know that there are competing theories, several of which are more widely accepted and based on more recent information and data than Spearman's.

Spearman's theory stemmed from the early development of factor analysis. Thurstone subsequently developed the technique of multiple factor analysis, and from his studies derived a multifactorial theory of intelligence (1938). Thurstone's theory regarded intelligence as being composed of a number of different factors, which did not have to bear any specific relationship to each other. While Thurstone allowed for the potential existence of g as a structural substrate, it was not an intrinsic part of his theory.

A prime example of the later development of theories of intelligence based on factor analysis is Guilford's theory of the structure of intelligence (1959-1967). This theory is the culmination of many years of work in the area by Guilford and his associates. The picture of intelligence generated is a multifactorial, multifaceted one that Guilford believes is reflective of the actual complexity of human beings. He says:

> *There are many individuals who long for the good old days of simplicity, when we got along with one unanalyzed intelligence. Simplicity certainly has its appeal. But human nature is exceedingly complex, and we may as well face that fact. . . . Humanity's peaceful pursuit of happiness depends upon our control of nature and of our own behavior; and this, in turn, depends upon understanding ourselves, including our intellectual resources. (1959, p. 479)*

In addition to these factorial theories of intelligence, there are various theories which derive from different lines of development. For example, Piaget's theory of intelligence derives from a developmental analysis of children's thinking (1952). One hallmark of the theory is the notion that intellectual development is intimately interwoven with the child's experiences: through the dual processes of assimilation and accommodation, the child comes to know his world, to incorporate this knowledge, and to modify his understanding in terms of new experiences and interactions. Piaget's theory is a "stage" theory, in the sense that levels of development are considered to be achieved in a fixed order, with each level building on the previous one. Whereas Jensen's notions of level are categorical and static, Piaget's reflect the idea of process.

None of these theories of intelligence has been "proven"; incontrovertible data have not been gathered to confirm any of them. However, each of the theories mentioned is as valid and prominent as *g*. Jensen's entire argument appears to be inextricably linked with the concept of *g*. Questioning *g* throws Jensen's whole line of reasoning into doubt.

Chein (1945) takes an altogether different approach in describing intelligence. He states:

> *Intelligence is an attribute of behavior, not an attribute of a person. Even though we may observe some constancy in how intelligently a person acts in different situations, we*

may, on this basis, speak of the person's characteristic behaviors and not of a genuine attribute of the person. (p. 119)

THE ATTRIBUTION OF ENVIRONMENTAL EFFECTS TO HEREDITY

Jensen's failure to discuss other theories of intelligence and the lack of any explication of his reasons for preferring the *g* theory is consistent with his unexplained selectivity of studies, theories, and literature throughout the article. Thus, in his brief discussion of the potential effects of pre- and paranatal variables on later development, Jensen refers to the studies by Stott (1960, 1966), but ignores the massive work in the area by, e.g., Pasamanick and Knobloch and their associates (1967, 1969). The fact that Stott allows for a genetic hypothesis, while the other investigators interpret their findings in social-environmental terms, undoubtedly is a factor in Jensen's preference. At the same time, the body of work of the others is so substantial that it can hardly be ignored in any discussion of this area.

Briefly, the Pasamanick-Knobloch group found a relationship between the socioeconomic level of the mother and the incidence of pregnancy and paranatal difficulties, including prematurity (specifically defined in terms of birth weight). In turn, pregnancy complications and birth difficulties are associated with a higher incidence of neonatal mortality, morbidity and brain damage, and subsequent learning and behavioral disorders. Montagu (1967) points out that maternal nutrition, especially vitamin and protein intake, is one of the variables heavily implicated in neonatal birth weight (prematurity) and condition, as well as in the other paranatal disorders mentioned. In his discussion, Montagu indicates that even the nutrition of a child's grandmother can affect the child, since the state of the grandmother's nutrition before and during her pregnancy would have influenced the quality of the mother's ova which were later fertilized. The same factors are operative for prenatal influences on the tissues which gave rise to the sperm, which subsequently fertilized the ova. Since low SES women typically have poorer nutrition than middle-class women, social and economic variables are clearly implicated. Montagu does allow for a potential genetic factor in susceptibility to the negative effects of poor nutritional status (i.e., not all individuals or groups need be equally adversely affected by the same degree of nutritional inadequacy), but the fact remains that such (possibly genetic) differential susceptibility would be operative only in interaction with (SES-related) poor nutrition.

Until such relationships are disproven (which seems unlikely), it would appear scientifically indefensible to discard social factors as major influences on pre- and paranatal events.

Jensen's discounting of the importance of social factors in this area is yet another example of his insufficient appreciation of the complexity of environment itself as a variable, and of the even greater complexity of organism-environment interactions. In sections of the article in which he discards environmental hypotheses (e.g., p. 84 f.) as a source of group differences, Jensen does little analysis of variables in the environment, but rather seems to regard the environment as a kind of unit. The variable he does separate out (p. 85) is a social-familial one: "father absence." Whereas in earlier writing (e.g., "Social class and verbal learning," 1968), Jensen discusses the need for "task analyses" and attempts to examine the differential verbal habits of different social classes, he does not deal with social variables on this level in his HER article. As a result, what emerges is a picture of some social-class-related holistic environment to which is attributed only a relatively small proportion of the variance of observed group differences. There is no consideration of a process of interaction between an individual and his environment.

MEDIATORS IN A
COMPLEX ENVIRONMENT

An exploration of the nature and effects of such interaction is found in C. Deutsch's discussion of environment and perception (1968). Using perception as an exemplar dependent variable, she analyzes the history and transformations of the "heredity-environment" controversy and asserts that, as long as the

issue was posed in such global terms, no specific data could emerge. Changing the terms to "nature" and "nurture," however, opened the way to specification of influential variables and to their hierarchization. On the basis of her analyses of both theories and data, she concludes that life conditions—including current social situations, past experiences, and socioeconomic factors—influence fundamental developmental processes. She hypothesizes that these influences operate through "mediating variables," which relate to environment on the one hand, and to behavior on the other. Referring to work in perceptual learning (e.g., Gibson & Gibson, 1955; E. Gibson, 1963; Covington, 1967) and to sensory-deprivation experiments (e.g., von Senden, 1932; Hebb, 1958), she emphasizes the role of the stimulus in learning and behavior. She suggests that the conditions of life for the individual are determinants of the quantity and nature of stimuli to which he is exposed, and that, therefore, one large class of mediating variables includes the actual stimuli which impinge on the individual.

These stimulus theories are consistent with a notion of modifiability of perception, as a result of particular stimulus presentations. From this point, Deutsch draws practical implications for the organization of classroom and school materials. Considering the prime importance of both visual and auditory discrimination in early learning and in the acquisition of foundation skills, such as reading, she believes that the school learning process could be greatly enhanced by appropriate organization of stimuli, so that the child could be provided with the greatest amount of relevant practice in building his discrimination skills. Slum environments, Deutsch suggests, do not provide young children with a sufficient variety of stimuli, and most especially do not provide the kind of figure-ground or signal noise ratio which is conducive to accurate and defined perception. Also, as compared with his middle-class peer, the slum child is less often told the names of the objects and noises he perceives and, consequently, he is further hampered in the development of stable discrimination skills.

Deutsch believes that the school situation can do much to remedy whatever perceptual discrimination deficiencies the child brings with him (providing, of course, he is not brain damaged or sensorily impaired). She proposes a "stimulus analysis" of classrooms and materials as a basis for formulating their appropriate organization and construction. Since perceptual processes play an important role in intelligence test performance, it is possible that remediable (and, according to these theories, environmentally conditioned) perceptual difficulties contribute substantially to observed SES differentials in IQ. Visual discrimination is an especially relevant factor in such tests as the Raven Progressive Matrices, on which Jensen places some emphasis; but he does not consider perception or perceptual development in his article. Neither does he consider the kind of operational role of the environment and its stimuli which Deutsch postulates.

In Jensen's article, heredity is similarly seen as a kind of global variable, but one which exercises a decisive influence on development. Further, this influence is seen as predetermined (from the time of conception) and as unmodifiable in its operation. The only kinds of interaction allowed for in Jensen's system are epistasis (interaction between genes) and the rather simple type of interaction exemplified by the attainment of height; the limit is set genetically, but factors such as nutrition and illness can prevent an individual from attaining his maximum stature. The implication of this position is that nature is unmodifiable, since it is considered as intrinsic to the individual. This simply means that people are locked into their individual life cages by their genetic blueprints, and environment has no influence except perhaps to interfere with the achievement of one's full genetic potential.[5]

My emphasis in this paper on environmental influences does not mean that I am discounting genetic factors. It is simply that they must be seen as interacting determinants, rather than as separate causative agents, especially when behavior is considered. For example, Hilgard and Atkinson (1967) explore the issue of the complex interaction of heredity and environment, and suggest that the methods of genetics may be applicable to

behavior as well as to structure. They believe that the chromosomes and genes must be responsible for the inheritance of various components of behavior, as they are for inherited structure. However, they make it clear that they are referring to behavioral components, rather than to complex developed behaviors. They also point out that some genes are dominant; some recessive; and some are sex-linked, so that predictions can be made only in terms of statistical probabilities.

In considering genetic influence on traits, it is important to make the distinction between genotype and phenotype. As Gottesman (1968b) states:

Genotype refers to the totality of factors that make up the genetic complement of an individual. Phenotype refers to the totality of physically or chemically observable characteristics of an individual that result from the interaction of his genotype with his environment. Environment must be broadly defined to include not only intrauterine and post-natal conditions but also a host of molecular factors within and between the embryonic cells (Waddington 1957).

Different genotypes may have the same phenotype, and different phenotypes may be displayed by the same genotypes. A lack of clarity is perpetuated in discussions of individual differences by a failure to specify the environmental circumstances when describing the phenotype of genes. And conversely, the attribution of an effect to an environmental manipulation may be misleading unless the genotype is specified. (p. 29)

Of course, in humans, specification of the genotype is extremely difficult, even for relatively simple traits, since each generation is so long, relatively few offspring are produced, and selective, controlled breeding is not possible. It is more possible, though, to develop analyses and methods of specifying environmental variables. As Gottesman points out, the more similar the environments, the more variability in traits can be ascribed to genetic factors. Perhaps the best approach to determining the genetic contribution to a given trait would be to describe accurately relevant environmental variables and then attempt to subject the varying populations under study to as nearly identical environments as possible. Since this has not been done, and since Jensen must recognize the differential environmental milieus of different social-class and racial groups, it seems inescapable that his main thesis of genetic structure as the major source of variance in intelligence test score differences between social-class and racial groups must be rejected on that basis alone. In considering Jensen's heritability formula in the light of these facts and definitions in modern genetics, Hirsch's (1968) statement is most apt: "Only when we consider the number of possible genotypes and the number of potential environments that may influence trait expression do we begin to realize how narrowly limited is the range of applicability for an obtained heritability measure (p. 42)."

Jensen relies heavily on kinship studies, particularly twin studies, for his estimate of the heritability of intelligence. While twin studies represent a logical and appealing approach to the heredity-environment question, they present several serious methodological problems. (For a more complete discussion of these problems, see Woodworth [1941], Essen-Moller [1963], and Vandenberg [1966].)

Fuller and Thompson (1960) point out that, "Methods of treating twin data cover a wide range of statistical procedures, some naive and others highly sophisticated (p. 109)." Unfortunately, Jensen's description of his procedure does not give the reader sufficient information to determine into which category his method falls. He may have used studies involving direct comparisons of monozygotic and dizygotic twins (a procedure to which there are many methodological objections), or he may have used twin studies employing other conditions. He states only:

I have presented elsewhere a generalized formula for estimating heritability from any two kinship correlations where one kinship is of a higher degree than the other (Jensen, 1967a). I applied this heritability formula to all correlations for monozygotic and dizy-

gotic (half their genes in common) twins reported in the literature and found an average heritability of 0.80 for intelligence test scores. (p. 51)

It would appear from this statement that he lumped together twin studies without reference to their widely differing levels of methodological adequacy.

Perhaps the most empirically derived twin studies in the literature on the influence of heredity on intelligence are those of identical twins reared apart. Jensen mentions three of the four existing studies. It is interesting to note that he gives most attention to Burt's (1966) study. It contains the highest estimates for heritability in this literature, and its findings are not completely substantiated by other studies.

While Jensen mentions intra-pair correlations for intelligence test scores of identical twins reared apart, he does not examine the mean intra-pair differences. In examining these differences, summarized in Table 2, we find that the average difference ranges from 6 points (Burt, 1966) to 14 points (Shields & Gottesman, 1965). Gottesman (1968) notes that at least 25% of Shields's (1962) sample of twins reared apart (N = 38) has within-pair IQ point differences of more than 16 points on one of the tests. In the studies cited in Table 2 the maximum within-pair difference ranges from 14 to 30 points. Such variation between co-twins, often significantly correlated with environmental differences, suggests the impact of environment on IQ test scores.

An example of the considerable influence of environment is seen in the frequently cited study of identical twins reared apart by Newman, Freeman, and Holzinger (1937). In this study it was found that the IQ scores of identical twins who were reared apart and who were separated during the first three years of life showed a correlation of 0.79 with educational advantage. Bloom (1964) analyzed these data, dividing the identical twins reared apart into two groups. In one group of 11 pairs with very similar educational environments, the rank order correlation of IQ test scores was 0.91, in contrast with a rank order correlation of 0.24 for the eight pairs of twins with less-

TABLE 2. Mean Intrapair Differences in IQ Test Scores

Study	N	Test	Mean differences in IQ points	Range of differences in IQ points
Newman, Freeman & Holzinger (1937)	19	Stanford-Binet	8.2	1-24
Shields (1962)	38	Combined score[a]	9.5	0-30
Shields (1962) as reported by		Mill Hill Vocabulary	14.0	–
Shields & Gottesman	38	Dominoes	10.0	–
Juel-Nielsen (1964)	12	Wechsler-Bellevue	7.3[b]	1-14
Burt (1966)	53	Stanford-Binet (London Standardization)	6.0	–

[a]From Dominoes and Mill Hill Vocabulary.
[b]Computed by P. Newton.

similar educational environments. From this analysis, they conclude that,

. . . if the identical twins are separated but placed in very similar environments, it is likely that they will have very similar intelligence test scores, whereas if placed in very different environments, their intelligence test scores will be quite different. (1964, p. 70)

Using the Newman et al. ratings of educational and social differences between pairs of twins, Stone and Church (1968) classified 10 pairs of twins as having "larger differences in educational and social advantages" (DSEA), and nine pairs of twins as having "smaller DSEA." They found that seven pairs of the twins in the larger DSEA group had IQ differences of 10 or more points, while only three pairs of twins in this group had IQ differences of less than 10 points. In the group with the smaller DSEA, all pairs of twins showed IQ differences of less than 10 points. In the larger DSEA group, four pairs of twins showed differences of 15, 17, 19, and 24 IQ points.

Results also suggestive of the influence of environmental factors on IQ test scores come from Juel-Nielsen's (1964) study of 12 pairs of identical twins reared apart. Examining his results for the seven pairs of twins who had had differences in educational experience, Juel-Nielsen found significant differences ($p \leq 0.005$) on the following parts of the Wechsler-Bellevue: Information, Digit Span,

Verbal Points, and Total Points. (Jensen did not cite this study in his article. The omission is unfortunate, as this study handles several of the methodological difficulties present in the other three studies of this design.)

Bloom (1964) suggests that a "conservative" estimate of the long-term effect of extreme environments may be about 20 IQ points. In supporting this statement, he notes that 20 points was the average difference for the three pairs of identical twins reared apart in the most dissimilar environments in the Newman, Freeman, and Holzinger study. He also cites a study by Sontag (1958) in which individuals changed as much as 20 points in what were termed as "favorable" and "unfavorable" environments. Burke (1928) suggested a similar figure for the effect of extreme environment.

These analyses of twin data indicate greater differences in intelligence test scores between identical twins reared apart then Jensen acknowledges in his discussion; implied is a greater environmental contribution to the performance of even the most genetically similar individuals.

As indicated at the outset, this article could not cover all the issues raised in Jensen's lengthy discussion. Instead, it has dealt, to a greater or lesser degree, with some of the most salient problems raised, and has pointed out and offered corrections for a sampling of the errors and inconsistencies found.

In review of the areas covered, one central thread seems to emerge: that is, that Jensen's main omission is the picture of a complex and multifaceted environment, with which individuals interact in highly complicated and differentiated ways. Once that concept is firmly fixed, it would seem impossible to hold a simplistic view of the respective roles of heredity and environment in influencing intelligence test performance.

The burden of the discussion in the present article is the necessity for looking more closely at our environment in order better to understand the aspects which most impinge on individuals and influence their development, and in order to maximize those factors which exercise the most positive developmental influence and to minimize the most negatively acting ones. This is a tremendous task, and one which could well involve a large number of social and behavioral scientists. For not only will it be necessary to develop the requisite knowledge and understanding; it will also be necessary to feed the new knowledge past the organizational barriers and into the structures of society's institutions, most significantly the school system. Wilensky (1967) points up the kind of difficulty to be expected:

> So often are accurate intelligence (i.e., information) estimates ignored—whether in the field or in the file of some subordinate department—that we might infer a general rule: the further we go from data collection to policy decision, the less knowledge and the more error—and indeed, standard treatments of intelligence imply some deterioration by stages. (p. 81)

Our society is in a very critical state of dysfunctioning. Unlike Rome, it could fall to a Carthage, either internal or external. The minds and knowledge of social scientists can play an enormous role in restructuring our social system as mediated through all human organisms. Through the socialization and education of children especially, it would seem that a significant degree of saliency could be reestablished between personal experience on the one hand, and on the other, social evolu-

tion founded in the gathering of knowledge and its correct and parsimonious utilization.

Unfortunately, Jensen's article, through its use by attorneys in some desegregation cases and by some legislators with respect to appropriations bills (aside from its overinterpretation in public media), has had a negative effect on social progress; less money for education cannot lead to better education; casting aside court desegregation decisions cannot lead to greater social equality.

As Dobzhansky said in the statement which was quoted more fully at the beginning of this paper: "Is a scientist accountable for misuses of his discoveries and utterances? He ought to be articulate enough at least to disown such misuses (1968, p. 129)."

Some years ago, I wrote an article on the concept of social courage, which I defined as an act ". . . taking place in a context of overt or covert social intimidation . . . (1959, p. 52)." The hypothesis was advanced that the manifestation of social courage would depend on the relationship between inner conviction (with respect to the issue around which the act would take place) and the punishment potential which the act would invoke. It would be in the social and scientific interest if Arthur Jensen would summon the social courage necessary to repudiate the positions which have been taken in his name; and to reexamine his thinking, reevaluate his sources of information, reassess his argument, and retract his genetic conclusions in the light of data about and understanding of environmental factors with which he was apparently not familiar at the time he wrote the article. In times of serious social crisis, when the barriers to social change are so enormous and when young people are venting such frustration, a senior social scientist's manifestation of the courage to reformulate a well-publicized opinion would be a positive example of the conquering of discomfort by the inner conviction of the necessity for scientific objectivity. It would be a positive act, too, because in the immense task which social scientists have with respect to our changing social structure, gifted experimentalists like Jensen can play important roles in generating new knowledge about the environment and the interactions individuals have with it

NOTES

[1] The opinions expressed here are mine, however, and do not necessarily reflect the views of the organization or its members.

[2] For an extensive discussion of test variables with respect to different groups of subjects, see Deutsch, M., Fishman, J., Kogan, L., North, R., and Whiteman, M., Guidelines for testing minority group children. *Journal of Social Issues,* 1964, 20 (2), 129-145.

[3] Actually, 75 is an unusual cutoff point in the mental retardation literature. Typically, 68 or 70 is used. The proportion of cases between 68 and 75 is not given in Jensen's report, but is usually substantial.

[4] The reader who goes back to check this should not be confused by an obvious proofing error: the captions for Figure 18 and 19 are reversed in most issues, correctly placed in the reprints.

[5] As C. Deutsch points out, however, modern genetics teaches that genic operation itself is responsive to environmental variation. For example, experiments show that incubating *Drosophila* larvae at one temperature will produce one color of adult fruit fly, while incubating larvae from the same genetic strain at a different temperature will result in adult individuals of a different color. The environment, then, affects the biological attributes of the organism by influencing the operation of the genes.

That the temperature has not simply produced a genic mutation is shown by the fact that offspring of the two sets of larvae, incubated at the same temperature, all develop into fruit flies of the same color.

REFERENCES

American Institutes for Research. *A study of selected exemplary programs for the education of disadvantaged children.* Final report, Parts I and II. September 1968 Palo Alto, Calif., Contract No. OEC-08-089013-315(010), Office of Education.

Blank, M. A. Methodology for fostering abstract thinking in deprived children. Paper presented at the conference on the problems in the teaching of young children Toronto, Ontario, March 1968.

Bloom, B. S. Letter to the editor. *Harvard Educational Review,* 1969, 39, 419-421.

Bloom, B. S. *Stability and change in human characteristics.* New York: Wiley, 1964.

Bloom, B., Davis, A., & Hess, R. *Compensatory education for cultural deprivation.* New York: Holt, Rinehart, and Winston, 1965.

Burks, B. S. The relative influence of nature and nurture upon mental development: A comparative study of foster parent-foster child resemblance. *Yearbook of the National Society for the Study of Education,* 1928, 27 (I), 219-316.

Burt, C. The genetic determination of differences in intelligence: A study of monozygotic twins reared together and apart. *British Journal of Psychology,* 1966, 57, 137-153.

Caldwell, B., & Richmond, J. The children's center in Syracuse, New York. In L. L. Dittmann (Ed.), *Early child care.* New York: Atherton Press, 1968.

Cass, J. Race and intelligence. *Saturday Review,* 1969, 52 (2), 66-67.

Chein, I. On the nature of intelligence. *Journal of General Psychology,* 1945, 32, 111-126.

Coleman, J. S., et al. *Equality of educational opportunity.* Washington, D.C.: U.S. Dept. of Health, Education, and Welfare, 1966.

Covington, M. V. Stimulus deprivation as a function of social class membership. *Child Development,* 1967, 38 (2), 607.

Deutsch, C. Environment and perception. In M. Deutsch, I. Katz & A. R. Jensen (Eds.) *Social class, race, and psychological development.* New York: Holt, Rinehart, and Winston, 1968. Pp. 58-85.

Deutsch, C. P., & Silfen, C. Effects of a longitudinal enrichment program on language skills of disadvantaged children. Paper presented at the Society for Research in Child Development, Santa Monica, California, March 1969.

Deutsch, M. Courage as a concept in social psychology. *Journal of Social Psychology,* 1961, 55, 49-58.

Deutsch, M. The disadvantaged child and the learning process. In A. H. Passow (Ed.) *Education in depressed areas.* New York: Teachers College Press, 1963. Pp. 163-179

Deutsch, M. Social intervention and the malleability of the child. Fourth Annual School of Education Lecture, Cornell University, Ithaca, New York, May 1965.

Deutsch, M. & associates. *The disadvantaged child.* New York: Basic Books, 1967.

Deutsch, M., Katz I., & Jensen, A. R. (Eds.), *Social class, race, and psychological development.* Holt, Rinehart, and Winston, 1968.

Dobzhansky, T. Genetics and the social sciences. In D. C. Glass (Ed.), *Genetics.* New York: The Rockefeller University Press and Russell Sage Foundation, 1968. Pp. 129-142.

Dreger, R. M., & Miller, K. S. Comparative psychological studies of Negroes and whites in the United States. *Psychological Bulletin,* 1960, 57, 361-402.

Dustman, R. E., & Beck, E. C. The visually evoked potential in twins. *Electroencephalography and Clinical Neurophysiology,* 1965, 19, 570-575.

Essen-Moller, E. Twin research and psychiatry. *Acta Psychiatrica Scandinavica,* 1963, 39, 65-77.

Feuerstein, R., & Shalom, H. Problems of assessment and evaluation of the mentally retarded and culturally deprived child and adolescent: The learning potential assessment device. Paper presented at the First Congress of the International Association for the Scientific Study of Mental Deficiency. Montpellier, France, Symposium No. 8, September 1967.

Feuerstein, R. The role of social institutions and subsystems in the causation, prevention, and alleviation of retarded performance: A contribution to a dynamic approach. Paper presented at the Peabody-NIMH Conference on Social-Cultural Aspects of Mental Retardation. Nashville, Tennessee, June 1968.

Fried, M. The need to end the pseudoscientific investigation of race. In M. Mead, T. Dobzhansky, E. Tobach, & R. Light (Eds.), *Science and the concept of race.* New York: Columbia University Press, 1968. Pp. 122-131.

Fuller, J. L., & Thompson, W. R. *Behavior genetics.* New York: Wiley, 1966.

Gibson, E. J. Perceptual development. In H. W. Stevenson, J. Kagan, and C. Spiker (Eds.), *Child psychology: The 62nd Yearbook of the National Society for the Study of Education, Part I.* Chicago: National Society for the Study of Education, 1963. Pp. 144-195.

Gibson, J. J., & Gibson, E. J. Perceptual learning: Differentiation or enrichment? *Psychological Review,* 1955, 62, 32-41.

Glasman, L. D. A social-class comparison of conceptual processes in children's free recall. Unpublished doctoral dissertation. University of California, 1968. Cited by A. R. Jensen, How much can we boost IQ a d scholastic achievement? *Harvard Educational Review,* 1969, 39, 1-123.

Gottesman, I. I. Genetic aspects of intelligent behavior. In N. R. Ellis (Ed.) *Handbook of mental deficiency.* New York: McGraw-Hill, 1963. Pp. 253-296.

Gottesman, I. I. Beyond the fringe personality and psychopathology. In D. C. Glass (Ed.), *Genetics.* New York: The Rockefeller University Press and Russell Sage Foundation, 1968a. Pp. 59-69.

Gottesman, I. I. Biogenetics of race and class. In M. Deutsch, I. Katz, & A. R. Jensen (Eds.), *Social class, race, and psychological development.* New York: Holt, Rinehart, and Winston, 1968b. Pp. 11-51.

Guilford, J. P. Three faces of intellect. *American Psychologist,* 1959, 14, 469-479.

Guilford, J. P. *The nature of human intelligence.* New York: McGraw-Hill, 1967.

Haller, M. Social science and genetics: A historical perspective. In D. C. Glass (Ed.), *Genetics.* New York: The Rockefeller University Press and Russell Sage Foundation, 1968. Pp. 215-225.

Hebb, D. O. The motivating effects of exteroceptive stimulation. *American Psychologist,* 1958, 13, 109.

Hefner, R. Personal communication (typescript), 1969.

Hilgard, E. R., & Atkinson, R. C. *Introduction to psychology* (4th ed.) New York: Harcourt, Brace, and World, 1967.

Hirsch, J. Behavior genetic analysis and the study of man. In M. Mead, T. Dobzhansky, E. Tobach, & R. Light (Eds.), *Science and the concept of race,* New York: Columbia University Press, 1968. Pp. 37-48.

Jencks, C. Some natural experiments in compensatory education. Unpublished manuscript. April 1969.

Jensen, A. R. Social class and verbal learning. In M. Deutsch, I. Katz, & A. R. Jensen (Eds.), *Social class, race, and psychological development.* New York: Holt, Rinehart, and Winston, 1968. Pp. 115-174.

Jensen, A. R. How much can we boost IQ and scholastic achievement? *Harvard Educational Review,* 1969, 39, 1-123.

Juel-Nielsen, N. Individual and environment. A psychiatric-psychological investigation of monozygous twins reared apart. *Acta Psychiatrica Scandinavica,* 1964 (Monog. suppl. 183).

Katz, I. Factors influencing Negro performance in the desegregated school. In M. Deutsch, I. Katz, & A. R. Jensen (Eds.), *Social class, race, and psychological development.* New York: Holt, Rinehart, and Winston, 1968. Pp. 254-289.

Katz, I. Review of evidence relating to effects of desegregation on the intellectual performance of Negroes. *American Psychologist,* 1964, 19, 381-399.

Klineberg, O. *Negro intelligence and selective migration.* New York: Columbia University Press, 1935*a*.

Klineberg, O. *Race differences.* New York: Harper, 1935*b*.

Klineberg, O. Negro-white differences in intelligence test performance: A new look at an old problem. *American Psychologist,* 1963, 18 (4), 198-203.

Knobloch, H., & Pasamanick, B. Prediction from the assessment of neuromotor and intellectual status in infancy. In J. Zubin & G. Jervis (Eds.), *Psychopathology of mental development.* New York: Grune & Straton, 1967. Pp. 378-400.

Kozol, J. *Death at an early age.* Boston: Houghton Mifflin, 1967.

Kuttner, R. E. Letters to and from the editor. *Perspectives in Biology and Medicine,* 1968, 17, 707-709. Cited in A. R. Jensen, How much can we boost IQ and scholastic achievement? *Harvard Educational Review,* 1969, 39, 1-123.

Lee, E. S. Negro intelligence and selective migration: A Philadelphia test of the Klineberg hypothesis. *American Sociological Review,* 1951, 16, 227-233.

Mental tests for 10 million Americans—What they show. *U.S. News and World Report,* 1966, 61 (1b), 78-80. Cited by A. R. Jensen, How much can we boost IQ and scholastic achievement? *Harvard Educational Review,* 1969, 39, 1-123.

Montagu, A. *Prenatal influences.* Springfield, Illinois: Charles Thomas, 1967.

Nelson, G. K., & Dean, R. F. A. The electroencephalogram in African children: Effects of kwashiorkor and a note on the newborn. *Bulletin of the World Health Organization,* 1959, 21, 779-782.

Newman, H. H., Freeman, F. N., & Holzinger, K. J. *Twins: A study of heredity and environment.* Chicago: University of Chicago Press, 1937.

Pasamanick, B. A tract for the times: Some sociobiologic aspects of science, race, and racism. *American Journal of Orthopsychiatry,* 1969, 39 (1), 7-15.

Pettigrew, T. Negro American intelligence: A new look at an old controversy. *Journal of Negro Education,* 1964*a*, 33, 6-25.

Pettigrew, T. *A profile of the Negro American,* Princeton, N.J.: Van Nostrand, 1964*b*.

Piaget, J. *The origins of intelligence in children.* New York: International Universities Press, 1952.

Powledge, F. *To change a child.* Chicago: Anti-Defamation League, 1967.

Rosenthal R., & Jacobson, J. *Pygmalion in the classroom.* New York: Holt, Rinehart, and Winston, 1968.

Scientists bar genetic study of the Negro. *New York Post,* April 30, 1969 (byline, Victor Cohn), p. 30.

Scott, J. P., & Fuller, J. L. *Genetics and the social behavior of the dog*. Chicago: University of Chicago Press, 1965.

Scott, J. P. Discussion: Race as a concept. In M. Mead, T. Dobzhansky, E. Tobach, & R. Light (Eds.), *Science and the concept of race*. New York: Columbia University Press, 1968. Pp. 59-68.

Shields, J. *Monozygotic twins brought up apart and brought up together*. London: Oxford University Press, 1962.

Shields, J., & Gottesman, I. I. Age at separation and IQ differences in identical twins reared apart. Unpublished manuscript, 1965. Cited by I. I. Gottesman, Biogenetics of race and class. In M. Deutsch, I. Katz, & A. R. Jensen (Eds.), *Social class, race and psychological development*. New York: Holt, Rinehart, and Winston, 1968. Pp. 11-51.

Shockley proposal tabled. *Science*, 1969, 164, 652.

Smilansky, S. *Progress report on a program to demonstrate ways of using a year of kindergarten to promote cognitive abilities, impart basic information and modify attitudes which are essential for scholastic success of culturally deprived children in their first two years of school*. Jerusalem: Henrietta Szold Institute, 1964.

Sontag, L., Baker, C. E., & Nelson, V. *Mental growth and personality: A Longitudinal study*. Monograph of the Society for Research in Child Development. 23, No. 2, 1-143.

Spearman, C. *The nature of intelligence and the principles of cognition*. London: Macmillan, 1923.

Spuhler, J. N., & Lindzey, G. Racial differences in behavior. In J. Hirsch (Ed.), Behavior-genetic analysis. New York: McGraw-Hill, 1967. Pp. 366-414.

Stoddard, G. D. *The meaning of intelligence*. New York: Macmillan, 1943.

Stone, L. J., & Church, J. *Childhood and adolescence* (2nd ed.), New York: Random House, 1968.

Stott, D. H. Interaction of heredity and environment in regard to measured intelligence. *British Journal of Educational Psychology*, 1960, 30, 95-102.

Stott, D. H. *Studies of troublesome children*. New York: Humanities Press, 1966.

Tanser, H. A. *The settlement of Negroes in Kent County, Ontario*. Chatham, Ontario: Shepard Publishing Co., 1939. Cited by E. R. Hilgard and C. Atkinson, *Introduction to psychology*, New York: Harcourt, Brace, and World, 1967.

Thurstone, L. L. *Primary mental abilities*. Chicago: University of Chicago Press, 1938.

U.S. Commission on Civil Rights. *Racial isolation in the public schools*. Vol. 1, Washington, D.C.: U.S. Government Printing Office, 1967.

Using speed of brain waves to test IQ. *Medical World News*, 1968, 9, 26. Cited in A. R. Jensen, How much can we boost IQ and scholastic achievement? *Harvard Educational Review*, 1969, 39, 1-123.

Vandenberg, S. G. Contributions of twin research to psychology. *Psychological Bulletin*, 1966, 65, 327-352.

Vandenberg, S. G. The nature and nurture of intelligence. In D. C. Glass (Ed.), *Genetics*. New York: The Rockefeller University Press and Russell Sage Foundation. 1968. Pp. 3-58.

Von Senden, M. *Raum- und Gestaltauffassing bei operienten Blindgeborenen vor und nach der Operation*. Leipzig-Barth, 1932. Cited by D. O. Hebb, *The organization of behaviour*. New York: Wiley, 1949. Pp. 28-31.

Wheeler, L. R. A comparative study of the intelligence of east Tennessee mountain children, *Journal of Educational Psychology*, 1942, 33, 321-334.

Wilensky, H. *Organizational intelligence*. New York: Basic Books, 1967.

Woodworth, R. S. *Heredity and environment: A critical survey of recently published material on twins and foster children*. Social Science Research Council Bulletin, 1941, 47.

B.
THE CAUSES OF PREJUDICE

38
prejudice and society

EARL RAAB and SEYMOUR M. LIPSET
Some students of prejudice have been interested in how severely prejudiced individuals acquire their attitudes. These theories were reviewed in the Introduction to Part V.
Other students have been more interested in what kind of society produces prejudiced individuals and what the effects are on the society of having prejudiced groups within it. This is the point of view of the authors of the following selection.
Earl Raab is the executive director of the San Francisco Jewish Community Relations Council, and Seymour M. Lipset is professor of sociology at Harvard University.

Prejudice as a social problem
    The term "prejudice" allows for many definitions; but as a social problem *in America today, prejudice can be defined exclusively in terms of human* behavior *which denies or attempts to deny equality of opportunity or status to certain racial, religious or ethnic groups.*

    The "problem of prejudice" emerges from the columns of the daily newspapers as one of our nation's most disturbing domestic problems. A sampling of news stories reported in the daily press in recent years might include the following:
* High schools in parts of Virginia are closed down to avoid compliance with a court order directing that Negro children be admitted to the same schools as white children.
* In Clinton, Tennessee, an integrated high school is partially destroyed by dynamite. A synagogue is bombed in Atlanta, Georgia. A synagogue in Miami, Florida, and another in Nashville, Tennessee, are dynamited on the same day.

Reprinted from Earl Raab and Seymour M. Lipset, *Prejudice and Society* (New York: Anti-Defamation League of B'nai B'rith, 1959). Reproduced by permission of the authors and the copyright holder.

* A report issued by the Anti-Defamation League reveals that some employment agencies in New York State have worked out particularly elaborate codes to screen out job applicants, in violation of the state FEPC law.
* As the first Negro family moves into Levittown, Pa., a suburban all-white community, violence erupts and state police are called in to disperse and arrest rock-throwing, cross-burning rioters.
* After being held for five days, two ministers are handed jail terms and twelve other Negroes suspended sentences for violating Birmingham's bus-seating law. The Negroes are charged with violating a new ordinance adopted in an effort to preserve segregated buses in Birmingham. It authorizes bus drivers to tell passengers where to sit and replaces the old ordinance requiring segregated seating.
* A survey of resort discrimination in the United States reveals that out of 933 resorts investigated, 214, or 22.9 per cent, discriminate against Jews.
* Two visitors to the United States, one from Ethiopia and the other from Ghana, are denied seats in a restaurant in Alexandria, Va., because they are Negroes. Both are members of a group studying at the United Nations and are touring the area.
* A report discloses that more than half of about 5000 cooperative apartments in Chi-

cago are believed to be discriminatory or, under an explicitly stated policy, maintain a strict quota limitation of Jews.

* Despite a boycott by 11 institutions, about 1000 delegates of a national educational society attend a conference at the Lake Placid Club which is known to practice discrimination against Jews through a restrictive membership and guest policy.

* A study of housing discrimination discloses that the Incorporated Village of Bronxville in Westchester County in the New York metropolitan area has earned a reputation for admitting to its precincts as home-owners or -renters only those who profess to be Christians.

* According to a recent report by the Commission on Race and Housing, no fewer than 27,000,000 Americans—nearly one-sixth of our people—are restricted in their choice of a place to live by their race, religion or ethnic origin.

* Studies by the Bureau on Jewish Employment Problems of 30,000 white-collar job openings in Chicago indicate that 98 per cent of these job openings bar consideration of non-whites. One-fifth exclude Jews, Catholics and members of various nationality groups. The bureau investigated the practices of 100 companies.

These items describe the face of prejudice as our society sees it and is concerned with it. All of the items describe some aspect of social *behavior.* They refer directly to ways in which men *act* toward other men. And these aspects of social behavior have one basic element in common: *the denial or attempted denial of equal status and opportunity to large groups of people because of their racial, religious or ethnic identity.*

It is precisely such acts of denial which constitute the social problem of prejudice. It is this behavior—legitimately termed "prejudiced behavior" no matter what its cause or motivation—which, in itself, forces organized society to consider prejudice as a serious problem. Prejudiced behavior treats individuals as though they were not individuals at all but, rather, indistinguishable parts of a classified group. Prejudiced behavior is not only irrelevant to the characteristics of the individual, but irrelevant to the characteristics of the

group. If an employer refuses to hire a Negro *because* he is a Negro, this is prejudiced behavior in itself, no matter what mental processes may be involved; it contributes equally, to the social problems delineated heretofore, no matter what mental processes may be involved.

Why is such behavior considered a social problem?

1. The Threat to Social Order: A society tends to break down when the "going rules" for relationships among its members become unacceptable to a large number of those members. One of the functions of an organized society is to let its members know what kind of behavior they may normally expect from each other. In our society, one man is not normally expected to assault another man; or to cheat him, at least not outrageously. Parents are normally expected to take care of their children. The children of manual workers expect to get into college on the same basis as children of white-collar workers. Some of these "rules of relationship" are formal and regulated by law; others are "unwritten" customs. In either case, they cannot be maintained in American society by police power; these rules of behavior must be accepted by the bulk of society. But whether these rules of relationship are accepted depends, partly, on whether they can satisfy the major goals or aspirations variously held by the bulk of society.

Thus, the question is not what these aspirations *should* be, but what they *are* in fact. In analogy: If a child has not learned to *expect* many gifts from his parents, he is not as disturbed by the absence of such gifts as is a child who has learned to expect them. Social expectations are learned; they differ in different times and in different places. Where a group has not learned to expect equal status or opportunity, the absence of such status or opportunity does not create an active intergroup relations problem for society.

This does not mean that group prejudice can ever be counted more or less moral. It is legitimate hindsight, for example, which labels "immoral" the bartering of human slaves in the market place, even though it may not have been considered immoral in early America.

izing of Jews in medieval Europe. If each man is born with a divine right or a natural right to human dignity which other men cannot legitimately violate, then he has always been so born. Basic moral concepts are not "adjustable" as to time and place, although our judgments about people who have committed immoral acts may be tempered by historical perspective.

In other words, the *moral* problem involved in the unequal treatment of racial and religious groups was always present; but where the expectations and aspirations of these groups did not seriously conflict with this unequal treatment, there was no serious *social* problem, i.e., there was no threat to the going rules of relationship. Robert E. Park has commented: "Where distinctions based on class, caste and race are part of the established social order . . . each caste and class lives within the limitations of its own world and accepts the definition imposed upon it as if it were part of the order of nature."

In short, the modern social problem of prejudice has sharpened in proportion to the growth of aspirations in traditionally subordinated groups.

Fifty years ago, for example, there was no notable expression of concern about the lack of equal housing opportunity for American Negroes. The industrial needs of the World Wars brought a substantial number of Negroes into the mainstream of the American economy—and also brought them to the metropolitan centers of the North where they gained political significance. They took their place alongside other Americans in the assembly lines and, eventually, in the armed forces. Their economic and educational status improved. They became more sensitive to the fact that the official values of this democracy were supposed to embrace them as well. This sensitivity was spurred by a growing leadership within the American Negro community and a civil rights movement in general. To reverse the hoary racist formula, the American Negro —a substantial segment of the American population—now "knows his place" in American life and is more intent than ever before to achieve this place.

These new aspirations of the Negro, which are in keeping with the official values of our society, conflict with many of the traditional "rules of relationship" for Negroes and whites in this country. Changes in these rules so that they may accommodate the new goals of the Negro community are seriously blocked by the kind of behavior described previously in the newspaper items.

The more a society is unable to accommodate mutual expectations and relationships among substantial numbers of its members, then the more it has an active social problem which threatens its functioning as an effective social order.

Therefore, it is a practical necessity for society to develop a new and harmonious order of relationships which will accommodate these new and legitimate aspirations. It is *this* growing necessity which is at the heart of the current ferment about the race relations problem.

2. The Waste of Human Resources: Modern industrial society increasingly depends on the development of new talents and energies within its population for its very life; it cannot afford to cut itself off from major sources of such talent or energy. The intricate economic and political machinery that has evolved to meet modern needs demands the fullest use of available industrial, scientific and leadership skills. There is a constant shortage of top-level scientists, technicians, executives and public administrators. The opportunity for every man to develop his capacities is no longer just an abstract ethical precept that attaches to democracy. It is a practical condition of a modern industrial society. Such a society can function efficiently only if opportunity for full development and participation is not arbitrarily removed from large groups of its population.

3. The Threat to Democratic Life: The ideological structure of our democratic order is based upon the principle of the equal worth and dignity of all human beings. If this principle is significantly breached, it is no longer an operative principle; and democratic life has lost the main underpinning of its rationale. Theoretically, the denial of equal status and opportunity to any single individual on arbitrary grounds should prick the moral conscience of a democratic society, but it is not necessarily a serious threat to the ethical foundations of that society. However, where there is a *mass* and institutionalized denial of opportunity, and where there is an open and substantial flouting of the principle of human dignity, such a threat does exist.

Under such circumstances, it is more difficult to teach children that the inviolable dignity of man is a sacred principle; it is more difficult to convince the world that America is dedicated to such a principle. The sharpening conflict between traditional relationships and new aspirations has made this value-conflict more blatant and dramatic, and therefore more threatening to the security of our democratic value system.

These are the practical threats that make prejudice a problem for society. These are threats that are posed by social *behavior* that denies equality of status or opportunity to racial, religious or ethnic groups: acts which frustrate the legitimate aspirations of members of those groups; acts which prevent members of those groups from developing or using their full talents; acts which openly flout the principle that each man is born with certain inalienable rights.

In sum, it is prejudiced behavior which in itself constitutes the social problem of prejudice. The state of mind or attitude which may accompany prejudiced behavior is not in itself the problem, unless it is discovered to have some significant causative relationship to that behavior.

The shifting nature of prejudice

Prejudiced attitudes do not predetermine prejudiced behavior. An individual's prejudiced behavior may be determined more by the social situation at any given moment, than by his pre-existing attitudes. Both attitude and behavior are highly susceptible to situational changes.

The problem of prejudice, as it presents itself to society, consists of overt acts which deny equal status or opportunity to people because of their racial, religious or ethnic identity. However, "prejudice" is often used in a specialized sense to describe an individual's state of mind or attitude. There has long been a popular tendency to reify "prejudiced attitude"; to conceive of it as a little mental package tucked away in a corner of the brain, waiting for the proper stimulus to bring it to life. According to this view, if a person has "a prejudiced attitude" against Filipinos, then when a Filipino brushes up against him, or enters the same room he's in, or applies to him for a job, or tries to move next door, this attitude would be triggered and the "prejudiced person" would act accordingly.

The evidence clearly indicates, however, that prejudiced attitudes are very far from being neat little mental packages; and that, at the very least, they do not predetermine prejudiced behavior.

Gordon Allport has partly defined an attitude as a "mental and neural state of readiness." The meaningful reference here is to the fact that an attitude is a "mental and neural" state and not just to the fact that it is a state of readiness. A mechanical jack-in-the-box, crouched on its springs, might be said to have an attitude of readiness. Its attitude is such that it will jump up when the cover is removed. But a human attitude describes an internal state that has an independent existence, apart from any resultant behavior. If a child were simulating a jack-in-the-box in a school play, his attitude toward jumping out of the box in which he was crouched might consist of a combination of elements, e.g., he may be displeased about the physical prospect of jumping out; on the other hand, he may have a strong fear of the derision he will face if he fails to jump. Both of these elements comprise his "attitude about jumping" at a given point. The attitude exists as a real fact even if the show is canceled and he never does have the opportunity of jumping or not jumping.

There is the possibility of at least two basic *kinds* of elements in any attitude: a cognitive element and an emotional element. The first has to do with the way we perceive or *think* of an object; the second has to do with the way we *feel* about an object. Both components usually are included in the typical definition of a "prejudiced attitude." A person may *feel* hostility or distaste toward Mexicans, for example. In addition, he may *think* of all Mexicans as lazy or uneducated or whatever. This cognitive element, this derogatory "picture" that we may have in our minds of a minority group, is most simply classified as an "overgeneralization."

The difference between generalization and overgeneralization is the critical difference between prejudgment and prejudice. We constantly find it necessary to prejudge objects, to generalize about them. We prejudge a lemon as sour without tasting it. We prejudge a tank of gasoline as combustible without setting a match to it. But when we prejudge a redhead as hot-tempered, we are overgeneralizing, or to put it more accurately, misgeneralizing. When we prejudge a Negro as lazy, an Oriental as sly, an Italian as noisy or a Jew as clever, we are similarly misgeneralizing. Neither intelligence nor qualities of character nor other aspects of personality are innate properties of any hair-colored, skin-colored, religious, racial or national groups. These identities of color or of religious, racial or national background are irrelevant to and therefore mistakenly used as a measure of qualities of intelligence or character. The fact that a lemon is yellow is irrelevant to its sourness, and would therefore be mistakenly used as a measure of the quality of sourness in other foods, such as the yolks of eggs. The religion or skin color of any human group is irrelevant to its distribution of innate aptitudes; more important, perhaps, the religion or skin color of any human being is irrelevant to his actual abilities as an individual. The overgeneralized image that we have of the members of any human group is called a stereotype.

It is common to think of the prejudiced attitude as consisting of both hostility and an overgeneralization or stereotype. It is even common to think of the hostility as flowing from the stereotype. But, in fact, it is possible for an individual to have the stereotype without the hostility, or the hostility without the stereotype. It is possible to cloak two groups with the same stereotype, and have different feelings about them. . . .

A negative stereotype may exist without hostility; hostility without a negative stereotype; a combination of both cognitive and emotional elements may exist with varying degrees of intensity and with varying targets. A prejudiced attitude is indeed not a homogeneous mental package. Prejudiced attitude Number 1 is different from prejudiced attitude Number 2, and there is almost an endless variety of possibilities.

Not only do prejudiced attitudes differ widely from one individual to another, but they tend to differ from one situation to another for any given individual. For an attitude is not a thing, it is a process; it is an interaction. It is an interaction involving not only the person and the object, but all other factors that are present in any situation. A crude illustration: In his own home town, Jones may have the deepest contempt for Smith, who lives up the block. He considers Smith a rough character with bad manners and worse taste, socially unacceptable and intellectually barren. Jones has a *feeling* of distaste when he thinks of Smith, and avoids him conscientiously. It happens that Jones, alone on an unguided world tour, has a transportation breakdown in a primitive village in a backward country. The villagers are unfriendly, unlettered and unsanitary. Into this unhappy and improbable scene, after a couple of days, rides Smith. Jones may well greet him with a joyful embrace, rather than with distaste. His image of Smith as a boor may be replaced by the image of a man who at least has the good sense to speak English and to wash his hands before eating. Whether or not this feeling and image will carry over in any way when the two men return to their home town is another matter— but the fact remains that a different external situation has evoked a different attitude. . . .

There are a number of different ways in which this "situational" character of prejudice may be described:

* A general attitude, about Negroes, for example, does not predetermine specific attitudes about Negroes. In other words, if a person has a general stereotype of Negroes, and a general hostility toward Negroes, this does not automatically mean that he will have an unfavorable attitude toward working in the same factory with Negroes.

* One specific attitude toward Negroes, e.g., working with them, may have a quite different

texture from another specific attitude, e.g., living next to them.

* The same person may have one attitude about working next to Negroes in one situation, and a different attitude about working next to them in another situation.
* In sum, a prejudiced attitude may shift from one moment and situation to another. . . .

It is true, of course, that the *expression* of an attitude may be different from, or at least only a surface part of an attitude. A person who is asked whether he would have any objection to rooming with someone of another racial extraction may honestly say, and honestly believe, that he is free of such prejudiced attitudes. But he may find, to his own shock, that when it comes down to it, he does have internal resistance to such a relationship; or indeed, without realizing it himself, he may find reasons and devices for avoiding such a relationship. Likewise, he may say that he *does* have objections, and when it comes down to it, he may not have these objections, or may not find them operative. His initial response may depend on the circumstances: who asks him and where. His ultimate reaction may also depend on the circumstances. This disparity between attitude as expressed and as it ultimately affects behavior merely re-emphasizes the *situational* character of the whole complex of prejudice. And it is the act of prejudice, not the attitude itself, which is the social problem of prejudice as earlier defined. . . .

Learning prejudice
Prejudiced behavior typically shapes and alters prejudiced attitudes. The learning of prejudice is effected primarily by the kinds of social situations in which people live.

The fact that attitudes do not necessarily predetermine behavior, does not mean that attitudes and behavior do not typically accompany each other. The human being is not a mechanical jack-in-the-box. We do normally have feelings and conceptions that accompany our behavior. But our feelings and conceptions —our attitudes—do not necessarily *precede* our behavior. The attitude of the boy who is going

to jump out of the box in the school play may be altered by the very fact that he is going to jump out of the box; just as his attitude immediately after his act may be shaped by the bare fact that he did jump out.

In brief, behavior typically shapes and alters attitudes. Cantril examined attitude polls on the subject of "lend-lease" assistance to the Allies before the United States was involved in World War II. He found that immediately after Congress actually passed lend-lease legislation, attitudes toward such legislation became more favorable by about 10 per cent. The point, according to Cantril is that public opinion tends to follow accomplished fact.

Stouffer and his associates asked white soldiers: How would you like it if your division had companies which included both Negro and white platoons? Seven per cent of those who already were in a company with Negro platoons replied that they disliked the situation; 20 per cent of those questioned who were in the same regiment but not in the same company as Negro platoons replied that they would dislike it; 24 per cent of those who were in the same division but not the same regiment as Negro platoons replied that they would dislike it; 62 per cent of those questioned who were not even in the same division as Negro platoons replied that they would dislike it. The further they were from the accomplished fact, the more they disliked it.

Many research studies show that specific attitudes change after the fact, e.g., attitudes toward living in the same neighborhood, serving in the same Army company. These studies are evidence that specific attitudes do shape themselves to specific behavior. However these studies do *not* indicate that a shift in one specific attitude toward a minority group will necessarily affect other specific attitudes toward the same group; or that a shift in a specific attitude will always affect the expression of a general attitude as it apparently did in the Deutsch and Collins study. . . .

In other words, evidence indicates that specific attitudes shape themselves to behavior. People who actually work with Negroes, especially as equals, develop attitudes favorable toward working with Negroes. People who actually are neighbors of Negroes develop attitudes favorable toward being neighbors of Negroes. Evidence also indicates that general attitudes shape themselves to behavior only if that behavior is itself general in nature. People who behave toward Negroes as full equals on every level tend to develop attitudes toward them as full equals on every level.

Thus, the mass of modern evidence runs counter to the "attitudes-first" fallacy, which holds that prejudice is a lurking state of mind that spills over into overt behavior. It might be more accurate to say that the prejudiced state of mind is typically a function of behavior; except for the danger that *this* formula might be oversimplified into a kind of reverse fallacy. Actually, there emerges an understanding that the key to prejudice must be found *outside* the realm of attitude-behavior relationships. The evidence has demonstrated how both attitudes and behavior are affected by the social frame of reference in which they occur. . . .

Perhaps then the most effective and workable approach to understanding the phenomenon of prejudice is through an investigation of the kinds of *social situations* which give rise to and sustain prejudiced behavior and attitudes. This is a sharply different approach from that which would investigate what kinds of *people* are prone to prejudice.

This is not to underestimate the special validity of an approach to prejudice from the vantage point of personality and personality differences. There are good reasons for making such a psychological approach. Prejudice serves an emotional function for many people. It helps them to shift blame from themselves to others, to rationalize their aggressions, or otherwise provides an outlet for their special emotional needs. Some people with special emotional needs have a special susceptibility to prejudice. . . .

The body of psychological knowledge which throws light on these reactions is extremely helpful in explaining individual differences and in helping to treat individual problems. Since certain emotional needs are universal, in one degree or another, this knowledge even helps to explain the special "attractiveness" that prejudice seems to have for human beings in general.

But it does not explain the specific *social*

problem of prejudice with which our society is currently burdened. . . .

Furthermore, the psychological approach, as valuable as it is, does not explain the preponderance of people who engage in prejudiced behavior, but do *not* have special emotional problems. It does not explain the widespread pattern of prejudice. It does not explain why prejudice is more intense in one place and time than in another. . . .

The prejudiced community

The pattern of community practices is the fountainhead of prejudice· of prejudiced behavior and of prejudiced attitudes.

The growing child learns his social behavior primarily by following the modes and models of behavior around him. Indeed, he has little choice. He learns how to behave toward people of other racial and religious groups by seeing how other people behave, and by automatically participating in the behavior patterns which already exist.

Consider the extreme but not atypical case of a community where the Negro population has been traditionally subordinate on every level. The Negro with whom the young child comes into contact is a domestic in his home or an elevator operator or janitor or a worker in some other menial capacity. The Negroes he knows are not as well educated as the white people he knows, nor as well dressed, nor as well housed. The white people in his community do not socialize with Negroes, nor share the same public accommodations with them. No Negroes sit down at the same dinner table with him or with the people he knows; Negroes are not customers in the restaurants or hotels to which he is taken. Negroes are addressed by their first name, but always address the white people as "Mr." or "Mrs." They do not go to the same school as white children. They sit in separate sections of the bus. They use different rest rooms in the bus stations. If there is a tight fit on the sidewalk, it is the Negro pedestrian who gives way.

These are the social situations, i.e., the overt sets of relationships with which the child is surrounded. He does not have to be *told* that Negroes are "inferior," or what his relationships to them are supposed to be. These are apparent. Even more important, he is part of the white community and necessarily he be-haves within the framework of these existing relationships. It is not just that his parents use a different rest room than do the Negroes. *He* uses a different rest room than the Negroes. *He* sits in the white section of the bus. *He* behaves toward them as social inferiors, and naturally comes to accept them as social inferiors. It isn't necessary to inculcate in him explicit attitudes about the social inferiority of Negroes. More likely, it is necessary for him to develop attitudes that do not conflict with his behavior.

Negroes conform to the prevailing patterns in such a community not only because they must, but also in part because they have accepted the values of the dominant community, and for the same reasons. They have been part of the same behavior patterns.

This process takes place at an early age. In one nursery school study, when preschool Negro children were given a white and Negro doll to play with, they almost uniformly preferred the white doll.

There is a tendency to believe that these kinds of prejudicial behavior patterns are to be found preponderantly in the Deep South. It is often startling to those in the northern and western parts of the country to find, by the most casual self-survey, the extent to which their own communities are "schools of prejudice" by dint of similar ongoing situations. . . .

These behavior patterns are not only the substance of prejudice as a social problem; they are also the breeding conditions of prejudice. In a very real sense, prejudiced behavior reproduces itself; carries within it, its own seeds of continuity. In the same sense, prejudice is a dramatic example of the "self-fulfilling prophecy." The prejudiced image of a Negro as a constitutionally menial worker is sustained by the prejudiced behavior which in fact freezes him as a menial worker.

The learning of prejudice is a natural result of actual participation in patterns of prejudiced behavior; or of firsthand observation of the patterns of prejudiced behavior in the community; but it may also result from

vicarious participation, or *secondhand* observation of the patterns of prejudiced behavior. A society provides many "cues" for social behavior, e.g., "white" and "colored" signs above public drinking fountains; or classified ads in the newspapers which read "gentile only"; or house-for-sale signs which read "white only" or "restricted."

During the War, 200 short stories were analyzed for their treatment of minority group characters. The Anglo-Saxon characters were usually shown as members of the more desirable occupations: bankers, businessmen and teachers. The ethnic minorities pursued lower-class occupations as peddlers, small businessmen or workers. The Negro characters were typically poorly educated, and even comic. More than that, the ethnic minorities were cast in those marginal and even illicit occupations which are found in disproportion among the socially dispossessed. When there were characters who were "menials," racketeers, thieves, gamblers, shady night-club operators, crooked prize-fight managers, such nonsympathetic characters were seldom Anglo-Saxon.

In some cases, these characterizations merely picture the prevailing conditions as they actually exist, e.g., the preponderant number of Negroes in menial positions, and thereby support the inference that these are the only kinds of positions for which Negroes are suited. The mass media, as the above analysis indicates, often accentuate and even exaggerate these conditions by failing to project representative counterimages, e.g., Negroes who are well educated and serving in high capacities in society.

These signs and images projected by the community are visible extensions of the basic behavior patterns of the community. They are part of the complex of social situations in which a young child finds himself. When a child sees a series of signs in front of houses saying "Gentile only," it is not so much that these signs *tell* him that Jews are socially unacceptable, but that these signs convey to him the way in which his elders behave, and the way in which *he* is expected to behave. These cues and vicarious experiences serve a supporting role for those who are directly participant in prejudiced behavior patterns toward minority groups; but they also provide "training" for those who have had less opportunity to participate directly in such behavior. . . .

Studies of the development of prejudice in children show that young children who have not yet been involved in prejudiced behavior patterns may pick up prejudiced talk, but this doesn't affect their unprejudiced behavior. Later, after having become involved in prejudiced behavior patterns, they may pick up democratic language in the schools or elsewhere, but this doesn't affect their prejudiced behavior. By the age of 15, Gordon Allport points out, "considerable skill is shown in imitating the adult pattern."

They are now able to rationalize their prejudiced behavior whenever necessary and resort to the prejudiced ideologies which do not precede but follow prejudiced behavior patterns.

In brief, the pattern of *community practices* serves as the primary source of prejudice in behavior and attitude. . . .

Family and group influences in the prejudiced community
The complex of prejudicial practices within a community provides the family and other traditional groups with the "frame of reference" which perpetuates these practices and sustains prejudice.

A community is not simply a collection of people. It is, for one thing, a collection of associations: families and other special groupings. It consists also of certain community institutions, such as schools, libraries and newspapers. It is characterized by laws and by common customs. It has an economic life, a residential pattern and certain leisure-time habits and facilities. A community exists on many levels. Prejudiced and prejudicial community practices embrace practices on all these levels.

These practices are not necessarily uniform in nature. There may be less prejudice in employment than in housing. There may be some churches that are segregated and others that are not. There may be some groups that promote prejudice and others that oppose it.

It is sensible, therefore, to talk about *prevailing* practices in a community. In generalizing about "community practices" the reference is necessarily to *prevailing* practices, with which certain specific group practices may conceivably be in conflict.

The child learns his prejudiced behavior and attitudes primarily from the modes and models of behavior around him; and the modes and models of behavior which are most influential on the child are normally those of the people or groups with whom he most closely identifies. The most potent influence on the very young child is likely to be at the family level. As a teen-ager, the most potent influence is often likely to come from his circle of peers. . . .

It is in the immediate family, of course, that the foundations for the young child's behavior patterns are most directly set. Here is built society's first wall of separation, when the family pointedly avoids contact with minority group members in the community. The family, of course, may take a direct hand in guiding the child into "proper" behavior practices toward minority group members. Eugene and Ruth Horowitz reported on the training methods used in two Tennessee communities. They found that white parents will often punish the children in order to get them to stop playing with Negro children. These white children will often verbalize reasons for not playing with the Negro children. Frequently they offer such self-serving reasons as "because I'm white and he's black." But these aren't really the reasons why they stop playing together. They stop playing with Negroes because they will be punished if they don't stop. It has already been reported that studies of the development of prejudice in children show that young children who have not yet been involved in prejudiced behavior patterns, may pick up prejudiced talk without acting in a prejudiced manner. Similarly, young children who *have* been involved in prejudiced behavior patterns may pick up prejudiced talk, but this talk does not necessarily have any effective relation to their prejudiced behavior. Their genuine acceptance of prejudiced talk and prejudiced attitudes often comes later, in the wake of established behavior patterns. They may even forget that they were ever punished for playing with Negro children.

In addition, the child will typically pick up "cues" from the family circle which family members may never have meant to provide. Parents are often shocked to discover, if they ever do, the extent to which young children are "cue-sensitive."

It is this cue-sensitivity of children that explains the impact of the "harmless" little jokes that father tells featuring comic, lazy and superstitious Negroes; or the insinuating little references that mother makes about the Jewish women who have applied for admission to her club. For the child these cues are "second-hand" evidence of the behavior that he may expect of his parents, and of the behavior which is expected of him toward minority group members.

Of course, such cues require an appropriate context of family behavior; even if it is the negative one of systematically avoiding contact with minority group members. Indeed, if father's behavior toward Negroes is in striking contrast to his stereotype stories about Negroes, these stories lose much of their significance as cues. This relationship between language and behavior is common to all human experience. We are likely to accept being made the butt of a joking remark by someone we know is friendly to us; we are more likely to be offended if the same remark is made by someone we know is unfriendly to us, or by someone of whom we are uncertain. Words often take on their meaning only within the context of behavior.

It is apparent that the family is uniquely in the position of being able to move *against* the community mainstream in shaping the initial behavior and attitudes of young children. If a family is ideologically and bitterly prejudiced, it can explicitly generate a prejudice that outstrips the general community temper. . . .

In other words, family and group practices are typically consistent with prevailing community practices. These community practices provide the "frame of reference," the social *situations* which are the key to the genesis and sustenance of prejudice. Such practices can be prejudicial by:

1. Prescribing the modes of behavior by which the individual himself will behave toward minority group members in various settings; i.e., as employees, as fellow-workers, as neighbors, as social acquaintances, as friends
2. Providing direct or indirect evidence of the modes of behavior which the rest of the community applies to minority group members in these various settings

In addition, the unfavorable images of minority groups projected by the community pattern, which support these practices, are themselves perpetuated by these practices.

39
variables related to resistance to desegregation in the south

BETH E. VANFOSSEN

Chapter 38 examined the position that prejudice results from the structure of and culture associated with a society rather than from personal traits. Beth Vanfossen, using "resistance to desegregation" as a measure of prejudice, tries to find those community factors most associated with prejudice. She is, of course, dealing with the South, and these findings could not be generalized to the North or West, where community traditions are much different.

Her findings concerning the percentage of blacks within the community and the differences in class between whites and blacks have implications for action. First, all those social programs that raise the class of blacks—education, employment, better housing—should reduce prejudice. Second, the continued migration of blacks from the South to the North and from the city to the suburb should reduce prejudice. Blacks are only 11 percent of the population, and if they were not concentrated in a few areas, they would be less than 20 percent in any single area, a figure below which prejudice seems to decrease. Blacks, however, are not sure this would happen and, as has been discussed earlier, feel that they might improve their position more through the political power they gain by being residentially concentrated.

Beth Vanfossen teaches sociology at Old Dominion College in Norfolk, Virginia.

The U.S. Supreme Court decision of 1954, the Civil Rights Act of 1964, and other legal and social pressures have recently been exerted to effect change in the system of Negro-white relations, particularly in the southern United States. The popular reactions which have been evoked point up the degree to which a populace may resist alteration of the social structure. In 1965, eleven years after the 1954 Supreme Court decision, about half

Reprinted from *Social Forces* 47 no. 1 (September 1968), pp. 39-44. Reproduced by permission of the author and publisher.

the southern states had virtually no Negro children in school with whites, while the other half had achieved significant integration rapidly and with little difficulty. This investigation centers on the problem of isolating and evaluating the variables related to the fact that some southern states have been inclined to desegregate much more extensively and willingly than others, with the ultimate purpose of examining the validity of several theories of discrimination. The relationship between selected socioeconomic variables and the incidence of desegregation which had occurred by 1965-66 in 17 southern and border states, as measured by the percent of the Negro student population attending school with white students, is examined.[1]

Although considerable knowledge and research exists in this area, a consensus concerning the sources of discrimination has not been reached. An enumeration of the various theories of the causes of discrimination and resistance to interracial change would include the following broadly stated ideas. (1) Prejudice, defined as unfavorable and/or inaccurate attitudes toward a minority group, may predispose a person toward discriminatory behavior; discrimination can thus be lessened through proper education and attitude reformation. (2) Psychological deficiencies, such as those which characterize people who are insecure, neurotic, afraid, or in other ways personally unstable, lead to prejudice and discrimination. Subcategories of the psychological explanation include the frustration-aggression hypothesis, the projection or scapegoat theory, and the authoritarian personality typology. (3) Ethnocentrism, a universal attitude which serves the function of supporting group morale and motivation, induces the individual to believe that he belongs to a superior race. (4) The widespread popular acceptance of the ideology of racism which maintains that certain races are innately inferior in a number of ways and that miscegenation results in biological deterioration, sustains and supports the already-established system of subordination. (5) Individuals with low levels of educational achievement, who thus have a limited view of life and are narrow in their perception of social issues, tend to be intolerant. (6) Members of the lower socioeconomic strata, the poor, the unskilled, and lower-level skilled workers are more likely to be "hard-core segregationists," and tend to discriminate more immediately and rigidly than other social strata. (7) Members of the majority group who feel that they will suffer economic loss if members of the minority group are allowed to compete occupationally will resist changes in the status quo—the "economic competition theory." (8) Rural background, both because it is important in its relationship to agricultural traditions and because it denotes the absence of urbanization

and industrialization with their accompanying emphases upon achieved universalistic characteristics, is related to resistance to change. (9) Urbanization and industrialization, which are associated with vertical and horizontal mobility, universalistic evaluations based upon achieved rather than ascribed statuses, economic prosperity, reduction of extended kin structure, decline of community and regional control, increase in frequency of secondary contacts, and decline in traditional values, mitigate against a rigid system of segregation.

These theories of the causes of discrimination have varying degrees of empirical support. Some have been subjected to little or inadequate testing, while others have been buttressed by a substantial body of cumulative research. All of them have at one time or another been presented in professional and educational literature, and are frequently offered in textbooks as accurate descriptions of reality. This paper reports the results of an attempt to examine the validity and applicability of the ideas listed above in points (5) through (9). The statistical support of the paper is presented in Table 1.

1. THE RELATIVE SIZE OF THE NEGRO POPULATION

Of the 15 variables examined, the percent of the population which is nonwhite proved to be the variable most highly correlated with degree of integration ($r = -0.78$). All of the states which have 20 percent or more of their population composed of nonwhites had little or no desegregation in 1965-66.[2] On the other hand, those which have 10 percent or less of their population composed of nonwhites had significant desegregation in 1965-66. This finding is consistent with earlier research. Several interpretations are possible. One is that the minority constitutes a greater threat to the majority in areas of high Negro concentration; consequently, the majority more strongly resists inroads on its means of superordination. In such a case, for example, the middle-class white parent, when he contemplates desegregation, might visualize a predominantly nonwhite school system, whereas the parent in a community with a small proportion of nonwhites might visualize a relatively small number of Negroes in an otherwise little-changed system. Another possibility is that those states with a high Negro population may also be states with the strongest tradition of white supremacy, resulting not only in attitudes disfavorable to the Negro but also in practices and institutions which insure his subordinate position. In support of this proposition is the fact that most of the states which had little desegregation in 1965 are in the Deep South and are states with a historical tradition of the rural plantation economy (Mississippi, South Carolina, Alabama, Georgia, Louisiana, and North Carolina); however, several others with little desegregation are border states which are not usually considered to be as strongly within the geographical complex of the Deep South states (Arkansas, Virginia, Florida, Tennessee, and Texas). Correspondingly, most of the states with substantial desegregation in 1965 are states on the periphery of the southern region (Oklahoma, Maryland, Missouri, Kentucky, Delaware, and West Virginia). Of the latter group, all have Negro populations of below 10 percent with the exception of Maryland and Delaware which have 18 and 16 percent respectively. A third possibility is that states which have a large percentage of nonwhites may also display other characteristics which are related to their resistance of integration. For instance, perhaps they have a lower socioeconomic level, are more rural, less educated, poorer, less industrialized, and less urbanized. However, as will be demonstrated later, all of these variables have much lower correlations with integration than does the proportion of nonwhites, and in some cases virtually no correlation at all.

It is plausible that the proportion of the minority group does, itself, constitute a significant and important variable in the dynamics of intergroup relations, given the already-existing subordinate status and disfavorable categorization of the minority group (without which it would of course cease to be a minority). Should this interpretation be correct, there are several practical implications. For instance, as the Negro population moves away from the southern states, not immediately dispersing equally throughout the country but concentrating in major northern cities, we can expect an increase in similar reactions toward integration and other forms of equality on the part of whites in those areas, even where little such resistance has previously existed. Along this line of thought, Laurenti found that the resistance of whites to buying or renting in integrated neighborhoods is less when the nonwhite group is small and when it is considered unlikely that it will approach the dominant group in size.[3] One might also anticipate that resistance to integration in southern states will decline as the proportion of Negroes in these states drops below 20 percent of the population.

2. THE EDUCATIONAL LEVELS OF WHITES

The empirical evidence on the question of the significance of education to discrimination is complex. On the one hand, Tumin, Stouffer, Bettelheim and Janowitz, and others, indicate that the higher the level of education the less the prejudice and discrimination.[4] On the other hand, prejudice toward Jews has been found to be more prevalent among middle- and upper-class individuals, and voluntary associations of middle- and upper-class status, such as country clubs, fraternities, and elite community groups, are quite frequently found to have discriminatory regulations. Robin Williams concludes that while the well-educated have more complex attitudes by having access to more facts, divergent opinions, and subtle distinctions and while their horizons are larger in the range of considerations taken into account in forming and expressing opinions, their prejudice may be harder, colder, more polite, and more thoroughly buttressed by rationalizations.[5]

Computation of the relation between the degree of integration and the median educational level of white adults in southern states reveals almost no correlation at all ($r = -0.10$). Clearly, if there is a significant relationship between amount of education and discrimination, it is not revealed in these data. One of the main functions of the elementary and secondary school systems is the inculcation of the cultural values of the local area, and one

TABLE 1. Correlation Coefficients, Fifteen Socioeconomic Variables, Southern States, 1960

Variable number	1	2	3	4	5	6	7	8	9	10	11	12	13	14	15
1		-0.78	0.44	0.72	0.75	-0.10	0.68	-0.18	0.45	0.15	-0.10	-0.14	-0.29	0.15	-0.30
2			-0.27	-0.66	-0.84	0.29	-0.65	0.20	-0.58	0.16	0.17	0.17	0.37	-0.33	0.40
3				0.82	0.35	0.50	0.22	0.61	0.81	0.10	0.71	0.73	-0.81	0.73	-0.83
4					0.81	0.07	0.39	0.27	0.84	0.03	0.39	0.43	-0.74	0.68	-0.76
5						-0.42	0.43	-0.19	0.57	-0.07	-0.08	-0.04	-0.43	0.39	-0.45
6							0.24	0.70	0.26	0.15	0.55	0.52	-0.12	0.29	-0.15
7								-0.21	0.24	0.23	-0.34	-0.35	0.04	0.00	-0.0
8									0.56	-0.15	0.88	0.87	-0.48	0.62	-0.42
9										-0.32	0.67	0.68	-0.82	0.87	-0.82
10											-0.28	-0.23	0.16	-0.36	0.01
11												0.98	-0.62	0.74	-0.56
12													-0.66	0.78	-0.62
13														-0.74	0.95
14															-0.73
15															

1. Percent Negro students in school with whites, 1965-66.
2. Percent of population which is nonwhite.
3. Median income of white males, 1959.
4. Median income of nonwhite males, 1959.
5. Nonwhite income as the percentage of white income, 1959.
6. Median school years completed, whites aged 25 and over.
7. Median school years completed, nonwhites aged 25 and over.
8. Percent completed 1-4 or more years of college, whites.
9. Percent of the labor force in white-collar occupations.
10. Percent of the labor force in manufacturing industries.
11. Percent of white males in professional and managerial occupations.
12. Percent of white males in white-collar occupations.
13. Percent of population residing in rural-farm areas.
14. Percent of population residing in urban areas.
15. Percent of labor force employed in farming.

should not in fact be surprised to find a negative relationship, as these data do show, between high school education and degree of integration in a community which has a history of ideological and structural discrimination. In order to determine if higher education might have a more liberalizing effect or might be more indicative, the correlation between degree of integration and the percentage of the white population aged 25 and over which had completed one or more years of college was computed. This correlation likewise turned out to be negative and minimal ($r = -0.18$), again giving no support to the theory that education decreases structural discrimination. Rather, these data suggest not only that formal education per se is not the panacea for prejudices, but also that it may instead be used to buttress and support them. The effect of an increase in average schooling for whites in the South may be that the white people can use their skills to express more effectively their anti-Negro sentiment.[6]

3. SOCIAL CLASS OF THE WHITE POPULATION

The correlations between desegregation and several indices of social class present an inconsistent picture. On the one hand, occupation is not significantly related to desegregation. The correlation between integration and the percent of the white male labor force in white-collar occupations (a category which includes professional, managerial, clerical, and sales occupations) is -0.14, and the correlation between integration and the percent of the white male labor force in professional and managerial occupations is -0.10. On the other hand, income displays a positive correlation with degree of integration ($r = 0.44$). Thus, wealthier states seem to be slightly more likely than poorer to desegregate, but the proportion of white male professionals, managers, clerks, and salespeople exerts little influence.

4. SOCIAL CLASS OF THE NONWHITE POPULATION

Basically, the phenomena of social class and race relations have much in common. Both derive from invidious categorizations on the part of the societal members; both involve differential statuses, and to some degree, differential roles; and both are related to life-styles and life-chances. Residential areas tend to be segregated according to both social class and race; the neighborhood school and the private school are used to ensure both racial and social-class homogeneity; and restriction on membership in formal associations may be used to prohibit admission to certain racial or ethnic, as well as class, groupings. The question occurs, to what degree is the resistance to integration on the part of some of the white population a resistance based upon social-class distinctions rather than racial distinctions? Further, if the Negro in the South is more likely to be characterized by lower-class attributes than the Negro in the North, could this not be one reason for the somewhat differing attitudes of northern and southern whites? It is probably true that the southern white is more likely than is the northern white to have repeated contact with lower-class Negroes such as maids, handymen, garbage collectors, etc., and less likely, because of segregation, to have such contact with middle-class Negroes that might be gained through formal educational or occupational structures. Would it be reasonable to anticipate that as more Negroes approach middle-class status and as the white population becomes aware of this, white resistance to certain forms of equality may decrease?

Further correlations show that where there are more Negroes in school with whites, the average status levels of the Negroes are much higher. The correlation between integration and median income of nonwhites is among the highest found (0.72) of all the variables measured. One might argue that this correlation is spurious because by considering only the median income of the nonwhite population neither the cost-of-living differential between states nor the income of the white population is taken into account. It is conceivable that in a very poor state, even though the income of the Negro population is low, it would not be much lower than the income of the white population, resulting in less possibility for invidious comparison on the part of the whites. This argument is nullified, however, because when nonwhite income as a percentage of white income is correlated with the degree of integration, an even stronger relationship of 0.75 appears.

The correlation between integration and the proportion of nonwhites (previously indicated to be quite high) drops from −0.78 to −0.42 when the factor of nonwhite income as a percentage of white income is controlled. This may mean that some of the high negative correlation between integration and proportion of nonwhites is a by-product and resultant of the fact that Negroes in areas of high Negro concentration are more likely to have incomes which are substantially lower than those of the whites.

Whereas the correlation between integration and the education of whites is nil, the correlation between integration and the education of nonwhites is considerable. Obviously, where there is much segregation, Negroes are less inclined to pursue formal education, and one could certainly maintain that it is the educational discrimination which brings about the low level of Negro education and thus contributes to their low status. The causes of the high drop-out rates in such areas are manifold, and the idea of the "vicious circle" is indeed appropriate. Regardless of the causes of low Negro education, however, the resulting present situation is that there are major social-class differences between whites and Negroes where there is the greatest resistance to integration, and these differences may, in turn, serve to perpetuate the discrimination.

These findings give strong support to the hypothesis that resistance to integration on the part of whites is related to the social class of the Negro population, and that the greater is the discrepancy between the general economic levels of whites and Negroes the more do whites resist integration of the public schools. These findings would also seem to offer some slight question of the economic-competition theory of prejudice which assumes that the greatest attempts among whites to maintain Negro subordination will be found where Negroes are closely enough related in their social-class composition to present a socioeconomic threat.

5. URBANIZATION AND INDUSTRIALIZATION

It is widely maintained that as the South becomes more urbanized and industrialized it will increasingly accept integration. Correlations between three partial indices of urbanization-industrialization and integration seem to give only limited support to these contentions. The percent of residents living in rural farm areas and the percent of persons employed in agricultural occupations are both negatively related to the percent of Negroes in school with whites ($r = -0.29$; $r = -0.30$); the percent of the labor force which is employed in white-collar occupations (including professional, managerial, clerical, and sales occupations), the percent of the labor force employed in manufacturing, and the percent of residents living in urban areas are positively but moderately correlated with the percent of Negroes in school with whites ($r = 0.45$, $r = 0.15$, and $r = 0.15$ respectively). These correlations are not as large as might be expected, although they are consistent in their direction with theoretical propositions, particularly if, as is often assumed, urbanization and industrialization must become expansive enough to exert major structural changes before they engender much attitudinal change. The strongest of these correlations, that between the percent of the labor force in white-collar occupations and the percent of the Negroes in school with whites, drops to zero, however, when the percent of the population which is nonwhite is controlled ($r_{19.2} = 0.00$). This would indicate that in areas of high Negro concentration, states with many persons employed in white-collar occupations are currently no more likely to desegregate than those with few persons employed in white-collar occupations. Similar findings were indicated by Matthews and Prothro in their study of voting registration. They found little or no correlation between their indices of urbanization-industrialization and the percent of Negroes registered to vote, and concluded that their analysis strongly suggests that urbanization and industrialization are vastly overrated as facilitators of Negro voter registration.[7]

SUMMARY

Several factors have been examined in an attempt to test theoretical positions regarding resistance to change in intergroup relations. The results tend to indicate that the reasons for resistance to integration are not necessarily the ones most frequently mentioned in the literature. Education of whites, for example, as measured by the median number of years of schooling completed, was found to have no correlation with integration, and college education was even found to be slightly associated with segregation. States with large proportions of white males employed in the higher-status occupational categories were no more inclined to desegregate than states with small proportions employed in these categories. Urbanization and industrialization show only a minimal relationship to the introduction of integration and the correlation between the proportion of workers in white-collar occupations and integration drops to zero when the factor of Negro concentration is controlled. There is, however, a fairly small positive correlation between desegregation and the median income of whites.

On the other hand, the proportion of nonwhites in the state and the social class of nonwhites show very strong relationships to desegregation. A segregated state is much more likely to display wide discrepancies between the socioeconomic standing of whites and Negroes; that is, the lower the social class of the average Negro, in comparison with the social-class position of the white in the same state, the less likely is that state to readily accept integration. It is also possible that the class position of Negroes is the relevant variable behind the very strong correlation between the percentage of Negroes in the state and the state's inclination to remain segregated.

NOTES

[1] The information on desegregation is taken from Southern Education Reporting Service, *Statistical Summary* for 1965-66, Nashville, Tennessee, 1965. All of the data for the independent variables were obtained from the U.S. Bureau of the Census, *U.S. Census of Population: 1960,* Vol. 1 (Washington, D.C.: Government Printing Office, 1962).

[2] D. R. Matthews and J. W. Prothro, in their analysis of factors related to Negro voter registration, think that the critical point is around 30 percent Negro population. "Social and Economic Factors and Negro Voter Registration in the South," *American Political Science Review* 57 (March 1963) p. 29.

[3] Luigi Laurenti, *Property Values and Race* (Berkeley and Los Angeles: University of California Press, 1960), p. 57.

[4] Melvin M. Tumin, *Desegregation: Resistance and Readiness* (Princeton: Princeton University Press, 1958), p. 180; Samuel A. Stoffer, *Communism, Conformity and Civil Liberties* (New York: Doubleday & Co., 1955); Bruno Bettelheim and Morris Janowitz, "Trends in Prejudice," in Bernard Berelson and Morris Janowitz (eds.), *Reader in Public Opinion and Communications* (2nd ed.; New York: The Free Press, 1966), pp. 100-105.

[5] Robin M. Williams et al., *Strangers Next Door* (Englewood Cliffs, N.J.: Prentice-Hall, 1964), p. 375.

[6] This correlation of −0.18 is similar to the Matthews and Prothro correlation of −0.26 between median school years completed by whites and Negro voter registration. *Op. cit.*, p. 38.

[7] *Ibid.*, p. 36.

40
white incubus

OTTILIE MARKHOLT

Most articles, including those in this book, deal with overt racism and discrimination. This article deals with residual racism: that which remains after one recognizes the biological equality of all men and the damage discrimination does to subordinate groups. The questions raised touch upon cultural pluralism, which has been discussed elsewhere in this text, and upon the implementation of community control, which will be discussed in Part VI.

That the attitudes Mrs. Markholt discusses are present is underlined by an incident that happened in a class on minority groups. Seven black students asked if they could form a panel in front of the rest of the class, which was white. They did so. One student asked: "Don't you think that the increasing adoption of black children by whites will go far to solve racial problems?" The answer: "I think adoption of black children by whites is murder."

Mrs. Markholt is a free-lance writer.

The white liberal was shocked that black people were not sorry to have been born black —that they considered themselves beautiful . . . his ego was shattered by black people's defense of the fearsome and alien ghetto.

The white liberal sits like a giant incubus on the black freedom movement. It has devoured the interracial civil rights organizations and waves their empty husks at the black people, trying to cajole them into fleshing out the dead organizations with their presence.

Probably it is futile to belabor the white liberal for his bland arrogance. He is so clearly incapable of understanding his present role in the civil rights movement that he professes to believe in and cherish. He is, after all, white—sharing the views of his white culture and by choice preserving his place in the white community. At best he was an innocent do-gooder whose presence in civil rights activities could be tolerated by the black community. At worst he has become the pawn of the white

Reprinted from *Negro Digest* 8, no. 8 (June 1969), pp. 4-14. Copyright © June 1969 by *Negro Digest*. Reprinted by permission of *Black World* and the author.

power structure in its desperate attempt to avoid facing and dealing with the emerging black strength in America.

Alone among white Americans the white liberal has a conscience of a sort. He believes that he is a moral man and America is a moral nation. This is essentially what separates the white paternalist from the white bigot. But the white liberal's conscience and his morality are inseparable from his white superiority. During the last decade the black revolt gained momentum, and the white liberal discovered that the hitherto nonexistent black people were being outrageously treated in America. He became indignant over their wrongs and he began to march. He picketed to integrate schools, jobs, neighborhoods. He crossed arms, locked hands and sang:

Black and white together
We shall overcome some day.

He gave time, energy, money, and occasionally his life. For years he was there—doing the right things for the wrong reasons.

The white liberal worked from several basic premises: that it was tragic to be born black, that black people should wish to be, and should be, exactly like white people, and that he knew at least as well as—probably better than—black people what they should want and how to get it. His morality, his social justice, consisted of deciding that people with dark complexions should share his white America on his terms: live in his neighborhoods, attend his schools, and work beside him. What more could they want? He did not question the basic values of white America, for they were his values and therefore absolute.

He argued with complete sincerity: "They are just like us. The only difference is the color of their skin." To himself he might add: "If some of them are culturally deprived, they are not to be blamed. They have been segregated so long. Integration will help them advance." To black people he said: "I'm completely color blind. I don't even think about it," and he tried earnestly to practice this enlightened outlook. When he socialized with black people he relished his own broadmindedness in offering himself as a true apostle of integration and giving his Negro friends the opportunity to associate with a white person. His Utopia was a completely integrated America, peopled by light-skinned white men and dark-skinned white men.

The black ghetto was alien. While he might fraternize in the civil rights movement with individual blacks, in the black community their numbers and strange closed faces frightened him. He ventured into the ghetto as a civil rights crusader, but at night he went home thankfully to his white neighborhood. This was the white man who marched and sang in Washington, D.C., and Selma: sincere, dedicated, paternalistic and completely white. He performed his good deeds with the blind arrogance of a white man dealing with black men.

The white liberal failed to ask the hard questions. He does not know they are there to be asked: "How can I know what black people want? What place in white America do they really seek? Am I bound to respect their right to make their own decisions? Or respect them as equals?"

There is a watershed of identity from which values arise. Almost all white Americans are glad they were born white, and they accept without question the superiority of their white Western culture. They feel sorry for people who were born black and who do not share freely in that culture. To them the black man must automatically wish above all else to lose his black identity and be completely assimilated in their America. When black people do not welcome this they are thought to be ignorant, backward or prejudiced. They think the black community and black institutions should dissolve as rapidly as opportunities for integration will permit.

For example, the persistence of the black church puzzles them, now that many white churches profess to welcome black communicants. When the Central Conference of the Methodist Church chose to retain its identity white liberals smiled knowingly and said it was because Negroes liked to flourish their bishops' titles, that the black Methodists were too self-important to give up their little empires for integration. They believe black clergymen are trying to keep their flocks out of white churches because the black preachers would surely lose their pulpits. Because white is right, they assume that white churches could serve black people better than black churches. They do not doubt that when black people have progressed sufficiently they will turn to the white churches. They have not the least understanding of the great and living strength of the black church.

The actions of black and white demonstrators were the same. Their motives were not.

The black man picketed a segregated school because he knew his child would have a better opportunity to learn in a predominately white school where it was assumed the pupils could and would learn, and the school was oriented toward that end. He knew that no matter how intelligent or gifted his child might be, the child would learn little in a segregated northern school where the staff considered black pupils culturally deprived and unteachable, and many of the children responded to this rejection with equal hostility. He was not seeking to thrust his child among white children because they were white, but because education was available in their classrooms.

The white man picketed because he

thought black children would be improved by attending white schools and mingling with white children. He knew his schools were better, and he was willing to be generous and dilute them with a few disadvantaged black children. The black child could only benefit from assimilating the cultural values of his white schoolmates. The relative merits of Bach and Rhythm & Blues were certainly not debatable.

The black man demonstrated for open housing because he wanted the opportunity to live wherever he chose—because the ghetto walls permitted landlords to charge him more for poor housing than he would have to pay in an open city. He did not wish to destroy the black community, but to breach the walls that surround it.

The white man picketed because the very existence of the ghetto, which he equated with both a slum and the black community, was the ultimate mark of humiliation and shame. He was trying so hard to help his dark-skinned compatriots forget they were not just like him—trying so hard to forget it himself.

During the late summer of 1964 I was associated with a CORE chapter in a large eastern city. It was the second chapter to be organized there, almost entirely black. National CORE had revoked the charter of the previous affiliate, organized and dominated by white university students. This black chapter had the confidence of many of the militants in the black community. A white social worker director of a large settlement house in a black neighborhood worked with the chapter. He was a small, intelligent, energetic man who loved power. He had been active in organizing the March on Washington in another city. He gloried in what he thought was his successful manipulation of this CORE chapter and its supporting groups. He told me as much. The black leaders watched this supposed exercise of power, utilizing the man's energy and talent, completely aware that they must retain control of policy decisions. They did.

The glimpse I had of National CORE was different and distressing. That fall I attended as an observer a regional CORE conference in New York City. It was dominated by three white experts on the national staff. Two of them were particularly assured white

men. I could not imagine them pausing to doubt their competence to tell the black freedom movement what to do. The black staff members had minor roles in the conference. I do not know what the black delegates thought of these white experts. This was two years before the black-white struggle in CORE became public.

I first saw Seattle CORE during the school boycott in the spring of 1966. The morning of the boycott in response to a last-minute call for additional help, I reported to the CORE office, the second floor of a vacant store building in the black community. I had been receiving the CORE bulletin and was impressed by the chapter's activity. A white woman was minding the office, coordinating activity for the freedom schools under CORE's direction. She sent me immediately to a large Catholic community center overflowing with children. Her daughter, a college student bubbling with excitement, drove me over. "Aren't they just adorable those little deprived black children," she cooed. I grunted. We reached the center before I could reply that the little black children were not deprived.

The principal of the freedom school was a strong black man. Most of the teachers were white liberal intellectual types. Some of the special features of the curriculum reflected white values. The white woman playing a gavotte on the harp was obviously a brief exposure to the better things for the deprived black children. A white man played southern racist songs on a violin for each class. Black music was ignored. There was no proud statement that black is beautiful. One learned black scholar lectured on the history of black people in America, concluding with Langston Hughes' "Rivers." Otherwise black culture was not recognized. The white students, almost a fifth of the enrollment, were largely the children of the white liberals who supported the boycott. They tended to be mouthy and self-assured seeking to monopolize the class discussions. They probably duplicated their public school roles.

Outwardly the boycott was successful in numbers of students who participated. But I'm not sure what it did for the black community. It appeared that whites dominated the planning, and certainly the teaching staff. Had the freedom schools grown from within the black community, I should think there would have been black Sunday school teachers to staff them. As it was, many of the white teachers showed little understanding of their black pupils, and the pupils had the experience of another white teacher rejecting them. The dominant mood among the white staff members was: "We are noble and benevolent in fighting for the right of these deprived black children to attend our schools and mingle with our children." I wonder how clearly the black children and their parents got the message.

A few months later I was appointed to our local NAACP executive board, protesting that I didn't think white folks should be making policy. I was told by friends (who privately agreed with me) that so many white faces were necessary on the board and if I declined some other white person would be appointed. So I began to attend meetings, resolved to say little. Shortly after that another white board member, concerned over the NAACP's lack of support in the black community, proposed we send representatives to various organizations to explain our program and invite them to discuss their problems. All board members, white and black, were expected to speak for the NAACP in the black community.

I objected to the idea of sending white members into the black community to tell black people what to do. This was arrogant and paternalistic. I tried to explain white people's limitations, their place in the civil rights movement as helpers and not leaders. The members present, black and white, were either firmly disapproving of or outraged by my statements that the black community would not and should not be expected to accept white NAACP spokesmen. Some denied angrily the "black racism" they thought I was implying the black community contained. A black woman warmly defended the white paternalists, citing Mary White Ovington and her spiritual descendants in the NAACP through the years. The two black board members who would have agreed with me were not present that night. The consensus was resolutely color blind. But the project of speakers before black organizations was not mentioned again.

I can only guess how the black civil rights activists felt during those years about their white liberal allies. The white liberal was talking about freedom—justice—equality, but it was freedom—justice—equality on his terms, as he chose to grant and administer them. This may not have been apparent at first. Possibly the black activists credited white liberals with more understanding and less arrogance than the whites possessed. Possibly they believed the whites would lose their paternalism as they came to know and understand the black community. I have often found black people more charitable in their assessments of whites than I thought was warranted. Judging by their own humane culture, they seem unable at times to believe that white folks can be so mean.

The deep cleavage between white liberals and the black community was dramatized when the concept of black power became an angry slogan hurled at white America. The white folks' illusion of allowing dark-skinned white people to share their white Western culture on their terms was threatened. White liberals had approved the humble and prayerfully supplicant posture of the nonviolent black demonstrators. To them it was right and natural that powerless black people should beg and powerful white people should decide to grant. They had accepted black people on the assumption they were trying to become white. Now they were forced to look at black men who did not beg and did not want to be white. Their treatment of Adam Clayton Powell revealed their inability to accept a proud black man. Socialists and other hitherto staunch civil rights supporters joined the white Establishment in attacking and reviling Powell. They could not understand black people's loyalty to him.

Then Stokely Carmichael shouted "Black Power," and the sorting out began. Many white liberals who had marched and sung in 1963 and 1964 retreated to silence. Those who remained, by their own definition, "dedicated workers in the civil rights movement," joined the Establishment to denounce the frightening new idea, or searched desperately for Negro leaders who would say the things they wanted to hear.

No wonder the white liberal was horrified and alarmed by the black power slogan and its attendant concepts. His paternalistic role was challenged. With all his blindness and disdain for the ghetto and for blackness, he had claimed the ancient white prerogative of knowing what was best for the Negro. Now that he **was** being told he could merely help, it was a deep affront to his white superiority. He could not accept a subordinate place, so he defended his paternalism by attacking black power. Assuming that black nationalism was indefensible he attempted to destroy blackness with it.

How did this white man suppose black people had lived for the last three hundred years in America: a complete negation and self-rejection, in limbo, waiting for the final day of integration when they could forget they were considered black first and American second?

The white liberal was shocked that black people were not sorry to have been born black —that they considered themselves beautiful. Most of all, his ego was shattered by black people's defense of the fearsome and alien ghetto. To him it was a slum, to be wiped out, bulldozed, as soon as possible. It was the supreme gesture of arrogance to question the precious gift of integration that the white liberal was working so hard to bestow. Not to want complete and immediate integration on his terms was separatism, racism, prejudice-in-reverse. Anything less than his kind of integration was antiwhite. He saw nothing valuable in the black community. He saw black culture only as a willful and misguided failure to become white. In the name of his mythical integrated Negro he would destroy the black community and its culture.

He was unaware of his double standard. For a black man to criticize white culture and defend black culture was antiwhite and biased. For him, a white man to criticize black culture and defend white culture was not antiblack, but objective.

Those white liberals who remained in the civil rights organizations fought the black militants for control. Black militants in the NAACP have charged that the United Auto Workers' faction in the 1967 and 1968 conventions used every tactic, from bribery to threats of physical violence, to retain control of the organization. Its declining membership nation-

ally reflects the black community's growing lack of confidence in it.

In late 1967 a group of leaders in the black community (Tacoma, Wash.) organized a strategy committee to press for certain goals. Among them were officers and members of the NAACP. Their first target was the personnel of the newly created Human Relations Commission, and particularly its executive director, a prejudiced white man in whom they had no confidence. They called for nonrecognition of the commission as constituted and appointment of a black director. The commission was characterized as "an instrument of appeasement controlled by the white power structure." This program was presented to the NAACP executive board with a request for NAACP support and implementation. Led by the white liberals, the board recommended rejection of the program. I reported the board's action in our monthly newsletter and wrote a signed "Letter to the Editor" that began: "It is time for a white member . . . to speak plainly." After reviewing the presentation to the board meeting I said:

The merits of the proposal are basically not at issue. Clearly the program was being brought to the NAACP by the leaders of the Negro community.

The Opposition . . . was led by three white board members. For all their lip service to the idea of respect for Negroes and recognition of their rights, these white members were displaying their superiority and paternalism in not recognizing the right of Negro leaders to make basic civil rights policy in this or any city. Anything less than our recognition, as whites, of the absolute necessity of Negro leadership is to bring our white paternalism with us right into the NAACP. We whites are not "equal" to Negroes in our understanding of and ability to communicate with the Negro community. How could we be? We have not walked the earth one day of our lives as Negroes.

Granted that these white members have worked hard in the branch, that they "mean well." This isn't enough. Unless they support loyally the Negro leadership they are doing more harm than good to civil rights. If they really respect Negroes let them accept this leadership and work to carry out the will of the Negro community. . . .

If the NAACP does not support the [committee] it will certainly alienate itself from the Negroes' struggle for human dignity. . . . I appeal to white NAACP members to move beyond their paternalism and join the struggle as loyal followers.

Just before the branch meeting the newly appointed director of the Human Relations Commission hastily joined the NAACP. He showed up at the meeting with a lengthy appeal for fair play and another chance before being condemned. (He had already bungled his first chance.) The white liberals were there in numbers, indignant at my attack, completely unmoved by my appeal. They voted down the proposals of the black leaders. The arrogance of the white liberals at this branch and their insistence on compromise and appeasement have tended to discredit it in the black community.

In the Seattle CORE election at the end of 1966, the white-supported moderate black candidate for chairman defeated the militant black candidate. The defeated faction withdrew and formed an aggressive black community organization. The whites may have saved CORE from the black militants, but they seem to have silenced it in the black community. In San Francisco's Fillmore District in 1968 I passed a vacant CORE office. I saw no evidence of its activity in the community. Maybe it, too, was saved from the blacks.

Recently a friend of mine, a black woman, related how impossible it was for a white man with whom she was associated in an interracial cultural organization to get along with his black peers. He seemed unable to avoid the appearance of patronizing them, and his feelings were hurt because they did not welcome him as a soul brother. He was aggressive in the affairs of the organization. The black men universally disliked him. "What can I tell him," she asked me, "to make him understand?"

"Tell him that he is a white paternalist," I replied. "He probably is incapable of under-

standing this, or he wouldn't behave as he does. White men are the lords of creation, and it is virtually impossible for them to be otherwise. Don't let the white paternalists dominate the organization, or they will drive the black people away." "They already are," she replied sadly.

During 1968 the civil rights movement has seemed to make some progress. Local white power structures are beginning to make concessions to the moderate civil rights organizations to avoid dealing with the black militants. They are engaging in sham battles with these organizations rather than recognizing the growing power of the black communities.

For years the Seattle school system resisted integration by changing boundaries or busing, while de facto segregation steadily increased under its open enrollment plan. The school board ignored appeals, picketing and the school boycott. Then in the fall of 1966 at I.S. 201, the new junior high in Harlem, black parents demonstrated for a black principal and community control of the school. In the summer of 1967 Seattle community organizations moved toward a similar program for their black schools. Early in 1968 the Seattle school board announced plans to close a black elementary and a black junior high school, to reduce the ratio of black students in the high school by transfers out, and to bus the children from the closed black schools to white schools. The NAACP and white liberals applauded the progress. The black community protested vigorously against busing its children out and demanded a black principal for the high school and community voice in its schools. The NAACP denounced this program as irresponsible.

It is true that the State Board of Education had finally established requirements for racial balance in school districts receiving state funds, but to me the real reason for the Seattle program is the changed options for the school boards. For years the alternative to the civil rights movement's demand for dispersal of black students throughout the white schools was to do nothing and keep the black children penned up in their black schools. Now the white community has realized that those black schools are the breeding ground for a continu-

ing crop of young black militants and the focal point around which the black community is uniting to demand community control and black administrators. Now the dispersal of these black students has suddenly become desirable—to stifle their rising black consciousness. The school board's program was not a victory gained by a strong civil rights movement, but an attempt to thwart the growing strength of the black community.

The same changed options were operating before and after the assassination of Dr. Martin Luther King, Jr. For years the white community had been opposing his demands and demonstrations. Then early in 1968, as the nation began to look forward to another violent summer, his nonviolent philosophy became a viable alternative to that of the black militants. Just before his death the *Saturday Evening Post* featured an article in which he said that the Poor People's March on Washington would be the last chance for nonviolence to prove its usefulness. He implied that one of the purposes of demonstrations was busy work to allow black anger and white guilt to be vented in harmless channels. (Malcolm X told us years ago the 1963 March on Washington was busy work.) Dr. King still believed white America had a conscience that could be awakened, and he preached love for all men. For these reasons he became the acceptable alternative to the black militants. The appeal to conscience could be ignored, as it had been for hundreds of years.

The lavish public mourning after his death by the same white power structure that had fought him during his life was a cheap attempt to buy time and appease black anger. That great opinion manipulator, the *Reader's Digest,* for June featured "Two Great Sermons by Martin Luther King" and a lead article, "Plain Talk About Hatred and Violence," by a white liberal. To me, passage of the Civil Rights Act of 1968 was not a tribute to Dr. King, but a comment on the flames in the sky over Washington, D.C.

White paternalism is inherently as racist as white bigotry. It stems from the same concept of white superiority and the same lack of respect for black people and black culture. The white paternalist, embodied in the white liberal, demonstrates his abhorrence for blackness by seeking to wipe out the black communities and assimilate black-skinned white men in his white Western culture. With increasing urgency the white liberal is being used against the black community. He is truly the last best hope of white supremacy.

41
a critical examination of textbooks on indians

CHRIS C. CAVENDER

Blacks have demanded courses in black history because they felt that commonly used texts in the public schools either ignored or misrepresented the history of both the Afro-Americans and Africa, the land from which they had come. As a result, not only do most schools that serve black students now have courses in black histories, but publishers have revised their textbooks and are providing a vast array of supplementary materials.

Much less has been done about textbooks handling of the histories of other minorities. Chris Cavender points out some of the most blatant kinds of distortions as well as the more subtle kinds in textbook discussions of American Indians.

Mr. Cavender works for the University of Minnesota and in the past has taught high school English and directed an Indian Upward Bound program.

INTRODUCTION

The main purpose of this paper is to show what I regard as the lack of a balanced perspective in history books dealing with the American Indian. This lack of a balanced perspective tends not only to sustain but also to strengthen stereotypes held by the non-Indian. This paper is also a mechanism by which I can express my own reactions—reactions of disgust, anger, resentment, etc., which I have felt when I have read such culturally biased material. Such reactions, I suspect, have been shared by many other Indians as well.

There are minor purposes of this paper as well. For example, I hope to include suggestions which would help to eliminate some of the cultural narrow-mindedness of many historians and educators. Also, I will include personal accounts of some of my ancestors

First published as "An Unbalanced Perspective: Two Minnesota Textbooks Examined by an American Indian," published by the Training Center for Community Programs, University of Minnesota (September 1970). Reprinted by permission of the author and publisher.

who were involved in the Sioux War of 1862, to show that there is more than one way of looking at a historical event or situation.

If the reader suspects that the writer is somewhat biased at times, his suspicions are entirely correct. Since I am a Dakota (or Sioux) by heritage, many of my comments will be concerned with things Dakota. I will be using the terms Indian, Dakota, or Sioux synonymously unless otherwise specified.

AMERICAN HISTORY TEXTS

To illustrate the thesis that there is a lack of a balanced perspective in history books dealing with the American Indian, I referred to several textbooks which were used in my college American history courses. One such textbook was *The United States Since 1865* (1959) by Foster Rhea Dulles.

It is interesting to note that in the 531 pages of this book, American Indians are considered important enough to have four full pages devoted to them. It is of further interest to observe that the title of the section concerned with Indians is "The Indian Menace."

One statement in this section says, "As the railroads reached out across the prairies, the construction gang grew accustomed whenever an alarm was sounded to throwing down their picks and shovels and seizing their rifles. They were never entirely safe from savage attack."[1] The terms "menace" and "savage" reflect a viewpoint which is entirely consistent with that of most historians and consonant with the treatment accorded to Indians in history. Too many times (I won't say all the time, because somewhere I believe there are objective historians) the Indian is presented as a "savage," a "barbarian," "a fiend," and in other such negative terms. The Indian is seen as subhuman, perhaps a step above the other animals. In some cases he is considered even in a worse way; he is considered to be an impediment to be gotten rid of immediately if not sooner. This is easily seen when one considers once again the title "The Indian Menace."

Another textbook used in college courses was *A History of the United States Since 1865* (1959) by Williams, Current, and Freidel. Out of 710 pages, approximately ten full pages are devoted to American Indians. The title of this section is "The Taming of the Tribes." Here again the use of the word "taming" implies that Indians are animals, like cows or dogs, to be domesticated. Over seven of the pages deal with the Indian wars. "A summary review of the principal Indian wars will suffice to illustrate the almost incessant conflict on the frontier from the sixties to the eighties."[2] This fact indicates the cultural bias of these historians. They regard the Indian as an impediment. In fact, they state this quite plainly in another of their textbooks,

Yet one of the Indians' greatest influences on American civilization was negative rather than positive. Despite their kindly aid to the first European arrivals, the Indian became an obstacle to the advance of white settlement, and life on the frontier derived many of its peculiarly "American" qualities from the Indian danger and the Indian wars.[3]

Note that in this statement the Indian is considered apart from "American civilization."

Apparently what the writers regard as "peculiarly 'American' qualities" applies only to the white settlers on the frontier. The following statement is particularly offensive to Indian people: "The white man, when he arrived in America, had much to learn from the Indian, but the Indian had far more to learn from the white man."[4] My immediate reaction to this is, "like what, for example?" The Indian was content with his way of life. Has this present American society, with its individual striving for success, with its materialistic emphasis, produced happy people? Another gem of these writers is "Even the most brilliant of the native cultures, such as the Mayan, were stunted in comparison with the growing civilization of Europe."[5] By whose judgment? By the judgment of the white, middle-class historians who write the books.

One of the gravest errors that are committed by historians is the belief that American history began in 1492 with Columbus' arrival on the North American continent. As David C. Bolin says, "This seemingly innocent lesson, usually encountered in kindergarten or first grade, is, in fact, charged with a cultural bias so monstrous and pervasive, yet so well disguised, that neither the student nor the teacher is inclined or equipped to challenge it."[6] Williams, Current, and Freidel are guilty of this error. Their first section in their American history textbook is entitled "Europe and the New World." As far as they are concerned, there is no American history before 1492. It begins in Europe.

Bolin has other noteworthy things to say, so I will quote him freely. "An entrenched cultural and racial bias, combined with an infinite delight in writing and learning about ourselves has allowed historians to ignore what should be a major branch of history; the history of the continent of North America." In another comment he states, "American history from the 16th century to the present should be taught as the most recent, rather than the only, development in the history of North America."[7]

In the textbooks that I have mentioned, nowhere are the accomplishments and contributions of Indians to the development of the United States mentioned. This again is another very serious error. Yet the virtues and accomplishments of white America are mentioned in superabundance, illustrating the truth that historians take "infinite delight" in writing about themselves.

RELATIVE TERMS

Words such as "hero," "traitor," "victory," and "massacre" are relative terms, depending on one's point of view. Since most of the present textbooks dealing with American history are written by white historians, these and other such terms have been used to portray the Indian in an unfavorable light. Thus, there is lacking a balanced perspective. However, I would like to show another point of view—how an Indian might use such terms.

Nathan Hale is considered a patriot and a martyr in American history, and rightly so. He was a man who was loyal to his people and country—a man who said "I regret I have but one life to lose for my country" and thus died a martyr's death. The 38 Sioux who were hanged at Mankato (in Minnesota) also were patriots. They had fought for their land. They fought because of the many injustices which had been wrought upon their people. Medicine Bottle and Shakopee, two Sioux chiefs, also died for the cause of their people. They were executed by hanging at Fort Snelling on November 11, 1865.

In the history books the term "renegade" is applied to Simon Girty, and the term "traitor" is applied to Benedict Arnold, and understandably so. These men turned against their own people and worked actively in the best interest of the enemy. John Other Day, a Sioux Indian who lived near the Yellow Medicine Agency, led 62 white people to safety at the time of the beginning of the Sioux War of 1862. Here is what one history book says: "And here is a portrait of that good Indian, John Other Day, who saved the lives of many white people during the dreadful Sioux Massacre."[8] To some historians a good Indian is a dead Indian. To this one, a good Indian is an Indian who turns against his own people and helps white people. To me, John Other Day was a traitor.

"Hero" is another term which is often applied only to white people in the history books. However, I would like to suggest some Indian heroes. Little Crow (Kangicistina) was a chief of the Mdewakonton (Spirit Lake) Sioux. Though he had been east and had seen many settlements of the wasicun (white men), though he knew the white men were as many as "the locusts when they fly so thick that the whole sky is a snowstorm,"[9] though he knew he would be fighting against overwhelming odds, he still led the Dakota in the defense of their homeland, against the dishonesty, injustice, and greed of the encroaching white man. Big Eagle (Wanmdi Tanka), another Sioux chief, also "had been to Washington and . . . knew the power of the whites, and that they would finally conquer us."[10] These men knew that they might win a battle or two, but would lose the war, and yet they fought. These men demonstrated courage and have the right to be called heroes.

The term "massacre" is used by many historians in a peculiar manner. If the white man wins a battle, it is a glorious victory. If the Indian wins, it is a massacre. Let us look at this term from another perspective. Two incidents from history will illustrate.

In 1863, Black Kettle led a friendly band of Cheyenne and Arapaho in to Fort Lyon on Sand Creek. This had been done at the request of the governor of Colorado. Black Kettle understood he was under official protection. Nevertheless, Colonel J. M. Chivington, leading the Colorado milita, treacherously attacked the unsuspecting camp in an onslaught that spared neither men, women, nor children. One white witness later testified of the fate of these Indians, "They were scalped. Their brains were knocked out; the men used their knives, ripped open women, clubbed little children, knocked them in the head with their guns, beat their brains out, mutilated their bodies in every sense of the word."[11] Some of the soldiers had cut off the breasts of the Indian women and had made skin pouches. Later these same men in Denver saloons would brag of their exploits and show off their trophies. This clearly indicates that white American soldiers are capable of committing atrocities.

At Wounded Knee, South Dakota, in 1890, another tragedy, another massacre occurred. Chief Big Foot and his band of Sioux men, women, and children had been apprehended by the U.S. Seventh Cavalry, and brought into Wounded Knee. The Indians were tired, hungry, cold, and some were sick, including Big Foot. It is reported that there was drunkenness in the cavalry camp. Though no one knows who fired the first shot, a deadly rifle fire broke out. Then the Hotchkiss guns opened up and no mercy was shown the Indians. The firing ceased when the targets were either down or they were beyond range. "A ghostly hush slowly crept over a field of the dead and dying. Only the mournful whine of a freezing north-wester, the chilling heartcry of a baby still clinging to the breasts of its mother who was beyond hearing, for she, too, was numbered among the dead, were the only sounds to break the numbness of the spell."[12] Approximately 120 men, women, and children were slaughtered and stacked into one long mass grave.

These things are not usually mentioned in grade school or high school textbooks because they run counter to the nationalistic pride and patriotism of the white historians and students. Only the savage Indians, the enemies, perform such horrible deeds. It would not be in the best interest of the American philosophy of education if white students were taught that in the 19th century the white soldiers "often excelled in the use of barbaric torture, brutality, and slaughter in their encounters with Indians."[13]

TEXTBOOKS ON STATE HISTORY

Texts on United States history are used throughout the country; but each state usually requires that state history also be taught. If Indians have played an important part in the history of that state, the misinformation and bias can be even more intense as the following examples for Minnesota show.

One of the textbooks on Minnesota history that is presently and frequently being used in classrooms throughout Minnesota is Theodore C. Blegen's *Building Minnesota.* What I am about to present are some personal reactions, criticisms, questions, and suggestions concerning this particular textbook.

I noted with great interest the statement made by Edgar B. Wesley in the "Introduc-

tion." He states that a book dealing with the people of a state should possess several outstanding characteristics, and one of these is, "The book should be free from partisan bias or social prejudices."[14] He goes on to say that he believed the author of this text had measured up to this standard. I do not think I believe that. However, keep this in mind.

In Blegen's opening chapter, titled "Woods and Waters Fair," which is nine pages long, Indians are mentioned twice. In the first instance, waterways are the main topic of the paragraph and Indians are mentioned as knowing the Minnesota system of rivers and lakes. In the second instance, Indians accept geographic conditions as they are. However, in the rest of that paragraph and the rest of the chapter, white people are discussed. In his text, Blegen makes what I regard as a very profound observation. He says, "The truth is simply that the Indian was human."[15] Many historians have not yet learned this truth.

I now want to concentrate on Chapter 23, "The Sioux Go on the Warpath." In this chapter Blegen is guilty of omissions. The settlers at Acton have been killed, and the chiefs and followers are deciding what to do. It would be helpful at this point to include excerpts from the speechs of various chiefs at this council, especially the speeches of Little Crow and Big Thunder. It would be helpful for the reader to know that the Indians knew they were at a tremendous disadvantage, that they knew the white man possessed an overwhelming superiority in numbers and weaponry. It would be helpful for the reader to know that the Indians reacted to injustice, dishonesty, greed, oppression, and prejudice. as any other people would react to these things. So they fought. These Dakota were a brave and proud people.

On page 210, Blegen finally does quote an Indian. Big Eagle, in talking about the attack on the white centers of Fort Ridgely and New Ulm, says, "We thought the fort was the door to the valley as far as to St. Paul, and if we got through the door nothing would stop us this side of the Mississippi. But the defenders of the fort were very brave and kept the door shut."[16] This is noteworthy, because when Blegen does quote an Indian, he does so to compliment white people.

Of course the same relative terms which speak favorably of white people and point negatively to the Indians appear in this textbook as well. Blegen uses the term "atrocities," and it is "Indian atrocities" naturally. The term "heroine" is used and this applies to a Norwegian, a white woman. Blegen does not mention white atrocities. Blegen does not name any Indian heroes. The hanging of Chief Shakopee is referred to; however, Blegen does not describe this Indian as a brave man, as a patriot who fought for his country, or as a martyr who died for what he believed. I suppose this task will have to be done by an Indian historian.

One last comment upon this particular chapter. A statement by Blegen reads thus: "We must remember that the Sioux were not civilized people."[17] This is perhaps the crowning insult to the Indian people in the whole book. No other statement reflects Blegen's cultural bias or his racist attitudes more than this statement.

In conclusion, there are many more statements which could be mentioned that speak derogatorily of the Indian. There are serious omissions, things which Blegen could have mentioned to present the Indians as humans, as people. In 510 pages, Blegen does devote one whole paragraph to the contributions of the Indians to American civilization. It is interesting to note that in this particular paragraph, it is not "American civilization" but "our own civilization."

Thus it is very obvious that Blegen does not possess a balanced perspective in his treatment of Indians.

Perhaps one of the most biased textbooks of all dealing with Minnesota history and Minnesota Indians is *Minnesota: Star of the North* by Antoinette E. Ford and Neoma Johnson. No other authors (and I hate to demean this term) display a more patronizing, a more superior, a more condescending attitude toward Indians than the authors of this particular textbook.

Let me illustrate how one group of Indians have reacted to this book. An Indian educational group, the Indian Advisory Committee to the Minneapolis Public Schools, requested the Minneapolis Public Schools to stop using this textbook because it presents

such a derogatory picture of the Indian. During the academic year 1968-69, the Minneapolis Public Schools responded in a favorable manner, and removed all copies of this text from the public schools' libraries and classrooms.

Why did the Indian Advisory Committee ask for the removal of this book from all libraries and classrooms of the Minneapolis Public Schools? What is in this book that is so repugnant to Indians? A few of the many examples of bias will serve to enlighten the reader of this paper.

The introduction of this book is entitled "Minnesota, Hail to Thee!" In this introduction the authors dwell at length upon the rich resources of Minnesota—the precious furs, the vast forests, the mineral treasures, the beautiful scenery, etc. Then the authors make this statement, "However, the most important of Minnesota's resources is not the rich farm land, the minerals, or the forests. It is the people themselves. . . ."[18] The Indian reader would think that of all the places where Indians could be mentioned, this would be the most logical or natural place to mention the first inhabitants, the Indians. However, no mention is made of Indians in this paragraph or in the entire introduction. This is an omission of the gravest sort. One can ask the question and ask it legitimately, do the authors consider Indians to be Minnesota's people?

In another place in the introduction, the customs of the Old World are referred to, "Happily some of the Old World folk songs, dances, games and holiday customs have been kept alive to give charm and color to many a social gathering and celebration in their American homes."[19] I find this statement rather ironic. For these white people from Europe to keep some of their customs, values, or part of their culture is regarded as positive in this statement. However, for an Indian to keep his language, to keep part of his customs, to dress in traditional garb, etc., is a trend not to be allowed. I consider the above statement to be ironic because for many years it was a high priority aim in government policy for Indians to assimilate into the dominant society. In some of the government schools, Indians could not speak their native tongue, could not dress in the traditional manner, could not act

"Indian"—and if they did so, they were punished severely. Could not Indian songs, dances, games and customs have added charm and color to the American scene?

The authors, at the close of the introduction, address a question to the readers of their textbooks: "Do you not feel proud of being citizens of Minnesota?"[20] How do the authors, after not mentioning Indians at all in the introduction, expect Indian readers to react to such a question? If the reader is white, then maybe he can be proud. Yet Indians definitely can be proud to be citizens, because Minnesota was and is their land.

On page 26 is found this statement: "Although one might tell of the cruelty of the Indians, you can see from this account that there is also much that is pleasant and interesting to learn of our red brother."[21] The authors later do tell of the horrible deeds of the "savages." However, this particular statement raises a topic which I would like to discuss in more detail—a topic which is directly related to the cultural bias found in this book. Much has been written about the Sioux War of 1862 and a body of literature has emerged which is known as the "atrocity stories." What is extremely repugnant about these stories is that the atrocities are committed by Indians only. The underlying assumption of these atrocity stories, and it is a loathsome assumption is that Indians are savages and white people cannot perform horrible deeds in war. I would like to recount two incidents which involve two of my ancestors and which clearly illustrate the cruelty of white soldiers.

My great-great-grandfather was a Dakota chief, whose name was Mazo-Mani or Iron that Walks. He was one of the chiefs who signed the Treaty of 1830. The first incident involves him. Soon after the Battle of Wood Lake, many Indians were tired of the war and did not wish to fight any more. Mazo-Mani was one such person, and after a council he was appointed to deliver a letter asking for a truce to the white soldiers. On the way to the white camp, he and others who accompanied him met some white soldiers. Even though Mazo-Mani carried a white flag, one of the white soldiers flagrantly disregarded the symbol of truce and treacherously shot him. Mazo-Mani did not die then but was brought

back to camp and died during the night. My great-grandmother would cry when she told of such things.

The other incident involves my great-grandmother when she was ten years old. Her name was Maza-Okiye Win or She Who Talks to Iron (her English name was Isabelle Roberts). She witnessed the killing of her grandmother. In the aftermath of the Sioux War of 1862, the feeling against the Sioux by the white people was so great that the Indians were forced to move from Minnesota. It was on the trip to Crow Creek in South Dakota that this incident occurred.

The killing took place on a bridge. The horses and other stock were very thirsty, and began to stir, so everyone stopped in order that the stock might drink. Maza-Okiye Win and her grandmother got out of the wagon in which they were riding. When the animals stirred, several soldiers came running to the scene and demanded to know what was going on. Since the Indians could not speak English, this irritated the soldiers, and they began to get rough and push the Indian women. The soldiers succeeded in pushing the grandmother off the bridge and into the water. The daughter and granddaughter (Maza-Okiye Win) ran down to the water and pulled the grandmother out. When they climbed up to the road, their wagon was gone. They decided to find a place that might be warm for the grandmother and safe from the soldiers. However, before they could get away, white soldiers caught up to them and one of them cruelly stabbed the grandmother in the stomach with a saber. She screamed in pain. The daughter stooped down to help her, but the older woman said, "Please daughter, go! Don't mind me. Take your daughter and go before they do the same thing to you."[22] Though this grandmother was in pain and dying, she was still concerned about her daughter and little granddaughter (Maza-Okiye Win) who was standing there and had witnessed all this.

These atrocities that I have described were commited by white soldiers. Such stories, however, are not mentioned in the textbooks, because they would destroy the myth that white people can do no wrong. My mother says, "Everyone in this day and age believes that in those days the Indian was a ruthless killer, but we know according to these accounts that some of the whites are just as ruthless and more so than the Indian. If one would stop and think, our people were fighting for what was rightfully theirs."[23]

The chapter which is perhaps the most offensive to Indians is the chapter entitled "The War with the Sioux." In this chapter Indians are referred to as "lazy," as "thieves," as "heathens," and almost constantly as "savages." The cultural bias of the authors is apparent to a revolting degree. Here are some obvious and obnoxious examples (Italics are the author's): "When you remember that for many years these *savages* had roamed the woods and plains" (page 157). "Always *lazy*, the Indians depended on the food and clothing, as well as money, supplied by the government according to the terms of the treaties " (page 157). "This last fort protected the trades carried on by the Red River carts against bands of *thieving* Indians" (page 185). ". . . for the *savages* were frantic with rage" (page 160). "At heart Little Crow was a *heathen* Indian" (page 161). This statement is particularly offensive to me, because generally the Dakota were a deeply religious people. "The *savages* were again repulsed, discouraged by the fire from the barricade" (page 166). By now, it should be quite evident to the reader that these authors are by no means objective.

In general the same criticisms that were leveled at Blegen can be directed at these authors. For example, the obvious attitude of racial superiority, the failure to mention Indian heroes, the failure to mention white atrocities, the omission of the Indians' role in the development of Minnesota as a state, and the omission of or slight attention to the Indian contribution to American society are quite apparent in this text. Of all textbooks, this by far demonstrates most clearly the thesis that most history books dealing with American Indians lack a balanced perspective.

NOTES

[1] Dulles, Foster Rhea, "The Indian Menace," *The United States Since 1865* (Ann Arbor: The University of Michigan Press, 1959), p. 40.

[2] Williams, T. Harry, Richard N. Current, and Frank Freidel, "The Taming of the Tribes," *A History of the United States Since 1865* (New York: Alfred A. Knopf, 1960), p. 155.

[3] Williams, T. Harry, Richard N. Current and Frank Freidel, "Europe and the New World," *A History of the United States to 1876* (New York: Alfred H. Knopf, 1960), p. 7.

[4] *Ibid.*

[5] *Ibid.*

[6] Bolin, David C., "North·America: The Blind Spot in History," *Random* (November 1969), pp. 26-27.

[7] *Ibid.*, p. 26.

[8] Ford, Antoinette E., and Neoma Johnson, "Henry Hastings Sibley," in *Minnesota: Star of the North.* (Chicago: Lyons and Carnahan, 1961), p. 112.

[9] Anonymous, "Tacyateduta Is Not a Coward," *Minnesota History* (September 1962), p. 115.

[10] Anonymous, "Chief Big Eagle's Story," *Minnesota History* (September 1962), p. 115.

[11] Dulles, *op. cit.*, p. 41.

[12] Excerpt from a brochure "Wounded Knee National Historical Site," printed by the Wounded Knee Museum of Wounded Knee, South Dakota.

[13] Bolin, *op. cit.*, p. 27.

[14] Blegen, Theodore C., "Introduction," *Building Minnesota* (Boston: D. C. Heath and Company. 1938), p. iii.

[15] *Ibid.*, p. 23.

[16] *Ibid.*, p. 210.

[17] *Ibid.*, p. 217.

[18] Ford and Johnson, *op. cit.*, p. 4.

[19] *Ibid.*, p. 6.

[20] *Ibid.*, p. 6.

[21] *Ibid.*, p. 26.

[22] Cavender, Elsie M., personal correspondence (1969), p. 2.

[23] *Ibid.*, p. 4.

VI.

proposed techniques for eliminating minority problems

introduction: some definitions

The selections in Part VI reflect a range of thinking about how minority problems in the United States might be diminished. Some of the programs advocated are broad philosophies of social change; others are minor steps toward changing a large section of American culture. A number of the techniques, especially legal remedies, have already been utilized and have proved their worth. Not since the end of the Civil War has there been such a great opportunity to eliminate one of America's major social problems as a result of both conscious effort and social changes occurring independently of minority problems.

Anyone in the over-fifty group has lived through a period of rapid social change in the relationships among ethnic and racial groups in the United States. Since World War II, all the indexes of social well-being—educational achievement, life expectancy, morbidity rates, infant mortality, better occupational distribution, earned income levels—have risen rapidly for all American minority groups; court decisions and new laws have removed official sanctions of segregation and discrimination. Action by voluntary groups and enforcement by government agencies have reduced the incidence of segregation and discrimination.

There is some evidence that blacks are aware of this improvement in their situation (data are not available for other groups). In the last part of 1967, Louis Harris reported that two-thirds of the nation's black population believed that racial discrimination can be ended, as compared with only 44 percent of the white population. A poll by Daniel Yankelovich, Inc. for *Fortune,* published in January, 1968, reported that three-fourths of blacks are convinced that conditions were better in 1968 than they were three to five years before; four-fifths (78 percent) believed their chance of getting a better job had improved. Increased hope for solving the nation's racial problems was expressed by 77 percent. (Polls summarized in *The Crisis,* January, 1968.)

Nevertheless, the papers are full of reports of riots, disputes over school desegregation, complaints against police brutality, and so on. Spokesmen for minority groups, both conservatives and militants, do not admit publicly that there has been any improvement. Young minority people do not remember segregation or the deep discrimination as their fathers do and measure present discrimination, not from the past, but in relation to the situation of contemporary whites.

Where does America go from here? It is hard to predict where American society is heading in 1972, but ignoring the possibilities of a nuclear holocaust or a full-fledged police state—because no suggestions for civil action would be useful then anyhow—one can assume that America will regain and keep peace in a society whose democratic procedures function at least as well as they have in the past. Given these two assumptions, what steps can be taken to hurry up the process of removing discrimination entirely from American society?

The suggestions to be made are all in the direction of reducing prejudice among whites.

Whatever the failings of the minority groups, they are *not* the cause of prejudice and discrimination; a great deal of recent discussion has proceeded as if this were so. One can hardly miss the fact that the disappearance of racism based on biology has been replaced by racism based on "culture," or family structure or poverty. Certainly, the culture and structure of minority communities are legitimate subjects for sociologists to study, but not if they are regarded as the "causes" of discrimination.

Before turning to the specific proposals of the social scientists, publicists, and organizers represented in Part VI, consider how the theories of prejudice examined in Part V can be translated into practical terms.

1. One step would be to give prejudiced people an intellectual appreciation that prejudice harms them financially and psychologically. They need to recognize that part of the gains that seem to come from discrimination is temporary and illusory. These gains (classified by John Dollard as economic, political, sexual, and prestige) divert the prejudiced person from more satisfactory and more permanent gains. Prejudiced people need to learn how they are exploited because of their prejudice.

2. The passage of laws by government and the adoption of rules by voluntary associations making overt discrimination illegal and unprofitable not only removes one motive for discrimination but also makes discrimination appear nonrespectable. Most people obey most laws if there is some effort at enforcement, and changes in behavior in compliance with civil rights legislation not only reduce discrimination directly but also indirectly reduce prejudice (under the social psychological principle that people rationalize their attitudes to conform to their behavior).

3. The provision of accurate information about minority groups breaks stereotypes and satisfies natural curiosoity regarding the causes of differences between minority and dominant groups. Facts of this kind are learned not only through books, newspapers, and speeches but also through personal contact on a friendly and equal basis. Some people's prejudices are based on misinformation, and correct information counteracts them. Correct information about minorities and about discrimination in American society is especially important for children because it will block the inculcation of prejudiced traditions.

4. One of the most important traditions to oppose is that of racism. This tradition can be attacked not only when it is applied to minority groups but also whenever biological explanations are presented as the sole cause of *any* social phenomenon.

5. Traditions on which prejudice is based can be maintained only by being transmitted to children. The transmission of prejudice through the home and play group must be counteracted by the school and church while the child's mind is still flexible. Also, if public opinion considers manifestations of prejudice to be shameful, many parents can be induced not to display their prejudice in front of their children. Insofar as this happens, children are less likely to acquire prejudice.

6. Direct efforts to solve major social problems can, at the same time, divert people from prejudice and remove some of the frustrations that create a psychological proneness to it. Providing economic security is the most important single step of this type.

7. Restoration of easy communication among people will enhance their sense of being able to overcome common problems. This security, in turn, will contribute to the solution of frustrating problems and reduce the general feeling that mysterious forces are manipulating society. Since minorities are the most frequent scapegoats for general frustrations and are frequently identified as the mysterious forces behind social problems, a diminution of these conditions should also diminish prejudice.

8. Demonstration that many of the fears about minority groups are imaginary might help

to dispel these fears. Probably a more basic understanding needs to be inculcated that fear or hatred of a minority group is a substitute for fear or hatred of some other object toward which people are unwilling to express their true attitudes. A general program of mental hygiene needs to be developed to get people to be honest with themselves. Frank discussion of the disliked or feared aspects of important cultural values would be the first step in such a program.

9. Public demonstrations—including marches, orderly picket lines, and sit-ins—can be effective ways of calling public attention to certain facts of discrimination and how minorities feel about them. They are specially effective if they are done on a mass scale and appear to have force and conviction behind them and are at the same time orderly and nonviolent.

A concerted program including all these activities would probably eliminate race prejudice in a generation or two. But many are difficult to put into practice. Further scientific research is needed to indicate just how important each of the causes of prejudice is and how they can be manipulated most easily. It must be recognized that worthwhile single efforts may have only the slightest of noticeable effects but that the steady pressure of social action changes the situation materially in a few years.

42
the future of the cities

THE NATIONAL ADVISORY COMMISSION ON CIVIL DISORDERS

The following piece is a chapter from the Report of the National Advisory Commission *on Civil Disorders. The commission was appointed by President Johnson following the urban disorders of the 1960s to try to find out why the riots had occurred and what could be done to prevent others from occurring. In its recommendations, the commission is torn between the realities of the situation—under even the most ideal situation, blacks are going to be living in the cities for some time to come—and the American melting-pot ideal. Blacks are also torn between the potential political power they can achieve by concentrating in the city and the desire for the educational and housing advantages of the suburbs.*

Very few people, except urban ecologists, realize the full extent of the decline of the cities. Many people think that the movement of whites out of the cities resulted from the in-migration of blacks and other colored minorities, particularly after the riots. The situation is more serious and has a longer history.

Out-migration from the cities to the suburbs started after World War I and has been continuing at an increasingly rapid rate, reaching epidemic proportions since World War II. The lures of the suburbs were single-family housing at a reasonable cost, low taxes, and uncrowded schools. Retail trade, then wholesale trade, and finally business followed residents to the suburbs. For the past twenty-five years, the migration has been entirely outward. The new suburbs are not all affluent; many are modest and house workingmen. Many people work in one suburb and live in another. The suburbs are connected one with another by a network of freeways. A new regional, ecological pattern is emerging, with the city losing its central and dominating position. If this continues—and there are absolutely no trends back into the city—the central-city inhabitants will be forced to support outdated and outworn facilities with a decreasing amount of taxable property and economic power.

As the following article suggests, it may be necessary to make major changes in government and financing of urban life, dealing with metropolitan areas as a whole rather than dealing separately with the cities and each suburb; but there is no certainty that this will be done and no certainty that America may not continue into two societies: one black, living in the central cities, and one white, spread out over the metropolitan areas outside the central cities.

INTRODUCTION

We believe action of the kind outlined in preceding pages can contribute substantially to control of disorders in the near future. But there should be no mistake about the long run.

Reprinted from *Report of the National Advisory Commission on Civil Disorders* (New York: E. P. Dutton & Co., Inc., April 1968), pp. 389-408.

The underlying forces continue to gain momentum.

The most basic of these is the accelerating segregation of low-income, disadvantaged Negroes within the ghettos of the largest American cities.

By 1985, the 12.1 million Negroes segregated within central cities today will have grown to approximately 20.8 million—an increase of 72 percent.

Prospects for domestic peace and for the quality of American life are linked directly to the future of these cities.

Two critical questions must be confronted: Where do present trends now lead? What choices are open to us?

1. THE KEY TRENDS

The size of the Negro population in central cities is closely related to total national Negro population growth. In the past 16 years, about 98 percent of this growth has occurred within metropolitan areas, and 86 percent in the central cities of those areas.

A conservative projection of national Negro population growth indicates continued rapid increases. For the period 1966 to 1985, it will rise to a total of 30.7 million, gaining an average of 484,000 a year, or 7.6 percent more than the increase in each year from 1960 to 1966.

Central Cities

Further Negro population growth in central cities depends upon two key factors: in-migration from outside metropolitan areas, and patterns of Negro settlement within metropolitan areas.

From 1960 to 1966, the Negro population of all central cities rose 2.4 million, 88.9 percent of total national Negro population growth. We estimate that natural growth accounted for 1.4 million, or 58 percent of this increase, and in-migration accounted for 1 million, or 42 percent.

As of 1966, the Negro population in all central cities totaled 12.1 million. By 1985, we have estimated that it will rise 72 percent to 20.8 million. We believe that natural growth will account for 6 million of this increase and in-migration for 2.7 million.

Without significant Negro out-migration, then, the combined Negro populations of central cities will continue to grow by an average of 316,000 a year through 1985.

This growth would increase the proportion of Negroes to whites in central cities by 1985 from the present 20.6 percent to between an estimated 31 and 35.6 percent.

Largest Central Cities

These, however, are national figures. Much faster increases will occur in the largest central cities where Negro growth has been concentrated in the past two decades. Washington, D.C., and Newark are already over half Negro. A continuation of recent trends would cause the following 11 major cities to become over 50 percent Negro by the indicated dates:

New Orleans	1971
Richmond	1971
Baltimore	1972
Jacksonville	1972
Gary	1973
Cleveland	1975
St. Louis	1978
Detroit	1979
Philadelphia	1981
Oakland	1983
Chicago	1984

These cities, plus Washington, D.C., (now over 66 percent Negro) and Newark, contained 12.6 million people in 1960, or 22 percent of the total population of all 224 American central cities. All 13 cities undoubtedly will have Negro majorities by 1985, and the suburbs ringing them will remain largely all white, unless there are major changes in Negro fertility rates, in-migration, settlement patterns, or public policy.

Experience indicates that Negro school enrollment in these and other cities will exceed 50 percent long before the total population reaches that mark. In fact, Negro students already comprise more than a majority in the public elementary schools of 12 of the 13 cities mentioned above. This occurs because the Negro population in central cities is much younger and because a much higher proportion of white children attend private schools. For example, St. Louis' population was about 36 percent Negro in 1965; its public elementary school enrollment was 63 percent Negro. If present trends continue, many cities in addition to those listed above will have Negro school majorities by 1985, probably including:

Dallas
Pittsburgh

Buffalo
Cincinnati
Harrisburg
Atlanta
Louisville
Indianapolis
Kansas City, Mo.
Hartford
New Haven

Thus, continued concentration of future Negro population growth in large central cities will produce significant changes in those cities over the next 20 years. Unless there are sharp changes in the factors influencing Negro settlement patterns within metropolitan areas, there is little doubt that the trend toward Negro majorities will continue. Even a complete cessation of net Negro in-migration to central cities would merely postpone this result for a few years.

Growth of the Young Negro Population

We estimate that the nation's white population will grow 16.6 million, or 9.5 percent, from 1966 to 1975, and the Negro population 3.8 million, or 17.7 percent, in the same period. The Negro age group from 15 to 24 years of age, however, will grow much faster than either the Negro population as a whole, or the white population in the same age group.

From 1966 to 1975, the number of Negroes in this age group will rise 1.6 million, or 40.1 percent. The white population aged 15 to 24 will rise 6.6 million, or 23.5 percent.

This rapid increase in the young Negro population has important implications for the country. This group has the highest unemployment rate in the nation, commits a relatively high proportion of all crimes, and plays the most significant role in civil disorders. By the same token, it is a great reservoir of underused human resources which are vital to the nation.

The Location of New Jobs

Most new employment opportunities do not occur in central cities, near all-Negro neighborhoods. They are being created in suburbs and outlying areas—and this trend is likely to continue indefinitely. New office buildings have risen in the downtowns of large cities, often near all-Negro areas. But the outflow of manufacturing and retailing facilities normally offsets this addition significantly—and in many cases has caused a net loss of jobs in central cities.

Providing employment for the swelling Negro ghetto population will require society to link these potential workers more closely with job locations. This can be done in three ways: by developing incentives to industry to create new employment centers near Negro residential areas; by opening suburban residential areas to Negroes and encouraging them to move closer to industrial centers; or by creating better transportation between ghetto neighborhoods and new job locations.

All three involve large public outlays.

The first method—creating new industries in or near the ghetto—is not likely to occur without government subsidies on a scale which convinces private firms that it will pay them to face the problems involved.

The second method—opening up suburban areas to Negro occupancy—obviously requires effective fair-housing laws. It will also require an extensive program of federally aided, low-cost housing in many suburban areas.

The third approach—improved transportation linking ghettos and suburbs—has received little attention from city planners and municipal officials. A few demonstration projects show promise, but carrying them out on a large scale will be very costly.

Although a high proportion of new jobs will be located in suburbs, there are still millions of jobs in central cities. Turnover in those jobs alone can open up a great many potential positions for Negro central-city residents—if employers cease racial discrimination in their hiring and promotion practices.

Nevertheless, as the total number of Negro central-city job-seekers continues to rise, the need to link them with emerging new employment in the suburbs will become increasingly urgent.

The Increasing Cost of Municipal Services

Local governments have had to bear a particularly heavy financial burden in the two decades since the end of World War II. All

TABLE 1. Local Government Revenues, Expenditures, and Debt (Billions of Dollars)

	1950	1966	Increase
Revenues	11.7	41.5	+29.8
Expenditures	17.0	60.7	+43.7
Debt outstanding	18.8	77.5	+58.7

United States cities are highly dependent upon property taxes that are relatively unresponsive to changes in income. Consequently, growing municipalities have been hard-pressed for adequate revenues to meet rising demands for services generated by population increase. On the other hand, stable or declining cities have not only been faced with steady cost increases but also with a slow-growing, or even declining, tax base.

As a result of the population shifts of the postwar period, concentrating the more affluent parts of the urban population in residential suburbs while leaving the less affluent in the central cities, the increasing burden of municipal taxes frequently falls upon that part of the urban population least able to pay them.

Increasing concentrations of urban growth have called forth greater expenditures for every kind of public service: education, health, police protection, fire protection, parks, sewage disposal, sanitation, water supply, etc. These expenditures have strikingly outpaced tax revenues.

The story is summed up in Table 1.

The fact that the problems of the cities are a national problem is seen in the growth of federal assistance to urban areas under various grant-in-aid programs, which reached the level of $10 billion in the current fiscal year.

Nevertheless, the fiscal plight of many cities is likely to grow even more serious in the future. Local expenditures inevitably will continue to rise steeply as a result of several factors, including the difficulty of increasing productivity in the predominately service activities of local governments, and the rapid technologically induced increases in productivity in other economic sectors.

Traditionally, individual productivity has risen faster in the manufacturing, mining, con-

struction, and agricultural sectors than in those involving personal services.

However, all sectors compete with each other for talent and personnel. Wages and salaries in the service-dominated sectors generally must keep up, therefore, with those in the capital-dominated sectors. Since productivity in manufacturing has risen 2.5 percent per year compounded over many decades, and even faster in agriculture, the basis for setting costs in the service-dominated sectors has gone up, too.

In the postwar period, costs of the same units of output have increased very rapidly in certain key activities of local government. For example, education is the single biggest form of expenditure by local governments (including school districts), accounting for about 40 percent of their outlays. From 1947 to 1967, costs per pupil-day in United States public schools rose at a rate of 6.7 percent per year compounded—only slightly less than doubling every ten years. This major cost item is likely to keep on rising rapidly in the future, along with other government services like police, fire, and welfare activities.

Some increases in productivity may occur in these fields, and some economies may be achieved through use of semiskilled assistants such as police and teachers' aides. Nevertheless, with the need to keep pace with private-sector wage scales, local government costs will keep on rising sharply.

This and other future cost increases are important to future relations between central cities and suburbs. Rising costs will inevitably force central cities to demand more and more assistance from the federal government. But the federal government can obtain such funds through the income tax only from other parts of the economy. Suburban governments are, meanwhile, experiencing the same cost increases along with the rising resentment of their constituents.

2. CHOICES FOR THE FUTURE

The complexity of American society offers many choices for the future of relations between central cities and suburbs and patterns of white and Negro settlement in metropolitan areas. For practical purposes, however, we see two fundamental questions:

Should future Negro population growth be concentrated in central cities, as in the past 20 years, and should Negro and white populations become even more residentially segregated?

Should society provide greatly increased special assistance to Negroes and other relatively disadvantaged population groups?

For purposes of analysis, the Commission has defined three basic choices for the future embodying specific answers to these questions:

The Present Policies Choice

Under this course, the nation would maintain approximately the share of resources now being allocated to programs of assistance for the poor, unemployed, and disadvantaged. These programs are likely to grow, given continuing economic growth and rising federal revenues, but they will not grow fast enough to stop, let alone reverse, the already deteriorating quality of life in central-city ghettos.

This choice carries the highest ultimate price, as we will point out.

The Enrichment Choice

Under this course, the nation would seek to offset the effects of continued Negro segregation and deprivation in large city ghettos. The Enrichment Choice would aim at creating dramatic improvements in the quality of life in disadvantaged central-city neighborhoods—both white and Negro. It would require marked increases in federal spending for education, housing, employment, job training, and social services.

The Enrichment Choice would seek to lift poor Negroes and whites above poverty status and thereby give them the capacity to enter the mainstream of American life. But it would not, at least for many years, appreciably affect either the increasing concentration of Negroes in the ghetto or racial segregation in residential areas outside the ghetto.

The Integration Choice

This choice would be aimed at reversing the movement of the country toward two societies, separate and unequal.

The Integration Choice—like the Enrichment Choice—would call for large-scale improvement in the quality of ghetto life. But it would also involve both creating strong incentives for Negro movement out of central-city ghettos and enlarging freedom of choice concerning housing, employment, and schools.

The result would fall considerably short of full integration. The experience of other ethnic groups indicates that some Negro households would be scattered in largely white residential areas. Others—probably a larger number—would voluntarily cluster together in largely Negro neighborhoods. The Integration Choice would thus produce both integration and segregation. But the segregation would be voluntary.

Articulating these three choices plainly oversimplifies the possibilities open to the country. We believe, however, that they encompass the basic issues—issues which the American public must face if it is serious in its concern not only about civil disorder, but the futures of our democratic society.

3. THE PRESENT POLICIES CHOICE

Powerful forces of social and political inertia are moving the country steadily along the course of existing policies toward a divided country.

This course may well involve changes in many social and economic programs—but not enough to produce fundamental alterations in the key factors of Negro concentration, racial segregation, and the lack of sufficient enrichment to arrest the decay of deprived neighborhoods.

Some movement toward enrichment can be found in efforts to encourage industries to locate plants in central cities, in increased federal expenditures for education, in the important concepts embodied in the "War on Poverty," and in the Model Cities Program. But so far congressional appropriations for even present federal programs have been so small that they fall short of effective enrichment.

As for challenging concentration and segregation, a national commitment to this purpose has yet to develop. This is seen in the history of national open-housing legislation, pending in Congress, which the President has again urged the Congress to enact.

Of the three future courses we have defined, the present almost 21 million Negroes— still much poorer and less educated than most whites—will be living there.

Can Present Policies Avert Extreme Polarization?

There are at least two possible developments under the Present Policies Choice which might avert such polarization. The first is a faster increase of incomes among Negroes than has occurred in the recent past. This might prevent central cities from becoming even deeper "poverty traps" than they now are. It suggests the importance of effective job programs and higher levels of welfare payments for dependent families.

The second possible development is migration of a growing Negro middle class out of the central city. This would not prevent competition for federal funds between central cities and outlying areas, but it might diminish the racial undertones of that competition.

There is, however, no evidence that a continuation of present policies would be accompanied by any such movement. There is already a significant Negro middle class. It grew rapidly from 1960 to 1966. Yet in these years, 88.9 percent of the total national growth of Negro population was concentrated in central cities—the highest in history. Indeed, from 1960 to 1966, there was actually a net total in-migration of Negroes from the urban fringes of metropolitan areas into central cities. The Commission believes it unlikely that this trend will suddenly reverse itself without significant changes in private attitudes and public policies

4. THE ENRICHMENT CHOICE

The Present Policies Choice plainly would involve continuation of efforts like Model Cities, manpower programs, and the War on Poverty. These are in fact enrichment programs, designed to improve the quality of life in the ghetto.

Because of their limited scope and funds, however, they constitute only very modest steps toward enrichment—and would continue to do so even if these programs were somewhat enlarged or supplemented.

The premise of the Enrichment Choice is performance. To adopt this choice would require a substantially greater share of national resources—sufficient to make a dramatic, visible impact on life in the urban Negro ghetto.

The Effect of Enrichment on Civil Disorders

Effective enrichment policies probably would have three immediate effects on civil disorders.

First, announcement of specific large-scale programs and the demonstration of a strong intent to carry them out might persuade ghetto residents that genuine remedies for their problems were forthcoming, thereby allaying tensions.

Second, such announcements would strongly stimulate the aspirations and hopes of members of these communities—possibly well beyond the capabilities of society to deliver and to do so promptly. This might increase frustration and discontent, to some extent cancelling the first effect.

Third, if there could be immediate action on meaningful job training and the creation of productive jobs for large numbers of unemployed young people, they would become much less likely to engage in civil disorders.

Such action is difficult now, when there are about 583,000 young Negro men aged 16 to 24 in central cities—of whom 131,000, or 22.5 percent, are unemployed and probably two or three times as many are underemployed. It will not become easier in the future. By 1975, this age group will have grown to nearly 700,000.

Given the size of the present problem, plus the large growth of this age group, creation of sufficient meaningful jobs will require extensive programs, begun rapidly. Even if the nation is willing to embark on such programs, there is no certainty that they can be made effective soon enough.

Consequently, there is no certainty that the Enrichment Choice would do much more in the near future to diminish violent incidents in central cities than would the Present Policies Choice. However, if enrichment programs can succeed in meeting the needs of residents of disadvantaged areas for jobs, education, housing, and city services, then over the years this choice is almost certain to reduce both the level and frequency of urban disorder.

The Negro Middle Class

One objective of the Enrichment Choice would be to help as many disadvantaged Americans as possible—of all races—to enter the mainstream of American prosperity, to progress toward what is often called middle-class status. If the Enrichment Choice were adopted, it would certainly attain this objective to a far greater degree than would the Present Policies Choice. This could significantly change the quality of life in many central-city areas.

It can be argued that a rapidly enlarging Negro middle class would promote Negro out-migration, and thus the Enrichment Choice would open up an escape hatch from the ghetto. This argument, however, has two weaknesses.

This first is experience. Central cities already have sizeable and growing numbers of middle-class Negro families. Yet as noted earlier, only a few have migrated from the central city.

The past pattern of white ethnic groups gradually moving out of central-city areas to middle-class suburbs has not applied to Negroes. Effective open-housing laws will help help make this possible. It is probable, however, that other more extensive changes in policies and attitudes will be required—and these would extend beyond the Enrichment Choice.

The second weakness in the argument is time. Even if enlargement of the Negro middle class succeeded in encouraging movement out of the central city, could it do so fast enough to offset the rapid growth of the ghetto? To

offset even half the growth estimated for the ghetto by 1975 would call for the out-migration from central cities of 217,000 persons a year. This is eight times the annual increase in suburban Negro population—including natural increase—which occurred from 1960 to 1966. Even the most effective enrichment program is not likely to accomplish this.

A corollary problem derives from the continuing migration of poor Negroes from the South to Northern and Western cities.

Adoption of the Enrichment Choice would require large-scale efforts to improve conditions in the South sufficiently to remove the pressure to migrate. It should, however, be recognized that less than a third of the estimated increase in Negro central-city population by 1985 will result from in-migration—2.7 million out of total increase of 8.7 million.

Negro Self-development

The Enrichment Choice is in line with some of the currents of Negro protest thought that fall under the label of "Black Power." We do not refer to versions of Black Power ideology which promote violence, generate racial hatred, or advocate total separation of the races. Rather, we mean the view which asserts that the American Negro population can assume its proper role in society and overcome its feelings of powerlessness and lack of self-respect only by exerting power over decisions which directly affect its own members. A fully integrated society is not thought possible until the Negro minority within the ghetto has developed political strength—a strong bargaining position in dealing with the rest of society.

In short, this argument would regard predominately Negro central cities and predominately white outlying areas not as harmful, but as an advantageous future.

Proponents of these views also focus on the need for the Negro to organize economically and politically, thus tapping new energies for self-development. One of the hardest tasks in improving disadvantaged areas is to discover how deeply deprived residents can develop their own capabilities by participating more fully in decisions and activities which affect them. Such learning-by-doing efforts are a vital part of the process of bringing deprived people into the social mainstream.

Separate but Equal Societies?

The Enrichment Choice by no means seeks to perpetuate racial segregation. In the end, however, its premise is that disadvantaged Negroes can achieve equality of opportunity with whites while continuing in conditions of nearly complete separation.

This premise has been vigorously advocated by Black Power proponents. While most Negroes originally desired racial integration, many are losing hope of ever achieving it because of seemingly implacable white resistance. Yet they cannot bring themselves to accept the conclusion that most of the millions of Negroes who are forced to live racially segregated lives must therefore be condemned to inferior lives—to inferior educations, or inferior status.

Rather, they reason, there must be some way to make the quality of life in the ghetto areas just as good. And if equality cannot be achieved through integration then it is not surprising that some Black Power advocates are denouncing integration and claiming that, given the hypocrisy and racism that pervade white society, life in a black society is, in fact, morally superior. This argument is understandable, but there is a great deal of evidence that it is false.

The economy of the United States and particularly the sources of employment are preponderantly white. In this circumstance, a policy of "separate but equal" employment could only relegate Negroes permanently to inferior incomes and economic status.

The best evidence regarding education is contained in recent reports of the Office of Education and Civil Rights Commission which suggest that both racial and economic integration are essential to educational equality for Negroes. Yet critics point out that, certainly until integration is achieved, various types of enrichment programs must be tested, and that dramatically different results may be possible from intensive educational enrichment—such as far-smaller classes, or greatly expanded preschool programs, or changes in the home environment of Negro children resulting from steady jobs for fathers.

Still others advocate shifting control over ghetto schools from professional administrators to local residents. This, they say, would improve curricula, give students a greater sense of their own value, and thus raise their morale and educational achievement. These approaches have not yet been tested sufficiently. One conclusion, however, does seem reasonable: any real improvement in the quality of education in low-income, all-Negro areas will cost a great deal more money than is now being spent there—and perhaps more than is being spent per pupil anywhere. Racial and social-class integration of schools may produce equal improvement in achievement at less total cost.

Whether or not enrichment in ghetto areas will really work is not yet known, but the Enrichment Choice is based on the yet-unproved premise that it will. Certainly, enrichment programs could significantly improve existing ghetto schools if they impelled major innovations. But "separate but equal" ghetto education cannot meet the long-run fundamental educational needs of the central-city Negro population.

The three basic educational choices are: providing Negro children with quality education in integrated schools; providing them with quality education by enriching ghetto schools; or continuing to provide many Negro children with inferior education in racially segregated school systems, severely limiting their lifetime opportunities.

Consciously or not, it is the third choice that the nation is now making, and this choice the Commission rejects totally.

In the field of housing, it is obvious that "separate but equal" does not mean really equal. The Enrichment Choice could greatly improve the quantity, variety, and environment of decent housing available to the ghetto population. It could not provide Negroes with the same freedom and range of choice as whites with equal incomes. Smaller cities and suburban areas together with the central city provide a far-greater variety of housing and environmental settings than the central city alone. Programs to provide housing outside central cities, however, extend beyond the bounds of the Enrichment Choice.

In the end, whatever its benefits, the

Enrichment Choice might well invite a prospect similar to that of the Present Policies Choice: separate white and black socities.

If enrichment programs were effective, they could greatly narrow the gap in income, education, housing, jobs, and other qualities of life between the ghetto and the mainstream. Hence the chances of harsh polarization—or of disorder—in the next 20 years would be greatly reduced.

Whether they would be reduced far enough depends on the scope of the programs. Even if the gap were narrowed from the present, it still could remain as a strong source of tension. History teaches that men are not necessarily placated even by great absolute progress. The controlling factor is relative progress—whether they still perceive a significant gap between themselves and others whom they regard as no more deserving. Widespread perception of such a gap—and consequent resentment—might well be precisely the situation 20 years from now under the Enrichment Choice, for it is essentially another way of choosing a permanently divided country.

5. THE INTEGRATION CHOICE

The third and last course open to the nation combines enrichment with programs designed to encourage integration of substantial numbers of Negroes into the society outside the ghetto.

Enrichment must be an important adjunct to any integration course. No matter how ambitious or energetic such a program may be, few Negroes now living in central-city ghettos would be quickly integrated. In the meantime, significant improvement in their present environment is essential.

The enrichment aspect of this third choice should, however, be recognized as interim action, during which time expanded and new programs can work to improve education and earning power. The length of the interim period surely would vary. For some it may be long. But in any event, what should be clearly recognized is that enrichment is only a means toward the goal; it is not the goal.

The goal must be achieving freedom for every citizen to live and work according to his capacities and desires, not his color.

We believe there are four important reasons why American society must give this course the most serious consideration. First, future jobs are being created primarily in the suburbs, but the chronically unemployed population is increasingly concentrated in the ghetto. This separation will make it more and more difficult for Negroes to achieve anything like full employment in decent jobs. But if, over time, these residents began to find housing outside central cities, they would be exposed to more knowledge of job opportunities. They would have to make much shorter trips to reach jobs. They would have a far better chance of securing employment on a self-sustaining basis.

Second, in the judgment of this Commission, racial and social-class integration is the most effective way of improving the education of ghetto children.

Third, developing an adequate housing supply for low-income and middle-income families and true freedom of choice in housing for Negroes of all income levels will require substantial out-movement. We do not believe that such an out-movement will occur spontaneously merely as a result of increasing prosperity among Negroes in central cities. A national fair-housing law is essential to begin such movement. In many suburban areas, a program combining positive incentives with the building of new housing will be necessary to carry it out.

Fourth, and by far the most important, integration is the only course which explicitly seeks to achieve a single nation rather than accepting the present movement toward a dual society. This choice would enable us at least to begin reversing the profoundly divisive trend already so evident in our metropolitan areas—before it becomes irreversible.

6. CONCLUSIONS

The future of our cities is neither something which will just happen nor something which will be imposed upon us by an inevitable destiny. That future will be shaped to an important degree by choices we make now.

We have attempted to set forth the major choices because we believe it is vital for Americans to understand the consequences of our present failure to choose—and then to have to choose wisely.

Three critical conclusions emerge from this analysis:

1. The nation is rapidly moving toward two increasingly separate Americas.

Within two decades, this division could be so deep that it would be almost impossible to unite:

*a white society principally located in suburbs, in smaller central cities, and in the peripheral parts of large central cities; and
a Negro society largely concentrated within large central cities.*

The Negro society will be permanently relegated to its current status, possibly even if we expend great amounts of money and effort in trying to "gild" the ghetto.

2. In the long run, continuation and expansion of such a permanent division threatens us with two perils.

The first is the danger of sustained violence in our cities. The timing, scale, nature, and repercussions of such violence cannot be foreseen. But if it occurred, it would further destroy our ability to achieve the basic American promises of liberty, justice, and equality.

The second is the danger of a conclusive repudiation of the traditional American ideals of individual dignity, freedom, and equality of opportunity. We will not be able to espouse these ideals meaningfully to the rest of the world, to ourselves, to our children. They may still recite the Pledge of Allegiance and say "one nation . . . indivisible." But they will be learning cynicism, not patriotism.

3. We cannot escape responsibility for choosing the future of our metropolitan areas and the human relations which develop within them. It is a responsibility so critical that even an unconscious choice to continue present policies has the gravest implications.

That we have delayed in choosing or, by delaying, may be making the wrong choice, does not sentence us either to separatism or despair. But we must choose. We will choose. Indeed, we are now choosing.

43
federal educational programs and minority groups

HOWARD A. GLICKSTEIN

Throughout this book, the importance of education in improving the economic position of minorities has been emphasized, as has the poor quality of education offered to the most deprived of minorities. The necessity of improving the education of blacks, Puerto Ricans, Chicanos, and Indians has not been overlooked either by these groups or by the government; or rather, one of the major pressures on the government by these minorities has been for better education. As a result the federal government has instituted two kinds of programs: those designed to enforce desegregation and those designed to try new educational techniques and supplement old ones.

Federal programs are always cumbersome and tied up in red tape. Much worse, if they do not immediately produce results, such as reduction of crime and economic advancement, they are often abandoned before they have a chance to prove their worth. Funds designed to help poor black children have often been diverted to the use of middle-class white children. Tax payers are aware that such money has been used for educational programs, usually in ghetto schools. They resent paying taxes out of incomes already lessened by inflation, and they are impatient when problems in the ghetto continue.

Nevertheless, more and better education offers the best hope for raising the economic level of minorities. The next selection evaluates the programs that have been tried and provides some guidelines for the future.

Mr. Glickstein is staff director of the U.S. Commission on Civil Rights.

INTRODUCTION

It is increasingly clear that this country has failed to provide equal educational opportunities to its minority groups. In fact, evidence suggests that schools actually injure the academic potential of disadvantaged and minority students.[1]

The statistics on minority children give

Reprinted from *The Journal of Negro Education* 38, no. 3 (Summer 1969), pp. 303-314. Reproduced by permission of the author and publisher.

an unequivocal indication of their plight: the drop-out rate of white students 16 to 17 years is 9 per cent; the rate for Negro students is almost twice as high.[2] In the Northeast, the average Negro student who does manage to struggle through high school has an achievement level nearly three and one-fourth years below that of his white counterpart by twelfth grade.[3]

The nation continues to deny even the most basic educational opportunities to several hundred thousand black children trapped in segregated Southern schools, despite the *Brown* decision of 1954 and Title VI of the Civil Rights Act of 1964. And, as the Commission on Civil Rights pointed out in its 1967 report, *Racial Isolation in the Public Schools,* de facto segregation, too, exacts a heavy toll in unequal educational opportunities. It is a stark fact that the richest country in the world is neglecting its most valuable resources—the mind of its youth.

It has been a top priority of the Federal Government since 1964 to provide "an opportunity for the best education which the Nation can offer each individual, suited to his abilities and interests and without regard to his family income, race, or place of residence."[4] This goal has not been realized. The Federal response to date, although precedent shattering, has been insufficient in providing quality education for disadvantaged minority students.

Significant Federal efforts to improve the education and subsequent life chances of the disadvantaged child[5] began with the passage of the Economic Opportunity Act of 1964, followed in 1965 by the Elementary and Secondary Education Act (ESEA) and the Higher Education Act.[6]

Several major problems trouble the Federal effort. First, the Congressional response to the national need has been piecemeal. A variety of separate programs has been established, all but one serving a very limited percentage of the total disadvantaged population. Second, these programs have not received adequate Congressional support. Appropriations have been cut or have been insufficient from the start.[7] In addition, appropriations have not been increased for programs that have demonstrated positive results, while vast amounts have been continued for Title I—a program that to date has been a substantial disappointment in improving education opportunities for disadvantaged minority students. This has been compounded by inopportune shifting of authority over promising programs from the Office of Economic Opportunity (OEO) to the Office of Education (OE)[8] while at the same time weakening the existing capability of OE to administer already-diffuse and inept programs under Title I.

The limitations of the Federal effort are further evidenced by the failure to provide impetus for major changes within the educational systems of this country, despite conclusive proof that our present public school systems have been unable to educate the poor.[9] As the discussion indicates, only one program, Teacher Corps, presently incorporates the objective of institutional reform. But this program has been prevented from realizing its full potential. In contrast, the large Title I program, which could have the most influence in the public school systems, has taken no decisive action to improve or to replace existing educational methods. Nor have the Federal programs sufficiently utilized community involvement.[10] Community participation has been practically nonexistent in the Title I program, and apparently the statutory requirement is being eliminated by Congress in its pending amendments to the ESEA. The shift of Head Start from OEO to OE also appears to signal the coming end of community involvement in that program as well.

Program evaluation, which has been either inadequate or nonexistent, presents an additional problem. Congress and administrators have little information upon which to base decisions. Few indications of success have been acted upon. The general picture is one of little accurate knowledge of what has happened or why.

Finally, programs have lacked coordination and adequate follow-up, which has precluded maximum benefit to students.[11] Gains made in one program tend to be nullified by a failure to continue intensive services through the later grades.

TITLE I, ESEA

Title I of the Elementary and Secondary Education Act (ESEA), the largest single educational program, presents a disappointing picture.[12] The program budget of over $1 billion a year represents nearly one-half of the Federal Government's commitment to disadvantaged children. It is designed to help districts meet the educational needs of children from low-income families. Under the administration of the Office of Education (OE), approximately

15,300 school districts are receiving Federal grants.

In some instances, Title I funds have been used by school administrators to carefully plan effective programs for the impoverished child, but in the majority of cases, the program is a federally funded, ineffectual free-for-all.[13] Since there are few Federal strings attached to the expenditure of Title I funds, school administrators have been able to spend the money in just about any way they wanted as long as it is spent on the poor. As a result, Title I funds have often been wasted. For example, in fiscal year 1966, 20 per cent of the total Title I appropriation was spent on educational equipment; 10 per cent on school construction.[14] In their 1969 report, the National Advisory Council on the Education of Disadvantaged Children, established by Congress to be the official monitor of the Title I program, observed that some local school systems continued "to enlarge equipment inventories or reduce class size by insignificant numbers."[15] The efficacy of such expenditures in improving the quality of learning is questionable. In addition, most school administrators have used and continue to use Title I funds to support the same old programs that have failed in the past. The National Advisory Council noted: "Our reports indicate that the bulk of Title I funds, . . . were spent on the intensification of existing approaches to the teaching of subject matter. Only a small portion was spent on genuinely new approaches to guiding and stimulating learning."[16] The Council further reported that a significant attempt to develop a curriculum "relevant" to the needs and experiences of disadvantaged children was observed in less than one-fourth of the 116 projects visited.[17]

The effect of Title I funds on the individual child also has been diluted. Despite the widely accepted view that a high per pupil expenditure is essential in providing quality education for the disadvantaged child, the majority of school administrators have distributed Title I money over a wide range of activities for a large number of children (9 million). The Office of Education reported that the average Title I per pupil expenditure dropped from $119 in fiscal year 1966 to $108 in fiscal year 1967.[18] The GETEMPO Study, in a sampling of 60 Title I schools, found that the majority of projects provided an expenditure of less than $5 per pupil.[19] One Title I official commented: "The range of services may look impressive, but in fact, a child may only get two of those 50 services—a pair of eyeglasses and a field trip."[20]

Finally, although all Federal education funds must be used in accordance with Title VI of the 1964 Civil Rights Act, in many cases Title I funds have been utilized in Southern states in opposition to the purpose of Title VI.[21] Many Southern administrators have had the "useful" misconception that Title I funds only can be expended in schools with a high concentration of children from low-income families.[22] Accordingly, these administrators have felt that Title I funds could not be used to support programs for disadvantaged children choosing to attend desegregated schools. As a result, Title I monies, in these cases, have perpetuated segregated schools. The Office of Education has encouraged local school systems to utilize Title I funds in a manner consistent with Title VI by emphasizing that "the money follows the child," but the problem still remains.[23]

Although State and local administrators are responsible for program planning, part of the onus for poor Title I programs lies with the Office of Education. Congressional authority gave most of Title I control to the State and local educational agencies, but the language in the Act is not so inflexible as to justify the Office of Education's lack of involvement in the program. For example, the legislation states that the Commissioner may establish basic criteria which the school districts must follow in designing Title I projects.[24] Yet, the Office of Education only has suggested, never insisted, that Title I monies be used for carefully planned, intensive programs that are appropriate to the needs of the target children. The National Advisory Council made this observation: "It is apparent the Office of Education guidelines urging concentration of funds have been disregarded in several States, possibly because these documents were unnecessarily liberal in their insurance of local autonomy."[25]

In addition, little effort has been made to establish direct communication with local educational agencies. There is no Federal monitoring of programs, nor any Federal technical assistance to help local agencies in the design of programs, although the ESEA legislation does not prohibit the Office of Education from engaging in these activites. In 1967, the Committee to Form Strategy for Improving Title I complained that the Office of Education

has not developed the capability for program, curriculum, or other substantive assistance to those administrators in local school systems who need help to find ways of doing something worthwhile for poor children . . . and we have not yet found ways to promote the Title I effort as a catalyst for educational change in poverty areas.[26]

The Office of Education has given very limited assistance to the State agencies in program administration, but no assistance has ever been given in program content. In effect, the Federal role in the administration of Title I has been to write the checks.

In part, this lack of involvement has been due to Congressional restriction on the size of the Title I staff. The Office of Education has made many requests for an increase of regional Title I staffs to enable them to give more technical assistance. Congress has consistently turned down these requests. Last summer, moreover, at the urging of the National Education Association, the American Association of School Administrators, and the Council of Chief State School Officers, Congress voted to withdraw all Federal Title I employees and all other Federal elementary and secondary education personnel, with the exception of Title VI compliance officers, from the regional offices.[27] This removed the one existing link in communication between the Office of Education and the State and local educational agencies.

Not only is the degree of Federal involvement inconsiderable, so too is the degree of community participation. Although the

ESEA legislation requires that local educational agencies work with the local community action groups in the planning of Title I programs, these groups are usually excluded from having any role in Title I program planning.[28] David Rogers, in his book *110 Livingston Street,* reported on the situation in New York City:

. . . The Title I programs for the 1966-67 school year had been planned by the board alone. Preliminary and later evaluation of the previous year's programs were not made available to citizen groups until after the board had developed its plans for the coming year. There were hearings in August, 1966, but all the structuring of programs had already been planned.[29]

The Office of Education was aware of this kind of violation of Title I legislation, and yet it took no action to correct it.[30]

A final shortcoming is the failure of the OE and State and local planners to provide an adequate framework for evaluation. Part of the difficulty is that State and local educational agencies, who are responsible for program evaluation, generally have neglected to establish clear program objectives or specific criteria by which to judge program success. The OE on its part has failed to make this a requirement. Evaluation is made more difficult because testing techniques vary from one school district to another and more frequently than not the statistical data collected by individual schools is incomplete. Consequently, a nationwide appraisal of Title I is virtually impossible. National efforts to identify successful programs for replication have been limited to an assessment of those programs which have adequate data.[31] These represent a small segment of the total number of Title I school districts. In addition, the lack of comparative data has made extremely difficult efforts to determine the factors that contribute to program success. In short, until a better evaluation system is devised, the overall effects of Title I will remain a question mark, and the OE will have less than a comprehensive picture of which programs should be continued and which ones should be discarded.

PROJECT HEAD START

Project Head Start provides more concrete evidence of program results. This program focused national attention on the need for special preschool programs for disadvantaged children. Each year, Head Start serves approximately half a million children in its summer prekindergarten program; its winter enrollment has expanded to over 200,000. The program's objective is to stimulate gains in the social and intellectual development of these children in order to strengthen the disadvantaged child's preparation for elementary school. Head Start operates on the premise that all the needs of a child must be given attention if improvement in intellectual development is to be effected. In keeping with this "whole child" concept, Head Start programs attempt to provide comprehensive medical, social, and educational services.

Results of studies, mostly of summer Head Start children, indicate that Head Start is making a promising first step toward raising the achievement level of deprived children.[32] The majority of studies have observed an increase in the test scores of children after the Head Start experience. The Office of Economic Opportunity has reported increments as high as 10 or more points in the achievement test scores of many Head Start children.

Evaluations of the long-term impact of the Head Start Program, however, are disappointing. These evaluations are based on follow-up studies of summer Head Start children only.[33] Although the OEO reports that summer Head Start children continue to demonstrate a greater interest in learning than non-Head Start children, there is a serious question in regard to the retention of achievement gains made during the Head Start experience once a child is placed in the regular school program. Follow-up studies of summer Head Start children show an eventual leveling-off in achievement test scores after they have been in the public school system for a while.[34] For example, one study, comparing Head Start with non-Head Start children from similar backgrounds, found that at the end of the kindergarten year, there was no significant difference in the test scores of the two groups.[35]

This would indicate that summer Head Start programs lose their effectiveness if adequate follow-up is not provided within the public school system to capitalize on these initial gains. (The Follow Through Program, which will be discussed later, is a limited response to this problem.)

Recently the Head Start program has attempted to expand its efforts through a new pilot program, The Parent and Child Center (PCC). This program is funded with Head Start money and is jointly sponsored by the OEO, HEW, HUD, and the Department of Labor. The OEO has observed that the very poor children in Head Start have developed serious handicaps by age 3. The Parent and Child Center program was started as a preventive measure to provide comprehensive services to children from early infancy. The program is distinguished from the Head Start Program in that it attempts to meet the needs of all members of a family in the program. It is premised on the notion that the psychological and physical well-being of the family unit affects the development of a young child. The PCC format includes educational services to the young child, parent instruction in the methods of stimulating the child's intellectual and emotional growth, assistance in job placement for adult members of the family, and comprehensive health care for all members of the family. Existing programs offered by the four sponsoring Federal agencies (e.g., Medicaid, Child Welfare, and Job Assistance) are utilized by the PCC Programs to provide many of these services.

At this time, the PCC program has had little significant impact since it is limited to approximately 3,000 children. At the beginning of this year, only 31 centers had been opened and many of these have been slow in becoming fully operational. Nonetheless, the PCC program shows promise because it recognizes the need to focus on the early years of childhood as a first and essential step in educational development. If the PCC pilot program can demonstrate that comprehensive family services have a decided impact on the rate of development of young children, the program should be expanded to serve a larger segment of the disadvantaged population.[36]

FOLLOW THROUGH PROGRAM

Follow Through, another extension of the Head Start program, was created in 1967 to provide a continuation of services to Head Start graduates through the primary grades. Since funding limitations prevented Follow Through from becoming a nationwide program as originally proposed,[37] the program focus changed to research and development of new educational models to determine successful alternatives to present educational systems.

Follow Through consists of 14 new educational models, including a community-school approach, which are being tested in 92 communities throughout the country. A careful evaluation of each program will be conducted by the community, the institution sponsoring the model, and the Office of Education. Eventually, those programs which demonstrate success will be expanded, while others which indicate failure will be discarded. This indicates a more intelligent method of seeking a solution to the education problems of disadvantaged children and promises a more effective and careful use of Federal money than has been the case with Title I.

Again, in contrast to Title I, Follow Through is well managed. Communities are given close supervision and assistance by the sponsoring institution as well as periodic assistance by the Office of Education in the development and implementation of the program. Each test project is expected to provide comprehensive services in keeping with the "whole child" concept embodied in the Head Start approach. The program operates on a high per pupil expenditure of approximately $1,200 per year.

Once successful programs have been identified, OE officials hope the Follow Through program will be able to fulfill two major objectives; the replication of successful models in school districts throughout the country under a heavily funded impact program, and a continuance of research and development of new education approaches on a smaller scale.[38]

TEACHER CORPS

The success of any education program, no matter how innovative, depends on those who are responsible for program implementation—the teachers. James S. Coleman in *Equality of Educational Opportunity*, found that "teacher quality seems more important to minority achievement than to that of the majority."[39] An official of the Office of Education noted of most Title I programs: "It's not just that the programs are unimaginative; the teachers are ineffective. Most of them are middle class teachers who don't understand these kids or anything about their backgrounds."[40]

In recognition of the urgent need for better teachers, the National Teacher Corps was conceived in 1965 to recruit and train the future teachers of economically disadvantaged children. The training emphasis is placed on sensitizing these teachers to the cultural and life-style differences inherent in the backgrounds of children from poor families. Varied techniques, from team teaching and individualized instruction to actually living in low-income communities, are employed in order to achieve the stated objectives.

The broader and more important goal of the program is to create change in existing patterns of teacher training. Colleges and universities that wish to begin a Teacher Corps program are required to give evidence that they plan to use the principles of the Teacher Corps approach to change their program for the training of all teachers. An educator at Temple University commented: "If the Corps should end tomorrow, the College of Education at Temple would never be the same. We are constantly incorporating the new techniques we've learned with Teacher Corps into the regular curriculum for all education majors."[41] Commitment to change is not limited to sponsoring institutions. Corps members are assigned only to those school districts that plan to use the Teacher Corps to help improve their method of teaching throughout their school system.

The Teacher Corps, regarded by some as Federal intrusion in the area of teacher education, was criticized from the outset. In response to objections from State and local sources, the word "National" was dropped from the Corps title. At the same time, in 1967, the authority to recruit, select, and enroll corps members, originally the function of the Washington headquarters, was transferred to the local school districts and training colleges in an effort to make the Teacher Corps more palatable to those who felt the program represented a take-over by the Federal government.

The Teacher Corps provides an example of Congressional failure to lend adequate support to its own education bills for the disadvantaged. For a period of seven months Congress refused to appropriate any money for the Teacher Corps. The original authorization of $34 million to train 5,000 Corps members in the first year was cut to an appropriation of $9.5 million, sufficient for only 1,600 corpsmen to begin their training in the Spring of 1966. The program suffered further setbacks because of late funding and uncertainty about Congressional intention to continue the program.[42] The tenuous existence of the program discouraged many interested students from applying, and late funding caused nearly 50 per cent of the corpsmen in the first cycle to drop out. (Many had gone without salaries for weeks, some for months.) The Teacher Corps was to have expanded to 10,000 corpsmen in 1967. The appropriation, however, again fell drastically short of the authorization figure and enrollment was limited to 1,150 interns.

Despite these setbacks, the Teacher Corps exhibits promising potential for educational change.[43] In its present size, however, it falls far short of meeting the need—only 657 interns graduated from the first two-year cycle. Richard Graham, Director of the Teacher Corps, expects at most, 1,500 new interns this summer. Although young college graduates appear eager to teach in poverty schools—the Teacher Corps had 13,000 applicants in 1966 and 10,000 in 1968—and the evidence strongly suggests that the Teacher Corps is a successful program, Congress continues to limit its support.

HIGHER EDUCATION

As our society becomes increasingly technological, a college education becomes a necessity. The Office of Economic Opportunity reported that approximately 600,000 disadvantaged high school students have the intellectual capacity for college, yet because of poor high school training, less than 8 per cent of these students go on to college.[44] Thus, thousands of young people are left behind with little prospect of sharing the benefits of this country. In an effort to alleviate this problem, the Federal Government offers a special college-preparatory program (Upward Bound), limited recruitment services (Talent Search), and financial aid to disadvantaged students.

Talent Search, a small program limited to a $4 million appropriation, attempts to seek out disadvantaged high school youth with potential, and to encourage and assist these students in gaining entrance to college. While the Office of Education reported 72 Talent Search projects in operation this year, they could not provide any information on the number of students served, or the number of students who have entered college as a result of Talent Search efforts.[45] After almost three full years of operation, the OE has no means of assessing or evaluating the merits of the program.

Upward Bound, a more comprehensive program than Talent Search, provides supplementary educational experiences in an effort to prepare high school students for college. The majority of the students served are "medium risk," i.e., students with a high school grade average of C—.

There is some tangible evidence of Upward Bound's impact. Over 10,000 Upward Bound high school seniors have entered college since 1965 and a majority of these students have stayed in. Again, the data is incomplete since many Upward Bound projects failed to keep up-to-date records of their students, but available figures for the program from 1965-1968 indicate that 65 to 80 per cent of Upward Bound high school graduates entered college and 74 to 82 per cent of these students have remained in college. Despite the program's apparent success, Congress has not increased Upward Bound appropriations. As a consequence, next year's enrollment will be limited to the 1968 figure of 26,000 students. Congress also has decided to shift the program's management from the OEO to the Office of Education. The period of transition will inevitably create administrative problems and will, in all probability, result in at least a temporary reduction of the program's effectiveness.

In 1967, the OEO sent questionnaires to 400 Upward Bound students who had dropped out of college. Only 50 students responded, but all 50 related their inability to stay in school to inadequate funds and the necessity for part-time jobs which caused them to fall behind in their studies. This may indicate that recruitment programs cannot obtain maximum results if sufficient attention is not given to assuring financial support commensurate to student needs.

The Federal Government offers three programs of financial aid to disadvantaged students—College Work Study, National Defense Student Loans, and Education Opportunity Grants (EOG). Total appropriations for these programs amounted to $473.9 million this past school year (1968-1969),[46] benefiting an estimated 710,000 individual students.[47] Individual student grants or loans, however, usually are too small to meet the disadvantaged student's need.[48] For example, the combined financial need of 7,000 Upward Bound students who entered college last fall was esti-

mated at $14.5 million. It was determined that the total financial assistance given these students (with Federal aid constituting the bulk of this assistance) fell short of the students' needs by $1.7 million.[49] In addition, the number of students to be served by these Federal programs has been reduced by a cut in EOG funding.[50] Again, inadequate appropriations have limited the effectiveness of Federal educational efforts.

CONCLUSION

There is little doubt that Federal involvement in the education of minority students will continue. To date, the impact of this involvement has been questionable. A few programs have had positive results and a few show promise for the future, but for the most part the overall Federal effort has been characterized by poor program management, a piecemeal legislative response, a splintered and uncoordinated approach and, most crucial, insufficient funding. Program appropriations must be increased, basic objectives broadened, program priorities set, and specific guidelines established. Otherwise, the lives and academic potential of America's disadvantaged minorities will continue to be wasted.

NOTES

[1] See for example, Kenneth B. Clark, *Dark Ghetto* (New York: Harper & Row, 1965), p. 124.

[2] James S. Coleman and others, *Equality of Educational Opportunity* (Washington, D.C.: U.S. Government Printing Office, 1966), p. 28.

[3] *Ibid.*, p. 273.

[4] *Special analyses, Budget of the United States*, Fiscal Year 1970, 114 (1969).

[5] The main thrust of the Federal Government's efforts to improve the education of minority groups centers on its programs for the economically disadvantaged. (The Federal Government funds only three programs for minority children per se: American Indian Education through the Department of Interior, a new bilingual program for Mexican-American children, and the Cuban Refugee Assistance to Dade County Program.) In recent years, large commitments of financial support have been focused on the poor. For example, in fiscal year 1968, nearly two-thirds ($2.3 billion) of total Federal outlays for elementary and secondary education was spent on programs for the economically disadvantaged child. The majority of the children served by most of these Federal programs are members of minority groups. In fiscal year 1967, for example, 76% of Head Start children and 64% of the children served by Title I (Elementary and Secondary Education Act) were nonwhite. Nonwhites comprised 67% of the students in the summer 1967 Upward Bound program. A more detailed breakdown indicates the following racial percentages: Head Start, fiscal year 1967: 51% Negro, 10% Mexican-American, 6% Puerto Rican, and 5% American Indian; Title I, ESEA, fiscal year 1967: 53% Negro, 6% Mexican-American, 3% Puerto Rican, and 4% American Indian; Upward Bound, summer, 1967: 50% Negro, 6% Mexican-American, 3% Puerto Rican, and 5% American Indian.

[6] Prior to these Acts, the Federal Government provided limited aid to disadvantaged students through the Vocational Education Act of 1963.

[7] Senator Bartlett of Alaska made reference to Congressional behavior: "Just at the point that we begin to transfer programs from paper to action, however, they have crashed to the ground in resounding failure.

The problem has been a familiar one; no funding or inadequate funding." 114 *Congressional Record* S10392, (September 6, 1968, daily ed.). In the beginning of fiscal year 1969, Congress chose to cut appropriations on the majority of educational programs for the poor and at the same time added $201 million to the "impacted area" program which, for the most part, serves the white suburbs.

[8] See discussion of the Upward Bound program, infra.

[9] See Coleman, *op. cit.;* and U.S. Commission on Civil Rights, *Racial Isolation in the Public Schools* (Washington, D.C.: U.S. Government Printing Office, 1967).

[10] Harold Howe II, former U.S. Commissioner of Education, believes community participation is "the only weapon that can bring about the revitalization that inner city schools need." (As quoted in Howe, Education Aided Social Changes," *The Washington Post,* December 8, 1968).

[11] See discussion of Head Start and the college financial-aid programs.

[12] Title III, ESEA, also serves disadvantaged children but to a limited extent. Although Title III is not a program specifically for the disadvantaged, it has funded some noteworthy projects, e.g., the METCO desegregation program in Boston and Project Concern in Hartford, Connecticut. For further information, see *Racial Isolation in the Public Schools,* pp. 152-53.

[13] The Committee to Form Strategy for Improving Title I, a committee of staff members from the Division of Compensatory Education and other OE officials, concluded: "The record shows that the Title I program is fast bogging down to nothing more than an extra teacher or two, a few more trips into town, or a few minutes a day with [a] remedial reading teacher. The Office of Education is in danger of losing its chance to provide leadership in the education of hard-core disadvantaged children as our program settles into fixed general aid." Report prepared for John F. Hughes, Director, Division of Compensatory Education, "Strategy for Improving the Effectiveness of Title I, ESEA, August 24, 1967, p. 5.

[14] The Congressional habit of late funding was a major cause of these expenditures. That year, funds were not allocated to the school districts until the end of the fiscal year. New equipment was a fast and easy way of getting rid of the money. (Commission staff interview, Office of Education, January 6, 1969).

[15] National Advisory Council on the Education of Disadvantaged Children, *Title I-ESEA: A Review and a Forward Look—1969* (Washington, D.C.: The U.S. Government Printing Office, 1969), p. 13.

[16] National Advisory Council on the Education of Disadvantaged Children, *Annual Report, 1968,* p. 9.

[17] *Ibid.,* p. 17.

[18] Office of Education, Division of Compensatory Education, *Statistical Report, Fiscal Year 1967, Title I/Year II,* 3 (1967).

[19] E. J. Mosbaek and others, *Analyses of Compensatory Education in Five School Districts,* Vol. I (Washington, D.C.: TEMPO, General Electric Co., 1968), p. 15.

[20] Commission staff interview, Office of Education, January 6, 1969.

[21] U.S. Commission on Civil Rights, *Southern School Desegregation 1966-67* (Washington, D.C.: U.S. Government Printing Office, 1968), pp. 80-86.

[22] Commission staff interview, Office of Education, November 7, 1968.

[23] Harold Howe II, Commissioner of Education, letter to chief state school officers, "Use of Title I Funds in Local School Districts Undergoing Desegregation or in Racially Segregated Attendance Areas," February 27, 1967.

[24] Elementary and Secondary Education Acts of 1965, Sec. 105.

[25] *Report of the National Advisory Council on the Education of Disadvantaged Children,* March 31, 1966, p. 20.

[26] "Strategy for Improving the Effectiveness of Title I, ESEA," p. 8, supra note 13.

[27] P.L. 90-557, October 11, 1968.

[28] An amendment to eliminate this requirement altogether from the Act was passed by the House of Representatives, 115 *Congressional Record* H3004 (April 22, 1969, daily ed.).

[29] David Rogers, *110 Livingston Street* (New York: Random House, 1968), p. 452.

[30] Commission staff interview, Office of Education, January 6, 1969.

[31] See *Report of the National Advisory Council on the Education of Disadvantaged Children,* supra note 15. The Council identifies 21 successful Title I programs and the components that distinguish successful programs from ones that have failed.

[32] See listing of studies in "Project Head Start: A Research Summary," *Integrated Education* VI (September-October 1968).

[33] At the time this article was written, no information was available on the long-term impact of full-year Head Start programs. Since then, the follow-up study of full-year Head Start children conducted by the Westinghouse Learning Corporation and Ohio University was released. This study concluded that graduates of full-year Head Start programs did not demonstrate significant gains over non-Head Start children.

[34] "Project Head Start: A Research Summary," *Integrated Education* VI (September-October 1968), p. 45; and Division of Research and Evaluation, Project Head Start: Evaluation and Research 1965-67" (Washington, D.C.: U.S. Government Printing Office, 1968), pp. 9-10.

[35] John Harding, "A Comparative Study of Various Project Head Start Programs" (1966). Paper presented at Cornell University for OEO.

[36] On February 19, 1969, President Nixon pledged a "national commitment to providing all American children an opportunity during the first five years of life." (President's Message to Congress on the Economic Opportunity Act.) In April, the President stated: "Toward this end, Secretary Finch has decided to expand the Parent and Child Center and Follow Through Programs. . . ." (Statement by the President on the establishment of the new office in the Department of Health, Education, and Welfare, April 9, 1969.) Secretary Finch issued this statement: "I plan to double, to $12 million, the size of the Parent and Child Center program which serves children under three years of age and their families." 115 *Congressional Record* E2888 (April 14, 1969, daily ed.).

[37] In its present stage, the program involves a very limited number of children, 15,500 children in kindergarten and first grade this year. The number is expected to double in school year 1969-1970 and again in 1970-1971 to 63,500 children. The program will have expanded through the third grade by 1970-1971. HEW Secretary Finch expressed his plans for Follow Through: "I will seek a substantial expansion of the Follow Through program which is budgeted to reach only 6 percent of Head Start graduates in F.Y. 1970, by encouraging greater use of existing Title I funds for this purpose." 115 *Congressional Record* E2888 (April 14, 1969, daily ed.).

[38] Commission staff interview with Dr. Robert Egbert, Director of the Follow Through Program, January 7, 1969.

[39] James S. Coleman, *op. cit.*, p. 22.

[40] Commission staff interview, Office of Education, October 22, 1968.

[41] Dr. Evan Sorber, Director, Teacher Corps, Temple University, Philadelphia, Pennsylvania (Commission staff telephone interview, May 1, 1969).

[42] An official of the St. Louis school system described the effects of late funding and uncertainty about the continued existence of the Teacher Corps: "In St. Louis we tried desperately to get a Teacher Corps program going, but in talking with the universities and colleges in the area, they felt that they wanted to be a little more sure of the future. There was a considerable cost in tooling up for the program, and getting the thing organized, and they were wary of getting into it when its future was so much in doubt." Testimony of Dr. Moeller, Director of Federal Relations of the St. Louis City School System, "Study of the United States Office of Education; Report of the Special Subcommittee on Education," House Committee on Education and Labor, 90th Congress, 1st Sess., H.R. Doc. 193 at 322 (1967).

[43] The Teacher Corps has been endorsed by Charles Cogen, President of the American Federation of Teachers, The National Advisory Commission on Civil Disorders, Braulio Alonso, President of the National Education Association, and many other educators. *Newsweek* magazine described the Teachers Corps as "the one imaginative program to shake the education establishment in decades sending enthusiastic teams of specially trained teachers into slum schools." For additional information see 114 *Congressional Record* S10375-92 (September 6, 1968). Also see National Advisory Council on the Education of Disadvantaged Children, *Special Report on the Teacher Corps* (Washington, D.C.: U.S. Government Printing Office, 1967).

[44] Speech by Dr. Thomas A. Billings, Director of the Upward Bound Program, before the American Educational Research Association Conference, February 9, 1968.

[45] Commission staff telephone interview, Talent Search Office, OE, March 18, 1969.

[46] Individual appropriations for 1968-69 were: College Work Study, $139.9 million; National Defense Student Loans, $193.4 million; and Educational Opportunity Grants, $410.6 million.

[47] College Work Study served 375,000 students; National Defense Student Loans, an estimated 442,000 students; and Educational Opportunity Grants, 271,000 students. Since some students receive a financial package of all three types of aid, the total number, 1.1 million, includes some duplications. The Office of Education estimates that 71% of the total number of students is unduplicated.

[48] In 1968-1969, the average Defense Loan was $660; the average earnings per student in the College Work Study Program, $475; and average EOG grant, $460.

[49] The American College Testing Program, *A Study of the Financial Need of Upward Bound Students, 1968.* (Report done for Upward Bound.)

[50] The fiscal year 1969 appropriation for the EOG program was set at $124.6 million, representing a $16 million reduction from the fiscal year 1968 figure of $140.6 million. As a result, fewer students will be receiving initial-year grants.

44
the white university must respond to black student needs

ROSCOE C. BROWN, JR.

Sixty years ago, W. E. B. Du Bois put forth his doctrine of "the talented tenth." He meant that the top students must be educated in the best universities to provide a leadership group for the black community. In these days of mass education, the relation of the university to black students is again in the forefront. White universities have responded to pressures from black students by establishing black studies programs that teach black history, literature, music, and often Swahili and African history. These programs vary both in organization and quality. Sometimes they exclude white students; sometimes black students are not concerned with them. But in general, they have provided a campus home, both intellectually and socially, for black students who have in the past been isolated.

Universities have also responded by recruiting black students, diverting funds to their tuition needs, reducing entrance requirements, and providing them with special tutoring. Both the establishment of black studies programs and special aids to black students have aroused opposition, particularly among marginal white students and their parents.

Dr. Brown presents the arguments for this compensatory treatment of black students. He is a professor in the School of Education at New York University.

On Thursday, April 4, 1968, Dr. Martin Luther King, Jr. was assassinated as he stood on the porch of a motel in Memphis, Tenn. With one shot, an assassin snuffed out the life and light of a black leader whom both his admirers and detractors respected. Within hours after King's assassination, riots and violence swept the nation's black ghettos. Almost simultaneously, black students on the nation's predominately white campuses began to hold demonstrations to present "demands" to college and university administrations. These demands were repeated as though they were being played on a phonograph record: "more black students," "more black professors," "more black courses," "all-black dormitories" and so on. In a real sense, the black students had awakened.

What is behind this awakening of black students throughout the country? Is it just a reaction to the King murder? Of course not! Black students have been in ferment for over a decade, first in the predominantly Negro colleges, and now in predominantly white colleges. We should remember that the Civil Rights Revolution really began when, in February 1960, a group of black college students sat down at a lunch counter in a Woolworth's store in Greensboro, N.C. (a thing unheard-of at that time) and refused to move until they

Reprinted from *The New York University Alumni News* 14, no. 4 (January 1969), pp. 1-3. Reproduced by permission of the author.

were served. The "sit-in" was the forerunner of the mass demonstrations, the marches, and now the angry confrontations that are part of the Civil Rights Revolution—and black students have been an important part of all of them.

If black students were in the vanguard of the Civil Rights Revolution, why did it take so long for the black students on integrated campuses to awaken? Possibly the answer to this question is the nature of the integrated university itself.

Many integrated colleges and universities have long sought Negro and other minority-group students and some have given a disproportionate amount of their scholarship money to minority-group students. These colleges and universities have insisted for the most part that the minority-group students meet the same standards, with minor revisions, as the white students. On the surface this looks good and seems fair, but it overlooks the educational disadvantages that most black students face in ghetto schools. Thus, the type of black student selected in the past has been a black counterpart of his middle-class white fellow student. Because he was in a definite minority (sometimes 2 per cent or 3 per cent of the entering class) and because he was more like the middle-class white student in background, the black student had little compulsion or desire to challenge even the most unfair aspects of his college life.

One such indignity that black students at integrated colleges have had to put up with for years is a kind of unspoken prohibition on interracial dating. Another has been the toleration of unknowing racial bias on the part of fellow students and professors concerning such things as racially tinted humor and the alleged rhythm that all Negroes are supposed to have. More painfully, they had to accept the inconsistencies about equality on campus and the existence of racially segregated fraternities and sororities.

Fortunately, many integrated colleges have now recognized that they have been servicing only a fraction of the talent among black high school graduates and have reached out to attract more black students from a wider variety of backgrounds. As more black

students come to the nation's campuses and have an opportunity to experience both the positive and the negative aspects of a university experience, the black students have begun to organize and discuss what they can do themselves to improve the situation. Most black students view their proposed improvements as of ultimate benefit to the white students as well. In more than one demonstration for more black courses, students, professors and white students who have tried to participate as members of the black students' groups have been told to go back to the white student body and begin to eradicate the racism that exists there.

Mention of the word "racism" in this context requires a brief clarification about what the black students mean when they use it. Racism is used to refer to an attitude, often not conscious, which causes an individual to respond to a situation in a different manner when blacks are involved than when whites only are involved. Thus, a question as to whether a Negro should quarterback the football team when he is the best quarterback involves a racist attitude. Similarly, concern about whether a qualified black student should be given a Rhodes Scholarship is a racist attitude. The black students feel that white students working among the white students to eradicate racist attitudes is a fundamental contribution that white students can make toward better racial understanding.

The black student speaks of relevance. He says that the curriculum must be "relevant to the black experience." While this sounds like so much jargon, and is spoken by some of the students with an almost ritualistic fervor, their concern is a valid one. What the black students mean is that the curriculum should give them some insights about the black man's role in society and help them to develop those skills which will enable them to improve life in the ghetto. Thus, the black students want courses in black art, black music, the economics of poverty and the economics of the ghetto. This does not mean that most black students want to go back to the ghetto as social workers or teachers. They want to become participating members of society in all of its aspects, and want to use their knowledge to help black people in many ways. The present generation of black students is aware of those omissions in their education which if rectified might help them to be more effective in their efforts to improve the lot of all black people, not just themselves. The cry for relevance parallels a similar cry by the student activists in colleges all over the nation. Those students are virtually concerned with poverty, racism, war and injustice. They, too, feel that the classical tools of scholarship have not been particularly helpful to them in dealing with these concerns. While they concede that a firm grounding in a variety of subject areas eventually might be helpful to them, the urgency of their youth and the urgency of the problems that society faces leads them to cry for more relevance in their education now.

The present emphasis on programs for black students offends many persons, white and black, because they feel that such an overt emphasis merely stimulates separatism and racial divisiveness. At a first glance, this proposition might appear to be valid. However, we must realize that self-respect and equaltiy are not bestowed on one group by another, but rather must be gained by the group being discriminated against by its own efforts. This is not to say that white people cannot play important roles in the process, but the black man must be his own spokesman, his own strategist, and must mobilize the sentiment among his own people for change. In the process, there is apt to be a strong overreaction by some black people. Thus, demands for all-black dormitories emerge, or statements are made that a white man cannot teach a course in black history. Those who aspire to a society in which black and white will live with mutual respect and opportunity must strive to understand the drives that cause some of these demands to be made.

In understanding the demands, the university must evaluate and analyze the consequences of accepting them or rejecting them. In many cases, such as the allegations about exploitation of Negro athletes that have been recently publicized in *Sports Illustrated* and *Newsweek,* the grievances of the black students have so much basis that some drastic action is needed. For example, the Negro

athletes' demand for a black coach is not unreasonable.

True, at the very moment of their demand, an appropriately qualified black coach may not be available, but the reason for this must be understood, too. With the large number of black athletes who participate in college sports, it is certainly more than an accident or oversight that few of them ever return to their alma maters to coach. Thus, the demand for a black coach is not as unreasonable as it may seem at first blush. Why not wait, then, until the college can take time to seek out one or develop one? This is, in a sense, the crux of the black revolution or black awakening. Blacks have been waiting for years for obvious grievances to be recognized and redressed—and since society has continued to ignore them, blacks are making demands for fulfillment now!

The intellectual, of course, recognizes that all demands cannot be met immediately, but a start can be made—even if on a basis that can be criticized as somewhat inadequate. The real task of the university is to begin to bridge the credibility gap that exists between the black students and society. The university can do this by attempting to understand the concerns and grievances of the black students and beginning to deal with them directly. In doing so, the university from its position of greater understanding and maturity must not try to always force the black students to function according to the university's rules—for in a sense it is some of the university's methods of operation that have created the situations from which the grievances stem. Just as the student revolts on campuses all over the country have forced universities to re-evaluate, and often change, policies that have been unchallenged for years, so should the black student awakening be viewed by the university as an opportunity to deal with the subtle and not too subtle effects of racism on the university.

Some observers of the changes in the college scene vis-à-vis the black student have wondered if this isn't racism in reverse. As I mentioned earlier, the whole black revolution is a reaction to grievances too often ignored and promises too frequently forgotten. Thus, there is the possibility of overreaction, on both sides. It is a painful experience for both the majority and the minority in a society to understand that so much of its fabric is interwoven with racism. The desire to eradicate it or to forget it (this is a much less feasible possibility in the context of modern society with its mass media and mass communication) can lead to many false starts and well-intentioned mistakes. The majority of blacks do not want an apartheid society, but many will stand with "black only" causes until society shows that it really means to include blacks in the society on an equal and meaningful basis. The black students are quite justified in demanding more coverage of black history and the contributions of blacks to society. Although some of the black students don't believe that white students should be admitted to these courses, black history courses will be of considerable value to white students also.

Certainly, the relatively inane treatment of slavery and the Reconstruction period by historians deserves correction in the minds of all. Some definitive works on Reconstruction, such as that of John Hope Franklin, chairman of the history department at the University of Chicago, have been written, but to a great extent these are not included in the basic history courses that are taken by most students. Black students are justified in asking that more black counselors and advisers be appointed. Not that only black counselors can counsel black students, but, black students should have black counselors available if they want to talk with one. Also, black and white students should be able to see blacks in a variety of positions in the university. Demands of the type that I have mentioned are not to develop an apartheid university; rather they are to provide for a valid recognition of black people and black students as a part of society and a part of the university.

The consideration of the black student as a special case in the university, particularly at an institution that prides itself on its democratic traditions, might appear to violate principles of equality and nondiscrimination. But the university, as one of the most important institutions of society, has a responsibility to help blacks and other minority groups achieve the position of social and economic equality that is implicit in our system. President James M. Hester of the New York University, for example, says that NYU intends to discriminate positively in favor of black students to help eradicate the effects of racism on them.

Although it can be argued that the university should merely reflect the values and traditions of society and create knowledge for the sake of knowledge, many people in society look to the university for leadership and guidance in the solution of a variety of social and intellectual problems. The university's concern with black students is clearly within this framework. Certainly, mistakes will be made. The black students will make mistakes and should be allowed to learn from them. University administrators will make mistakes and should also be allowed to learn from them. The black student awakening and the contemporary student activism on America's campuses point the way for the enhancement of the university as an important institution in our society. Those of us in the university should really hold ourselves in their debt for so forcefully bringing this challenge to us.

45
the federal government and protest

DAVID MARS

This writer must confess to surprise and dismay to find that protests ranging from college sit-ins to mass marches to the capital city are regarded by a considerable proportion of the citizenry as dangerous, subversive, and un-American. The coincidence of protests with riots in large cities and on some campuses, causing property damage, casualties, and deaths, may account for some of the negative attitudes. Riots and protests are, however, very different phenomena. Riots usually occur spontaneously; if, as on some campuses, they are deliberately started, there must be widespread dissatisfaction before they will spread and involve large numbers of people. Protests, on the other hand, are organized, have deliberate aims and goals, and involve no violence. The large-scale marches to Washington have involved up to half a million people and were, with minor exceptions, dignified and orderly.

The basis of democracy is that the governed shall control the actions of the governing. When government is far away in Washington or a state capital or buried in bureaucracies absolutely impervious to communications from outside, there is no way to get to those governing except to come physically into their presence and impede action until your plea is heard. Protests started first among racial minorities and moved to campuses; but other groups—workers, taxpayers, middle-class citizens concerned about environmental destruction—have adopted the protest techniques of the younger and more radical groups.

To the extent that neglected interest groups succeed in being heard through protest, protests can be seen as safety valves that prevent conditions from becoming so bad that they explode in riots. To the extent that even protests do not produce change, more disorder and dissatisfaction can be expected.

Mr. Mars, who is director of the School of Public Administration at the University of Southern California, discusses the extent to which the federal government responded to protest in the sixties.

Early in April 1968, on one Los Angeles radio station's two-way-radio-conversation program, a caller asked an interesting question. She wanted to know why the various civil rights acts and related measures which had

Reprinted from "Protest in the Sixties," *Annals of the American Academy of Political and Social Science* 382 (19 March 1969), pp. 120-130. Reproduced by permission of the author and publisher.

been enacted during the past several years had been put on the books only after great struggles and widespread protest, rather than having been based on principle and "what was right." The commentator (or "communicaster," in the local-communications-media jargon), whose opinions were rather conservative, tried to respond to the question, remarking finally that more civil rights legislation had been passed in the past few years than had been passed in the entire previous history of the nation. To this, the caller answered quietly that we have also had more protest during the past few years than at any other time in the nation's history.

The relationship between protest and response to protest is an interesting and very important one to explore; it is also frequently a relationship extremely difficult to establish. On many occasions, it is almost impossible to discover whether an action undertaken by a governmental body is indeed a response to protest or whether it was actuated by an altogether different motive.

BASIC NATURE OF THE RIGHT TO PROTEST

In a fundamental sense, the right to protest lies at the very basis of a free and democratic system of government. The revolutionary leaders who played such an outstanding role in the civil rights movements of the 1770's and 1780's, and those who were responsible for moving the amendments which subsequently became the Bill of Rights, seemed to be well aware of the connection, at least insofar as it extended to nonviolent protest. Hence, they enshrined this right in the First Amendment, together with the other basic rights of free speech, free press, and free religion (both in its exercise and in freedom from state-established religions).

Significantly, these early leaders were apparently not interested in protecting a merely academic right of protest. They realized that for protest to be meaningful, there must be an expectation that the reasonable demands stated and embodied in the protest will be responded to and dealt with meaningfully by the state. Thus, while free speech, free press, free exercise of religion, and freedom from established religion stand alone as rights (and are connected by "or"), the right of protest was linked closely with the right to expect implementation of steps designed to meet the protest (and connected by "and"). Accordingly, the First Amendment speaks of "the right of the people peaceably to assemble, and to petition the government for a redress of grievances."[1]

It hardly needs to be emphasized that the Constitution clearly does not countenance violent protest, nor does it guarantee a right to the type of protest which has come to be called civil disobedience.

The connection between protest and democracy is as clear and as important today as it was in the earliest days of the Republic. Within the past year, we have seen the statement made boldly and unflinchingly that "when a presumably democratic government fails to respond to dissent or protest, it has become a dictatorship."[2]

CIVIL VERSUS SOCIAL RIGHTS

The record of the federal government's response to protest during the 1960's has, in general, been marked by presidential and congressional concern for, and action in, the field of civil and political rights, and by considerably less action in the field of social and economic rights. By the late 1960's, there was general recognition that the civil rights struggle, bitter and protracted though it had been, would prove to be far less difficult than the achievement of social and economic justice for all Americans. The civil rights movement had focused largely on the black communities of the United States, where political inequality, and the injustices related thereto, had been long-standing, patent, and a very obvious blotch on America's image, both at home and abroad. In contrast, the question of social and economic justice was clearly not limited to one racial community. Though a large percentage of America's poor are, in fact, black people, by no means all of them are. In addition, the condition of poverty was—and is—not as apparent to many Americans as earlier civil and political abuses and malpractices (for example, lynchings, exclusion from the franchise, and the like) had been: witness such expressions as "the other America" and "the invisible poor." Finally, while the color of one's skin could not be hidden, one's economic condition could be, and frequently was as a matter of pride and self-respect: it was demeaning to admit that one was poor.

Martin Luther King had been fond of pointing out that it had not cost one cent to desegregate lunch counters and other public facilities (he might have also mentioned housing in the same category, except that congressional action here did not occur until after his murder), and predicted that the struggle to win social and economic rights would be a far more difficult one.

A major reason for the difference in difficulty of achieving civil rights and social-economic rights is that the latter will require substantial attitudinal changes. It is one thing to permit a person with a different skin to vote in the same election (and have his vote counted equally), or to serve on a jury; it is a totally different thing to permit him to put his children into the same school as one's own children, or to dig deep into one's pocket to pay the taxes necessary to support a decent living standard for him.

President Johnson had recognized that though legislation in the area of civil rights was an important step along the path toward "liberty and justice for all," it was not the only step. In his 1968 civil rights message to the Congress, he said: "The more we grapple with the civil rights problem . . . the more we realize that the position of minorities in American society is defined not merely by law, but by social, educational, and economic conditions."

We will focus here on three points: (1) the civil rights legislation of the period 1957-1968, especially those enactments viewed as being particularly in response to protest, (2) the report of the National Advisory Commission on Civil Disorders, and (3) the Poor People's March and the action by Congress in 1968.

CIVIL RIGHTS LEGISLATION

Of the three branches of the federal government, the Congress was the slowest to move in the field of civil rights. During the 1940's and 1950's, both the Supreme Court and the President took substantial action to try to end racial discrimination and segregation. But the Congress did not move until 1957, when the Civil Rights Act of that year was adopted, the first federal legislation in the field since the days of the post-Civil War Re-

construction era. During the decade since then, a number of other civil rights measures were enacted: in 1960, in 1964, in 1965, and in 1968.

In one sense, perhaps none of this legislation was a direct response to protest. In another sense, at least three of the measures do seem to have borne some relation to previous actions of protest. We shall look at all the measures briefly, focusing particularly on those which may be said to have constituted responses to protest. It is a tragic irony that, in two of these cases, the assassination of a very prominent American political leader played a part in the final passage of the legislation.

Of great interest also is the point that the three statutes which appear to have been responses to protest were the more recent enactments. Thus, it might be concluded that the Congress has been growing more responsive to protest. As will be shown below, however, Congress' very recent action—or inaction—raises some doubts on this point, or at least suggests that there is still a long way to go.

1. The Civil Rights Act of 1957 was an outgrowth of President Eisenhower's proposals of 1956, embodied in his State of the Union message of that year and in a draft program submitted to the Congress in April. The package as finally approved by the Congress was somewhat narrower than the President's. The major contribution of the act to civil rights was the provision designed to enforce the right to vote, by empowering the Attorney General of the United States to seek an injunction in every instance where an individual was deprived, or was about to be deprived, of his right to vote. Also important was the creation of the Commission on Civil Rights and of the Civil Rights Division of the Department of Justice, the latter to be headed by an Assistant Attorney General.

Of significance were the series of political events which took place in 1956, including the adoption of civil rights planks in the two major party platforms of that year: the Republican plank specifically endorsed and supported enactment of Eisenhower's civil rights program. Another important political event was the national election, in which the Negro vote reached substantial proportions. The Act may thus be viewed as having been, at least in part, a response to the visibly increasing political power of the Negro, though not specifically a response to actual protest.

2. In early February 1959, President Eisenhower submitted a seven-point civil rights program to the Congress. The only legislative action taken by the Congress during 1959 was an extension of the life of the Civil Rights Commission for two years (until November 1961).[3] But the stage was set for the enactment of the next piece of civil rights legislation: the Civil Rights Act of 1960. This Act simply amended and supplemented some of the provisions of the earlier Act. The major new provision authorized judges—after a proceeding in which a pattern or practice of depriving Negroes of their right to vote had been determined—to appoint referees to help these Negroes to register and to vote. Among the other provisions of the Act were criminal penalties for obstruction of court orders, transportation of explosives with the knowledge that they would be used to explode vehicles or buildings, use of interstate facilities to threaten bombings, and crossing state lines to avoid prosecution or punishment for bombing or burning vehicles or buildings. (These provisions were not tied specifically to racial incidents.)

Civil Rights Acts as Responses to Protest

3. The Civil Rights Act of 1964 was the first enactment by the Congress during the period 1957-1968 which may be said to have been, at least partially, a direct response to protest. During 1963, demonstrations and boycotts by Negroes had taken place in eight hundred communities across the antion. The climax of these demonstrations came on August 28, when 200,000 persons, black and white, participated in the "March on Washington for Jobs and Freedom." It was on that occasion that Martin Luther King delivered his most famous speech, when he spoke of his dream of an America rid forever of racial inequality, with blacks and whites living peacefully together and sharing in the nation's opportunities and abundance.

Prior to this, however, the federal government had begun to take steps to process the protests. These protests had not been confined to Negro groups; many white persons, especially church groups and college students, had made common cause with the Negroes, and had expressed themselves forcefully in favor of racial justice and equality. In June, President Kennedy greatly broadened his civil rights program (originally submitted to the Congress in February), proposing rather sweeping legislation. He was fully conscious of the need for legislation to respond to the protests. In a nationwide television address, given a week before submitting his legislative package to the Congress, he had warned of the dangers in a situation in which legal remedies were ineffective or nonexistent. In these cases, he said: "Redress is sought in the streets, in demonstrations, parades and protest which create tensions and threaten violence—and threaten lives."

By late November, the bill incorporating the civil rights package had been formally reported but had not been cleared for floor action. On November 22, 1963, President Kennedy was assassinated in Dallas. In one of his first actions as President, Lyndon Johnson pressed for enactment of the legislation, saying: "No memorial oration or eulogy could more eloquently honor President Kennedy's memory than the earliest possible passage of the civil rights bill for which he fought so long."

Despite the urging of the new President and the connection of the proposed legislation with the martyred President, it was not until mid-year that the legislation finally cleared the Congress (and was signed by the President on July 2).

The Civil Rights Act of 1964 was the most comprehensive piece of civil rights legislation enacted in the country's history. In eleven titles, the Act broadened the guarantees of the Negro's right to vote; barred discrimination in public accommodations; authorized suits by the federal government to desegregate public facilities and schools; broadened the responsibilities of the Civil Rights Commission and extended its life for four years; barred discrimination in any program or activity receiving federal assistance; outlawed discriminatory practices in employment and created the Equal Employment Opportunity Commission to enforce these provisions; and created a Community Relations Service to aid communities in resolving disputes growing out of discriminatory practices.

Though designed originally as a response to protest, the question may be fairly raised whether the Civil Rights Act of 1964 would have been so sweeping—or would have passed at all—without the additional political and sympathetic impetus provided by the assassination of President Kennedy.

4. The Voting Rights Act of 1965 is the second of the three civil rights enactments of the 1960's which may be regarded as responses to protest. In fact, it represented the most direct response of the three. In this instance, the response was to a series of demonstrations protesting voting discrimination in the South. Though demonstrations, marches, and sit-ins were held in various places throughout the country in early 1965, the main focus of the protests was Selma, Alabama, where peaceful demonstrations soon gave way to violence, which, in turn, aroused much public attention and sympathy for the civil rights cause.

The depth of this sympathy, as well as the direct and obvious connection between the protest and the response, may perhaps be measured best by regarding the relative speed with which the Congress moved. On March 17, President Johnson submitted a draft voting-rights proposal to the Congress, and by August 4, the bill had cleared both houses; it was signed by the President on August 6.[4]

The Voting Rights Act of 1965, considered to be the most sweeping such bill of modern times, contained a number of provisions bearing upon the right to vote. The most important provision, constituting a departure from the pattern of earlier civil rights legislation, was that calling for direct action by the federal government in the electoral process. This action took the form of authorizing federally appointed examiners to determine individuals' qualifications to vote, and to enroll voters, after specified findings made by a federal court or by the Attorney General, or after certain facts had been established.[5]

Five days after the President signed the Voting Rights Act of 1965, Watts exploded into bloody violence, in the worst racial disorder in American history. The six days of violence caused 34 deaths, 856 injuries, over 3,000 arrests, and nearly $200,000,000 in damages.[6]

The Civil Rights Act of 1968

5. For those persons who were getting accustomed to a new piece of civil rights legislation every year, 1966 must have been a disappointing year. The key section of the administration-backed civil rights bill of that year, a provision calling for open housing, quickly aroused a great deal of controversy, and became the focal point for the opponents of the bill. It was to prove the proposal's undoing. Though the bill passed the House (by a roll-call vote of 259-157), a group of Republican senators, led by Senator Dirksen, focused their attack on the open-housing provision, and prevented passage by the Senate.

The next year, the first year of the Ninetieth Congress, was to prove almost as disappointing to civil rights supporters. The only action taken by Congress in this area during 1967 was to extend the life of the Civil Rights Commission for five years.

President Johnson's 1967 civil rights package, in substance, closely resembled the comprehensive bill introduced in 1966, which the Congress had turned down. However, in an attempt to win Congress' approval of the rights legislation in 1967, separate bills were proposed for each item. The law extending the life of the Civil Rights Commission was regarded as the least controversial of the items in the President's civil rights package. Two other parts of the package were passed by either the House or the Senate, but not by both.

In January 1968, President Johnson's civil rights message asked the Congress to enact five measures not acted upon during the previous year, including open housing, which subsequently was attached as an amendment to a civil rights bill passed by the House in 1967. Since the Congress appeared to be in a more conservative mood than it had been while passing the rights legislation of 1964 and

1965, most observers felt that the civil rights bill of 1968, especially since it contained an open-housing provision, would not pass.

After the Senate had approved it by a generous margin (71-20), the bill ran into trouble in the House. The dramatic switch which eventuated in the final passage of the bill came in the Rules Committee. First, the committee voted to delay the bill. After the delay, the committee was scheduled to vote on whether to approve the Senate-passed version or to send the bill to a conference committee. Before this next action could be taken, however, Martin Luther King, Jr., was assassinated in Memphis, and violence broke out in over a hundred American cities. The vote in committee was taken on the same day on which King's funeral was held in Atlanta. Republican John B. Anderson (Illinois) decided that sending the bill to a conference committee would seriously jeopardize its chances of passage, and unexpectedly switched his vote to favor bringing it to the floor of the House. On the next day, the House approved the bill, putting on the books the first federal open-housing legislation since 1866.

What effect King's death and the resulting disorder had on the vote is impossible to gauge accurately. It is possible that the bill would have passed eventually anyway, without the tragic events of April; it is also possible that the rioting subsequent to King's death lost supporters for the bill in Congress. Commenting indirectly on the possibility of such a "backlash" effect, Representative Anderson, who had played such a key role in the passage of the bill, said at the time of his vote, "I legislate today not out of fear but out of deep concern for the America I love."

In general, it was felt that King's death did contribute positively toward the bill's enactment. As in the 1964 Act, the legislation came to be viewed as a fitting monument to a fallen political leader.

It is interesting to record that the Civil Rights Act of 1968, though it did incorporate the first federal open-housing legislation in over a century (and dealt with other rights as well), also included some antiriot provisions and penalties for specified riot activities.

THE REPORT OF
THE KERNER COMMISSION

The work of the National Advisory Commission on Civil Disorders (Kerner Commission) and the fate of its report provided an interesting and revealing story. The creation of the Commission itself was clearly a response to protest, which, in this instance, had been articulated in the violent civil disorders which had swept through 128 American cities during the summer of 1967.

Commission members were so impressed with the urgency of the racial problem in the United States, and with the likelihood that the summer of 1968 would bring more violent protest in the mode of the previous summer, that they released their final report earlier than had been anticipated. Originally appointed by the President on July 29, 1967, members of the Commission had been instructed to make an interim report on its findings of fact by March 1, 1968, and a final report by July 29, 1968. Instead, they issued their final report on March 1, five months before the date that it was due. They expressed themselves as having "worked together with a sense of the greatest urgency" and, as a result, having decided that the "gravity of the problem and the pressing need for action are too clear to allow further delay in the issuance" of the report.

The report and its urgent tone apparently touched a responsive chord in the American people. Within the short space of three weeks, 740,000 copies of the report were sold (mostly on newsstands), probably qualifying it for the record of the fastest-selling book in history.

In sharp contrast, the response by both the President and the Congress was generally disappointing. The President's noncommittal statement (some persons described it as cool) at the time of the release of the report disappointed many who felt that major changes were needed in order to alleviate the situation in the nation. Several weeks later, the President was asked at a press conference to comment on the report and on the criticism that he was not acting quickly enough on the recommendations contained therein. At that time, he elaborated on his view of the report, indicating that he found it to be very thorough and very comprehensive, and that it included many good recommendations. His extended remarks, however, again failed to reflect any urgency, and again disappointed many persons.

In a television broadcast about two months after the report was published, an attempt was made to trace its short history and its fate. Governor Kerner of Illinois, who had chaired the Commission, expressed keen disappointment at the general lack of action on the recommendations which had been made, pointing out that, up to that time, there had been no discussion of it, either in Congress or in congressional committess. Mayor Lindsay of New York City, the Commission's vice-chairman, agreed. He felt that the country was not moving fast enough, or far enough, to process the recommendations. He also felt that there had been insufficient action by the federal government, a failure which he identified as the responsibility primarily of the Congress.

Perhaps the most eloquent appraisal of the report—and a cogent comment upon protest in the American system—was made by a black resident of Newark, one of America's most riot-torn cities, who said: "The riot commission report didn't change anything; it's the riots that changed things."

THE POOR PEOPLE
AND THE CONGRESS

The very day on which the words here were being written (in July 1968) brought an announcement from the Ninetieth Congress of the United States that that body, in which is vested "all legislative powers" granted by the Constitution, had announced that, in order to make possible an early adjournment, no further legislation authorizing new programs or commitments would be considered. The early adjournment was, of course, being contemplated with a careful eye on the calendar, for 1968 was a presidential election year, and the supreme legislative body of the nation had to cede the spotlight and the forefront of the stage to the national nominating conventions to be held in August.

Earlier, the Congress had approved a twofold measure designed to check inflation: an income-tax surcharge and a cut in spending by the federal government. It was widely felt that the measure would result both in increased unemployment (at a time when unemployment was a critical problem in urban ghettos) and cuts in domestic social welfare programs (at a time when it was becoming increasingly clear that the money committed to such programs had not been adequate to do the job).

In short, in the summer of 1968, the Congress of the United States had indicated that its stance toward protests based on pleas for social and economic justice would be: business as usual.

Reflective of this stance was Congress' reaction to the outstanding nonviolent protest made during the second half of the decade: the Poor People's March and Demonstration, in May and June of 1968, which was originally conceived by Martin Luther King as a dramatic move to symbolize the plight of the poor people of America.[7] The leadership of the protest march and demonstration had devolved upon Ralph Abernathy, King's disciple and assistant, who had taken over the latter's role as leader of the Southern Christian Leadership Conference (SCLC), a major sponsor of the march. Abernathy possessed neither King's control over SCLC, nor his ability to evoke the confidence of the poor people, nor his level of political skill. It is clear that, in many ways, the Poor People's March and Demonstration, and their experience in the construction and management of Resurrection City, were badly handled by a divided and mutually suspicious group of leaders. Most to the point here is Abernathy's lack of political skill, as exhibited in his presenting the national government with what was generally regarded as an inordinate and impossible set of demands. We can speculate that King would have made demands which would have been easier to obtain, would have achieved some success in getting a fair number of these demands met, and then would have been able to ride out the protests of the militants among the poor, who would have been unsatisifed with the partial success.

But whatever the internal problems of

the Poor People's March, our main point of concern here is the response by the federal government, and particularly the Congress, since it was the Congress which was the focal point of the protest. One newspaper commentator appraised the over-all accomplishments reflected in Congress' response, dealing with the question on two bases for measurement: measured against the demands made by the poor, he termed the record "abysmal"; measured against the President's proposed program for the poor, he characterized the record as "modest."[8]

In fact, the Congress did manage to take some action in mid-1968 in the fields of social and economic welfare, some of which action was presumably in direct response to the poor people's protest activities. In a number of instances, the Congress went even beyond the President's request, or took action without specific suggestion by the President. For example, in early July, the Congress added $28 million to a presidential request, in order to provide more summer-job and educational opportunities for the underprivileged than the President had programed. Further, the Model Cities Program, designed to spur upgrading and redevelopment of urban ghetto communities, was given more generous financial support in 1968 than it had received the previous year. In addition, as this article is being written (July 1968) there has been affirmative action by one house of Congress, and final action is expected before adjournment, in a number of other areas, including a large new program of housing subsidies and a large addition to the federal budget to provide free or low-cost school lunches to needy children.

In considering the positive steps taken by Congress during mid-1968 in response to protest, two separate points need to be made, the former pragmatic, the latter philosophical or a matter of policy. The first point is that the President has been charged by Congress with reducing federal spending by $6 billion during the next fiscal year. Accordingly, regardless of the number and the variety of programs which have been enacted and budgeted, the real question of how much federal money will be actually spent in their implementation has not yet been settled. It is clear that a

spending cut of $6 billion cannot be effectuated without severe cuts in many federal programs, and we can predict that at least some of these cuts will come in the social welfare area.

The second point, setting aside the question of the looming spending cuts, is whether the action taken by Congress in 1968, parts of which were described briefly above, were, in fact, sufficient, in light of the real needs of the nation. These needs were perhaps most graphically portrayed in the Poor People's March (and in the activities and statements which preceded and accompanied it), and were also reflected in the grim statistic that by mid-year, 1968, serious disturbances related to racial conflict and the cause of the poor had occurred in over two hundred cities and towns across the United States.

The question of whether Congress' action in 1968 was sufficient raises still another question, even more fundamental: whether the people of the United States, taken at large, have reacted or responded sufficiently to the needs of the nation, particularly the disadvantaged portions, as expressed in the various protest movements. Both questions are closely interwoven and cannot, in fact, be separated, given the basic assumption of a democratic representative government. The question thus becomes: Could the Congress have done more than, in fact, it did given the present level of concern and commitment of the American people? The answer is: Probably not. While there is a significant role for leadership by a representative body in a democratic system, that role must be delicately played, and can never be permitted to grow too far beyond the bounds set by majority opinion.

We might conclude with the opinion that, by mid-1968, the American people had not yet been aroused to that level of concern and commitment which would bring them to exert consistent pressure on federal legislators, executives, and administrators,[9] to cause these, in turn, to undertake the major—and very costly—changes required to meet the present challenge and to respond to the protests of the 1960's. Until that concern and commitment are widespread and at a high level, we can expect little success in bringing about these major changes.

NOTES

[1] Two comments are in order here, both of which merit fuller exposition. First, much of what we would today call protest is also covered under other rights guaranteed by the First Amendment, notably free speech and free press. Second, though we are concerned here with the response to protest by the federal government, we should recognize also a corresponding responsibility laid upon the states by constitutional interpretation. In a long succession of decisions, the Supreme Court has established the doctrine that most, or all, of the rights guaranteed as protection against the federal government by the First Amendment have been "incorporated" in the due process clause of the Fourteenth Amendment, and thus have also been applicable to the state governments. See particularly *Palko* v. *Connecticut,* 302 U.S. 319 (1937), where Justice Cardozo indicated that the due process clause of the Fourteenth Amendment has incorporated all those guarantees of the Bill of Rights which are "implicit in the concept of ordered liberty" and "so rooted in the traditions and conscience of our people as to be ranked as fundamental."

[2] James W. Douglass, "Politics Without Violence?," *Christian Century,* June 28, 1969, p. 836.

[3] The extension was not voted on as a separate measure, but was attached as a rider to—of all things—the appropriations bill for the Mutual Security Program.

[4] The signing ceremony took place in the President's Room, off the Senate chamber, where, exactly 104 years earlier, President Lincoln had signed a bill freeing slaves impressed into the Confederate armed services.

[5] For example, if the Director of the Bureau of the Census determined that less than 50 per cent of the voting-age population living in an area was registered to vote.

[6] Partially obscured by the tragic news from Watts was the eruption, on the same day (August 11) of violence in Chicago, where two days of fighting between Negroes and police brought eight injuries and over a hundred arrests.

[7] It is interesting and ironic to remember that on the Sunday before his death, speaking in the Washington Cathedral, King indicated that he was willing to call off the march if Congress would promise action, but doubted that Congress would be interested in such a trade.

[8] Vincent J. Burke, *Los Angeles Times,* July 7, 1968, sec. G, p. 1.

[9] We have not discussed here the various steps taken by federal administrative agencies during the 1960's. Whether or not these steps were specifically in response to protest, they represent, in total, some important changes and concessions. A review of the record would show that it has been easier to get action from federal administrative agencies than from federal legislative bodies. This raises some interesting questions both about some of the assumptions and about the underlying theory of democratic representative government. The point is too important to be dealt with cursorily; it clearly deserves separate treatment.

46
ethnic groups and education: towards the tolerance of difference

NATHAN GLAZER

This book started by posing the problem of how to obtain consensus in a society composed of a variety of groups with different cultures and religions and control over economic and political power. Should cultural diversity be encouraged or suppressed? This final essay comes back to the same subject.

In a low key, Dr. Glazer points out that cultural differences persist much longer than social scientists had supposed and that they encourage those within the culture into diverse pathways. Cultures are internally consistent, and if one set of culture traits is lost or changed, other sets will be lost or changed. Over a long period of time, the culture becomes another culture; in the short run, the culture holders may undergo disorganization and anomie. Dr. Glazer argues for an acceptance of differences, particularly in education, to the end that ethnic groups can change at a slow-enough rate to bring their cultures into harmony with one another without inducing anomie in their members.

Dr. Glazer is professor of education and social structure at Harvard University.

History and social research convince me there are deep and enduring differences between various ethnic groups, in their educational achivements and in the broader cultural characteristics in which these differences are, I believe, rooted; that these differences cannot be simply associated with the immediate conditions under which these groups live, whether we define these conditions as being those of levels of poverty and exploitation, or prejudice and discrimination; and that if we are to have a decent society, men must learn to live with some measure of group difference in educational achievement, to tolerate them, and to accept in some degree the disproportion in the distribution of rewards that may flow from differences in educational achievement.

I am not sure actually that men can do this; that the conflicts between liberty (which inevitably produces differences) and equality (which inevitably means their reduction) which have lain at the heart of American democracy can be compromised (and compromise is all we can hope for, and the best we can hope for) in any permanent and decent way. But at least a first step is to explore this dilemma.

As to the argument that there are deep and enduring differences in the degree to which different ethnic groups achieve educationally: To speak of the differences between groups is to raise incredibly difficult problems. The study of national and ethnic differences, which became popular during World War II

Reprinted from *The Journal of Negro Education* 38, no. 3 (Summer 1969), pp. 187-195. Reproduced by permission of the author and publisher.

and which continued for some years after that war, fell into decline during the fifties. The excitement of the work of Ruth Benedict, Margaret Mead, Nathan Leites, Geoffrey Gorer, David Riesman, and others on national culture and values wore off. In part, people lost interest in the work on national differences because of the methodological excesses of some of the practitioners. The explanation of these differences in terms of child rearing and various kinds of psychoanalytic and psychodynamic models seemed far-fetched. To establish the differences in the first place seemed difficult. To shift the techniques and theories that had been developed in the study of small, isolated, primitive groups to large, complex, and differentiated societies was questionable. There was also the serious problem of dislike and antagonism between nations that could be fanned when scholars of one nation analyzed the intimate life and resultant character of people of another. Thus, the studies of Germans, Japanese and Russians in the early postwar period began to look embarrassing a few years later.[1]

I think in the end the attempt to define differences between groups in a global way, to specify the main trends of their culture and character, must always be in large part an exercise in literary and artistic skill and imagination. But this is much less true when we come to specific differences between groups living under similar historical circumstances. I believe educational achievement represents such a specific area of difference, though still of course enormously complex, and the experience of ethnic groups in America provides us with a natural laboratory in which to study some of the enduring differences between groups and the specific mechanisms which make them up. The study of such specific areas of difference is in part an outgrowth of an interest in ethnic groups as such. In defining and exploring the differences between groups, certain areas of human experience seem particularly illuminating. One of the most illuminating, for example, is mental health—what symptoms are defined as abnormal, what diseases are recognized, how are they treated and responded to? The beginning of studies of ethnic differences in mental health owes as

much to the desire to explore ethnic difference and its significance as such as it owes to the desire to learn something about mental health by looking at its cross-cultural manifestations.[2] Another such area is undoubtedly achievement in education.

Thus, there are some striking ethnic differences in educational achievement for which we have good enough evidence. One of the best documented (though still insufficiently for scholarly purposes) is that of American Jews (specifically Jews of East European origin), who since the turn of the century—this is, a period about midway between the onset of heavy East European immigration in the early 1880s and the end of this period in the early 1920s—have shown a remarkable and disproportionate degree of educational achievement. For example, by the turn of the century East European Jews already dominated the free City College of New York, to which entrance was obtained at that time only by formal educational achievement.[3] Teachers in schools reported to researchers for the Immigration Commission that Jewish children almost uniformly did well in schools.[4] Jews, at a later stage, dominated lists of winners of New York State scholarships. While a simple summary of East European Jewish educational achievement is not easy to provide—since Jews are not identified in census returns—the case for Jewish educational achievement, from various kinds of statistical evidence, is overwhelming and generally taken for granted.

Perhaps even more striking is the achievement of such a group as the Japanese Americans. The contrast between these two immigrant groups could not be greater. The preimmigrant experience of one is urban and small town, the other peasant and agricultural. One defined itself as a priest-people, and placed a high value on formal study of religious classics; the other defined itself as a peasantry of inferior status. In this country, one group settled in New York and other large cities, the other in the California countryside. One showed early evidence of educational achievement, the other was defined as an educational problem. But by 1950 (and this after a period in which the entire Japanese community had been uprooted, lost is property, had

been sent to concentration camps in the
Western desert, suffered intense persecution,
all this coming upon the heels of decades of
discrimination and persecution), Japanese
Americans in the state of California were
already the best-educated racial group in the
state. Japanese Americans have been represented on the elite University of California
campuses in proportions far greater than could
be expected by chance.[5]

On the other side, we can point to ethnic groups which have done poorly educationally—the case of the Italian Americans has
been studied in some detail.[6]

All this is common knowledge. The question is, what does this mean? What do we
make of it? One thing it means—and one reason why these differences have been studied
—is that it leads us to suspect there must be
differences in areas other than educational
achievement that help explain educational
achievement. If large numbers of Jews and
Japanese Americans go to college, we are by
that token interested in why this phenomenon
arises, what factors in family structure, value
teaching, disciplinary practices, goals set before children, the role of voluntary organizations, etc., etc., might explain it, and what
thereby we might learn about the group. These
educational differences help support the argument that there are cultural differences of
significance between groups. And in order to
support the argument of the importance of
cultural differences it is important to examine
groups that have received no particular support from the general American environment
(who have indeed been subjected to various
degrees of discrimination, prejudice, and persecution, such as the Japanese and Jews)
because then the argument as to distinctive
cultural reasons for high educational achievement become all the more powerful.

A second question arises—are these
really cultural differences or genetic, racial
differences? The study of genetic, racial differences between groups went into eclipse, for
political as well as scientific reasons, with the
rise of Hitler. It has led a shadowy and almost
underground existence since. The analysis of
genetic differences between groups as a basis
for educational achievement has suddenly

achieved both new notoriety and a greater
measure of scientific respectability as a result
of the work of Arthur R. Jensen.[7] I think we
can for the purposes of this article avoid such
disputed ground, because the differences between ethnic groups, to my mind, need owe
nothing to genetic differences. We have a good
way to go before we sufficiently expose the
cultural and social background of the varying
educational achievements of American ethnic
groups. Two such valuable works as Mark
Zborowski's *Life Is With People* and Leonard
Covello's *The Social Background of the
Italo-American School Child* assume that cultural differences with no relation to genetic
factors can be taken as sufficient explanation.
We need more work of this kind, on both these
and other groups. We do not understand well
enough how the social and cultural differences
that we hypothesize play some role in leading
to educational differences actually work. At
this stage, to my mind, it is hardly necessary
to resort to genetic differences. But I also
believe we cannot rule possible genetic factors
out of court and refuse to give them any hearing or status. For myself, my interest and concern is with the cultural differences. I feel they
are more accessible to study and are more
proximate as "causes" that permit us to understand differences in educational achievement.
They are attractive on other grounds—they
will not raise the fierce passions and the political dangers that we know are inherent in racial,
genetic explanations of group difference. On
the other hand, we know well enough by now
that scholars will not escape political attack
even if they restrict themselves to cultural and
social differences. At this point in our history.
to discuss cultural and social differences between groups opens one to the charge of
"racism" almost as much as if one discusses
genetic bases of difference. Consider the case
of Daniel P. Moynihan.[8]

There is another and somewhat disputed
reason why one may prefer to emphasize at
this stage social and cultural reasons for differences in educational achievement rather
than genetic reasons. If we are interested in
raising levels of educational achievement in
certain groups it seems reasonable to assume
that social and cultural factors that hamper

educational achievement may be more accessible to policy intervention than genetic factors. Yet there are problems to this approach. First of all, if we deal with causes that are very intimate, rooted in family culture, for example, it is not easy to see how cultural factors may be any more accessible to intervention than genetic. Secondly, if we deal with such intimate factors in public discussion we inevitably raise a powerful defensive reaction. No one—except perhaps for Jewish novelists—is going to accept coolly or objectively an analysis of his family structure as being damaging and defective in producing some commonly agreed on valuable objective. Either it will be denied that the family is defective in this way, or it will be denied that the hitherto thought-to-be desirable objective which is hampered by that family structure is indeed desirable.

We have seen both reactions in the case of the question of the Negro family and its relationship to educational and occupational achievement. Nevertheless, despite the political dangers that accompany any discussion of group differences, it has generally been accepted that to emphasize social and cultural factors means to be more "liberal," to be more positive about change and more optimistic that it can occur, than to emphasize genetic factors. This was certainly the understanding of Franz Boas, Ruth Benedict, and other anthropologists when they opposed racial interpretations of cultural differences. And yet, there are ambiguities. The cultural differences analyzed may be so deep-going, so integrated in a complex supportive structure, that it may be scarcely possible to see what policy action might change it. How would one have changed Kwakiutl culture—or Hopi, for that matter?[9] And beyond any political reasons for preferring social and cultural explanations to genetic and racial ones, there remains the question of scientific truth—the fact may be, as Jensen argues, that the social and cultural factors contribute only a small part of the variance or difference. Yet it may also be the part we can get at.

Beyond the "conservative" or "reactionary" racial explanation, and the "liberal" social and cultural explanation, there lies yet another possibility—the economic and political explanation, which is perhaps best called "radical." This would argue that the genetic differences are nonexistent or irrelevant, that the cultural differences are epiphenomenal, that only political and economic differences (in wealth, power, and status) lead to the differences between ethnic groups—and that these can be changed, and not by the subtle measures of social policy whereby liberals might try to modify differences in social structure and cultural orientation. How much guidance science and scholarship can give us in determining which of these interpretations we select is an open question.

A third question arises. What is the importance, after all, of the differences in educational achievement and the presumed differences (let us grant for the sake of the discussion they are social and cultural) on which they are based? The argument as to the importance of educational achievement is too obvious to rehearse. These days it is based on such grounds as the importance of skills and capacities to achieve a decent income and a satisfying occupation and the economic resources for a good life. Somewhat muted today is the argument that skilled manpower is needed for national economic development and military strength. Still further in the past (and yet perhaps to be revived) is the argument that educational achievement is an important part of personal fulfillment, giving one the powers and capacities (and not in this case economic, but cultural and political) to lead the good life as a member of the good society.

But very powerful arguments today attack the notion of educational achievement as a desirable objective, and by extension the presumed desirability of the cultural and personal traits that make it possible. Certainly there is little need to explore the recent devastating criticisms of American national policy—many critics today would consider it desirable that American economic and political power were less than it is. There is a powerful attack, though to my mind less well founded, on the need or desirability of every individual taking up productive economic work in an affluent society. There is even an attack on the idea that schools as now constituted can do anything but thwart the personal fulfillment of a free individual and the creation of a good society.[10]

Since these critical views are so widespread, it is understandable that those traits that presumably lead to educational achievement should also be subjected to searching criticism. Thus the argument that educational achievement is based on some inherent valuable capacity has been attacked. Perhaps, the attackers suggest, it is based on the exaggerated overdevelopment of some capacities and the suppression of other capacities. Suppose educational achievement is based not on differences of intellectual capacity but on differences in motivation, in ambition, in work habits. Suppose it is based on differential ability to adapt to the environment of schools and to the desired expectations of teachers—which are various and only one of which is intellectual capacity and creativity.

Educational achievement might then relate less to intellectual capacity than to the ability to make use of schools and what they have to offer instrumentally, so as to achieve various desired ends—money, position, prestige, etc. Or perhaps we have yet another kind of relationship between personal traits and educational achievement—one in which educational achievement is not seen as an instrument but comes as the consequence of certain uncontrollable or unconscious trends of character, for example, docility, the desire to please, the preference for passive sitting as against active physical movement, etc., etc.

Obviously educational achievement can be seen in a variety of ways—and one will judge the ethnic differences that seem to be related to it differently as one judges educational achievement. If one sees it as the consequence of an ability to tolerate a repressive and authoritarian environment, one will have one point of view. If one sees it as the ability to make use of a variety of environments of varied qualities for instrumental ends, one will have another point of view—depending on how one judges the ends. If one considers it the simple consequence of abilities and talents, one will have yet another point of view. There are other possibilities.

While I share in some degree all three of these interpretations, I lean most strongly to

the last—capacity determines achievement; and next to the second—a strong desire for the things educational achievement can give determines achievement; and least to the first—uncontrollable traits of character determine achievement. And while I see some virtue in such arguments as those of Theobald and others that the puritan ethic or work ethic as taught in the schools unfits people for the society they are entering, actually I think this a rather exaggerated and distorted argument.[11] I believe what most people want from their lives (and legitimately want) requires, for as long as we can look ahead, a society in which there are more opportunities in the form of useful and satisfying work than there are people to fill them. I think of these wants not only in terms of gross consumer needs that are now attacked by young radicals in such countries as Germany and France, as well as the the United States, but in terms of needs for education, for cultural activity, for knowledge, for health, for recreation—all of which demand enormous numbers of trained people. Even the desires for consumer goods are hardly as gross as radical critics think they are. The French workers, many of whom live without indoor baths and toilets, were mystified by the student radicals' attack on "the consumer society." American workers, who might still look forward to a better house or to a hunting camp or a motorboat might still be mystified. The demands for work in society are not only determined by the desire to minister to our pleasures but by the needs of a still overwhelmingly poor world, and by more than that, the simple satisfaction that men take in productive labor, something that one would hesitate to see go. Men who can avoid work often choose to define a work life for themselves—even if that consists of politics, charity, philanthropy, sports, or art collecting.

The fact that one can define humanly valuable and humanly satisfying work does not mean that most work men do today is of that kind; or that educational achievement is the best test for sorting out people for various kinds of higher education and work; or that the qualities needed for educational achievement in the kind of school system we have, which has been so devastatingly described by

Friedenberg and others, are themselves more humanly valuable or desirable than their opposites. These are all serious questions, and to answer them involves serious and extended effort. And yet, to make a brief answer, I think that educational achievement in our schools reflects qualities that can be put to various valued uses, and would appear in varied settings. Thus, for example, those groups—to return to the ethnic problem—that do well in school do well in a variety of schools, for example, conservative and progressive, in a variety of educational systems. Now even all the schools we know do not sufficiently tap the possible variety of schools to convince us that the capacities that lie behind present school achievement are more than a narrow range of limited talents. It is still impressive that those groups that do well in one school system will very likely do well in another; that in effect they have talents that can be displayed in a range of settings. For example, to take the case of East European Jews again—helpful not because they are the only group that shows high school achievement (we have pointed to the Japanese; there are also the Chinese, the Armenians, etc.), but because they live in a wide range of social settings. We will find that Jews do well in Soviet Russia as well as in the United States. Now the differences between the contemporary Russian school system and the American school system are fairly large, if not as large as those between either of them and the kinds of schools Paul Goodman and Edgar Friedenberg would like. In other words, if a group shows high achievement in a school system that some of us may consider unduly repressive and destructive of decent human traits, and gains an advantage in taking up work in a society some of us consider the same, this does not mean the same group will not show high achievement in a revolutionized school system, in a revolutionized society. Indeed, it probably means it will—because we have good evidence of the enduring character of differences in educational achievement under varied school systems and social systems.

It is this enduring quality to which I turn, and which is our most serious problem. If we believed—if we could believe—that edu-

cational achievement was fully a matter of concrete economic opportunities, concrete characteristics of the home, or if we believed that home differences in occupation or income could be compensated for fully by remedial measures in school, then we would not find differences in educational achievement between ethnic groups such a serious matter. We would find such differences; but we would believe that, if our measures for social reform succeeded in narrowing the gaps in occupation and income and style of life, as they have done to some extent, this would be a problem we could solve. The fact is that while there are correlations between occupation and income—class, in a word—and educational achievement (and these are terribly important correlations), class factors are not the only ones that affect school achievement. It is not because of the class-location characteristic of an ethnic group that it shows a certain distinct level of educational achievement. Ethnic factors play an independent role. When we say ethnic factors, we say cultural factors. We know by now something of what makes up the cultural factors relevant to educational achievement—language styles in the home, interaction between mother and child, the degree of encouragement and stimulation provided the child, expectations for him, etc., etc. These form a complex that is to some degree subject to intervention, but forceful intervention—perhaps of the kind that is undertaken in Cuba and China, and was undertaken in Russia early in the revolution—would certainly conflict with other values we possess, values which favor individual privacy, familial integrity, and even the desirability of maintaining cultural styles and characteristics that may directly hurt educational achievement. Who, for example, was to determine that the tight South Italian family culture and peer group, which we know had negative consequences for educational achievement, was to be broken up in order to increase educational achievement?

One of the most impressive demonstrations of the distinctive character of ethnic styles as they affect capacity for educational achievement is in the work of Stodolsky and Lesser.[12] By inference, their work also demonstrates how enduring these styles are. They have studied, using various tests, children of four New York ethnic groups—Chinese, Jews, Negroes and Puerto Ricans—of two class levels, They find a distinctive pattern of mental ability (as defined by scores on their tests of reasoning, verbal ability, number ability, space conceptualization) for each group. The striking thing is that the profile is the same for lower-class and middle-class children in each group, although the level of performance is higher for middle-class children in each group. Since working-class children show the same pattern of performance as middle-class children of the same group, we can assume that when most Jewish children were working class rather than middle class (let us say forty years ago), they would have showed the same pattern of performance too.

A great deal of imaginative work is now under way on changing levels of achievement; e.g., directly through new types of curricular materials, teaching approaches, changing school environments and administrative patterns, by going into the home, working with parents, working with children, etc. It is scarcely possible to summarize all this. It is possible to take the position that different levels of ethnic achievement will crumble under the impact of such changes in education, if they are sufficiently extensive and sustained. But it is also possible, and this is the position the evidence to date leads me to, that these differences, which have endured under such varying social circumstances in the past (conditions of deprivation and of affluence, of prejudice and its absence, of rigid schools and permissive schools, of strict patterns of child rearing and loose patterns, etc., etc.), will continue into the future, even if reduced.

The question that troubles me most is what attitude we are to take to these differences. Are we to view them as the consequences of ill will—that of teacher, administrator, the society in general? How elaborate are we to make the efforts to wipe them out, and how successful can we hope to be no matter how elaborate our efforts are? Are our measures to equalize to include the restriction of the opportunities to those groups that seem to find school achievement easy? Or are we to develop a set of values that accepts within some measure differences as desirable and expectable, and tries to mitigate the negative consequences that society imposes for them? These are hard questions, and they are questions to which we do not have answers. Nor are they questions for the United States alone. They are questions for every ethnically diverse society in which some groups show distinct patterns of educational achievement, whether in Malaya, Nigeria, Indonesia, or what have you, in which all these questions are real and live.

They are questions that can destroy a society, and we are already halfway there. We need to press not only our research on these differences, their origins, their extent, their causes, the measures that reduce them, but also develop and strengthen a political and social philosophy that permits a society to accept them, to live with them, and be stronger because of them.

NOTES

[1] For a review of this work, see Alex Inkeles and Daniel J. Levinson, "National Character," in Gardner Lindzey (ed.), *Handbook of Social Psychology* (Cambridge, Mass.: Addison-Wesley, 1954), pp. 977-1020.

[2] See, for example, Marvin K. Opler, *Culture and Mental Health* (New York: Macmillan, 1959); Anthony de Reuck and Julie Knight (eds.), *Transcultural Psychiatry* (New York: Little, Brown and Co., 1965).

[3] On this specific point, see Moses Rischin, *The Promised City, New York's Jews, 1870-1914* (Cambridge, Mass.: Harvard University Press, 1962).

[4] Nathan Glazer, "Social Characteristics of American Jews," in Louis Finkelstein (ed.), *The Jews* (3rd edition, New York: Harper & Row, 1960), p. 1705. See, too, Meyer Weinberg, "A Yearning for Learning: Blacks and Jews Through History," *Integrated Education* VII (May-June 1969), pp. 20-29.

[5] The Census of 1950 showed Japanese in the state of California with more years of education than any other racial group, including whites. The observation on the University of California is based on estimates

of students there. For a general view of the Japanese American experience as a case of success under adverse conditions, see William Petersen, "Success Story, Japanese-American Style," *The New York Times Magazine*, January 9, 1966. See, too, Harry Kitano, *Japanese-Americans* (New York: Prentice-Hall, 1969).

[6] Leonard Covello, *The Social Background of the Italo-American School Child* (Leiden: E. J. Brill, 1967).

[7] Arthur R. Jensen, "How Much Can We Boost I.Q. and Scholastic Achievement?," *Harvard Educational Review* XXXIX (Winter 1969), pp. 1-123. See the critiques of his work in the *Harvard Educational Review* XXXIX (Spring 1969).

[8] For the dispute surrounding his report on the Negro family, see Lee Rainwater and Martin Yancey, *The Moynihan Report and the Politics of Controversy* (Cambridge, Mass.: M.I.T. Press, 1967).

[9] For further discussion on this point, see my introduction to the 1966 University of Chicago, Phoenix Books edition of E. Franklin Frazier, *The Negro Family in the United States.*

[10] The chief critics are Edgar Friedenberg, *Coming of Age in America* (New York: Random House, 1965) and other books; and Paul Goodman, *Compulsory Miseducation* (New York: Horizon Press, 1964), and other books. But their thinking is now diffused to the high school level, and below.

[11] I am referring to the argument of Robert Theobald (in many books) that expectable and near technological achievement will make the need to work for most people unnecessary.

[12] Susan Silverman Stodolsky and Gerald S. Lesser, "Learning Patterns in the Disadvantaged," *Harvard Educational Review* XXXVII (Fall 1967), pp. 546-593.

index

72 73 74 75 76 9 8 7 6 5 4 3 2 1